Smithsonian Institution Secretary, Charles Doolittle Walcott

Charles Doolittle Walcott 1850–1927, by Helen Breese Walcott Younger, 1927. Oil on canvas, 127 x 101.80 cm. Gift of artist's granddaughter, Catherine Ann Younger, to the National Portrait Gallery. Smithsonian Institution S/NPG.94.27. Reproduced by permission of the National Portrait Gallery.

Smithsonian Institution Secretary,
Charles Doolittle Walcott

Ellis L. Yochelson

The Kent State University Press

Kent, Ohio, and London

©2001 by The Kent State University Press, Kent, Ohio 44242
Library of Congress Catalog Card Number 00-010267
ISBN 0-87338-680-9
Manufactured in the United States of America

06 05 04 03 02 01   5 4 3 2 1

Library of Congress Cataloging-in-Publication Data

Yochelson, Ellis Leon, 1928–
    Smithsonian Institution secretary, Charles Doolittle Walcott / Ellis L. Yochelson.
        p.   cm.
    Includes bibilographical references and index.
    ISBN 0-87338-680-9 (alk. paper)
    1. Walcott, Charles D. (Charles Doolittle), 1850–1927.
    2. Paleontologists—United States—Biography. 3. Smithsonian Institution
    I. Title.
    QE707.W35 Y64 2001
    560'.92—dc21

                                            00-010267

British Library Cataloging-in-Publication data are available

Composed in Adobe Minion by Em Studio, Inc.
Printed on 50-pound Supple Opaque natural stock (an acid-free, recycled paper)
and bound by Thomson-Shore, Inc.

Once more, to my dear wife, Sally, who has put up with me—
in marriage—for more than fifty years. I could probably retire
from retirement if I had paid her a dollar each time she said,
"Why don't you go upstairs and work?"

Contents

Preface

I find three principal motivations behind writing a scientific book: to unify questions, solutions, advancements, and discussions on a particular topic; to summarize one's lifetime work; and to have fun.

—A. A. Zaniest, 1998

History shows that if all else fails, the best course is to tell the truth. Accordingly, I admit to at least one mistake in my study of Walcott's earlier career (Yochelson 1998); there are others, but that is my secret. The introduction indicated that I first became interested in him when attending the International Zoological Congress in London in 1959. I miswrote, misspoke, lied, or whatever, for the date was 1958. With this correction, the record is now clarified: it was forty years from Walcott's death to the National Academy of Sciences biography (Yochelson 1967) and forty years from my first interest to published book.

Much as one likes uniformity, forty more years to complete a study of the last part of Walcott's life is not feasible in the face of the three score and ten years in one's allotted span. I have passed that mark.

To continue the biblical theme, in my moving from one computer system to another, the heavens fell in. I ended with no disks and six hundred single-spaced pages to be scanned. Simply to remove the new glitches inserted by that process took forty days and forty nights, at least, and provided a glimmering into Noah's state of mind while he was helplessly drifting. Accordingly, assembling this volume should better be considered a millennium project. The millennium begins either in 2000 or 2001 and thus provides some wiggle room. An added benefit is that I brag about a project that took more than one century to complete.

One invaluable lesson I learned in writing a book about Walcott's earlier years is that the world truly does not want to know every jot and tittle I have learned or inferred about him. Seriously, I have tried to curb my prolix prose, but it is not my fault that he kept taking on new challenges in areas far removed from paleontology. I also may have cut a few corners on research to meet the deadline, but again, whether this is true, and if so, what corners and where, is my secret. To cite one example, there are 105 boxes of official office correspondence covering most of his tenure as secretary of the Smithsonian Institution. A true scholar would have read everything; I have read a reasonable, scientific sample. Most letters are routine answers to inquiries from taxpayers, but there are other, more interesting items to be uncovered. All a future investigator would need is endurance.

Walcott kept a small pocket diary and for more than fifty years scribbled a few lines in it each day. The diary provides an account of his travels, some of his activities, and, very rarely, his inner feelings. That he did not miss a day of entries tells volumes concerning his self-discipline. Time was in limited supply for Walcott and was quite important to him; this document provides a time line to follow through his life.

I have quoted quite liberally from the diary. My aim was to reproduce faithfully all its details, such as capitalization, abbreviations, spelling, and punctuation. There are idiosyncracies in spelling and obscure abbreviations, clarified by the use of "[sic]." Similarly, the italics in Walcott's diary reflect his original, occasionally inconsistent, underlining.

I am exceedingly lucky to have year after year of uninterrupted diaries as a resource to supplement Walcott's letters and finished papers. Some who undertake biographies of famous personages have scanty original sources or must rework that which has been published earlier. I nearly foundered from too much.

To return to Walcott himself, several reviewers of his pre-Smithsonian life have noted the lack of spice in my earlier account, published in 1998. In one sense, Walcott's life was dull. To be fair to myself, how many different ways can one write that a workaholic worked hard? During the final twenty years of his life, he continued to be a workaholic and as much a "straight arrow" as he had been in his earliest days. Fortunately for me, though sadly for him, in those two decades there was far more human drama to recount. These years included travel through the finest scenery in North America, romance, a beautiful debutante, an incredible discovery, a national scandal, and great personal tragedy. Nevertheless, all these events are played out against a background of detailed and never-ending scientific work.

Walcott's scientific work was basic to his character. He was not an administrator who studied rocks and fossils but a scientist who did administration. The distinction is fundamental, not trivial. In the prologue I have included a few pages on the nuts and bolts of fossils and strata, in the hope that this would make parts of the text more intelligible. One colleague thought there should be a glossary, but I am concerned with recording a life, not preparing a textbook. Even if one cannot follow all the notes in Walcott's tune, it is easy enough to hear the beat of unremitting labor.

Almost every reviewer of *Charles Doolittle Walcott, Paleontologist* (Yochelson 1998), Walcott's life from birth until 1907, has commented that it contained no discussion of the Middle Cambrian Burgess Shale fossils, and some nearly accused me of fraud for not including this point in the title. Among other comments I might make is that if you want people to read a book, they should, as a bare minimum, be able to lift it easily. To have tried to put all of Walcott's life in a meaningful manner into a single volume would have produced an unpublishable document.

For published material that I have quoted, a parenthetical reference to author, date, and page is given; when the reference is more general, page numbers are omitted. For unpublished sources of quoted material, only a superscript reference to a chapter note is given. These notes simply indicate the location of material; I see no reason to remove interesting or useful comments from the text and hide them in small type at the end.

In the text I have intermixed names of organizations with their acronyms, using both in order to break up the monotony. After all, "Carnegie Institution of Washington," "the Carnegie," and "ciw" mean the same thing; the last is the shortest. Walcott went to innumerable meetings of the executive committee of that institution. In his diary he referred to it as the "Ex Comm," with or without periods. I prefer the simplest form, as does the printer; the paper saved may not preserve a tree, but it will help a twig or two.

Surely "the gwma" is no harder to understand than the "George Washington Memorial Association." The National Advisory Committee for Aeronautics has disappeared, but during its lifetime it was "the naca" to almost everyone. Likewise, shortening "National Academy of Sciences" to "nas," "National Academy," or even "Academy" is obvious. Almost everyone in Washington refers to the nrc, not the National Research Council. The Research Corporation is not so much a household phrase, but there is nothing else in the discussion to be confused with "the rc." Despite the merit of abbreviations, however, the Washington Monument Society is associated with such a venerable and prominent part of the Washington skyline that any acronym might be considered disrespectful to the man, the city, and the nation.

The first building and headquarters of the Smithsonian Institution (si) is a remarkable piece of architecture and deserves to be a capitalized "Castle" (Hafertepe 1984). "Museum," capitalized, refers to the new natural-history building, which opened in 1911 (Yochelson 1985). During Walcott's tenure it was part of the United States National Museum, informally called the "new National Museum." Curiously enough in the Washington scene, that federal agency, when not abbreviated to usnm, was written out in full, whereas U.S. Geological Survey (usgs) was the conventional usage for more than a century.

The Burgess Shale is the most important fossil discovery ever made. I have made that remark as a preface to several dozen lectures, and no paleontologist has disputed me. If Walcott had done nothing more in his life, his discovery and description of these fossils should have ensured him a place in history of science, or at least the history of geology. Why this is so important will be made clearer later in the present volume. Still, Walcott was a forgotten figure until 1989, when the Stephen Jay Gould's *Wonderful Life: The Burgess Shale and the Nature of History* was published (by W. W. Norton). It brought this outcrop to the attention of the general public, discussed modern work being done to re-describe the fossil material obtained there, and propounded a view of the evolution of life. Along the way, Professor Gould made a few harsh judgments concerning some of Walcott's traits and, especially, the quality of his science. This makes for an awkward situation in writing a biography of Walcott.

Nothing is to be gained by arguing with those interpretations. Walcott would prefer to have the facts of his life and his work speak for themselves. More pragmatically, there is no logic in being drawn into an argument that one is guaranteed to lose, regardless of the right or wrong of the matter. Point-by-point refutation is both dull and pointless. In the final analysis, I have won no medals or prizes, have written little in history of science (and almost nothing of a popular vein), and my opinions on the course of evolution have not always been those of the mainstream of evolutionary biologists. So taking the high road is sensible.

On the other hand, I have published more papers in paleontology than has Steve Gould, and I would be less than human if I did not take a few pokes at him, especially near the end of the story. Still, they must be viewed in light of the fact that Steve gave me one of the first five copies of his book to come off the press, with a nice inscription that I knew more about Walcott than he did. I do.

To return to business at hand—fortunately for me, during Walcott's years as SI secretary Walcott's geologic and paleontologic investigations were more focused than earlier in his career. Geographically, except for a couple of seasons in Montana and Wyoming, almost all of his field work was in Alberta and British Columbia. His stratigraphic work was confined mainly to the lower Paleozoic, and especially the Cambrian—a somewhat mystifying attempt at clarification of what these words mean is in the prologue. His paleontologic work was confined mainly to trilobites; again, peruse the prologue. The one glaring exception was his description of the organisms of the Burgess Shale. The classic television series *Star Trek* said it well: in investigations of that remarkable discovery, he went where "no man had gone before."

To balance partially that geologic simplification, his administrative efforts were more diverse than in earlier years. Why should a paleontologist become so deeply enmeshed in aviation that he set up a government agency to advance the subject? What possesses a geologist to work with a strange inventor and develop patents, so that any profits can be given away? These are good questions, without obvious answers. Add to all that a few organizations that took up Walcott's time, and one has a full plate. If there are too many tangents and details, for heaven's sake do not blame the author—it is not my fault Walcott had his finger on the pulse, shoulder to the wheel, and nose to the grindstone of a great part of American science policy. Even in that peculiar posture, he never stopped working.

Acknowledgments are the next item to consider. Previously, I had indicated a debt to many librarians and archivists (Yochelson 1998, xii). That really is a pale and poor thank-you, but there are no words really appropriate for dozens of people, known and unknown to me, who for decades assisted with replies to inquiries. David and Martha in the Natural History Branch of the SI library occasionally lifted eyebrows at some of the books I wanted, for it was obvious these had nothing to do with dead snails, my erstwhile field of specialty, but they never said a word, and they always produced what I wanted. For backup, my daughter Abby, at the reference desk of the Library of Congress, always provided answers to impossible inquires. The government documents room at the University of Maryland, McKeldin Library, was a quiet place to work, with a librarian enlightened enough to allow one young grandson to use the microfiche machine for printing while I searched through and cursed the systems used to index congressional documents.

Computers are also helpful, but they have given new depth to the concept of "mixed blessings." Most of the time I'm grateful to my son Jeffrey for taking away my KAYPRO and, despite my protests, upgrading my software and changing the hardware. Still, leaving the KAYPRO left me with a dozen disks that could not be converted and a dot-matrix manuscript that was not easy to scan. Fortunately, earlier in life I had developed a basic vocabulary for recalcitrant situations, though on this occasion I added new words. My other son, Chip, must bear responsibility for at least one of the chapter subheadings.

The Automatic Data Processing group in the National Museum of Natural History, mainly Kurt Luginbyhl, has saved the day more times than I care to mention. Kurt is a soccer player and coach, yet not once did he threaten to kick me around the room for pushing the wrong keys. My Le Ducharme, Department of Palaeobiology, was of tremendous assistance in scanning documents, an arcane skill known to few.

In my study of Walcott's life from birth to 1907, I noted the cooperation of many institutions. It is still appropriate to thank them all again, but for brevity, I limit the list herein to those places whose material provided background for this particular study or at least searched on my behalf. These include the archives of American Art, Smithsonian Institution, Washington D.C.; the American

Legion, National Headquarters, Indianapolis; the Freer Gallery of Art; the National Zoological Park, Washington, D.C.; the offices of Architectural History and Historical Preservation, Washington D.C.; the general counsel and the treasurer, Smithsonian Institution Library, Department of Transportation; the Naval Historical Center, Washington D.C.; the Metropolitan Museum of Art Archives, New York; the archives of the Canadian Rockies, Banff; the Canadian Pacific archives, Montreal; the Rockefeller Archive Center in North Tarrytown, New York; and the Western Reserve Historical Society in Cleveland, Ohio.

To extend this list further, I acknowledge with many thanks those places and institutions from which unpublished material has been quoted, with permission. These include the Academy of Natural Sciences, Philadelphia; the Carnegie Institution of Washington, D.C.; the government of Canada's archives, Ottawa; the Huntington Library, San Marino, California; the National Academy of Sciences, Washington, D.C.; the Natural History Museum, London; the New York State Library, Albany; Princeton University, Princeton, New Jersey; the Royal Ontario Museum, Toronto; the Swedish Academy of Sciences, Stockholm; and Yale University, New Haven, Connecticut. Of course, it is really the individuals in these organizations who should be thanked.

Permission to use illustrative material was generously given by the Canadian Pacific Archives; the Geological Survey of London; National Portrait Gallery and Smithsonian Institution Archives. Letters and manuscripts in the National Archives and Records Service are in the public domain; those in the Library of Congress and the Smithsonian Institution archives may be. Whether acknowledgment is formally required or not, I would be a rotten human being if I did not include appreciation for assistance given me by the staffs of these places. I have spent so much time at the SI archives that there was talk of either giving me a desk or charging me rent.

William Cox always brought what I wanted and always added that perhaps I should look in Record Unit such and such. He was always right. After the fact, I need to acknowledge several people. By accident I discovered that Kennard Bork of Denison University was a reader for Kent State University Press; without his enthusiastic comments, Walcott from birth to 1907 might never have come about. He did far more for me than just write a dust-jacket "blurb." Friend Hatten Yoder, Geophysical Laboratory, CIW, has to be applauded for another blurb, as well as for steady encouragement and insight into the CIW. The person I must really thank for past effort is Michele Aldrich. She deserves my gratitude for carefully reading the first manuscript and going over it with both hobnailed boots and a fine-toothed comb; I hope that after reading this she will accept my statement that I learned what she was trying to teach. Alan Leviton of the California Academy of Sciences, and Tom Dutro, U.S. Geological Survey (retired), former boss and longtime friend, cheered me on to write this volume, as they had earlier cheered on Michele to cut me down to size; there is more than one meaning to that phase.

Geologists and paleontologists need not be historians to be of tremendous assistance.Thanks to a grant in 1993 from the American Philosophical Society, James D. Aitken of the Geological Survey of Canada, retired, guided me along many of Walcott's footsteps in western Canada. I mentioned this earlier, but it bears repeating; it was invaluable to see the rocks in Canada and hear his comments on geology, camping, and a host of other matters; I think he has forgiven me for hitting an elk while driving at night, nearly killing him in the process. Desmond Collins, Royal Ontario Museum, has been indefatigable not only in quarrying the Burgess Shale but in running down references and leads, all of which he has generously shared. William Fritz and Brian Norford, both also retired from GSC, provided further insight into Walcott's scientific work in western Canada and improved my knowledge of Paleozoic stratigraphy. Professors Harry Whittington and Simon Conway Morris of Cambridge and Professor Derek Briggs of Bristol—the mafia of the Burgess Shale studies, if you will— have answered innumerable questions and provided penetrating insight. The late Gunnar Henningmoen of the Paleontologisk Museum, Oslo, taught me a little about trilobites, which have more parts to worry over than nice snail shells.

Ever cheerful, LeAnne Freidy, Geological Survey of Canada, found documents, gave me leads, and was generally helpful. W. S. Bacon, Research Corporation, Tucson, Arizona (retired), deserves a significant amount of appreciation. Earle Spamer of the Academy of Natural Sciences of Philadelphia, and Dove Menkes of Fullerton, California, have continued to inform me about Grand Canyon history. Brenda Coen, National Park Service, Glacier National Park, provided some useful documentation. William Massa of the Sterling Library, Yale University, enlarged his reputation as a helpful archivist. C. Hennessey, archivist of Sackler/Freer, was of considerable assistance. Janice Goldblum, National Academy of Sciences Archives, answered question after question.

Dr. T. Cornell, Rochester Institute of Technology, allowed me to examine parts of a manuscript in progress, as did Dr. Lois Fink, National Museum of American Art (retired). Sidney Phillips kindly sent me a copy of his story of his growing up in Banff National Park. John C. Miles also allowed me to use a copy of his book manuscript, since published and herewith recommended for those interested in our national parks.

Thanks to e-mail I was able to make inquiries overseas. Dr. Annie Dhondt, Institut Royale, Brussels, Belgium, advised me that there was nothing to be found concerning an inquiry; even negative answers are helpful. The late John Thackrey, a fine man, discovered a hitherto unknown 1888 photograph of Walcott.

He also put one of his associates on a search for me, and Pamela Hutton, of the library at the Natural History Museum, London, found a choice item.

Although Sidney Walcott is long departed, he still deserves my thanks for the letters and material he sent me years ago. The late George Vaux and Henry J. Vaux, nephews of Mary Vaux Walcott, added human interest that would otherwise have been lost.

I owe a special debt to Erin Younger for allowing me to quote from the reminiscences prepared by her grandmother Helen Walcott Younger. Former secretaries the late C. G. Abbott and A. Wetmore gave me their time, as did the Walcott chauffeur, the late Alphonso Jones.

G. Arthur Cooper (1902–2000), during his fifty-seven years at the Museum, came about as close to being a role model for the kind of effort Walcott devoted to paleontology as anyone I have ever met. Were it not for him, I would not be a paleontologist and certainly not a historian of a paleontologist.

Rodney Feldman of Kent State University, an excellent person and an equally excellent paleontologist—especially if one's taste runs to crab, shrimp, and lobster—and an all-around decent human being, was my original entrée to the Kent State University Press. Editors are to authors as dogs are to cats. Still, I deliver a reluctant but sincere thanks to Pelham Boyer, my copyeditor. No one enjoyes having mistake after mistake and inconsistency after inconsistency pointed out; still, better to be humiliated in the manuscript stage than after a book is printed.

Those who produce books have the good sense not to ask for author input in a book's design. Thus, I was most surprised and most pleased in 1998 to see a drawing of the Middle Ordovician trilobite Triarthus becki atop each page. This sketch was taken from one of Walcott's early papers, and it was an exceptional choice as a hallmark of his scientific work. The idea was so good that I asked to repeat it for this book. Thus, atop each page is a drawing of *Marrella sepndans,* the most characteristic fossil of the Middle Cambrian Burgess Shale. Mary Parrish, officially a scientific illustrator, but really an artist, in the Department of Paleobiology, National Museum of Natural History, drew this little gem.

As with my 1998 study of Walcott's life, director John Hubbell and his group did a job that Walcott would have approved of—pardon—"a job of which Walcott would have approved." Managing Editor Erin Holman was patient with most of my foibles and questions. Editor-in-Chief Joanna Hildebrand Craig, who had to deal with me through the 1998 publication stayed in the background and smiled as we negotiated. I suspect that John issued instructions for his editors to allow me an occasional win during arguments on the use of virgules, single and double quotes, brackets, and ellipses.

Well, here it is.

Smithsonian Institution Secretary,
Charles Doolittle Walcott

Prologue

As quiet as Powell was flamboyant, Walcott translated ideas into institutions. That the U.S. Geological Survey became the prototype of the Progressive Era technocratic bureau, that as the "Mother of Bureaus," it spawned new offspring almost annually was largely a tribute to Charles Doolittle Walcott.

—S. J. Pyne, 1998

IT IS NO SIMPLE TASK to condense fifty-seven years into a few pages and still produce something coherent (Yochelson 1998). On the other hand, it is exceptionally poor policy to start any story in the middle. The best way to begin is to begin at the beginning. Notwithstanding that sage alliteration, this prologue can be ignored by a reader without too much difficulty, or referred to later. One may also read the paragraphs on Walcott's life and skip the rambles among the rocks, though this will probably lead to skipping nearly every other paragraph of the narrative.

For Charles Doolittle Walcott, the beginning was March 31, 1850. At the time of his birth, he had two older brothers and an older sister. When he was two, his father died. His grandfather, Benjamin, to whom the lad was quite attached, was a very rich man, having opened the first knitting mill in New York State. When Walcott was seven, about the time his grandfather retired and his uncle William took over the mills, the widow Walcott moved her brood a few miles east, from the hamlet of New York Mills to the city of Utica. It is likely that young Walcott was pampered and perhaps a little sickly. He had trouble with teachers in grammar school and dropped out of the Utica Academy before graduation. Walcott's formal schooling lasted from age eight to eighteen.

During the Civil War, the family spent one or more summers in the area of Trenton Falls, a few miles to the northeast. At the time this was a famous vacation area, noted for the scenery along West Canada Creek and for fossils that could be collected from the limestone rocks of the region. Walcott fell in love with fossils and met a local farmer/paleontologist, William Palmer Rust, who had a magnificent collection. According to Walcott, by the time he was sixteen he was familiar with the local fossils.

This, then, may be as good a place as any to mention a few elementary facts about geology, for Trenton Falls was where Walcott learned his craft. It is even harder to condense three centuries of scientific investigations than half a century of a life, but his life story makes little sense without the geologic underpinning.

Sedimentary rocks, those formed from sediments carried by water, are characterized by having been deposited in layers. Although there are exceptions among continental beds, most stratified rocks were deposited in marine waters. There is a plethora of marine invertebrates; some of them have hard parts, and their remains are sometimes preserved after death. To tie this to common experience, many people have walked along a beach and picked up shells. If the individual sand grains were cemented together, the beach would be a sandstone, from which the shells could be broken out, if one had a hammer.

Not as many people stroll along mud flats, for the walking is more difficult, the water action is less dramatic, and the shells may not be as pretty. If geologic forces squeeze most of the water out of mud, the resulting rock is a shale. Even fewer people have walked through the shallow areas around the Bahamas Islands. Unlike most muddy areas where clays are deposited, in these tropical islands lime mud is being deposited today. Squeeze lime mud, and limestone is formed. Modern experiments in mechanically compressing the mud have shown that it flows around any enclosed shells and commonly does not deform them. So much for the rocks of limestone, shale, and sandstone.

Now consider a meal of crepes or pancakes. Pancakes are better, for they are easier to see, being thicker, and they are commonly are piled up rather than rolled. A standard stack and a short stack can easily be differentiated by counting the number of pancakes. It is also possible to stand a ruler on the plate and measure the height (or thickness) of the total pile. This is no different from measuring the total thickness of a pile of sedimentary rocks. Depending on the skill of the cook, some pancakes will be thinner and some thicker, some slightly undercooked, and some a delicious, golden black. Observing the details of individual pancakes is no different than describing the individual strata within a pile of sedimentary rocks.

Standard pancakes, blueberry pancakes, and those containing chocolate chips are readily differentiated; one may use sight, smell, or taste to do so. Although fossil remains occur in sedimentary rocks, not all rocks contain them, and when they are present, not all are the same. Distinguishing kinds of fossils is far more complex than picking out varieties of pancakes, but the basic principles are similar.

Assume that several restaurants offer pancakes. They might all serve the same number of pancakes for the same price. Nevertheless, one restaurant may prepare thicker pancakes than another. The seemingly inane behavior of using a ruler to measure the thickness of a stack would then have an economic basis—determining which place gives the most for the money. Plotting trends in the thickening and thinning of layers is one tool geologists use in the economic quest for oil deposits. Because a lot of rocks have similar physical characteristics, determining whether the fossils are chocolate, blueberry, or something else, allows one to be confident that one is still tracing the same layer one started with.

The scientific professions, which were just developing a few centuries ago, learned from medicine men the importance of jargon to ensure that unenlightened folk are properly awed. What has been illustrated by pancakes is *stratigraphy*, the study of strata. In *correlation*—that is, the matching of individual pancakes from place to place—geologists commonly use *lithostratigraphy*, studying the physical features of strata. When they become confused because many pancakes look similar, geologists are forced to call in the expert on finding blueberries or chocolate chips. To overgeneralize, the geologist looks for the broad picture, and the *paleontologist* looks for the details.

Going back to young Walcott—with the help of farmer Rust, he learned to read the layers of limestone and the fossils they contained. Some places are better to collect in than others, because of the original conditions under which the rock was formed and the organisms lived. Within the walls of Trenton Falls gorge, the exposed strata lie nearly flat, yet one can see that the rocks are slightly tilted and in places broken into blocks that moved up or down; such complications have to be considered by a geologist measuring a section. Whether one measures two hundred feet of rock layers in Trenton Falls or two miles of rock in the Grand Canyon, the principles are the same. During his career, Walcott measured and collected at both places and many others. (As an editorial aside, use of the shibboleth "a host of others" has been shunned to facilitate simplicity in communication.)

To pursue rocks a little farther, geologists apply geographic names to strata. The Trenton Limestone is named for Trenton Falls, and the Utica Shale for the city of Utica. Both units can be correlated to other places in the state and to other regions. To write of the Utica Shale at Albany, New York, sounds like an oxymoron, but it makes good sense to a geologist.

In the realm of confusing geologic terminology, the words for time rank high. The concept of time has been a subject for metaphysicians, philosophers, and physicists, not quite since time immemorial but certainly for hundreds of generations. Even that interval is short compared to the age of rocks. It has now become fashionable to designate geologic time as "deep time." Whether this oxymoron was coined to play on the concept of deep space, another oxymoron, or is a product of the Department of Redundancy Department is uncertain; accordingly, the term *geologic time* is used here.

Time, whether it is short or long, is a continuum; processes are intermittent, either in duration or in the strength of their effects. Because rocks are a result of processes, there are breaks in the sequence, both short intervals and longer intervals termed unconformities—often marked by dramatic changes in the inclination of underlying layers relative to those above. One aspect of geology has been to apply time to the rock sequence and impose artificial breaks on the time continuum. Because this is such a specialized field, a terminology has had to be invented.

Starting from the bottom of the predominantly fossil-bearing rocks, three great divisions have been named for ancient, middle, and modern life, respectively: *Paleozoic, Mesozoic,* and *Cenozoic.* Forget about the latter two, as they are younger overburden, in many places covering up the more interesting Paleozoic strata. The Paleozoic stack contains seven pancakes. From the bottom upward these different flavors are: *Cambrian, Ordovician, Silurian, Devonian, Mississippian, Pennsylvanian,* and *Permian.* Outside of North America, the stack has six layers, with *Carboniferous* combining Mississippian and Pennsylvanian between Devonian and Permian. Actually the U.S. Geological Survey (USGS) did not formally adopt Mississippian and Pennsylvanian for about three decades after Walcott's death. These terms should not all be completely forgotten, but the older Walcott concentrated almost entirely on Cambrian, and he hardly ever went above the Ordovician rocks.

"Precambrian" is used today for rocks below the Cambrian; in Walcott's day it was spelled "pre-Cambrian." Today, "Lower," "Middle," and "Upper" are supposed to refer to rocks, whereas "Early," "Middle," and "Late" refer to the times when those rock subdivisions were deposited. Walcott was not consistent in his usage, let alone in more mundane matters like capitalization. Likewise, today words like "Limestone," "Shale," and "Sandstone" are capitalized in names of formations, but that was not the practice in the past. Apparent discrepancies in the later pages should be assumed to be either quotes or following early-twentieth-century convention; this presumption also has the positive effect of hiding any authorial errors.

What has been considered in the discussion above is relative time; for example, this rock layer in the middle is younger than the one below and older than the one above. During Walcott's lifetime radioactivity was discovered; the rate of decay of radioactive elements was used to provide numbers for ages. With considerable hubris, this procedure is now called *absolute time,* rather than radiometric time. It turns out to be an "absolute" that changes. Do not bother with the concept, for this in no way affected Walcott's geology. He summed up the thickness of the geologic rock column and the proportions of the three main kinds of sedimentary rocks, guessed at the rate of deposition of each kind, and arrived at a figure of about a hundred million years for the age of the earth, with the pre-Cambrian being the longest span (Walcott 1893; Yochelson 1989). From what we know today, five times that amount would about cover the Paleozoic, Mesozoic, and Cenozoic combined.

With the simple stuff out of the way, now the fossils must be considered. There are ninety-two naturally occurring chemical elements, and these combine in various way to make a few thousand minerals. Plants and animals are far more complex, and as a result there are myriads of different kinds of living forms around today. In the mid-eighteenth century, Carolus Linnaeus began to systematize their study by emphasizing two ideas. His first was the notion of generic and specific names, which were simply names and not actual long, detailed descriptions. His second idea was the concept of a hierarchical arrangement beginning with species, one or more species being placed within a genus. Genera were combined into a family, and families, in turn, were grouped into still higher, or more general, categories. Linnaeus had four main categories of animals. The living world is now recognized as having about forty phyla of animals, and the increase in many of the number of lower categories has been far more than tenfold. The terms *taxonomy* and *classification* are often used in discussing the arrangement of organisms into appropriate categories.

Generic and specific names are italicized, but Walcott lapsed on that point in his diary. When used to indicate a zone, the scientific name is not italicized, so at least in theory there are no inconsistencies in presentation. "A foolish consistency is hobgoblin of little minds," or whatever. Finally, nomenclature is a written language, not a spoken one, so no one should be concerned about trying to pronounce any italicized words.

Before the nineteenth century, a few geologists recognized that different strata contained different fossils. Whether this discovery was based on recipes of pancakes being also different seems unlikely, but one never knows what inspires a great idea. Rocks that looked physically similar could be differentiated and correlated from place to place by the fossils they contained. The result was that *biostratigraphy* was born and flourished for more than a century. Shortly after the middle of that century, the lapsed geologist Charles Darwin wrote his big book, and the concept of evolution began to pervade both biology and geology. *Paleobiology,* which considered fossils as former living organisms rather than just curiously shaped objects in rocks, began to be a concern. For a long time, this view was more the province of the vertebrate paleontologists, but the outstanding invertebrate paleontologists had commonly majored in biostratigraphy and minored in paleobiology. Walcott, as a good paleontologist, took care of the bread and butter of correlation by fossils, but he occasionally added some jam of morphology (description of structure) and classification.

There is a far better record of occurrences through time of clam shells than of worms. It does not take much observation to know that the exterior of a worm is much softer than the exterior of a clam. During his career Walcott described a variety of hard-parted creatures through the Paleozoic strata, but by the mid-1880s he was beginning to concentrate on rocks of Cambrian and Ordovician age and on the fossils of two phyla. For the first, he had some interest in the brachiopods. (There is no common name for these fossils, so brachiopods are referred to herein as brachiopods.) They have two shells and look like clams but are not related to them. Most clams live with one shell on the right side of the body and one on the left; most brachiopods live with one shell down (the ventral position) and one shell up (dorsal).

Walcott's great interest was in the Arthropoda. There are more kinds of arthropods than all other living creatures; there are almost as many kinds of living beetles as all other living creatures combined. In addition to the Insecta, the phylum Arthropoda contains many other classes. In the marine realm, the most prominent class is Crustacea. Crabs, shrimps, and lobsters are well-known crustaceans and are readily distinguished from each other, even if one's concerns are gastronomic rather than biologic.

In the Paleozoic one finds trilobites, members of an extinct class of arthropods. These have a head, a thorax with a number of segments, and a tail. The thorax is characteristically raised in the center and flattened laterally, giving another three-part effect. A centipede has many segments, but a better model for a trilobite is a "sow bug," whose body has three distinct parts. When disturbed, sow bugs tend to coil up, and many of the trilobites also had the ability to enroll.

The Cambrian and, to a lesser extent, the Ordovician, was the heyday of the trilobites. Arthropods have a hard outer shell, and to grow they have to molt; consider that Maryland delicacy, the softshell crab. Trilobites molted, and in places one finds one body part but not another. A fine brachiopod is not exciting to the general public, but a complete trilobite looks like an ancient extinct creature. Some amateur collectors use trilobites as a standard of currency—such as, this *Olenellus* trilobite is worth a hundred *Orthis* brachiopods. Professional paleontologists who study brachiopods should not take offense, but with all respect, trilobites do have more general appeal.

Walcott may not have learned all that has been mentioned above, but by eighteen he knew enough to take a short trip to collect in central New York. What the young man did for the next year or so is unknown, except he did not go to college. He had a year of clerking in a hardware store in Utica; though the proprietors liked him, he hated the work.

With no prospects, he left the hardware business and moved to the Rust farm at Trenton Falls. He received occasional sums from his mother, and in return for work around the farm he obtained room and board, plus some time to study local fossils and collect more. He "went in partners" with William Rust, and in the fall of 1873 they sold a collection of fossils to Louis Agassiz of the Museum of Comparative Zoology. The few days Walcott spent with Agassiz while he was unpacking the collection were sufficient inspiration to carry him throughout his career.

Another inducement to Trenton Falls was Lura Rust, William's younger sister. She was seven years older, and his mother was concerned, but they became engaged and married. Briefly, married life was idyllic for the couple, but Lura soon became sick and was intermittently worse; a reasonable guess is tuberculosis. Two years after marriage Walcott was a widower, his spirits further flattened by the never-ending farm chores.

Whether it was the inspiration of Agassiz, encouragement from his bride, or other factors, before Lura's death Walcott somehow made a great transition from the profession of collector of fossils to that of paleontologist. In 1875, he published his first four papers; two of them are quite short, but the latter two are respectable studies of a Trenton Falls trilobite and its occurrence.

In November 1875, Walcott left the farm for Albany, New York, where he became the special assistant to James Hall. Hall was both state geologist and state paleontologist. He published an enormous series of monographs, collectively known as *Palaeontology of New York*; in terms of volume of publication, he was the second most prolific paleontologist in history. He was ruthless and relentless in the pursuit of fossils. Hall was also director of the New York State Museum. Walcott worked in his private laboratory and at the museum. In addition, Walcott worked at the state capitol, lobbying for support of this science and watching over bills of interest to Hall.

If Rust taught him the basics of field geology and collecting, Hall gave him an enormous education in many ancillary fields. Besides paleontology, Walcott learned how to run a museum, how to assemble a major publication through all stages, including printing, and most importantly, how to stay on the good side of those who supply money. After two years of faithful service at seventy-five dollars per month, however, Hall did not renew his contract. Walcott remained at Albany for more than half a year, without income but pursuing fossils and publishing scientific papers.

A key point in understanding Walcott's makeup is that he published while in Hall's employ. Hall had a string of assistants, and there are papers by Hall and Meek, Hall and Whitfield, Hall and Clarke, etc., etc., etc.—with, of course, the younger, second author doing all the work. There are no joint Hall and Walcott papers, and that reflects considerable strength of character on Walcott's part. In fact, Walcott published only one joint paper in his life.

The first paper Walcott published in Albany was a short description of the legs of trilobites. The work is in two parts, one with a Trenton Falls address and a few concluding paragraphs from Albany. There is no question that the ideas are those of Walcott, developed before Hall enmeshed him. Walcott knew Hall all too well. This modest-length publication is the first ever to demonstrate conclusively that trilobites had legs and that these legs were segmented. To rephrase this, by this discovery Walcott proved that the trilobites were arthropods, an incredible accomplishment for an unknown from the backwoods. Throughout his career, Walcott made contributions to paleobiology, interspersed among his biostratigraphic efforts.

In the early summer of 1879, Walcott once again had no prospects whatsoever, and he planned to return to the farm. Lightning struck: the USGS had just been organized, and its director, Clarence King, offered him a job as a temporary geological assistant at fifty dollars per month, two-thirds of what Hall had paid him. Walcott became employee number twenty, was administered the oath of office on July 17, and immediately thereafter was in Kanab, Utah—that is, as soon as train and stagecoach could transport him. His assignment was to measure the thickness of the section of rocks from what is essentially Bryce Canyon, Utah, southward to the Colorado River. Three months and two vertical miles of rock-measuring later, he was back in Washington. King was so satisfied that Walcott became an assistant geologist, at $1,200 per year.

Meanwhile, Walcott completed a major study of the biology of trilobites (Walcott 1881). Next, he was part of a team sent to work out the geology of the Eureka, Nevada, mining district. After four months in a tent, he took his collections to the American Museum of Natural History and spent more than a year writing a monograph. Less than two years after the new organization had begun, Clarence King left, and John Wesley Powell took over as director.

Walcott was ambitious and no shrinking violet. He wrote privately to Powell,

> In our conversation at the Brunswick in May you mentioned that my salary was too small and should be increased. I gave the subject no more thought thinking it would come up in making out the estimates for the present year. As the check for July is at the old rate of $1200 per annum, it appears that no action was taken.
>
> While I need the money an increase of salary would give, I feel much more keenly the effect of the nonrecognition of an attempt on my part to do earnest and through work. That is, in the sense a business man looks at it.[1]

It was not until September 1882 that Walcott's salary increased to $1,800. What Powell gave immediately was field money to do more collecting in the Eureka district. Walcott moved to the north rim of the Grand Canyon for more field-work. In November Powell had a trail built, and Walcott spent seventy-nine days in the Grand Canyon measuring a section and looking for fossils. After another two and one-half miles of vertical rock-measuring and seven months in the field, Walcott moved to Washington. The city became his permanent home.

Walcott had his office in the United States National Museum building, the brick structure east of the Smithsonian Castle. From 1882 onward, when he was not in the field, he was almost always in that building, Sundays at church being the only exception. When the new fiscal year began on July 1, 1883, Walcott received a statutory position as paleontologist and a salary of two thousand dollars (Rabbitt 1980, 76).

Even before the Eureka report was completed (Walcott 1884), Powell sent him off to the Northeast. In 1838, a geologist had proposed the term "Taconic System" for a series of rocks in eastern New York and western New England. For the next forty years, there had been argument as to whether this was a discrete part of geologic time. In 1887, Walcott resolved the problem, and the Taconic disappeared. It may have been meeting Helena Stevens that year which inspired him. His efforts also inspired Powell, and as of May 1, 1888, Walcott received $2,400 per year.

In June 1888, the thirty-seven-year-old widower married the fair Helena and took her off to Newfoundland for a honeymoon. A Norwegian paleontologist had insisted that American paleontologists had confused the Cambrian, calling Lower Cambrian "Middle" and the Middle Cambrian "Lower." Helena had a great deal of fieldwork under her belt by the time Walcott found the evidence to prove that the Norwegian geologist was correct. This was such exciting stuff that Walcott took Helena to London and reported to the International Congress of Geologists that American geologists, including Walcott, had been wrong in the matter of the Cambrian.

Their first child, Charles Doolittle Walcott, Jr., was born in Washington on May 17, 1889, a fruit of the trip to Great Britain. Two years later Helena had a miscarriage, but a second boy, Sidney Stevens, was born October 2, 1892. Throughout much of this period, the Walcotts moved from house to house, slowly working their way into the better neighborhoods. Walcott kept going into the field each summer and writing nonstop when in Washington. In 1891, the International Congress of Geologists met in Washington, and Walcott again made a splash, with a massive compilation on the Cambrian of North America (Walcott 1891), plus a tidbit that pushed the record of fish back into significantly older rocks than had been previously reported (Yochelson 1983). He was now world famous; there is no reason to give references to every one of Walcott's many papers, bulletins, and monographs, for the interested person can find them with little difficulty. Meanwhile, Powell had seen merit in combining the paleontologists into one unit, and Walcott became chief paleontologist, "at a salary of Three Thousand dollars per annum to take effect July 1, 1891."

While Walcott was progressing with geology, Powell was involved in social engineering, concerned with irrigation in the western United States. It is a complex story, but in effect the scientist was sandbagged by politicians and bureaucrats (Stegner 1954). Congress punished Powell and his organization. The year 1892 was a terrible one for the USGS, but Powell had the good sense to call Walcott from the museum to the Hoe Iron Building and place him in charge of geologic and paleontologic activities. In July 1893, Walcott's salary jumped to four thousand dollars, though even that was hardly in keeping with the extra responsibility.

The 1879 USGS Act fixed the salary of the director at six thousand dollars. To further encourage Powell to leave, in 1894 Congress reduced it to five thousand. That spring, Major Powell finally retired, and almost immediately Walcott was nominated and confirmed as director—at the lower salary; Powell spent his waning years at the Bureau of Ethnology, across the street from the USGS.

It was no certainty that Walcott would receive the position of director, and he cannot be accused of celebrating early, yet Helen Breese Walcott was born on August 20, 1894.

"Walcott had become Director in inauspicious times, with the Survey under attack in Congress, and regarded with disfavor by segments of both the mining industry and the profession, and with the most serious economic depression of the 19th century underway" (Rabbitt 1986, 57). Walcott put things on a businesslike basis, restoring first the confidence of the employees and then the confidence of Congress. He expanded activities in topographic mapping, reinstituted studies of water—the subject that had destroyed Powell—and, notwithstanding some congressmen, actively supported paleontological research. He also fathered the couple's final child, Benjamin Stuart, born July 8, 1895.

George Brown Goode, assistant secretary in charge of the National Museum, died in 1896. Smithsonian Institution secretary Samuel Pierpont Langley, who had succeeded Spencer Fullerton Baird, persuaded Walcott to take on another chore; for nearly eighteen months beginning early in 1897 he also served as an acting assistant secretary in charge of the United States National Museum. Still without enough to keep him fully occupied, Walcott spent several years helping develop and build several luxury apartment buildings in Washington.

Life got even more complicated in late February 1897. With a stroke of his pen, lame-duck president Grover Cleveland established essentially half the present-day national forests. This tying up of natural resources was not the sort of action that the incoming William McKinley administration would favor. When the dust settled, however, Walcott had persuaded the new president and the new Congress that the forests should be saved (Walcott 1898). Until 1905, when the Forest Service was formed, the USGS was essentially the government agency for rocks, wood, and water. Meanwhile, Walcott kept studying fossils.

As might be expected after becoming Geological Survey director, Walcott was elected to the National Academy of Sciences, and almost immediately he became its treasurer. Meanwhile, he was moving through the ranks of organizations; he became president of the Cosmos Club in Washington and the Geological Society of America. He became interested in trying to promote a building for higher education and helped found the Washington Academy of Sciences (Yochelson 1996). All his activity finally came to someone's attention on Capitol Hill; on July 1, 1901, Walcott's salary became six thousand dollars.

In December 1901 Walcott met Andrew Carnegie, who was smarting because Congress would not grant a national charter for the proposed Carnegie Institution of Washington (CIW). Walcott convinced him to pursue this project, got a local charter, incorporated the organization, and by the end of January 1902 had the CIW going, with himself as secretary (Yochelson 1994).

In 1904, Walcott was able to steer a national charter for CIW through Congress (Yochelson 1994), and steering anything through Congress is never easy. Consider this sentiment about Carnegie, delivered by Senator John D. Works a decade later when John D. Rockefeller was arranging a national charter for the Rockefeller Foundation. "Even the charities of the present day have become commercialized. ... One of the millionaires of the day conceived that an easy and convenient way of ridding himself of some of his useless and burdensome millions and at the same time exalting himself would be the giving away of public library buildings. They are always distinguished by having his name attached to them."

In an example of history repeating itself, once again this overloaded man now had more bales of straw thrown on his back. The new president, Theodore Roosevelt, considered reclamation of western lands a key project for his administration. The Newlands Act of 1902 set up the Reclamation Service as part of the USGS. Where dams and reservoirs are to be built, and in what order, is a political minefield; Walcott walked through it unscathed. Walcott produced few scientific publications in 1902, hardly any in 1903, when Roosevelt had him on two special committees, and none in 1904. Nevertheless, Walcott was still somehow looking at fossils and preparing manuscripts.

Even as director, Walcott was in the field almost every season. Despite all these activities, there is every indication that he was a good father and good family man. In January 1905 the family made their final move, to a house that Walcott had designed and had built. He had realized his dream of a home of his own; it is in an excellent neighborhood, on the crest of a hill at the corner of S and 22d Streets, Northwest. Along the way to building this dwelling, Walcott accumulated a number of honorary doctorates, starting in 1898, and a few medals.

Before Walcott left the USGS in 1907, he had developed "the best geological survey in Christendom" (Rabbitt 1980, 299). It is hazardous to generalize among institutions, but under Walcott's tenure the USGS was without argument the best geological survey in the world, and the largest. It may have been the largest scientific research organization in the world. If one can compare the apples and oranges of various branches of science, worldwide the USGS was near the top in terms of scientific productivity and new ideas; it might even have held the premier place.

Late in February 1906, long-ailing Smithsonian Institution (SI) secretary Langley died; Walcott was one of his pallbearers. The Smithsonian Board of Regents delayed replacing Langley, placing Assistant Secretary Richard Rathbun in the position of acting secretary; he soldiered on, bearing responsibility without authority. On December 4, the regents met, not having done their homework, and offered the position to Henry Fairfield Osborn, vertebrate paleontologist and president of the American Museum of Natural History.

Within a few days, Osborn turned them down. This turned out to be a stroke of luck for the SI. The USGS Pick & Hammer Club, which had a keen sense of humor, in later years would parody him as Henry Fairly Boresome. After Osborn declined, Walcott let it be known that he would be available if asked; how much active campaigning he did is uncertain, but with many friends on the board and with his reputation, he would not have needed to do much. On December 18 he submitted his resignation as chief of the Reclamation Service. There were many good reasons for that action, but it might have been a step toward election by the regents.

After receiving informal word on January 23, 1907, of his election as SI secretary, Walcott had an understandably busy time. The next day, Thursday, he told President Roosevelt of this honor; the election was no secret, but it was appropriate protocol for him to inform his superior prior to accepting the appointment. Six days later, he wrote a formal letter of acceptance.

As to why Walcott took the secretaryship, one reason may have been affection for the place. In 1882, the second SI secretary, Baird had appointed him an honorary assistant curator—no money—of the United States National Museum, and two years he later promoted him to honorary curator; Walcott had spent many happy years in the building. Another reason lay in the challenge of building up an organization, a function at which he excelled. During his stint as acting assistant secretary under Langley, he had seen many things to improve but had been powerless to act.

A minor factor in his decision may have been prestige and recognition of his efforts. The secretary of the Smithsonian is far above a bureau chief; he or she is approximately on a par with the members of the president's cabinet. (No one knows exactly what the first Board of Regents discussed, but it chose the title of "secretary," and the word has a particular meaning in Washington.) Answering only to the Board of Regents, the secretary has more independence than even the cabinet secretaries, who have to be confirmed by Congress and answer to the president.

Finally, being head of that institution entailed far less administration than had been demanded of Walcott up until then. Compared to the manifold activities and size of the USGS and Reclamation Service, Walcott could run the SI sitting down, with both eyes closed and one hand tied behind his back. The time thus gained might be devoted to fossils, and if there was one preeminent factor in his decision, it would be that.

Congratulations on the appointment poured in, in some measure because Walcott had shown himself to be a miracle worker as an administrator, and the SI, if not directly in need of a miracle, at least needed a great deal of assistance. Osborn's refusal to leave New York had been a clear indication to anyone who was paying attention that the once-illustrious reputation of the SI was becoming tarnished.

Secretary Langley may have been an excellent scientist, but his failure to launch a man-carrying aircraft in 1903, followed almost immediately by the success of the Wright brothers, had not been good publicity. A new museum was being built; the architects had had fanciful ideas, and one of Langley's last acts had been to call in another architect. As a result, a Roman dome surmounts the Natural History Museum building, rather than the ornate cap originally planned. This squabble and delays in construction had further eroded his support among the board. An embezzlement of funds by a trusted employee had been a great embarrassment, and though Secretary Langley had vowed to draw no salary until the loss was repaid, his death shortly thereafter had made this a hollow vow.

At the USGS, Walcott had G. K. Gilbert and Bailey Willis as an informal brain trust. Similarly, the SI had two assistant secretaries, who served as sounding boards. Richard Rathbun had followed Walcott and was in charge of the United States National Museum; he was small in stature but big in heart, so far as dedication to his position went. Dr. Cyrus Adler had been hired as librarian in 1892 and in 1904 had moved up to help the failing Langley. He was a great scholar and as much of a workaholic as Secretary Walcott.

For three months, Walcott officially ran both the SI and the USGS, but the latter engaged most of his attention; there was little Walcott could do at the Castle. Notwithstanding this load, somehow he found time to plan for a field season of camping in western Canada. In early February, Walcott was at the White House with Theodore Roosevelt. Three senators, J. A. Holmes, and Gifford Pinchot were present. The topic is not mentioned, but it is a safe bet that the future of the USGS and the prospects of separating off a Bureau of Mines were discussed. Teddy Roosevelt gave a White House dinner in honor of Secretary Walcott on February 9—not bad for a lad who had started as a clerk in a hardware store.

Thereafter, Walcott was busy with appropriations matters. Some members of Congress mounted an attack on the Geological Survey, which kept growing; despite Walcott's efforts, that year the topographers took a budget cut. Walcott accepted the inevitable and went to talk to the Johns Hopkins alumni association. His increasing number of honorary degrees gave him access to more alumni associations than any college graduate could aspire to. He ended the month trying to raise funds for George Washington University; he was on its board of trustees. Anything that Walcott was involved in, he took seriously. Surprisingly, George Washington University never awarded him an honorary degree.

Early in March, James A. Garfield, son of the assassinated president took office as secretary of the interior, and Walcott's resignation from the Reclamation Service was accepted; F. H. Newell moved up from the number-two spot. Walcott was a bit older than Garfield, but the three Garfield boys approximately matched the Walcott sons, and all became playmates. There was a great deal of business for their fathers to do. "At Survey 9–11 A.M. Call 6 topographers together & notified them of reorganization of topographic branch" (March 21, 1907).

Walcott ended the month by meeting with Pinchot and Garfield on the question of who was to succeed him as USGS director. Several obvious choices had declined the position. Pinchot was a great supporter of young Dr. George Otis Smith, as was Garfield. Smith might have been selected in any event, but the part these two played in saddling the USGS with this bureaucrat for nearly twenty-four years should be recorded. He would not have obtained the position without Walcott's tacit approval, but at least Walcott does not bear all responsibility for the selection.

April was even busier. For a man about to leave office, Walcott was still heavily involved in Interior Department affairs. He "settled work between geol—& Technical branches of Survey" (April 1, 1907). This was the penultimate step leading to a bureau of mines, for all that was needed now was congressional action, which was to come in three years. Joseph A. Holmes was placed in charge of the Technical Branch; he acted as though he was already a bureau head. Five days later, the appointment of Smith as the fourth director of the USGS was announced, and Walcott made plans to leave his office as of May 1. It was an emotional event for him.

Even at the end of April, the USGS did not release its grip. One of the more powerful of the Smithsonian regents wrote him inquiring as to why one of the topographers had been reduced in salary from $2,400 to $1,800. Walcott responded that budget cuts had forced him to drop five men and downgrade the positions of others, reducing their salaries. Rather than leaving it at that, Walcott added that he personally felt friendship toward the person involved, "but in administrative matters, I have made it a rule not to permit my personal relations to interfere with decisions that appear to me to be for the good of the service."[2] Probably this letter was written from Walcott's new office in the Castle.

There was still a tie to the old organization. Late in January, Walcott wrote Secretary of Interior Hitchcock requesting that he be given status as a geologist: "The object of the appointment is in order that I may be able to carry on and complete certain investigations that I have had in hand for the last twenty years, and upon which I have given more or less time during my directorship. A quarto volume is now nearly ready for the printer, and I expect to be able to complete further studies and preparation of material in the future."[3] In this instance, Walcott could not predict the future very well. It took five years for the volume mentioned to be published, as USGS monograph number fifty-one.

1

The Kindly Years (1907–1910): Great Family, Grand Fossils, Good Fortune

It was the best of times . . .

—Charles Dickens, *A Tale of Two Cities*

DRAMATIC CHANGES were coming to the Smithsonian. Secretary Abbot, who succeeded Walcott, would write, "When Dr. Walcott became Secretary of the Smithsonian Institution we all saw that a man of very different temperament from Secretary Langley was with us. Where Langley was shrinking from publicity, Walcott enjoyed it. He was an athletic, breezy type of man, who would go for a brisk early morning walk in Rock Creek Park and turn up for breakfast with some influential Representative or Senator, or perhaps the President. Without apparent guile, and with a cheerful humorous talk, he would put in just the right words to lead his host in the way of promoting some good thing he had at heart" (Abbot 1958, 97).

January 31, 1907, began the Walcott era at the SI, which was to last for two decades. His formal letter of acceptance was the first step in the physical and psychological transition from one organization to another. Walcott had considered resigning from the board of the Carnegie Institution of Washington, but he convinced himself he could carry on CIW responsibilities without harm to the Smithsonian. One extra benefit of the change was that his salary was increased from $6,000 to $7,500 by the Board of Regents; he was receiving more money for less work. In December 1910, the salary was raised to ten thousand, but by then Walcott was as heavily engaged as he has been on the USGS.

As to "regents," the boards of most organizations have "trustees." However, the University of the State of New York is governed by regents, and, seemingly, this term dates back to the early Dutch influence in that state. During 1846, in the closing days of the congressional debate on establishing the SI, a congressman from New York used "regent," and the term stayed. (In framing a definition for the word, the *Oxford English Dictionary* mentions its use in connection with the Smithsonian "Institute," not Institution; shame on it.) Earlier, in 1904, Walcott had been appointed an honorary curator and head of a new Department of Mineral Technology; for a few years he also retained that title, along with that of secretary.

In his first meeting with the Board of Regents, Walcott directed attention to the tradition of personal research by the three earlier secretaries. "The Secretary added that his own research work had been in the line of geology and paleozoology, and that he desired to continue it as opportunity and time permitted" ("Proceedings" 1908, xxv). A year later he remarked, "I wish to take the opportunity of saying here that my going to the charge of the Smithsonian Institution by no means indicates any break in interest in research work in geology and paleontology. Indeed, I am looking forward to devoting a greater share of time to research work than I have in the past, for it has been a well established custom that the Secretaries of the Smithsonian Institution shall carry on researches in the particular subject to which they are devoted, and the organization, large as it is, is of such a nature as to render this reasonably possible."[1]

At the March regents' meeting, only six members were present. The main new business was negotiating with the new museum building's architects, who wanted more money. Walcott, ever the businessman, had noted that only the Superintendent of Construction could disburse funds and that if he were incapacitated, all work would stop; before the meeting, Walcott had arranged for the Sundry Civil Bill to include a provision giving the regents the power to act, and he requested their approval after the fact. This is a trivial point, but Walcott saw details that escaped others and worked behind the scenes to achieve his ends; it is a cameo of his style.

There was good news after the regents' meeting. William Evans made a significant donation of painting to the new National Gallery of Art. As the gallery was a paper organization, with no space of its own, these pictures hung for a time in the private Corcoran Gallery of Art. Walcott also arranged for summaries of research and abstracts of some articles in the *Annual Report* to be distributed to the press.

Again, this was an action that no one else had thought of; a bit of history is behind it. The Hoee Iron Building, which housed the USGS, was close to what was then "newspaper row," and Walcott cultivated the press. He probably taught F. H. Newell, who was in charge of water investigations, to issue press releases on activities in guaging the flow of rivers. One Washington legend is of a reporter on Pennsylvania Avenue fleshing out a feature story by offering to sell silver dollars for a penny to passing tourists, all of whom suspected a trick and refused. When the USGS director came along, he immediately made a purchase and humorously asked for five more to augment the appropriation. Walcott knew how to stroke reporters just as well as the politicians.

Social life at home and in the city continued. Cousin Fred Walcott came from New York to dine and brought along his fiancée; "She is a sensible, home-like appearing woman & apparently a good mate for Fred" (March 10, 1907). March 13 brought Walcott a "great dinner," mounted for him by the USGS. L. L. Nunn of Provo, Utah, came to town, and his business necessitated a quick trip to New York; there will be more of Nunn, no pun intended. Before that trip, however, Walcott had to attend the funeral of W. J. Rhees. Rhees had joined the Smithsonian in 1852 and had been chief clerk almost forever. What we have of the early days of the institution was preserved due to his efforts, and he deserves to be remembered.

The New York trip took the edge off the emotion of leaving the Geological Survey. Walcott had E. H. Harriman, the railway tycoon, and Nunn meet; whatever the issue, Walcott loved putting people and pieces together. His commercial business out of the way, Walcott attended to Carnegie Institution of Washington business at the Ex Comm meeting. Board president John Shaw Billings was the most faithful attender of these meetings, but Walcott ran a close second.

Other Andrew Carnegie interests then caused him to travel on to Pittsburgh. Walcott represented the SI at the opening of new laboratories and buildings at Carnegie Tech. He took along Joseph A. Holmes, head of the new Technologic Branch of the USGS (and no relationship to the Smithsonian anthropologist-artist William Henry Holmes). The two men looked at the heating plant, the picture gallery, and the new laboratories. This order reflected, in a way, Walcott's eclectic interests.

The secretary was in Washington in time to attend the National Academy of Sciences annual meeting; he was elected vice president, a point not worthy of notice in his pocket diary, or else he was so busy he forgot to jot it down. Near the end of the month, Walcott contributed to a memorial meeting for the late minister of the Church of the Covenant. He took an unusual tack in his remarks, but one that provides insight into how Walcott viewed the world: "From the inception of religious thought men have to a greater or less degree magnified the temporalities of their religion. The spiritualities have often followed rather than dominated. With Dr. Hamlin there was such a strong sense of the reality and power of his religious belief, and he so clearly manifested it, that few fully realized the business sagacity and common sense with which he treated all matters pertaining to the temporal affairs of the church and to the educational and charitable organizations with which he was connected" (Walcott 1907, 32).

On May 1, the USGS was officially behind him. On that day Walcott was back in New York, on an art initiative. The Frederick Church painting *Aurora Borealis* was being considered as a donation to the new National Gallery of Art. Walcott inspected it and called in William Henry Holmes for his opinion. They agreed on its merits, and eventually this magnificent canvas came to Washington. Walcott got back to Washington in time to put in a few Saturday afternoon hours at the office.

On what was essentially his first full day in the Castle, Walcott wrote: "Spent the day at the Smithsonian engaged with administrative matters & the monograph on the Cambrian brachiopoda. Much work remains to be done on the latter" (May 6, 1907). He was tired, but the brachiopod investigations had to go on to completion. Fortunately, young Lancaster Burling agreed to transfer from the USGS to the Smithsonian; Walcott would not have to train a new research assistant. Arthur Brown, officially a messenger but actually far more than that, also came from the USGS. "A son of a slave, he had been a waiter on a dining car, worked at the White House under Grover Cleveland, and had known presidents and many other distinguished people. His fund of stories was unlimited, and his judgement of human nature exceedingly keen."[2]

Interior arrangements within the Castle had been modified in the past (Hafertepe 1984) and have since been changed again; at this late date it is uncertain where anything or anyone was placed, though it seems reasonable that Arthur Brown had only a chair outside Walcott's inner office. It is hard to tell where Burling sat, though probably he was on the third floor. One source suggests that before 1910, Walcott also occasionally used the services of A. Dickout, a USGS preparator in the brick museum building, to help extract fossils from the matrix.

The Ex Comm of the Carnegie met, but with Robert Woodward as president, meetings were increasingly routine. There was another trip to New York, to attend a reception for a senior Japanese officer. Walcott took the time to see Dr. Billings and George Kunz, the gemologist at Tiffany Jewelers, and to begin to cultivate Henry Frick. Walcott returned just in time to say goodbye to Charlie, his firstborn. Charlie had gone to Provo, Utah, the previous June, for work and school at Nunn's establishment and had come home for a visit.

An old Albany friend came to town; Walcott "called for Prof. J. M. Clarke of Albany, N.Y. & took him over to see my work at Smithsonian on Cambrian fossils. Next took up plans for National Museum work for 1907–8 & in afternoon drove out to zoo to look over plans for its administration. Spent the evening with ex-Senator Cockrell" (May 22, 1907). Clarke's visit meant a great deal, for there were few people who could appreciate the grinding work that went into the production of a monograph. As one who had also worked with James Hall on volumes of the *Palaeontology of New York,* Clarke knew what labor was involved.

By the next day, remaining plans for the Smithsonian and its various bureaus had been examined. Sunday School for the children and church continued as in past years, but occasionally Walcott would go to his office on a Sunday afternoon. The brachiopod work crept forward. Late in May, he was off to New York again to see the Frick art collection and to talk to railroad magnate Harriman. Being a trustee of George Washington University and presiding at the University Club filled in a few of the "spare" evenings. "About one half of my time is taken with administration & the remainder with Cambrian brachiopod studies—The latter will not be completed before I leave for the west" (June 10, 1907). This is the first indication in his diary of coming fieldwork, though there must have been a great deal of planning and letter writing in advance.

Walcott dropped by 1600 Pennsylvania Avenue to say goodbye to Theodore Roosevelt, who, like everyone else of importance, left Washington in the summer. He made a quick trip to see Mr. Harriman; it was a combination of SI and Southern Pacific business matters, not quite so far-fetched as it sounds when one is trying to obtain donations. Back in Washington, Walcott presided when the University Club finally decided to build. The result, in 1911, was a six-story building at 900 15th Street NW. Later the club built on 16th Street next to the Russian embassy.

When summer officially began, the Washington heat wave was already in full swing. Administration slackened, but odds and ends of monograph fifty-one kept coming up. Another quick trip was needed to New York to talk over electric power in Utah with Nunn and Harriman. After all, no law said that just because one was a scientist and an administrator, one could not also be a businessman. Walcott went back to Washington and sent the new puppy "Scald" north to Aunt Helen in Oneida, New York. Finally, on June 30, he put on his scientist's hat; wife Helena and children Helen and Stuart accompanied their father west.

The party took the train to Buffalo and transferred for Toronto, Canada. The Canadian Pacific route was to Sudbury, Port Arthur, and then through the Canadian plains to Winnipeg. Independence Day was celebrated en route by hanging American flags from the coach window and the children setting off firecrackers. The next day they were in Calgary, and from there it was up into the mountains, by way of the Bow River Valley, a route to be traveled many times in the future. The train went through Banff and Laggan, the station for Lake Louise. They crossed the Continental Divide at Kicking Horse Pass and descended through the spiral tunnels completed that year. (These tunnels are a marvel of engineering, and they eased the railway slope on the west side from perilous to merely hair raising.) At Field, the first station in British Columbia, they were met by Mr. and Mrs. Lancaster Burling.

Walcott had a solid geologic reason for starting at this point. "The presence of the genus *Olenellus* in the Rocky Mountain regions of British Columbia has long been well known. In 1886 I identified for Dr. Geo. M. Dawson of the Canadian Geological Survey, among the fragments of fossils found at Kicking Hose Pass, a species of *Olenellus* that appeared to be *Olenellus howelli Meek*" (Walcott 1910, 317). From other collectors Walcott obtained more specimens from that area and correlated the faunas across a thousand miles to those he had collected from the Highland Range of Nevada (Walcott 1888). The correlations of the two sections were essentially correct, except that when he wrote the paper he had been still under the mistaken impression that *Olenellus* was an indicator of Middle Cambrian, not Early Cambrian. The 1907 trip allowed him to correct that error, obtain more material, and put this trilobite on record as a new species.

Camp gear was overhauled, and the party moved up the northwest slope of Mount Stephen to "rough ground about 1350' above the valley. Put up tents &

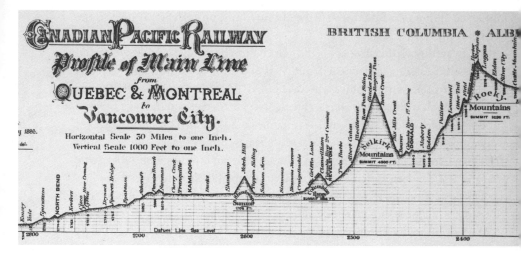

The last portion of the Canadian Pacific Railway, prepared in 1886 when the route was completed. The territory Walcott traveled repeatedly during his fieldwork lies to the far right. The railway climbs sharply at Banff and continues up past Castle Mountain, Silver City, Eldona, and Laagen to the highest point, Stephen, at the provincial boundary. Hector is just beyond the crest of the dramatic grade down to Field. Westward along the line from the town of Field are Otter Trail, Leanchoil, Palliser, and Golden at the east floor of the Rocky Mountain trench. Glacier House, where Walcott measured glacial retreat with Mary, lies just west of Rogers Pass, at the summit of the Selkirk Mountains. Some of the marked locations are recognizable in the generic and specific names bestowed by Walcott on Burgess Shale fossils. Reproduced by permission of the Canadian Pacific Archives.

made snug for the night. This is a beautiful spot in the heart of the mountains" (July 6, 1907). No one who has ever seen the Canadian Rockies will quarrel with Walcott's aesthetic opinion. By the next day, early Sunday morning, Walcott had tried out the new camera and had a promising lead for his collecting. He dashed off a hasty letter to Assistant Secretary Rathbun in Washington: "A clear beautiful morning. Frosty last night. Snow banks above & below us—All well. Will you not have *Mr.* Smilie [the Smithsonian photographer] develope [*sic*] the accompanying film at *once*. Report result to you & then will you telegraph to Field B.C. whether the result is good, bad or indifferent. Found a slab of rock last eve with 6 entire trilobites averaging 3 *in* long. Will stir more up tomorrow."[3]

As soon as the letter was dispatched, serious fieldwork began. Walcott took young Stuart up the west slope of the mountain to locate the fossiliferous beds, about 1,500 feet above the camp. There ensued several days of collecting Middle Cambrian fossils, but Walcott decided that the section was too broken by faults to measure. Burling and Walcott found a slightly younger fossil horizon, and while Burling collected there, Walcott and family concentrated on the main bed. Helena located a fossiliferous loose block and proceeded to do her own collecting, for two days; everyone participated in finding fossils. After ten days in camp, they took the packed fossils to the train and treated themselves to a few nights at the hotel. It was a wonderfully interesting section for him, but Walcott felt understandably "sore and crooked." He had been doing some long climbs and bringing down substantial loads of rock. He and Burling went east on the Canadian Pacific track by freight train and spent the day in a quick examination of a section.

Following this first session of collecting and measuring, Walcott paused in his geologic labors. All campers went west to Revelstoke, where the ladies—Helena, Mrs. Burling, Helen—and Stuart left them. The men went to Sicoumous, as the first stop on a complex trip. Walcott was a member, along with two appointed by Canada, of a commission to inspect the markers placed along the international boundary. It was an enterprise that had to be done; there is nothing so boring as a straight line, but until officials certified that the line was properly run and properly marked, no one would know for certain where the forty-ninth parallel lay. With railroads going back and forth across it, to cite only one example, the border's precise location has economic consequences.

Walcott left Field July 19 and was back on August 6. At the start of this jaunt, Burling and Walcott "walked over to the Similkameen river & let the mosquitoes tease us" (July 22, 1908). (There are pros and cons of work in the north compared to other regions. Two major cons are the mosquitoes and blackflies.) Walcott took a couple of geologic photographs, but otherwise the trip was limited to looking at boundary posts, beginning with number 108. This involved riding on construction trains, visiting Nighthawk—which still only barely exists— and Oroville, Molson, and Midway. There was nothing that ran parallel to the boundary on either side, nor is there today. They went to Grand Forks, Cascade, and Rossland, none of which is a household word. At Nelson, it was a switch to a river steamer and then back to a buggy. Burling and Walcott were in Port Hill and Bonner's Ferry, Rexford, and Gateway. Then it was back to Canada at Fernie, where Mr. Burling left to set up camp again. Walcott went up the Arrow Lakes and caught the train east to Field. Lake steamers and railways have changed, and the precise trip could not be repeated today.

Walcott got into Field at 5:45 A.M., and after breakfast he and Burling went out to collect; by noon, the steady drizzle had driven them back in. Time for fieldwork is always limited, and if one can possibly go out, one does. "Rain early in the morning. At 10 A.M. we went up the Ry [railway] 3 miles & worked on the Lower Cambrian zone near the Mt. Stephen Ry tunnel. Ret'd at 5 P.M. wet & tired—showers & mist all day" (August 7, 1907). They moved camp to the slopes of Mount Bosworth but otherwise continued on the Lower Cambrian rocks, finding fossils three hundred feet below the limestone, which two decades earlier had yielded *Olenellus* to geologists of the Geological Survey of Canada.

The ladies and Stuart returned, brightening the new camp. Sunday came and went, with Walcott out pursuing the *Olenellus* zone. This was followed by "a day of collecting in the Olenellus zone—Helena found a drift block with Zacanthoides fauna, same as on Gordon Creek Lewis & Clark forest Reserve— Montana. She found many fine specimens in it—I measured the lower 600 feet of the section of Mt. Bosworth" (August 12, 1907). This is what stratigraphic paleontology, or *biostratigraphy*, or whatever the latest buzzword may be, is all about. Finding the same fossils in two different places allows one to correlate them as being of the same age. When Walcott named the new genus *Albertella*, the type species was *A. helena*. "The specific name is given in recognition of the discovery by Mrs. Walcott, in 1907, of this species and the accompanying sub-fauna on Mount Bosworth in the Canadian Rockies" (Walcott 1908, 22). Almost always, Walcott gave credit where credit was due; he named the genus *Burlingia*.

Walcott and Burling continued on the section, only to be forced down by bad weather, walking back for three hours in a snow squall; the rest of the party had taken the train to Banff for the day. Conditions did not improve: "Rained all night & all day—Snow on higher parts—About camp resting & keeping fire going—A very disagreeable day—Helena, Helen & Stuart are good campers and do [not] whimper or complain" (August 14, 1907). There is no consensus as to which is worse, bad weather at the beach or in the mountains, but some authorities that suggest the higher the altitude, the more the misery. The next day they engaged in a wet session of collecting.

The Walcott party broke camp. Most went to Laggan, though Burling and Walcott stayed in Field. There is a prophetic note in his diary wherein Walcott mentions meeting Mr. and Mrs. George Vaux and Miss Mary M. Vaux of Philadelphia. The Vaux family had been coming to western Canada since the 1880s. They did some of the earliest measurements in North America on movement of glaciers and were equally pioneers in photography of the area (Cavell 1983). They will return to the story later.

While Burling was moving camp gear to Castle Mountain station, east of Lake Louise, Walcott fretted at Field, for trains were not going east, as a result of a wreck. He finally got to Laggan and Lake Louise that evening. Walcott and his family had dinner with Mr. William Whyte, vice president of the Canadian Pacific. No doubt one subject was the virtue of railroad cuttings, artificial rock exposures, and the kindness of the track-building crews in helping to push back the frontiers of geologic knowledge.

Lake Louise, with a dusting of snow from the previous evening, was superb, as Walcott put it, but the aim was geology, not scenery, and that evening they were settled in the new camp and ready to study the local geology. "With Stuart, Mr. Burling & Berman [packer] went upon east end of base of Castle Mountain. Found Olenellus fauna—also Zacanthoides—below first massive silicious lm. Returned to camp 7 P.M. We had a hard trip thru fallen & burned timber & rock slides" (August 19, 1907). They were out again the next day measuring to the base of the high cliffs. The party assembled a small camp outfit, measured 1,065 feet of the massive limestone, and camped out in the Helena amphitheater. It took another day to complete the section of 4,132 feet of rock to the summit of Castle Mountain. Because rocks are often tilted, altitudes and thicknesses of selected strata seldom coincide.

They hung about the main camp a day, resting and waiting for a train that never came. They did get out the next day and set up near Laggan, taking time to collect from siliceous shales of the Bow River. It rained, and the Walcott family hopped a freight train to the Mount Stephen House in Field. The rain continued unabated. The dreary day was made drearier when Helena, Helen, and Stuart left for Rochester, and Mrs. Burling went to Seattle; the two bachelors were left to pack collections and write letters. The next day, they rode the train up-grade for three miles, dropped off, and then hiked up Mount Stephen to collect and measure the higher beds. The following day, they were at the lower beds near the tunnel. Rain was intermixed with fog. They spent part of the next day on Mount Bosworth, collecting *Zacanthoides helena* until the rain drove them back to the track, where they spent several miserable hours waiting for the next freight train.

Surprisingly, the next day there was no rain, and they were off "measuring upper silicious limestone of Mt. Bosworth section—found interesting Cambrian fauna at summit of lime—in shales" (August 30, 1907). (For sharp-eyed, editorial-minded readers, Walcott's spelling of "silicious" does not follow current usage; it means "sandy," no matter how "siliceous" is spelled.) Walcott decided that at least three more days would be needed to work out relationships in this Castle Mountain Group. The weather held for one day, and on the second they did a little climbing to get photographs of Mount Stephen. They then continued the section up to the overlying Ordovician rocks before the rain returned.

A day in camp did not help Walcott's disposition—so many fossils and so little time! The weather improved, and they rode horseback up Mount Stephen. Walcott continued his section and located the *Ogygopsis* bed in place. Most of the earlier descriptions of fossils from the area had been from isolated samples, whereas one of Walcott's interests was to find the correct sequence of faunas. This was an important discovery, and his mood improved with weather. The next day on Mount Bosworth, Burling and Walcott measured three thousand feet of section of the Mount Whyte Formation and established that the sequence there was *Olenellus* followed by *Albertella helena*.

It was time to pack; the result was 825 pounds at the freight depot. Sunday was a busman's holiday. They took a three-hour ride on a freight train west to Glenogle, looked at the section, and then for a treat came back in the caboose of a special mail and baggage train. There was time for a nap before getting on the train west to Vancouver. They looked at a couple of more boundary monuments, near the town—an eight-mile walk—and Walcott went on to Seattle; Burling joined his wife at Tacoma but caught up several days later.

By September 12, Walcott's train had passed Pocatello, and he disembarked at Alexandra, Idaho. He went to the Grace Plant of the Telluride Power Company and found number-two son, Sidney, well. Sidney had also been sent west for schooling and work with Mr. Nunn. Next, Charlie came in from Salt Lake City. They hired a teamster and cook and, thus augmented, went via Alexandra to Montpelier, Idaho, and thence to Ovid and Liberty into Mill Canyon, where they settled into camp about one and a half miles south of the Spence Shale bed. A few years earlier, Walcott had had good collecting here, and he wanted more material.

It took a day to locate a key horizon below a great band of shale, but then the fun began. "With B[urling] Cha[rles]'s & Sidney began systematic work on the Spence Gulch fossil bed. We met with fairly good success. Found a fine cystoid & a lot of trilobites" (September 17, 1907). (A cystoid is an extinct echinoderm, a very distant relative of a sand dollar.) To a paleontologist or even a paleontologist's child, there really is nothing to equal the thrill of collecting at a place rich in fossils. For a break, Charlie hunted grouse, and Sidney looked in the underlying sandstone, finding only fragmentary fossils.

The field party went back to Montpelier and continued to Salt Lake City. After the fossils had been shipped and the crew paid off, Burling and Sidney went to Washington. The two older Walcotts went to Provo and the Battle Creek and Olmstead plants of Telluride Power. There was sociability and business, but soon the Telluride Power Company transported Charles and Charlie back to Salt Lake City by automobile. They boarded the Union Pacific to Chicago, for what turned out to be a bad trip; the single-track line was overloaded, and there was delay after delay. They finally got to the Windy City by the first of October and to Washington the next day. Walcott actually took the rest of the day off before going to the Castle.

In less than a week, he polished off the mail and various loose ends and was back writing the introduction to his work on Cambrian brachiopods. The family was all under one roof again. Sidney was attending Western High School. Helen was at Holton Arms, a private school for girls. Stuart was plugging away at the France School, another private academy. Charlie was studying Spanish, in anticipation of a trip to Mexico with Mr. Nunn. The October days were fine, and the time was relaxing; fall is the best season in Washington.

Other duties called, and there was another trip to New York. Walcott spent the afternoon at the country place of Jacob H. Schiff; it never hurts to know better the people who have money, particularly if they wish to be friendly. The next day there was a meeting of the CIW Ex Comm, with a few words beforehand in Dr. Billings's ear, and then a quick trip to the American Museum of Natural History.

Then it was back to Washington and the routine of administration and research. The Ex Comm of the Carnegie generally alternated meetings between New York and Washington, and this time he did not have to go to New York. The CIW budget for the coming year was fixed, and Smithsonian administrative chores were taken care of. Maud Adams came to Washington to play the lead in *Peter Pan*, and that was a must for the Walcotts. There were a couple of lunches at the USGS, partly for old times' sake, though mostly to obtain information from the Technical Branch.

In mid-month, Walcott took a steamer south on the Chesapeake Bay. He saw the Jamestown Tricentennial Exposition, but his business was more important than checking the SI display. Walcott spoke to the National Advisory Board on Fuel and Structural Material Testing on two topics: the need for increased testing of material and fuel, and the need for research on materials. Back in Washington, the end of the month saw a big family social event, when Sydney Stevens,

Helena's half sister, married. Notwithstanding the wedding, Walcott got a bit of work on trilobites done at home.

November came and brought more interruptions to the work on monograph fifty-one. First was the CIW Ex Comm meeting in New York. Walcott also saw Mr. Harriman and, not wanting to waste more time when there were new fossils to be described, "wrote draft of new genus & species of trilobite on the train" (November 12, 1907). Next, only five days later he was back in New York to see Nunn and Harriman, on strictly commercial business for one day.

It was also the season for the National Academy's fall meeting. Walcott warmed up by giving a talk to A. W. Grabau's class at Columbia University, and then he lectured the NAS on a "Summary of Studies of Cambrian Brachiopods." On the train home with Helena and Charlie, who had come to New York for an eye examination, he wrote a draft description of a couple more of his Cambrian brachiopods. On the following days he seized scattered hours here and there for the monographic work.

Walcott recorded a crick in his back as a result of working in a cold attic room; this is the only indication of where his laboratory was located in his house. The Burlings dined with the Walcotts on Thanksgiving. A few days later came the "Regents meeting. I presented many matters of business all of which were acted upon" (December 3, 1907). It had taken little time for the new secretary to organize the board to his satisfaction.

That year, the dinner after the annual meeting of the CIW Board of Trustees, was in honor of Andrew D. White, the man who had steered Andrew Carnegie toward educational activity in America. White had helped Erza Cornell found Cornell University; White had wanted another university but was content with the research institution that had been created. Thereafter, the grippe laid Walcott low for two weeks. He did finally get to the office but, outside of testing several panorama cameras, did not accomplish much. Charlie left before Christmas; his father missed him. The annual meeting of the Ontario Apartment House Company took place, and 1907 ended.

In his annual summary at the back of his diary, Walcott remarked on his election as Smithsonian Institution secretary and his resignation from the USGS and the Reclamation Service. 1907 had been a year of major change. It had also been Walcott's third-poorest year as far as publications were concerned. Time spent on preparation matters a great deal, as witnessed by the ponderous monograph fifty-one, but there still was not much to show. Comments in *Science* rebutting Professor Branner's complaints about USGS work in Arkansas, a tribute to his pastor, and a eulogy to Louis Agassiz constituted his printed contributions; annual reports do not count. Even if they did, he did not write one for the U.S. Geological Survey, though the organization did mention his work in Canada;

the Smithsonian annual report for 1907 did not appear until 1908. If one needs a measure of how busy Walcott had been with administration, this lack of significant publications is it. A measure of his continuing interest in geology is the flood of publications after 1907.

Being a careful man, Walcott always put his address in the front of his pocket diary. For most years, it had been the USGS office. In 1907, he used 1743 22d Street, Washington, D.C., and for this new year of 1908, it was Smithsonian Institution, Washington, D.C. The twenty-six official calls he paid on the first day of 1908 set a record for him, but then he was traveling alone and could move faster; Helena was receiving at the home of Mr. and Mrs. James Garfield. Walcott also measured his children, for the record. Charlie was six feet, three inches, slightly taller than his father; Sidney was five feet, nine inches, and 135 pounds. Helen had likewise inherited a tall frame and was two inches taller than Sidney, though at the same weight. Though he still had some years to grow, young Stuart had reached four feet, ten inches, and ninety pounds.

Wasting no chance this new year for his politicking, the next day Walcott took the Speaker of the House, "Uncle Joe" Cannon, to see the new Museum building on the Mall. The year 1908 would be the first time Walcott appeared before the Appropriations Subcommittee in his new position, and he was not one to leave things to chance. Still, science had to have its share of time, and just before leaving for Philadelphia, he was arranging on plates drawings of trilobites.

On January 7, 1908, Dr. and Mrs. Walcott took the train to Philadelphia, where he was to be given the Hayden Memorial Geological Award by the Academy of Natural Sciences of Philadelphia. Ferdinand Vandeveer Hayden had been the head of one of the territorial surveys that had coalesced in 1879 to form the Geological Survey. Upon being notified of the award, Walcott wrote: "I remember that this medal was first awarded, in 1890, to my distinguished preceptor and patron, James Hall, whose memory will be dearer by this association with him through the action of your academy. And when I turn to read the names of those who have since likewise been honored . . . my pride and gratification become greater, I fear, than my deservedness. Yet I must not omit to recognize the fact that your award is, in part at least, a recognition of the service of our national geological survey."[4]

These particular words were written late in 1905. For a decade from 1890 onward, the medal was awarded annually. Then the committee decided that it should be awarded every three years; Sir Archibald Geikie, retired director of the Geological Survey of Great Britain, received it in 1902. Next it was decided to redesign the medal and strike it in gold. Unfortunately, the country was suffering a gold shortage—in other words the Hayden fund did not have enough money; the 1905 medal was delayed three years.

No matter. There was a first-rate dinner, and Prof. Persifor Frazer, the man who had not delivered on hosting the 1891 International Congress of Geologists in Philadelphia, did deliver some stirring words. He indicated that Walcott would have received the medal in 1899 except for the crime of being a young man. Honorary Dr. Walcott was up to the occasion. After thanking the academy and his associates and assistants on the Geological Survey, he praised that organization, went on to discuss his current position, and got to Hayden's character and work. Toward the end he waxed poetic, if not exactly grammatical: "I have often, when lying in my blankets on the great desert plains of the west, thought of the quality of the men, who like Dr. Hayden, alone, single handed, pushed their explorations, season after season, farther and farther into the unknown area, was sufficient to be able to commune with her and learn some of the secrets of her innermost existence."[5]

Helena went back to Washington and Walcott went on to New York City. "Talked with Mr. Russell Sage 5–6:30 P.M. on question of endowment for S.I. research" (January 8, 1908). Even after less than a year as secretary, Walcott was acutely aware of the small size of the SI endowment and was trying to raise funds. Next on his calendar was a diplomatic reception at the White House, and the following evening a musical. Meanwhile, he sent off the introduction to monograph fifty-one to Charles Schuchert at Yale, one of the few people who knew anything about brachiopods; Schuchert had also worked for James Hall and had spent a decade in the old USNM building. Of course, Walcott had to attend board meetings for the Iowa and Ontario apartment house corporations and meet with the board of the Washington Academy of Sciences; that academy too was trying to raise money for a building.

During the middle of January, Walcott went through the ritual of reelection to presidency of the WAS (Yochelson 1996). Then it was off to New York City once more to obtain John Cadwallader's advice regarding an advisory committee for the National Gallery of Art; a few days later, the committee was organized. While in New York he saw Mr. Carnegie again, which was pleasant and might eventually be profitable. The meeting of the regents went "smoothly & harmoniously."

At odd moments he crammed in work on monograph fifty-one, still not completed. It was far enough along so that he could give the revised introduction to E. O. Ulrich of the USGS. (Ulrich has been described as an outstanding paleontologist and a dreadful geologist.) When Ulrich finally returned the introduction, it was with more than fifty pages of comments, which says more about Ulrich than it does about Walcott's ideas.

There followed another quick trip to New York. He saw Harriman and conducted some Telluride Power Company business, but the prime reason was to join John Cadwallader at a dinner of the "Crew of the Half Moon." It is not clear what this takeoff on Henry Hudson's ship did, perhaps it was the seagoing equivalent of the Boone and Crockett Club, but it was one of those men-only social engagements that the secretary had to attend in his quest for money.

It took Walcott a Sunday at the office to catch up, for once again the Carnegie Ex Comm was meeting, and a new regent had to be appointed to the SI board; the latter was more complicated than one might imagine, as the specified geographic distribution of the regents was and is complex. Mid-February, he finally gave the British Columbia fossils some uninterrupted time. Among social events noted was a dinner Secretary of Interior Garfield gave for Theodore Roosevelt: the Garfields were becoming increasingly good friends. After dinner, Walcott took the night train to New York; this time it was Telluride Power business between Nunn and Harriman.

George Washington's Birthday was appropriately celebrated by a meeting of the Washington Monument Society. One can never say how various contacts will turn out to be useful. The geologist George F. Becker was interested in stress-and-strain effects in rocks. He wanted to hang a wire inside the monument and measure how much it stretched under its own weight. Walcott supported a grant from the CIW and no doubt whispered in the ear of Secretary of War William Howard Taft, who had ultimate jurisdiction over the monument, that this was a good idea and that Dr. Becker would not injure the structure.

Walcott kept on with monograph fifty-one but took time to speak to a senator concerning a monument for Major Powell. The major deserved one, and Walcott made it a point of honor to pursue this task. Nunn and Eugene Steigmeyer of Telluride Power came into town briefly and then left for Chicago. Walcott had "a busy day at the office & at hearing before Secretary of Interior Garfield on hydroelectric power rights in forest reserves" (February 26, 1908). This was not a conflict of interest, for Walcott was no longer involved with the Departments of the Interior or Agriculture. That night, the University Club had its annual dinner, and any impression that Walcott was using influence at a hearing faded under the effect of fine wines and good cigars, even if Walcott did not smoke or drink.

Walcott wrote the next day, "Am trying to complete a little paper on Mount Stephen B.C. for Canadian Alpine Club" (February 27, 1908); a week and half later, despite numerous interruptions, the manuscript was nearly complete. Among the interruptions was a visit by Mr. Charles Freer of Detroit (immortalized in the Freer Gallery of Art.) Another interruption was a quick trip to New York. He and Helena had been invited to the Harriman's daughter's wedding. Back home, Nunn and Mr. Green of the power plant in Ontario came to call.

There were more complications for Walcott from his former positions. The Southern Pacific, owned by Harriman, had instituted a claim for its efforts in staunching the flow of the Colorado River into the Salton Sea. Railroad car after railroad car of rocks and dirt had had to be dumped into the break before the flow stopped (Newell 1908). Of course, if the SP had not fixed the break, the Southern Pacific would have been out of business; as it was, the railroad had to move its line several times as the waters rose. It was going to take a White House conference to sort out how much the company should be paid for its efforts. That chore done, Walcott went back to his British Columbia fossils and completed his Alpine Club paper (Walcott 1908a).

This little paper is a curious item. It is a popular account in three pages of the geology of the Mount Stephen area, followed by eight detailed pages of measured section and faunal lists. Walcott probably remembered his days at Trenton Falls, when fossil collecting was a pursuit of the tourist; he now indicated both by word and illustration where the best fossils were and included five plates of line drawings of the more common forms. Walcott knew how to assemble a popular paper; among his panorama photographs was a shot of Stuart and Helen collecting fossils.

This may be a good place to digress and discuss places of publication. Members of a governmental organization, such as the New York State Museum or the USGS, would ordinarily use their own outlets. Walcott earlier also had many papers in professional journals. His journal of choice was the *American Journal of Science*; more of his papers appeared there than in any other journal. In the context of those times, "choice" may be a poor word, for until 1887 there were essentially no other American journal outlets for geologic papers. When the Geological Society of America began publishing its *Bulletin*, Walcott contributed several manuscripts (Yochelson 1988). More or less coincidentally with the death in 1895 of James Dwight Dana, longtime editor of *AJS*, the *Journal of Geology* began; Walcott gave it three papers in five years.

One reason an author might submit a manuscript to a journal rather than his organization's outlet is size. In general, the USGS did not publish extremely short works. Another is the hope, sometimes realized, of faster publication. One more reason was distribution to a somewhat different audience. When Walcott became Smithsonian secretary, he moved into the best of all possible worlds, at least from the standpoint of publication. The *Smithsonian Miscellaneous Collections* were issued quarterly, like a journal. The editing was of high quality, and funds for publication were assured. As with a journal, the quality of illustrations was excellent by the standards of the time. An author could also obtain reprints of individual articles to distribute to those who might be interested.

Walcott had a manuscript slated for a volume of the *SMC* in 1907, but he withdrew it and delayed a few months so as to have this little paper start another volume the next year. Even better, Walcott could have an overall, general title; so five entire volumes of SMC are called "Cambrian Geology and Paleontology." So much for the outline of Walcott's next two decades of publication.

Along with his contribution in the *Canadian Alpine Journal*, in 1908, Walcott put five papers into volume 53 of SMC; thereafter he almost never thereafter published in scientific journals. The first of these five works was a short paper that gave new formation names, so that they could be used in monograph fifty-one; the last, a longer one, gave measured sections and correlations for the new formations. A paper on Cambrian trilobites was followed by two on Cambrian brachiopods. The first indicated that the manuscript for the monograph was in the hands of the editors and was to appear in 1909 (Walcott missed by three long years). The second brachiopod paper was based largely on material drawn from the introduction to the large work. Ever mindful of proper procedure, Walcott put in this paper a footnote indicating that it had been published with the permission of the USGS director.

With the Alpine Club paper behind him, for once, Walcott recorded feeling well and not driven by any fixed engagement. Still, with his temperament he simply could not sit still; if there was no outside pressure on him for action, he would initiate something. Two days later, he was talking to the local gentry about art organizations in Washington, gradually building support for the new National Gallery of Art.

On March 25, 1908, Secretary Walcott in his new office first appeared before the House Appropriations Subcommittee. The previous year's budget had been assembled by Acting Secretary Rathbun and had been defended before Walcott really appeared on the scene. Walcott wasted no time in getting the committee's attention, and his words are still pertinent to any attempt to understand the complexities of the Smithsonian Institution.

> Mr. Chairman, I have long been acquainted with the Institution and its branches, having been a member of the Museum staff since 1884, and on assuming the secretaryship I looked very carefully into the conditions and workings of each branch in charge of the Institution. I noticed, first, the peculiarity in the institution that Congress to a certain extent shares in its government. There is a Board of Regents of fourteen. Three members of the House, three members of the Senate, and the Vice-President and Chief Justice of the United States are members of that board, and in addition Congress confirms by its election the six citizen members of the board, so that it has a voice in the organization of the board, and of course through its membership from the House and Senate it can keep in full touch and take part in directing the operations of the branches of the Institution. I think this is a peculiarity not shared by any other Government organization. The Congress

in making appropriations for other Government purposes turns the money over to the Departments and organizations, and after that has no control or supervision over it whatever. (Walcott 1908b, 105)

Walcott then immediately threw in a few sentences about the Fish Commission, a predecessor agency to the Fish and Wildlife Service. The message was obvious that investigations by Secretary Baird had led to the creation of a bureau in the Department of Commerce and Labor, which now paid economic dividends. He went on, even more briefly, to the Weather Service, which had been started by Secretary Joseph Henry. It made good economic sense for Congress to invest in the Smithsonian.

Next, Walcott moved to the National Zoological Park; after getting started, he turned matters over to Superintendent Frank Baker. Baker and Walcott joined forces to impress upon the committee the limitations of the National Zoo, compared to its rival in New York City. Then came the work of the Bureau of American Ethnology and its involvement in native races of Hawaii and Samoa, a consequence of American expansionism; William Henry Holmes carried this ball. Walcott spoke of the coming Museum building and made a pitch for funds to turn the SI Castle into an art gallery. Mr. Rathbun filled in details concerning the new Museum building being constructed and its furnishings. Assistant Secretary Adler defended the International Exchange Service, and Charles Greeley Abbot ended the hearing with a discussion of the Astrophysical Observatory.

Walcott delegated testimony to those who were in charge of spending the funds, quite a break with the tradition of Secretary Langley. Langley had replied to every question, but he had often left the room to ask his staff, waiting in the hall, for the answers. Some years, committee members vied to see who could make the secretary leave the room the most times.

Not only were the hearings dramatically different from Langley's day, but the entire atmosphere had changed. One incident, probably either in 1907 (when the astronomer George Ellery Hale lectured to the NAS) or in 1908 (when he spoke at the SI) is worth mentioning. "Calling on Secretary Walcott one day, Dr. Hale found his door open and Walcott full of jokes with his feet on the table. Hale told me the contrast with his "moon visit" to Langley in the "dim religious light" of the Regent's Room with a corps of stenographers to record his words of wisdom, and the chief men of the Institution all about to listen to them, was indeed startling" (Abbot 1958, 97–98).

Once when George Ellery Hale had brought photographs of the moon for Langley to see, Langley had kept him for hours; Mrs. Hale twice tried to get a messenger to contact her husband, but the man had been too terrified of Langley to interrupt. Walcott was a breath of fresh air.

To return to 1908, Walcott went to a Hamilton College alumni dinner and exchanged remarks with politician Elihu Root about the old days in central New York. He discussed a National Academy of Arts with a few people who might be able to make such an organization viable, and then went to the annual Boone and Crockett dinner. A couple of days later, "Sister Josie came at 4:15 for a visit. This is my 58th birthday. I am in good health & busily engaged in administrative & scientific work. Am planning for ten years [sic] work & hope that I can continue at it longer" (March 31, 1908). Walcott would live up to his plan and in fact nearly double it.

The first Sunday in April was another family milestone. As Walcott phrased it, the youngest child, Stuart, was "united" with the Church of the Covenant. It was a satisfied father who took the increasing familiar train to New York. Among the items was a meeting with Cousin Fred Walcott, who just happened to work for the General Electric Corporation, not a bad connection for someone associated with the Telluride Power Company. Walcott gathered up William Henry Holmes, and they went off to Detroit and the home of Charles Freer for two days. Walcott wrote, "I greatly enjoyed my visit with Mr. Freer & have a bit of an impression of the great collection he has given to the Smithsonian" (April 10, 1908).

It was back to Washington, and to the comments of Professor Schuchert on the introduction to the Cambrian brachiopods. Switching gears, the Walcotts gave a formal dinner for the new Advisory Committee on the National Gallery of Art, introducing them to several of the regents. There was a little time to switch back to Middle Cambrian fossils from Malad, Idaho, and then came the Carnegie Ex Comm meeting; Walcott saw to it that Speaker Cannon and Secretary of Agriculture Wilson were guests at the CIW dinner. The NAS academicians came for their annual meeting. A quick trip to New York ensued. Fred Walcott went with him to see Harriman, and then Cousin Charles talked to two trust companies; the electric power business in the West was getting serious. Back in Washington, Walcott studied the Cambrian brachiopods from the Blacksmith Fork section in southern Idaho.

Walcott began May with a nearly uninterrupted day writing up the geologic sections of Idaho. On another day, he spent the morning looking at Cambrian fossils from the House Range in western Utah, and the afternoon at the home of Mrs. James Pinchot, speaking to a group of ladies interested in the fine arts; if anything, the stretch in activities was getting wider. From fine arts, he went to the White House, where Roosevelt had convened his famous conference of governors on the subject of conservation. Walcott noted that TR gave a fine address. He spent the next three full days listening to the formal speeches and working behind the scenes for protection of America's rivers and forests.

Mr. Harriman came to town, and this provided the excuse for a small dinner to welcome a new ambassador. The Walcotts did not entertain as much at home as they were invited out to dine, but they did their fair share in the Washington social whirl. Walcott observed Charlie's nineteenth birthday, a bit sad that he was away in Olmstead, Utah. Judging from his diary and a few letters, Walcott was evenhanded and loving to all his children, but his firstborn and namesake must have had a special place. If any twinge of missing Charlie was present, Walcott buried it in describing stratigraphic sections of the Cordilleran area.

On the first of June, Helena and Helen went to Madison, Wisconsin, for a wedding, leaving Walcott with Sidney and Stuart. In the role of bachelor father, the secretary did surprisingly well. He took the boys out twice for rifle practice and once horseback riding. They entertained Joe Iddings, Walcott's tentmate at Eureka, Nevada, at dinner. Walcott managed to work in these events between the Washington Academy of Sciences board, a meeting of the trustees of George Washington University, and another visit from L. L. Nunn. He also looked at Lower Cambrian fossils from Nevada and had the office shipshape when he and the two boys left for Buffalo on the 19th.

Mr. Burling joined them in Toronto, and the Canadian Pacific moved them to Winnipeg. Walcott wrote to Helena on their anniversary and told her how happy his twenty years of marriage had been. At Medicine Hat, between trains, they saw a ball game. The train crossed Crowsnest Pass and headed for Fernie; Walcott and the boys looked at the coke ovens and then reboarded for Belton, Montana. The canyon cut by the south fork of Flathead River exposed a fine section of the Precambrian rocks, so Walcott and Burling walked the tracks to examine them. Unlike the field season of the year before, this one was to be mainly in older rocks of the Precambrian.

It took a day to gather supplies and get organized, but Walcott, Burling, Sidney, Stuart, Reuten the packer, and Ward the cook finally started north with the pack string of ten animals. Outside of initial saddle soreness, the first part of the trip to Kitla Lake was fine. They had to clear some trail to get to the Continental Divide so that Walcott could take panorama pictures. For a point of reference, the party was in what is now Glacier National Park.

They went back west to the Flathead River Valley, north into British Columbia, and then into the drainage of Old Man River across the Continental Divide. The Altyn Limestone yielded some fossils, or perhaps pseudofossils. After a few more days of poking around, Walcott pronounced, "As far as I can see there is no Cambrian or 'Castle Mountain series' strata in this area or south to Lake McDonald or north beyond the Crows Nest Pass line of the C.P. Ry" (July 15, 1908). The party continued moving, looking at rocks and taking an occasional photograph. By the third week in July, it had come 284 miles by horseback and was in its thirteenth camp. The men spent a day or two more around Waterton Lakes in Canada.

Burling brought in the mail; that may sound trivial, but it involved a fifty-two-mile ride. Walcott had wanted news, and he got it from the acting chief clerk in a three-page letter. Among other items, he learned that the coming International Tuberculosis Congress was developing well, the only question being whether Walcott's august presence would be necessary. Walcott wrote a hasty note to Assistant Secretary Rathbun. (If there was any doubt that the secretary had a happy administration, this letter is addressed to "My dear Sir Richard.")

> I am sitting on a rock (cold) while the men are finishing the packing of the mules. We start in a few minutes *via* Waterton lake trail for the u.s. Expect to reach Belton by Aug *4th–5th*. Will get supplies there & probably work south.
>
> Will you not ask Mr. Adams to send me 4–$50 checks—on acct personal salary? Will need cash in Aug. All well & all going well. Only one troublesome problem remains that I expect to get at tomorrow. We have had 5 days of heat & wind but this morning the air is cool—bracing & from the west. A perfect late Sept. day at home.
>
> Trust you are well & all is well with you & yours.
>
> I have ridden some 300 miles thus far & feel fine.[6]

While the Walcott party gradually moved south, Assistant Secretary Adler was preparing to leave the Smithsonian for academia. He contributed enough to the institution during his tenure that a few words are appropriate; his own words are best.

> Walcott and I were good friends, and I was very glad to continue to be of service to him and to the Institution, as I had been under Langley, but I did feel that Walcott had not the same need of me as Langley had. He himself was an experienced administrator and devoted his time to the administration of the Institution, except during the summer, when he went to the Rocky Mountains, whereas Mr. Langley's scientific work occupied him virtually every day of the week and quite a number of hours a day.
>
> One of the last incidents of importance concerning the Smithsonian Institution occurred in the summer of 1908, when I was Acting Secretary, and had to do with the expedition of President Theodore Roosevelt to Africa. Some time in June, Mr. Roosevelt[,] who had already gone from Washington to his home in Oyster Bay, telegraphed the Smithsonian that he intended immediately after the 4th of March [1909], when his term of office would expire, to do a year's big game hunting in Africa, that he would get up an expedition, take his son with him and pay his own and his son's expenses, but that he could not afford to pay the expenses of the taxidermist and the

shipment of specimens, and if the Smithsonian Institution could supply these two things, he would give all these specimens to the Smithsonian, if not, he would offer them to another museum. I was in a quandary. Owing to the system of government appropriations, item by item, there was not a single cent free in our budget for expeditions. I assembled the few curators connected with the Zoological Department, who told me that it would be very important if the collection could be obtained for the Institution, because Roosevelt was a good naturalist and there would be éclat connected with the collection made by a former President of the United States.

It was a very hot day in June and it was not my custom to go home for luncheon, because our apartment was several miles from the Institution. However, I thought I would take the best counsel a man could obtain, go home and ask my wife's advice as to whether she thought there was any possibility in Washington of my raising the money toward such an expedition. She told me I ought to try, whereupon I did try; and the first man I went to was Oscar Strauss. I told him the story, and he at once said to me: "I will give you $5000 towards that." This start so encouraged me that I telegraphed Mr. Roosevelt that the Institution would accept his proposal. Four days after that, we got in telegraphic communication with Secretary Walcott, who approved my action, and when he came back in the autumn, he successfully collected the rest of the fund. (Adler 1941, 270–72)

Not only did Walcott fully approve of the action, shortly thereafter he sent Adler a chatty account of his field activities. "We arrived at Belton, last eve after a 9 (nine) hrs ride—on trails—Breakfast at 5 A.M. a rest of 3½ at noon & dinner at 8:30." He noted that the packer was taking half the string of packhorses to his ranch, as Sidney and Burling would be leaving that Sunday. Young Stuart would continue with his father for the rest of the season. "All has gone along finely—Weather good—Scenery superb. Geology on a grand scale." Burling had gone to Fernie to pick up the trunks, but a forest fire had wiped out several railway bridges and burned two stations. "The air is hazy with smoke—Days hot—nights cool. Four (4) blankets over me last night. We are camped about 100 feet above the river in a [*sic*] open grove—a cold rivulet runs near by & the grass is fine for the animals—The boys look tough but they are happy & well. Stuart will have much to do on the next trip. Sidney has been a good asst. packer the past five (5) weeks. He is strong, willing and active—Sorry to have him return."[7]

Earlier, Adler had written Walcott about errors in one of the stratigraphic papers, concerned with conversion of feet to meters and miles to kilometers. Burling wrote Washington acknowledging his mistakes, but the paper had already been printed. "B. told me about the errors in the proof of my papers—It was the one thing I left entirely to him. Will be more guarded in the future—I am very thankful that Chester caught the blunder-Please thank him."[8] A small sheet of errata for volume fifty-two was mailed by the SI to correct the errors. However, Burling redeemed himself by recovering the trunks before the train station burned.

The reduced party moved east to the Continental Divide and crossed at Gunsight Pass. Walcott took photographs and "with Stuart searched for fossils in the lower portion of the Siyah limestone. We found fine Cryptozoon sp. but nothing else—All conditions point to the pre-Cambrian age of the Siyah & overlying formations" (August 7, 1908). Walcott's views on Cambrian and older had changed since his 1882–83 winter in the Grand Canyon, where the supposed Cambrian rocks seemed to extend downward practically forever. They moved upward to the Sperry Glacier; the huge panorama camera required an animal by itself. The trip was good, and after returning to Belton for supplies, they packed into the mountains again, up the south fork of the Flathead River. In the cliffs near Spotted Bean Creek, Walcott collected Cambrian fossils and then moved to Big Salmon Creek, where again the Cambrian limestones capped the Algonkian red beds. The party moved once more. "Did not get any new varieties of fossils on Gordon Creek but freshened my knowledge of their mode of occurrence etc. preparatory to going at the section on Gordon Mountain" (August 22, 1908).

A toothache laid Walcott low for a day, but he had come too many miles not to go on to Gordon Mountain. "I found the *Albertella* fauna extended down to within 40 feet of the contact of the Algonkian & Cambrian. Driven in at 3 P.M. by strong snow squalls" (August 25, 1908). To translate this into English, in British Columbia Walcott had found a great thickness of beds containing the older *Olenellus*, but here, if *Olenellus* was present at all, it occupied only forty feet or less of strata. This is the sort of data needed to plot the extent of ancient seas. Stuart and his father were assisted by the packer in gathering trilobites; in the Walcott camp, everyone collected.

They moved to White Creek and up to the Continental Divide for more photographs. Walcott enlisted someone from the Forest Service for this jaunt, as the weather was turning nasty; Stuart aided the packer in moving the camp once more. By the end of the month, they were back at Spotted Bean Creek and in the thirty-sixth camp of season. Setting up a camp is no mean feat; moving camp every other day is quite a chore. Walcott went up-slope again for photographs and spent the night in a spike camp, leaving the main camp and camps a night or so with the minimum of equipment. "Returned to camp on Spotted Bean Creek. A tedious work as there are no trails & there was much sidehill & windfall work. . . . Have not had a haircut since June 16th" (September 3, 1908).

This was an exciting trip for Stuart. One afternoon he helped catch twenty trout for dinner. The next day he helped shoot and butcher a buck elk. Thereafter, it was mist and rain as the party went back to Belton; camping and trail riding is not all fun. Walcott caught up on the mail, and they were off again, following the route of the Great Northern Railway to Nyack, where Walcott and Mr. Weeks had worked a decade earlier. It took two more days of riding to reach the Continental Divide, where more photographs were the order of the day. Anyone who has been in Glacier National Park knows just how spectacular the scenery is, be it sunshine or mist. Of mist and rain there was plenty, as they slowly returned west, looking at the geology all the way. "Went up 2700 feet on N.E. side of river N.E. of Paola—Could not see peaks of main range" (September 17, 1908).

Rain or not, they had a schedule to keep and a couple more hard rides to meet it. When the two Walcotts caught the train from Belton to Helena, Walcott's report for the summer included forty-nine camps and 957 miles on horseback. Naturally, Walcott had to spend part of a day looking at the section east of Helena before they went on to Butte and saw the copper-reduction works, while waiting for a connection to the eastbound train.

The next stop was Salt Lake City and Stuart's big brother Charlie. Then they called at the office of Telluride Power and went south to Provo. Walcott conferred with Nunn concerning permits for dam construction in national forest reserves. He walked up Provo Ridge with Charlie, perhaps to explain a letter he had written. Charlie had offered to hunt bear and elk for the new displays, but Walcott had declined, in part because there was no money, and in part because it would be inappropriate for Charlie to take the time away from his employer, Telluride Power. Oldest and youngest brother had only a short visit. On the trip to Chicago Walcott wrote up field notes and labeled his photographs, but the trip was more tedious than usual. October was at hand when Helena, Helen, and Sidney met the two travelers.

Walcott registered for the International Tuberculosis Conference, held in the unfinished New National Museum (Yochelson 1985). Construction was suspended for a week while temporary displays were installed and the auditorium was used for the first time. It was a major event both for Washington and in the history of the "white plague." Walcott called on Teddy Roosevelt to finalize Smithsonian participation in his African trip, gave his views on the merits of a bureau for health and education under the secretary of interior, and four days after his return was correcting page proofs.

October 11, the peripatetic Walcott was off to New York for the Ex Comm of CIW, but also to conduct a bit of Telluride Power business. He went on to New York Mills, packed the trunks of ailing sister Josie (who was coming to Washington), and put flowers on his mother's grave. In Washington, he met with the Commission on Organization of Government Scientific Work and accepted money from a regent for a flight cage at the zoo, but he could not concentrate on SI affairs, for his sister was failing rapidly. The day William Howard Taft was elected president, she died; Walcott and Helena took her body to upstate New York. Otis Tufts Mason, head curator of anthropology, also died while Walcott was away. Brother Ellis came to Utica for the funeral and returned to Washington with them. It was a good visit with an older man whom he rarely saw, and that partially healed the loss of Josie.

After Ellis left, the CIW Ex Comm met, and then the fall meeting of the NAS, in Baltimore, ensued. Routine further helped in healing. Back to New York again, he saw cousin Fred and Mr. Harriman on business. There was more than electric power in Walcott's New York business dealings: "With the latter [Stilwell] I called on Prest. Underwood of the Erie Railroad to present the Hackensack Meadows scheme to him" (November 20, 1908). It will be for others to trace the many paths of Walcott, business tycoon.

Walcott was after Harriman to speak at an upcoming mining congress. This took yet another trip to New York, but Walcott landed him. The first week in December, Charlie came back from Utah; Walcott hardly had time to say more than hello before he and Helena were in New York again, to attend a wedding. By now, things were running so smoothly that one day Walcott had a meeting of the CIW Ex Comm in the morning and the Smithsonian Institution regents in the afternoon yet found hardly anything from either to note in his diary.

The first month of winter brought another family milestone, when Helen went out to her first dinner party. Walcott worked a little on a lecture to be given a couple of weeks later. Christmas was a happy time, and the following day he was able to look at some Grand Canyon fossils. On the 28th, in Baltimore, the joint audiences of the American Association for the Advancement of Science and Geological Society of America heard about the "Influence of environment on Early Paleozoic Faunas." "Walcott followed conservatively the lines of classification laid down in his earlier papers on the Cambrian of North America. He felt obliged by the state of investigations to confine his discussion largely to evidence afforded by the brachiopods and indicated that more elaborate conclusions might be suggested by a similar thorough study of the trilobites and other elements of the fauna" (Gulliver 1909, 749).

That comment might have summarized the talk, but the paper, short as it was, covered more ground. Walcott used the word "evolution" in his title. He did not speculate on origin of the Cambrian fauna but was content to analyze what was known of the diversity and distribution of fossil forms. He concluded that the Early Cambrian seas had been warm, because of the presence of corallike organisms, archaeocyathids; that the Middle Cambrian fauna had been more diverse, because the seas were more widespread; that part of the reason for this diversity had been the development of provincial or isolated faunas; and that after the Middle Cambrian, interchange of currents had resulted in nearly cosmopolitan faunas. "In other words it is evident that the evolution of the early Paleozoic faunas was profoundly influenced by their environment" (Walcott 1909, 202). These generalizations still hold.

New Year's Eve was quiet, and Walcott chose not to sum up his year. New Year's Day was quite different, for instead of official calls, he returned to Baltimore for meetings. The next day he toured the new Museum building, still not finished, and later heard Bailey Willis recount his adventures in China. Walcott set a new record date for his first trip of the year to New York. By January 3 he was chasing J. P. Morgan for a donation; he saw Morgan's pipe organ and new library but missed the man himself on this occasion. Still, the trip was not a total loss, as he called on Carnegie, Harriman, and Schiff; eventually there would be money to support Theodore Roosevelt's collecting in Africa.

Thereafter, it was "a busy day at my office getting various matters of administration closed up & mail attended to. Did not get time to work over any personal scientific papers until after dinner at home" (January 7, 1909). He had his first committee meeting of the year, concerned with matters of the NAS; that organization had not occupied much of his time since he had resigned as treasurer, but now in his role as vice president it was to take increasing amounts of his time. Another trip to New York followed, for yet another meeting of the CIW Ex Comm, which ate up two days.

Walcott prepared a note for a popular magazine on future activities of the SI: "While the history and achievements of the Smithsonian Institution are widely known, it is not generally understood that it receives no grants of money from the United States Government, but is wholly dependent for its maintenance and operations upon means derived from private sources. Nor do the American people realize fully that the Institution was funded by a bequest to their nation, formally accepted by them. A conception of the true position of the Institution is perhaps slightly confused by the fact that it directs research in several government agencies" (Walcott 1909a, 585–86).

He suggested that if the Smithsonian endowment were to be increased, the institution could undertake research into earthquakes, study the American people in detail, explore in Central and South America, and undertake various less costly research subjects. Walcott never thought small. His last line hints at the distinction between the Smithsonian's private funds and congressional appropriations for government agencies, and for generations these two sources of money were kept rigidly separate, even if the outside world called it all "Smithsonian."

By mid-month Walcott was able to get back to looking at Grand Canyon Cambrian fossils, for two hours. His annual reelection to presidency of the Washington Academy of Sciences came and went. The last week in January, the family was again split up. "Sidney left for Olmstead Utah—He is not strong & the west will do him good" (January 26, 1909); it would be a long while before Sidney was home again.

On the first of February, Walcott went before the Subcommittee on Appropriations, as always with the hope of increasing funds. A few days later he took the SI regents on a tour through the New National Museum, nearly complete on the outside but with much interior finishing still needed. This month, on another trip to New York, he had a late-evening meeting with Harriman, and the next day saw other monied folk—De Forest, Schiff, and one or two more. The Walcotts gave a dinner for Secretary of Interior Garfield. A few evenings later they dined with the secretary of agriculture to honor outgoing President Roosevelt; Walcott looked over the Rough Rider's plans for the African trip. The evening after that, the George Washington Memorial Association (GWMA) gave a dinner for Vice President–elect James S. Sherman. Walcott always seemed to have luck as well as skill. Although he knew incoming President Taft well, his relations were not as close as those he had had with TR. However, it turned out that Sherman was an old Utica boy, so there was another channel to 1600 Pennsylvanian Avenue, if Walcott ever needed it. Besides, Sherman would be another friend on the Board of Regents.

Walcott wrote his second son in Utah, "We are thinking of changing our horses etc., into a White Steamer [automobile,] 20 H.P. Mother would miss her slender Proctor—but we could get about town easily & not feel for the muscles of the horses. The auto has limitations but not those of horses. Perhaps we will long for old Jack & Frank. . . . Keep up *deep* breathing morning—noon and night. Strong lungs mean good blood & that means good blood & nerves. With love from all & from your father."[9] Less than two weeks later, Walcott jotted, "At my office during the day. Time for a little work on Cambrian trilobites. Began using a new White Steamer automobile" (February 21, 1909).

It was off to New York once more. The GWMA was moving toward receiving congressional approval to build on government land. That action required pulling lots of strings and seeking lots of funds. This was also the occasion of a Peace Dinner honoring Elihu Root.

The first of March brought a formal call to bid farewell to President Roosevelt. When President Taft was inaugurated, the weather was so bad that Walcott and Charlie witnessed the ceremony in the Senate chamber. It was not a bad omen, as the following day "Congress increased appropriations for S.I. branches

$251,000 = $740,00 total" (March 5, 1909). It was a happy Walcott who went to New York to speak to the Pen & Brush Club. Modifying by-laws of the GWMA and the executive committee of that organization took another day; a scheme was evolving for the proposed building, when built, to be placed under the control of the Smithsonian. Walcott attended a dinner in honor of William T. Evans, an art patron of the Smithsonian, at the National Arts Club. For a physical scientist, Walcott was working the arts circle in a diligent manner.

Perhaps he was working a bit too diligently. After a dinner for the German ambassador and one day with the beloved trilobites, Walcott's sciatic nerve in his right leg acted up so violently that he went to the Washington Sanatorium. A dinner had been planned for his fifty-ninth birthday, but Walcott could not move. It was more than a week before he was even able to arrange figures of trilobites for the plates of part 6 of his *Contributions*. Two weeks passed before he wrote, "Am very glad to get back to our home & family" (April 12, 1909).

> A week after I called upon you in New York, I was so unfortunate as to wrench my leg in stepping on a street car, and the next morning was laid up with an acute attack of sciatica. This continued for two week, the doctors treating me at the sanatorium with the usual remedies for such trouble, including hot baths, electricity, etc. I then notified them that [they] did not know what my trouble was, and returned home and sent for Doctor John Dunlop, a young man trained at Johns Hopkins and in Boston. He soon located the source of the irritation to the nerve by finding the hip bone had been slightly displaced at the sacral joints. He then drew the bone back into place with strips of plaster, and in twenty-four hours the sciatica was a thing of the past. I lost sixteen pounds in weight, and was generally pulled down by the two weeks of pain.[10]

Walcott hobbled off to the NAS council meeting, grateful to be up, and he was still moving slowly at the Academy annual meeting. Near the end of the month, a meeting ensued with Gifford Pinchot, two Forest Service lawyers, Sen. Reed Smoot, and Nunn and Steigmeyer of Telluride Power. It does not take great power of divination to figure out that Telluride wanted to put dams in forest reserves in the state of Utah. It does not take much more to predict that all went smoothly. Walcott ended the month with CIW business.

On May day, Walcott signed the budget estimates for 1910 and left for New York; probably it would have been cheaper for him to buy his very own seat on the train, since he was on this run so often. After lunch with the Harrimans, Walcott left to pursue various folk concerning the actual building of the GWMA structure. Walcott also got in a few hours with Nunn and Harriman, discussing water power.

It was back to Washington to clear up a few points with the Forest Service and then home, sick from overdoing. Walcott got in a morning at the office but lunched at home and attended to the affairs of the GWMA. That evening he received a portrait of Adm. George W. Melville from the American Society of Mechanical Engineers for the National Gallery of Art. Sick or not, he came up with the appropriate words for the occasion (Walcott 1909b) and kept moving.

Sunday came, but the ailing Walcott ducked church and went to York, Pennsylvania, to see Prof. Atreus Wanner and tramp the hills in the sunshine. They looked at Lower Cambrian shales near town; Walcott was pleased to find the large, bottom-dwelling trilobite *Olenellus* and the tiny floater *Agnostus* in the same bit of rock. Professor Warner had sent Walcott a growth series of *Olenellus* collected around York, and Walcott wanted to see the rocks that had yielded these fossils. An interested collector who lived on the outcrop and would donate his collections was the best of all possible worlds. Small wonder that Walcott coined the trilobite name *Wanneria*. He moved from York to Professor Justin Roddy at Millersville and continued his working holiday.

It was a refreshed Walcott who returned to Washington a week later. He called on President Taft, and he prepared estimates for fiscal year 1910. That out of the way, it was off to New York City. Friday and Saturday were given to hydroelectric power concerns in the west. On Sunday he saw Dr. Billings on CIW business, and Monday he devoted to the GWMA. He came back to correspondence and "odds and ends."

The second of June saw Walcott in New York once more, meeting with directors of Telluride Power for a day; on July 1, Walcott became a company director in name as well as in fact. He went home, collected Helena and trunks, and returned immediately to New York. Charlie was left in charge in Washington; Sidney was still at Olmstead, Utah; Helen was in Lynn, Massachusetts; and Stuart was with the Garfield family in West Mountain, Ohio. With the family scattered but safe, Helena and Walcott departed on the *Celtic* for their second trip to England—and a great event. Letters, shuffleboard, and fiddling with plates for a coming publication took some of the time, but most of it went to napping as the Walcotts steamed toward Liverpool. The last vestige of sciatica vanished— at least for now.

The Walcotts were dutiful tourists, seeing Melrose Abby and Walter Scott's home Abbotsford before taking the train to Edinburgh. Walcott spent part of the day talking to geologists, while Helena shopped. Then they headed north with two British geologists, Dr. B. N. Peach (in charge of the Edinburgh office of the Geological Survey) and a Mr. H. Brantwood Muff. They spent a couple of days looking at Lower Cambrian rocks and actually found a few *Olenellus*

(Yochelson 1997). The Walcott party moved on to Skibo Castle and spent the night with the laird and Mrs. Carnegie; Mr. Muff vanished. The next day they toured the grounds and went to services dedicating a new organ that Mr. C. had given a local church. Dr. Peach took them back to Edinburgh, and Walcott had nearly a full day examining Cambrian fossils at the Geological Survey and the Royal Scottish Museum; Peach lent him specimens for his coming paper. Walcott wrote, "He rendered great service to Scotland in visiting the best localities in the North-West Highlands where the *Olenellus* fauna occurs in our Cambrian rocks. He was so much impressed with our specimens that he arranged to have a special collection made at the best locality and sent to himself. He also helped us in determining a collection of doubtful fossils found in altered rocks along the eastern border of metamorphic rocks of the Scottish Highlands. At my request he readily undertook to do this service if the collections were sent to him for determination. His opinion regarding the probable age of the fossils was highly valued."[11]

After Walcott's stint at the museum, the couple took the sleeping car to Cambridge. At the university Walcott spent the day in the Sedgwick Museum looking at fossils, as he had done in 1888. This time he was not a struggling geologist but a distinguished one, invited to receive an honorary degree on the occasion of the fiftieth anniversary of the publication of Charles Darwin's *The Origin of Species*. This time Walcott received a doctor of science degree, as befitted the occasion, not a doctorate of laws. The three days at Cambridge made a profound impression, and Walcott repeatedly commented on how well the affair had been organized. He asked Regent Henderson to translate the Latin citation for him, and whenever there was an opportunity, he wore his scarlet robe. His first honorary degree, from Hamilton College in 1898, may have meant more at the time, but he remembered Cambridge for years.

The finale was a day in London, where, not surprisingly, Walcott was to be found at the museum in South Kensington. The Walcotts were dined and taken to the grand opera. The next day, it was a bit of a struggle to get packed in time for the train to Southampton and the *Minewaska*. The couple had had a scant two weeks in Britain, but the trip had produced a storehouse of pleasant memories. On the return voyage the weather was indifferent to poor, and there was little opportunity for him to work. Walcott noted averaging twelve hours of sleep a day.

When the *Minewaska* steamed into New York Harbor, Jacob Schiff met the couple and took them to lunch at his country place, where they could regain their land legs. They returned down the Hudson by boat. While Walcott called on the wealthy and the well-to-do of New York business society, Helena went north to investigate the Westover School at Waterbury, Connecticut, and other private schools in Massachusetts. She could move through business as promptly as her husband. Two days after landing they were home.

During the time the secretary was away, the *Annual Report* for 1908 had been published. Such documents tend to be dull and unread, but one sees here the ability of Walcott's touch to make even that document more interesting. Under Langley, the reports would begin with proceedings of the Board of Regents, followed by accounts of the Executive Committee, adding figures to dull further the numbing prose; for the secretary's report, Dr. Langley's name was set in thirty-point type. Walcott put the secretary's report first and saw to it that his name was in smaller type than the rest of the title. He listed the "Establishment" and the "Regents" but also the scientific staff of the bureaus; Charles D. Walcott was included as one of the USNM curators. In later years, he also had the title of "Keeper *ex officio*" of the Museum; that may have been a result of his trip to London—the British Museum has keepers rather than curators. There is a slight difference in philosophy reflected in the title.

On July 8, Walcott decided what was to be done about a sea-lion pool at the zoo; with that decision, SI matters were resolved and future problems left to Mr. Rathbun. A short motor-car ride provided relaxation, and two days later Walcott was on the B&O railway, accompanied by Helen, Helena, and Arthur Brown. At Chicago they recovered Stuart and went to St. Paul to take the Soo Line and the Canadian Pacific west. By 5:00 A.M. a couple of days later, they were in Banff, where the ladies went to the Canadian Pacific Railway Hotel.

Walcott, assisted by Stuart and Arthur Brown, got supplies and shipped the camp outfit to Laggan. Arthur set up the camp on a site across the lake outlet from the hotel, on Lake Louise. Arthur stayed in camp while Stuart and Walcott went to the hotel. As virtually the only black man in western Canada, Arthur Brown attracted attention. So far as Walcott was concerned, Arthur was in camp to guard equipment, not because he would not be welcome in the hotel as one of the Walcott party. At the hotel, Charles introduced Helena to the Vaux family of Philadelphia: George Vaux, the noted mineral collector, his son and daughter-in-law, and daughter Mary. A day or two of fossil collecting ensued, but Helena badly sprained her leg. Walcott thoughtfully brought in a packload of shale so that Helena could sit around camp and search for trilobites in the rock without climbing. Walcott never wasted an opportunity.

Most of the summer was spent within a day or two's horseback ride of the camp. Walcott concentrated on panorama photographs and on the lower part of the Bow River Valley, measuring the Precambrian and tracing the contact with the Cambrian.

During the summer of 1909 I continued my study of 1907 on the Cambrian formations of the main range of the Rocky Mountains on the line of Bow

Valley, in Alberta, with the view of discovering a base to the Fairview formation of the Lower Cambrian, and if possible, of finding fossils in the shales and sandstones beneath that formation in the Bow Valley. When measuring the Cambrian sandstone on the northeast slopes of Mount Fairview and Saddle Mountain about 2.5 miles southwest of Laggan, a fine quartz conglomerate about 100 feet in thickness was found, and below it a gentle, forest covered débris slope without rock outcrops. Knowing that there were shales and sandstones in the Bow Valley to the northwest, I went up the slopes of Mount Saint Piran, and from there examined with a strong fieldglass the valley and mountains to the northeast. I could see that the Fairview sandstone formed a cliff on Mount Hector and Fort Mountain above slopes that were evidently clear of débris, and that there was a marked change in the character of the rock where the cliff and slope met. A week was next spent at Fort Mountain and vicinity, and with the information secured there as to the presence of a massive bedded conglomerate at the base of the Fairview formation, a trip was made along the southwest side of Bow Valley in search of contacts between the basal conglomerate and the shales below. (Walcott 1910a, 423–24)

This is solid, workmanlike geology, not earth shattering, but basic. Those few sentences required a lot of riding and scrambling up and down slopes. Walcott presented information in clear terms, accompanied by half a dozen panorama photos and a simple map. In the conglomerate he found pieces of limestone that could have come from an underlying unit like the Siyah, a Precambrian limestone outcropping in Glacier National Park, but no longer exposed here. This study reinforced his view that much of the Precambrian strata may have been deposited under nonmarine conditions and that there was a major break between Precambrian and Cambrian rocks.

After the first group of collections had been shipped to Washington, Arthur Brown and Walcott moved the camp to Field. They rode up the beautiful Yoho Valley with eight animals to Takakkaw Falls, reported to be among the highest in the world, and pitched a tent. An early morning rainstorm roused them to pitch the second tent. After the day in camp, Helena felt up to her first climb in four years. The upper Yoho Valley is exquisite, but snow squalls and rain took some of the edge off the scenery. The weather cleared, and the men "went up to Burgess Pass & took photographs. Found the Stephen formation trilobite bed. Returned to camp 7 P.M. Helen is ill[.] Helena is just recovering for a severe cold & I am nearly all in with cold & fatigue" (August 28, 1909). It had been a long, tough field season.

The next day, equally unpleasant, Walcott took two horses up and camped on the north slope of Burgess Pass. Following that, Walcott "was out collecting on the Stephan formation all day" and reporting finding many interesting fossils. The

rest of the party—Helena, Helen, Arthur, Stuart, and the packer Jack Giddie—
came up late that afternoon (Yochelson 1996a). August 31 was a fine day from
the standpoint of the weather and an incredible day for paleontology: today the
fauna of the Burgess Shale came to the attention of a scientist for the first time.

To put it as briefly as possible, the Middle Cambrian Burgess Shale may be
the single most important fossil find ever made. Among other points, it dramatically expanded the number of animals known in the Cambrian, for it preserved many unique forms, particularly soft bodied organisms, which were
totally unexpected in the fossil record.

Various stories have appeared as to how this locality was discovered. The most
common one is that Walcott was leading the pack train and encountered a large
piece of rock that had slid downhill onto the trail. Walcott got down to move it
and, as was his custom, hit it with his hammer; a remarkable fossil fell out. This
is incorrect, for if Walcott was already at the pass and the others were coming
up, he could not have been leading them. In later years Burling, who was not
even present, was to comment that if he had been leading, he would have found
the fossils. All Walcott wrote in his official report to the Regents was that "a most
interesting discovery of unique Cambrian fossils was made near Burgess Pass"
(Walcott 1911, 12). There simply is no first-hand documentation of exactly how
the find was made.

Still, there is one more account, written by Helen in 1955 for her granddaughter. The account does not match the Walcott diary, and several trips are
probably combined. "That was the summer we spent six weeks on Burgess Pass
[probably 1910], about Field B.C. The summer before we were at Emerald Lake
and Yoho Valley. Father and Mother were returning to camp one day, by way
of Burgess Pass. Father wanted to see an outcrop at the base of the cliffs on
Mt. Wapta, so mother waited on the trail while father made the steep climb up
the scree. She began to split open the shale by the side of the trail, and by the
time father returned she had several very remarkable fossils.[12] If this is correctly
recalled, Helena Walcott was the one who first found the Burgess Shale fossils.

On August 31, Walcott mentioned in his diary a "remarkable group of phyllo-
pod crustaceans" and made several drawings in his notebook. The next day, he
noted some sponges in place in the rocks and not in loose blocks. Following that
he worked up the slope, looking for the level that had produced the arthropods,
while Helena broke up rock near the trail. Part of the group left, but Walcott remained another day to keep collecting this incredible material.

When the weather deteriorated, Walcott retreated to the other side of Kicking
Horse Valley. Jack Giddie and Arthur Brown had set up a camp on Mount Stephen,
even though much of the outfit had already been packed up for the season.
Enlisted a visiting tourist from New York to assist, he searched up the slope,

unsuccessfully, to see if these spectacular fossils could be found. The relationships between the beds on Mount Field and those on Mount Stephen are sub-
tly complex (Fletcher and Collins 1998). Walcott scribbled a note to the chief
clerk of the Smithsonian to alert the Treasury Department and pass the word
to the customs officials to move his shipments promptly. "All well—Have had
great success collecting the past ten days."[13]

Packing was frantic for a couple of days, as a number of slabs were being sent
to Washington, and the camp outfit was in disarray. These chores were finished
in time to board the *Seattle Special*. Everyone, but especially Walcott, was tired.
Walcott sent another note to Washington to make certain the boxes of fossils
were placed in his working room. "The collections are large & full of interest—
We bro't them 800 feet down the mountain slope & they were then packed 3000
feet down grade to Field."[14]

At Seattle, Helena, Stuart, and Helen went out with him to the fairgrounds
to see the Alaska-Yukon Pacific Exposition. This was work related, for the Smithsonian Institution had a display there, as it had at most of the national expositions from the time of the 1876 Philadelphia Centennial. After a day at the fair,
they took the sleeper to Portland and the next day headed east to Ogden, Utah.
When they got to Salt Lake City, Charlie met them at the Telluride Power Office,
and the augmented family went to Provo and to see Sidney. For the first time in
nearly two years, the family was together. It was to be one of the last times.

The four days around Provo were excellent. Walcott and Stuart tried fishing,
but the trout did not bite as they had in Montana and Canada. Walcott walked
up the canyon with his sons, while Helen was enjoying herself with the local
boys. In odd moments Walcott caught up on his mail and talked business with
Mr. Nunn. He and Walcott took Senator Smoot to see the Battle Creek power
plant. The idyll ended, and on Saturday the senior Walcotts and accompanying
teenagers boarded the train for Denver. "We left Charles & Sidney at Olmstead
with Telluride Power Co. where they are to study & work for the winter" (September 19, 1909). The family took fast trains and in a little over four days were
home. It is indicative of the couple that they agreed to bring back with them the
body of a Washington boy who had suffered a fatal accident in Utah.

Almost the first order of business after Walcott returned was President Woodward showing Walcott the new headquarters building of the Carnegie Institution of Washington, at 16th and P Streets, N.W. For the next order of business,
Walcott "unpacked a number of specimens brot back in our trucks. A few of
those collected Aug 31 (*ante.*) & Sept 1" (September 23, 1909).

There was also a council meeting of the NAS in the three days Walcott was in
Washington before going off to New York. On Monday in New York he saw a
number of people, not the least of them John D. Rockefeller, the largest money

giver of them all. He also ran a few errands for Telluride Power. Cousin Fred and he went out to Governors Island, where they examined the flying machines of Wilbur Wright and Glenn Curtiss. He was on the reviewing stand the next day for the Hudson-Fulton Pageant. The secretary mixed in more business for Telluride, saw the impressive naval review, and tried to find investors. He paid his respects to Mrs. Harriman—her husband had died the month before while the Walcotts were still in the West—and went on to New Haven, Connecticut.

There were enough people that Walcott knew at Yale to make the visit a bit like old home week, but mainly he saw Charles Schuchert. "Advised Dr Schuchert not to use controversial & disputed names in his new scheme of geologic nomenclature" (October 3, 1909). Schuchert was in the process of writing textbooks that influenced a full generation of geologists, as had James Dwight Dana before him; Walcott's remark was directed at some of the stratigraphic notions that E. O. Ulrich of the USGS Survey was propounding, but that is another story entirely (Weiss and Yochelson 1995).

Walcott spent most of another day with Schuchert, looking at the paleogeographic maps Schuchert had been compiling and talking over the work on Cambrian brachiopods. He went to Boston, to Cambridge, and specifically to the Museum of Comparative Zoology. Over the years, Walcott had learned more about trilobites than he had known when he first started at Trenton Falls, New York, and he wanted to look again at the slides of appendages he had made in the 1870s. (In natural history, one has to keep going back to look at old material. This is why museums are so valuable, as places to keep collections safe from harm. Systematics is an additive science, a point that somehow seems to escape most chemists and physicists, but especially present-day administrators.)

Walcott wore his Cambridge gown at the inauguration of Lawrence Lowell as the new president of Harvard University. While at Harvard he talked to Reginald Daly about the geology of the forty-ninth parallel. The United States and Canada had sent joint geologic parties as part of the boundary survey, but Canada had eventually published the results, whereas America, to its shame, had not. Dr. Daly was a Canadian expatriate and had been to Canada more or less what Bailey Willis had been to America. Daly was a man of large ideas, a man whom Walcott respected, even though they differed about the Precambrian. As often happens to a visiting dignitary, the following day Walcott had to give a brief address, before heading south to New York.

Helena met him after taking daughter Helen to Mrs. Porter's School in Farmington, Connecticut. Walcott tackled a few more people about financing for Roosevelt's African expedition, and the two paid their respects to Mrs. Harriman at her country place. The Walcotts returned home, but in a couple of days the secretary was back in New York. R. A. Franks gave a sizable donation to the African expedition. On quite another level, Judge Lovell suggested that Walcott act as an advisor to the Southern Pacific and Union Pacific on natural resources.

Mulling that offer over, Walcott went back to the District of Columbia, while Helena went to see Aunt Helen Sanford in Oneida; it was she who had brought the couple together. Walcott spent his days dictating letters and his evenings at the University Club council on the matter of the new building. It now being mid-October, Arthur Brown started the furnace fire to warm the home place. Helena returned, but it was a big house for only three Walcotts. Walcott picked up the threads of his manuscript on the Mesonascidae—that is, *Olenellus* and its close cousins—and helped Helena clean the walls of their home. Mrs. Hubbard, widow of Gardner Greene Hubbard, who had founded the National Geographic Society, was killed in an automobile accident, one of Washington's early victims of the road; Walcott acted as a pallbearer, as he had done for her husband a dozen years before.

Finally, he had more fossils to examine. One of his shipments from Canada had come through promptly, but the other had vanished. Copies of the bills of lading had been sent several times, to no effect. In one his rare displays of exasperation, Walcott had then stopped dealing with underlings and expressed his anger to the assistant secretary of the treasury over the inability of the Customs Service to find his boxes. Not surprisingly, there had been an answer in forty-eight hours. Fortunately for the u.s. customs, the fossils had been sitting in a warehouse in Alberta rather than North Dakota.

The secretary was as keenly interested in the future as he was in the past, and after a day in the office, he went to College Park, Maryland, some ten miles from downtown Washington, to see the U.S. Army test the Wright flying machine, in two flights of two hours each. He was so impressed that the next day Walcott brought Helena and Stuart out to see. After that, office routine continued for a couple more days, but then it was time for another train trip, only this time the destination was Cleveland, not New York. He saw the friendly Garfield family briefly and went into a two-day session with the other directors of Telluride Power before heading back to Washington science and administration.

Some days, Walcott was able to spend mornings at home toiling on the Lower Cambrian trilobites and afternoons at the Castle, generally on Smithsonian matters. To illustrate once again the breadth of his activities, one morning it was describing a new species, *Holmia rowei*, followed by a committee meeting on hygiene and demographics. The second week in November, Walcott was back in Cleveland for another two-day session on Telluride Power. He switched from science to business to science as easily as flicking an electric switch on and off. On Sunday, after church, Walcott traveled again, to the nas fall meeting. He jotted a note from New York: "I am going up to Utica tonight to visit the resting place of my parents & sister. Will return here—Monday morning. Will you not have mail sent to the Belmont up to Sunday evening. The meeting at Princeton on the 16th & 17th was a very pleasant & instructive one—I may stop in Philadelphia on return trip."[15] While at Princeton, he dined with Woodrow Wilson. Walcott had met him several years earlier when Wilson had spoken at the University Club.

There were no faxes in 1909, and long-distance calls were rare, but it took only one day for a letter to go from New York to Washington. Despite his travels, Walcott was always on top of his mail, even when in the field. Whether he started his career at the Smithsonian with one clerical assistant is not known, but he soon followed the tradition of Baird in having two secretaries, because the burden of correspondence was so large. Back in New York after his sentimental pilgrimage to Utica, Walcott saw John Hay and other folks from Wall Street; he returned to Washington the day before Thanksgiving. Mr. and Mrs. Burling shared the turkey.

As Stuart had the following day off from school, Walcott took him to the Castle and put him to work unwrapping Canadian fossils. A new British ambassador was a reason to dine out. The GWMA came up again, but notwithstanding his busy schedule, Walcott found the time to give a lecture to the public school teachers of Washington. After church, he went to Philadelphia to confer with Cyrus Adler and S. Weir Mitchell, on topics not specified, but likely Smithsonian and Carnegie matters, respectively. The German ambassador was the reason for another dinner out, causing Walcott the loss of another evening. Social duty called even though he was "endeavoring to catch up with odds & ends of work at home in the evening" (December 9, 1909).

The Carnegie Institution of Washington opened its new headquarters building on December 13, the Ex Comm meeting being that morning. The next day the regents met in the morning, Walcott lunched with the CIW trustees, meeting with the Ex Comm again before the annual Carnegie dinner. It was a physical and mental grind, on which Walcott seemed to thrive. Charlie came in, and Walcott waved hello as he left for his last trip of the year to New York, trying to raise more money for the African expedition. "Went downtown with intention of seeing a number of men. Secured $1000, but found most men out" (December 17, 1909). Walcott gave up fund-raising for the year, saw the aquarium and a few cousins, and went back to his office. At home, the Christmas tree was lovely, and in the afternoon it was quiet enough to look at some of the fossils collected near Lake Louise.

The outside world intruded on the trilobite study. There was money to be made from natural resources, but Walcott declined an opportunity. An official of the Union Pacific–Southern Pacific Railway System asked for a report on how the railways might best exploit the Permian-Age phosphate deposits in Utah and Wyoming. The short reply from Walcott was that such a report would take a great deal of time to prepare. This crossed another letter in the mail: "I am glad to learn from our President of your appointment as Consulting Expert on the development of natural resources in the areas tributary to the Union and Southern Pacific Systems. . . . I understand that the arrangement dated from October 1st, 1909 and enclose voucher for $6000.00 in payment of one year's salary to October 1st, 1910."[16] Walcott wrote on December 27 and again the following day, declining the offer. Within a few days, he went to New York, consulted with Judge Lovell about this matter, and returned the check. It was an incident not mentioned in his diary.

The penultimate day of the year Walcott spent getting organized to return to work on the Mesonascidae; fortunately, fossils are dead and will wait in a drawer until one can get to them. On New Year's Eve, Walcott reflected, "1909 has been as a whole a kindly year to our family. The children are growing strong & well physically but none show a desire to study for the love of it" (December 31, 1909). He did not mention the Burgess Shale fossils. Likewise, he did not mention his degree from Cambridge; somewhere along the line, Walcott had also become a fellow of the Christiania Scientific Society and an honorary member of the Astronomical Society of Mexico.

The absent Sidney, still in Olmstead, was missed when Dr. and Mrs. Walcott gave a dancing party for Helen and Stuart to end 1909. The year 1910 began busily enough, for the children's party did not break up until 1:30 A.M., but by 9:30 Walcott was in his office. He made a New Year's Day call on President Taft at noon, went to meeting of the Washington Monument Society, and then paid official calls for four hours. Perhaps this busy start was a portent. The next day, after the church service, Walcott was off to New York City, breaking his record of the previous year. Apart from returning the check to the railway, it was a trip to look for money for the si and to renew acquaintances. He saw Cornelius Bliss, George Perkins, Henry de Forest, Cleveland Dodge, Andrew Carnegie, Mrs. Harriman, and others. Just how much money he collected is not recorded. Then it was back to Washington and back to the Mesonascidae paper.

Helena went off, returning daughter Helen to Miss Porter's School in Farmington. For his part, Walcott went to see President Taft, to whom he recommended Henry Graves, who had been hired by the USGS in 1897 to work on the forest reserves, as chief of the Bureau of Forestry. Those who are up on their conservation history know that Gifford Pinchot was then engaged in a fight with Secretary of Interior Ballinger concerning disposition of natural resources. Had Pinchot not been such an extremist, Taft might not have released him, Teddy

Roosevelt might not have gotten so upset with Taft, Wilson might not have been elected, and World War I might have ended sooner. Who can say how events interconnect and affect the future?

As was a January tradition in Washington, Walcott was reelected president of the Washington Academy of Sciences. When Helena returned, the Walcotts gave a dinner for the French ambassador. This was followed by several small dinners, the main purpose of which was to push along the GWMA's effort to obtain a site in Washington. Once these dinners were over, it was quiet in the evenings. At a Geological Society of Washington meeting, L. D. Burling had the opportunity to explain what he had been doing to help along the slow-moving monograph fifty-one (Bastin 1910). Stuart and Charles helped arrange photographs, and Walcott labeled his collections of the past two years. Helena came down with influenza, and to get some quiet in the house, Walcott took the boys to an auto show—no doubt about it, the horse was being replaced. A week later Helena was still sick, and Walcott was out running errands and making social calls on her behalf.

Late in January, Senator Joseph Dixon asked Walcott for photographs taken in the area of the proposed Glacier National Park; Walcott obliged with several panoramas. George Bird Grinnell is considered the father of that park and deserves almost all of the credit, but Walcott added his moiety. Joseph Dixon said on the floor of the Senate: "If the Senator from Mississippi so desires, I will read from the report, but I have in my hand 7 feet of a better and more eloquent speech, taken with a camera by Mr. Walcott, formerly Director of the Geological Survey, of merely one corner of this wonderful country, which, if any Senator is interested, gives in better language and with more eloquence than I can command a description of this wonderful country. . . . I would be glad if other Senators who seem to be interested in this matter would examine the 3 yards of camera reproduction made by Mr. Walcott, of the Geological Survey, who has been one of the ardent and original promoters of Glacier National Park.[17]

On the 28th of January there was a quick trip to New York for a dinner of the Rocky Mountains Club, another of those gatherings that might pay dividends in the future. Walcott dropped in at the White House, but President Taft was in conference. A few days later he cornered Taft, who agreed to give a speech. The next day, Walcott corralled Senators Lodge and Burton. On the 19th of February these three worthies descended on the assembled schoolchildren of Washington. The aim was to enlist the children of America in collecting their pennies for the patriotic purpose of building the memorial to George Washington. The scheme almost worked.

Before that event transpired, Walcott was off to Cleveland again; the board of Telluride Power was meeting. Then it was back to Washington for two days and then off to the American Museum of Natural History in New York, where a statue of the late museum president, Morris K. Jessup, was to be unveiled. "Met Prof. Alfred S. Bickmore, my friend since 1868" (February 9, 1910). Bickmore remembered their meeting, when the schoolboy from Utica with a knapsack on his back had come to collect fossils near what is now Colgate University. In 1879, three months before he joined the USGS, Walcott had tried to sell his collection to Bickmore, who was then in charge of the American Museum; the offer had been declined, because the purchase of Professor James Hall's collection had taken all the museum's funds.

The secretary came back to Washington immediately, for on February 10 the Langley Medal was presented to Wilbur and Orville Wright. At their December meeting in 1908, the regents had instituted this medal, "to be awarded for special meritorious investigations in connection with the science of aeronautics and its application to aviation." At the same time, they had also authorized a memorial tablet for Professor Langley, to extol his contributions to aeronautics. Because the Wright brothers had been engaged in a lawsuit, the medal presentation had had to be delayed a year, until they could get to the Washington.

It was absolutely right and proper that the Wright brothers received the medal. The ceremony itself was relatively small and fairly private. Chief Justice Melvin W. Fuller presented the medal, and regents Alexander Graham Bell and Henry Cabot Lodge spoke. No doubt the brothers were pleased with the medal, though they thought that too much recognition was given to Langley.

Octave Chanute was on the committee that had selected the awardees. He had been advisor, mentor, and all-around encourager as the Wrights struggled to resolve the many problems involved in manned flight. Subsequently, his high opinion of the brothers had cooled a little. "Now the results obtained by the Wright brothers are far superior to any others, but the resolution mentions 'meritorious investigations'—not achievements, and this seems to imply that those investigations should be given to the world, a thing which the Wrights have hitherto declined to do."[18]

Cousin Emma died, but Walcott did not go to Utica for that funeral. It was better to stay home, write up his manuscripts, and listen to Charlie and Helen sing around the piano. The year was settling in. "A quiet busy day at my office with correspondence & many matters—Obtained 4 hours on my research work. At home in the evening. Mr. John William Smith dined with us & explained a scheme for quarrying limestone etc in Michigan. Meeting of Board of University Club 4:30–6 P.M. My term as president expired today" (February 18, 1910). The schoolchild penny scheme came and went, and it was time to consider more substantial funding at the appropriations hearing. Walcott "explained estimates for government work in chg of Smithsonian Institution" (February 25, 1910).

The confused relationship between the SI itself and the government agencies administered by it was, as it still is, a never-ending source of misunderstanding.

By the first of March, fund-raising for the GWMA was becoming a major preoccupation, and Walcott was on a committee to canvass the city, coordinating efforts with those in other cities. A pioneer seismologist, H. F. Reid came down from Johns Hopkins University to help Walcott formulate his efforts to have the SI and eventually the federal government develop major roles in seismology.

Research with fossils went on, notwithstanding such interruptions. "At Smithsonian 9 A.M. to 5 P.M. Routine and work on *Mesonacidae*. Worked over paper in relation to development of limestone quarries in Michigan in the evening" (March 7, 1910). (Like the business enterprise of slate quarries in Newfoundland that Walcott had considered years earlier, the limestone quarries in Michigan can be left for someone else to delve into.) In mid-week, Walcott went to the Capitol to listen to an application from the Rockefeller Foundation, a friendly rival, in a sense, of the CIW.

"At church A.M. with Charlie & Stuart. In the afternoon went to the New Museum Building to receive friends who came to get a first look at Nat. Gallery of Art—at home in evening" (March 13, 1910). Walcott had started the process for a new museum building in 1898, and now, twelve years later, it was opening (Yochelson 1985). In the middle of the three great hallways, pictures and sculpture were installed, for Congress had not provided funds to convert the Castle to an art gallery. The general opening was on St. Patrick's Day. Walcott spent the afternoon talking to "people who came to see pictures & groups of peoples in cases" (March 17, 1910). Displays of life-sized figures that William Henry Holmes had made for the Chicago Exposition flanked the National Gallery of Art collection, for ethnology, presumably, was related to art. It is curious that a natural history museum would encompass art, but the art was to remain within the building for half a century. The other museum halls would open as they were completed over the next several years, but at least a start had been made.

A letter to the American ambassador to France forms a nice summary of events.

> I think of you every time the matter of the Smithsonian African Expedition comes up, or any of the collections arrive. We have received a superb lot of material thus far, and there are two or more shipments on the ocean now. It has been a great expedition, and Colonel Roosevelt and his associates deserve the greatest credit for thorough systematic work.
>
> The condition of mind of most of the American people in regard to public matters is fairly well expressed by a paragraph in a speech Carnegie made yesterday in Los Angeles when he said "Taft will yet make good." There is a general feeling of unrest throughout the country, and it will require very wise action to prevent a political revolution at the next election.

You may be interested to learn that today we open for the first time the National Gallery of Art, which has been installed in the central section of the new National Museum building. It is a very creditable exhibit for a beginning, and I am sure will attract the hearty cooperation of many American citizens interested in the fine arts.[19]

Walcott went back to writing his introduction to the Mesonascidae. It was a strange time in Washington; Walcott noted that in Congress "Joe Cannon" was voted down for first time in many years. There was no time to ponder this political development, for he was off to Cleveland. Telluride business dealings took four full days, but the trip included a visit to see Stuart at the Garfields'. When Walcott finally did get back to Washington, part of the Telluride board accompanied him and stayed around for several days. They went en masse to New York for a meeting. While in New York City, Walcott went to visit the White Motor Company, for gasoline was now replacing steam on the roads. He got back to Washington and discussed with the Daughters of the American Revolution their new building; the DAR would later offer its use to the Smithsonian.

A bad cold took the secretary out of circulation for a few days but provided the opportunity for him to collect his thoughts for his next project. In mid-April Walcott started on a paper for the International Geological Congress meeting in Stockholm; the name had changed slightly over the years. Walcott would not attend, but his younger colleague, Waldemar Lindgren—a transplanted Swede who had joined the USGS in 1884, survived the bloodletting of the 1890s, and had become the bureau's expert on the formation of mineral deposits—would present the paper at the August meeting.

It took Walcott three weeks to complete the draft and another month for the manuscript to be edited and polished. This was one his more theoretical papers, but it was grounded entirely on his field observations. One of the features of the Stockholm congress was a symposium on the start of the Cambrian fossil record. "Abrupt Appearance of the Cambrian Fauna on the North American Continent" was directly on target. Although all other papers eventually appeared in the *Compte Rendu* of the congress—that is, two years later—Walcott's did not. The same day that Dr. Lindgren spoke in Stockholm, August 18, 1910, the manuscript was published; the convenience of having *Smithsonian Miscellaneous Collections* directly at hand was obvious. This little paper started Walcott's second full volume in that series.

"I have for the past eighteen years watched for geological and paleontological evidence that might aid in solving the problem of pre-Cambrian life" (Walcott 1910b, 1). All there was to show for the effort were the curious stromatolites that Walcott attributed to the efforts of single-celled protozoans, a few presumed worm trails, and *Beltina*, which currently is not considered to be an arthropod, as Walcott had thought (Walcott 1899). "There is nothing about the crustacean remains incomparable with their living in fresh water, in fact the fragments indicate a form more nearly related to the fresh-water *Branchiopoda* with very thin test, rather than the strong *Merostome* (*Eurypterus*, etc.)" (Walcott 1910b, 13). Walcott emphasized the profound break between the Algonkian and the Lower Cambrian and refined his views on the encroachment of the Cambrian seas from the east and west (Walcott 1891a). He mentioned that the trilobite-bearing Lower Cambrian in the west was older than that known in the east, still a valid observation. Walcott called on interpretations of the young Cenozoic in the west, including some notes that he had made in 1879, to document the occurrence of freshwater limestones. He did not doubt that a marine Precambrian fauna existed somewhere, but he was satisfied that it did not appear in the Algonkian of North America.

To Walcott it seemed clear that no rocks had been deposited on the continent during a span of time between the Algonkian and the oldest known Cambrian. "Lipalian is proposed for the era of unknown marine sedimentation between the adjustment of pelagic life to littoral conditions and the appearance of the Lower Cambrian fauna. It represents the period between the formation of the Algonkian continents and the earliest encroachment of the Lower Cambrian sea" (Walcott 1910a, 14).

Walcott gives the Greek derivation, though no locality, but one might note that Lipan Point at the Grand Canyon is an ideal place to see the unconformity, or break, between Precambrian and Middle Cambrian strata. "I fully realize that the conclusions above outlined are based primarily on the absence of a marine fauna in Algonkian rocks, but until such is discovered I know of no more probable explanation of the abrupt appearance of the Cambrian fauna than that I have presented" (Walcott 1910b, 15).

That is not a bad ending for a paper. Walcott explained his observations and the conclusions that he drew from them, but certainly he did not paint himself into a corner. G. F. Matthew, the customs collector at St. John, New Brunswick, had found a few fossils below *Olenellus*; the way Matthew presented this data, Walcott had felt justified at the turn of the century in placing these beds in the Cambrian. A few geologists strong on hindsight have criticized Walcott for a cavalier attitude toward Matthew. The two frequently exchanged letters, and on the scale at which Walcott was working, he was correct.

Another point not known at the time was the great age of the Algonkian in the west, relative to the Cambrian. Until radiometric dating of sedimentary rocks became common, no one knew that hundreds of millions of years separated the strata called the Belt Supergroup rocks from the Cambrian. Decades later, animal fossils were found in the much younger portion of the Precambrian, but such deposits were found first on other continents. Most geologists agree that some of the Belt is nonmarine; how much is still a matter of argument. If a summary is needed, Walcott wrote a neat paper for Sweden that explained the abrupt appearance of trilobites, based on the information he had.

Having a significant manuscript in the formative stage was no reason for the secretary not be involved in stirring other pots. A local citizens' committee to raise construction funds for the GWMA had to be organized. The same evening he entrained to New York with Mr. Nunn of Telluride Power. He saw Dr. Billings the next morning and then charged back to Washington for the annual NAS meeting. Before that gathering, a word or two more is in order about L. L. Nunn, Telluride, and the schooling of Charlie and Sidney—for they are all interconnected.

Nunn, three years younger than Walcott, had made big money in the mining boom at Telluride, Colorado. He saw the potential of electric power and at one time had the largest power plant in the world tucked away in the Rockies. From there, Nunn had moved to Utah and started the Olmstead plant, capitalizing on the river in Provo Canyon and steadily expanding his electrical web. Nunn made electricity into money, but he was also a visionary. Walcott had explained this a few years earlier to a friend:

> Charles, Junior, is working for the Telluride Power Company, a large hydro-electric company that has plants in Colorado, Idaho and Utah. They employ quite a number of young men to whom they give Twenty dollars a month and their board. The boys do all kinds of work. During the winter months they are at the headquarters near Provo, Utah, where they are under instruction at the Telluride Institute; this means real study and work in the shops.
>
> The manager of the Company is Mr. L. L. Nunn, Provo. . . . The work of the company is hard; and the whole spirit of the organization is to work and overcome all obstacles in the way of development of any projects that may be in their charge.[20]

When Charlie and later Sidney went out to Olmstead for what Walcott described as study and work, this is precisely what they did. In its way, Olmstead for a brief time was a fine engineering institution.

Naturally enough, some members of the board of Telluride Power thought that the reason for a company was to make money, especially for them, not to fritter away funds on education and character building. This difference of opinion eventually led to the sale of the Olmstead plant and several other properties to Utah Power. The eleemosynary aspect of electricity generation appealed to Walcott and explains why he and Nunn became so enmeshed.

After the sale, the Beaver River plant in Utah remained to Nunn, and Telluride Power carried on in education. Late in life, Mr. Nunn started and endowed Deep Springs College, in extreme western Nevada, to carry on his ideas of work and study. Walcott suggested to him this remote ranch site at the foot of the Inyo Mountains. In addition to his educational-philanthropic activities in Utah, Nunn also had a stake in Cornell University, where he provided first-class accommodations for the young men who became part of the Telluride Association. It is a reasonable bet that this may have been part of the reason that Sidney later went to Cornell; Walcott's name is recorded in the house guest book. An important thing about Walcott was the interesting people he knew and interacted with.

So much for digression. There was one day in which to catch up on NAS council affairs before Walcott "presented my paper on development of *Olenellus* 4 P.M. illustrated by lantern slides" (April 20, 1910). Projected illustrations were not new, but they were still uncommon enough to warrant mention.

The *Olenellus* study was being completed, but perhaps a point or two still had to be checked in the field. As an alternative explanation, Walcott may just have needed some rest and relaxation to order his thoughts. Whatever the reason, Walcott took the train to Lancaster, Pennsylvania, and the trolley to Millersville. He and Professor Roddy had a good Saturday in the field. The rains came, and Walcott went back to Washington to listen to rain on his own roof. The sound of the drops falling on a solid roof—meaning that one is not being rained on in the field—can be very soothing.

Mr. and Mrs. Carnegie came to town, and Walcott shepherded them around when the building of the Bureau of American Republics was dedicated; this later became the Pan-American Union and, still later, the Organization of American States. He went back to routine letter writing and administration; also, he completed his Stockholm manuscript and selected for illustration a few Burgess Shale fossils found the previous year. These were phyllocarids; think of a clam shell with a shrimp extending out both ends, and one has an approximation of this group.

It was time for another quick trip to Cleveland—ceremonial, not business, though Walcott passed the time in the cars talking to executives of the Santa Fe Railroad he happened to meet. Cleveland was another opportunity to rub elbows with Charles Freer, but the official ceremonial activity was a dinner in honor of Dr. James Angell; Walcott spoke of his many years of service as a regent of the Smithsonian. The next day Walcott spent more time with Freer and then visited the Garfield family. Then it was back to Washington.

"Administrative matters, correspondence and completion of paper on 'Abrupt appearance of the Cambrian fauna.' Began preparation of Pre-Cambrian rocks of Bow valley, Alberta, Canada. At home in the evening" (May 12, 1910). The end of one manuscript was the signal to start another, especially if it could be knocked into shape before the field season. "At my office 9–10–11 A.M.–2:30 P.M.—Called on President Taft 10:15 A.M. to speak of head of new mining bureau At 4 P.M. talked to meeting of American Federation of Arts on National Gallery of Art. Many members visited gallery 4:30 to 6 P.M. An hour at Parson's reception 10–11. This is Charlie's 21st birthday. He is a fine strong young man" (May 17, 1910).

President Taft's term was not a happy one and one of his main sources of difficulty was conservation. The year before, Pinchot had been fired. The day before this meeting, the Bureau of Mines had finally come into being, but there had been some question as to who would head it. Holmes, rightly or wrongly, was viewed as an ally of Pinchot. Taft temporized by appointing the director of the USGS as acting head. Later, sixty-seven senators signed up to support Holmes, and Taft eventually recommended him for the position. Walcott does not record what was discussed, but it is a reasonable assumption that he recommended Holmes be appointed. Taft should have immediately accepted Walcott's candidate and saved himself the embarrassment.

Walcott went off to New York to pursue odds and ends and to stroke a few rich men, and then up the line to Farmington to visit with Helen. After checking on his darling daughter, the secretary went to Utica to see a few elderly cousins and view the family graves; he picked up an 1838 pocket almanac his father had carried and placed it in his diary. Walcott spent the night at Scanandoa, near Oneida; Aunt Helen Sanford was responsible for Walcott's happiness with Helena, and he never forgot it. Back home, he and Helena observed the joint spectacle of the return of Halley's Comet and an eclipse of the moon from their front porch. It was a moment to remember.

At the end of May, Walcott consulted with Senator Dodge about the appropriation for the USNM; it never hurt to lay groundwork. He also suggested that Mr. Carnegie endow a library in Wyoming. Being secretary is not all fun, and his next stop was a Baltimore courtroom in the suit of *United States vs. Graham*; the construction of the new Museum building had not been smooth affair with respect to some of the contractors. Three days into June, Walcott gave the Smithsonian editor his manuscript on the Bow River Valley (three weeks is not quite a record for writing, but it is close), and a copy of the Cambrian boundary paper to Lindgren to present at the International Geological Congress in Stockholm. Psychologically at least, Walcott had cleared up all matters and was ready for the field season.

Charlie took his entrance examinations for Yale University, and naturally he passed. The first of Walcott's children was to go to college. Then came a day of proofreading; this is always a boring process, but it is one that a scientist must do. The idea that a mistake in a paper is the printer's error is not the sort of excuse fellow scientists generally accept. If one's name is on the paper, one is responsible for the contents.

That out of the way, Walcott was off to Cleveland. Getting ready for the field can be a complex process; on this trip, Secretary Walcott was accompanied by the house dog, Scald, and Garfield, Stuart's canary; the James Garfield family provided safe summer housing for the animals. That important mission fulfilled, Walcott could concentrate on the future of the Telluride Corporation at the board meeting.

Walcott also scored a major art coup in Detroit. He convinced Freer to have a temporary display in Washington of some of his rare objects. Freer was a complex man, and to persuade him to show a few of his treasures to the general public before they were displayed in Freer's very own building was really a feat. So it was that on the west side of the new museum building, where later mammals had stood for years, Chinese vases appeared briefly. By mid-June Walcott was back in Washington. He arranged for someone to look over the house and cut the lawn—cost, $1.50 per week. At the other end of the scale, Mr. Rathbun was to be in charge of the si, with F. W. True to supplement him, if necessary. The loose ends were tied up.

Helena had left several days earlier to collect daughter Helen at school. Walcott took Stuart, and they assembled in New York City. The family were guests on board the *Mohawk*, one of the ships that steamed out to welcome ex-President Roosevelt back from Africa. Like all good tourists, that night the Walcotts took the children to see the Great White Way. They rested on Sunday in Walcott's favorite New York place, the Hotel Belmont, at Park Avenue and 42d Street. On Monday the family attended the wedding of Theodore Roosevelt, Jr.—needless to say, an elaborate affair.

That would have been enough excitement for the average American family, but it ought be clear that these were not average folk. Walcott took his wife and brood to New Haven for the night. The following day was "Yale Commencement day—Received degree of L.L.D. along with Jas. J. Hill & Gov. Freer of Hawaii" (June 22, 1910). Walcott spoke for a few moments at the alumni dinner that night. What effect, if any, Walcott's sixth honorary doctorate had on his two youngest children is not recorded. Coincidentally, the date was the Walcotts' twenty-second anniversary, and one can almost see Helena beaming at what her serious young man had accomplished since they first met.

They went back to New York and caught the train to Buffalo. From there it was the familiar route to Toronto and then west across Canada. Somewhere along the line, in June, the family was weighed. Walcott recorded a chubby Helena at 186 pounds and an equally sturdy Helen at 145. Young Stuart was a surprising 124 pounds; the tall, thin, sixty-year-old Walcott was a trim 174. "Sidney is to meet us at Calgary en route from Provo Utah. We have not seen him since the winter of 1909" (June 26, 1910).

June still had four days remaining when the five Walcotts arrived in Field, British Columbia, and linked up with packer Jack Giddie. Somewhere en route, perhaps in New York, Arthur Brown had joined the expedition. With the best camp cook in the world and an excellent packer in tow, they collected the new flies which had been ordered to cover the tents. Anyone who doubts that Walcott was not both experienced and meticulous in detail should read the specifications he sent the tentmaker detailing the kind of canvas, grommets, stitching, and a host of other significant features.

Two days after her arrival in Field, Mrs. Walcott wrote to Harry Dorsey, the chief clerk of the Smithsonian, "The pack train has just started off—and we are to follow shortly. We met Sidney at Calgary, well and happy—as we all are. This is a glorious, bracing mountain day—a relief after the intense heat of the journey out."[21]

The first day they went west, passed the Leanchoil station on the Canadian Pacific Railway, left some of the gear, and camped on an island in the Kicking Horse River. Near the mouth of the Beaverfoot River, at Wapta Falls, Walcott found little agnostid trilobites and fragments of larger forms in nodules. These nodules were in a green shale like that seen the year before in a valley east of the Beaverfoot Range. To build up further his local geologic section, he took Stuart and Jack Giddie up the Beaverfoot to the Ice River Valley. The scenery was grand, but the section was no better than at Leanchoil, so back they went.

Next was a quick exploration between Mount Vaux and Chancellor Peak. "Found fossils at several horizons, but not worth much for study" (July 4, 1910). The climb up Mount Vaux proved to be difficult, with lots of brush and downed timber. Walcott, Arthur, and the ladies took the train back east to Field and left the others to bring in the pack string; the nice weather had given way to rain.

"Up at 6 A.M. Went up Yoho valley & camped in Noahs valley under east slope of Mr. Wapta (Camp 8000 feet above sea level) a beautiful camping place in full view of Cathedral Mt. (10,454) good water & fire wood. Feed for animals. All well but very tired at night" (July 8, 1910). The next day, he and Helena went down Yoho Canyon and found a nice locality for Lower Cambrian fossils, sort of a reprise of their honeymoon in Newfoundland in 1888. This was all well and good, but what Walcott wanted to do was get to the Burgess Shale; Jack Giddie and Stuart scouted ahead and reported heavy snow at the campsite.

The rocks on Mount Wapta were too broken up by faults for Walcott's taste. "Moved camp up to Hector at foot of Mt. Bosworth. A rather dangerous trail on account of traveling on railway tracks. Helena went to Field for supplies &

came up to Hector with Arthur on evening train" (July 12, 1910). This combination of fieldwork by horseback and train is unusual, to say the least, but it was an efficient way to examine the country. If there were any unsung heroes of Walcott's time in western Canada, it was the railroad men who let him on and off freight trains and made special stops for his convenience.

The weather continued glorious for most days. They looked at the strata at Sherbrook Lake and climbed the slopes of Mount Odaroy to collect fossils from the Cathedral Limestone. At McArthur Lake a few more Lower Cambrian fossils were found. The weather permitted photographs from the slopes of Mount Odaroy. "With Stuart went to Lake Ocra under Mt. Lefroy—Found traces of fossils at base of Wiwaxy Peaks on Lake O'Hara. Same horizons as on Vermillion Pass in 1909 about 2000 feet down in the St. Piran formation" (July 20, 1910). Walcott spent another day confirming this correlation by beating three species out of the tough quartzite. His knowledge of the local stratigraphy and structure was increasing.

> All well in camp—warm July days—cool nights. Photographed floating ice in Lakes McArthur & O'Hara yesterday & day before—Am tired, footsore & restless today—Will attend to mail & rest up for a long tramp tomorrow around Mt Odaroy—a fine point that goes up to over 10200 feet above sea level. I wish to learn what its s.w. ridge has to say.
>
> Will probably move camp down near Field about the 25th.
>
> Ten days ago the snow was four (4) feet deep at our Burgess Shale camp where I wish to spend ten days collecting. Hope to make camp there by Aug. 7.
>
> Has the paper for the geol. congress at Stockholm been put in type? Ask Mr. Clark to send me copy of No 6. Vol. 53 & No 7. as soon as issued. Also proof of Stockholm paper.
>
> Remember me to all in the office.[22]

They moved the camp to Hector, on the railway, though not before a sudden snowstorm forced reerection of the tents they had just struck. From this new camp, Walcott was "out on Mt. Bosworth with Sidney & Stuart taking photographs. Beautiful day. Helena returned at 8 P.M. to camp. Took a number of views of the Bow valley & mountains Northeast & south of Mt. Bosworth" (July 25, 1910). Photography done, Walcott spent two days collecting *Albertella*, one of the trilobites he had named, near the Hector station. The rest of the camp outfit came in, and the Walcott party headed up Yoho Valley again. No one who has not done it has any idea of the problems involved in packing horses and moving a camp.

Two days before July ended, Walcott, Sidney, and Jack Giddie reestablished the camp at Burgess Pass. Now the real effort of the summer could begin. Walcott and Sidney started the proceedings by going to the top of Mount Field to measure a section and look for fossils. After that, Helena and Walcott went up to the cliff face on the north side of Mount Burgess to scout the ground. August began with "all out collecting the Burgess formation until 4:00 P.M. when a cold wind & rain drove us in to camp" (August 1, 1910). "Out collecting with Helena—Stuart & Sidney. We found a fine lot of 'lace crabs' & various odds & ends of things" (August 6, 1910). The lace crabs were specimens of *Marrella*, the most common Burgess fossil; eventually Walcott was to obtain about fifteen thousand specimens of this genus.

Walcott reported back to Washington:

> Our first continuous rainy day enables me to look over mail and perhaps papers. Have been putting every available hour into collecting and necessary work of camp. Mrs. Walcott is enjoying the collecting & and is now breaking up rock for "lace crabs." The crustacean (crab) fauna is most remarkable. If weather permits we will work the locality very thoroughly—It is 1200 feet up the mountain side from camp in a broken cliff & debris slope. We have to dig out places to stand & sit in. Have a supply of dynamite, etc. & will attack the beds *in situ* as soon as the blocks on the slopes are worked up. The boys are strong & active & we take down slabs of the richest rock for Mrs. Walcott to split up. Helen & Arthur look after camp. Jack Giddie the packer is kept busy looking after the horses—going out for supplies to Field, etc. Field will be headquarters for mail during August unless unforeseen conditions arrive.[23]

There are many myths concerning the Burgess Shale. One, that Walcott used dynamite, is absolutely true. A spinoff that he was promiscuous in its use and destroyed many fine fossils is not true. At Trenton Falls, New York, his brother-in-law William Rust had a rock quarry to fill his lime kiln; there Walcott had learned to blast rock. Another myth is that at the end of the collecting, Walcott dynamited the quarry so that no one else could collect—absolutely false.

Walcott took a couple of days off to take photographs of the area from adjacent slopes, but otherwise the collecting continued more or less as outlined in this letter. There were occasional showers, but still the collecting continued. As a pause from this frantic activity, which was turning up novelties by the double handful, the rest of Walcott's letter to Mr. Dorsey should be mentioned.

> My paper No 7. should be sent to some of the Canadian Alpine Club members. Send a copy to Mr. Arthur A. Wheeler Alpine Club—Banff—Alberta, Can. & ask him to send you a list of 50 members of the club to whom the paper should be sent. Also ask the Director of the Geol. Sur. Can. Ottawa for a list of the members of that Survey & send No 7 to them. Many may be on our regular list. No. 6 (1934) should be sent to the *leading zoologists* of the world.

We were glad to hear about the house. Also of the lot in Whitney Close. Will consider the matter closed when the check comes in. Let me know how the sub-s [subscriptions] to G.W.M.A. building have come in from S.A.R. etc., etc. Will you not kindly remember [me] to Mrs. Burnside & tell her that I hope she will soon be out & well as usual—Tell Mr. Traylor that I miss his news letters such as he sent me last year. All well & happy in camp.[24]

To go to the last paragraph first, the enigmatic "SAR" is the Sons of the American Revolution. After all, what better group could there be to contribute money in honor of George Washington? With all the years of effort and prodding, the memorial was never to come about; on the land authorized by Congress now sits the National Gallery of Art. It is surprising that with incredible fossils to occupy him, Walcott could still fret about this project.

The first paragraph concerns two parts of *Smithsonian Miscellaneous Collections*. Walcott had increased this series so that it was no longer published as a quarterly; thus, each manuscript in turn could be published and there were no restrictions on the length of a manusript. That benefitted everyone in the SI, and Walcott not the least. A great many other people produced profound works in these volumes, but in some way it was Walcott's private journal. His filling an entire volume allowed continuous pagination, a table of contents, and an index devoted entirely to his papers. In business terms, all this was ideal vertical integration. In the field, Walcott gathered the raw materials that he then worked up in his own factory, describing the rocks and fossils. Manuscripts were processed by the Smithsonian Press, and the finished product was sent out through established outlets, with extra copies for special distribution. What a magnificent machine for research had been assembled.

Number seven of volume fifty-three was the little paper on the Bow River Valley Precambrian that Walcott had knocked out in the spring. Because date of publication is a key point in systematics, Smithsonian publications used to be dated; purists may be disappointed that seven bears only the month of August, not the day. Actually number seven was out before number six appeared, on August 12, 1910, but Walcott did not object in the least; the main point was that his completed works appeared promptly. Up to number six, bearing 1934, all Smithsonian publications were numbered in consecutive order as they appeared. The numbers occasionally are cited in references, and they now baffle all librarians, including those of the institution.

Number six was quite a different matter than number seven, for it was a large work, containing forty-four plates, on the principal group of Early Cambrian trilobites. Walcott treated exhaustively of *Olenellus* and the other nine genera he included in the Mesonascidae. This work picks up the trilobites where Walcott

(1890) left off in his early effort on the Olenellus Zone and includes specimens collected as late as 1909. Assignment of all the reports of occurrence in the literature as Walcott had revised them occupies a table twenty pages long. Walcott divided the Early Cambrian into four zones depending on which trilobites occurred. A few years after Walcott's study appeared, a Norwegian paleontologist, also studying the Olenellus zone fossils, commented on this "admirable survey ... which is equally notable for its excellent descriptions and illustrations, and its fruitful impulses."[25]

Paleontology includes both geological and biological aspects. One reason that Walcott wanted to send the paper to leading zoologists was its discussions of the morphology of the various parts of these trilobites, his findings on their eyes, and his views of their interrelations, some of them based on interpretations of larval stages. Few people in the profession produced papers as thorough as this. It was of interest to those who studied arthropods, and that was a sizeable segment of the taxonomic community.

Number six may have been the last word for the moment on trilobites of the Early Cambrian, but the new and incredible Middle Cambrian fossils were at hand. Increasingly, the routine was to bring large pieces down to the camp for Helena to break up. This was more efficient than for her to make a daily climb, and it saved her the effort. The camp was moved up-slope; later Walcott was to record that the fossils were 750 feet above camp, and he would not have made that sort of mistake.

Operations became more complicated when Stuart pierced his shoe and instep with a dropped rock. He was out of action for nearly two weeks. Sidney carried on with Walcott for a couple of more days of collecting. Father and second son rode to Field for a day; Jack Giddie brought down a packstring of three horses loaded with fossils, and off these went to Washington. It was back to camp and a brief excursion with Helen and Sidney to the upper part of the Yoho Valley for photographs of the Presidents Range. Walcott had thoughtfully provided Helena with lots of rock to break up, and he found some magnificent fossils when he returned.

This last part of August brought snow squalls, but the work of bringing slabs of shale down the mountain continued. A break in the weather allowed some photographs of the local area, a pause in the ten-hour days of splitting rocks on the mountain. Fortunately Sunday was a nasty day, so everyone caught his breath. The weather did not improve much, but five more packs of fossils went out to Field. "Squally & cloudy. Went up to fossil bed with Sidney but was driven in by cold & snow squall—Warmer & fine rain at night. We packed up a lot of specimens of crustaceans etc. Helena not feeling well but she worked out 65 specimens" (August 30, 1910). When one looks at drawer after drawer of nicely trimmed Burgess Shale fossils in Washington, one tends not to realize the human effort involved in their collection.

On the last of the month, the two boys and Walcott brought a final load of "worm" rock into camp; most of these slabs were taken down by rope. Weather alternated between fair and terrible, but the strategy of bringing the large slabs down rather than preparing them on the outcrop turned out to be a good one. Nasty days were spent in camp swinging hammers; good days were spent on the outcrop swinging hammers. Good weather became rarer as September moved along. One more letter from camp set the tone: "Four inches of snow yesterday at camp & more up at the quarry. I had a supply of the fossil bearing rock at camp wh. kept me from getting grouchy. All the morning the snow swirled & floated everywhere so I moved up from the "fly" to the big tent & at 10 A.M. was settled for work. . . . The collection is great. Worthy of monographic treatment. It has more fine, new things than I had supposed could be found. . . . I have no time for writing & my hands are so cut up and stiff that it is difficult. Rain, snow, mud add greatly to the physical discomfort but it all passes out of mind after a bath & clean up.[26]

"Clear frosty day. Trail frozen. With Stuart went up on the mountain & cleaned up all rock we had piled up to break for fossils. Found a few good things. Cleaned up after 7 P.M.—Last day of field work for 1910" (September 12, 1910). The outfit still had to be moved to Field, the fossils still had to be shipped, and the bills settled, all in two days. "The season has been a mixed up one. Very little geology but big results in paleontology" (September 14, 1910). Now here is a thought to ponder. In the face of the most significant find of fossils in the world, Walcott was still a bit concerned that the basics of measuring sections and correlating were being neglected. He was not a paleontologist and not a geologist, but a true geologist-paleontologist.

They got an early start from Field to Calgary. Helena, Helen, and Stuart waited for Number Forty-six east to Washington and school. Walcott and Sidney spent the night in Lethbridge. From Lethbridge, Alberta, the route was to Shelby, Montana, then to Great Falls and a night in a hotel. The train wound its way through Montana to Butte, and Charlie got on at Beatles, Idaho. The next stop was Salt Lake City.

This was hardly a social time, though Walcott did see his two older boys again at the headworks in Provo Canyon. It was a quick hello, for he and Nunn went to call on Senator Smoot in Salt Lake City. Walcott judged him to be a fine man, both as senator and citizen. From there, the two went west across the valley to Bingham, Utah, to consult with the Bingham Copper company, a major user of electricity, and then to Millard in southwestern Utah, where Nunn showed Walcott the Beaver River Power Company plant. They then moved back to Salt Lake

City for the trip east. Nunn, several of the other Telluride stalwarts, and Char-lie accompanied them to Chicago. At the Windy City Charlie left for college, and the rest went on to Cleveland. Two hasty days of meetings of the Telluride Power Company ensued, and Walcott finally was home.

He was just in the house for a day. At the end of September, Walcott rented it to Mr. Arthur Emmons of Newport, Rhode Island. Rent from October 15 through June 1 was four thousand dollars; today a comparable house in Wash-ington would rent for more than that a month. The other big excitement was that on October 10 the family went for its first drive in the new Oldsmobile, chauffeured by Alan Drew. Three days later, Walcott was driven out to Bennings on the east side of the Anacostia River to see Graham White fly both a mono-plane and a biplane. That was an impressive performance. Hardly had they moved into an apartment building than Walcott was in New York for a CIW Ex Comm meeting.

Back in Washington after his quick trip to New York, Walcott used the phrase he so often recorded, of pursuing "odds and ends." Walcott most emphatically was developing new initiatives in science. "Had a talk with President Taft on Biological Survey of Panama Canal zone. He approved" (October 27, 1910). Two days later, Walcott was conferring with the assistant secretary of commerce and labor and the assistant secretary of war on this survey. The SI secretary did not let any grass grow under his feet. The Smithsonian Tropical Research Institute in Panama is a relatively new name for what has been a longtime interest in the region.

Walcott also took time to see Interior Secretary Ballinger on behalf of Mr. Nunn and the Beaver River Power Company. Two days later he wrote, "Attended to mail & a few administrative matters. Also put in a little time on Chinese Cam-brian fossils. Am getting behind with my scientific work owing to trivial incidents taking so much time. At University Club smoker 8–10 P.M." (October 31, 1910).

Having made that private complaint, Walcott began November by agreeing to serve on a committee to help his church resolve its debts. If ever there was a self-inflicted wound, it was the time Walcott spent getting into organizations or starting them. He maintained a community of interests, for a few days after his complaint, the chauffeur drove him to Baltimore to witness an aviation meet. A couple of days later, Helena and Stuart accompanied husband and father to hear Theodore Roosevelt present a rousing lecture on savage men and beasts in Africa. The next day Walcott showed TR the new Museum and accompanied him to a men's dinner. One of the highlights of the new mammal hall was to be a pride of lions that Roosevelt had annihilated and brought back to be stuffed.

Late November brought an adventure of sorts (recall that this was still 1910). Mr. and Mrs. Walcott, accompanied by son Stuart, decided to motor to New

York City. The first night the chauffeur got them safely to Chester, Pennsylvania. They completed the second leg of the journey in time to attend the theater. Thanksgiving dinner was at the Van Dusens', and Charlie came down from Yale to join them. Walcott called on various folk, and they dined with the Schiffs'. Helena went north to see Helen, and despite a late start at 2:40 P.M., that evening the car was in Philadelphia; the following day, father and son came home without incident. Elapsed time from Philly to D.C. was nine and one-half hours; perhaps the motorcar was here to stay.

With Helena away, Stuart and Walcott took their meals in the dining room of the Brighton Apartments. Being without a house did not prevent one from being hospitable. H. F. Reid again came from Johns Hopkins to talk to Walcott about the need for more earthquake investigations. Walcott did not have to be sold on the subject; the only questions were ways and means. Reid spent the night, as did other occasional visitors. The secret was another apartment for the use of Stuart and those who dropped in. This was not a bad life for a teenager.

Father and son continued to go to the office on Saturdays. After some two months' delay, the last of the fossils had finally arrived. Stuart unpacked most of the material collected that past summer and reported that almost all had come through transport in good condition. The regents' meeting went so smoothly that it hardly warranted a notice; Walcott's friend Vice President Sherman was elected chancellor. Smithsonian affairs were in good order.

Helena finally returned the day before the CIW Ex Comm met and their annual lecture was held; Carnegie affairs also were in good order. Walcott spent part of the next day showing his Canadian fossil medusa to Dr. Alfred A. Mayer, who was running the Dry Tortugas Station for CIW, and to Dr. T. Wayland Vaughan, a promising young man on the USGS, also interested in corals. Imagine placing a jellyfish on a book and bearing down on top of it with another book. Notwithstanding this flattening, some of the internal details are preserved. Whether Walcott told Mr. Carnegie of his latest fossil finds at the Board of Trustees dinner that night is not recorded.

Mid-December brought disagreeable weather, but despite that, Walcott had to undertake another trip to Cleveland to advise the modified Telluride Power Company on some of its difficulties. He came back via Ithaca, New York, where he saw the Telluride House and the twenty-two "boys" of the Telluride Association. "At 4. P.M. to Attorney General Wickenshaus office to listen to L. L. Nunn present Beaver River Power Co's case. Senator Reed Smoot, S. A. Bailey & Nightingale were present" (December 19, 1910). This really was a political minefield. Pinchot had withdrawn water rights in forest reserves, Ballinger had restored them. Ballinger had been under attack for months and was obviously not going to be accused further of supporting special interests. In the face of all this, Nunn made a fine presentation, and whatever legal qualms there might have been about the installation of the Beaver River power plant disappeared; presumably the u.s. senator and the secretary of the Smithsonian were only present in case Mr. Nunn needed a character witness or two. Telluride Power affairs were in good order.

Four days before Christmas, Charlie came down from Yale. Occasionally Walcott referred to him as Charles, as befitted a young man in college, but old habits are hard to break. Serious administrative problems seldom appear just before holidays, and Walcott had a full day to look over his plates of Chinese fossils. Since coming back in September—despite moving, despite Telluride problems, and despite other tasks—Walcott had been examining fossils from Manchuria to supplement those Willis and Blackwelder had collected in China while he was still director of the Geological Survey.

Christmas Dinner on Sunday was excellent, except that "we all miss Sidney very much" (December 25, 1910). Then the family scattered. Stuart, growing up, went to Cleveland alone and then on to Meteor, Ohio, to see the Garfield boys; Helen had friends in Buffalo. Charlie headed north to enjoy the winter snows of Lake Saranac with the Blagden family. Walcott took part of a day to look over the Burgess Shale medusa again, and then he went to Pittsburgh, leaving Helena with Mollie the cook and Scald the house dog.

The Paleontological Society, organized in 1908 as an offshoot of the Geological Society of America, held its first meeting in 1909. Walcott was at the second meeting of the society and made quite a splash. This was the first professional presentation of his sensational Middle Cambrian fossils. He spoke for twenty minutes about the medusa and another twenty minutes on the antennae and other appendages of the trilobites.

Although his offspring were dispersed, the main point at the close of the year so far as Walcott was concerned was that all were well.

The children have made good records during the year for work, conduct and physical development. The principal items with me were—Degree at Yale in June—great find of Cambrian fossils at Burgess Pass B.C. in association with Helena—Sidney & Stuart. Recognition by Board of Regents of my work at the Smithsonian by raising my salary $2500 to $10,000—In all I have assisted by the hearty cooperation & sympathy of my wife Helena & our children. May 1911 be as kindly to us all as 1910.

We rented our house for the winter of 1910–11 for economic & physical reasons. Economic to get extra money on account of school expenses. Physical to be relieved for a year from the care of housekeeping (December 31, 1910).

Walcott also took the time to write a five-page letter to eighteen-year-old Sidney, alone in Utah. This letter reveals quite a bit about the secretary.

I am at my new desk (made 30 yrs ago) in the Brighton Apt House 2123 California street. We are comfortable & happy altho it was a pull to leave the old home. It is all in a day's work so we will be content here until June 1st 1911—if all is well.

Sorry you feel homesick. I knew the feeling long ago many times but my work & duty were plainly before me and [I] tried each day to get out of that day all there was in for me—and to do what I had in hand as well as it was in me to do it. The result was that I have had a very happy life and succeeded far beyond any expectations I may have had. In fact I have been so occupied with the work of each day that I did not trouble about the future more than to shape events as they came along so as to work into a general plan I had to do certain work if I could.

Knowledge is power and life to the individual so get what you can each day from books—men—nature and your own reasoning on the things that you hear & see. Study the relations of cause & effect. A good life, a decent energetic life leads to one type of manhood. A dirty, unbalanced life leads to degradation, failure and contempt of oneself & life. I think life is worth living & that we can make or unmake it as we wish. We can draw nearer & nearer to our ideals of right, or slip back and see them vanish one by one as we deteriorate.

Physical condition has much to do with the mental & moral nature of man but he can do much to strength the physical if he *will*. You have done well these past two years & I am proud of my boy Sidney & of all our boys.

Mother is a bit tired. She had done a lot of hard tedious work in getting the house in order & in fixing up here & we have had hot, damp weather for two weeks. Now that we are settled I hope Mother will soon get rested & be as light hearted as in 88—when we started in at housekeeping

We enjoy your letters & think of you every day.

With love from all & from your affect[ionate] father.[27]

2

The Dreadful Years (1911–1913): It Is Always Darkest before It Becomes Pitch Black

> Overriding everything else, the *Titanic* also marked the end of a general
> feeling of confidence. Until then, men felt they had found the answer to
> a steady, orderly, civilized life.
>
> —Walter Lord, 1955

THE NEW YEAR began on a Sunday and, naturally enough, the Walcotts attended church services. Afterward, Helena and Walcott had their own private celebration in his office, feasting on a lunch of tea, hardtack, and apples. Monday was the day for official calls, beginning with President Taft and ending with a meeting of the Washington Monument Society. Tuesday, Walcott accompanied Helena to call on the wives of cabinet members. There was a little time for work on the plates of Chinese Cambrian fossils before he had to leave for Cleveland. Businessman/educator Nunn was voted a five-year contract as manager of Telluride Power; that was a problem resolved.

Back in Washington, Walcott was into administration, continuing with the Chinese Cambrian fossils, going to meetings of the Iowa and Ontario Apartment corporations, and eating at a diplomatic reception or two, plus the National Geographic Society dinner. He examined the design for the memorial for John Wesley Powell, the second USGS director, to be built on the south rim of the Grand Canyon; Colonel H. C. Rizer, still handling all the paperwork of the USGS, and William Henry Holmes were the others on the committee. Walcott also attended a meeting of the University Club building committee. All in all, it was a typical first half of January for him, except for one minor point: Walcott had completed his eleventh year as president of the Washington Academy of Sciences and chose not to seek reelection.

The month rolled on. In addition to his other activities for the organization, he published two papers in its *Proceedings*, which, of course, he had helped found. The Appropriations Committee hearing took only part of one morning, which allowed plenty of time for Secretary and Mrs. Walcott to relax before dinner and theater as guests of the vice president. After the performance, they took the sleeper to New York, and Helena went north to Helen's school for a couple of days' visit. Walcott made the rounds in New York, drumming up interest in the GWMA and gathering support for more Smithsonian emphasis in the art field. He heard Theodore Roosevelt expound to the Boone and Crockett Club and was present at the formal opening of the African Hall at the American Museum of Natural History. Then it was back to Washington and the Chinese Cambrian fossils. Major museum-hall openings are not typical, but otherwise this was a representative latter half of a January.

Notwithstanding all the running about, Walcott still had time for his local friends and colleagues. At the second meeting in January of the Geological Society of Washington, Burling (1911) described his new method of photographing the Burgess Shale fossils, and he exhibited examples of his skill. Walcott then showed lantern slides of panoramas he had taken in Glacier National Park. Linking the two on the same program was an indirect boost to the young man.

Late in 1910, *Economic Geology* published an editorial suggesting that more effort be devoted to general problems of ore deposits and less to individual mining districts. Walcott joined a host of others commenting on general principles and views related to that point.

> I believe that in most states and certainly in federal scientific and technical organizations, the authorities would willingly acquiesce in the expenditure of 25 per cent, or more of appropriations for special work, provided it is made clear that the purpose is the discovery of fundamental principles that will be of service in the development of science and natural resources. . . . [T]here are usually a few men, who, by their own initiative, begin special investigations, and all that is needed to obtain large results from them is encouragement and support by the administrative officials. In rare cases men of great originality and force will succeed despite neglect and antagonistic administrative influence. I am very glad that you called attention to the importance of working on special problems in economic geology, as it applies not only to that field but to many other fields of research. (Walcott 1911a, 71–72)

Here are words of wisdom from a man of initiative.

Paleontologist Walcott broadened his horizons farther and joined the Seismological Society of America, formed in the wake of the San Francisco earthquake. Interestingly enough, John C. Branner of Stanford University sponsored his application, yet only a few years earlier the two had exchanged stiff letters in *Science* over geologic investigations in Arkansas (Yochelson 1998). Time changes many things.

"At my office during the day. Called on Vice-President Sherman & Senator Lodge at noon—Worked on descriptions of plates of Chinese Cambrian paper until 6 P.M. In the evening put in two hours 9–11 P.M. on sections of trilobites of my paper of 1881" (February 2, 1911). The remarkable preservation of the Burgess Shale trilobites necessitated his going over his original work on trilobite legs in the light of new information; and Walcott had borrowed his thin-sections, slices of fossiliferous limestone that can be studied under a microscope, from Harvard. Science is not a straight-line process leading to the truth. As to the other manuscript mentioned, "The Report on the Chinese Cambrian is moving along slowly, but I hope to have the 'dead work' completed this month, and the Introduction out of the way and the paper completed in March. As it includes 240 species, it will make quite a contribution."[1]

All was not quite so well with Mr. Nunn as it had seemed in Cleveland, for Senator Smoot told Walcott that the attorney general was considering a suit against the Beaver River Power Company. That bad news was counterbalanced by a visit to Washington by the Vaux family; they all went to hear Gifford Pinchot, former chief forester, speak; Walcott added a few informal remarks. The SI regents met, but Walcott had matters so well in hand that but for the mailing of the announcements, the meeting itself might not have occurred. Despite the smaller size of the SI relative to the USGS, Walcott was busy—only partly as a result of time spent on research—and he wanted a second assistant secretary. Mr. True, the head curator of zoology, was approved for the position, starting in the new fiscal year.

The secretary of the navy had the Walcotts to dinner, but there were so many dinners to attend that there was hardly time to write all of them down. Walcott dashed off to New York for a Carnegie Ex Comm meeting, dashed back, changed in his office, and was able to get to the annual Gridiron Club dinner, wherein all Washington politicians are put on the griddle; it still continues today, a political "roast." Most of the dreary month of February was quiet. "Grinding away all day at various matters and interviews. Completed review of description portions of mss [manuscripts]—on Chinese Cambrian faunas. With Helena attended a very pleasant dinner party at Mr. & Mrs. Sloat Fassetts" (February 21, 1911). Stuart came to the Castle one Saturday and started trimming the Burgess fossils, cutting away the excess shale with a bandsaw. Meanwhile, Walcott described a few of the trilobites. Research was not uninterrupted, for he had to spend some time with his old nemesis Congressman James A. Tawney concerning the appropriation; later he attended the University Club dinner with Mr. Taft. Still, all in all, February began and ended uneventfully.

"A quiet busy day at my office 9 A.M. to 5 P.M.—Decided to work up large 'Sidney Crab' from Burgess Pass B.C. that we found last August—Sidney found the first one" (March 1, 1911). He wrote of that fieldwork: "For thirty days we quarried the shale, slid it down the mountain side in blocks to a trail, and transported it to camp on pack horses, where, assisted by Mrs. Walcott, the shale was split, trimmed, and packed, and then taken down to the railway station at Field, 3000 feet below. Among the finds there were a number of specimens of a beautifully preserved Merostome which will be the subject of this paper, and the first species to be described in a preliminary manner from the new locality" (Walcott 1911b, 18). The extinct merostomes are vaguely related to horseshoe crabs and even more distantly to lobsters, though they are all kissing cousins among the phylum Arthropoda.

Inside of a week, the manuscript was virtually complete (Yochelson 1996). One secret behind such speed was that Walcott would marshal his thoughts and then dictate the text. Generally there was little revision of his draft needed. Burling was available to photograph the fossils, check the references, make sure the figure numbers on the plates were in the proper places in the manuscript, and other niggling and time-consuming details.

Walcott sent a note to his second son, in Utah:

Dear Sidney: I am sending you herewith a photograph of the "Sidney crab" that we found on the ridge near Burgess Pass last summer. Also one of his claws, which has a very complex structure.

The paper describing and illustrating this new form will be published in about two weeks.

You will be interested to know that it represents the highest type of life living in *Middle Cambrian* time. It was before the development of fish, or any animal with two backbones. (About 17,000,000 (17 million)) years ago.

The paper will have a number of illustrations beside the old animal, its mouth parts, breathing apparatus, and different forms of claws.

Much love—Very busy these days—Father.[2]

The letter must have been dictated and typed by a secretary, judging from the syntax in places and the "two," instead of "true," backbones. The underline for emphasis—italicized here—the parenthetical date, and the final paragraph are handwritten. Sidney always addressed Walcott as "Father" when they wrote or spoke. Years later, Sidney told a geologist in Canada that his father had been trying without much success to make a geologist out of him. "On the day the first specimen of *Sidneyia* was discovered, Sidney had climbed as high as he cared to and was relaxing. He idly fingered a piece of rock, broken from the outcrop and there was the fossil."[3] Sidney wrote his own account of his experience collecting from the Burgess Shale, without quite that emphasis on his disinterest in geology (S. S. Walcott 1971).

This discovery pushed the record of merostomes back from Ordovician to Middle Cambrian. Much more importantly, it showed the presence of a fierce predator earlier in the fossil record than had been considered the case. The notion that the earth was of great age, which was being generated by investigation of the decay of radioactive minerals, was still a long way from general acceptance by the profession; Walcott probably derived an age for the Burgess Shale from the numbers he had calculated in 1893 when he considered the rates of deposition of strata.

Another point to be emphasized, one that seems to have been lost on some later workers, is that at the start of his text Walcott was quite emphatic that it was a preliminary report, not a definitive study. The press cooperated in speeding the manuscript, and by April 8 the text, with six plates, was distributed. As regards speed, one minor myth of the Burgess Shale is that *Sidneyia inexpectens* was so named because Walcott was in the field and a baby Sidney came sooner than expected.[4] Since Sidney was eighteen and with father and mother at the time, this story shows how much some folks can read into an innocent scientific name.

Secretary and Mrs. Walcott, reciprocating an invitation given them in February, had twenty-five to dinner in honor of Vice President Sherman. Charlie came down from New Haven for a couple of days; being a college man seemed to agree with him. Calls at the White House were less frequent than when TR had been in residence, but President Taft did consult with Walcott about the River Regulation Board. Walcott was also watching closely Senator Francis Newlands, of irrigation fame, for a bill on forestry research was floating around on Capitol Hill. The latter part of March brought nice weather, and Walcott commonly walked to work. One significant change on the Washington scene was that he no longer took Speaker Cannon on buggy rides; the chauffeur drove them in the Oldsmobile (Yochelson 1998).

"Attended to routine and getting Cambrian material from Burgess Pass ready for illustration. This involves deciding on genera and species and selecting specimens to be photographed" (March 22, 1911). What with interruptions for administration and visitors, it took Walcott four or five days to pick out the specimens to be photographed. The soft-bodied fossils in the Burgess Shale "are pressed flat so that the animal is represented by only a thin film. Fortunately this is darker than the shale and usually shiny, and the contents of the animal are often preserved as a glistening silvery surface, even to the fine details of structure. How clearly the specimens exhibit both external and internal characters is shown by the plate figures which are reproduced from photographs made by reflected light. As it was impossible to bring out all the characters through light falling from one direction, the photographs were touched up by pencil, but not to such an extent as to introduce interpretation of structure not shown by the fossil" (Walcott 1911c, 110).

Another myth of the Burgess Shale is that photographs were so heavily retouched that body features were modified and that Walcott even added nonexistent structures. These are serious accusations; restudy of Walcott's original specimens has destroyed them. He described what was present, and he did not change the morphology—period! For the earliest photographs, shale slabs were propped up on a window sill and photographed late in the afternoon, when the sun's rays fell obliquely on the surface. However, Burling (1911) improved the method by using reflected artificial light, a shrewd and then-novel technique.

March would have been almost an ideal month, except for the death of S. F. Emmons. This senior geologist had been a link to Clarence King, and it must have been a wrench to see the link broken. Still, life goes on, and Walcott celebrated his sixty-first birthday by playing pool with Helena, Stuart, and Helen, who was back from school. Indeed, for almost a week the routine was examining Burgess Shale fossils by day and playing pool at night.

Peculiarly enough, one incident in late March was never recorded in Walcott's diary. On March 26, there was an airplane on the old Polo Field at Potomac Park. In the afternoon, passengers were taken up for brief flights. According to the newspaper account, Mrs. Walcott was present, but when she turned her back, Walcott took a ride. Afterward, it was reported that he declared there was nothing like it, that he only wished that Langley had had the opportunity to experience the flight. This is the only evidence of Walcott ever having flown, and it is indeed strange that he did not mention it.

Early in April, Sir John Murray, a noted British oceanographer, came to Washington; Sir John had made his reputation on the *Challenger* voyage, a major expedition in the history of oceanography (Deacon 1997). They spent several hours studying medusalike forms from the Burgess Shale. The Washington Academy of Sciences held a dinner to honor this distinguished visitor. More or less simultaneously, in mid-April, Charles came from New Haven, Sidney came in from Utah, and the four children were together with their parents—for the last time.

"Routine & started paper on Holothurians of Middle Cambrian from Burgess Pass" (April 15, 1911). Sir John and Walcott agreed that the circular forms were not jellyfish but only looked like medusa. This short preliminary paper, again with six plates, described five new genera of holothurians. Those who have been in the Orient may have eaten sea cucumbers or *beche de mer*; alive or dead, holothurians are not particularly appetizing. They are related to sea lilies and starfish, but they lack the grace and symmetry of those creatures. Later workers doubted that these fossils were holothurians, but still later ones have confirmed

Walcott's interpretation. Isolated plates of individuals occur in beds as old as Late Paleozoic, so this description of soft-bodied forms was a sensation.

Walcott also named *Peytoia* as a jellyfish. This has turned out to be the mouth part of a predator more fierce than *Sidneyia*. Everyone makes mistakes, and until a specimen with the circular mouth in place was discovered, that was a plausible assignment. Before June was half over, this second preliminary paper on the Burgess Shale fossils was published.

Life held much more than fossils for Walcott. "*Easter Sunday* Helen united with the Church of the Covenant in the morning. This completes the list of our family as members of this church. Helena & I are very happy and proud of our clean cut, decent family of children—May all grow into strong, self respecting men, & our Helen, woman" (April 16, 1911). A couple of days later, Charles and Helen left for school. Not knowing it was never to be, Walcott hoped for as happy a reunion in 1912.

While the children were still in town, the NAS annual meeting began. One highlight was a lecture by Sir John Murray in the auditorium of the new Museum, followed by a reception in his honor. Not only was that a resounding success, but Charles Greeley Abbot of the SI was awarded the Draper Medal by the NAS, and Walcott presented a thirty-five-minute talk on his geological reconnaissances in British Columbia. At the final council meeting, Walcott proposed Sir John as a Foreign Associate. Approval came moments before Walcott was called to the telephone, to hear Sir John offer the Academy six thousand dollars to award an Agassiz medal in honor of his late friend. Skill in dealing with people and luck in timing seemed to be intermixed throughout Walcott's career.

"Sidney left us in the evening for Olmstead, Utah via Chicago Salt Lake City & Provo—He is a fine boy and we miss him more & more at each parting. The same is true of Charles & Helen & will be true of Stuart when he goes off" (April 21, 1911). Late April involved another trip to New York City. Walcott was the featured speaker at the dinner of the Aero Club of America. He waxed enthusiastic on Langley's accomplishments with his models, mentioned his part in obtaining funds for the professor's ill-fated man-carrying aerodrome, as Langley termed his machine, pointed out that federal support in purchase of planes had been invaluable, and ended on the note that the government should be involved in research in the field.

After the dinner, Walcott spent two days in New York seeing those with money and checking specimens at the American Museum. His self-imposed internal pressure to publish research was building, and with all the distractions of New York City at hand, the secretary spent the evening looking over his plates of Chinese Cambrian fossils. Seeing Charlie for a day was a pleasure and relieved some of his pressure, but once again Walcott was wearing down from pursuing too many different interests. Worn down or not, Walcott scored another coup. Mr. Albert Kahn of Utah Copper was interested, or had been persuaded to be interested, in setting up a foundation under the Smithsonian to provide funds, drawn from investments overseas, for foreign travel for researchers. It was a grand idea at the time, though inside of a few years the firestorm in Europe was to wreck it before much could be accomplished.

Back in Washington, Vice President Sherman had him to dinner again, though it was more business than social. Mr. Sherman was chancellor of the Smithsonian, and the two had a great deal to discuss about this new foundation. Another distraction from the fossils was a display of flying machines at Bennings, a flat area on the east side of the Anacostia River, the same day that "Kranstrand was painting a sketch portrait of me" (May 7, 1911). (This artist seems to be unknown today.)

"Routine, callers, and administrative matters. Turned in paper on Middle Cambrian Holothurians & medusae—Also an illustrated paper on BC for National Geographic Magazine. Am now taking up Chinese Cambrian Memoir. At my rooms with Stuart in the evening" (May 9, 1911). Helena had gone to Rochester for a few days to see friends, leaving the two bachelors. Walcott used the quiet time to concentrate on the proofs of the Burgess Shale worms paper, and almost immediately the manuscript was back in the hands of the editor. When it was finally completed, eleven plates of photographs accompanied the text.

The worm paper did not appear until September, but a few words here from the author may not be amiss: "I have often searched the fine shale of pre-Cambrian and Cambrian strata for remains of annelids but it was not until the summer of 1910 that anything more than trails or borings were found. The fact that from one very limited locality there have been collected eleven genera belonging to widely separated families points clearly to the conclusion that the fundamental characters of all the classes had been developed prior to Middle Cambrian time. . . . Thus far the annelids collected were incidental to other fossils rather than a direct object of search" (Walcott 1911b, 111). In the paper ten of the new genera are given geographic names, but right in their midst the long-dead A. H. Worthen, state geologist of Illinois, is honored with a patronym. Why this name appeared where it did is a mystery. Worms are difficult, and most of those that Walcott described he placed in new families. One wormlike creature, *Pikea*, is now thought by some to be a chordate, an ancient form in a long line leading to backboned animals and to us.

Walcott began his Burgess Shale publications with description of a sensational arthropod; arthropods were his strong suit among fossils. Still, he then switched to two other major phyla. If one can speculate on the developing research program, Walcott was properly impressed with how incredible and striking was the Burgess Shale. Therefore, he wanted to put on record as soon as possible the remarkable preservation and long geologic range of soft-bodied animals not known before to be preserved in ancient rocks. Anyone faced with such exciting material would have reacted in the same way.

This is also the place to comment on a contribution for popular consumption, "A Geologist's Paradise." As was appropriate for the *National Geographic Magazine*, half the pages were photographs. These included much scenery but also an eye-catching reproduction of one of his plates of *Sidneyia*; in the caption he gave its age as fifteen million years. Walcott added a photograph of another slab of trilobites and also because human interest is important, of the tent camp, with Walcott at his camera and the fair young Helen posing beside a horse.

Walcott was as skilled in popular accounts as he was with technical material. For example: "It is a curious and instructive feature of the geology that the strata of the Rockies, although crowded eastward and thrust out over the later rocks of the plains of Alberta, have not suffered nearly as much dislocation, injury, and alteration as the apparently more massive bedded rocks of the Selkirks. The latter are crumpled, broken, and altered in about the same manner as large blocks of brittle paper would be if subjected to side pressure in a hydraulic press" (Walcott 1911d, 509).

Walcott touched on geology, but it was a very light touch, and anyone who can read the magazine can follow him. In the midst of technical detail, he did not neglect the personal approach. "I well recall stepping off the limestone onto the snow, thinking it hard and secure, and dropping in up to my armpits within a few feet of the rocks" (Walcott 1911d, 515). The secretary ended with a discussion of photography and his panorama camera, plus a few tips on camping. The spectacular part of this article was a 109-inch-long illustration. "A panoramic view of the Canadian Rockies, printed on a strip more than eight feet long and 7 inches wide, and issued as a supplement to the June, 1911, issue of the National Geographic Magazine, represents an outstanding publishing achievement. . . . It remains to this day one of the most marvelous mountain views ever photographed. Twenty peaks, passes, canyons, and other features were distinctly captioned on the supplement" (Grosvenor 1948, 77). The editor did not exaggerate; he also mentioned Walcott as one of the distinguished lecturers to the society.

This is also the appropriate place to mention a 1912 publication. Walcott conceived of another new departure, like his earlier idea of issuing press releases, for the Smithsonian. Probably it was germinated in the spring of 1911, for it takes time to compose a new-style effort, edit text, and print it. Walcott recognized the need to publicize field research so as to encourage the flow of money. For instance, fund-raising for Theodore Roosevelt had been successful; his African safari had paid scientific dividends, and even more importantly, it had brought good publicity to the institution. Walcott's article in *National Geographic* on the Canadian Rockies had provided a model of what to do.

One of Walcott's early actions was to free the *Smithsonian Miscellaneous Collections* from the straightjacket of a quarterly format to publication of manuscripts as received, thereby allowing shorter papers. Each issue of SMC was to be divided into parts, printed separately so they could be distributed widely. Starting in 1912, each year one part of SMC was on "Explorations organized or participated in by the Smithsonian Institution in . . . ." The first installment of this informal series covered 1910 and 1911. This issue was produced on coated paper to ensure that the numerous photographs were reproduced well. The basic message was in the first paragraph: "In recent years, as in the whole of its past history, the Institution has had the aid of public spirited citizens" (Walcott 1912, 1).

To return to the narrative, in mid-May Mr. Freer from Detroit called at the Castle; soon a temporary display of his treasures began to take shape, a real coup by Walcott for the art world. Walcott spoke to the American Federation of Art on the future of the National Gallery of Art: "The United States is the last of the great nations to establish a national gallery. The Smithsonian Institution is popularly regarding as existing 'for the increase and diffusion of knowledge among men' and until recently applied its energies chiefly to this field, but it is also the legalized conservator of the nation's treasures of art."[5] He mentioned the Harriet Lane Johnson bequest, given by the niece of President James Buchanan, he follwed with a great pat on the back to Charles Freer for his generosity (Rathbun 1909). No one could accuse the secretary of neglecting any part of the SI enterprise. Even though art was still a new departure for him, Walcott was pushing it hard.

The Walcott family moved back from the Brighton Apartments to their house, which was just as well, what with hot weather coming on. The apartment was stuffy, and one had to go to the roof to cool off. The Walcotts also took time to see Stuart perform in his high school's Company H of the City Cadets Corps. People outside Washington tend to view the city only as the site of the federal government; in those days, for those who lived there, high schools were of great interest, and they were judged by their cadet companies. Competition between the companies was more important than any of the intramural sports. Today, high school football approximates the rivalry and enthusiasm that the cadets generated.

Despite these high points, the weather in mid-May was bad, remarkably hot even for Washington; on several days it was almost too hot for even Walcott to work. The Walcotts made use of the car, going for afternoon drives in the hope of finding a cool place. A Washington summer cannot be described; to be believed, it has to be experienced. Regardless of the heat, Mrs. Henry F. Dimock came down from New York to lobby for the GWMA building, and Walcott had to see more people than he had anticipated. Helen was going off to visit a school friend, Helena was to be away; this would have been a fine time to concentrate on his research. Fortunately, the lobbying took only a day.

Although monograph fifty-one was still not out, it was in press, and therefore Walcott was no longer confined to the USGS, as far as professional affiliation was concerned. He received a letter from R. W. Brock, director of the Geological Survey of Canada. "On the authority of the Hon. William Templeman, Minister of Mines, I have pleasure in appointing you Collaborator in Geology, with special reference to the study of the Cambrian and Lower Ordovician rocks of the Rocky Mountains. I wish to thank you on his behalf for your generous offer to work with us in the matter, and to furnish us with the important result which you will obtain in your study."[6] One tangible benefit was that this opened to him the prospect of publication in the series of the Geological Survey of Canada; Walcott would avail himself twice of this outlet.

As June began, Walcott was putting the finishing touches to the Burgess Shale annelid worms. Mr. Nunn came to town, and more or less coincidentally, Stuart left to join brother Sidney in Provo; the youngest Walcott was growing up. This left Walcott all alone for one day, which he devoted to his fossils. Telluride affairs took Nunn and him to Cleveland for two days, and he returned home by way of upstate New York. Aunt Helen Sanford was getting old, and Walcott helped her draft a will. Next stop on his itinerary was Wall Street in New York City to see Hayden, Stone & Company and D. C. Jackling to arrange for Telluride Power financing.

He was relieved to get back home. "Prof. J. A. Holmes & Prof. Cottrell of University of California came in after dinner for a talk on assigning certain patents to the Smithsonian" (June 16, 1911). Actually, this is scene two of an important story. At the regents' meeting in February, Walcott had mentioned the "desire of a gentlemen" to present royalty-bearing patents to the institution; the regents put the matter in the hands of the permanent committee to sort out. For the moment this is simply a stray note, but that visit was the first segment of a thread leading to the space age.

"A busy day at my office. Paper No 4 vol 57 S.I. Misc. Coll on Chinese Cambrian fossils came out to day. Monograph 51—of Geol. Survey is progressing finely & I am working on the annelids of the Middle Cambrian of Burgess Pass. Helena & I dined at the Charles J. Bells at Twin Oaks" (June 17, 1911). A few times, Charles—not Charlie, as that did not befit a Yale man—met him at the office, and they walked home the two miles together.

The paper on the Chinese material deserves a few words. First, since Walcott had effectively his own journal, he could fill it with whatever manuscripts he completed, in whatever order he chose. This *SMC* volume already contained the Stockholm paper and two Burgess Shale fossil papers when the Chinese one popped up. Second, the Cambrian of China was very poorly known, and material collected by Bailey Willis and Elliot Blackwelder a few years earlier had been invaluable. Walcott knew more of the Cambrian of China at the time than almost anyone else in the world. Third, if one has good fossil material, one always wants more. Joe Iddings had gone to China and brought back more for his friend. Fourth, this paper would come out sooner than the more detailed, larger monograph.

One result of the study was a three-page list of species previously named that were to be reassigned to other genera as a result of this study. Another result was a page on new specific and generic names. These represented much work, and it is small wonder that references to Chinese fossils kept reappearing in his diary for several years. Because Walcott had a solid grasp of the literature and many comparative collections at hand, his research could be wide ranging. Thus, one should not be surprised to see within the pages of this work a genus named for the Coosa River in Alabama that has a new species from Manchuria assigned to it. The paper does not look nearly as striking as that on the annelids, but it was immeasurably harder to construct.

"Our wedding anniversary 22 years of comradeship and happiness has been our lot—Four fine, decent children we have to love and educate. Helena busy with personal matters & I spent the day at my office" (June 22, 1911). Two days later, Ned Hollister, director of the National Zoological Park, left for British Columbia on an Alpine Club–Smithsonian expedition to Mount Robson, taking Charles along as an assistant. Walcott also completed his paper on the Burgess Shale annelid worms, which was on its way to the printers by the 27th of June, after only three days in the editor's office. What more could one ask of life? A fantastic wife, a namesake son following in one's footsteps, and research on fossils undreamed of before. The weather was disagreeably hot, but one cannot have everything.

The research machine was running at full throttle. "Began work P.M. on fossil crustacea from Burgess Pass. Conference in the evening with Joseph A. Holmes & Prof. Cottrell of California" (June 26, 1911). Cottrell was a brilliant chemist/inventor—he appears in dictionaries under "Cottrell precipitator"—that Holmes was trying to recruit for the new Bureau of Mines. (Place an electrified grid across a smoky chimney, and smoke and dust will coagulate rather than go up into the atmosphere. It is actually a complex process, but that is the essence, and Cottrell had done what no one else could. Without Cottrell, the industrial world might have choked on its air pollutants decades sooner.)

Because Walcott had familiarity with coal-burning power plants, cement manufacturing, and metal smelting, plus a smattering of knowledge about the generation of electricity, he immediately realized what might be involved in Dr. Cottrell's discovery. Cottrell, however, was not interested in making money. He wanted to give the proceeds away to support science. He had some notion of what good might be done with funds freely given. This offer of patents was a most tantalizing prospect and one that Walcott was able to develop.

A couple of days later, Walcott's sentimental side came to the fore. He jotted in his diary, "This is the day we met in 1887 & learned the old old story" (June 28, 1911). Helena and Walcott embraced, and Helen went off to Massachusetts for a few days' visit; it was just as well, for by July 4, the Washington summer was at its worst—106 degrees. Walcott had to spend some time fussing with the University Club Building Association, but little otherwise interrupted his research.

"Have had a quiet week. Made progress on Cambrian crustacea paper. A good time with Helena" (July 8, 1911). The next day was a "hot, muggy day—In house until 7 P.M.—when Helena & I went for a motor ride. We had a long talk during the day on family & personal matters. Helena prepared draft of her will and memoranda relating to her personal belongings in the house" (July 9, 1911). Who can say what brought on this discussion, unless it was Aunt Helen's age and her drafting a will. On the 10th, Helena left for Boston to meet Helen, for the two ladies were to spend the summer with friends in New England.

"Helena killed at Bridgeport Conn[ecticut] by train being smashed up at 2:30 A.M. Did not hear of it until 3 P.M. left for Bridgeport 5:35 P.M. accompanied by George Otis Smith" (July 11, 1911). News of the tragedy sped through Washington. Half a century later, the retired president of the McLaughlin Bank could recall being given an envelope of cash by his father with orders to hand it to Dr. Walcott, who would need it for the trip; the boy was not to worry him by asking for a receipt.

The New York, New Haven, and Hartford train had been crossing a viaduct on which a switch had been left open. It had plunged to the ground, killing those in a day car behind the locomotive, as well as some of the occupants in the sleeping car following that. Helena may have been killed by a blow to the temple, but some accounts were far more gruesome. It was hours before the bodies were identified; the first newspaper account listed Helena with residence unknown. Walcott brought the body back to Washington. "I went home where Helena lives in everything about it—My love My wife—my comrade for 24 years—I thank god I had her for that time. Her untimely fate I cannot now understand" (July 12, 1911). "It is difficult to reason why or how. The problem is unthinkable" (July 14, 1911).

Helen left an account of the tragedy. She had been visiting the home of Albertine Hoyt, her roommate at Farmington school.

> After a week or so, we left for their summer camp of Lake Muskoma in Canada. Happy days of fishing, sailing, swimming picnics, passed rapidly. In a few days I was to join mother in Northeast Harbor, but late one morning Mr. Hoyt turned up unexpectedly from Buffalo. I was soon sent for; went in to see him alone, the whole procedure rather frightening and strange. He told me my father needed me very badly. There had been a wreck in Bridgeport of the Congressional Ltd. from Washington. . . . Her nightgown [had] had her name on it so a newspaper man who knew of Daddie, [had] called him in Washington about four in the morning. . . .
>
> Father was upstairs when I arrived and when I went in, he put his head on my shoulder and cried. I had never dreamed my strong wonderful Daddie could break down. . . . [T]here seemed to be no end to the telegrams, letters, and flowers. There were over a thousand. The heavy scent of the flowers permeated the house, and to this day I do not like cut flowers very much.
>
> Charlie, on a surveying trip in British Columbia, did not get word until a month later. Then a trapper went through with one of the many telegrams that were sent. It merely said that mother was killed in a train wreck—that was all. I was supposedly with her. No word from me, of course for no one remembered that he thought I was with her. He started back to civilization for details—short-cutting over passes where horses couldn't go—fording rivers, sleeping in his wet clothes. It took him three days and three nights and father always thought his terrific exertion at that time weakened him.[7]

Before the tragedy, the Alpine Club of Canada had planned a major expedition to chart the essentially unknown area around Mount Robson, the highest peak in the Canadian Rockies. The leader had searched for Canadian geologists and zoologists to join the group, to no avail. "Failing there I applied to Dr. Walcott who is a personal friend of my own. He took the matter up with enthusiasm, arranging to come himself for the Geology and to send Mr. N. Hollister of the United States National Museum and Dr. Walcott's son for the other branches of natural history" (Wheeler 1911, 182). Apparently Helena and Helen had meant to stay in the northeast the summer that Helena was killed.

The SI sent a short obituary announcement to several foreign journals, which noted that in 1888 Mrs. Walcott had helped her husband collect in Newfoundland and had accompanied him in the field for eighteen seasons. Mr. Rathbun was ill and trying to recover in Maine, where the weather was cooler. He offered to return, but Walcott wrote insisting he stay in Maine until he was healthy.

Assistant Secretary True wrote Assistant Secretary Rathbun, "Mr. Walcott's condition is truly pathetic. She occupied, and ably, so large a share of his life. It was only through her activities that he secured the time for his special scientific work. I am glad to know that he will go west. It is the only thing for him to do. He needs the diversion and the work to occupy his thought."[8]

A week after the funeral, Walcott went to New York City. His cousins and L. L. Nunn offered what comfort they could. He went to New York Mills and then on to see Aunt Helen Sanford. The train took him to Cleveland. Helen, Sidney, and the Garfield family helped settle him a bit, and he got enough of a grip on life to attend a Telluride meeting. (It was agreed to build a plant at Oneida Rapids if $500,000 in bonds could be sold; Walcott subscribed to five thousand dollars.) He took the steamboat to Buffalo and looked at the Niagara Falls plant run by Nunn's brother, boarded the train to Toronto, and began the long, lonely ride west. Sidney and Helen were present, but the trip was lonely, notwithstanding; he wrote letters and a manuscript, but that did not fill the loneliness.

"Arrived in Field 9 A.M. went to Mt. Stephen House for lunch & to change clothing. Mr. Burling met us & we all went up to our old Burgess Pass camp. Found Mrs. Burling & Arthur there. All is natural except that Helena is not here to welcome us. Rain & mist" (August 6, 1911). The field group included George Hawkins to help with the heavy work, and packer Howard Coleman. Work began at the quarry. "All but Arthur upon fossil bed. We found a fine lot of fossils & greatly enjoyed the sunshine & dry air" (August 10, 1911).

Through good weather and not-so-good weather, the quarrying went on. Like the year before, great slabs were slid down the mountain and broken up in camp. A school friend of Helen's showed up for a few days, which enlivened activities. When the weather was good, ten-to-twelve-hour days were put in on the mountain. "Out on the fossil bed all day with Sidney & Hawkins. We found a few good fossils & made preparations for work next week by blasting out a lot of rock" (August 26, 1911). Even with all the exciting fossils at hand, Walcott was still restless with memories. "This is our third week in this camp. Will be glad to move on next week to some other spot" (August 27, 1911).

Helen's account adds more personal detail. "I was not quite the gangling string bean I had been. I was very close to Daddie that summer. I remember one evening we walked up to Surprise Point on Burgess Pass. . . . It was very beautiful, and as we sat there, Daddie began wondering about Mother[:] . . . where she was . . . how all the laws of Nature were against her just being snuffed out like a candle . . . but where was she? How would he know her? He had faith that there was something else, but what? Where? That was my first realization that father, grownups, didn't know all the answers; that they, too, questioned, and sought help."[9]

Burling left for a short trip to scout other localities. After another ten days with Helen and Sidney, Walcott reported, "We found a lot of fine things. Trilobites with legs the most noteworthy" (September 2, 1911). The weather began to deteriorate, and they took a tent up to the quarry for occasional shelter for the last few days of work. "At noon Sidney, Hawkins & I completed work at fossil quarry & went down (800 feet) to camp where we broke up *"Marrella"* rock until 6 P.M." (September 8, 1911). "Today closes five weeks at Burgess Pass camp. We are all stronger & happier than when we came" (September 9, 1911). In this five weeks, Walcott put in twenty-eight days on the mountain in hard physical work, not a bad record for a sixty-one-year-old bureaucrat. Once the fossils had been packed to Field, the party moved to the Imasco River, near Otto Creek, to look at Van Horn Mountain, scouted out earlier by Mr. Burling; the Burlings had moved on.

Now comes a small distraction. On September 12 Walcott wrote that he was "not at St. Andrews University," referring to the five-hundred-year celebration of that institution in Fife, Scotland. Apparently the secretary of the Smithsonian had been scheduled to represent the Smithsonian and receive a degree; Dr. Leonhard Steininjer, a vertebrate zoologist on the staff, went in his place. St. Andrews had a policy against awarding honors in absentia, but late in December Walcott received a doctorate of laws; seven other degrees were also conferred on individuals who could not attend. It is the policy of that university to destroy all papers bearing on honors, so one cannot today determine whether Andrew Carnegie may have jotted a note to move things along.

Back in British Columbia, several days of rain necessitated moving the camp. On the other hand, the trout particularly liked the cloudy weather, and Walcott had a great time fishing. When the group finally got to Imasco Pass, its members were rewarded for their trouble with some Middle Cambrian fossils. The weather was too poor to do geology, but father and son went fishing and brought back a few trout. Snow began again, and the party retreated to Field. "This closes our camping for 1911" (September 21, 1911). The Walcotts stayed around for two more days. As regards the field season, "It has been a half hearted one for me & my interest & strength have not returned in full force" (September 23, 1911).

While Walcott was still in the mountains, another honor was heaped upon him. September 6, 1911, marked the hundredth anniversary of the Universitat i Oslo, celebrated in grand style. That institution had begun as Christiania University and had became the Royal Fredericks University, changing its name when Norway emerged as a sovereign nation and Christiania became Oslo. This was not quite as noteworthy as the five hundred years for St. Andrews, but it was a major event for the new country. Walcott received another honorary doctorate in token of his work on Cambrian fossils; there is little doubt that his longtime friend W. C. Brøgger was responsible. Few people receive honorary degrees, and very few receive as many as Walcott did; to be awarded two honorary doctorates in one year is most unlikely. One cannot say that with Helena gone such honor was ashes in his mouth, but he made no reference in his diary to the degrees from either Norway or Scotland.

The mountains were soothing, but it was time to go. At Calgary, Arthur Brown arranged to store the equipment, said goodbye, and headed home. From Calgary, it was on to Lethbridge. Walcott spent the time from Lethbridge to Great Falls writing an introduction for his delayed manuscript on the Burgess Shale crustaceans. Sidney and Helen found less intellectual entertainment.

There were still two days left in September when the Walcotts' train finally got to Salt Lake City and continued south to Provo. Sidney stayed until the first of the month before heading east. Helen kept Walcott company at Olmstead, although there was so much Telluride business that he hardly had time to pine.

The company was negotiating a ten-year contract with the Utah Light and Railway Company. Added to that were the complications with Beaver River Power Company and possible federal problems, plus the untangling of this holding from the rest of Telluride. That was not the only problem. "In 1911 a committee was appointed to arbitrate the complaint by James Campbell, a shareholder, that the expenditure of Telluride Power money for education by L. L. Nunn was not beneficial to the stockholders' interests. The committee included O. M. Stafford, C. D. Walcott, A. T. Perry and D. T. Perry. The disagreement resulted in the sale of Telluride Power to Utah Power & Light in 1912."[10]

Business was partially straightened out in a week, and father and daughter headed to Chicago. They distracted themselves with a day's sightseeing in the Windy City and then were forced to return to Washington. "Oh! but that Helena could have welcomed us. Her home her children—her life & she not here. Why! Why! Why!" (October 10, 1911). Sidney and Helen helped Walcott select a lot in Rock Creek Cemetery, and Helen enrolled at Holton Arms School in Washington. Walcott took a trip to New York and saw a few people, but he was more interested in going on to see Charlie. He sat through a Carnegie Ex Comm meeting and came home to the house—the home without Helena. In his diary, Walcott reported that matters were in hand except for many personal letters to write, but one senses he was not much interested in affairs.

Professor Schuchert of Yale had a "chat with Charlie and learned of his summer work in the high mountains of British Columbia. I was delighted to hear from him that your health is good and that Miss Helen is keeping house for you. It must have been a great deal of comfort to you to have your daughter and two sons with you in the camp."[11] Charlie/Charles Jr. was apparently doing well in New Haven.

About the only distraction was when one of his neighbors, the French ambassador, called to discuss parking on 22d Street. Charlie had come down from Yale to share his grief when his mother was interred, but he left the next day. Walcott began unpacking the Burgess Shale and started looking at the crustaceans, the ancestors of today's shrimp and lobsters. The fossils helped sooth his soul a bit. He took up work on his study of the Chinese Cambrian fossils, to be published by the Carnegie Institution of Washington. Joe Iddings came for a visit, and Whitman Cross dropped in to talk over NAS financial matters.

He poked over a few fossils from the Potsdam Sandstone in eastern New York in connection with other Upper Cambrian faunas. Walcott did not resist being elected to the board of managers of the University Club. "Work on Burgess shale fossils of B.C.—began by sawing out specimens collected of 1911" (November 10, 1911). One of the myths that has grown up is that Walcott knew no zoology and did not consult with those who did. Like the other myths mentioned earlier, it is wrong. The invertebrate zoologist A. H. Clark had come to Walcott and practically begged to restudy *Eldonia* so he could refute A. H. Clark and show that this fossil really was a holothurian (Clark 1912, 1913). Clark did not hesitate to deal with the secretary on zoological matters.

> My comments are given in a series of memoranda, some of which refer to marginal numbers on the proof.
>
> Of course I assumed when you handed me the paper that you wished me to give it exactly the same kind of criticism that I would a paper published by someone unconnected with the Institution; it will get this sort of criticism anyhow, and it is much better to have it now than after publication.
>
> If any of my suggestions appear unwarranted, or too batheresque, I am of course willing to discuss the matter in detail and explain the position taken.[12]

There is a little tongue in cheek here, for F. A. Bather was an eminent worker in the British Museum.

Despite reading proofs and soliciting critical comments, Walcott was far from settled in his mind. He went to Arlington Cemetery to look at various styles of gravestones. Mr. Nunn came in for a day or so. The real savior was Mrs. Garfield, Helena's best friend, who left her family in Ohio to organize the disorganized household and sooth the widower. She took Stuart back to Cleveland when she left. Walcott followed, in part to try to resolve Telluride difficulties. After a few days of visiting the Garfield family, Walcott finally had a grip on his changed life.

Walcott went up to New York City for the NAS fall meeting. Apparently he took Burling, for CIW president Billings wrote that Burling had forgotten his briefcase. As part of the proceedings, Walcott presented a memorial to Samuel Pierpont Langley (Walcott 1912a). Much of this had been written by A. H. Clark, and the paper duly notes that point. While in the city, he called on Mrs. Henry F. Dimock. She was a real sparkplug, a person who might be able to keep the GWMA project moving; it was a worthy effort, and such a building in Washington could have many uses. The problem was that Walcott could only pursue so many items at one time, and this association was no longer at the top of his list.

Walcott was finally sleeping better and, despite the cold weather, still used the sleeping porch at the back of the house. He visited the cemetery several times but apparently could contain his grief. He accepted election as president of the Board of Trustees of the Church of the Covenant, perhaps because Helena would have wanted him to undertake this job. He also motored to Annapolis, Maryland, for Stuart was considering the Naval Academy and wanted to see the facilities.

"Conference with Holmes, Cottrell & Parsons in re. Patents" (December 3, 1911). An indication of Walcott's continuing distraction is that he did not use "Dr." or "Prof." in referring to these men. The same day he met with Judge George Gray, a key Smithsonian regent. Cottrell was his guest at dinner two days later, and likely it was here that they began to discuss what to do if the Smithsonian would not accept Cottrell's patents.

He also had a scientific visitor, Prof. William Patten from Dartmouth College, who discussed the origin of vertebrates with him. This man had devoted most of his life to study of *Limulus*, the living horseshoe crab. According to one story, during a summer lunch at the biological station at Woods Hole, Massachusetts, the conversation turned to the issue of which of the invertebrate group had given rise to the vertebrates. Patten decided it was a fruitless topic, and to show that similarities could be found in any group of invertebrates, he compared the features of horseshoe crabs and vertebrates. He presented this as a preposterous hypothesis the following day but became so charmed with his idea that he was to spend the rest of his life pursuing it.

Walcott had to go to Cleveland again to smooth over the sale of Telluride Power to Utah Light and Railway; that took two days of his precious time. Walcott was not, meanwhile, neglecting his duties as a father. Helen was interested in a European tour, and Walcott discussed this with Miss Anna Horsey, a forty-year-old traveling companion and niece of a Supreme Court justice. As to Stuart and the Naval Academy, they went to see President Taft—not every father can take his son to talk to the president about a presidential appointment to Annapolis. There may have been a bit of quid pro quo in this conversation.

Someone had arranged for Taft to give a presentation to the American Institute of Architects; Walcott and his neighbor the French ambassador filled out the program.

The Permanent Committee of the Board of Regents had met prior to Walcott's trip to Cleveland. In effect, the three members wanted the money that Cottrell's patents might produce but not the complications that might come from the si's actually owning the patents. Regent Alexander Bell had experience with the problems of patent infringement and lawsuits. Secretary Walcott, the fourth member of the committee, had the solution. Thus, at the annual meeting the regents resolved to decline the offer yet resolved to accept freely any money that the owners of the patents might wish to present.

Walcott was back in his old form, in that he proposed setting up a corporation, to be run by disinterested men, to oversee the patents. "In this connection, it would seem desirable to have the moral support of the Institution back of the company, to the extent that the secretary and the Permanent Committee, if desired, could take up with the members of the company the questions of the appointment of the members of this board."[13] The regents never voted but tacitly agreed that Secretary Walcott could go out and make money for them. The performance was Walcottian manipulation at its finest. Cottrell was given the opportunity to appear and explain his proposed gift after the secretary had set the stage. It all went so smoothly that that same afternoon, Walcott was at the CIW Ex Comm meeting; again, not a ripple disturbed the formal proceedings.

Formal meetings done, there were lots of odds and ends to be pursued, and Walcott was still distracted, but some of his attention was finally focusing again on fossils. Earlier Dr. A. C. Lawson, then of the Geological Survey of Canada, had sent some intriguing material from Steep Rock Lake in Canada; Walcott finally decided that the objects were sponges. The rocks were old, and sponges are considered among the most primitive of animals. It was just possible that these objects might be the oldest fossils in the world.

"Christmas day. We (Charles, Sidney, Stuart, Helen & I) had our Christmas tea at 10 A.M. with Mollie, Arthur, Catherine, Nellie & Fred Kennett of the household" (December 25, 1911). It was a sad time, and Walcott was ill on top of that. The annual meeting of the Geological Society of America was in the new Museum building, but Walcott was sufficiently sick to miss the first day. He struggled to give a talk the next day, with A. C. Lawson, on the Steep Rock material. The following day he presented a lecture on his Burgess Shale crustaceans to the Paleontological Society.

The year was over. "Am glad 1911 has passed. It robbed me of my loved wife & comrade—The children are all well & we have much to be thankful for but our home life has received a blow that for us all cannot be less than a practical crushing out of the happy conditions of the past twenty-three years" (December 31, 1911).

This New Year's Day there were no official calls. "A quiet day for me. At my laboratory except for a meeting of the Washington Monument Society 1–2 P.M. at home of Theo. W. Noyes. Conference with L. D. Burling on his future work A.M." (January 1, 1912). Mr. Burling was becoming restless. Charles, Helen and several of their young friends took the secretary to hear the Yale Glee Club that evening. Sidney and Stuart came home from the Garfields' in Ohio, and the family, less Helena, was together again; once more, Walcott did not know this was a gathering of his children not to be repeated.

In the first work day, he was able to get several hours for research on the Burgess Shale arthropods. Also, he talked to Cottrell, for it was now time to pick up the patent problem and resolve it. Walcott may still have mourned, but he was back to full steam on his research. "Working on revision of Middle Cambrian Burgess Shale Crustacea paper in galley proof. This & mail took up most of day. I have four papers under way. Wish to complete memoir on Chinese Cambrian this month" (January 3, 1912).

Five days after his comment concerning four papers, Walcott began a short paper on the Cambrian-Ordovician boundary in British Columbia. J. A. Allan of the Geological Survey of Canada came down to see Burling. They had found some key fossils in the right place, and, with Walcott's identifications, this helped determine the stratigraphic position of a particular rock unit.

That out of the way, Walcott saw to the affairs of the Iowa and Ontario Apartments; these required only one meeting a year, but Walcott showed up consistently to ensure that all functioned well. Next he started the preparations for his daughter's coming trip. Miss Horsey of New York and Helen were to leave on the 24th of January on the *Cedric*, bound for Italy. Presumably the trip was to put a European polish on his western mountain girl. One of the local papers carried a little note about the secretary's daughter leaving for Naples; Walcott clipped it and put it in his diary. Later that month another parting took place, when Sidney finally decided on Cornell University.

Walcott met Cottrell in Boston. They spent two days discussing with various people their scheme for a corporation, both to make money from the precipitation patents and to give it away. Boston is just across the Charles River from Cambridge, and Walcott took time for a Burgess Shale problem. Walcott had described holothurians in 1911, and H. L. Clark, one of the few holothurian specialists in the world, had objected in print; a visit to see him was appropriate. Walcott caught up with Cottrell at the Chemists Club in New York. They spent three more days talking to prospective trustees, looking at laboratories, and drawing up rules and regulations for their proposed company.

Although Walcott was occupied with SI administration during the following week, he still found time to prepare a report for Congress on the Newlands bill concerning America's waterways. He also polished off the short boundary paper documenting the occurrence of fossils. Helen and Walcott now left for New York City. The next day, Charles joined them for breakfast, and father and son saw Helen under way for Europe. Walcott spent another day discussing the precipitation company with various New Yorkers and then headed home.

He had not quite five full days in Washington. During that time, besides all the administrative routine, Walcott completed a short paper on a trilobite not hitherto known in America. For good measure, he took Mrs. Dimock to the Capitol for a final conference on the site of the George Washington Memorial Association building; a few days later, Sen. Elihu Root would submit a bill to Congress for a donation of the land. The first of February saw him back at his favorite hotel in New York, the Belmont, for the night. "At 2 P.M. meeting of men to organize 'Research Corporation' 2–5 P.M." (February 2, 1912).

This does not sound impressive, but what Walcott and Cottrell had done in a very few days during January was to locate people willing to serve on the Board of Trustees. The trustees all agreed to serve without any compensation. More than that, they agreed to finance the company; if all went well, they would get back their original investment, but nothing more. Finally, they agreed that all profits from the company were to be given away. Dr. Walcott and Professor Cottrell were persuasive men.

Walcott reported his activities to the SI regents. "After discussion, it appeared to be the informal opinion of the regents that it would be well to have Mr. Walcott on the Corporation in his individual capacity. His name, therefore, will be added to the list of incorporators before the charter is filed."[14] Walcott could not know it at the time, but the Research Corporation would turn out to be quite a handful. The patents could not simply be licensed, for each installation had its own set of problems. In the end, the corporation went into business building and installing precipitators. This presented more of a managerial problem than anyone on the board had bargained for.

With the RC out of the way for the moment, Walcott could look at some fossils. These were ancient history, not in that they were old but because this was the Upper Cambrian fauna from Saratoga Springs, New York, that Walcott had first seen in 1878. After a day or so on this fauna, Walcott moved to working on the Late Cambrian of Wisconsin, the subject of his first job for Professor Hall in the fall of 1876. The interest now was in a detailed study of the Dikelocephalidae, trilobites with large, flat tails.

The Ex Comm of CIW did something unusual that February, in that they met in Philadelphia, probably because the eighty-two-year old S. Weir Mitchell could not travel. Walcott attended the meeting at which Mrs. Dimock was reelected to head the GWMA, but during the middle of the month Walcott mostly worked at home, trying to complete the introduction to his Chinese Cambrian memoir. He did go out to Arlington National Cemetery, where a monument at the grave of Major Powell was unveiled; whether this monument had been thought of before the one for the Grand Canyon rim is not clear, but Walcott had been involved in raising funds for both.

Mr. Freer called again. He was a meticulous man and one who had to be treated with extreme care. According to some authorities, Freer had contracted syphilis while he was a young man in the Far East and was erratic, verging toward crazy; over the years Walcott kept him on the rails in Smithsonian dealings. Walcott also had a couple of conferences with E. O. Ulrich of the USGS about Late Cambrian–Early Ordovician fossils. Walcott mentioned about this time in his diary that he was wearing down; from what is known of Ulrich's notions on correlation and his method of discussion, it may be that these conferences were what wore him out.

The day after March began, Walcott did something most unusual. He went on vacation, to Jeckyll Island, off the coast of Georgia. While there he did nothing—wrote no manuscripts, prepared no annual reports, nothing. It was entirely atypical; this week was unique in his life. One nice aspect of science is that once the author has corrected the printer's proofs of his paper, the rest is automatic. While Walcott loafed on a beach, part 8 (on the new American trilobite species which had migrated in from Sardinia) of his volume fifty-seven came out.

As to part 7, which appeared on the same day, earlier at the Geological Society of Washington meeting, "Mr. K [*sic*] D. Burling described the reexamination by Mr. J. A. Allan and himself of the Mount Bosworth (British Columbia) section described by Dr. Charles D. Walcott in 1908, in an attempt to determine the position in that section of a series of 2300 feet of Cambrian shales and limestones measured by Mr. Allan in the Ice River Region, and announced the finding of typical Upper Cambrian (Sherbrooke) fossils in the "Ordovician" beds forming the top of the exposed section, a discovery which enabled them to place the Ice River beds in the interval between the Sherbrooke and the true Ordovician" (Anderson and Richards 1912, 357).

Field geology consists in part of ever-finer correlations and divisions of strata. Burling had made a useful contribution.

Purists will note that part 6, "Middle Cambrian Branchiopoda, Malacostraca, Trilobita, and Merostoma," was published five days after parts 7 and 8—close enough not to trouble anyone. Part 6 is quite a respectable piece of research, with eleven plates and nearly sixty pages of text. It was still called a preliminary paper, but in it Walcott delved fairly deeply into the relationships among the various groups of arthropods. The details of the highly technical discussion can be followed by only a limited number of paleontologists. However, the new information provided by the diversity of forms in the Burgess Shale was of general interest to all biologists.

Right in the middle of the descriptions are several pages devoted to limbs of trilobites, a consequence of the material quarried in 1911. This provides a further indication that Walcott's primary goal was to produce illustrations and descriptions in a timely fashion, without waiting for monographic treatment. "In the near future I wish to review the conclusions published in my paper of 1881, and those that have been entertained regarding *Triarthrus becki* and the new material from the Burgess Shale" (Walcott 1912b, 192).

The new arthropods got some exotic names. As in prior papers on the Burgess Shale, almost all of these generic names were based on Canadian place-names, but Walcott also honored a Swedish paleobotanist, and *Marrella* recognizes a British colleague. That genus is the most common form in the fauna, yet only one letter between Walcott and John Marr can be found. The best guess is that Marr had been instrumental in Walcott's receiving the Cambridge 1909 honorary degree and that Walcott was showing his appreciation. (Because of the lack of critical papers, the life of a historian of science is not always easy, though it is certainly far easier than that of a scientist worthy of investigation by a historian.) That is as good a note as any on which to end a week of relaxation.

Because there is such an abiding interest in these fossils, it is worthwhile to repeat a few comments that Walcott sent to Schuchert, Schuchert having read part 6 written to him about it.

> *Marrella* is certainly a most interesting animal. It is not a trilobite. It appears to have more points in common with the Trilobite, as I now understand it from specimens here, than with *Apus*. I have recently discovered some wonderful gills in the Trilobites from the Burgess Shale. The Trilobite has both the broad setiferous lobes on the exopodite, and also peculiar, elongate, slender gills.
>
> I do not wonder you stumble over *Opabinia*. An additional number of them have turned up in the collections of 1911, none of which lead me to change the conclusion that they are crustaceans.[15]

"*Opabinia* had five eyes at the front of the head and a long flexible proboscis that ended in an array of grasping spines" (Briggs, Erwin, and Coller 1994, 210). Everyone stumbles over *Opabinia*.

Of course, two days after Walcott arrived home from his vacation, he was on a day trip to New York with Cottrell to further the interests of the Research Corporation. Naturally enough, Walcott was elected to its executive committee, but he was able to resist being shanghaied into the presidency; at the time no one took that office.

Following that New York City stint, Walcott came home for a couple of days to catch up on paperwork and play pool with Stuart. His next stop was in upstate New York to see Aunt Helen. While he was in the neighborhood, Walcott gave a talk at the City Club of Utica on the Smithsonian Institution; it was a case of a local boy making good and coming home to be feted. Notwithstanding, Walcott indicated in his lecture that more money was needed in the endowment.

On his way south, Walcott stopped at Philadelphia. "Lunched at the Academy [of Natural Sciences]. Went to Bryn Mawr with Miss Mary Vaux to visit the farm. Returned to supper with her & her father" (March 20, 1912). That was a bit of a detour, for next he doubled back to New York for a CIW Ex Comm meeting. Philadelphia, the city of brotherly love, was beginning to hold some interest for widower Walcott.

In Washington the hearing before the Appropriations Subcommittee was straightforward and took less than two hours. As a ceremonial duty—such things are a significant part of the responsibilities of any secretary of the Smithsonian—Walcott accepted a portrait of John Ericsson, designer of the famous uss *Monitor* during the Civil War. Walcott was just getting back to his Chinese Cambrian fossils when the Congress called with another interruption. Someone had had the bright idea of transferring the Naval Observatory to the si; Walcott was able to scotch it.

For a change from the Chinese material, Walcott went back to the Burgess Shale by day and playing pool at night, a reprise of the previous year. Early in April, Walcott went to Rock Creek Cemetery to see the monument that had been installed at the Walcott gravesite. Charlie came down from Yale, looking livelier than on his past visit, and Sidney came in from Cornell; life was looking up. "At church A.M. with Charlie, Sidney, Stuart. All well & strong. I felt the absence of Helena & Helen most keenly. After luncheon went to the cemetery with Sidney & Stuart" (April 7, 1912).

No sooner had the two older boys left than Freer came in from Detroit to look over the temporary display of a few of his treasures. He was satisfied with the exhibit. (For those who wonder where it was, for thirty years a life-size model of a blue whale hung over the area in the central hall on the southwest side of the Museum of Natural History where Mr. Freer's delicate vases sat for a few months [Yochelson 1985].) In mid-April the NAS council had a dinner and a first view of the Freer collection. Walcott went to the first day of Academy meetings and had a delightful time meeting old friends.

The next day, he was less pleased when Charlie arrived from New Haven ill with fever; Walcott called it bronchitis. The day after that, Walcott could not devote much time to his son, who apparently only needed a few days' rest; there was the NAS meeting and the Daughters of the American Revolution, who had to be shown Freer's treasures. Charlie's situation did not improve, but it did not seem serious. "Charlie with bronchitis & fever is a sick boy. Miss Macafee came as nurse P.M." (April 19, 1912).

Going north again, Walcott stopped in Philadelphia. Although he had been elected a member of the American Philosophical Society years earlier, he had not attended many meetings. Now he presented "Illustrations of Remarkable Cambrian Fossils from British Columbia." "The marine worms are so perfectly preserved that they show not only the exterior form, but the interior intestine and the long proboscis which the worms thrust out through the mouth to secure food and to aid in drawing themselves through the mud" (Anonymous 1912, 334). Certainly, the paleontologist had remarkable and interesting information to impart to the scientific community. Still, there was also an opportunity to meet the Vaux family members on their home ground and explain his scientific efforts.

One reason Walcott had new information to impart is that by the end of the 1911 field season, a great deal of rock at the Burgess Shale site had been moved and searched for fossils. "The fossil quarry is now 65 feet in length on the steep slope of the ridge, with a floor extending back into the ridge 10 feet, and a vertical wall on the back side from 10 to 12 feet. About 150 cubic yards of shale have been quarried and split up. The fossils are scattered more or less irregularly, and are rarely very abundant, with the exception of a few species" (Walcott 1912c, 189–90). The Burgess Shale continued to be an astounding find of spectacular fossils.

The Philadelphia stop was short, for Walcott had to go to New York as a member of the RC executive committee. He returned to Washington and then immediately back once more to New York, for problems with Telluride Power had popped up again. During Walcott's years, the railroads made money; he certainly contributed his fair share (or is it fare share?). By the end of the month, Walcott could finally get back to the fossils, and Charlie seemed to be improving.

May saw another day trip to New York for the Research Corporation; once the RC had been established, Cottrell devoted his full time to the Bureau of Mines and had nothing to do with running the corporation. Another item of note was a Langley Memorial meeting held at the Chevy Chase Country Club; what marked it as special was a flight over the club by four airplanes, which had come miles from an airfield in College Park. (For those interested in trivia, College Park is where the Wright Flyer was officially demonstrated to the U.S. Army;

it is also the site of the first commercial airport, which remains in operation.) Walcott also entertained the Japanese delegation to the International Red Cross; the activities of an SI secretary are many and varied. Charlie was still very ill.

Walcott was one of the speakers at a memorial meeting for Francis David Millet, chairman and one of the original members of the Smithsonian advisory arts council. Millet had drowned on the *Titanic*, which sank that year—though, curiously enough, the tragedy was not recorded in Walcott's diary. This meeting was in the Museum auditorium and demonstrated once more the value of such a facility in Washington, a point Walcott had argued for years in pushing a memorial for George Washington.

After the Millet memorial, Walcott went to Princeton for the inauguration of a new president of that university, and then on to Cleveland; the problems of the Telluride Corporation seemed to be unending. As partial compensation, he came back via Philadelphia, specifically Bryn Mawr, where he and Mary Vaux looked over many photographs of the Canadian Rockies. He pushed on to New York City to see John Shaw Billings, president of the CIW board and still a power in CIW affairs; he also attended to RC matters.

Charlie was no better, and though Walcott never wrote the words, it was obvious by now that his firstborn might have tuberculosis. The disease had killed his father in 1852; the concern Walcott had showed for the physical well-being of Charlie, Sidney, and even Stuart in sending them west indicated that worry about tuberculosis had never been far from his mind. He had thought that a hot, dry climate might stave off the "white plague." "At my office much of the day looking after Charles getting off to California [to a sanatorium in Monrovia, near Los Angeles] tomorrow. At home in evening wrote to Helen. Am feeling tired and long for the mountains" (May 29, 1912).

Late Cambrian trilobites once more came to the fore. A discussion of them with his younger friend Schuchert, a grammar school dropout but now a solid Yale professor, reveals several interesting points.

> I have been studying the specimens of *Dicelocephalus*, and this afternoon asked [Ray S.] Bassler to come and go over them with me. We concluded that if the extremes represented by *D. minnesotensis* and *D. lodensis* are compared, it will be very easy to consider that two genera were represented, but with the intermediate forms that I now have illustrated, it is not practicable to separate them.
>
> I expect the latter part of the week to take up the description of the species of the genus, and in this connection would like to have the best illustrations that can be made of the specimens you have, to put on the plates. If you will send the material down I will have it photographed and send you back the specimens and prints of the photographs to use in description of species, which you can publish before my paper comes out.[16]

One point about this letter would be methodological: it shows that once Walcott had made preliminary examination specimens, he had illustrations made up. James Hall had had illustrations prepared in advance of the final text when writing the many volumes of the *Palaeontology of New York*, and Walcott seems to have followed this approach more or less consistently though his career. It had made good sense at a time when drawings took a long time to prepare; now, however, photographs were supplanting drawings. A second point would be that whereas Walcott has been accused of building fences and keeping others away from the Cambrian, here is a generous offer to help speed Schuchert's own work on Cambrian fossils.

The letter, further, reinforces the point that Walcott did not work in a vacuum but when necessary consulted with others on difficult paleontologic problems. Whether one genus can contain all the species of a particular morphology is a difficult problem; the questions of "how different is different" and "how similar is similar" are not readily quantified. Of course, Bassler, who did not work on trilobites, may well have given Walcott the answer he thought Walcott wanted.

A great deal was happening that late winter and spring that Walcott did not record in his diary. Almost as soon as Helen arrived in Europe, she lost some checks. Walcott sent replacements and some advice about safeguarding money, and he informed her that Mary Vaux wanted to be remembered. There was a fairly large correspondence between the children. So far as Italy was concerned, Helen wrote her younger brother, "It makes America seem a little shiny and new but I'd prefer Burgess Pass to anything I've seen yet."[17]

Despite a few rough edges to be rounded off, Helen rapidly became the world traveler, and inside of two weeks Walcott was cautioning her about spending too much money on clothes. He pointed out that finances were difficult with two sons in college and Stuart to go the following year. Nevertheless, he "wrote her she might spend fifty dollars extra for music, etc. at Munich. . . . Charles is very slowly but steadily improving. I do not anticipate that he will resume active life before October."[18] There is no indication that his world was to be shattered again. (As an aside, the correspondence between Helen and Walcott, especially the letters written to Walcott by her older companion and erstwhile temporary guardian, make for interesting reading. The term "high-spirited" does not do justice to the young lady.)

Walcott wrote Helen again to tell her that Charlie was very sick indeed. The illness had been diagnosed as typhoid, but Walcott still was not especially worried. Unfortunately, inside of a couple of weeks he had to report to Helen that her brother had contracted pneumonia, which had resulted in serious damage to his left lung. It was so bad, Walcott wrote Helen, that he doubted Charlie could live anywhere except in a dry climate. Charlie did seem to improve at first in the California sanitarium, but the cost was two hundred dollars a month, and Helen kept coming up with elaborate travel plans. She wanted to return early in October; her father pointed out that if she waited two weeks the fares would be less. Eventually, it was decided that she spend more time in Europe and go to school.

Thus, Walcott carried a burden of family cares all that spring, as late May segued into early June; almost every Sunday he visited Helena's grave at Rock Creek Cemetery. Walcott called at Capitol Hill to hurry along the final stages of the appropriation, and he struggled to finish his research on the Upper Cambrian fossils from Saratoga Springs, New York. He took "Uncle Joe" Cannon for an automobile ride and found stray hours to work on the plates and plate descriptions for the Dikelocephalidae, finishing the latter just before he left for the summer.

Notwithstanding all he had to do and worry over, Walcott spent time to write Joseph Holmes, who had just sent him the first *Annual Report* of the Bureau of Mines, and pass on some advice: "It has occurred to me that now while the Bureau is very popular and you can get almost any reasonable request granted, you had best establish it on strong, conservative lines so that it will become a feature of the Government Establishment just as the Geological Survey is. You will probably find that Dame fortune will be more or less fickle as far as support in Congress is concerned. But if each step is taken with the view of obtaining practical and sound results there will be very little difficulty."[19]

Twice in June he wrote to Miss Mary Vaux. Long ago, Walcott had dropped the habit of recording in his diary to whom he sent letters, so there is some significance that he listed these. On his last day in Washington that spring, Walcott was up at 5:30 A.M. to take down his awnings and screens—so much for his august position. He worked away until it was time to see a baseball game with George Otis Smith and Secretary of Interior Walter L. Fisher; the chances are that they discussed more than the game. He had dinner, packed his bags, and left on the Baltimore and Ohio Railroad for Pittsburgh. With all these varied activities, he was still "glad to leave as memories of Helena last June and July are still fresh" (June 18, 1912).

Walcott spent most of the day in Pittsburgh. An LL.D. was conferred upon him by the University of Pittsburgh, and such ceremonial events cannot be hurried. He got away that night to Niagara Falls and took the boat to Toronto. At Port Arthur, the standard route changed; he went west only as far as Atikokan, Ontario. Walcott was exceedingly interested in the material that A. C. Lawson had found and they had reported on the previous December, for it seemed to push the record of life back into the distant past; correlations were uncertain, but these rocks were probably older than those of the Belt series in Montana.

After a few letters back and forth, arrangements had been made for J. D. Trueman of the Geological Survey of Canada to meet him there.

It was Sunday when Trueman and Walcott left town, and the weather was hot, but neither factor deterred Walcott from looking over the outcrops of limestone near their camp. The next morning day he examined more limestone until "at 10:30 A.M. we went up the bay to see Steep Rock Falls & study limestones. Canoe upset in Seinne river 2:20 P.M. Knox & I escaped and Trueman drowned" (June 24, 1912).

Years later John Knox, at the time the geological assistant to Trueman, gave his account.

On that day in June we took along our passenger, Mr. Walcott, sitting in the bottom of the canoe. I was in the bow, the chief in the stern. We made the point and viewed the falls. But wind and spray made it a poor place for photographs and Walcott wanted a photo. Then, instead of heading downstream and running the rapids as we had previously done the chief said "Let's go across and try from the other side." . . . One moment I was kneeling in the bow of the canoe; the next moment I was somewhere between the surface and the bottom of the river, rapidly being swept toward the lake. . . . In a moment a head broke water, Walcott's, a short distance away. He floundered a bit and I called "Are you OK?" "No" he answered, "I can't swim." As a matter of fact he was doing a good job of staying on top as we bobbed up and down over the waves but it was evident that he could not swim. And we had to stay in the water till we reached the lake [through the rapids]. We couldn't get out anywhere along the shore. It was only a moment's work to catch the canoe as all three of us were close together and to get Walcott a good grip on it and settle down for the rest of the trip to the mouth of the river where the banks were lower. Then I looked around for the chief. There he was, back up the stream some distance. . . . We never saw him again. Walcott was an old man [sixty-two], as old as I am now. How he spent a lifetime in the open and never learned to swim I will never understand. But he had learned one thing, and completely. He had learned never to let his fears upset his reason. The mouth of that river is a most unpromising place to get to shore. The water is deep, over forty feet as we found later. The banks are of smooth, glaciated granite with nothing in the way of a finger hold or toe hold except a few cracks. And the water was cold, very cold, for it came from recently melted snow. Walcott could never have got out by himself and he realized this. He said to me "What do I do now?" We were circling around in a big eddy, Walcott clinging to the canoe, and I trying to push or pull the canoe to the shore as we swept by it. I realized my clothes were too much of an encumbrance and that I must get rid of them. It was nearly thirty minutes from the time our canoe swamped until I had Walcott on the shore with his head touching his feet [bent double] on the smooth steeply pitching rock. If he had not been wearing a belt I could never have got him from the water. With toe hold and finger hold in the cracks of the rock I dragged him from the water by his belt. He was unconscious but he soon came to. He was a remarkable old man. Never once in that 30 minutes did he show a sign of fear and never once did he hesitate to do what I asked as long as his strength held out.[20]

The next day they searched for Trueman's body, but without success. "Am no good & cannot sleep or write" was Walcott's diary entry (June 25, 1912). After that, Walcott and Knox went back to Atikokan. At Port Arthur he met Director R. W. Brock of the Geological Survey of Canada, and Walcott recounted the details of the accident. The terrible heat made this bad situation worse. This violent death of a geologist who had been assisting him shook Walcott. The next year Walcott would name *Olenellus truemani* "in memory of the most promising young geologist who was drowned" (Walcott 1913, 316).

Walcott's paper describing the supposed sponge was published the year of Trueman's death (Walcott 1912d). Two years later, irony was added to tragedy when a British scientist suggested that the apparent fossil was inorganic; Walcott agreed (Walcott 1914). Still, there really were fossils in the Steep Rock Limestone, though not animal remains. The year after Trueman's death, an Austrian paleontologist, August Rothpletz visited the site and later Walcott at the quarry; he named a new species of algae *Cryptozoon walcotti*. (The lake would be drained during World War II to allow iron ore to be mined; huge domal structures were seen in the limestones, along with undoubted stromatolites; Walcott's "sponge" is still relegated to the realm of pseudofossils [Wilks and Nisbet 1985].)

Walcott moved on to Winnipeg on the second leg of his field season. The Canadian Pacific was getting some competition from the Grand Trunk Pacific line, which was being built westward. Walcott saw their public-relations man, R. C. W. Lett, and arranged to meet him in the field. Over the next few years photographs by Lett appeared in Walcott's papers. The two men were to make a good team.

Meanwhile, Walcott pushed on to Field, and on July 1 packer Tom Martin took him to the Burgess camp set up a few days earlier. In the camp were Herrick B. Wilson, whom Assistant Curator Bassler had recommended to Walcott as an assistant (Yochelson 1996). W. S. Stevenson, a local worker, was also in the camp. Arthur Brown had come out from Washington and was to cook for another season. Rain kept Walcott in camp and gave him a chance to catch a bit of rest. "Tom came up & brot letters. Charlie is still in miserable shape but has a fighting chance for health & life" (July 2, 1912). The next day Walcott accompanied Wilson and Stevenson to the quarry.

They put up a small tent for shelter. "Foggy & occasional light showers made things nasty" (July 3, 1912). The group celebrated the 4th of July with more work in fog and mist. Three days of rain suspended work; Walcott made the best of it by writing letters and talking to John Allan of the Geological Survey about the joint work that that geologist had done with Burling. There was more rain; after that, a couple of good days produced new fossils, including a large worm. For a change, one morning there was snow.

Walcott caught the Pacific train west for Glacier, and at Glacier House he met Miss Mary Vaux. "We looked over photographs after dinner" (July 14, 1912). She took him on a walking tour on one of the glaciers; "My first tramp this year & a very enjoyable one" (July 15, 1912). No doubt Miss Vaux told him of her work keeping careful records of the movement of the glacier, but there was more happening than just a geologic lecture.

Then it was back to Field. Sidney had come in from Utah, and, with Arthur Brown, they all left for Calgary and then north to Edmonton, from where the Grand Trunk took them back west to Fitzhugh. (For those who look for this town on a map, it is now Jasper, in Jasper National Park.) The reason for the trip had in part to do with Charles Jr., who had been in the area in 1911. "My son Charles brought back a few Cambrian fossils picked up while hunting, and told me that ridge after ridge encircled the great Robson Peak with rocky layers, all sloping back toward the mountain" (Walcott 1913a, 629). Mount Robson is the highest peak in the Canadian Rockies, and Walcott was the first geologist to study its strata.

Sidney described Fitzhugh: "The hotel there consisted of a wooden, one-story shack with a large kitchen stove and dining room in one end and a big room divided into cubicles in other end with partitions about eight feet high and open above to a high ceiling. Heat from the stove warmed the whole place in winter. We were glad it was summer. Each room contained a double bed, a wash stand with towels that had seen much hard use, one chair, and a commode under the bed. The town was in keeping with the hotel, and there wasn't much of it. It was a small edition of Edmonton, which in 1912 was a way station that gave little promise of days to come."[21]

As soon as possible, the party, augmented by Harry Blagden (Sydney's friend from Washington), Clawson Otto (a packer-guide), and Doc Burgen (packer and keeper of hunting dogs), got on the train for mile seventeen, the end of track. R. C. W. Lett joined them for two weeks. The seven riders were accompanied by an eleven-horse packstring as they headed north along the Moose River. Once the group left the track, it encountered no one else until it returned to the track on August 24; this was wilderness.

The first week brought much rain and difficult travel. "We reached the permanent camp across from Berg Lake. Mt. Robson was above us to the right and

Hunga Glacier flowed down eastward from the summit and ended at the lake where great chucks of ice would drop off into the water and float for days or weeks as icebergs. My Father was busy every day on the geology of Robson and the surrounding mountains, and when he was not measuring the thickness of formations or searching for fossils, he was taking panoramic pictures of the area."[22]

While Walcott was taking pictures and breaking up rock, Sidney and Harry were out hunting. Many ptarmigan and squirrels went to the collections in Washington, along with a fine series of mountain goats. Rather than discuss his geologic efforts, Walcott would later tell an appropriations committee, "Last year I sent an expedition to British Columbia into an area never hunted over by anyone, practically, connected with any American museum. That party found a new caribou, a new species, new type, the largest and most prominent one found. They also obtained other small forms. They were sent there more especially to get the typical goat, sheep, and grizzly bear of the Canadian Rockies. . . . They succeeded in obtaining these specimens" (Walcott 1913b, 394). For more than half a century, the goats were on display in the Museum, with a painted panorama of the mountains behind them.

Because this was a huge mountain and there was no professional help, once Walcott had climbed the adjacent slopes to take pictures and get a general view of the land, he began to look at the moraines, rocks piled up by the glaciers. He identified the age of the fossils in these loose blocks and then climbed to locate the layers that had produced them. Given the conditions, it was an efficient way to operate. One such discovery was especially notable: "Harry Blagden & I went up to north face of Munn Mt. On the glacier found fine, entire *Olenellus canadensis*. Traced shale to base of mountain. We returned to camp 8 P.M. The discovery of the fauna in such good condition is now best fossil find in this region" (August 12, 1912). "The locality is high up where rain, fog, and snow squalls may be expected nearly every day of the year" (Walcott 1913b, 310).

There is no question as to the Early Cambrian age of these fine fossils, but apparently the original collection was from material moved by ice, not really from outcrop; two different trilobite zones are intermixed in the collection. Walcott would revisit the locality the following year, and later Burling was to come several times. Walcott named too many formations in this area; he could not trace some of the rock units, and the fossils were not from where Burling thought they should occur. Nevertheless, sixty-nine years after the original publication, when a more comprehensive study came out, Walcott was still given a great deal of credit for his endeavors (Fritz 1992).

Walcott summed the work up fairly well. "The time available for actual fieldwork was greatly limited during the season of 1912 by the unusual rainfall. This condition and also the necessity of making a general reconnaissance before determining where to establish the typical section prevented careful measurements and the working out of detailed sections. Several horizons [or rock layers] were found containing fossils and rather careful estimates made of the thickness of the various formations between Tah Pass and the summit of Robson" (Walcott 1913c, 329). Walcott estimated that twelve thousand feet of Cambrian rocks were exposed and at least three thousand feet of Ordovician. The section was thicker than at Mount Bosworth, to the south. As regards speed of publication, his paper on the stratigraphy was out less than eleven months after the fieldwork at Mount Robson.

Once the party got to civilization, such as it was, at mile seventeen, they went east to Yellowhead Pass, where the Grand Trunk and Canadian Pacific were both building. Walcott saw a nice unconformity of tilted Precambrian Belt age rocks surmounted in an angular relationship by Early Cambrian, but again there was lots of rain. All in all, this was a difficult trip. Walcott caught up, however, on the large accumulation of mail. Seemingly Charlie was holding his own. Walcott cabled Helen to go to school in Florence. He read of the Progress Party convention, Teddy Roosevelt's break from Taft's Republican Party—"A great movement for the American people. Hope it will win out" (August 28, 1912). They had one more day in the field, in poor weather; it was so miserable that even Walcott noted, "Bad day for work in field & camp" (August 29, 1912).

Labor Day is as big a holiday in Canada as it is in the United States. They all celebrated in the way that one does on that occasion in a place like Fitzhugh. Harry Blagden left for home. Sidney, Walcott, and Arthur caught the midnight train for Field. Jack Giddie, the packer in 1909 when the Burgess fauna had been first found, met them.

The next day, "Wilson reports bad weather & very few fossils as bed appears to have given out" (September 4, 1912). Snow kept everyone in camp. Sidney and Wilson went goat hunting, and Walcott scoured the slope several hundred feet below the quarry. It was a fruitless quest, cut short by snow squalls. The weather finally allowed them to get to the quarry. "We cleaned away snow & began taking up rock. Found a number of good fossils" (September 7, 1912). They had three more good days of collecting, ducking into the tent when snow squalls hit. Wilson's bad weather was not the same as Walcott's. "I find Wilson exceedingly slow mentally & physically & told him so today. Am greatly disappointed in him" (September 11, 1912). Walcott and Sidney shared a sunset, and then Sidney headed for Cornell, leaving Walcott with Wilson.

They pushed along though ten-hour days in the quarry. "Found a few good specimens & a lot of duplicates" (September 16, 1912). "Am about ready to stop collecting at the fossil quarry for this season. Very little new material is turning up" (September 17, 1912). "Arranged to have Wilson sent home" (September 19,

1912). With Wilson gone, Stevenson and Walcott carried on for two more days. Walcott wrote to Wilson, formally discharging him; he sent a copy of the note to the chief clerk of the Smithsonian, along with a cover letter.

> The enclosed is self explanatory. Tell Mr. Adams to hold Wilson chk for last half of Sept until accts are settled. Everyone in camp was glad to have him [Wilson] go.
>
> I now expect to reach Washin Oct. *1st* or *2d* (P[ay] P[eriod]) Closed up at the quarry yesterday as a wild driving bank of mist swept down from the *Presidential* range. Have had 10 days of fine weather. Wilson collected 10 pkgs fossils in 49 days. With the same quarry man & a little mechanical help from Wilson I sent down over 50 pkgs in 13 days. He wrote me that the quarry was exhausted. Stevenson the quarry man tells me that he ordered him to throw most of the rock over the dump. If Mr. Bassler has returned call him over & show him my letter to Wilson & tell him we will have to try again.
>
> At the quarry I asked Wilson why he acted so grumpy & worked with so little life. He said that his mother was ill & he was worried. I remarked that I had not known of it & that I sympathized with him. He retorted that he not did not consider that it was any of my business if his mother was ill & and that he did not wish my sympathy. I told him that if he acted at the Smithsonian as he had been doing for several days the men would not have anything to do with him & and that he would have difficulty in getting ahead. He replied that he did not care what they tho't of him. Stevenson tells me that he has been in the same mood the past month.
>
> I would have sent him home at once but I wished to study him & also learn more of his general bearing & influence. All the men regard him with amused contempt. Curious how camp life brings out the characteristics of a man.
>
> I have put in 60 hrs work the past week at the fossil quarry and enjoyed every hour of it. Resting today & writing letters. Have a lot of choice rock to break up tomorrow here at camp. Sent it down by packer at odd times from quarry.
>
> Am feeling fine. Remembrance to all in office.[23]

A desperately ill son in California, and a daughter not very well organized in Europe; an almost unbroken spell of bad weather at Mount Robson; and an inept assistant at the Burgess quarry—combined, all this made for a memorable summer. Walcott and Arthur broke up rock for another day, cached the heavy tools, and dismantled the camp. Arthur headed for Washington; Walcott lingered in Banff to have film developed and settle various accounts. As a fitting finale for the season, many of his photographs did not turn out, because the company had sent the wrong film for the panorama camera. He spent a day in Winnipeg looking at Lett's photographs. From there it was more or less due east.

By the first of October, Walcott had reached Toronto. The university had a new museum to examine, and he also wanted to talk to Professor William A. Parks, who over the years had lent him many specimens from the collections of G. F. Matthew, purchased by the university. The route was to Buffalo, to the si, to New York City for an Research Corporation meeting, and back to the si in time to tackle a problem at the zoo and attend a formal dinner. Two days later, after church, he placed flowers on Helena's grave and proceeded to resolve accumulated Smithsonian paperwork.

Some secondhand comments on the field season from Professor Schuchert may be in order.

> I am delighted to know that you have again been so successful in the far west and that you have got a new lower Cambric horizon with fine trilobites. I am sorry to hear that your field assistant, Mr. Wilson, has not turned out well but of course I hardly expect that you [will] ever find anyone to dig out fossils in so large a quantity as yourself. You have the reputation of collecting very rare things by the ton. I am very sorry to hear that Charley is still in bad [shape] but I rejoice with you in the thought that he is improving and may soon be himself again. Undoubtedly he has the very best surrounding that can be given him and the splendid climate of California will surely build him up.
>
> I can readily imagine that your accident in the Steeprock Lake region must have affected you seriously mentally and physically, but I was not aware that your lumbar muscles had been tied up for so many weeks. However, as you say you are again strong and well. I am delighted with this information.[24]

While Walcott had been away, in September the si had ground out two more parts of *smc* volume fifty-seven. Part 10 is a scanty three pages long, but in it Walcott suggested "Waucouban" as the term for Early Cambrian. The term that had been used was "Georgian," a reference to the section containing trilobites at Georgia, Vermont. With all his work in western Canada, the best sections Walcott had ever seen were still in the Inyo Mountains of California, near Waucona Spring. His 1897 measured section, published a decade later, was the type; some things cannot be hurried. For the Upper Cambrian he proposed to use "St. Croixan," from Wisconsin, rather than "Saratogan," from eastern New York. The reason for the latter change was the question of priority, as Saratogan had been used earlier in the literature in connection with much younger rocks.

Part 9 was on what he had called the Saratoga fauna in his diary but was now officially St. Croixan. Walcott started his paper with a bit of history. "When engaged in reconnaissance work in Saratoga County, New York, during the summer of 1878, I found a small group of fossils in a thick-bedded, hard gray siliceous limestone at Hoyts quarry, 4 miles west of Saratoga Springs" (Walcott 1912e, 252). He had described several species, but without illustrations; a few years later a plate with figures of these fossils was made up and distributed to a few paleontologists.

"The 'Saratogan' fauna of New York was correlated with the *Dicellocephalus* fauna of the Upper Mississippi Valley in 1879" (Walcott 1912e, 253). A few more localities in New York had been found in 1886 and 1888. Additional species had been described in 1890, and Walcott had given a summary of the stratigraphy in his 1891 correlation program. It was time for another more definitive paper on the fauna. To engage in a bit of speculation, the discovery of Late Cambrian fossils by J. A. Allan and Burling may have triggered Walcott into doing more with fossils near the Cambrian-Ordovician boundary.

The fauna Walcott described was a very mixed bag; it actually began with flora. Cabbage-shaped growths that Walcott had seen in Precambrian limestones of the West occurred in the Upper Cambrian limestone, and James Hall had given them the name *Cryptozoon*; these structures were also in the limestones at Steep Rock Lake. At this time Walcott redescribed *C. proliferum*; he classified it under Protozoa, as a growth of simple, single-celled organisms.

Following the *Cryptozoon*, Walcott described a trail that he attributed to a giant worm, a couple of brachiopods, and half a dozen mollusks or mollusk-like shells. He ended the paper with descriptions of nine trilobites and an exposition on a curious trackway; on the basis of trilobite appendages found in the Burgess Shale, he concluded this had been formed by a trilobite walking around—not a bad piece of paleobiology. In fact, this little paper was a good, solid contribution, and it tidied up a number of small issues in paleontology and added new data. Like so much of invertebrate paleontology, it was not dramatic science, merely fundamental.

At some point that summer arrangements had been made to rent the house again, and Walcott packed up the dresses of Helen in Italy and the clothes of Charles in California, almost as far away. For some reason the rental did not take place, however, and Walcott stayed in his own house. Actually, he more or less camped out in it, taking his meals elsewhere to cut down on household expenses. Helen was still spending more than had been anticipated.

The International Geographical Congress met in Washington again. Walcott took interested members to Great Falls on the Potomac, just north of Washington, and to the Museum to view the fantastic Burgess Shale fossils. With that exposition as a warm-up, by mid-month he was going at full speed again. He went to Albany, New York, to see the new State Education Building. State Geologist/Paleontologist John M. Clarke had engineered this structure; in his way, he was the Walcott of the Empire State. Although much of Albany has since been torn down for the vast Empire State Plaza, this building, which has the longest colonnade in the world, still stands to one side of the state capitol.

At the congress, Walcott extolled Albany and the birthplace of Joseph Henry: "I likewise esteem it a personal privilege and honor to appear here today, the third successor to Secretary Henry, for it was my pleasure about a third of a century ago to be engaged in some geological studies in New York under the direction of your honorable body, a field of work in which I still take a special interest in connection with the United States National Museum. As Keeper ex-officio of the Museum, placed under the direction of the Smithsonian Institution, I bring to you today the greetings of that great National Museum."[25]

From Albany, Walcott made a point of going to Scanandoa to see Aunt Helen; returning, he visited New York Mills and Utica to see the few remaining friends and relatives—there were no more visits to Trenton Falls of his youth. In keeping with his mood, he made arrangements for his father and long-dead brother to be moved from the family tomb and reburied next to Josie and his mother. The RC met in New York City and the CIW Ex Comm at the new Carnegie Laboratory, at Cold Spring Harbor on Long Island. The trip home was interrupted by a stop to see Miss Mary Vaux. (Just when Walcott decided to remarry is uncertain, but it must have been a cautious and somewhat painful courtship for both parties.)

"Began work on text of *Dikelocephalus* paper" (October 24, 1912); that was a project that had been hanging fire for some time. (For those who worry about trivia, sometimes *Dikelocephalus* was spelled with a *c* and sometimes a *k*; people still argue today.) The research was almost immediately laid aside, for Walcott had to be on the special train from New York City to Utica accompanying the body of the vice president. "The Smithsonian Institution has lost a strong supporter & I an old friend by the death of Mr. Sherman" (November 2, 1912).

This was the last of the problems and miscalculations that marked the one-term presidency of William Howard Taft. For the first time since Grover Cleveland, the Democratic Party, under Prof. Woodrow Wilson, would now be in charge of the White House. The philosophy of administration does not change, however, and the rule is get what you can when you can. Walcott called on Secretary of Interior Fisher. "Talked to him about man for Indian Commission & Supt. Glacier Park and work of Reclamation Service" (November 9, 1912). Secretary Walcott was a gray eminence who could put his finger in every pie in Washington.

Having been in Washington for almost three weeks, it was time for Walcott to take yet another train trip. Stuart was at the Taft School in Watertown, Connecticut, and his father visited him briefly before the NAS fall meeting in New Haven. Clarke was there from Albany, and, with Schuchert, they probably traded stories about James Hall. Walcott presented a talk on the Cambrian rocks of the

Mount Robson region. He got to Washington about the time the fossils from the region finally arrived from the field; no one sent rocks by express. First on his agenda was a quick look at the fossils hammered from the Lower Cambrian rocks of Mount Robson.

Before November ended, he was back in New York City. A formal dinner was being held for Mrs. Dimock. The early plans for a GWMA building had been put aside, in the hope that somehow there could be an arrangement with the Carnegie Institution of Washington, founded in 1902 (Yochelson 1998). Then Columbian College had transformed itself into George Washington University; that hope for GWMA cooperation with academia had also withered. Finally, the decision had been made to proceed alone. Now that the GWMA had a site in Washington, all that was needed was money, and this seemed a place to raise some.

On the train ride home from Mrs. Dimock's dinner, Walcott worked on photographs and maps of the Mount Robson area. Some of his photographs, especially panorama views, greatly reduced in size, are in the "Explorations for 1912" (Walcott 1913d); that, however, did not count in his mind as a scientific publication. Worry about promptly producing scientific papers always seemed to be with him; in these weeks, worry about the health of Charles never left him either. Of the strange ideas that had been offered to the RC since its formation had been announced, Walcott was strongly interested in "Oxo," a protein source that its inventor thought would be easy to digest. Walcott saw it as a way to help his firstborn regain his strength.

In another letter to Helen, Walcott wrote about the election results and mentioned that the new president and his wife would make an interesting couple in the White House. A few other items followed before he got to the main point, Helen's finances. "I think if there is such a thing possible it would be well for you to take a course in Economics and Book-keeping. Unless you obtain some cash sense it would be a hopeless task for me to think of having you take charge of our home as you will bankrupt us the first six months!"[26] The same theme continued in letters the next year; in what has become a rapidly changing world, the teenager has tended to remain constant. Walcott also told Helen that he planned to visit Charlie in December. "I am thankful for life & health for Sidney, Helen, Stuart and myself & that Charlie has not succumbed to his illness. That our country is at peace & prospering. It will take the wisdom of great men to guide our people the next 25 years."[27] Perhaps it was thought of a coming Democratic administration that engendered these reflections.

A map of Mount Robson with new topographic names added was sent off to the director of the Geological Survey in Canada; new geographic names were needed, because new geologic formations were to be named based on these localities. That was effectively the end of geologic studies for the year, though examination of fossils went on. He conferred with regent and senator Henry Lodge on the Langley memorial tablet, which was taking an inordinate amount of time to complete.

Speaking of inordinate delay, USGS monograph fifty-one now finally appeared. Burling (1913) performed one last service for his longtime employer, by clarifying that a few copies had been distributed in December 1912 and listing who had received them. This 1912 date was a key point with respect to priority, even though most copies left Washington in 1913. Early that year a letter from Walcott left Washington: "Monograph No 51 of the Geological Survey, 'Cambrian Brachiopoda,' was issued in December, 1912. I received, as author, one copy, and have none for distribution, but I learn from the office of the Survey that if you will make an application to the Director of the U.S. Geological Survey, Washington, D.C., a copy will be sent you. The Monograph is in two volumes, one of text and one containing 104 quarto plates."

There is no need to cite a repository for the quotation, as the collected letters of almost all stratigraphers and geologists with whom Walcott corresponded contain copies of this form letter. Geologists from all over the world responded enthusiastically to the offer. The government was charging four dollars for monograph fifty-one, in two bound volumes. Granted, four dollars in 1912 is not four dollars today; even so, the price was ridiculously low for the size and quality of these books. Who knows how many free copies were sent out as a direct result of Walcott's form letter?

The reviews of this opus were ecstatic. Clarke (1913) rambled on for four pages. Other reviewers were shorter but no less generous in their praise. "Dr. Walcott has had this monumental monograph on the Cambrian brachiopods of the world, his *magnum opus*, in hand since 1898. In it are described 536 species and varieties, grouped in 44 genera and 15 subgenera" (Schuchert 1913, 331). "Rarely, perhaps never, has there been published a paleontological monograph so complete in every detail as this great work. . . . Through the publication . . . the records of Cambrian brachiopod life are made more complete than for any other geologic period" (Weller 1913, 568–69). "This monumental work of 872 quarto pages would seem to include all the information possessed up to the present upon all Cambrian and some Ordovician Brachiopoda—not only of North America but the rest of the world" (Shimer 1913, 564).

There is not a great deal more one can add to such statements, except to note that at least one newspaper gave the monograph twelve inches of column space, headed "Fossils are to be found here—Monograph is prepared by Uncle Sam—Study of Paleontology now highly important."[28] One seldom has the opportunity to use the old expression "it boggles the mind," but even in 1913 government publications hardly ever rated mention in newspapers, let alone headlines indicating that fossils were important. For anyone, this monograph would be the work of a lifetime.

Walcott had written, "In this paper the Brachiopoda are treated in three ways—historically, geologically, and zoologically"; he succeeded admirably in all three fields. The work was not as complete as he might have wished on the relationship of Ordovician brachiopods to their ancestors, but "my main purpose has been to make the results of the investigation of value to the student of Cambrian faunas and to the stratigraphic geologist" (Walcott 1912f, 11).

As good as it was to see his neck finally freed of the millstone of the monograph, that was ancient history; current events were more meaningful. Early in December, Walcott took the train to Philadelphia and once more looked at photographs with Miss Mary Vaux. Bad news from western California, however far outweighed a pleasant day in eastern Pennsylvania: Charlie had written to say how homesick he was. Walcott made the decision that Charlie should come home, for the desert air was effecting no cure.

By letter, Walcott railed to Helen that for months he had begged Charlie to save his strength and not write letters but that Charlie would not listen. It was a classic case of denial. There was nothing Helen could do for her older brother, and Walcott urged her to stay in school, build up her strength, and not worry about "coming out"—a process that for a debutante was exhausting and for a father was incredibly expensive. Indeed, if Helen did come back early, Walcott urged her to stay out of town and not get into the social whirl.

On a more positive note, Walcott could report to the SI regents in December that eight commercial installations of the new Cottrell precipitator had been made and that others would be installed soon. The implication was that money would be rolling in. (Life was more complicated than that, however, even for one who planned as carefully as Walcott did; it was to be years before the RC made money.) Nothing else of note transpired with the regents. The annual CIW board meeting was equally uneventful.

"Charlie returned home with nurse from *Monrovia Cali.* He is still very weak & ill" (December 20, 1912). Walcott wrote a moderately cheery letter to Helen that Charlie's spirits were up for the first time in months and that he had had nine invitations to dine out during the first half of January. It was whistling in the dark. Walcott's concern for his dying son is even more painful to read in his diary than his shock at Helena's death. Christmas was quiet, with little gifts for the staff and the much-reduced family. The American Philological Association, Archaeological Institute of America, and Society of Biblical Literature and Exegesis came to town. Despite his distraction over Charlie, Walcott had to welcome these worthies to an informal smoker at the University Club. "1912 closes with Charles seriously ill. Tuberculosis. Sidney & Stuart at home for holidays Helen at school in Florence Italy" (December 31, 1912).

1913 started with a traditional New Year's Day. President Taft received a formal call, as did the members of his cabinet, soon to depart official circles. Likewise, as had become traditional, yet another job arose to eat into the secretary's research time. "At organization of Committee for American School of Archeology [*sic*] in Pekin, China 10 A.M. [At] 1:30 P.M. selected as Chairman of Committee & executive Committee. Mr. Charles L. Freer & others present" (January 3, 1913); one could hardly say no to Freer, with a major art collection and a building hanging in the balance. A diplomatic reception at the White House did not prevent Walcott from noting again in his diary that poor Charlie was very sick.

Walcott saw Mrs. Dimock and the daughter of Grover Cleveland; the GWMA was bubbling along. He conferred with Secretary of Treasury I. W. MacVeagh on Smithsonian business and, despite all these conferences, still got in a few hours looking at *Dikelocephalus*. The big scientific-social event of January was the National Geographic Society dinner, at which Robert E. Peary of North Pole fame presented the society's medal to Roald Amundsen of South Pole fame; this was before news of Capt. Robert Falcon Scott and the four men he led to their deaths reached the outside world. In a two-week interval, Walcott was at three formal dinners significant enough to warrant mention on the society pages of the local papers. He slipped away from the social scene for a quick meeting of the RC and managed a stop at Bryn Mawr on the way back.

The hearings of the appropriations subcommittee rounded off a full three weeks of the new year. "Mr. L. D. Burling said goodbye as he goes to Ottawa to join Geological Survey of Canada" (January 25, 1913). Probably it was time for Mr. Burling to pursue his own interests, but his departure did put a crimp in Walcott's efforts. "Not having any assistant I am trying to get the collections of 1912 unpacked and ready for study" (January 27, 1913).

Occasionally gossip helps explain events. After coming to the USNM as an assistant to Schuchert, Bassler had slowly worked his way upward. Whether he was one reason that Burling left Washington is problematic; Bassler eventually got a doctorate from George Washington University and taught there part-time, but Burling is little known, in part because he never received that advanced degree. At least one factor was that Bassler would not lend specimens when Burling was trying to write a thesis in absentia. It says a great deal about the man that other members of the Museum staff referred to Bassler as Walcott's pet, and that for years he repeated it as if it were a compliment.

In regard to Walcott's great desire to continue intensive research on fossils, he was his own worst enemy. The school of archaeology in China was very far afield from his interests; such things had to be balanced against his duties as secretary.

Freer had been to China again and was prepared to will more of his objects to the Smithsonian. Freer was also concerned about a proper building in which to display his treasures. Somewhere along the line, perhaps after the enthusiastic reception of the temporary exhibit, Walcott planted the seed that it would be nice for Freer to build the structure during his lifetime rather than will the money upon his death. It was an idea that had to be developed with the greatest of care, but the secretary did in fact develop it.

Walcott now decided to move into the field of aviation. At an Aero Club of America dinner in 1911 he had suggested that the government should sponsor research in aviation, but nothing had happened. Walcott was determined to make something happen. "Conference with Dr. Zahm and Capt. Chambers in re Aeronautical Laboratory" (January 30, 1913). (Dr. Alfred H. Zahm taught at Catholic University and his name was to come up again as this matter developed.) He met with them again on the first of February, and inside of three days a more formal title was in use: "Meeting of Aeronautical Commission at Carnegie Institution 3–5 P.M." (February 4, 1913).

It is a bit hard to understand the roots of this interest in aviation, but it went back a long way. In some part, the interest was loyalty to Langley's memory. Less than two years after his appointment as secretary, Walcott had written to Octave Chanute, the most widely respected engineer in America who was concerned with aeronautics. His reply to an inquiry concerning the Langley aerodrome: "My judgement is that it would probably be broken when alighting on hard ground and possibly when alighting on water, although the operator might not be hurt in either case.If the institution does not mind taking this risk and suitable arrangements can be made about the expense, I believe that it would be desirable to make the test, in order to demonstrate that the Langley machine was competent to fly and might have put our government in possession of a type of flying machine, which, however inferior to that of the Wrights, might have evolved into an effective scouting instrument."[29] Quite apart from differences in size, there were major differences between the biplane of the Wrights and the tandem wings of Langley.

In a larger sense, Walcott's aviation interest was more likely the result of vision. Walcott saw the need for conservation of raw materials, he saw the potential of electricity and of motor cars, and he saw the potential for aerial transport. Perhaps the thousands of miles and hundreds of days that he had spent in railway cars triggered his imagination as to alternative transportation. Whatever the motivation, Walcott was to spend a great deal of his time making the formalization of aviation research a reality.

Meanwhile, Walcott was still dining out fairly frequently, and a dinner in February also made the society column. Just possibly it was too painful to remain for hours in the house with Charlie, but they did eat together on occasion. Walcott knew the awful truth—that Charlie was failing and that there was nothing that he could do. The si regents' meeting in February was routine, and he was still spending a few minutes here and there on the Dikelocephalidae. As NAS vice president, and as a man on the spot in the city, Walcott was heavily involved in the local arrangements for the fiftieth anniversary of the National Academy of Sciences that spring. Yet these were only minor distractions from his worry over Charlie.

"Took up usual routine work & also study in laboratory. Many matters of interest come and go every day" (February 25, 1913). One should avoid the temptation to read too much into remarks, but these inane comments, like his lumbago, which began to act up, could have a psychological basis in the tragedy daily enfolding at home. By the latter part of February, Charlie was rapidly weakening.

Not unexpectedly, Walcott was invited to a final White House dinner that President Taft gave his cabinet. Needless to say, less than a week later Walcott was also at the inauguration of President Wilson. Inside of two days, he went with Zahm and Chambers to present their cards at the White House. Aviation was to be brought promptly to the attention of the new administration.

Walcott began his article on Mount Robson for the National Geographic Society. Walcott was clinging to straws: "Charlie very ill but not as low as a week ago" (March 9, 1913). The issue of new regents to be appointed as a result of the new administration took him to the Capitol. "Jogging away all day at my office with the result of getting odds & ends of things caught up with" (March 11, 1913). He seemed to be just putting in time at the office to avoid the growing terror at home: "Charlie not as well as I wish he were [*sic*]—Dear boy is thin & weak" (March 13, 1913). Attending the funeral of John Shaw Billings, with whom he had shaped the CIW, could not have helped his mood.

"A very busy day at the Smithsonian. Nearly completed short paper for geographic magazine. Meeting Trustees of Church of Covenant. Dined at Mrs. Henry F. Dimock" (March 20, 1913). Fortunately, there was simply too much to do for Walcott to concentrate on Charlie's struggle. The CIW Ex Comm met, practically for the first time without Dr. Billings present. Walcott stole off to Philadelphia and Bryn Mawr, where he accompanied Miss Mary M. Vaux "when she showed lantern slides of the Canadian west at Darlington School." The trip was rationalized—that may be the correct word—by a meeting with the Philadelphia Academy of Fine Arts to talk about the growing National Gallery of Art. After church that Sunday, he went once again to the cemetery with flowers for Helena's grave.

"Completed paper for Geog—Society & began preparation of geologic report of Robson Peak District" (March 25, 1913). He attended the meeting of the local archaeological society, yet the Philosophical Society, the Geological Society, and the Washington Academy seemed no longer to hold his interest. Walcott celebrated his sixty-third birthday at the home of Dr. and Mrs. Whitman Cross. Mrs. Eldrege was there to keep the lady of the house company; Joe Iddings, who had shared a tent with Walcott in 1880, and young F. D. Adams from Montreal completed the group. There were no paleontologists of Walcott's stature in Washington; it is a bit ironic that his three closest acquaintances on that occasion were all experts on igneous rocks.

On April Fools' Day, Walcott was on the train to New York for another quick RC meeting. He revised his account of the trip to Mount Robson on the way up, and he filled another day with meetings. "Conference with Dr Zahm on Aeronautical Laboratory, Dr Arthur L. Day on Nat. Acad. Celebration. Committee Board of Trade on G.W.M.A. building" (April 3, 1913). These were just distractions from tragedy. Against all logic, Walcott took Charlie with his nurse, a Miss Conway to a hospital in the Catskills, but what does one do when one's oldest son is dying? "Charlie's condition is serious & disheartening. No apparent chance for him now" (April 6, 1913).

"Charlie passed away 6:20 A.M. very quietly in Miss Conway's arms" (April 7, 1913). Sidney and Stuart met the body at the train station; Mrs. Garfield came in from Ohio. "Many friends sent beautiful flowers & after a fine service we laid Charlie beside his mother in Rock Creek Cemetery. God knows why—I do not—that he should leave us" (April 9, 1913).

He gave his paper to Gilbert Grosvenor for publication in the *National Geographic Magazine* and just wandered around, pursuing odds and ends. Sidney went back to Cornell, Stuart back to his school in Connecticut, and Miss Conway back to Los Angeles. Only Mrs. Garfield stayed for a few day longer. It was a horrible reprise of Helena's death, less than two years earlier.

The next week Walcott went to the office; there was nothing else to do. The swirl of duties carried him along, talking to a senator about the Fish Commission, going to the CIW Ex Comm meeting, and seeing Freer on the issue of support of the American School of Archaeology in Rome; what a long way archaeology in Italy was from the trilobite *Triarthrus becki* from near Rome, New York. The funeral of Director George Otis Smith's young daughter cast more gloom.

Duty called, and Walcott appeared at an NAS council meeting. The great semicentennial celebration began. "On acct Charlie's death did not go to reception at Nat. Museum" (April 22, 1913). The next day there was an official reception at the White House, and later Walcott hosted guests at the CIW headquarters; neither event could be ignored. "Business meetings of the Nat. Acad. 9 A.M. 12:15 was reelected vice president altho' not wishing it. The Academy drifts along without any fixed policy. The members went down the Potomac to Mt. Vernon & dined together in the evening" (April 24, 1913). One need only read the history of the first fifty years to see how little impact the Academy had had (True 1913).

By various chatty letters, Walcott kept encouraging the members of the unpaid RC board to keep working on its behalf. "Last evening at midnight we closed a week's celebration on account of the semicentennial of the National Academy of Sciences. As Chairman of the General Committee I was kept fully occupied night and day."[30] The letter does not mention Charlie's death, for Walcott's grief was both deep and private.

During a quick trip to Philadelphia, Walcott spoke, for the second year, at the American Philosophical Society annual meeting on the Burgess Shale fossils; the program had been arranged months in advance. "The fossils are most beautifully preserved and include such delicate forms as medusae (jellyfish), holothurians (sea cucumbers), finely preserved marine shells of various kinds and a large variety of crustaceans. . . . Altogether over 80 genera of invertebrate fossils have been found from a bed not over 5 feet in thickness" (Goodspeed 1913, 724–25).

Walcott shuffled furniture around at home. The study on the second floor became Helen's new bedroom, ready for her when she returned from Europe, and he made her old, smaller room into his study. He was very much depressed and at loose ends. Sunshine and fresh air were in order, so off he went to Professor Roddy at Lancaster, Pennsylvania. A class from Princeton University arrived, and he showed the students how to collect trilobites. Two days in the field helped settle him. Mrs. Garfield finally had to go back to Cleveland. Fortunately, the next day there were major distractions. "Annual meeting of Aero-Club of America & Langley Day. The Smithsonian presented gold medals to Glenn Curtice & Gustav Eifel [sic]. Also unveiled Langley tablet in the Smithsonian building. At home in the evening" (May 6, 1913). Langley Day was a splendid affair (McCurdy 1913).

The Wright brothers had received their medal at a meeting of the regents, a small private affair, whereas these medals were given as part of a grand public ceremony. Just to add another little twist, the new laboratory being organized by the Smithsonian was at Walcott's suggestion to be named for the professor. Whatever Langley had or had not done to provide a theoretical basis for flight, he had not flown. The Wright brothers *had* flown, and in the growing adulation for Langley, this basic point was being ignored. No doubt, all this rankled Orville Wright, the surviving, younger brother.

As May moved along, Walcott joined the Chevy Chase Club, still one of the better country clubs of the area. Likely this was for Helen's sake. He had a conference with Mr. Nunn and spent a day in Philadelphia. That was en route to the

CIW Ex Comm in New York. The RC occupied two more days; he made a few calls on relatives and friends and saw Charles M. Manly, who had been the pilot of Langley's ill-fated aerodrome. Back in Washington, the NAS council met to consider what the semicentennial had accomplished and to start thinking seriously about a building of its own. Walcott had another conference with Zahm, picked up work on a manuscript, and, just possibly, the worst effects of Charlie's death began to fade.

"Meeting of Aviation Committee of Smithsonian 10–1 lunch 2:30. Orville Wright[-]Glen Curtis-John Hays Hammond Jr. came—in addition to Washington members" (May 23, 1913). Walcott had launched his aviation initiative. He also spent two days with Mrs. Dimock and an architect. For the last several years, Mr. Dimock had rented a house in Washington for the season rather than stay in New York City; this was a straw in the wind of the growing importance of the federal government and of the Washington social whirl. Mrs. Dimock was certainly the driving force needed if the GWMA was ever to succeed.

Walcott's *National Geographic* article came out; he had proved again he could write as well for the public as for the scientist. "Robson Peak rises majestically cliff on cliff for 7,000 feet (2,136 meters) above Berg Lake to its summit, where the vapors from the Pacific gather nearly every day of the year. . . . A new fossil find was made by chance. Mr. Harry Blagden and I were sitting on a huge block of rock at the lower end of Mural Glacier, munching our cold luncheon, when I happened to notice a block of black, shaly rock lying on the ice. Wishing to warm up, for the mist drifting over the ice was cold and wet, I crossed to the block and split it open. On the parting there were several entire trilobites belonging to new species of a new subfauna of the Lower Cambrian fauna" (Walcott 1913a, 635–39). This was the famous find that subsequently provoked argument as to its precise location in the section. It is yet another example of Walcott's possessing a combination of skill and luck.

As far as photography goes, he was also lucky with Mount Robson itself. The article is supplemented by a panorama of mountains, glaciers, and lakes eighteen inches by forty-six inches; this may not be quite as fine as that published two years earlier in the magazine, but it is close. (The thought of dragging that camera up the slopes is scary.) Between this article, "Explorations" (Walcott 1913d), and part 10 of his second SMC volume, the scenery of this incredible area is well documented.

Mr. Nunn, a perennial visitor to Washington, came and went; Decoration Day, Memorial Day of the present calendar, came and went. Walcott celebrated by taking time for two baseball games in three days. He was braced again for work. The committee on archeological exploration in Central America took part of a day, and Zahm took the rest. He got in a few solid days on the dikelocephalid trilobites; at the final stages of a manuscript, uninterrupted time is critical. Problems with the Beaver River Power Company had to be explained once more, for it was a new administration, and Walcott stopped by the office of an assistant secretary of agriculture—national forests were and are under Agriculture—to clarify matters for Mr. Nunn. (Just how Nunn would have fared without Walcott as a partner is an interesting question.)

He took a day off for a quick trip to Philadelphia; the reason is not spelled out, but it may have been to visit Vaux relatives. Sidney came back from Cornell, and friends took both Walcotts to Rock Creek Park for a picnic supper, a nice event during a nice time of year in Washington. A few days later Sidney took his father to the train station, and Walcott headed for Boston. A letter written two months earlier provides the background for this trip: "It gave me great please to read your [P. Lowell] note of April 14th, as I have a particular fondness for Harvard, although I have not had the privilege of being directly connected with the University. In the fall of 1873 I spent a week with Professor Louis Agassiz and obtained from him and the various biologists and geologists at the University an inspiration that has always influenced me."[31]

"Attended Commencement Exercise of Harvard College. Received degree of *Dr* of Science" (June 19, 1913). This was Walcott's penultimate honorary degree. He now had been granted an LL.D. from Hamilton College, the University of Chicago, Johns Hopkins, The University of Pennsylvania, Yale, St. Andrews, and Pittsburgh; a D.Sc. from Cambridge and Harvard; and a Ph.D. from Royal Fredricks University. His long-dead mother Mary would have been proud of her "little stone breaker."

On the way back, he took care of RC business and made a stop in Philadelphia to see "M.M.V."; affairs were developing. A couple days later was a "Meeting of Advisory Committee L[angley] A[eronautical] Lab. 10 A.M. to 2:30 P.M." That evening Walcott spoke a few words on aeronautics at the Army and Navy Club, when the McKay Trophy was presented to Lt. Henry H. Arnold. (Lieutenant Arnold would go on to become Gen. "Hap" Arnold, Army Air Corps chief of World War II fame.)

Walcott rushed off to New York for another RC meeting. Stuart joined him, and the two spent the following day roaming around the zoo and other parts of the city. The *Princess Irene* arrived from Genoa in Hoboken, New Jersey, the next day, and they escorted Helen home. It was a busy three days in Washington unpacking and repacking for the trip west.

This trip was a little different than in past years, for a couple hours west of Niagara Falls, the party left the railroad and took the *Huronic* to Port Arthur, landing there in time for their own, private Independence Day picnic. On the trip to Winnipeg, the Walcotts were on the Grand Trunk Railway rather than the Canadian Pacific. In Winnipeg, Walcott took care of transportation, a few supplies, and other odds and ends. "We called on Miss Mary Vaux & visited with her during day more or less" (July 5, 1913). This was to be a repeat of the 1912 investigations; they connected with Sidney at Edmonton. Mr. Lett lent Walcott his railway car for the overnight trip from Edmonton to Jasper; the name Fitzhugh had disappeared from the map.

This short trip may have been the basis for another of the myths that surround the Burgess Shale. This story is that every year Walcott traveled west in a private railway car and lived in grand style, using up all available funds so that no one else from the Smithsonian could go out. If a private railway car was used later, that certainly is not evident from his diary. Years earlier, when Walcott had gone with Secretary Langley to South Carolina to observe an eclipse, he had noted that mode of travel. To beat this particular horse a little more, a tent camp in the Rockies may be great, but it is never grand. Walcott kept excellent accounts, and there is no indication he spent lavishly ever, let alone on fieldwork. He had first-class equipment, but good camping gear is a necessity, not a luxury.

A couple of lost trucks delayed them, but finally the four Walcotts were off to the Mount Robson station. Mr. Lett showed up for one day to reclaim his car and take a tramp with Walcott. "The Otto Bros. horses came by train 10 A.M. After luncheon Clawson Otto & Jack packed our supplies & camp outfit on the horses and moved them over to Grand Fork river where we camped" (July 12, 1913). They were only a couple of weeks into the field season when parts 11 and 12 of Walcott's second SMC volume, mentioned earlier, came out. The first was description of the fossils found on Mural Glacier and traced to Mumm Peak, and the second discussed the new geographic and geologic names of the Mount Robson area. In less than a year, Walcott had laid out the general geologic section of this area and had documented it.

3

The Healing Years (Last Half of 1913–1915): Not All Ups and Downs Are in the Canadian Rockies

The ground around the geyser's mouth is covered by a broad, gently sloping cone of pearly gray rock. The rock has two names: it is called either sinter or geyserite. It is made largely of silica, dissolved by hot water from stone deep beneath the ground, then carried up to harden on the surface. Other minerals, especially sulphur and iron, sometimes add hushed tones of yellow, purple, rose, lavender, and other colors.

—Susan J. Wernert, 1989

THE 1913 FIELD SEASON at Mount Robson was superior to that of the previous year. For one item, Walcott had all three of his remaining children with him; the pain of Charlie's death was easing. For another, he had some familiarity now with the local geography and geology; visiting an area without any prior knowledge of it is a real test for a geologist. For a third, the weather was better; no one has control over this, but it axiomatic that good fieldwork cannot be done in bad weather. One result of the good weather is that he took some nice pictures—though when they were published, all his panoramas were reduced to fit on a page (Walcott 1914a).

The pack train took four days to reach the Robson Peak camp of last year, with stops to collect and to photograph; some mornings carried mist and rain, but not so bad as to halt their efforts. They pitched tents, considered building a trail over Hitka Pass to the Mural Glacier, and proceeded with their tasks. "With Sidney & Stuart went up on s.w. slope of Titkana Mt & took panoramic photographs A.M. After the boys found & killed a kid & goat. I found a horizon of Upper Cambrian fossils" (July 21, 1913).

Almost every day, Walcott either found a new locality for fossils or was able to re-collect from those discovered the previous year. With each collection, he was getting an ever better grasp on how to divide the immense pile of rocks.

Near the end of the month, Mr. and Mrs. Lett and Miss Mary Vaux came to visit. The Alpine Club of Canada had established a camp at Berg Lake, and these three were in the party enjoying the wilderness. One day Miss Vaux went up Hunga Glacier with him to collect Upper Cambrian and Lower Ordovician fossils. She was quite an able assistant; unfortunately, at the end of the month she had to return to Philadelphia to help nurse her elderly father, who had become ill.

Before Mary left, she joined a group that climbed Mount Robson. As one of the first women to perform this feat, she made good newspaper copy. She sent a clipping to Walcott, annotated on the bottom: "What does thee think of such a lot of stuff as this? Many eastern papers published it this morning! If only they would stick to the truth."[1] (Philadelphia Quakers do not use "thee" lightly in addressing non-Quakers, so matters were progressing.) Several days later, Secretary Walcott presented a lecture on local geology to the Alpine Club campers at the mountain.

Helen was amusing herself by climbing most of the peaks in the area and was "qualified" by the Alpine Club. The boys were either off hunting or assisting Walcott. They went back to Mural Glacier to try for more of the fine Early Cambrian fossils. The group put in two days, and then came "a misty showery day. Regret as I wished one more day on the collection" (August 6, 1913). Where there are good fossils to be obtained, the paleontologist is never satisfied without at least one more day than he has already been able to collect. This is a difficult spot to reach, and the wonder is the size of the collection that was assembled and carried out.

It took a day to return to the main camp. They rested and then headed for Mount Robson station and the luxury of Lett's private railway car. For two days they repacked, took a few photographs of Mount Robson in the distance, and then waited for a locomotive to pull them to Edmonton. After a day in Edmonton visiting members of the Alpine Club, they caught a sleeper to Calgary. Early in the morning the four Walcotts, plus Arthur, caught the train to Field; after lunch they left for the Burgess Pass camp with the two packers of the season, Frost and Tupper. Nineteen horses were used, so this was no small affair. William Stevenson, the quarryman of last year, was in the fossil quarry, as was R. M. Mesler. Rick Mesler had come out from Washington to assist with the collecting. He was E. O. Ulrich's assistant, totally devoted to the man—he would die on the day of Ulrich's funeral. (Generally, he was mentioned as Mr. Mesler in Walcott's diary, but occasionally he was Mesler, more an indication of haste than of familiarity.) It was the first and only time that Walcott had the help of a trained collector who was not a family member.

The weather was poor the first day in the quarry, with mist and occasional showers. "The outlook for collecting good things is poor except by a great amount of hard work" (August 13, 1913). The next day snow drove them in early, and the following day was equally bad. Then the sun came out, they put in ten hours in the quarry, and "a number of good fossils were found" (August 16, 1913).

Sunday and Monday the work continued, despite rain, and Walcott decided that the quarry really would yield significantly more fossils. Anyone who has seen a strip mine knows that the rock deposited above the coal has to be moved in order to reach the coal. Most strip mines are in areas where the rocks are flat lying; the problem here was the steep mountain slope, which increased the amount of rock overlying the productive layer the farther one quarried back into the hill. The amount of this overburden to be moved was daunting, but the crew was undaunted. "The boys—Stevenson, Sidney & Stuart are stripping the upper layers while Mr. Mesler and I attempted to collect fossils" (August 19, 1913). Because of the steep slope and the slight inclination of the strata into the hill, an additional foot of overburden had to be removed to make the quarry a foot wider. It was a great deal of hard work, but the results were worth the effort.

A group of visitors brought a pause. "Went down to Field to meet excursion of geologists—Found many old friends. Visited with them & in the evening talked to about 75 at the hotel" (August 22, 1913). The excursion left, but Prof. August Rothpletz from Munich stayed for a day to collect. He became the motivating force for a Walcott publication a few years later.

A digression is needed to explain this gathering. Walcott had made a name for himself internationally with his appearances at the 1888 (London) and 1891 (Washington) meetings of the International Congress of Geologists. The organization had prospered, metamorphosing very slightly into the International Geological Congress. Walcott (1901) had contributed a little-known paper to the 1900 Paris meeting, a summary of his 1899 work on the Precambrian fossiliferous rocks and geology of North America. Finally, as mentioned, he had had a paper presented for him at the 1910 Stockholm meeting. The twelfth meeting of the International Geological Congress was in Toronto, and Walcott could easily have attended. He had a relatively clear-cut choice either to listen to talks and speak himself or go again to Mount Robson. There was no simply no contest; on the one hand, Walcott's reputation did not need any enhancement, and on the other, field time was precious.

Walcott made a small contribution to the guidebooks, discussing his work decades earlier along the St. Lawrence River, where he had found Cambrian fossils within conglomerates (Walcott 1913e). Now, he was also contributing as a local guide for the western excursion. It must have been quite a pleasure for him to show the Burgess quarry to a group who could really appreciate the significance of these marvelously preserved fossils. At the very least, it was a day off from the hard work.

Because of the volume of rock to be moved, Walcott hired another local to assist Stevenson. "A long day at the quarry with Mesler, Stevenson & McCullen. We are blasting down thru the massive layer above the fossil bearing beds" (August 26, 1913). Frost was busy either packing rock to camp to be split up or packing the wrapped fossils down the trail to Field. The boys were off hunting with Tupper, and Helen helped in the quarry when she was not entertaining tourists. The director of the Geological Survey of Russia and a distinguished geologist from Germany came into camp for a day, collected a bit, and left. The hard work went on and on. "All working at the quarry getting down to fossil bearing layers & finding many good specimens" (August 30, 1913).

Walcott wrote Richard Rathbun, holding down the si in Washington. "We are now down to the fossil bearing layers at the quarry. Blasted 12 feet of rock from off the 'Medusa' zone. Big job & the last one. All well."[2]

They reached the productive layers. "We found lots of fine specimens but nothing unusual" (September 1, 1913). The boys came back from the hunting trip; their guide had gone on a drunk. Unfortunately, three days of terrible weather prevented Walcott from immediately exploiting this extra help. The group got in two more good days of collecting, but snow came, along with cold wind. Lots of rock was broken up in camp; conditions were not ideal. "Up at quarry cold & unpleasant in the morning & cleared up in the afternoon. We found some fine fossils" (September 11, 1913).

Two more days, one of good weather and one terrible, and it was time for the Walcott children to leave. Walcott wrote how sorry he was. The work went on. "Clear, cool day. We worked at the quarry 8 A.M. to 6 P.M. Found many rare & good fossils. Put up 9 pkgs—Our *biggest* day" (September 15, 1913). It had been a difficult decision to extend the quarry farther into the slope, but the physical effort had paid off. The next day the wind was so strong in the quarry that they had to put up a shelter, but, to compensate, a new annelid worm was discovered. The season was late, and one day the trail was frozen hard. Still the heavy work at the quarry went on. Mesler and Stevenson put in a final day, while Walcott stayed below in camp breaking up the accumulated rock.

The season more or less ended on a peculiar note: "This afternoon Sept 22/13 local game warden Henry came to camp & notified me that the permit you issued to me & party was illegal & that he was to take chg of any skins etc that I had & I was to stop hunting. This was under instructions issued by A. Bryan Willain through Avery at Golden. I had not thot of hunting more this season so no plans are interrupted. Please wire me at Field on receipt of this letter what to do. I plan to pack fossils & camp outfit the *25th* & *26th*. There are three skins and two skulls."[3] Eventually the matter was straightened out, and Walcott was able to export his material and later continue hunting for scientific purposes. A habitat group of Big Horn sheep in the Museum, also on exhibit for years next to the mountain goats, was credited to Walcott. Scattered through the mammal and bird research collections are various skins and skulls gathered during his travels.

The quarry was closed for 1913, the rock that had been carried down was broken up, and the camp was dismantled. Mesler left for Washington. Arthur and Stevenson spent two days packing up, as Walcott had outlined in his letter, and then Arthur went home to Washington. Walcott left the following day via Lethbridge and then south to Great Falls, Montana. There was business to be conducted with Nunn at Provo, Utah.

No sooner did he arrive than he and Nunn left for western Utah. They were off across the Sevier Valley so that Walcott could see the Lower Fish Creek power plant, especially the flume. They moved on to Richfield and to the Beaver Creek plant and then back east, on what was a hard trip. "We are both half sick with grippe cold" (October 5, 1913). The next day was better; "Clouds cleared away at sunset. The stars were beautiful in the dark blue sky" (October 6, 1913). That sentiment may have been what brought on a bad cold; he finally left Salt Lake City on the 8th.

It was late on October 10 when Walcott finally got to Washington. His house staff—Mollie, Arthur, and Teddy—greeted him; whether this was Mollie the cook who had first appeared when the children were little is not clear. Faithful Arthur Brown had been around almost forever, but Teddy is an unknown. In any event, that there are three names gives some notion of the expense of running an upper-class household prior to the First World War.

While Walcott was still out west, a press had produced yet another of his tomes. His ciw monograph, containing 295 pages and 29 plates, was based primarily on the collections that Bailey Willis and Elliot Blackwelder had brought back from China, supplemented by the fossils collected by Joe Iddings in 1909. Both of these collections had formed the basis for preliminary publications in smc, but for this monograph the thorough and methodical Walcott had contacted several German professors to obtain additional specimens or illustrations of species from China that had been described years earlier. It was a great relief to see this work finally published; Walcott had been at it, off and on, since 1905, when he had supplied preliminary identifications for Bailey Willis.

> The chief results . . . are the discovery of portions of the upper part of the Lower Cambrian fauna and a great development of a Middle Cambrian fauna of the same general character as that of the Cordilleran Province of western North America; also an Upper Cambrian fauna comparable to that

of the same general character as that of the Cordilleran Province and Upper Mississippian Province of the United States. The fauna of the upper zone of the Lower Cambrian was found to be of the same general type as that of the Cambrian of the Salt Range of India, and we were thus enabled definitely to locate the faunal horizons in India which have heretofore been referred to Upper Cambrian and post-Cambrian formations. . . . A noteworthy addition to the knowledge of the Cambrian faunas was the discovery for the first time of a true cephalopod in a fauna referred to the Upper Cambrian. (Walcott 1913f, 2)

Incidental to this, Walcott deduced that the Cambrian seas had flooded China later than Siberia, another important point in the growing study of paleobiogeography. The last quoted sentence reports a discovery that would have been the subject of a special paper by almost anyone else. This is still the oldest known cephalopod in the world (Chen and Teichert 1983). As another indication of Walcott's luck, in the 1970s a team of Chinese paleontologists went back to recollect from this key locality. After a week of work by five people, two specimens were found; Walcott had more specimens in the collection that had been made for him. Walcott had been lucky in sending Willis to China and skillful in recognizing what he brought back. Chinese paleontologists view this publication as fundamental, the start of detailed studies of Cambrian rocks and fossils in their country. It is the benchmark against which all their subsequent studies of the Cambrian fauna are judged.

Walcott later wrote a colleague: "I regret that I am unable to send you the "Cambrian Faunas of China" as published by the Carnegie Institution, owing to the fact that I received but one copy as author, and none for distribution. I suppose this also applies to the reports by Professor Girty and Professor Weller, which formed a part of the volume. The introduction to my report was afterward published, however, as No. 1, Vol. 64, Smithsonian Miscellaneous Collections, and a copy will be sent you. . . . The volume of the "Cambrian Faunas of China" is for sale by the Carnegie Institution of Washington at $5.00. As the edition was a limited one, the cost was proportionally great."[4] Five dollars is not an inordinate price for this work, even in 1913 dollars, but it shows what an incredible bargain was to be had with USGS monograph fifty-one, at four dollars.

Walcott had four days to catch up on accumulated institution paperwork before his first trip of the fall to New York City. Duty, in the form of the CIW, called him again; with the deaths of both Billings and Mitchell, he was the senior scientist on the Ex Comm. Elihu Root moved from vice president to president of the board, and Walcott took his old position. Then it was back to Washington to escort the prince of Monaco around the new Museum and show him the Burgess quarry treasures.

After a day or two of administration, Walcott was off to Princeton, with a brief stop to see Miss Mary Vaux. The occasion in Princeton was the dedication of the graduate school, a far weightier assignment than one might imagine; the site for this school had been a source of argument for years on the campus. Afterward, Stuart cut a few classes and went with his father to New York City for a mild shopping spree. It was back to Washington to engage in several days of complex discussion with Ulrich concerning detailed correlation of the Upper Cambrian in Wisconsin and Minnesota. Ulrich had a talent for making complications, but Walcott needed the information if he was ever to complete the investigation of the dikelocephalid trilobites.

November was relatively quiet. Early in the month, both the Research Corporation and the Carnegie Ex Comm needed him in New York, but otherwise he stayed at the office and mainly worked on fossils. At mid-month, he and Helen went to Baltimore, she to a dance and he to an NAS council meeting. Throughout his vice presidency of the academy, Walcott was a fairly faithful attendee at the fall council sessions and meetings. Helen also accompanied him to New York. Walcott sat in on the RC and Ex Comm meetings, while Helen shopped. The next day, Mary Vaux came up from Philadelphia for a few hours, and the three of them went to the zoo. It was a delicate matter for spinster Mary, but she was trying to get to know Helen.

Besides affairs of the heart, Walcott had affairs of the head to consider. "At 5— had interview with Mr Platt—Architect for Chas. L. Freer building" (November 21, 1913). If Secretary Walcott had done nothing else for the Smithsonian during his tenure, his handling of Freer and ensuring that the collection and appropriate housing for it came to Washington should have been sufficient to give him a place in the history of the institution. It was to be nearly a decade before the building opened, but that portion of his art initiative was a resounding success. Carnegie Institution business in anthropological research kept him busy for a day, but otherwise, when administrative duties permitted, he was working on a major address. Charles Schuchert had arranged for a series of seven lectures to honor the hundredth anniversary of the birth of James Dwight Dana, one of patriarchs of American geology, and Walcott had been invited to participate. A month after he noted this project in his diary, he sent a first draft to Schuchert. Not incidentally, the lecture brought an honorarium of five hundred dollars.

"At my office all day interviewing callers & trying to revise my paper on Cordilleran Cambrian" (December 4, 1913). The Washington scene and the SI in particular were quiet; indeed a meeting of regents was canceled for lack of a quorum. The annual meeting of the CIW Board of Trustees ensued. "Presided at Trustees dinner 8–11 P.M. Escorted Mrs. Carnegie. Helen at dinner as my *lady*"

(December 12, 1913). The emphasis is that of an exceptionally proud father. Contrary to what he had feared, Helen had settled well into running the house, and the following night she handled a formal dinner for eight.

Secretary Walcott went off to New Haven and spent the night with Schuchert. "Fixed up lantern slides & illustrations for lecture given at 5 P.M. on Cambrian of Cordilleran Province" (December 15, 1913). It was a great success, and the generalizations that Walcott presented still hold. While traveling home, lunch in Philadelphia added an extra fillip to the occasion. Schuchert, perhaps best known today for his textbooks, later wrote, "Two years ago I thought I knew what the Cambrian succession was, at least well enough to state it for undergraduates. Since then Walcott has delivered a lecture here in our Silliman course commemorating Dana's centenary, and after reading the manuscript of this lecture two weeks ago it was quite evident that I had to rewrite my entire Cambrian section."[5]

The paper by Walcott is not the longest in *Problems of American Geology*, but Yale University got its money's worth. If there is one minor problem with this summary, it is in the use of "Ozarkian" and "Canadian" (Weiss and Yochelson 1995). These are the names of two proposed geological systems that Ulrich wanted to insert into the geologic column between Cambrian and Ordovician time. There is a chance that he might have been able to convince at least the American geological community of the validity of one of these, but the two together were too radical a change, and Ulrich was too undiplomatic for his notions to be generally accepted. Walcott was one of the few who used his nomenclature. Usage of these divisions in no way disturbed the account he presented; it simply placed boundaries above the lower part of the Middle Cambrian in different places.

Walcott began by noting conditions in the Precambrian before encroachment of the Early Cambrian sea; he went on to movements of the land that had seemingly limited the extent of the flooding during various parts of the Cambrian. He considered the past climate, summarized the general pattern of sedimentation (both by thickness and kind of rock), and listed main elements of the fauna. He discussed the boundaries between Lower and Middle Cambrian and between Middle and Upper Cambrian, and he indicated the problems to be examined in the future. For good measure, Walcott included four panoramas and two other photographs of the Canadian Rockies.

This is still a good summary, but in light of Walcott's later field activities the paper contains one unexpected statement: "When we closed the field season in British Columbia, after several years' research in that region, I realized that I was ready to go back to Nevada and take up the study of some of the problems of the southern Cordilleran Cambrian from the twentieth century point of view.

This I hope soon to do myself in a limited way and will leave to others the task of pressing the work forward in the future" (Walcott 1915, 163).

A logical interpretation is that Walcott, having accumulated sufficiently detailed biostratigraphic data in Canada, now wanted to look for finer subdivisions, or zones, in the sections he had measured decades earlier. Nevertheless, the secretary continued field investigations in Montana and western Canada. Except for a few local studies, the Cambrian of the southern Cordillera area remained static for a full generation, until a new group of geologists tackled the stratigraphy; that is quite a different story, far removed from 1913.

Three days after Walcott's return from New Haven, Miss Walcott was hostess at a dinner party for ten—better and better. What is surprising is a note on science in the diary for the same day. More will come later, but the comment is worth recording, for this sentence has the aspect of a major new idea that has suddenly made a number of isolated observations mesh: "At all possible moments worked on question of algae being the agent for the formation of the pre-Cambrian limestones" (December 19, 1913). One can never tell when a new idea will hit. Perhaps compilation for the Yale lecture or a chance question asked of him had suddenly cast light on the mysterious.

The next day, the two boys were home from college. A few days later, fossil collections of the summer arrived, and everyone worked unwrapping, when they were not Christmas shopping. Christmas was a fairly quiet holiday, but following it Helen managed a dinner for eighteen members of the social whirl. One can almost see Walcott beaming as he clipped notices from the local paper and placed them in his diary: "Dr. Charles D. Walcott . . . and his debutante daughter, Miss Helen Walcott, entertained at a charming dinner party . . . in honor of Miss Nona McAdoo, daughter of Secretary of the Treasury. As the entire party after attended the Draper Renaissance ball they wore their fancy costumes, and the effect about the dinner table was most brilliant. . . . Miss Helen Walcott was charming as Queen Clotilda, of France, and her costume was one of the handsomest at the ball."[6]

Several days later, "Mrs. Henry F. Dimock gave a ball for Helen. I went & remained until 2 A.M. leaving Helen Sidney & Stuart to dance it out" (December 29, 1913). This too was written up in the society columns. There was no summary for the year, for after the ball Walcott left for the Geological Society of America meeting at Princeton. On the last day of the year, Walcott "gave address on Cambrian of western America 2:30–3:45 outlining subject matter of Dana Memorial address. Presided at meeting of Paleontological Society P.M." (December 31, 1913).

This last item involved a most curious situation, but then scientific societies occasionally do curious things. As a result of changes in the constitution when the Paleontological Society became affiliated with (or split off from, or whatever) the Geological Society of America, Walcott as president of the Paleontological Society also became third vice president of the Geological Society of America, a decade and a half after being second vice president. No one in the world outside of the organizations would understand or even care. Walcott did not mention his election to the presidency of the Paleontological Society in his diary, nor was it listed in *Who's Who*.

New Year's Day was good, for the route back from Princeton included a long stop in Philadelphia and a visit to Fairmount Park with Mary Vaux. Thereafter the month fairly flew by. Administrative duties were light, which left a great deal of time to pursue the flat-tailed trilobites. It was mid-month before major meetings significantly interrupted research. Between the SI Board of Regents and the CIW Ex Comm, Walcott sandwiched in a meeting with William Henry Holmes and W. B. Parsons; this meeting took place long after the start of archaeology in Central America, but it began another phase of study in the region. Holmes also wore so many hats that sometimes it was hard to know which piece of business he was pursuing.

Being the father of a debutante can be difficult work; Walcott noted, "We have very little home life these days" (January 18, 1914). Either they went to formal dinners or Walcott was invited out to dine, while Helen was invited out to dance. His idea of a quiet life and hers were understandably different. It was almost an escape to get to New York overnight for a Research Corporation meeting and to see cousin Fred.

Walcott was involved in comparing the Late Cambrian trilobites to those slightly younger in the Early Ordovician when Cousin Libbie Pettibone died. Walcott went to New York for the funeral and to Utica for the burial; it was sad to lose one of his dearest friends. Fortunately, after he returned to Washington, Mary Morris Vaux came down for the day, accompanied by a lady friend—it was important to observe the proprieties. Despite all the dancing, Helen pulled off another dinner for fourteen. She was indeed becoming a Washington hostess.

February passed nearly as swiftly as January had. Helen left for a few days in New York City, and the SI remained quiet. Walcott concentrated on research "and at odd times took up questions connected with my studies of Cambrian faunas" (February 16, 1914). This was a reference to his manuscript of the Yale lecture. Still, the man who could not say no lost more research time when he agreed to be chairman of the GWMA finance committee. Helen organized another formal dinner for eight, plus a dinner for "young people," to close out the short month.

March began briskly. "Had a brief interview with Prof. Woodrow Wilson 12:15–12:30 about several matters affecting the Smithsonian" (March 2, 1914).

Relations with the president were cordial, but Walcott was no longer the close policy advisor that he had been under Teddy Roosevelt. Nevertheless, that did not deter him from making policy where it seem to be needed, as will be seen with aviation research. He took C. G. Abbot to the Washington Navy Yard to see the testing of aeronautical instruments; Walcott was determined that the government would have a policy in aviation.

"Turned in for printing paper on *Dikelocephalus* & rounded up paper on Cambrian of Cordilleran" (March 7, 1914). Less than a month later, the last part of Walcott's second SMC volume was out (Walcott 1914b). With forty-five pages of text and ten plates, it is the sort of work a paleontologist teaching at a university might be expected to produce three or four times during his career. Like so many of Walcott's works on Cambrian fossils, this was nothing spectacular, but it was a definitive paper, basic to future study of this family of trilobites.

Paleontology is based on similarities and differences and, therefore, must of necessity be a matter of opinion as to their significance. "Berkey (1898), at Franconia, Minnesota, describes from one sandstone bed several growth stages of the one trilobite *Dicelocephalus misa* Hall, from the Cambric rocks. Walcott appears to describe the same forms severally as so many separate species, of different genera even, from Franconia, of course, but by picking up a piece at a time here and there, for Wisconsin, Texas, Canada, etc., and describing them separately and at different times"(Sardeson 1929, 283).

Obviously, not everyone agrees with everyone else as to what constitutes a species. The Dikelocephalidae have been revised at least twice since Walcott first worked on them, and probably he was closer to the truth (if truth be defined here as the number of species and genera present in the rocks) than most other interested parties. Disagreement in science is not limited to the study of fossils.

About this same time, Walcott must have decided to print the introduction to his Carnegie monograph as the first paper of his third SMC volume. It is virtually identical to the pages of the monograph, with list after list of species assigned to other genera, but Walcott could not miss an opportunity to improve and tinker, so there are a couple of photographs of the rocks and a little more information on Cambrian fossils from what was then Indochina.

It was just as well that these varied items were out of his hands. "Busy with hearings on Smithsonian Institution appropriations 10 A.M. to 5 P.M. Suggested organization of an Aeronautical Bureau under S.I. direction" (March 10, 1914). The suggestion was not immediately accepted, nor did the final product come out quite the way Walcott had planned, but this was another stepping-stone along a new direction for American aviation.

Here is the place to mention some of the ancient history surrounding Walcott's aviation initiative and what was to become the Wright controversy. The two became intertwined, but they began quite separately. The involvement of the SI in early efforts at aeronautical research is a story that has been told several times, yet it continues to hold fascination, in part because so many different aspects and so many complex personalities are involved.

Walcott's serious interests in aviation can be documented at least as early as the spring of 1910, in a letter written to him by Smithsonian regent Alexander Graham Bell.

> In your note of April 19, you requested me to have a talk with Prof. Zahm [Catholic University] and Major Squier [Army Signal Corps] in relation to conducting such experiments on the physics of the air, etc., as will be of service in the development of aerodynamics....
>
> I quite agree with Prof. Zahm and Major Squier in thinking that America needs a National Laboratory relating to aerodynamics, supported at government expense, to investigate all the scientific questions involved in aerial locomotion.
>
> As Major Squier has pointed out experiments relating to aerodynamics have been, and are being carried on in a desultory fashion in several of the government departments independently of one another; and it is certain that as the work broadens there will be considerable duplication of work unless some steps are taken to secure the co-operation of the several departments with one another, and a proper co-ordination of the work.[7]

One clue to Walcott's interest lies in the Hodgkins Fund, a donation given to the Smithsonian Institution decades earlier to study air. (To state that how the fund was to be used was obscure is to state the minimum.) Another clue may be found in that the Langley laboratory had been closed at the professor's death and had remained closed. The small building was just south of the Castle, and every day Walcott could see it from his window and reflect that it was his efforts in 1898 to promote a man-carrying machine that had led Secretary Langley to his debacle in 1903. A third clue may be found in the concept of duplication of effort in the government; after all, Theodore Roosevelt had appointed Walcott to a committee to reduce such waste.

On the other hand, it does not seem likely that Walcott was attempting to build an empire of new bureaus. The SI model had been to start an investigation in a neglected field and then spin off the project. The weather service had become a separate weather bureau. Museum investigations of fishes by Baird had led to the Fish Commission. Judging from his past actions, Walcott saw the role of the SI as starting aeronautical research and simply guiding its course for a few years as a separate bureau evolved. Under Walcott, the USGS had followed the same model in giving birth to the Forest Service, the Bureau of Reclamation, and the Bureau of Mines.

With respect to Walcott's motivation, his efforts in founding the CIW Geophysical Laboratory provide some insight (Yochelson and Yoder 1994). Problems of formation of igneous and metamorphic rocks and megatectonics are not the concern of the stratigrapher and certainly not of the paleontologist. Walcott, however, determined that they were important to the field of geology as a whole, if not to his disciplines. He therefore set out to organize such a laboratory. He persisted through several defeats and administrative roadblocks until he eventually got the facility established. It was a parallel to his efforts to establish a national laboratory for aeronautical investigations.

In the spring of 1911, as noted, Walcott gave a talk at the Aero Club of America—a booster club, if you will—concerning research in aviation. President Taft was invited to attend, and he was supposed to announce that the Bureau of Standards would open a laboratory to be administered by the Smithsonian Institution (Roland 1985, 4–5). Unfortunately, this did not happen, in part because the Navy Department felt that it was better equipped to conduct experiments than the Bureau of Standards; Taft said nothing, so as not to raise a fuss in his cabinet.

Perhaps as a reaction to this defeat, or more likely simply as a result of enthusiasm, in 1911 the Aero Club of Washington started a May 6 "Langley Day" celebration. The event was to honor the anniversary of the flight of Langley's steam-powered model in 1896. In 1912, a more elaborate celebration was held, and by 1913, Langley Day and the second presentation of the Langley Medal had become a major event (Walcott 1913g). There was no celebration of a Wright Day; once the Wright brothers had received their Langley Medal, they more or less disappeared from mention in Washington aviation circles. They had been the first to fly, they were acclaimed throughout Europe, and more practically, and they had sold to the army an airplane that met difficult specifications, yet it was Langley on whom adulation was poured by the aviation establishment of rich sporting enthusiasts and government bureaucrats.

It is generally well known to aviation history buffs that Alexander Bell, "Casey" Baldwin, Lt. Thomas W. Selfridge—later to become the first fatality of an airplane accident—and Glenn L. Curtiss formed an association to experiment with aircraft, four years after the Wrights flew. The Wrights had seen the basic problem of flight as that of control and had developed the technique of wing warping, allowing them to turn the machine while aloft (Crouch 1981). Once Curtiss became involved, he eventually came up with the concept of control through flaps on the tail surfaces.

Bell's association dissolved in 1909, and Curtiss opened a factory to build aircraft to his new design. By January 1910 the Wrights had placed an injunction on Curtiss for patent infringement; their claim was upheld in court (Crouch 1989).

One legend of the RC is that Smithsonian regent Bell, who had been involved in the patent fight concerning the telephone, saw what was happening in aviation and advised against the SI's taking Cottrell's patents directly, for fear of litigation. To make matters still worse, in 1912, Wilbur Wright died of typhoid fever; the family was convinced that the struggles and testimony in court had so weakened him that he succumbed to the disease. Most of those who have studied the Wright brothers agree that Wilbur was the more outgoing of the two and the easier brother with whom to discuss matters.

Capt. W. Irving Chambers was the Navy Department's advisor on aerial matters. As noted in Walcott's diary, he and Zahm met several times with Walcott in 1912. (Just who initiated these meetings has not been established, and at such a late date it is no longer important.) Chambers generated a fair amount of interest by starting a national campaign for an aeronautical laboratory, needed because "the methods of scientific engineers have replaced the crude efforts of the pioneer inventors" (Roland 1985, 7–8). Neither Orville Wright nor Glenn Curtiss would have considered themselves "inventors" in the slightly pejorative sense used by Captain Chambers; it is fortunate that Chambers was not in the diplomatic service.

President Taft, during his lame-duck months, appointed a commission to study the matter. The group was under the chairmanship of CIW president Robert S. Woodward, and it included Walcott as one of the nineteen members. The commission agreed fully on the need for a laboratory but disagreed fundamentally on who should run it. The discussions and actions were a classic case of interdepartmental rivalry; Walcott's attempts to use the SI as a neutral headquarters failed. In addition, Congress exercised its prerogative and refused to grant funds, indicating that that august body should have been consulted before the commission had been formed. The correct Washington word describing the result is "shambles."

It is against this background that Walcott's efforts in the spring of 1913, following the death of Charles Jr., have to be measured. He persuaded the regents to reopen the Langley facility, and he organized a committee to supervise its efforts. If any indication is needed of the secretary's powers of persuasion, consider what must have been involved in getting Orville Wright and Glenn Curtiss to sit down at the same table on May 23, 1913. Curtiss had lost his patent suit and was involved in an appeal. Curtiss felt that Wright was acting as a roadblock to progress in aviation and implacably pushing him into bankruptcy. Wright was sure that Curtiss, in addition to being a cheat, was responsible for the death of his brother. Wright was essentially being ignored as a crank inventor, while Curtiss was the darling of the SI and, for a time at least, the pet of Alexander Graham Bell.

To use a pre–information age sociological term, if Wright and Curtiss had anything in common, both were essentially "blue collar." In marked contrast, John Jay Hammond represented the exceedingly rich sporting element who thought flying was great fun; it does not impugn his interest in encouraging the art of flying to point out that most people with lots of money fail to understand why those who were not born to money are so concerned about potential money-making schemes. Now add to this an army-navy rivalry fueled by the prospect of a new weapon; put in a pinch of the old fight about civilian against military control, as concerning the position of the Weather Bureau; and one has a fine brew. Zahm, who was then employed by the Smithsonian, was on the committee; to provide a little extra spice, he had testified as an expert witness in favor of Curtiss at the patent-infringement trial (Crouch 1987). Notwithstanding this mixture, the committee met again in June and December. Not much got accomplished, but at least some investigations into the state of the art were conducted; it was a beginning.

There were a couple of meetings, and then bureaucracy cracked down. A bean counter in the Treasury Department determined that government employees could not officially serve on the SI committee, because that committee had not been authorized by Congress; this was the same stumbling block that had produced complications a year earlier for the commission under Woodward. Walcott called this problem to the attention of the regents, and they (as he instructed them to do) advised him to get the matter straightened out on Capitol Hill. This was to bring the secretary to the Appropriations Committee and his setback of 1914. However, that is enough about aviation for the moment, more than enough.

A couple of days after the Appropriations Committee hearings, Walcott took a jaunt to Philadelphia. He and Mary Vaux went to Elkins Park and saw the Widner Museum paintings—a fine collection of old masters, according to Walcott, though the interest for him was more in the heart than in the art. The next day, in Washington, Walcott "fixed a lot of Algonkian fossil algae for photography" (March 14, 1914). His brainstorm of last fall about algae as the source of Precambrian limestone was being pursued seriously and rapidly. "Algonkian" had become the accepted term for the rocks below the Cambrian that were neither extremely metamorphosed nor exceedingly ancient; the present-day term is "Proterozoic."

Another funeral interrupted research. Aunt Helen Sanford died, and Walcott went to Oneida for the burial service. In a way, she was the final link to the departed Helena. Just possibly, this indirectly put him in a mood to reflect on the past and not think carefully about aviation; if so, it was the spark for what was to develop into a major problem. The day after the funeral in New York City,

Walcott had a "conference with Glen Curtice [*sic*] and Manley [*sic*] respecting Langley Aerodrome" (March 19, 1914). From there he went to the Aero Club of America dinner, where he was one of the speakers, lecturing on the work done the previous year by the Smithsonian Institution. (As an aside, there had been a "Curtice" twenty years earlier, an early and excellent assistant, so the misspelling of "Curtiss" makes sense.)

This meeting may be where the Walcott-Wright controversy had its start. To go back a bit, in mid-January 1914, a U.S. Circuit Court of Appeals had, as noted, ruled in favor of the Wright Company. That was effectively the end of Curtiss as a manufacturer. Scarcely a week later, Lincoln Beachey contacted the SI to request an opportunity to rebuild and test-fly the Langley aerodrome. Beachey had learned to fly from Curtiss and was a stockholder in the company, in addition to being a stunt flyer. Not to ascribe base motives to someone without any proof, but it is perfectly obvious that if the Langley machine could be put into the air, even then, somehow that might be interpreted as predating the Wright's first flight in 1903, or at least cast a shadow on the validity of the Wright brothers' patents. Beachey was not a disinterested party, by any interpretation. Richard Rathbun recommended against granting the request, and Walcott concurred (Crouch 1987).

Thereafter Curtiss wrote to Bell, "There has been some talk of reproducing the old Langley machine and having it flown. I should like to know what you think of this plan, as it would be any easy thing to do, provided it is worthwhile."[8] A flight of the old machine would certainly be worthwhile to Curtiss, if to no one else. What talk there was of flying a replica of the old machine was being generated by Curtiss and his associates; just how much Zahm, who was in charge of the SI Langley Aeronautical Laboratory, contributed to it is not certain, but again it would have been in his interest to see a flight made. Bell's reply to Curtiss is not known, but Curtiss was not discouraged; otherwise, he would not have talked to Walcott on the subject. The RC meeting kept Walcott in New York for another day. Mary Morris Vaux came up from Philadelphia; they dined and went to the theater, and he escorted her back to Philadelphia the next day.

The next week in Washington passed more or less in a blur, because of an attack of the grippe, but during that time Walcott telephoned Bell. (Fortunately, Bell was in the habit of keeping a summary of his important calls.) Walcott reported that Curtiss was anxious to make a copy of the Langley aerodrome. Curtiss had claimed that he could have it in the air in time for the May 6 Langley Day celebration. Furthermore, Curtiss had declared that expenses would not exceed two thousand dollars. Would Bell approve of the institution's undertaking this expense?

Bell indicated that he liked the idea but doubted that it would be appropriate to consider SI funding. Secretary Walcott replied, "I was thinking that I might chip in myself personally to the extent of a $1000."[9] Bell responded that he would also contribute and that it was better for the funding to come from outside parties than from the Smithsonian. Bell was a longtime close friend of Langley. Walcott also was a friend, and he was exceptionally loyal to the memory of his former chiefs.

So there it was! One had simply to show that the old machine could have flown to wipe out the stain on Professor Langley's character cast by the press after his failures in 1903. To this could be added the simple curiosity of finally determining whether the professor had been correct; if Curtiss was willing to risk his neck in the interest of science, as it were, he should be given the chance. Bell, if anyone, should have seen the potential for trouble, but he did not.

The end of the month brought two conferences that had fateful results. "A quiet busy day at the Smithsonian. Had a talk with Glen Curtis [sic] P.M. respecting Langley Flying machine" (March 30, 1914). "Talked further with Glen Curtis [sic] about testing out Langley Flying machine. My 64th birthday & all is well" (March 31, 1914). Helen arranged for a nice dinner with friends.

April 1 brought a note from Dr. Bell: "I have not yet heard what has been decided in relation to Glenn H. Curtis's [sic] proposed attempt to fly a machine built upon the Langley model. I sincerely hope that the attempt will be made with a duplicate and not with the original machine. I do not wish to express an opinion upon the propriety of aiding the expenses by an appropriation of Smithsonian funds as I am, in a measure, associated personally with Mr. Curtiss, as member of the AEA [Areal Equipment Association]."[10] "So far so good" does not quite express it, but if a replica were to be built with private funding and trials financed privately by Walcott and Bell, no one should seriously object. If nothing else, this trial might give a boost to the effort for a national laboratory for aeronautics. "It may be recalled that this man-carrying aeroplane was begun in 1898 for the War Department, and in the interest of national defense" (Walcott 1915a, 10).

To leave the air and return to the earth, the same day that Bell wrote Walcott, "Mr. Charles E. Resser came & began work as my assistant" (April 1, 1914). That date may have been felicitous, in the light of some of Resser's latest publications, but certainly after all that effort devoted to the air, it was time to return to something tangible, like fossils. Eventually, Resser was to obtain a doctorate from George Washington University. All accounts are that he was a kindly man and deeply religious, two traits of which Walcott would have approved.

He was also, at least until Walcott's death, not exceptionally active in a scientific sense. The only joint paper Walcott ever published was with Resser.

Resser published nothing else while Walcott was alive, at which point the floodgates opened. Resser's publication record leaves a great deal to be desired, and it just may be that he chose not to attempt any publications while Walcott was alive, because he knew his limitations. What he published has not generally been well received; in fact, correcting his publications in which he "corrected" Walcott's efforts has given rise to a large number of publications by many workers. Still, so far as Walcott was concerned, Mr. Resser gave faithful service, and that was sufficient. Resser would even arrange the manuscripts for two posthumous Walcott publications, a particularly onerous task.

Walcott immediately started Resser on examining trilobites from the southern Appalachians, and he had Dr. Cooper Curtice (Yochelson and Osborne 1999), he who had been Walcott's assistant for three years in the 1880s and whose name he would miswrite for Glen Curtiss's, come over for a day from the Department of Agriculture, next door, to clarify locality data. That the collections and information from 1885 were still significant shows the extent to which stratigraphic paleontology is an additive science. One does not discard collections and start fresh every decade with a bold new notion, as in some sciences.

With Resser in place, Walcott could dash off to New York. In one day he managed to see Nunn on business, meet a group of students in town from the Telluride Association at Cornell University, take care of RC business, attend the Kahn Foundation board, and still get to Philadelphia in time to take Miss Vaux to dinner at the Wissahickon Inn.

Walcott must have been preoccupied, for somehow two interrelated aviation items slipped past the executive committee of the SI regents that should not have. First, time was passing, and if the Langley aerodrome was to fly by Langley Day, a replica could hardly be built. If no harm would ensue, why not let Mr. Curtiss use the original? Second, there was a new member of the executive committee, and if the more experienced members thought it was appropriate to use Smithsonian funds for the trial, why not use them? The fatal mix occurred. During April, the machine was shipped off to Hammondsport, New York. By the time of the regents' annual meeting in December, the flight tests had been made.

After his New York meeting marathon, Walcott had a week in Washington to catch up on odds and ends. These included Nunn and his troubles with permits, the CIW Ex Comm, the American Association for the Advancement of Science, and the NAS council, with a few licks of research interspaced. The fiftieth anniversary of the academy had stirred an interest in history, and Walcott became chairman of a committee to collect historical portraits, manuscripts, and instruments (Day 1915); there was always something new to interfere with the fossils.

The highlight of the NAS annual meeting was a lecture by Sir Ernest Rutherford, the distinguished British physicist. Rutherford and radioactivity had broken the short time-scale that Lord Kelvin had attempted to impose on the geologists in the latter part of the nineteenth century (Burchfield 1975). Eight years before, Schuchert had written to the USNM's head curator of geology, "The Rutherford letters are replete with interesting information. Geologists need no longer ask the physicists for time. R. is willing to grant us all we want and more."[11] Geologic time, time by the double handful, was and is a dramatic aspect of civilization (Albritton 1980; Toulmin and Goodfield 1982).

At the Academy annual meeting, Walcott "presented preliminary rept on the Algonkian algae of Big Belt Mountains, Montana" (April 22, 1914). He was pursuing his idea with the zeal that he had shown a quarter of a century earlier when he had resolved the problem of the position of the *Olenellus* zone. Walcott was an old dog with a new trick, one that was important to the early history of life.

Thus, this seems as appropriate a place as any to discuss "Precambrian Algonkian algal flora," the second part of Walcott's third SMC volume; it was distributed late in July while he was busy in Montana collecting more of the algal flora. The nineteen plates and thirty-seven pages of text, nearly half of them descriptions, packed a great potential.

Walcott's notion that the banded hummocks and lumps in the Precambrian limestones might have been formed by algal secretion was absolutely fundamental; he may not have been the first to suggest an organic origin for stromatolites, but he was the first to demonstrate this point conclusively. John M. Clarke had described limestone balls that were forming in Canandaigua Lake in New York, where Walcott had spent the summer of 1903. Walcott made a close comparison between these undoubtedly organic structures and the Precambrian examples. If the present was the key to the past, stromatolites were formed by algae and bacteria.

Walcott also reasoned that the algae and bacteria that produced these nearly spherical deposits might also be the sources of the lime that formed the even-bedded limestone units. There is general agreement today that both inorganic and organic constituents form limestones. The relative importance ascribed to one or the other depends on the investigator and the area studied, though perhaps a majority of sedimentologists would agree that organic processes are more important overall.

All this came about as a result of Mr. M. Collen, who had accompanied Walcott in his 1905 trip over the Precambrian rocks in northern Montana. (Despite determined looking, several interested people have found almost nothing about

Collen's life.) In 1906 Collen wrote, "During last May I sent you about 1,000 lbs. of fossil material from the Algonkian of the Big Belt Mts. A careful study of this material will probably throw some light upon the origin of the very early limestones. Some of the specimens show the *Stromatopora* forms uprooted and piled together in a confused mass, and subsequently cemented into a crinkled, concretionary-like limestone."[12]

Apparently this material just sat around after it arrived in Washington. Walcott had plenty to do in the summer and fall of 1906, and then had come the appointment as SI secretary and the prospect of fieldwork in Canada. There really was no adequate place to lay out the material, or equipment to cut some of the large pieces, until the move into the Museum in 1910. An exceptionally important aspect of museums is that material may be accumulated and stored safely in them until it can be studied.

One of the elements of Walcott's study was a recognition that the lumps were not coral. He also recognized that these lumps had definite features, allowing one to differentiate genera and species. He named *Collenia* and distinguished it from *Cryptozoon*, deciding that the latter was confined to Cambrian and younger beds. He named four other genera from the Newland Limestone. A British sceptic was not impressed. "The general belief among American geologists and several European authors in the organic origin of *Cryptozoon* is, I venture to think, not justified by the facts. . . . It is clearly impossible to maintain that all such concentrically constructed bodies are even in part attributable to algal activity" (Seward 1931, 86). This view delayed further study of the field for about a generation (Schopf 1999).

Subsequent workers have suggested that some of these forms are the result of inorganic processes and are not distinct genera and species after all (Fenton and Fenton 1934; Gutstadt 1975). The operative word here is "some," for Walcott did include true organically formed structures. "If [the structures are] not biogenic, perhaps unique physicochemical or environmental conditions existed, or were more widespread, to promote formation of such structures at this particular interval of geologic time" (Walter 1992, 506). More than half a century after Walcott (1899) directed attention to these forms in the Glacier National Park region, they were investigated and found to be stratigraphically useful (Rezak 1957); the literature on stomatolites as biogenetic structures is one of the great themes of paleontology in the last half of the twentieth century.

Even allowing for some structures being inorganic, Walcott built a strong case for the organic origin of the growths and compiled what had been a scattered literature. He discussed in some detail his concept that the majority of the Belt rocks were terrestrial. The limestones had been deposited either in lakes, like the temporary playa lakes of the desert, or formed in restricted incursions of the sea, rather like estuaries. What is particularly interesting is that this concept flies in the face of the classic doctrine that the present is the key to the past. Essentially, the only stromatolites known in the American fossil record at that time were the "cabbage heads" in the Upper Cambrian at Saratoga Springs, New York. These were associated with trilobites, brachiopods, and other accepted marine fossils.

In effect, what Walcott proposed was that stromatolites could have formed under a variety of conditions. The environment of deposition of the Belt limestones has been argued ever since, and there simply is no consensus on whether they are marine, freshwater, or something in between (Fenton and Fenton 1931). Interpretation of these sediments is a difficult problem, and Walcott did remarkably well in producing a coherent story from the information that was available. In the early 1930s, stromatolite growths were to be found alive in the Bahamas, and suddenly fossil stromatolites were interpreted as marine. Now the pendulum seems to be swinging back to Walcott's view that at least some of the Precambrian forms were nonmarine.

So much for this grand concept. No sooner was the NAS meeting concluded than Walcott took off for the American Philosophical Society meeting in Philadelphia. "Gave a talk on the Burgess Shale fauna after luncheon" (April 25, 1914). Inasmuch as one of the members of the American Philosophical Society was Mr. Vaux, Walcott just might have had a bit more in mind than simply telling the membership once again of the treasure he had found. He pushed on to Princeton, spent the night with Stuart, and the next morning was impressed with the sight of the assembled young men in the chapel. From Princeton, it was easy enough to get to meetings of the Carnegie Ex Comm and the RC in New York.

Mary Morris Vaux came to Washington, and Walcott took her to see Great Falls. Coincidentally, perhaps, Helen came back from a trip to New York and took this proper Philadelphia lady to lunch. In addition to the pleasure for him of the two ladies' getting together, Walcott the next day showed the first sketches of the GWMA building to the finance committee. A major problem this time was that Mrs. Dimock was seriously ill (though she was to recover and renew her efforts). The plan was to raise a million dollars in about a year for the construction. Try though Walcott and other parties might, the building kept slipping away; it never materialized.

A more weighty matter, closer to home, had to be considered. After church on Sunday in early May, Walcott apparently worked out with Helen one aspect of a major issue, his remarriage. "We took a walk in the evening & talked over family questions of interest to us" (May 3, 1914). A scientific problem was also being pursued: "Attended to various matters & wrote on dep'ts of fossil algae"

(May 5, 1914); "Worked on algae paper" (May 8, 1914); "At odd times working on Algonkian flora" (May 12, 1914).

Affairs of the heart warmed considerably on the next trip to Philadelphia. "Met M.M.V. & went up the Wissahickon for a picnic supper. We had a heart to heart talk about the future" (May 16, 1914). The talk was satisfactory enough to allow Walcott to concentrate afterward on science. "A long busy day at the Smithsonian. Rounded up my algal flora paper so that only the microscopic work remains to be done & describing of the cells" (May 16, 1914).

It was about this same time that Walcott decided that his comments on stopping field investigations in the Canadian Rockies and moving operations to southern California, mentioned in his Dana lecture at Yale, had been premature. He wrote his faithful quarryman, Stevenson, in Field: "The things upon the mountain can remain in the trees [at the camp site], as they are of no special value, and will be needed in future work in the quarry. It might be well, if you are up on the mountain, to bring down the big crowbar, as it belongs to the Park Service."[13] There was to be no work in the quarry that year, but it is equally clear that regardless of how many specimens Walcott had accumulated from that spot, he wanted more. It is almost as clear that since Mary loved the Canadian Rockies even more than Walcott did, her desire to visit there must have influenced him.

He spent a day looking at the Burgess Shale collections of last year, seemingly as much for relaxation as anything else. Then it was off to Philadelphia and a meeting with George Vaux, Jr., three years younger than Mary; brother William had died in 1908 of tuberculosis, providing another bond between them. Walcott rushed back to Washington and spent time "grinding away all day on routine & the last touches on Pre-Cambrian Fossil Algae Flora Paper. Turned in paper in P.M." (May 21, 1914).

He rushed again to Philadelphia, this time seeing Mrs. George Vaux, Jr., and meeting Helen at the train station; father and daughter went on to Ithaca. Stuart joined them for the Cornell homecoming. A joint Yale-Cornell glee club sang. The next day Cornell beat Yale at baseball and Princeton at rowing. Chapel that Sunday, given the losses the family had suffered, could not have been a finer family occasion, at least as far as Walcott was concerned.

From Ithaca it was easy to get to Hammondsport, where Glenn L. Curtiss had his shop. "Found the Langley Aerodrome nearly ready for trial" (May 25, 1914). The machine was moved out the next day, but bad weather prevented any tests. When finally put in the water, it planed well with the wings removed. The wings were attached, and Curtiss took the controls. "Langley machine launched 6:20 A.M. It planed & lifted from the water. 9:30 A.M. another short run. Motor trials. After dinner two trials. Motor weak" (May 28, 1914).

Zahm was on hand to observe and record the trials, as the official Smithsonian Institution representative. He provided glowing accounts of the accomplishments and downplayed the changes that Curtiss had made, apart from the addition of pontoons; this was the penultimate ingredient of the later feud.

Walcott did not hesitate to share his enthusiasm with Freer. "Yours of May 22d received while I was absent in central New York in connection with certain tests being made of the Langley flying machine. We had the pleasure of seeing the machine rise from the water into the air, with everything the same as when Mr. Langley built it, except that an additional weight of 345 pounds was added so as to provide for pontoons, in order that it might be tried out over the water."[14]

Walcott hung around Hammondsport for a few more days, but bad weather was followed by a broken transmission on the aerodrome, and that was the end of trials for a time. A photograph documents Curtiss and Walcott in the cockpit of the Curtiss seaplane *America*, but if Walcott went on a flight, he did not note it in his diary. He stopped in Philadelphia on the way home.

June in Washington that year was a fretful time—"the hottest, dampest, most trying day of 1914" (June 8, 1914). Even motor car rides did not help abate the heat. Most of Walcott's immediate scientific interests had been resolved. Nothing was doing in Congress, and both the si and ciw were running smoothly.

It was also a waiting time. A newspaper printed the headline, "Announcement Is Made in Philadelphia of the Engagement of Miss Mary Morris Vaux of Bryn Mawr, Pa. to Dr. Charles D. Walcott."[15] On a Sunday, at the Friends Meeting House, Walcott gave Miss Mary a ring to make the announcement official. He hurried on to Princeton and saw his three children. They stayed around the following day for a ball game. Then Walcott went to Philadelphia early, Helen and the boys coming later. All lunched with the Vaux family; Helen stayed on briefly, while his sons went to Washington. Three days later, the boys went west with Mr. Nunn. They were grown, Walcott was certainly grown, and the boys had business in the west so they skipped the nuptials. Before the ceremony, Walcott saw a senator and a congressman concerning aviation legislation. He put the finishing touches on the si budget and went to a ball game. The happy waiting time became gloomy when Assistant Secretary True died; still, two days later, Helen took her father to Philadelphia. Charles Doolittle Walcott married for the third time on "a perfect June day" (June 30, 1914).

The ceremony was held at the home of Mary's brother George. It was quiet, in the tradition of the Friends, yet there was more than a bit of tension. When Walcott filled out his application for a marriage license, he had listed Lura Rust (Yochelson 1998), the bride of his youth in Trenton Falls. Everyone knew of the tragic death of Helena, but that Walcott had been married earlier was a shock. What is curious is that for Walcott, Lura had become a nonperson. Except for this one mention on the application, her name had not appeared in his papers for years, and it did not appear again. None of the biographical sketches prepared for *American Men of Science, Who's Who,* or various foreign societies mentions her; she was not noted in most obituaries. It was a door slammed shut and nailed tight.

Time has inflated the reaction of Mary's father to the discovery of this first marriage, to the point of his calling the secretary of the Smithsonian Institution a fortune hunter and cutting Mary out his will. This is another myth; it is not true. What is true is that Mary's father did not walk across the yard from his house to attend the ceremony. Whether it was personal objection to Walcott, the loss of his homemaker at an advanced age, or an admixture of the two is trivial. For an independent-minded spinster fifty-four years and eleven months old, marriage was a courageous and delicate step.

In a reprise of his 1888 journey with Helena, the married couple went first to Montreal and the Redpath Museum at McGill University. Walcott could not introduce his new bride to Prof. William Dawson (Sheets-Pyenson 1996), now deceased, as he had done with Helen, but he could look once again at Dawson's "Eozoon canadense" and, working from his newly acquired information, interpret the specimens—incorrectly—as having been formed by algae. Afterward, instead of heading east toward Newfoundland as the new Walcott couple had done decades earlier, these newlyweds boarded the train west, seeing friends in Winnipeg and Banff before stopping at Glacier, British Columbia.

From 1884 onward, the Vaux family had systematically photographed and systematically surveyed the advance and retreat of the ice there (Cavell 1983). One general method was to place a series of markers across a glacier and then remeasure their position in subsequent years. Like river water, glacial ice moves faster near the middle than near the edges, but, again like a river, movement may be complex. Glaciers always flow forward, but the front edge of the ice may either advance overall or retreat, depending on whether the climate is getting cooler or warmer. Worldwide, mountain glaciers have been in retreat, and the data provided a century ago by the Vaux family has been exceptionally useful.

Mrs. Walcott now had a willing assistant to train, the reverse of Walcott's 1888 honeymoon with Helena. "Went up on the Illecillewaet Glacier with Mary and assisted her in taking photographs & measuring position of foot of glacier" (July 7, 1914). He included a panorama of the Asulkan glacier in the "Explorations" (Walcott 1915); this fold-in increased the cost of publication, but it was a dramatic photograph. They did spend a few hours one day searching for Upper Cambrian fossils, but apart from that, the Canadian trip was Mary's. The weather cooperated beautifully; there was no rain until the last evening.

The couple took the train west to Vancouver, took a boat to Victoria, and another to Seattle, enjoying the sunsets and the people they met along the way. From Seattle, the newlyweds headed east across Washington, through the Bitterroot Mountains of Idaho and ultimately to White Sulphur Springs, Montana, where the trip became Walcott's. "Left White Sulphur Spgs. at 6:20 & drove out to camp on south fork of Birch Creek. Found Arthur Brown & Chas. E. Resser. Fred Strange,—teamster drove team. A fine camp and all going well" (July 19, 1914).

Getting the camp established had been a complex operation, though more or less representative of earlier years, and setting it up demonstrates well Walcott as organizer. The secretary had spoken with a USGS geologist who had warmly recommended as a packer one Fred Strange, who had worked in eastern Washington. He had also contacted George Otis Smith, USGS director, and received permission to use nine government horses pastured at Hall, Montana. Walcott had then contacted the War Department and had been authorized to use army wagons from Fort Missoula. He had written William Stevenson to ship the camp equipment from Field, British Columbia, to Drummond, Montana. All the pieces had come together at the same time. Incidental to these logistics, Walcott had also gathered the latest maps and permission to work in five national forests.

Shortly before Walcott left for Philadelphia, Resser and Arthur Brown had each received identical travel orders, "Sir—you are authorized to. . . ." Walcott had written Strange: "I will send Arthur Brown, who has been out with me as cook for sixteen seasons, to meet you at Drummond July 1st."[16] (Even in the summers in which Arthur Brown was never mentioned in Walcott's diary, he was at hand to cook his famous pancakes.)

What Walcott did not mention to Strange, or in any of the few letters that mention the efforts of Arthur Brown, was that the man was black. It must have been an interesting meeting in Drummond between packer and cook, yet as in past seasons, Arthur surmounted or ignored all local difficulties caused by being nonwhite in the West. Walcott had many good mental attributes, and one of his best was that so far as race was concerned, he was color blind—both in the field and in a city that was Deep South in its attitudes. There is no need to elaborate on this subject, but it is fundamental.

The first day in the field near White Sulphur Springs, a fierce thunderstorm drove the party back to camp, but on the second they were able to gather a large collection of the Algonkian algae along the south fork of Birch Creek. Walcott measured the section, and Mary made sketches of the algal bodies in place; having an artist in the field has advantages. There were several algal beds, and Walcott was finally able to discover the locality in the Newland Limestone from which Collen had sent him the specimens he had named *Newlandia*.

After collecting and seeing what there was to be found geologically along Birch Creek, the Walcotts went by buckboard to Newland Creek. They collected a few concretions, lumps of limestone that are not formed by algae, locally called fossil turtles, and returned to the main camp; the weather was almost unbearably hot. It was time to pack up specimens, and they sent a ton and a half back to Washington. The algal colonies are large and are solid rock; one accumulates bulk and weight rapidly—the antithesis of the Burgess Shale collecting.

"Mary is strong & a great help to me in various ways" (July 31, 1914). Obviously their marriage was standing the test of fieldwork. They moved camp a couple of times in Deep Creek Canyon, looking for a slightly cooler spot, along with the proper rocks. "With Mary, Resser & Fred went up to summit of Mt. Edith (9200±). Found a base for the Algonkian series & decided to measure section east to Black Butte. A long tiresome day owing to rough ground the last mile to the summit" (August 3, 1913). The heavy collections continued to accumulate, for they had camped near a good exposure. There were two beds of specimens in the Newland Limestone, and Walcott sampled each liberally.

The use of names in Walcott's diary is interesting. Previously all assistants had been "Mr." almost every time; "Resser," however, mostly appeared alone. It is possible that Mr. Wilson of the 1912 season had soured Walcott just a bit on being friendly too quickly. An alternative interpretation is changing customs, for in the old days the use of last names had been a sign of familiarity, whereas now it had become an indication of a slight distance.

"Resser & Fred went to White Sulphur Springs for lumber & supplies & brot back papers telling of great European war. England, France & Russia against Germany & Austria" (August 8, 1914). The world would never be the same, though that was not evident as yet in rural Montana. Walcott's team boxed up another 1,200 pounds of algal limestone for shipment. "Began work on the stratigraphic section from Mt. Edith east. A batholite of 'granite' forms the base of the mountain. Measured over 5000 feet in thickness of shales & sandstones. A very hot tiresome day" (August 10, 1914). All field days were long; this one was thirteen hours.

The sections of Algonkian rocks were incredibly long, and measurement of the thickness of the units within them took days. Eventually, the campsite was moved to Wall Mountain, where Cambrian rocks were exposed above the Belt series. Resser looked for fossils in these beds, while Walcott finished up his section of the Algonkian. "With Mary, Resser & Fred went along Wall Mountain & over to Sixteen Creek Canyon 7:10 to 4. P.M. The Cambrian rocks are most disappointing. Shales not well exposed and limestones very much broken up. Found a few fossils of little importance" (August 19, 1914).

Camp was moved to the forest ranger station at the head of Dry Creek, and the party went after more algal specimens; the ranger was happy about the company and an occasional meal that he did not have to cook. In three days, Fred and Resser had to take another large shipment to the railroad station. They moved camp down the valley of Dry Creek and onto the east fork of the Gallatin River. "Out 6:40 A.M. to 5:30 P.M. Measured section of Algonkian rocks from E. Gallatin river to the base of the Cambrian on the high hills to the north. Obtained 3028 ft in thickness and several algal limestones" (August 29, 1914). As with his work in younger parts of the geologic section, Walcott did not simply collect but determined the stratigraphic position of his collections of fossil algae. He also used their occurrence at several levels as markers to allow him to correlate the sections from one locality to another. The result of his labors was another thirteen boxes shipped to Washington.

"Moved camp via Manhattan to Cherry Creek 5 *mi* above Madison river. A fairly long drive 35 *mi* & a hot one—No rain since July 6 & roads are deep with dust" (September 1, 1914). Walcott caught up on his correspondence and rode out from this base to look at the Cambrian; he found the trout to be more elusive than in Dry Creek. They moved to the vicinity of Ennis—few fossils, but less wary trout.

Notwithstanding the cooperation of the trout, they moved again to near Logan, the unrelenting heat making conditions for travel less than ideal. "With Mary & Resser went out on the Cambrian section on the N. side of Gallatin river. We collected a few fossils from the Wolsey shale" (September 10, 1914). One insightful story about Resser concerns a trip he made in the early 1930s with a German geologist and a Japanese couple. They drove to this area, and Resser pointed out that just across the river, which they could wade, was the type locality of the Wolsey Shale—all the while assembling a fly fishing rod.

"Out collecting with Mary & Resser in the Algonkian. After luncheon we ran into a fine lot of *Gallatinia* & *Newlandia*" (September 11, 1914). The weather finally broke, and while it stormed they caught up on mail. Walcott wrote to Washington, Mary serving as amanuensis, as shown by the fine penmanship. "Our six weeks of hot weather closed last evening with a hurricane that blew it south. Today it is snowing and we are having our first stormy day in camp. Yesterday we collected an usually fine lot of fossil alga, which is resting on the mountain side about three miles from camp. Much depends upon the length of this storm as to further movements. If it continues we will not get far north of Helena this season."[17]

The Walcotts took the buckboard and moved their tent to a nearby ranch house. "Fred, Arthur & Resser marooned on road by mud" (September 16, 1914).

The camp was finally reestablished on Boulder Creek, and Walcott spent several days roaming the rocks in that vicinity, to little effect.

The weather improved, and they moved camp to near Helena. "Went into Helena early with Mary & Resser. Obtained supplies & at 11 A.M. started up Ten Mile canyon. Crossed over to Seven Mile canyon. Caught up with baggage at foot of Muller Pass & camped by the roadside. A very interesting days [*sic*] ride. Noted Helena limestone near mouth of Ten Mile Canyon" (September 24, 1914). The party crossed the Continental Divide the next day and camped near Avon. The next camp was near Drummond; Walcott commented on having been there fourteen years earlier with Helena and the children.

The hardworking USGS horses were finally put out to pasture at Drummond, and the party moved on toward Missoula. Walcott examined the Precambrian rocks but found no remains of algae. "A fine section of the Camp Creek series of the Algonkian but no fossils. Caught mess of trout after lunch. Returned at 6 P.M. to camp. Three months ago Mary & I were married" (September 30, 1914). The Montana field season had been an excellent one from several different aspects.

They had one more day of good weather before moving to Fort Missoula in a driving rain. It took a couple of days to dry equipment, pack up, and straighten accounts with the army. Walcott took Mary and Arthur to Drummond then to Helena in a snowstorm. The party tried for another day of fieldwork in Ten Mile Canyon, but snow and mud made that impractical. The season was over, and they headed east on the Great Northern Railway.

In Minneapolis, Walcott and Mary visited the University of Minnesota and the Walker Art Gallery; Arthur probably went straight on to Washington. The couple stopped at Onalaska, Wisconsin, where brother Ellis and his wife welcomed them. It was a cordial visit, though Walcott did not have a great deal in common with his remaining brother. Walcott had been fifteen when this veteran had come back from the Civil War and found himself unable to settle back into life at Utica, New York. Still, family was important, and Walcott wanted Mary to meet his sole surviving sibling.

The couple returned to Washington without incident. "Mary & Helen getting things settled at the house" (October 13, 1914). The first order of business was a reply to one of the forest rangers whom Walcott had met and who had sent in some rocks that he thought might be of interest. "I was glad to hear from you. If it had not been for the snowstorm Mrs. Walcott and I would probably have driven out from Helena to spent two or three days at the Deep Creek Station. . . . The specimens from the east slope of Bridge Gulch are the kind we were looking for last summer. The others, 2, 3, and 4, are of concretionary origin and not fossils."[18] Some of Walcott's supposed algae may have been inorganic, but Walcott was too good a geologist to be confused by typical concretions; if he truly was in error—there is still no agreement—the sedimentary processes that formed the structures in the Newland Limestone were atypical of concretions in younger rocks.

The month moved along quickly, for, as might be expected, even though lots of SI paper had accumulated while the secretary was away, nothing of great excitement had occurred. Walcott had to go twice to the New York for Research Corporation business, Mary had to go to Philadelphia a couple of times to pick up various personal items and settle her affairs, and Helen went off with friends. Walcott was once again a pallbearer when Bernard L. Green, the man who had built the Library of Congress and the new Museum, died after half a century of government service. Henry Gannett, geographer, and A. C. Peale, geologist and great-grandson of the painter C. W. Peale, were both seriously ill; two more links to the old USGS were breaking.

Walcott took his bride to the Church of the Covenant, but on the second Sunday in November, they played hooky. The chauffeur drove them west, across the Blue Ridge and into the Great Valley of Maryland. "5 *mi* s. of Hagerstown we collected a lot of fossil algal remains from the Conococheague limestone (upper Cambrian)" (November 8, 1914). (For those who are vitally interested in stratigraphic correlation, this limestone is fairly close to the same age as the limestone at Saratoga Springs, New York, which shows the wonderful *Cryptozoon* "cabbage heads.") The Walcotts spent two more days touring the immediate area and collecting algae. One may deduce that the weather was exceptionally fine for them to have gotten over the mountains and then around by car, and also that the interest in ancient algae was running exceptionally high.

Perhaps a break from paperwork and setting up house was also in order. Walcott took Mary and Helen to see Stuart and attend the Junior Prom at Princeton; Helen and Stuart seem to have enjoyed themselves thoroughly. They all saw the Princeton-Yale football game and cheered for Princeton. Walcott went off to New York to attend RC meetings, and Mary went to Philadelphia. They met at home and then went to Baltimore to hear a lecture on mountain climbing. There seemed to be hardly any staying at home, even relative to the days of Helen's limited housekeeping, but the pace and activity were definitely to Walcott's taste.

Walcott went off to New York again for a one-day triple-header—the CIW Ex Comm, followed by the RC executive committee, followed by a full board meeting. "Research Corporation is doing finely & is a success according to financial returns" (November 19, 1914). After that, he went to Brooklyn to see the survey ship *Carnegie*. This vessel was a major investment of the Carnegie Institution of Washington, built without iron to cruise the world making magnetic observations.

Walcott's diary notes that on November 23 Arthur began cutting excess matrix off the Burgess Shale fossils, leaving them on squares or rectangles; he was indeed a man of many parts. (Apparently a room on the third floor of the Castle housed a trim saw.) Thanksgiving Day for Walcott with his new family was quite nice. He ended November on a good note. "At my office during the day attempting at odd moments to do a little work on Cambrian faunas. A quiet happy evening at home" (November 30, 1914).

Early December took Walcott to New York again, this time for the committee of the American School of Archaeology in China. It was a satisfactory meeting. When he returned, one of Mary's lady friends came down from Philadelphia, and Walcott toured her around the Museum. That too was a satisfactory visit. The Red Cross took up part of a day; this was a bit less satisfactory, for it was becoming painfully clear that the conflict in Europe was not going to end soon and that there were a great many people who needed relief.

Notwithstanding the clouds over Europe, Walcott took the annual meeting of the SI Board of Regents and the CIW trustees in stride, with hardly a comment. He did mention to the regents the difficulty posed by the inability of federal employees to serve on the aeronautical advisory committee. The regents, taking the proper Washington action, appointed a committee. By mid-December, Walcott had recorded only one scientific event for the month: "At my office most of the day. Arnold Hague called. Also David Fairchild. Talked about fossil algae & botanic garden with Fairchild" (December 14, 1914). Dr. Fairchild was a plant explorer for the Department of Agriculture, in his way the Walcott of fruits and vegetables.

The Botanical Garden is one of the anachronisms of Washington. In 1842 Cdr. Charles Wilkes had returned from his around-the-world exploration expedition, bringing various exotic plants with him. There being no other place to put them, Congress had assigned the plants to a small botanical garden adjacent to the Patent Office; Congress has supervised the Botanical Garden ever since. Had the Wilkes expedition returned four years later, the SI would have been established and probably would have been placed in charge of the exotic vegetation.

Stuart came in for the holidays, followed by Sidney. "Am glad to have all three children at home" (December 23, 1914). The next day, Walcott was "Busy with fossil algal specimens A.M. as office was closed at noon" (December 24, 1914). Ever since the Civil Service had come to the federal government, working conditions had improved, and occasionally even a bit of compassion had crept in: the clerks were given a free afternoon. "*Christmas*—We had our gifts 10:30 A.M.

all happy & well—After 12 noon Mary & I went with the boys to the Smithsonian. Mary & Stuart developed photo plates & I put away a lot of algal fossils collected last July—all home for dinner & the evening—a very happy day" (December 25, 1914). Different families celebrate in different ways. They all went to church, and Walcott took the boys to Rock Creek Cemetery.

Walcott filled in the hollow time between Christmas and New Year's by getting his lantern slides ready to go with Mary to Philadelphia. No one in Philadelphia would have been particularly interested in Algonkian algal remains, but Walcott could speak on other subjects as well, and the husband of Mary Vaux would be well received. "The old year finds us all well. Sidney in 3rd year in Cornell University. Stuart 2nd in Princeton. Helen will remain at home with us—Mary & I are very happy & contented at home" (December 31, 1914).

The Walcotts spent the morning of New Year's Day at his laboratory, before going to a luncheon. Stuart took them for a drive that afternoon, and the family gathered for dinner. The next day Walcott and Mary went to Philadelphia. "Mr. Walcott, who was accompanied by Mrs. Walcott, was the guest of honor at the annual dinner of the Alpine Club of America."[19] Walcott addressed the club on "The Call of the Mountains." "The mountains are essential facts of the continents in connection with the welfare of the human race. To them we owe the local circulation of air and water; the possible development of mineral resources, and indirectly the wonderful fertility of our soils. Again, the best physical, mental, and moral development radiates from the mountain races to invigorate and stimulate the lowland peoples. Such is the lesson of the mountains to a geologist, and to one who has wandered among them for thirty years seeking answers to problems that came in his pathway as a boy."[20] The next day, being Sunday, Mary took Walcott to a meeting of the Friends and then back to the Washington grind. "A very busy day at the Smithsonian. Managed to get a little done on Cambrian trilobites" (January 4, 1915). Despite the large collections made in 1914, Walcott did not write another paper on Precambrian stromatolites. There were too many other duties pressing. Like the bulk of the Burgess Shale collections, these were a legacy for the next generation, and again like the later Burgess Shale collections, the algal remains were to go unstudied for decades.

The Walcotts were in demand socially; Washington society wanted to meet the new wife. Distraction from research came in the form of discussion about the site for Freer's building. All members of the special regents' committee agreed that this could be on the Smithsonian reservation, west of the Castle; the si had title to part of the Mall around the original building. That site obviated congressional approval and also some of the other obstacles to building in Washington. The annual meetings of managers of the Iowa and Ontario Apartment Houses passed without incident; these had both been shrewd investments.

The Walcotts went to New York City, their first such trip of the year. Walcott was the guest of honor at the annual dinner of the Aero Club of America, and like the Alpine Club of America dinner, it was an appropriate recognition of his accomplishments; on some published biographical statements, Walcott listed his clubs as "Cosmos, University, Aero Club of America." The next night was a reciprocation of sorts; they attended a dinner the Research Corporation gave in honor of Cottrell. The Walcotts also visited cousins in Brooklyn, spent the night in Philadelphia, went to the Sunday Friends meeting, and came home. Walcott was still content.

Back in Washington, one of Walcott's responsibilities for the year was presiding at what he called the Archaeological Society meetings. This was the Washington chapter of the Archaeological Institute of America. The chapter was not a major organization, even by the standards of the local scientific societies, and unfortunately most of its early history has been lost. Walcott was apparently president from 1914 through 1917, and he seemed to enjoy attending its meetings. He listed his membership in a biographical sketch from which other comparable memberships were omitted. It was a new field for him, and that always held interest.

The appropriations committee took only two hours of his time, but more effort was going toward aeronautics. "Meeting of Smithsonian Committee on aeronautics at Senator Stone office 3:30" (January 30, 1915). Alexander Bell was there, along with Representative E. W. Roberts. This gathering decided strategy and produced a letter to Walcott on the same day asking for a report on SI activities. The next day Walcott had a reply ready, but then, what else would one expect from a master at lobbying Congress? Had he ever taken up tennis, Walcott would have played both sides of the net.

Walcott's reply not only explained the problems the SI faced in setting up a committee but discussed what various government bureaus might do in the field if they worked together. Walcott emphasized the efforts of other countries in promoting aviation and contrasted them with the American approach. "With no central body or clearing house for the various agencies, no place to meet and discuss problems of research, no place to try out new ideas, and no body of expert advisers for the Government and civil interests, aeronautics in America will be simply drifting and trusting to luck that all will come out well through sporadic and scattered efforts. . . . At the present time the thought of aviation is in connection with war, but there is no apparent reason why, as in the case of the automobile, the flying machine will not of far greater service in peaceful pursuits than in war" (Walcott 1915c).

During this time of congressional activity about aviation, Glenn Curtiss put landing skids on the Langley aerodrome, to replace the pontoons and tested it on the ice of Lake Keuka. Not much was accomplished; eventually the machine was changed back to more or less its original configuration, shipped back to Washington, and placed on display in the Arts and Industries Building. That was the final piece of the coming Walcott-Wright confrontation: next to the restored machine was placed a lengthy informational sign claiming that this was the first machine proved to be capable of manned flight. There was no indication of the failed attempts by Langley; likewise, there was no indication of the modifications made by Curtiss.

The flight of the Langley machine was a triumph for the Langley aeronautical laboratory. Those who had the most to gain from its flight were Curtiss, in his hope of breaking the Wright patents, and Zahm, in cementing his place in aeronautical investigations. No one knows now who wrote the text of the exhibit label, but all lines of inference point toward Zahm.

Even earlier, an attempt to obtain one of the Wright planes for display had been bungled, and both brothers had been insulted by the way the matter had been handled. When the Langley aerodrome was placed on exhibit with its misleading label, that was the end for Orville Wright. Walcott was in error, and for the rest of his life, the Smithsonian would receive unfavorable publicity as a result.

If there is anything to be said by way of mitigation, it is that Walcott was defending the reputation of a dead man. Langley had been pilloried by the newspapers after his failure in 1903. Walcott had at least been indirectly responsible, for he had exerted effort to obtain funds to continue Langley's work after his steam-driven model had flown. Orville Wright, however, was also defending the reputation of a dead man: it had been Wilbur Wright's dream to fly, and his younger brother had helped make this happen (Crouch 1981). Neither side would admit to slighting the feelings of the other. Added to that was the image of the SI Goliath in the nation's capital against the inventor David from smalltown America; eventually this became a public relations nightmare for the Smithsonian.

Fortunately for the SI, the country was being increasingly distracted by European events; still, there was a great deal of concern by Orville Wright and those who recognized that the Wright accomplishment was being virtually ignored. The problem simmered from 1915 onward, and if anything could have made it worse, this delay did so. Fortunately, that is enough for now on the Langley aerodrome.

Walcott had kept the congressional ball rolling for aeronautical research, but this year the spread between aviation and algae was too much for him to bridge, and he never produced a major paper based on his 1914 collections. The first month of 1915 had gone by with virtually nothing of paleontological interest accomplished by Walcott, but at the start of the next month he "took up study of trilobites of Upper Cambrian *Crepicephalus*" (February 1, 1915). This was a logical step, following his publication on the dikelocephalids. He had studied the Cambrian brachiopods in short papers, more or less a family at a time, and the same strategy could be used to gather the information for a monograph on all Cambrian trilobites. Unfortunately for science, there was little time for work in the evenings. Dinner parties away from home took his research time, and dinners out called for parties in. The Walcotts entertained in honor of Judge Oliver Wendell Holmes and later in honor of Chief Justice Edward Douglas White; Helen had a tea dance between these dinners, to add a little levity to the house.

By mid-month, Walcott was reflecting on the difficulties of carrying on research. "Routine work at my office & a little research work. A few callers & the hours of opportunities were passed" (February 15, 1915). Walcott had a rule that he was not to be disturbed before 10:00 A.M., but this may not have been enforced as rigidly as it should have been. The ladies left for a couple of days— Mary to her old home, Helen to friends in Baltimore—leaving Walcott "jogging along as usual except for a hearing before the Naval Committee [of the] H.[ouse of] R[epresentatives]. 10:30–12:10" (February 21, 1915). The use of the term "usual" is fascinating, but it could have been appropriate, for after all, Walcott had been appearing before congressional committees for more than two decades.

To go back a step or two, on February 12, Acting Secretary of the Navy Franklin D. Roosevelt had approved an advisory committee on aeronautics, but he had suggested a few modifications of the number and arrangement of the committee. Walcott took care of this detail in his testimony, leaving time as the only problem. "So Walcott used a tactic he had learned in the Geological Survey in the 1880s, 'a period when legislation normally got through only by stealthily clinging to appropriation bills.' . . . The naval appropriations bill, [which was already in the Senate and had the provision attached] containing the joint resolution . . . passed both House and Senate on 3, March 1915, President Wilson signed it the same day, . . . the last day of the 63rd Congress" (Roland 1985, 24). It was not bad footwork for an elderly man, albeit one who knew the rules and the playing field. Passage of this bill was not worthy of mention in Walcott's diary.

The Washington Monument Society met on Washington's birthday and found all well with the structure. Following this, Walcott had "a quiet busy day at the Smithsonian. Am still busy with the Cambrian trilobites at all odd moments" (February 23, 1915). Mary joined him at the office occasionally to print pictures. She was a remarkable artist both with a camera and in the darkroom, at a time when a lady simply did not indulge in such activities. Photographs in Alberta and British Columbia were generally credited to the Vaux family, not to one or the other of her brothers, so that Mary could at least indirectly receive some of the credit. In those days, women's liberation would have been a stranger concept than space satellites.

March began with a formal dinner at the Walcotts to honor the hardworking Mrs. Dimock. The next night they had an even larger dinner for the vice president. Walcott rushed from dining table to New York, polished off meetings of the RC and CIW Ex Comm, and raced back to Washington. "At my office most of the day, except for one hour at the U.S. Senate to bid goodbye to Senators Root, Perkins & Burton. Old friends who go out of Senate. Met Prest. Wilson and members of his cabinet" (March 4, 1915). Washington was a much smaller town in those days than it is now, but even so, having three senators one could claim as friends must have been atypical for a scientist.

Two days later, Walcott helped William Healy Dall celebrate fifty years of SI association with a dinner at the Cosmos Club. Dall had been hired by a telegraph company to explore in Alaska, then he had worked for the Coast Survey, and finally for the USGS. The Smithsonian was for him more of a moral commitment and a helping hand than a source of salary; the symbiotic relationship of the institution to Dr. Dall was typical of its association with many in the government bureaus of Washington.

Not all was going smoothly with family matters. After church Walcott had "a long talk with Helen about her future & home relations" (March 7, 1915). Helen had been mistress of the household, but now Mary was in charge. Helen was a glittering young thing, but Mary had been a sober old maid. Helen was at loose ends, with no obvious goal, except perhaps to marry, and there was no one she particularly fancied.

Walcott's other concern was the actual organization of an aviation advisory committee, now that legislation had been passed. He devoted nearly all of four days to talking with various officials in Agriculture, Commerce and Labor, and of course the Navy and War Departments, before he worked out an arrangement. Finally, he "sent letters to President en re members of the Advisory Committee for Aeronautics. Had two hours for my own research work" (March 11, 1915).

Walcott had written to a member of the Research Corporation asking for help on a project and in reply now got a long letter pointing out how many extracurricular activities the member was already involved in. Walcott's reply is interesting, especially in light of the effort he had put into an advisory committee for aviation.

> I see nothing for you to do but to get out of one-half or two-thirds of the boards and committees on which you are serving. I was in your position a few years ago, and began systematically to cut my connection in such matters. If a board would not accept my resignation I systematically remained

away from it. . . . I do not believe in cutting out and running, but there comes a time in every man's life when he must decide whether he will be an effective force for the remaining portion of his life or break down and become a burden to himself and to all interests with which he is connected. From long experience in Washington I have learned that no man is indispensable in any organization, and that if he gets out some one else will take his place and carry the work forward, perhaps not as well, but usually it does not suffer any permanent setback.[21]

Walcott could provide excellent advice to others on removing oneself from distractions, but he could not follow it himself. The next day was mainly given over to the GWMA, a hearty perennial. Walcott complained that he was "making very slow headway with research work owing to many interruptions and the spring lassitude" (March 13, 1915). No matter how much might be accomplished in other fields, the standard for Walcott was how much he accomplished in paleontology. One fundamental technical detail to Walcott was publication, for no matter how much one may know in a scientific field, it counts for nothing unless it is shared in print with other scientists. "Once when I was at the Smithsonian which then served as headquarters for the [National] Academy [of Sciences] I did ask him [Walcott] how he kept up his scientific work so well with so much executive work to do. He said he had two different but adjacent offices and all executive work stayed in one and all scientific work in the other. He took 15 minutes or so to show me both offices and how he did his work. His scientific office was really a geological & paleontological laboratory."[22] Likely, Walcott established this working place shortly after moving into the secretary's office. Discovery of a picture of Walcott at his research desk has established that this laboratory was in an anteroom on the south side of the building.[23]

The rest of March went quickly and well. Dr. and Mrs. Walcott took a quick trip to Philadelphia to see friends and discuss farm matters. Walcott had left the Rust farm at Trenton Fall in 1876, but he still knew which part of a cow to milk and how to do it. In late March, a snow squall hit Washington and allowed Walcott to spend most of the day in his laboratory without interruptions. The weather improved, and the couple celebrated spring by an auto trip to Great Falls, on the Potomac River north of Washington. When Congress was not in session, the Washington pace slowed. "A quiet day at the Smithsonian. Had several hours for study of Cambrian trilobites from the southern Appalachians" (March 29, 1915). On his birthday, Walcott recorded, "All has gone well this past year. All well at home & I am very happy with Mary" (March 31, 1915).

Early in April, a meeting date for the Advisory Committee for Aeronautics was finally set, and Walcott could concentrate on science. The secretary gave a talk to the Botanical Society of Washington. "Mr. Walcott described the stratigraphic position of the great Prepaleozoic Beltian series of Central Montana, which he considered to be of fresh or brackish water origin. Photographs of thin sections of both the fossil and recent deposits showed similar chains of cells which are characteristic of the blue-green alga" (Spalding 1915). All Walcott wrote in his diary was that he had "announced the discovery of fossil bacteria in Beltian algal limestone of Montana" (April 6, 1915). One might assume that the discovery had been made only shortly before Walcott wrote his diary entry.

Less than two weeks later, he presented this discovery to the National Academy of Sciences. One positive result of the NAS semicentennial celebration was an arrangement to publish a monthly *Proceedings* (Wilson 1966). Volume one, number one, was issued on January 15, 1915: "Pres. Walcott sent us a brief note on his discovery of Algonkian bacteria. It came with a letter from A. L. Day, then Home Secretary, saying that it was very important and should be published promptly. I received it on April 9 and it appeared in our issue of April 15. Normally it would have appeared in the issue of May 15, 1915, but I thought I'd try to see what I and the press could do in the way of speed. Dr. Day had said the Ms. was letter perfect and that proof could be waived."[24]

This may be the place to mention several aspects of scientific procedure. One point is that fortune favors the prepared mind. Walcott suspected that bacteria were important in deposition of stromatolites, so he looked for them. Consider the following part of a letter he wrote:

> Your memoir on the Salton Sea is most interesting and valuable and I have looked through it with great pleasure. The chapter on the behavior of certain microorganisms in brine is of special interest, as it has a bearing on the problem of the algal remains which I have been finding in such great abundance in the Pre-Cambrian (Algonkian) rocks of Montana. I think these rocks were deposited in an inland sea probably of fresh water but possibly in the later stages brackish and eventually with salt. I concluded from my studies last winter that the algal deposits were made by blue-green algae, and I think the associated limestones may owe their origin to unicellular algae and probably bacteria.[25]

A second point is that Walcott did not have the necessary skill or background to identify bacteria, and he knew it. Thus, he enlisted the services of a microscopist in the Department of Agriculture. "You will be interested to learn that Dr. Albert Mann, whom I asked to search the thin sections of the Algonkian algal deposits for bacteria, has recognized two forms. This was to be expected from the known part played by the bacteria in the recognition [apparently a typing error for "deposition"] of recent calcareous deposits, but it is very satis-factory to find them in the Pre-Paleozoic limestones."[26]

That letter bears on the third point of the apparent rush to publish. Some-time before December 3, 1914, five months before his announcement to the Botanical Society of Washington, Walcott knew ancient bacteria had been identified. There is almost no detail given in his two-page note, except that nu-merous thin-sections had been cut from specimens collected in 1914 and the bacteria had been found in colonies of *Gallatinia* (Walcott 1915d). A superficial interpretation is that Walcott published in haste, yet that is certainly not the case.

The year 1915 was a skimpy one in Walcott's publication list, but this discov-ery could have been a bombshell to more than match the normally large num-ber of pages published each year by him. Sadly, the geological profession ignored this announcement and a few years later also ignored evidence of bacterial action in deposition of Precambrian iron ores.

Three decades later, amidst great excitement, fanfare, and press conferences, bacteria were rediscovered in the Precambrian (Schopf 1999). Today, simple life is being found in ever-earlier rocks, and each discovery is rushed to the press as soon as it is made. Pressure for grant money and the need for a "big score" is the norm. A discovery such as Walcott made would never be delayed. Times change, and the change is not always for the better. Meanwhile, the current thinking on Walcott's actual material is that the slides show "mineral grains or possible filamentous prokaryotes" (Mendelson and Schopf 1992, 877).

Lest the lack of the interest in fossil bacteria be taken too seriously, there re-ally was interest in Walcott's efforts with stromatolites. An Australian paleon-tologist wrote him a glowing letter: "Your very interesting and able work on *Pre-Cambrian Algal Flora* reached me a few days ago. What a remarkable repos-itory your Cambrian and Pre-Cambrian rocks are in the early forms of life. I have met with numerous examples of concretionary structures—both big and little—in our Cambrian limestones and have been disposed to regard them as nodular travertine incident to an arid climate. Your researches throw a new light on such structures and will be duly considered in dealing with forms of this kind. Oolitic, pisolitic, discoid ("biscuit") and other concretionary form are forming at the present time in some parts of South Australia."[27]

Between the time of his announcement to the Botanical Society and the NAS talk, stromatolites came to the fore once more. Walcott took Mary and Arthur Brown back to the Great Valley of Maryland (for those who want details, William Dohman was the driver). They spent five days extracting stromatolites from the Conococheague Limestone to supplement the collections made the previous year. A half-ton of material was shipped back to Washington. Walcott never worked this up for publication, but it was described by Bassler. Nowhere in Bassler's discussion, however, is there a mention of Walcott's collection.

The NAS meeting carried a harbinger of coming disruption. The concept of redescribing every species, especially those that had never been illustrated, had been a concern of some paleontologists. In 1914, John M. Clarke organized a U.S. committee under NAS to aid this international effort; Walcott was a member. A few cards showing a picture and text of a particular fossil were produced by Walcott and a few other paleontologists; these are extremely rare items. In 1915, Clarke recommended that the committee be discontinued as a result of the problems in Europe.

During the meeting Walcott received word that his elderly father-in-law had died. Mary went immediately to Philadelphia. Walcott gave his paper, showed the algal specimens to John M. Clarke, and left the next day. After the interment, Walcott and his wife came home, "Mary tired & sore—mainly by tongue lashing of her brother George" (April 23, 1915). Funerals have a way sometimes of bringing out harsh feelings. Apparently, Mary should have remained a spinster and cared for her father rather than impetuously dash off to get married at age fifty-four. It took Walcott a few long car drives and wildflower-collecting sessions to soothe Mary, but soothe her he did.

"Resumed routine at office & study of Appalachian Cambrian fauna" (May 2, 1915). This requires a bit of an explanation. When geologic mapping had started in the southern Appalachians in the 1880s, it had soon become apparent that many of the sections were faulted in such a way that some rocks was cut out, and in other places thrust faults repeated the sequences. The western Canada sections of Cambrian were very much less disturbed, and a sequence of trilobite faunas could be established. With that information, it was possible to determine better the relative position of various isolated collections made by Cooper Curtice in 1885 and by later workers (Yochelson and Osborne 1999). Walcott could have devoted his time to fossils from the Burgess Shale. He chose to go back and refine earlier paleontological determinations, work that would allow for more detailed mapping and a better understanding of the structural complications.

The war in Europe kept intruding on the United States, the latest event being the sinking of the *Lusitania*. It was evident how outraged Walcott felt: "About 1100 civilians killed or rather murdered under guise of a war measure" (May 7, 1915). Involvement in the war was coming closer.

The Walcotts went to New York, and first on the agenda was a party in honor of Mrs. Dimock. An ever-widening range of interests was now becoming a family matter. While Walcott was at the RC meeting, considering the merits of making railroad ties from concrete, Mary was attending a meeting of the Guernsey Cattle Club. There was also a gradual fusing of their interests, evidenced by Walcott's speaking to the American Federation of Arts.

Spring in Washington, though short, is possibly the prettiest time of year in that city, and Walcott and Mary developed the habit of early-morning walks either along the Potomac or in Rock Creek Park. It was precisely the sort of routine that Walcott enjoyed. Meanwhile, he was working away "as time permitted" on Upper Cambrian trilobites from the Appalachians. Helen had been out of town for a few days but seemingly was finding herself, as her return was reported in Walcott's diary with a great deal of pleasure. The month ended on "Decoration Day. Mary & I spent the day at the Smithsonian & I worked on Cambrian trilobites" (May 31, 1915). In their own ways and their own time, each of Walcott's two previous marriages had been excellent; he was now blessed a third time.

Sidney came from Cornell, and Walcott was delighted to have the young man home again. He attacked the problem of making up the plates of figures for his trilobite paper with reviewed vigor, for the more of his family Walcott had at home, the better his spirits. Perhaps Mary had made him more aware of the good qualities of his children. He had a standard for comparison, as nearly the first thing Mary had done upon coming to Washington was to get involved with the board of a reform school for girls; charitable activity was a strong tradition in the Vaux family.

The executive committee of the National Advisory Committee for Aeronautics met in Walcott's office. Walcott could not attend the organizational meeting in April due to his father-in-law's death. Brig. Gen. George P. Scriven was elected chairman, and to balance the services, Naval Constructor Holden C. Richardson, the youngest man present, was elected secretary. "National" was added to the organization's name as the first official action of the meeting. The main committee tinkered a bit with the draft rules Walcott had written and designated that an executive committee would have power to act between the two stated yearly meetings of the NACA. The executive committee met, elected the absent Walcott as its chairman, and then adjourned.

Walcott had definite ideas as to the way the NACA should operate: "The Main Committee had deleted from the draft of rules and regulations sent to President Wilson the original suggestion by Walcott that the NACA should appoint subcommittees chaired by members of the Main Committee but including outsiders as well. Scriven had been opposed. . . . Walcott appealed directly to President Wilson, at whose request the provision was restored. . . . Probably no provision in the original rules and regulations would be more important than this one" (Roland 1985, 29–30). For three more years, Walcott continued as chairman of the NACA executive committee.

There is anecdotal evidence of his ability with that group. Navy Constructor Richardson was given authority to hire an assistant, and John Victory became NACA employee number one; he was the last person to leave when NACA was abolished to make way for the National Aeronautics and Space Administration. Victory had framed pictures of all committee members in his office; that of Walcott was larger than the others. One of Victory's sons was named after Walcott, just as Cooper Curtice had named a son after him. Even if the SI secretary was far afield in the technical aspects of aviation, he still knew how to make an organization function and how to gain the admiration of those who worked for him.

L. L. Nunn came in town for yet another conference with Walcott; they made an odd pair but worked well together. Had it been otherwise, Sidney would not have been in the Telluride House at Cornell. The Telluride Association also was aiding the SI by financing an expedition to Siberia. Bailey Willis dropped in to report that he was leaving the USGS for a professorship at Stanford. Walcott's link to the U.S. Geological Survey and the past was not totally broken, but it was no longer tight.

As mid-June approached, Walcott in his traditional manner rushed to finish one odd job after another before leaving Washington. His last spring day at the SI, he "turned in paper on Cambrian trilobites for printing" (June 18, 1915). "Cambrian Trilobites" (Walcott 1916) had taken seven months from leaving Walcott's desk to publication, a bit slower than some previous papers, but still quite fast, especially by today's standards.

One reason for the time lag was that it had fourteen plates. These are all well reproduced, and printers do not handle high-quality plates rapidly. Another cause of delay was a detailed index; that may not sound like much of a problem, but making an index is a difficult chore for an editor. Walcott had many new species and new genera, and in addition, he discussed and redescribed many other taxa already in the literature. Once one has determined that a form is new, description and discussion is relatively straightforward. With a previously described form, however, one should examine the original types or at least specimens from the same locality, consider all the pertinent literature, and compare and contrast the new find to other species. This means a great deal more work to write the same number of words; about the only place the extra effort shows up is in the index, where all uses of the fossil name are listed.

In this paper Walcott described the species in sixteen genera of trilobites. They ranged in age from Early Cambrian to Late Cambrian and included both eastern and western occurrences, with a bit of effort on Scandinavian and

Chinese trilobites to add a cosmopolitan patina. The paper is rock-solid paleontology; having turned the manuscript in, Walcott could go west in a happy frame of mind. Helen and Stuart joined the senior Walcotts and Sidney en route.

Not every loose end had been completed in Washington. Sunday, on the train west, Walcott was "resting & reading over Mss [manuscripts] of general paper of my work of the past 3 years for Ann. Rept. of S.I. Mailed it back to office from Chicago" (June 20, 1915). On trains there were no visitors to interrupt concentration, nor in those days did the trains carry telephones. From Salt Lake City, the boys went to Provo for a few days. Nunn squired them around, conducted some business with Walcott, and introduced them to the vice president of the Ogden Short Line. As a result, the next day at Idaho Falls they boarded a special car and had "a beautiful ride" up the west side of the Teton Range to Yellowstone station.

The freight boxes had not come in, and more importantly, the horses had not arrived. Walcott had hired C. D. Flaherty of Cold Spring, Montana, as teamster and packer. He had given fairly precise specifications as to the route to take, getting into such detail as instructing Flaherty to contact the blacksmith before he went out to the ranch where the horses were pastured. He wrote Flaherty that he would meet the cook. "Arthur is a good teamster and will drive the buckboard."[28] Arthur was given instructions as to how many tent poles of what size to cut, and Flaherty was told to make certain the poles were cut before they reached the park, but not early in the trip. These were all details, and some were quite minor, but collectively they ensured that few things went wrong in camping; it was very hard-won experience.

The party relaxed for a day, walked by the Madison River, and met some of the army officers running in the park. Flaherty and Arthur made it to Yellowstone National Park that evening. Walcott cooled his heels for another day; he was "tired of waiting for outfit but there is not much use of worrying so will rest in peace" (June 26, 1915). With the luxury of a private railway car at hand, Walcott still would have preferred to be in camp. When the boxes arrived two days later, he mentioned, "Am glad to be under canvas" (June 28, 1915).

Walcott had been in Yellowstone National Park in 1897 and 1898 and had collected Cambrian fossils and advised the secretary of the interior on the roads. One may properly ask why, with all the interesting rocks and fossils in western Canada, even allowing for the spectacular geologic phenomena in the park, one would want to go back. "First: to determine, if possible, the extent to which the lower forms of algae and possibly bacteria contributed, through their activities, to the deposition from the geyser and hot-spring waters of the contained carbonate of lime and silica. Second, the securing for the National Museum of a series of geyser and hot-spring deposits, also silicified wood from the petrified forests and certain types of volcanic rocks" (Walcott 1916a, 6).

Walcott succeeded admirably in both these objectives. The Smithsonian secretary had written the secretary of the interior for permission to collect: "I find that it is very desirable that illustrations of some of the forms of hot springs deposits be collected for exhibition in the National Museum. Despite the numerous Government expeditions that have been in the park, the material in the Museum is inadequate for exhibition purposes. I also wish to obtain specimens illustrating certain types of deposits, for comparison with supposed deposits of similar origin in some of the rocks forming the Belt Range, east of Helena."[29]

This was the last season that the army would be in charge in Yellowstone, and the last season before the National Park Service was formed.

The Walcott party collected tons and tons of geyserite, silicified wood, obsidian, and other volcanic rock. Present-day preservationists would probably be appalled, but the specimens went for scientific and educational purposes and had been taken from areas where tourists did not normally venture. (This was also the first season that a motorcar was allowed into the park [Shankland 1951, 66–67]. It was a momentous decision for the park, as it meant the end of the stagecoaches and the decline of the stranglehold the railroads had had on the tourist trade [Albright 1985].)

The boys showed up a few days after the boxes arrived from Washington. In his account of the expedition, Walcott would credit them and Mary with assistance; Helen was present throughout the excursion but is not noted. It was a good season. Three weeks into it, Walcott wrote to "Dear Sir Richard," the assistant secretary, faithfully on duty in Washington.

> Just in from a hard days work. We—Mrs. W., Sidney and Stuart,—examined the Norris Geyser Basin and made two rich strikes. Collected over 100 specimens of (Hello! A black bear just walked into camp....)... [A] very beautiful geyserite.... Near the 'Growler' the boys cut out amidst clouds of steam two large specimens.... Helen and Flaherty rode over the Gibbon Basin and report some unusual deposits. We will visit them tomorrow. We have ten fine horses that thus far have behaved as well as cayuses can.... Mrs. W. and Stuart have come to change photo plates in our tent, so this must come to an end. We rig up a dark tent inside the big tent.... Skeets and noseeums are very abundant and trying to ones patience.... All well and happy. Flaherty is the best camp man we have had in years, and a gentleman too.[30]

"Skeets" is a fairly clear reference to mosquitoes; "no-seeums" are swarms of tiny, dreadful black flies.

Walcott had planned on two to four weeks in the park, but the collecting was so good that they stayed on until the first of September. He scribbled to Washington, "All ready for next trip—wish boys could continue with me."[31] "Sidney,

Helen & Stuart left at 7 P.M. for San Francisco, San Diego, Grand Canyon & home" (September 1, 1915).

The horseback mileage was about 675 miles in the park, and the camp was moved seventeen times, but it was nonetheless a leisurely field season. Perhaps the most pressed member of the team was Flaherty, who had to transport the boxes of specimens to the railroad station. Although there were one or two difficult days when the trout simply would not bite for Walcott, on other days he could not get his line back into the water fast enough to satisfy them. The only incident worth mentioning was the smashing of a camera box in August during one of the climbs. To summarize this part of the season, a good time was had by all, except Helen.

Walcott was much ahead of his time in studying life of the hot and cold springs. In one sense, it is a shame that other events prevented him from further efforts. Nothing was published except a generalized account of the collecting (Walcott 1916a). On the other hand, new techniques were needed to study in detail living algae and bacteria. "Work in the last 30 years has documented direct fossil evidence of microbial evolution through the Proterozoic, and this is now being importantly supplemented by various geochemical techniques" (Walter 1992, 507). Walcott really was better off pursuing rocks and Cambrian trilobites.

The reduced party came out of the park on the west side, where it had entered, and moved north-northwest toward Three Forks, Montana; that spring Walcott had anticipated going back to Glacier National Park, perhaps for more algal collections, but Yellowstone had presented too many opportunities. The day after the children left, it rained. Walcott, Mary, Arthur Brown, and Charlie Flaherty traveled two days in the rain, had one fair day, and more rain. Finally Walcott reached Castle Mountain, on the Gallatin River, in the rain.

Walcott read proofs of the trilobite paper for one day while it rained. They did get a few Cambrian trilobites the next day before the snow came. Mary and Walcott drove on to Belgrade, Montana; Arthur and Charlie took the wrong road and ended up near Manhattan. They joined up north of Three Forks. "We are heartily tired of rain, mud, bad roads" (September 15, 1915). Some seasons are like that. The next day snow came again. It was windy and cold when the party finally reached the Deep Creek Ranger Station beyond Townsend, but afterward Walcott could record "Fine Day" with a double underline. "With Mary & Flaherty went up north fork of Deep Creek. Found that limestones of Deep Creek crossed canyon & extended for a long way E & W" (September 16, 1915). Prospects for algal stromatolites were good.

Mary wrote at Walcott's dictation to the chief clerk. "We are at last having beautiful weather, clear & bracing & all are happy in camp; even the old hens have braced up, and are laying eggs every day in the baggage wagon. I fear it will break Arthur's heart to kill them at the end of the season."[32] That is an interesting comment. Nowadays, one would never think of dragging chickens all over the countryside, but if one is camped in the wild and needs eggs, how else can one get the eggs? Arthur was a man of many abilities.

They moved camp one more time and began serious collecting of Precambrian algae in the Black Butte Canyon. They ended up with fifteen boxes of specimens. "Mary and I took 12 photographs in Black Butte Canyon 1–3 P.M. of lower algal limestone" (September 25, 1915). The field season was over; Ranger Orin Bradeen agreed to store the camp gear at Deep Creek Ranger Station and take care of the horses. Among his other titles and connections, Walcott was officially a "collaborator" with the U.S. Forest Service.

A year after Walcott began to collect in Yellowstone, his Australian colleague Walter Houchin wrote again. "Some time ago you stated in correspondence that you intended shortly to make a special examination of the genus *Cryptozoon*, and asked if I could let you have one of our specimens for comparison. . . . Since writing you last the same gentlemen who had forwarded the original specimens sent me others from a new locality. As *Cryptozoon* is of such abnormal type and difficult to assign to any definite zoological position, there remains the doubt as to whether it be of organic origin or not. For this reason I am sending you a series to aid you in your determination of its true character."[33]

It was some time before Walcott responded. Houchin had sent the specimens with library books on an international exchange. The method was slow, because a large crate had to filled before it was sent off, but it did avoid the cost of a shipment. Years ago, this kind of international exchange between libraries was basic to the diffusion of knowledge. Walcott kept a few specimens and returned the remainder, via the same route.

Since writing to you about a year ago I put aside the study of the supposed Algonkian algae, as it was necessary to give all my spare time to work upon the Cambrian trilobites in order to obtain data for stratigraphic determinations.

During the summer of 1915 we made large collections of both siliceous and calcareous deposits in the hot springs and geysers of the Yellowstone National Park. The field study led me to conclude that much of the deposit was made through algal and bacterial agencies, but the final form of deposit was controlled to a considerable extent by the action of concretionary or other forces that were independent of the forms governed by algal growth. In some instances, however, the algal growth clearly controlled the form. This taken in connection with the so-called "lake balls" [see Walcott 1916a, pl. 4, figs. 1 and 2] leads me still to conclude that *Cryptozoon* and a number of other Paleozoic and Pre-Paleozoic forms owe their shape to algal growth.[34]

It is evident that Walcott had a good idea of research to be pursued on the Precambrian stromatolites and limestones. Nevertheless, the little paper on bacteria was the last word. The only products of the Yellowstone work are the photographs published in "Explorations" for 1915. No one can say what might have resulted from this line of inquiry. Later, one more algal paper was written, though it was on the Cambrian Burgess Shale, and not the Belt material. Concern for aviation and the press of the Great War ended this inquiry.

On the last Sunday in September, after all the Precambrian specimens had been shipped from Deep Creek and the camp had been dismantled, the Walcotts drove the buckboard to Townsend and took the train to Helena. They called on Walcott's old friends, saw the forest supervisor, and left for Butte. In that metropolis they examined the copper smelters and a mine before going south to Ogden, Utah. On the westbound main line, it was only twenty-eight hours to San Francisco.

4

The Busy Years (End of 1915–mid-1917):
Every Silver Lining Has Its Cloud

> The human organism has rarely been subjected to a severer test than the
> study of scientific problems, nor is there a truer hero than an investigator
> who never loses heart in a life-long grapple with the powers of the uni-
> verse. It is courage of the highest order to stand for years face to face with
> one of the enigmas of nature; to interrogate patiently, and hear no answers;
> to try all known methods and weapons of attack, and yet see the lips of the
> sphinx compressed in stony mobility; to invoke the utmost powers of
> imagination; to fuse the very soul in the fires of effort, and still press the
> listening ear against a wall of silence. It is easier to die in the breach.
>
> —Clarence King, 1892

THE AFTERNOON of their arrival in San Francisco, Secretary and Mrs. Walcott
were at the Panama-Pacific International Exposition. "The grounds & buildings
of the exposition are fine and beautiful and exhibits unusually good" (September 30, 1915). Walcott had been attending such gatherings since the Philadelphia
Centennial Exposition in 1876, so his praise was not given lightly. As in the past,
the Smithsonian won awards for its displays. In a way, this was nearly the last of
a string of fairs and expositions dating from Philadelphia. What with movies
and the automobile, people no longer had to visit such gatherings to see the
wonders of the world. There were a few expositions in the United States during the 1920s and 1930s, but Smithsonian participation became increasingly
limited, and the entire character of such events was to change.

One part of the SI exhibit was Langley's steam-driven model of 1896. Professor Langley was noted on the Column of Progress; this was simply more fuel
thrown on the fire of insult to the achievement of the Wright brothers. Almost
immediately, going to the fair became like old home week. Dr. Cottrell was conducting some experiments in dissipating the famous San Francisco fog by use

of electric currents (Cameron 1952, 130–31). The next day they ran into Mr. Lett of the Grand Trunk Railway. It was a long day for the tourists who stayed until the evening fireworks.

The Walcotts spent almost four more days in the San Francisco area. Two days at the exhibits were broken by a trip to see the Cottrells, then living in Berkeley. Of course, Walcott had to call at the California Academy of Sciences museum before they left for southern California. Helen met them in Pasadena, for in September she had telegraphed that she was not going east with the boys as had been arranged.

Years later, Helen was to write about "What Grandma Did" for her granddaughter. In it, she would mention the summer in Yellowstone. "It was not a success. As children will, we discovered Mary's weak points and I think we made their summer pretty miserable."[1] After a few weeks on the West Coast, Helen had persuaded her brothers to go east without her and had enrolled in an art school, where she had a fine time being squired around by several young men. "The final straw came when I received a letter from Dad, saying that I had been impossible all summer, I had not behaved like a daughter should, that unless I mended my ways he didn't want me at home. He was absolutely right, but I immediately thought 'that woman' and went into a complete tailspin."[2]

Helen took all her money and bought a steamship ticket to New Zealand, having no idea what she would do when she arrived. Meanwhile, her brothers had stopped in Ohio, and Mrs. Garfield had pried out the information as to Helen's state of mind. She immediately telegraphed Helen and her father. "I went meekly east with them, first to the Grand Canyon, then to Cleveland where I spent the winter with Aunt Helen. Dad really did love me—Mary wanted to be friends. We were just oil and water and would not mix."[3] In September Walcott resigned from the Chevy Chase Club, but apart from that action and not acknowledging assistance from Helen in Yellowstone that summer, nothing of this discontent of his daughter appears in his diary. Private as the diary was, there were still some matters that were not mentioned.

All Walcott wrote about his day in Pasadena was a conference with George Ellery Hale, a visit to the astrophysical laboratory, and a passing reference to a letter to Mrs. Garfield. The secretary went on to the Panama-California Exposition in San Diego; competition between northern and southern California is not new. "The grounds are more attractive than those of the P.P.I. Expo. at San Francisco" (October 7, 1915). When the San Francisco extravaganza closed, the Smithsonian exhibits were moved to San Diego for the 1916 season.

Mary and Walcott moved on to Los Angeles. The day was split between Cottrell's colleagues who held patent rights on the West Coast, and the vertebrate remains from the La Brea tar pits—again, quite a range of interests. Walcott took

Mary to Catalina Island overnight; this might have been to celebrate the truce between Mary and Helen, but in any event, Mary had more than earned a modest treat after all the fieldwork. "The trip to Avalon was an enjoyable one despite the tossing about in boat & no fish biting" (October 10, 1915). They met Helen again in Pasadena and took her with them to see the Mount Wilson Observatory, another part of Andrew Carnegie's largess to science.

Then the three were on the eastbound train to the Grand Canyon. The Grand Canyon still had the status of a national monument, assigned it by Theodore Roosevelt. The area was administered more or less by the Department of Agriculture; it would not become a national park for another four years. (One would have thought that this scenic wonder would have immediately been placed in that status once the concept of such parks was established by Yellowstone. Politics are as much a part of the nation's park system as they are of the national forest system, and a few local interests preferred to have parts of the area in private hands. It was not a good area for sheep, but if one cannot fleece sheep, one can fleece tourists.)

The geologist and accompanying ladies went down the Cameron Trail (now the Bright Angel Trail) to Indian Garden Camp and spent the night. Helen and Mary hiked down to the river, while Walcott collected "a fossil bed about 100 feet above the Tonto Sandstone. Found a few good cystoids & trilobites" (October 15, 1915). It is likely that Walcott also took a photograph of "the great unconformity" (Walcott 1916d). The next day they walked around on the Tonto Plateau, the Cambrian sandstone that forms a flat esplanade on either side of the steep inner gorge. When Walcott went down from the north rim in 1882, the Tonto had been at the top of the two-mile-thick section of Precambrian rocks that he had measured.

This was more nostalgia than serious collecting; after the morning stroll, they rode back out on horseback. Walcott took Mary to the rim, where they could see the monument to Major Powell that was being constructed. This monument is a little story of bureaucracy and persistence, buttressed by a four-inch-thick pile of letters in the records of the secretary of the interior. In 1904, when the International Geographical Congress met in Washington, a resolution was passed urging a Powell memorial. That was fair enough, for he had made known the course of the last major unexplored river in the United States. After a mere five years of behind-the-scenes effort, Congress both authorized the monument and appropriated five thousand dollars; authorization without money is commonly nothing more than a gesture—witness the difficulties the GWMA encountered.

Events had moved swiftly at this point. William Henry Holmes was appointed chairman of a committee that included Walcott and Col. H. C. Rizer, the chief clerk of the USGS. Holmes was heading west, and in less that two months the committee had selected a site on the south rim of the canyon and had given consideration to the kind of monument it wanted. This was phase one.

Next came phase two, which consisted of six years of design, revision, discussion with the Commission on Fine Arts, opinions of the secretary of the interior, and manifold other aggravations. Walcott had a hand in getting movement started again, writing directly to President Taft that the words "Soldier, Explorer, Scientist" be placed on Powell's gravesite monument in Arlington National Cemetery. "If ever a man deserved to have such a recognition he certainly did. He was my chief for twelve years as Director of the Geological Survey and I learned to appreciate and admire his unusual character and qualities."[4] It is an indication of the size of the government of that time that the White House was involved in such a matter. It is a further indication of Walcott's loyalty to those he served. This trait served him well with the memory of Major Powell, but not so well with the memory of Professor Langley.

When the design of an Aztec-like altar for the West was finally approved, phase three, the site, presented fresh difficulties. The Grand Canyon National Monument was under the Department of Agriculture, yet it was Steven Mather, assistant to the secretary of the interior, who went out in the summer of 1915 to clarify matters. Several land claims had been filed by those who wanted to exploit the tourist trade. Mather, in effect, said to build the monument where it had been planned, regardless of those claims.

By now the five-thousand-dollar appropriation had been reduced in size, and costs were rising. Railroads were asked to carry freight for free, and cement companies were asked to donate. Fortunately, at this point the Bureau of Reclamation stepped in. Arthur Powell Davis, the major's nephew and now second in command of the bureau, assigned one of his engineers to assist. This man had all material on the job by early September and was to complete the monument a week after Walcott viewed it. The correspondence, however, continued, with a fight as to whether the Bureau of Reclamation should pay the salary of the construction engineer, who was caught in between the gears of the government and went unpaid for months. Fortunately, the behind-the-scenes problems do not show on the finished product, which is a noble monument in an appropriate place; Walcott could view it with satisfaction before boarding the train.

They had breakfast at Winslow, Arizona, and dinner at Albuquerque. "Crossing Kansas. A warm day. Nothing of note occurred" (October 18, 1915). At Chicago, Helen left them to spend the winter with Mrs. Garfield, which may have been just as well. They got to Washington, looked over the mail, and were back on the train that afternoon, Mary to Philadelphia and Walcott to New York. The CIW

Ex Comm was meeting, and Walcott resumed his frantic administrative routine as though the four months away had never happened.

Fortunately, the meeting in New York went quickly, and the Walcotts could return immediately to Washington. "We are delighted to be at home & where we can rest a little in a quiet orderly fashion" (October 22, 1915). Four months away is a long time, no matter how enthusiastic one is for fieldwork, and one must pay the piper simply for having been gone. "At Smithsonian all day attending to correspondence etc.—Field collections have all come in & the work of fall & winter is all ahead of me" (October 25, 1915). Mary helped unpack fossils and with him called on the British ambassador—two worlds widely separated in time. Honors continued to accumulate; Walcott was elected an honorary member of the Imperial Society of Naturalists of Moscow.

The month of November began. "With Mary continued unpacking Yellowstone Park collections. Finished 4:30 P.M. 100 drawers exclusive of rocks" (November 1, 1915). Within a very few days, Walcott got the NACA papers in order and attended to other administrative loose ends. "Looking after unpacking of Black Butte Canyon fossil algal remains dictating letters and incidentally getting in touch with Cambrian trilobite material that is still undescribed" (November 3, 1915). He began examination of the trilobite "*Bathyuriscus,* as it is of stratigraphic importance in Cambrian sections" (November 5, 1915).

The NACA Executive Committee went smoothly, but then, meetings Walcott chaired seldom got out of hand. He again was elected president of the local archaeological society. Walcott got in a day on fossils, mixed between Precambrian algae and trilobites.

Mary took him off to Philadelphia for a Sunday meeting of Friends, and they went on to New York. Walcott was tied up one day with the RC, now seemingly a moneymaker. He presided at the NAS fall meeting and ended the week with a meeting of the Carnegie Ex Comm; this was easier than three meetings in one day. Still, home looked very good when he and Mary returned to Washington.

Walcott's youngest came in for the Thanksgiving holiday. The next day, "Stuart assisted me in photographing slabs of algal deposits" (November 26, 1915). The mood was darkened by a telegraph that Walcott's last brother was seriously ill; Ellis died the following day. Walcott, when not thinking about the past, got ready for the regents' meeting, while Mary was busy enlarging photographs.

By the end of the month, the secretary was back in New York for more meetings. "Conference with Charles L. Freer 9:30–11:30 A.M.. He told me that he had placed $1,000,000 cash in Trust Co for an art building under Smithsonian administration" (December 1, 1915); one cannot ask for much better news than that. An astronomer associate of George Ellery Hale had seen Mr. Freer's collection in Detroit in 1906 and had noted carefully the news that it had been given to the nation but was to stay in Freer's possession until his death. Still later, came the announcement that the collection would be transferred to Washington as soon as a suitable building could be prepared. Years later an associate remembered, "I asked him [Walcott] what lay behind the change in plan. 'It really was a very simple matter,' he replied. . . . We had only to point out to Mr. Freer that if the collection could be transferred to Washington in the near future, it would be of immense value to us during the period of construction and installation. We thought, too, that he might find satisfaction if the collection could be displayed during his lifetime in a manner that met his approval."[5] Walcott also noted that he would be able to draw on Freer's intimate knowledge of the history of the objects and their significance and to have his advice as to the best method of their presentation to the public.

This sounds simple, but assuredly changing Freer's mind was no easy task. The glow caused by Freer's gift continued through lunch with Eugene Meyer, one of Freer's younger confidants. Next, an RC meeting went smoothly, and then Walcott was on the southbound train once more. He was back in good time to take up one of the ceremonial aspects of the position of secretary, formally welcoming the Red Cross the first week in December.

The auditorium of the Museum was in almost constant use. It was one of the very few large auditoriums in Washington and was in a particularly convenient location; the foyer, used for temporary displays, was ideal for large receptions. According to some authorities, the reason that the restrooms are at the far end of the foyer rather than near the auditorium was a fear that the bathroom noises would interfere with the presentations. As a result of debate on the construction of the Castle, one of the original regents, Richard Owen, had written a piece on public architecture; the addition of indoor plumbing added a new dimension to the subject.

Committee meetings came in droves as the year was closing. The annual meeting of the SI Board of Regents was more a formality than anything else but still had to be held. The NACA Executive Committee was becoming more active. The Carnegie Institution of Washington Ex Comm and the annual meeting of the Board of Trustees followed. Walcott presided at the trustees' dinner; no mention is made in his diary of work on fossils. The first snow of the season came, but it brought no joy. "European war overshadows our lives. It is a terrible calamity & full of thot as to the curse of having ambitious irresponsible rulers" (September 13, 1915). A meeting the next day with Charles Platt, architect for the Freer building, helped lighten the mood. Walcott got in most of a day on trilobites and had the pleasure of taking $650,000 of Mr. Freer's money to the bank, but he could still worry that "between callers & routine I am not getting much of my own work done" (December 18, 1915).

There was little prospect that Walcott's concern for his own research would be gratified. Two days later, the Pan-American Science Congress opened in Washington, a major event made larger for Walcott by a joint meeting with the Archaeological Society of America (the society later transformed itself into the present-day Archaeological Institute). Walcott was involved in ceremonial activities, but he stole a few hours to begin preparation of a scientific presentation; lecturing to one's geologic colleagues requires more preparation than extending greetings and welcome to groups of distinguished visitors. Just as Walcott could run the Smithsonian with a minimum of fuss, he could say the appropriate words at almost any gathering, regardless of its size; this is not easy, for the proper quality of spontaneity requires a great deal of thought and planning.

The day before Christmas, the Smithsonian clerks were again generously given half a day off; Walcott spent the quiet afternoon sorting through accumulated reprints and arranging them for filing. Christmas was quieter than normal with Helen not there to spark the proceedings. The day following, Walcott and the boys went to Rock Creek Cemetery with flowers in what was becoming an annual tradition for them. What little remained of December was exceedingly busy. Not only was the Pan-American Scientific Congress still proceeding, but the Geological Society of America came to Washington to interact with some of the South American geologists. Walcott spoke at the GSA dinner, and he and Mary received 1,285 people at a congress reception; for a nonpolitician, this is a large number of handshakes.

The day before the year ended, Walcott spoke on the hot spring deposits he had studied the previous summer. On December 31, he attended the International Congress of Americanists and formally closed that congress, yet another gathering in conjunction with the Pan-Americanists. The final reception for them was in the Great Hall of the Castle, smaller than the foyer of the Museum but larger in tradition.

> The year 1915 has been full of activity & in general of results but none of unusual importance. Smithsonian building renovation completed for large hall. Freer Art Gallery assured by deposit of $1,000,000. Our family well. Helen is at Cleveland, Ohio. Sidney & Stuart at home for holidays. Stuart goes to Cleveland to visit Helen at the James R. Garfields.
>
> The Great European War is the one great catastrophe of the year. May it wear itself out before the close of 1916. Civilization suffers from it but in the long run it will be fully restored & advanced far beyond that of the first decade of the 20th century.

> My brother Ellis died at Onalaska, Wisconsin Nov. 29 1915. He was the last of my family and altho we have never been closely associated in life I shall miss him. (December 31, 1915)

The new year began with a late breakfast out, followed by formal calls at the homes of cabinet members; this year the White House was skipped. That evening the Walcotts attended an excellent reception of the Pan-American Science Congress and the next day rested after church; when the Walcotts were not in Philadelphia on a Sunday, Mary accompanied him to the Church of the Covenant. The week was devoted to research, interspersed with attending a few sessions of the scientific congress. "President Wilson gave a fine address on Monroe Doctrine" (January 6, 1916).

The long scientific congress finally adjourned, and Walcott could concentrate more on the fossils. He had never been to Labrador, but Professor Schuchert had made collections from there and western Newfoundland for him, and these were next on the research agenda. The annual meetings on the apartment houses took him across the river to Alexandria; a NACA meeting took him to the War Department. Mary and he gave a small dinner for eight. In terms of busyness, 1916 appeared to resemble 1915.

Joseph A. Holmes, the first director of the Bureau of Mines, and according to some the best ever, had died the previous July while Walcott was in Yellowstone. Walcott met with others to organize a "Safety First Association" in his memory. Holmes would have liked that, for one of the first things the Bureau of Mines had done was investigate explosions and reduce the terrible death toll in the coal mines. While Walcott was thus engaged, Mary was arranging for the Philadelphia Symphony to play in Washington, and entertaining some of its members.

The couple went to a British embassy dinner before they took the night train to New York. The CIW Ex Comm transacted its business, and in the afternoon Walcott conferred with Henry Fairfield Osborn at the American Museum. It is a wonder that Walcott and Osborn were as close as they were, for Osborn was far more of a patrician, impressed with his own ability, than Walcott ever was. They dined with Eugene Meyer and family; Mr. Freer must have been a topic of conversation. The next day was occupied by the RC Executive Committee and, later, the board. The flood of war orders from Europe had increased the need for Cottrell's precipitators, and the corporation had expanded dramatically. That night, Mrs. Harriman entertained the couple; Walcott had the knack of retaining friendships for years despite his busy schedule.

They returned home in good time to attend a banquet of the Security League, yet another organization concerned about America and the European conflict.

A carload of furniture arrived for Mary from Philadelphia. The Spanish ambassador called to inquire about platinum. Attending a luncheon in honor of a new president of Johns Hopkins University was another obligation that could not be shirked. Walcott's time was expended by others as though it were an inexhaustible commodity.

Somewhere along the line, Walcott did find time to write a one-page summary of his latest contribution on Cambrian trilobites, completed in 1915; that work had been published in January by the Smithsonian. The first paragraph of this abstract gives the rationale for that particular publication. "The writer has assembled data to aid in clearing up some of the problems of formations of the Appalachian region by a careful comparison of portions of their contained faunas with those of the Mississippi Valley, the Cordilleras, and other localities. No thorough study and comparison of many genera of the Cambrian faunas has been made, though collections from many outcrops have been in the writer's possession for years, awaiting the opportunity to make these studies so necessary in his work on the Cambrian trilobites" (Walcott 1916b, 101).

The summary was submitted to the new NAS *Proceedings* on the last day of January. It and the Precambrian bacteria piece were the only words of Walcott recorded in that particular journal. The same day this note reached the editor, Walcott finally was able to spend a few hours with the long-neglected *Bathyuriscus* and get farther into his next contribution on Cambrian trilobites.

This social season was atypical in that there were more dinners in than out; the Walcotts had two large gatherings before February was well started. Apart from that, the trilobite studies moved along at a good pace. Virtually the only item noted in this interval was the NAS involvement at the Panama Canal. Because of the persistent landslides, President Wilson had asked the NAS to investigate, and Charles R. Van Hise, an eminent geologist who was also the president of the University of Wisconsin had taken a group south in December (Cochrane 1978, 205–6). Walcott dropped by the White House to make certain that Wilson had an informal copy of the results as soon as they had been prepared.

Sidney was ill, and Walcott went to Ithaca. No one should suggest thoughts that might have been in another's mind, but surely he must have recalled Charlie's death. Fortunately, this illness was not as serious as it seemed at first. Walcott gave a talk to the Telluride Association boys, and his daughter came in to solidify peace with her father. "Had a long talk with Helen—She wishes to return home while Mrs. Garfield is in California" (February 10, 1916). "Sorry to leave Sidney and to have Helen go (to Buffalo)" (February 11, 1916). L. L. Nunn accompanied Walcott back to Washington, but fortunately for the study of fossils, he continued onward. Walcott could get back to "routine & a couple of hours on Cambrian fossils" (February 15, 1916). Such virtually uninterrupted time lasted for only a couple of days.

"Annual hearing before H.[ouse of] R.[epresentatives] Committee on Appropriations. Committee in a hurry & our men worried" (February 16, 1916). He had an informal meeting with several members of the NACA. "The days come & go with a rush that would be disheartening if it were not for getting a little done every day" (February 18, 1916). In this comment may lie the secret of Walcott's productivity: no matter what the press of other business, he stole a few minutes each day for science. To balance that, it may well be that this time spent away from administration made him such an able administrator. Administration was a means to an end, not an end in itself; Walcott knew this and tried to ensure that everyone under him knew it.

Helen came home, and two days later, on a Sunday after church, Walcott remarked how pleased he was to have her home; the debutante had become a young lady. The Washington Monument Association met on the first president's birthday and found all well with his monument. Life got very serious again when Walcott appeared before the Naval Affairs Committee. By the end of the month Walcott was commenting on the unsettled relations with Germany over the submarine warfare that belligerent was waging.

At the office it was possible to get through the routine quickly and back to the Cambrian trilobites. Home life was definitely better; though in the first week in March Mary and Helen held a tea for two hundred, which was followed by a dinner for some members of the NAS in honor of Dr. Bell. The social whirl of past months then slackened dramatically. "Quiet day—Managed to get quite a little work done on Cambrian mss [manuscripts]" (March 9, 1916).

The quiet did not last long, however, and the horde of callers increased. Mary got in the habit of picking him up in the car—that is, directing the chauffeur—and taking him for an evening walk by the river. The Holmes Association was organized under the auspices of the Bureau of Mines. Chairman L. P. Padgett of the Naval Affairs Committee received a visit from NACA members S. W. Stratton and C. D. Walcott. It was as though the entire world conspired to keep Walcott from the trilobites. Yet he referred to it all as the usual routine.

Helen, who could generally not sit still, went off to Buffalo, briefly, leaving things very quiet in the house. "Very quiet at Smithsonian so put in half a day on Cambrian work" (March 22, 1916). Thereafter, Walcott had aches and pains, leading to a bout of the grippe, all of which he attributed to the bad weather. He skipped a musical at the White House, but Mary and Helen attended. The weather and his health got better the next day, as March was ending. "Began preparing a paper on an article by [Prof. August] Rothpletz attacking my work about Helena Montana. My 66th birthday. Still effective & full of the future" (March 31, 1916).

That hopeful note was a little too hastily, for Walcott had a relapse and had to cancel two dinner invitations. He struggled to get a little done on the Rothpletz paper, and he struggled to get to a dinner in honor of the secretary of state. He did attend the celebration of the hundredth anniversary of the Coast and Geodetic Survey. Then Mary took him off to Spring Lake Beach in New Jersey. Professor Rothpletz was much on his mind, and he spent most of the week away on the manuscript. Before he left the seashore, it had been mailed to Washington for typing.

The Walcotts returned to Washington to attend the reception at the Daughters of the American Revolution convention. One official duty of the secretary was to transmit to Congress the reports of the American Historical Association and the Daughters of the American Revolution. This particular chore had been arranged by George Brown Goode when he was assistant secretary; it has since vanished even from the Smithsonian corporate memory. For those interested in comparisons, Helena had been an active member of the Daughters of the American Revolution, whereas Mary belonged to the Colonial Dames; the Vaux family was long settled in America and saw no sense in becoming involved with an upstart organization. Stuart came home from Princeton on his spring break. Another harbinger of spring was the annual NAS meeting. This was followed by a meeting of the NACA Executive Committee.

That gathering, in turn, was followed by a CIW Ex Comm meeting and one of the few times Walcott commented on its proceedings. "Woodward violently opposed to grant for Int. Cat. Sci. literature" (April 20, 1916). The International Catalogue of Scientific Literature is another long-forgotten SI activity. The project had been organized in 1901 in London, and the Smithsonian had become the focus of collecting and cataloging American literature. As might be expected, each year the volume of literature had expanded, and the line between pure science, the original goal, and applied science became less and less clear. The war put a further strain on the project, particularly as to funding. Woodward was adamant; Walcott could not obtain CIW money.

"Your Secretary succeeded in interesting the Carnegie Corporation of New York, in the project and through the generous assistance of that establishment it was made possible to publish the fourteenth annual issue" (Walcott 1917, 32). When Andrew Carnegie decided that he could not give his money away fast enough, he set up the Carnegie Corporation to take over the chore. H. W. Pritchett, an old acquaintance of Walcott's, was in charge of the corporation. One should never overlook the importance of knowing many people; the concept was developed eons before the term "networking."

Despite the complication imposed by Dr. Woodward, Walcott seemed serene. "Correspondence & administrative matters & review of my paper in mss [stage] on Rothpletz memoire kept me busy" (April 21, 1916). If there was any anger on the matter of the catalogue, it was lost in the upset that Professor Rothpletz (1915) had caused.

In that connection, this may be the appropriate place to touch on Walcott's article in the *Annual Report*, which he had completed in 1915 en route to the field. For generations, the report had been significantly expanded by the addition of a series of papers on a variety of subjects. Traditionally these had been reprints of papers published elsewhere, but deemed important. Under Walcott, original contributions were encouraged, and though the number of them was still small, it was increasing. Walcott was not one to ask others to do that he would not do himself, so "Evidences of Primitive Life" had been written (Walcott 1916c, 235–55). It is an excellent summary of Walcott's scientific career, even if he concentrated more on the Precambrian than on any other facet. The paper is profusely illustrated from his earlier publications and mainly written in a popular style, such as Walcott used for his *National Geographic* articles. Only one example need be cited. "Friends have often asked me how I happened to take up geologic work in the Rocky Mountains. The reason is a very simple one. As a boy of 17 I planned to study those older fossiliferous rocks of the North American Continent which the great English geologist, Adam Sedgwick, had called the Cambrian system on account of his finding them in the Cambrian district of Wales" (Walcott 1916c, 235).

Walcott began with the notion that the earth is quite old; noted the retreat of Algonkian seas from the continent; and emphasized the unconformity between these older rocks and the Cambrian. He then discussed the Precambrian limestones and considered the importance of algae and bacteria. The occurrence in these rocks of "Beltina," which Walcott still judged to be a possible early crustacean was still a problem, but he was now interpreting it as having lived in brackish, or fresh, water. This article is an excellent review of his findings and his interpretations of the deposition of the Belt rocks. "Beltina" is no longer considered an animal and may have been based on broken fragments of some sort of algal remains.

With that base laid, Walcott moved up to the Cambrian and discussed the differences between Lower and Middle Cambrian faunas. He touched on the early studies of the Cambrian of China and the need for more comprehensive stratigraphic data; "This project was held in abeyance for 18 years" (Walcott 1916c, 245). Walcott then moved on to some of his finds in the Burgess Shale and emphasized the discovery of soft-bodied holothurians and annelids. He slipped into a bit more technical detail in a section on the relationships within the Arthropoda, but he gave a nice nontechnical account of his efforts at Mount Robson. That is followed by more personal material from his Trenton Falls days. He ended by taking the reader to the Cambrian/Ordovician boundary, before his concluding remarks: "How much earlier than the pre-Cambrian and Algonkian faunas the study of primitive life may be extended will depend very largely upon the discovery and study of now unknown fossil faunas and floras. . . . Students and investigators everywhere are invited to cooperate with the writer in his studies of the evidences of primitive life, and in his effort to correlate all procurable data on the subject and make them available for study and research by all those interested in these fascinating problems" (Walcott 1916c, 255).

This also the place to touch on Professor Rothpletz; the dating of this last sentence could be helpful in considering Walcott's attack on the man. Rothpletz published on June 5, 1915. Walcott could not have seen that paper before he had finished writing "Evidences." The Rothpletz paper was translated for Walcott, according to a note from the translator, on March 23, 1916. Unfortunately, it is not possible to determine when the *Annual Report* for 1915 was published. The formal letter of transmittal is dated December 15, 1915; commonly that is the last item prepared. In theory, Walcott might have seen the Rothpletz article and then added the final sentence to his paper, but it is far more likely that the thought was in his manuscript before he obtained the translation of Rothpletz's work.

"Crime" may be a bit too harsh a word to use in dealing with matters of science, but then again it might not. In the summer of 1913, Professor Rothpletz had attended the International Geological Congress in large part to participate in the field trips and gather material for his investigations of limestone masses, possibly formed by organic agencies. This was what Walcott was interested in as well, and it is an example of more or less simultaneous investigation. That phenomenon happens more times in science than is generally realized; when a certain level of information is reached, several scientists are likely to have the same ideas. The literature is full of arguments as to who deserves priority for discovery of a new idea.

Rothpletz went to Steeprock Lake and stayed on for a couple of days after the field trip. In a later publication (Rothpletz 1916), he complained about the map, the lack of outcrops away from the lake, and a few other matters. He concluded that "Atikokania" was a sponge. The war had made a mess of communications, and no one can fault him for not knowing of the discussion in *Nature* wherein Walcott concluded he was in error and that this form was not a fossil. Rothpletz then proceeded to make the generalizations that the fauna was relatively young and that most of the Canadian Shield was younger than dozens of geologists had worked out. These generalizations were basically wrong, and they were presented in what might be considered a rather arrogant matter, but after all, people have their own writing styles. The naming of a species *Crytozoon Walcotti* by Rothpletz in this paper may have been the only scientifically correct part of the work.

After Steeprock, Rothpletz had gone on to western Canada. As noted, he was with the Congress excursion to the Burgess Shale and had stayed on to collect with Walcott. Later that summer, Rothpletz went to Helena, Montana, to collect, and then to the Grand Canyon, where he hoped to obtain some of the material Walcott had collected in 1882. The real "crime" was that Rothpletz did not tell Walcott what he was planning for the rest of the season. Had he done so, Walcott could have given him advice.

It is one thing for two people to stumble into the same problem without knowing of each other's interests; sometimes they subsequently cooperate, and sometimes they fight in public. It is not uncommon for a later worker to decide that an earlier worker made a mess of things and rework the problem, even when the earlier worker is still alive. Nonetheless, to move into an area of research being actively pursued by a scientist and not mention that one is doing so is unethical; it is no different from poaching. To spend time with the first worker and listen to his ideas without comment, with the intention of immediately going out to test them, is incredible.

Once a manuscript is written, it may be extensively reviewed by colleagues, or it may be sent directly to the press. Nothing—except organizational administration—requires review, but prudence suggests that having other parties examine one's work before it is published is a way to eliminate errors. Rothpletz spent four days in the field at Helena, Montana, and wrote up his results. He may have had a European colleague review his work, but the first Walcott knew of this venture was when the Rothpletz publication appeared. Thus the importance of the last sentences of "Evidences," offering and asking for cooperation.

To be brief, Rothpletz identified a limestone outcropping on the east side of Mount Helena as the Helena Limestone. He then proceeded to collect fossils from the unit, identify them as Early Cambrian, and, using that as a basis, cast doubt on the age of much of the Belt rocks. He complained about a poor topographic map published by Walcott and the difficulty of locating a generalized cross-section of the strata. These comments are interspersed with jibes about poor advice he was given on collecting in the Grand Canyon, and about how he therefore could not obtain material.

The language used by Walcott in his rejoinder is restrained. "If the limestone he identified as the 'Helena' is not the Helena, then the elaborate deductions and conclusions he [Rothpletz] has drawn are therefore without foundation" (Walcott 1916d, 261). Walcott then went at great length to point out that Rothpletz had indeed misidentified a Cambrian limestone as the Helena Limestone. He mentions several key pieces of literature that Walcott could have referred

Rothpletz to, had he been asked, or that Rothpletz could even have seen after his trip to America. Walcott included data from a number of sections to demonstrate the major unconformity between the Belt rocks and the overlying Cambrian; he also reproduced several pictures of the Grand Canyon showing this unconformity to hammer home the point. As a finale of sorts, he noted that the fauna Rothpletz had described was Middle Cambrian in age, not Early Cambrian. Walcott had started on his rejoinder to Rothpletz on March 31, and he had a draft ready for typing in two weeks; a week later he was polishing it up.

The paper was published on June 24, 1916, so little, if anything, was added to it after the three-week interval mentioned in Walcott's diary. There are quotes from earlier Walcott papers and quotes from Rothpletz; also, the pictures of fossils had been published previously; still, this is a thirty-eight-page paper with seven plates. Walcott must have been working at white heat in writing this! There are no direct attacks, but this paper is the only one in which Walcott set out to destroy the work, and perhaps the reputation, of another. There were other disagreements with other paleontologists, but nothing ever approached this level. So much for the fourth part of Walcott's third SMC volume.

Two days after Walcott reviewed the manuscript of the Rothpletz rejoinder, Nunn was back in town. This time he had a scheme for a big spread in Texas under the auspices of the Telluride Association where boys would live to study and farm; nothing came of this notion. After Nunn left, George Ellery Hale called the following day. He and Walcott had a long talk on NAS affairs and went for a motor ride to continue their discussions. Two days later came a significant gathering. "Administrative matters & routine with a little research work kept me busy most of day. Called on Prest. Wilson with Committee Nat. Acad. Sci. 12:45 P.M." (April 26, 1916).

Clarifying this cryptic entry requires a great deal of background, most of it concerning George Ellery Hale. A brief summary is not easy, as at least two books have been written about him and his accomplishments in science (Wright 1966; Wright, Warnow, and Weiner 1972).

The time to begin is 1902, when an advisory committee on astronomy was established by the new CIW. Thirty-four-year-old Hale was secretary of the four-man committee (Wright 1966, 162–63). Hale was the only one interested in astrophysics, and the draft report of the committee hardly mentioned the subject. That summer, Walcott called, unannounced, on Hale at the Yerkes Observatory.

Walcott liked what he saw and what he heard concerning a possible solar observatory. He wrote a committee member to suggest major changes in the astronomy report. Walcott wanted concern focused on what problems were to be studied, not how much they might cost. "I have suggested to Professor Hale that he make up a draft of the report in accordance with this plan, and submit to the advisors in Astronomy."[6] In effect, in a polite way, Walcott overruled the three senior members of the advisory committee.

The death of Abram Hewitt, first chairman of the Board of Trustees, shortly after the founding of CIW caused problems. Hale was enthusiastic in his hopes that Vice Chairman John Shaw Billings would become chairman and that as a result, within a few months, Hale would receive funding. "Walcott is a hard-headed businessman, who takes a very practical view of things."[7]

The revised report and modest funding it generated resulted in Hale's moving to California and setting up his equipment on Mount Wilson. It also led to his overextending himself financially and spending more than had been allocated by the CIW; Hale lived by overextending himself, promoting ever-larger telescopes and ever more expansive schemes. In 1904, Hale was in a torment over the funds he had spent, torn as whether to ask for more money, and concerned that Billings, now chairman of the board and the strongest single power in the CIW, would be upset.

Billings was not quite what Hale had expected. "With Dr. Walcott, on the contrary, there were no reservations.... Dr. Walcott advised me to revive our original project for the solar observatory, including the 60-inch reflector and present it personally to the Executive Committee."[8] Hale decided to present both his original plan, which required less money, and his new plan. Two weeks later Walcott informed Hale that money for his new plan had been approved, subject to the approval of the Board of Trustees. At that meeting Walcott steered the proposal through, despite some serious objections (Wright 1966, 193–96).

In his correspondence with Andrew Carnegie, Walcott kept emphasizing the solar observatory in particular and the need by astronomers in general for larger instruments. Carnegie finally visited Mount Wilson in 1910, and early in 1911 he bestowed on the CIW another ten million dollars. On some subjects Carnegie was not an easy man to convince, but between Walcott's logic and Hale's enthusiasm, he was persuaded.

Needless to say, Walcott and Hale were by now fairly well acquainted. In addition, in 1910 Hale became the foreign secretary of the NAS and was on the council with Vice President Walcott. Before Carnegie's gift was received, Hale had had a nervous breakdown, and he was traveling abroad when the new CIW endowment was announced. Despite this incredible boost to his research, upon his return he spent months in a sanitarium. Hale recovered sufficiently to plan how to spend Carnegie's money, and then he had a relapse.

Hale pulled himself together for the 1913 NAS semicentennial. "The Academy celebration was a decided success, especially because Welch was elected President.... In many respects he will be a better president than Walcott would have been, and I am delighted with his election."[9] This is an interesting characterization by Hale, considering how much time and effort Walcott had devoted to bringing Hale's schemes to fruition; without the support from the CIW that Walcott garnered, Hale's notions would have been grandiose schemes rather than grand successes.

That fall, the visionary Hale wrote an article suggesting that if the Academy was to be more effective, it needed a building, a journal, and better international ties (Cochrane 1978, 194–99). Rather early in his career, Hale had had a brush with the military side of German nature, and events on his trip in 1910 confirmed his fears as to the desire of the kaiser for conquest (Wright 1966, 285–86). By 1915, he was writing to President William Welch of the NAS trying to convince him that the Academy should offer its services in the event of war (Cochrane 1978, 208). The same day he wrote, a Naval Consulting Board was set up under Thomas Alva Edison; its members were inventors, not scientists. To put it mildly, Hale was upset that no one in Washington would take him seriously.

By 1916, the situation had changed dramatically, and more NAS members believed that America would be in the war. Hale was reelected foreign secretary and was able to steer through a resolution that the president of the National Academy of Sciences was to offer its services to the president of the United States in the event of a break in diplomatic relations. At the subsequent council meeting, a committee was formed to call on President Wilson. This consisted of Councilor Edwin G. Conkin, Foreign Secretary Hale, Vice President Walcott, President Welch, and member and CIW president Robert S. Woodward.

President Wilson listened and suggested that the NAS form a committee to enlist cooperation among the scientific community, but he asked that his oral acceptance of the idea be kept private (Wright 1966, 287–89). Hale contacted a number of persons and received offers of support but felt strongly that the effort should be made public. He then managed to make a campaign issue out of it by forcing Wilson to acknowledge his support for a National Research Council. Such details tend to be lost in official histories (Barrows 1933).

The mercurial Hale has properly received credit as the founder of the NRC. Having said that, one might ask how it was that the NAS committee received an appointment to visit the White House so promptly, let alone got listened to, to say nothing of having its ideas accepted immediately by a president under a great deal of stress. For this, one might go back to a handwritten letter from Walcott to the president, written in camp along the Madison River in Montana while he had been enjoying his honeymoon.

"A passing Forest Ranger told me of Mrs. Wilson's serious illness and later delayed papers told of her passing onward—I sympathize with you most sincerely. She was an exceptional woman of the best American type and the country loses [*sic*] by her going—I wish I could help you. Steady systematic work is one's salvation at such a time of trial and surely you have more than enough of that."[10] Anyone who could write such a letter to the president could pick up the telephone and arrange an immediate appointment. No one else on the committee, including NAS president Welch, had such access, and no one else of that committee had the confidence of the president.

In the first account of the NRC (Day 1917), Hale and Conkin were joined by three others to form an organizing committee for a research council. Walcott was not on this committee, yet he became first vice president, a member of the executive committee of the NRC, and chairman of the military committee. Because of one key organizational item, it seems logical to assume that Walcott played his usual role, behind the scenes. As noted earlier, once the NACA was set up, Walcott insisted that subcommittees be established that included persons who were not members of the NACA, and he went to President Wilson to get what he wanted. The point for the NRC was that like the NACA—it could include persons who were not NAS members. It is an interesting parallel, and while it might have been pure coincidence, Hale and Walcott had their heads together before the meeting with President Wilson. All this suggests that perhaps Walcott deserves more of a share of the credit in founding the NRC.

This long digression has tended to break the narrative thread at April 1916; it is past time to return to the end of that month. Before Stuart returned to Princeton, he mentioned a girlfriend; the family was growing up. The Archaeological Society met again, but otherwise, with the youngest in the family gone again, life became quiet. Despite the war clouds, May brought "fine weather & all nature joyous with new life" (May 1, 1916). It marked the start of an uneventful week, devoted almost entirely to fossils. "Another week should close up Cambrian trilobite paper for this spring" (May 8, 1916).

Despite Walcott's trying to focus on his beloved fossils, the war in Europe kept intruding. The Walcotts attended a garden party to raise money for British soldiers; Helen took part in the tableau. A few days later, the conflict came closer. "Mrs Jas [James] R. Garfield talked with us about Helen's going to France to work in hospital. She dined with us" (May 13, 1916). A week later, Helen had determined to go to France, and father and daughter had a long discussion. Helen had metamorphosed from willful debutante to young lady; when she returned from France, she was to be a young woman in the finest early-twenty-first-century use of that term.

Walcott met with Cottrell to discuss his investigations into producing nitrates, which were in short supply and were critically needed for both fertilizer and explosives. From that meeting, he moved to a conference with the Fine Arts Commission concerning Freer's proposed museum. If there is any ultimate power in Washington, it lies in the Fine Arts Commission; no one can overturn its rulings. A day later Walcott was speaking to the American Federation of Arts and that evening welcoming its members to a reception. Between these events, he met with Senators Lodge and William J. Stone. Freer had been forced to pay taxes on the money he was giving for his building; Walcott arranged for a special bill to be introduced in Congress to restore the Federal tax money to the building fund. The breadth of his efforts seemed to get wider each year.

Walcott went from the American Federation of Arts reception to the midnight train and a full day of meetings in New York. The RC and Ex Comm were taken care of before he went to see and soothe Mr. Freer. As if that were not enough, he was part of a NAS committee to meet with engineering groups. The next day he and Hale discussed their results in attempting to forge an alliance between scientist and engineer. He saw cousin Fred, dropped in at the RC office, and went home.

The three senators who were SI regents held an informal meeting, and Walcott was back on Capitol Hill with them. Two days later he was in the office of the secretary of war, briefing him on problems in aviation and in nitrate supply. The Walcotts got to Philadelphia for the weekend to see Mary's brother and attend the Friends meeting.

Decoration Day was a holiday, which meant that Walcott devoted full time to the Cambrian trilobites. Early June was as badly chopped up as late May had been, with two meetings on aviation, a jurisdictional problem concerning police coming onto Smithsonian grounds, an issue at the zoo, some concerns of E. O. Ulrich, and a visit with Mary to the National Training School for Girls. It was a whirlwind.

"Sent in paper on Cambrian trilobites" (June 4, 1916). What makes this a little unusual is that this was a Sunday. Walcott's one week in May to finish the paper had become four, and he was pressed for time. If there is any rule in writing a paper, it is that everything takes longer. This is not a complete sentence, and it is grammatically incorrect, but every scientist will understand it.

"Cambrian Trilobites," a second use of the same title, came out September 29, less than four months after Walcott completed the manuscript (Walcott 1916e). The paper—actually, book may be more appropriate—contains twenty-three plates and more than a hundred pages of text. The genus *Bathyuriscus* has more pages and pictures than any other single genus, but a number of genera are included. To make a rough comparison, this work is to the Early and Middle Cambrian trilobites what "Cambrian Trilobites" published in the spring had been to the Upper Cambrian forms.

The paper is not a monographic treatment, with extended discussion and long summaries to provide general information. Rather, like so many publications in paleontology, it consists of descriptions of species and genera—dull to read, unless one is a paleontologist interested in trilobites. It is the occurrences given for the species that are vital, for they are the key to the correlation of widely separated formations. Walcott calls attention to only one correlation of similar trilobites, in the St. Lawrence–Newfoundland area and the Mount Whyte Formation of western Canada; the other details are left for the careful reader to cull out. This was not the end of such effort. "I now have a considerable series of undescribed Cambrian trilobites that have been grouped under genera and species, and of which figures have been made for illustration. These will be studied and descriptions prepared for publication as opportunity permits" (Walcott 1916e, 308).

The publication of this large descriptive work and the rejoinder to Rothpletz marked completion of the third full volume of *Smithsonian Miscellaneous Collections*. That event engendered a three-page summary review. The reviewer gave proper credit to the wonders of the Burgess Shale but began by putting Walcott's work in perspective. "To the student of Cambrian geology, the writings of C. D. Walcott are always matters of enlightening study, not only for the matter they contain, but also because they combine that admixture of stratigraphy and palaeontology in which the latter, though accorded a prominent position, is always used to the full to subserve the wider claims of the former" (Illing 1917, 25). This is a remarkably fair summary, for Walcott was not interested in the fossils in a vacuum but in where the fossils occurred within the geologic framework.

One more comment might be germane about "Cambrian Trilobites." For Walcott to have put aside this comprehensive manuscript, which was to close his third volume, when it was so nearly complete in order to write his comments on Rothpletz's paper is a further indication of how upset he must have been. Now, with two papers in press, Walcott could attend to other affairs, and there were important matters to pursue in other fields. "Meeting of Executive Committee of N.A. Com. Aeronautics 9:30 A.M. to 4:30 P.M. Lunch at Smithsonian— After good motor for aircraft" (June 8, 1916).

A historian of NACA judges that the one great American aeronautical achievement in World War I was "development and production of the Liberty engine" (Roland 1985, 186). It began at this particular gathering. "The meeting was an overt attempt to bring together the consumers and the producers, to identify what was holding back engine production in the United States, and perhaps to decide on a remedy. Chairman Walcott stated the problem bluntly in his opening remarks. 'There is not a good American motor made.' It was, he said, up to the people in that room of the Smithsonian building to correct the deficiencies" (Roland 1985, 34–35).

After that opening statement, the meeting became increasingly acrimonious. Auto manufacturers blamed the government for being difficult to understand

and to deal with; military blamed civilians for not understanding the need and responding to it. The transcript records deep and bitter differences (Roland 1985, 34). A lunch soothed feelings, and eventually agreement was reached.

There is more to this event than that bland statement. The oral tradition is that shortly after the meeting started, Walcott recognized that it might soon break up in disarray. He sent a messenger to Mary to have a luncheon prepared. Then, at the first opportunity, Walcott started speaking and kept the floor for hours, until it was time for lunch. He began with the founding of the Smithsonian by James Smithson, mentioned Henry and Baird, went to Langley's selection as secretary, reviewed his experiments, and brought in every item he could think of to force the group to stay together. Whatever the precise details, the group did not disband, there was cooperation that afternoon, and the Liberty engine was the eventual result.

Laying the groundwork for a more powerful engine was an achievement of which Walcott could be proud. Completing two manuscripts that spring was another satisfactory accomplishment. A pleasant family milestone was reached that June, when Sidney graduated from Cornell University; unfortunately, Walcott was too busy with the NACA to attend. When Sidney came home, he announced his engagement. The children had had various girlfriends and boyfriends over the years, but this was the real thing. Another aviation conference took more time, along with the usual scramble of leaving for the field. A new item that had to be taken care of this year was paying income tax.

Sidney left for Brooklyn about the time that Mary and Walcott boarded the train west. "Sorry to leave Helen behind. She is to sail for France June *24th*. Stuart hopes to go to Belgium for the summer" (June 23, 1916). In Chicago, they looked at an art gallery and strolled in Jackson Park before catching the night train to La Crosse, to call on Ellis's widow, Elizabeth. They had a long talk with her before heading west on the Great Northern Railroad in the evening.

Train service was getting better, and in only a day and a half they were in Shelby, Montana. Walcott occupied the time by reading proofs on his trilobite paper. One job that never diminished was proofreading. The SI *Annual Report* had to be read each year, and future years would bring annual reports for more organizations. On the other hand, there is some satisfaction in returning proofs to the printers and knowing that one is finally finished with a particular manuscript; it is not quite the satisfaction of turning in the manuscript, but it comes close.

The Walcotts "watched the sunset over the snow capped Rockies & turned in early" (June 17, 1916). The next day, they met Arthur and Alex Minton, a new packer for the season. There had been a lot of letter writing to arrange their meeting with these two, and then more when the question of using an army buckboard, or buying a new one, came up. Eventually, Walcott bought a new one. The next day the outfit of wagon, buckboard, and a dozen horses headed north. They made thirty miles the first day. The second day they made thirty-two miles, despite steady rains and the border crossing. Even though Canada and the United States have the most open international border in the world, one cannot easily move livestock from one to another, to which must be added the fact that Canada was at war. That they crossed so rapidly is a tribute to Walcott the planner and letter writer.

Walcott had spent several years collecting from the Burgess Shale, but those remarkable fossils were not now immediately on his mind. He had spent a season collecting Precambrian stromatolites and another season studying living algae and hot spring deposits, but that subject also was not on his mind. Late in May he had written to an RC member, "I expect to get away about the middle of June for British Columbia, in order to complete work that I was engaged on in 1913."[11]

Stratigraphy and biostratigraphy were the order of the day. Burling had now been working for several years for the Geological Survey of Canada, and in a 1914 paper he had suggested that beds that Walcott had dated as Early Cambrian might be Middle Cambrian in age. This was a puzzle and, if Burling was correct, potentially a major problem.

Even with mud underfoot, they made another thirty miles the first full day in Canada. This is close to the extreme for a team and loaded wagon, and they rested a day before pushing on to Calgary; by the time Walcott reached that town, he had ridden 250 miles, and the fieldwork had not even started. The trip was physically hard, yet Walcott enjoyed it, especially after the rains stopped. "Two years ago Mary & I were married at Bryn Mawr, Penna. at noon. We have had two very happy years together. This is a bright beautiful day & the views of the Rockies are superb as we wind in & out in the rolling slopes" (June 30, 1916).

They started up the Bow River valley, and their twelfth campsite was, finally, in Banff. Rain and high wind assaulted them. "Felt tired so moved slowly" (July 3, 1916). The weather cleared, and they packed into a forest-ranger cabin on Healy Creek. The pack train moved up toward Simpson Pass, but there was too much snow to camp. They moved again; "All tired including animals" (July 8, 1916). The Walcotts rested a day, and, leaving the camp in the hands of Arthur and Alex, returned to Banff and caught the westbound train to Glacier.

Mary Walcott's research concern remained the movement of mountain glaciers. She took her assistant to Illecillewaet Glacier. The ice front had melted back 617 feet from where it had been in 1910. Rainy weather for a couple of days gave the couple a bit of rest. Then Mary measured and photographed the foot of the Asulkan glacier. That done, it was back to Banff to meet Robert Chapman, out for a summer's fun.

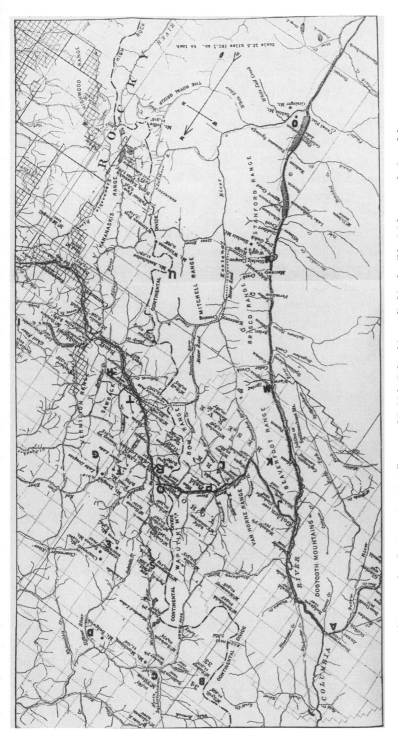

This map of geologic sections in Alberta and British Columbia studied in detail by Walcott, exclusive of the Mount Robson area. The area shown in approximately 165 miles by 75 miles; because of the reduction, the original scale below the north arrow should be ignored. Published in *Smithsonian Miscellaneous Collection* 75, no. 1 (1924), and reproduced in no. 5 (1928).

Not only was there a new helper, but Walcott treated himself to a new horse. Unfortunately, the first morning Buckskin slipped away, and it was noon before he could be caught. They finally got on the Assiniboine Trail, and camp sixteen was pitched a mile below the Continental Divide. On the other side of the divide, fallen timber made the trip toward Simpson Creek something of a nightmare; more rain made bad conditions worse. The party finally got to Lake Magog at the foot of Mount Assiniboine. "Up at 6 A.M. Sky nearly clear—Taking photographs of Mt. Assiniboine & adjoining mountains until noon. We exposed 32 8½ x 6½ plates and 4 8-foot 8-*in* films. After 3 P.M. went up to foot of Mt. Assiniboine & found Cambrian fossils (Mt Whyte) (Stephan) in moraine from mountain" (July 23, 1916). When the weather was good, Walcott did not waste a minute.

"The very heavy snowfall of the previous winter together with frequent snow and rain squalls during the summer, had made the conditions unusually favorable for taking photographs, the air being exceptionally pure and clear during the season—conditions, however, very unfavorable for geologic investigations" (Walcott 1917a, 4–5). As a result, the "Explorations" pamphlet for the year has many pictures but almost no text. Still, Walcott's aims were to determine the position of the Lower and Middle Cambrian boundary and to find the *Albertella* fauna in place, and he accomplished both of these goals; actually, they were intertwined into the questions of where *Albertella* occurred and what it meant for age determination.

Walcott rode through Wonder Pass, finding the basal quartzite and the *Olenellus* beds eight hundred feet higher on the west side, and Middle Cambrian limestones on the east side. "One of the important incidental results was the discovery at Wonder Pass of the great overthrust fault by which the basal Cambrian rocks forming the mountains on the west [right] side of the pass are have been thrust eastward over upon the limestones of the Devonian," shown on the slope to the east (Walcott 1917a, 15). In earlier "Explorations," Walcott had had many panoramas, reduced to page size. Here he included one that approached his effort for the National Geographic Society in 1912. It is well worth framing.

Walcott, accompanied by Chapman, rode to Assiniboine Pass, where he dated the rocks as the younger Silurian and Devonian, confirming his interpretation of the geologic structure. While the men were away, Mary Walcott painted wildflowers. This is the first mention in Walcott's diary of Mary's painting, though she must have done it in previous summers as well.

"Measured section of Cambrian rocks above Lake Gog—1860 feet to top of Whyte formation. Mr. Chapman climbed up with me. Mary down by lake painting wild flowers. Several snow squalls during day" (July 28, 1916). More summer was to come in the Rockies that season, but on days such as this, that was not obvious. The weather did get better, and they collected Middle Cambrian fossils in the glacial moraine and took a few more photographs. The elusive *Albertella* could not be located. "Except for the 'nasty' weather July 1–29 inclusive we have had a fine trip. This Assiniboine camp is one of the most attractive known to me. Marys [*sic*] birthday. May we have many returns together" (July 31, 1916). Walcott was to enjoy another decade of happy returns with Mary.

"Moved camp via camp 17 & down the Simpson river to the brook leading up to Simpson Pass—A very poor trail & a long day. On trail 9:30 A.M. to 7:30 P.M. & up 5 A.M. to 10 P.M." (August 1, 1916); it was a difficult fifteen miles that day. They moved through the pass and onto a plateau east of Monarch Mountain. That night it rained, and the following day brought sleet and rain. Walcott maintained his enthusiasm in the face of the wild weather. "Went out for a look over the ridge west of camp. Driven in by snow squall 3 P.M. This is a most attractive mountain upland" (August 6, 1916).

The weather turned fair, and Mr. Chapman and Mary helped him measure a section of the Mount Whyte Formation near Pharea Peak. That was sufficient for the geology, and they moved down to Healy Creek, the twenty-first camp of the season and one laden with mosquitoes. Alex had left the day before for Banff and had brought in a lot of mail. Friends from Banff came out to visit, while Chapman headed for a telegraph station. For him, it had been an interesting summer of rain, snow, sleet, and mosquitoes, along with the magnificent scenery.

They moved up the Bow River Valley to Baker Creek. From Baker Creek they moved farther up the Bow River and up the Ptarmigan Trail to the foot of Ptarmigan Peak. "Am glad to camp here with Mary as it is a beautiful spot & Stuart & I camped here about 1909" (August 8, 1916). This ride had been difficult, and a rainy morning gave a good reason not to pursue geology the next day. "Fog until 10 A.M. cold wind 38°. We went up on Ptarmigan Pass & search [*sic*] for fossils all day with little success. Determined that my section of 1909 was in error in including upper portion of thin bedded limestone" (August 10, 1916).

A bit of explanation is needed. Walcott was not in error on the total thickness of rocks that he had measured. However, with more experience in the area and a better knowledge of the vertical distribution of different fossils, he now determined the beds that had been considered the same from bottom to top were better treated as two separate units. It is a general rule that as an area becomes better known, the stratigraphic breaks—that is, changes or interruptions in deposition—become clearer, and more units are recognized within what had originally been considered a single formation. The more one learns, the finer the subdivisions recognized; this is not unique to geology.

They moved on to Consolation Lake. Walcott examined the fallen blocks in the talus, that is, the broken pieces of rock that tumble down a mountainside, for fossils, but he found few specimens and decided the cliffs were too difficult to climb to reach the Mount Whyte Formation. They moved on to Paradise Valley, arriving in time to get the tents up just before the rain. Despite snow and sleet in the morning, "Mary & Alex went to Lake Louise Chalet for supplies. Chapman & I went up on the horseshoe glacier in the rain & sleet 2 to 6 P.M." (August 17, 1916). Some days in the field are nicer than others.

The next day the rain was sufficient to warrant an underline and two exclamation marks in Walcott's diary. While Walcott cut firewood, wrote letters, and napped, the faithful Alex took five horses to be shod. Moving a bunch that size is no mean feat. Snow squalls and mist were the order of the day following. "After 1 P.M. I went up on the east slope of Mt. Aberdeen. Cold wind & light squalls of mist & hail assisted in inducing—my return at 5 P.M." (August 19, 1916). Some days in the field are even nastier than other days.

Walcott rested, wrote letters, and fussed around camp for a day while Mary painted. The next day he went off to take pictures, only to have the mist roll in. Instead, he measured a section on Mount Temple; it was "a cold, windy, disagreeable day." July weather at Mount Assiniboine was looking better in retrospect. Fortunately, conditions improved again. Mary and Walcott rode over to Lake Agnes so he could reexamine the section of the Mount Whyte Formation that he had measured in 1909. Walcott was fairly confident from the presence of *Olenellus* that the Mount Whyte Formation was Early Cambrian in age. However, Burling had suggested that the genus *Albertella* occurred in the Middle Cambrian and that *Olenellus* occurred with it. In British Columbia *Albertella* had only been found in loose blocks, and until the paleontologists could determine where this form occurred in the section, the argument could not be resolved.

After that little jaunt to Lake Agnes, Mary and Walcott went to the head of Paradise Valley to take photographs. "We should have some good ones as the wind was strong" (August 23, 1916). In addition to haze from the trees, smoke from forest fires was not uncommon. Clear mountain air is not always the norm. They moved via Lake Louise to the head of Wapta Lake; camp twenty-six was near Hector on the Canadian Pacific Railway. Finally came success. "Located 'Albertella' fauna in Mt. Bosworth section about 1 *mi* w.n.w. of Stephen on C.P. Ry. This is the same as Mt. Whyte. Out 7:10 A.M. to 5 P.M." (August 25, 1916).

That December Burling would write, "The inability of either Mr. Walcott or myself, jointly or severally, to find this bed during the years in which search has been prosecuted is due to the fact that its reference to the Lower Cambrian led us largely to confine our efforts to the series of thin beds underlying the Cathedral formation" (Burling 1916, 470). Walcott wrote of its occurrence: "The band of shale is from 7 to 11 feet (2 to 3.3. m) in thickness, and the little terrace formed by it is almost always covered by dirt, broken rock, trees, and brush" (Walcott 1917b, 13–14).

Finding the bed that August seems to be a case of independent discovery, for Walcott later wrote, "The exact stratigraphic position of the typical *Albertella* fauna was unknown to me when I went to the field in June, 1916, although Burling had stated in a general way that he had found it on Mount Bosworth in the Cathedral formation and I had a specimen from the Cathedral limestone of Castle Mountain" (Walcott 1917b, 11). Walcott made his find west of Burling's locality. To make sure there was no misunderstanding, Walcott included a double-page spread of Mount Bosworth in his paper, with all the formations labeled on the photograph.

The day after his discovery on Mount Bosworth, he and Alex went up Ross Lake Canyon and found the *Albertella* zone; everyone was tired, and all rested up for a day. "With Mary & Alex went to Ross Lake canyon. Mary collected fossils & I measured section above on west side of canyon. Found Albertella zone high up" (August 28, 1916). They came back the next day and collected more fossils from loose rocks. After that, Walcott finished his section measuring, while Mary went to Field for supplies.

This trilobite zonation is a complex story, but it was finally unraveled. *Albertella* had been found in loose blocks in Canada. In the Mount Whyte Formation, considered Early Cambrian in age by Walcott, there were isolated trilobite heads that Walcott thought were *Albertella*, or at least closely related, and therefore Early Cambrian. "I did not fully appreciate that trilobites with almost identical cranidia might have a dissimilar thorax and pygidium and belong to quite different genera" (Walcott 1917b, 11). Now, there is a statement to ponder! Formal study of the systematics of animals dates from the work of Linnaeus in 1758. Trilobites had been scientifically examined for more that 150 years, yet here was a fundamentally new concept.

One result of the study of *Bathyuriscus* was to bring this point to the fore, and it was a lesson Walcott never forgot. "Another result was to question the identification of *Albertella* in the Mount Whyte formation as it was based only on specimens of the cranidium" (Walcott 1917b, 11). Until Walcott realized that different trilobites could have similar heads, he was wrong, if for the right reasons.

Meanwhile, Burling had decided that *Albertella* was so different from the Early Cambrian trilobites that it must be younger, and in this he was right. He reviewed the first discovery of *Albertella* in Montana by Walcott in 1905, considered work that he had done east of Salt Lake City, and reviewed the literature of its occurrence elsewhere in the West. It was a thorough piece of work. Burling suggested that collections from Nevada might have been mixed, because of the apparent conflict in age of the trilobites in the assemblage. "Even this conclusion may be wrong, however, and we should be loth [*sic*] to adopt it if it had not already been forecasted by Mr. Walcott" (Burling 1914, 123). Walcott almost never wrote in his reprints, but he scribbled a marginal note that there was no need for Burling to be sorry. When he described the fauna in 1917, he indicated "Mr. Burling's paper was a through and admirable study" (Walcott 1917b, 10).

Because *Albertella* appeared to be a younger form, Burling then suggested that at least the upper part of the Mount Whyte Formation was Middle Cambrian and that *Olenellus* extended into the Middle Cambrian; in that conclusion he was wrong. In some ways, this scientific argument is comparable to that of the 1880s when the stratigraphic position of *Olenellus* had been of concern. It is an indication of what three decades of investigations had produced by way of precision in relative dating by fossils. This argument was not over the position of an entire series of the Cambrian but rather over whether a particular fossil indicated late Early Cambrian or early Middle Cambrian. Walcott would have much to do in the laboratory to document his findings, but the biostratigraphic problem was resolved.

The following spring, after Walcott had completed his detailed study of the *Albertella* fauna, he presented his results at the annual NAS meeting. In the abstract of his talk, he more or less turned Burling's arguments around and, understandably, emphasized the correctness of his own earlier work. "The stratigraphic position of the Mount Whyte formation of the Cambrian system in the Canadian Rockies having been questioned, I searched for evidence of its place during the 1916 field season and found that it forms the upper member of the Lower Cambrian terrane both from the evidence of its contained fauna and its stratigraphic position. This conclusion is supported by the successions of the Cambrian faunas in the Lake Champlain and Lower St. Lawrence valleys" (Walcott 1917c). Just to end the story, the Albertella zone is now accepted as the second time division above the base of the Middle Cambrian (Resser 1933).

A rainy morning provided a bit of rest after the *Albertella* collecting, and a bright afternoon allowed a bit of blackberry picking; Alex took three of the horses for new shoes. Chapman was still in camp, but his zeal for geology seemed to have diminished. The next day Alex and Walcott collected more *Albertella*, and the secretary commented on his excellent assistance.

Several more days of rain stopped that effort; Walcott and Mary went to Field for the day by local train and saw the superintendent of Yoho National Park. "Went up to Ross lake 10 A.M. & dynamited a big block of Albertella rock. Rain came about every hour so we finally gave up & returned cold & wet at 5 P.M." (September 5, 1916). If nothing else, this proves that Walcott was deadly serious about trying to collect as much as possible.

The following morning was nasty and a good time to stay in camp, but Walcott "went up on Mt. Bosworth P.M. & found Albertella shale *in situ*" (September 6, 1916). Mary and Alex helped him collect the next day until heavy rain came. They broke camp, moved to Field, and left fossils and cameras for shipment to Washington. They moved on to Castle Mountain. The trout were biting in the Bow River, but otherwise generally nasty weather made for miserable camping.

They moved on toward Banff and camped at the Buffalo corral. "A busy day attending to errands—making arrangements for hunting trip etc. Mary assisting in every way—A beautiful frosty day" (September 14, 1916). Zoologists at the Museum in Washington thought it would be nice to have a western Canadian moose or two to compare with those in the United States. Walcott summarized this endeavor. "We have now used up 6 beautiful days & not caught a fish or shot at an animal. Country appears to be stripped of game" (September 21, 1916). Mary had sensibly gone off to measure glaciers. Walcott finally got some fish one day, but the next day nothing would bite. They moved back to Banff. "The hunting trip was the most complete fizzle I have ever experienced" (September 25, 1916).

The Walcotts spent a couple of days in Banff with friends, packing and arranging to store the camp equipment. "Mary & I walked out to the Buffalo corral & saw Arthur & Alex Minton start for Morley with horses & wagon" (September 29, 1916). Some of the horses were left in Canada, and Walcott thoughtfully arranged for the USGS to pay for their board. The wagons had to go back to the army.

Alex Mitton later wrote to Walcott about his trip. "I arrived home Wednesday morning and found the weather much more pleasant on this side of the mountains. I lost the rubber robe some where north of Shelby, and the axe east of Townsend, also my raincoat. I stoped [*sic*] over a few days and did the most that I could in helping to sell these horses. They did not sell very good [*sic*], but they were so poor that no one seem [*sic*] to want them."[12]

Walcott wrote back a humorous letter suggesting a rope be purchased to tie down the camp outfit the next time Alex traveled. They settled accounts, Mitton reminding Walcott of a fifty-dollar payment that Walcott had forgotten. The six poor, worn-out horses sold for twenty cents to $1.50 apiece; they deserved better, but that is the fate of working government horses.

The Walcotts left Banff on the 6:00 P.M. train and two days later were in St. Paul, where they admired the state capitol building while waiting for their connection. In Chicago, Walcott made a series of calls at the university. In all, the trip back was fairly swift. Sidney met them at the train station. "Unpacked baggage & in early" (October 3, 1916). "Mr. Walcott arrived day before yesterday, apparently entirely well, though he lost 20 pounds, as did also Mrs. Walcott. His work was greatly retarded and cut off suddenly at the end by cold, rain and snow."[13]

Walcott had one day to catch up on three months' worth of events at the si before the NACA annual meeting, a gathering he judged "interesting." A major concern of the NACA was to establish its own facility for research and not simply serve as a coordinating body. That would be an item high on the agenda for the coming months, inasmuch as Walcott had arranged for congressional funds, despite opposition from the secretary of the navy. Naturally, Walcott was chairman of the site-selection subcommittee (Roland 1985, 31–32).

The following day he was driven to Virginia. Mr. Nunn's scheme for a Texas farm had collapsed, and now he was out with Sidney and Stuart looking for eastern land. Most of the properties he examined were covered by scrub oak and worn out from too many crops; eventually Nunn would settle on a place on the California-Nevada border, hardly prime farm country. A meeting of the NACA executive committee called Walcott back to Washington.

Aeronautics was now running his life. Walcott had to confer with the secretary of the navy and later the assistant secretary of the army. For a switch, he next talked with a CIW botanist about proposed work in South America. The NACA Executive Committee met again to hear formally the reports from the army and navy that Walcott had lined up. Nunn dropped in again. Sidney was also back and available to drive Walcott to Baltimore.

"Motored to Aberdeen [Maryland] & looked over lands to south as a possible aviation proving group. We found an area that is very promising" (October 15, 1916). That Walcott would be so engaged on a Sunday is an indication of the seriousness of the European crisis. Walcott conferred with three other members of the executive committee on the merits of this land, but the owner declined to sell, and the NACA had to look elsewhere. Walcott must have mentioned the site to others, for this later became the U.S. Army's Aberdeen Proving Grounds, a few miles north of Baltimore.

Mary took him north to the monthly meeting of the Friends, after which he went on to New York; regardless of the NACA, the CIW Ex Comm and the RC still demanded his time. He saw cousin Fred before leaving the city. "Dr. Geo. E. Hale called for conference on Nat. Comm. for Research" (October 20, 1916). The National Research Council was beginning to gear up, though even its name was still not clear.

A group of NACA members, Walcott included, took a trip to Buffalo to inspect the Glenn L. Curtiss factory, found it satisfactory, and returned to Washington. The days continued to be crowded with conferences and correspondences, but on the last Saturday of the month, assistance arrived. "Miss Gardiner began work in my laboratory" (October 28, 1916). Finally, Walcott had a personal research assistant again; Resser had been called on repeatedly, but he was on the museum staff and on the other side of the Mall from the Castle. Miss Julia Gardner received her Ph.D. from Johns Hopkins in 1911; after a relatively short time with Walcott she would go off to France to drive an ambulance.

From today's perspective, some might accuse Walcott of sexism for waiting so long in his career to hire a woman; actually, the reverse is true. Miss Julia was one of the first professionally trained women paleontologists in America, if not the first, and Walcott gave her a position worthy of her skill. After the war, she would go on to a long and distinguished career with the Geological Survey. Walcott had a knack for picking talented people; Wilson of 1912 stands out as the one glaring exception, and he might have been suggested by Bassler.

"Puttering around with Cambrian fauna P.M." (November 1, 1916) was the first mention of fossils since Walcott's return from the field. Mary began to take him for walks in Potomac Park on as regular a basis as his schedule permitted; despite the lateness of the season, Walcott continued to sleep on the porch rather than in the house. Sidney came home for a few days until Nunn arrived, and they both went off to Richmond, still looking for land. "I am beginning to make a little headway in research work but it goes very slowly as there are many interruptions" (November 4, 1916).

The Walcotts went downtown to hear the presidential election results, but the outcome was not clear. The following day, it was still not clear that President Wilson was to have a second term. By the time the NACA Executive Committee met the next day, that issue had been decided; this meeting resulted in individual conferences with the secretaries of war and of the navy. The NACA facility, if there was to be one, would have to satisfy both of these worthies. Having smoothed some of the interservice rivalry, Walcott left for the NAS fall meeting. "Dr. Geo. E. Hale presented report on work of Nat. Research Council at evening session" (November 13, 1916). While Walcott was in the Boston area, he became a committee of one to inspect local automobile and aircraft factories and report back to the NACA.

On the way home, he spent a day in New York City. Not only did the Research Corporation and the Carnegie Ex Comm call him, but Sidney was now employed there. The visit was short, for Walcott had to get back to Washington and immediately take the steamer down Chesapeake Bay to Norfolk, Virginia, with other NACA members. The result was agreement on the area that was to become Langley Field.

Walcott got back to Washington in time to leave with an NACA group for Detroit. They looked over the auto plants with an eye toward conversion to airplane manufacture, inspected another possible area for a proving ground, and rushed back to Washington. When he returned, Mary finally had a chance to develop the photographs taken last summer. (When Mary arrived in his life, the number of field photographs Walcott took increased; they were always good throughout his life, but one might argue that the quality improved a little under her artistic eye.)

The Executive Committee of the NACA met again. Notwithstanding this increasing drag on his time, Walcott "planned to take up my investigations of Cambrian faunas" (November 24, 1916). On Thanksgiving Day, "we missed Sidney & Helen but are thankful that they are both well" (November 30, 1916).

December began with a great occasion, a dinner in honor of William Henry Holmes's seventieth birthday. The National Gallery of Art would never be established in its own building during his lifetime—Dr. Holmes continued to work at the Museum into the early 1930s—but it would not be for lack of trying. Meanwhile, his colleagues celebrated his many accomplishments in anthropology with a large volume of essays, privately printed.

There were a few quiet days, allowing a bit of research time, until Walcott "spent most of day at H.R. Committee on Naval Affairs explaining needs of Aviation" (December 7, 1916). The committee needed a great deal of education. Among many items, Walcott had to explain the nature of air as a fluid and why air currents should be studied. Even the simple points had to be explained. The level of committee inquiry did not improve in later years.

> Mr. Roberts: I have read that on some flying machines in use on the Continent they fire through the propeller apparently without hitting the blades of the propeller or injuring it
>
> Dr. Walcott: Yes sir; the rapidity of the motion of the propeller is such that the chance of hitting the blades is slight and the shots are so synchronized through the driving shaft they will not hit the propeller.
>
> The Chairman: How can they arrange them if they go through the sphere of the circle of the propeller blades; how can they arrange them so as not to strike?
>
> Dr. Walcott: That is an engineering problem worked out so that the bullets will not strike the blades, and there is also a device to make the bullets glance off in case of their striking the blades.
>
> The Chairman: It would just be a matter of whether the two came into the same space at the same time?
>
> Dr. Walcott: Yes, sir. (Walcott 1917d, 533)

Congressional hearings can produce some monumental inanities. They can also, occasionally, produce an insightful comment. When the chairman asked Walcott about commercial possibilities, he remarked that there had been an increase in the safety, stability, and speed, of airplanes to the point that "it is almost inevitable that for certain purposes they will be used. Just to what extent is difficult to say now, any more than you could have said in 1890 to what extent the automobile would be used" (Walcott 1917d, 519).

Walcott wanted NACA money appropriated in three broad categories, not itemized. "I was Director of the United States Geological Survey for some fifteen years, and during that time we had many 'lump sums' as they were called, and I found that we could get more effective work and get more out of the money by arranging it in that way than we could possibly get if the salaries were fixed by law" (Walcott 1917d, 531).

Walcott eventually got his money, and with minimum congressional strings. The next day he dropped the NACA papers off at the White House, to ensure that the appropriation got an extra little push. That evening he was involved with the nitrate-production problem; the war was pressing ever closer. Cousin Fred came to town for a Red Cross gathering, which Walcott addressed. (Shortly Fred would be deeply involved with Herbert Hoover in relief efforts; years later he would serve one term as a senator from Connecticut.) After the Red Cross came the meetings of the SI regents and the CIW Ex Comm. Just keeping track of Walcott's schedule must have been a formidable job for his secretaries.

The annual CIW meeting brought more complications to Walcott's busy life. "I was elected Chairman of the Executive Committee" (December 15, 1916)—it has been said somewhere that the way to get a job done is to give it to a busy man. Stuart came home for the holidays, and Dr. Stratton dropped in to talk over NRC activities.

That fall, Walcott had summarized some of the developments in Washington. "Just now I am somewhat puzzled by various agencies the President has appointed for mobilizing the technical and scientific men of the country. Between the Naval Consulting Board, the Council for National Defense, and the National Research Council, there is more or less a duplication of effort. There should be somewhere a clearinghouse, so as to avoid duplication."[14] Walcott put Stratton at ease and resolved one problem of duplication rapidly: members of the NACA constituted simultaneously the NRC committee on aviation. That way, any inquiries or problems directed to the NRC came to the correct group immediately. This sounds simple and elementary—it even causes a smile for those who are not familiar with organizations—but it was profound. There are many empire builders both inside and outside Washington, and with this stroke one potential empire was eliminated. Only someone like Walcott, who was determined not to increase his own empire, could cut such a Gordian knot.

The day before Christmas, Sidney arrived with his fiancée Helen and her family. "Helen (2d) appears to be a capable, fine type of woman" (December 24, 1916). It was a correct first impression. After Christmas, Walcott planned for the Geological Society of America meeting and looked forward to attending with

Mary, but a cold knocked him out. The meeting was in Albany. It would have been an old home week for Walcott, and he had been going to talk about the *Albertella* fauna. Burling was giving a paper, and this would have provided a chance for them to discuss their different views.

In addition, the New York State Museum was opening, and it would have fine to reminisce about the old days in the Agricultural and Geological Hall under Prof. James Hall. As it was, his talk, read in his absence, did tend to glamorize the past just a little. "Fifty years ago a boy of central New York looked to this Capital City for inspiration and guidance in those things that were to shape his career. Through the notable publications of the scientific and educational organizations of the State and the generous aid of its able investigators and scholars, that youth received more than he had dreamed or hoped for and grew to respect and honor his native commonwealth for its efficiency in scientific research" (Walcott 1917e, 19).

The cold that laid him low improved enough so that at the end of the year Mary dragged him to the National Training School for Girls to hear the choir. Walcott summed up the year: "The year 1916 has been a happy one with us at home but the European war & the children being away has cast a shadow all year through. Sidney has graduated from Cornell University in June & is now working in New York. Helen is working in a French war hospital (since July), Stuart is studying at Princeton University. May god [*sic*] watch over them in 1917 & may He bring peace & joy to the warring nations of Europe" (December 31, 1916). This was another set of wishes not to be fulfilled.

The New Year was quiet enough. The Walcotts spent the morning in his laboratory in the castle, had a late breakfast with friends, and made a few calls. January 2 was more lively; the five-day National Parks conference began in the Museum; that evening Walcott hosted a reception in the National Gallery of Art, one floor up from the auditorium (Yochelson 1985). The Museum was the site of many conferences, but this one must have been fairly close to Walcott's heart. During the 1890s, Walcott had investigated conditions in Yosemite and Yellowstone National Parks and had reported to the secretary of the interior. He wrote another report to Interior Secretary Franklin K. Lane in the fall of 1915 after his season in Yellowstone.

The National Park Service was authorized in 1916, but after the appropriation bills had already been passed, so that it was a bureau without money. In November 1916, Steven "Mather proceeded to make arrangements for another national-parks conference, the biggest yet. It was at the bottom only an elaborate pep meeting, but since the Park Service appropriation was due to come up for study, that was what the strategy called for" (Shankland 1951, 108). A biographer of

Mather, the first director of the National Park Service, lists a host of important people who talked but does not mention Secretary Walcott.

Walcott spoke January 3 on "National Parks as a Scientific Asset." "When I came in I told our chairman that the subject assigned to me was one which could be dwelt upon for an hour or more with ample illustrations or descriptions, or limited to five, or seven minutes, and under the circumstances I prefer the five minutes. I have prepared a brief note, and I am going to read a paragraph at the beginning and a paragraph at the end, with some comments as to the first" (Walcott 1917f, 112).

Walcott then proceeded to extemporize about the territorial surveys. He mentioned John Wesley Powell, William Henry Holmes, earlier geologists at the Grand Canyon, and his own work in that area and in Yellowstone and Glacier National Parks, along with references to the investigations of other geologists in the West. He read his last paragraph and ended: "Whether we will or no, the scientific method and divine spirit must rule humanity in the future, and as a great source of training and inspiration the national parks will be a mighty asset, both scientific and spiritual, through the centuries" (Walcott 1917f, 115).

It was a good speech, and the long conference was an overall success, in that Congress appropriated money for the National Park Service; the agency has been busy ever since. (The strain of organizing this meeting, however, was the last straw for an overworked Mather, who immediately after the conference suffered a nervous breakdown that lasted for months.) Associated with the conference was a fine art show of paintings of national parks, though Walcott has never received any credit for assisting with that either. The secretary has the final say on what the Museum may display and who may use the auditorium. Walcott's tenure as secretary was most enlightened, and almost every major group that asked to use the auditorium was accommodated.

The meeting was tiring, yet there was little prospect for rest in the future. "Meeting of Ex. Com Nat. Council for Research 10 A.M. to 3:15 P.M. with Military Def[ence] Comm. I was elected chairman of latter" (January 6, 1917). The new duties did not affect Walcott's attending church, but afterward he was at his office working on NRC papers. The Walcotts gave a dinner for the Military Defense Committee, "Genl's Gorgas, Crozier, Col. Squier, Admirals Taylor, Griffen, Drs. Gatewood, Stratton, Mannino, Marvine" (January 9, 1917). All of them Walcott knew well.

Despite the fighting in Europe, some groups there attempted to continue to function with a semblance of order. Early in January, Walcott was notified that the Royal Geographical Society of London had elected him an honorary member, "in consideration of his eminent service to geography." His dramatic panoramas of the Canadian Rockies must have had something to do with this. Nice as this recognition was, it was a minor ripple in the stream of mail, calls, and interviews.

The NACA Executive Committee met again, using up most of a day. The appropriations hearings took only two hours, and much of the remainder of the day was spent with Frank Springer. Springer was a lawyer who had become interested in fossil crinoids and had an enormous collection of these stalked animals, called sea lilies. In 1912 he had retired from law practice in New Mexico and moved east to become a research associate of the Museum. The fossil collection and his portrait came to the Museum after his death in 1927. Springer had stipulated that his collection should be placed, and his portrait hung, in a separate room, and his wish has been honored. The Museum hoped that the collection would be accompanied by an endowment; it turned out to be smaller than anticipated, but such is life.

Walcott was doing his duty as secretary in cultivating Springer as he had Freer, but there was little time for such activity; the tail was really wagging the dog. "As a whole the extra work of the Aeronautical Committee takes much of my spare time usually given to research work" (January 16, 1917). There was no prospect whatsoever of relief from NACA duties. The matter of the bill to recover the money Freer had paid in taxes, and an effort to transfer paintings from the Capitol to the National Gallery of Art, took more time. Admiral George Dewey died, the government was closed, and Walcott was able to get in an uninterrupted full day in his laboratory.

Walcott completed a short report on his summer's activities. He looked again at the Appalachian Cambrian trilobites with a far more critical eye. On the social side, he gave a dinner for fourteen in honor of Secretary of the Navy Josephus Daniels. Afternoon walks with Mary, church on Sunday, and a visit from an eighty-one-year-old former neighbor at New York Mills provided diversions from the grind. The month ended. "Mary & I gave afternoon tea to about 350 members of Smithsonian staff & their families" (January 31, 1917). Such an event would never have occurred while Professor Langley was secretary, and the staff, especially the older employees, appreciated their invitations.

From this social event, it was back to business in the strictest sense of the word. "Meeting of Aeronautical Committee 10:30 to 1:20 in relation to aeronautic patent situation" (February 1, 1917). Shortly after Curtiss had lost his patent appeal in count, the Wright Company had been purchased from Orville (Crouch 1989). Since the new management of Wright-Martin held the basic patents for a flying machine, anyone who built an airplane was infringing. There was money to be made in enforcing the patent rights, and the company was bound to make it. The result was that not very many airplanes were being built, especially in the light of potential need in time of war.

While a resolution of the patent situation was simmering, social life in Washington went on. The Walcotts had a small dinner in honor of Vice President Thomas R. Marshall. The next evening was an event even more to Walcott's taste, the stag dinner for Colonel Rizer, who as the USGS chief clerk had long kept the USGS on course and the funds in order through several generations of young field geologists. Rizer knew that his function was to maintain the organization with a minimum of disturbance to those who were actually out studying geology. If he had a motto, it was that paperwork was only a means to an end, not an end in itself.

Another meeting of the NACA brought Walcott back from pleasant memories of the past to present-day realities. This was followed by a special Sunday meeting at his house. The patent pot had gone from simmer to boil, and a solution had been agreed upon by the NACA. The next step was to convince the various parties of the merit of the plan. "Called on Secty of War Baker, Sect'y of Navy Daniels & at White House *en re* legislation for clearing up patent situation on aircraft manufacturers" (February 5, 1917).

That evening, Walcott presided at the local archaeological society. Just when it would seem the limit had been reached, the breadth of his activities widens still farther, leaving even less time for his central interests: somewhere during this busy month, Walcott received notice he had been elected a corresponding member of the Reale Academia della Science dell' Instituto di Bologna (Royal Academy of the Institute of Science at Bologna). Despite their preoccupation with the war, scientists in Italy saw the merit in his work. That was all well and good, but if one person never rested on his laurels, it was Walcott. This was yet another certificate to put on the growing pile of honorary memberships.

With the patent situation moving forward, the next day was devoted to the NRC Military Committee. After that, the Naval Committee of the House of Representatives had to hear of the plan to break the patent logjam. Then it was off to New York City for the Aero Show. Walcott presided at a session on scientific developments, looked at the Curtiss autocar, and did a great deal of behind-the-scenes discussion concerning the patent situation. He came back to his office for yet another gathering of the NACA Executive Committee on patents; the situation was serious. "Read papers as war with Germany is close at hand" (February 11, 1917). Notwithstanding the various committees, memoranda, and items to pursue, he actually got in a few hours looking at Cambrian trilobites. That braced him up for another full day discussing NRC activities with J. J. Carty and Stratton.

The early days of the NRC laid the foundation for explosive growth in the spring of 1917. The fertilizer needed for growth of almost any human endeavor is money, and the money trail here is interesting. The NAS did not have two nickels to rub together and essentially gave the NRC only moral support. Before the NRC could receive any government money for investigations, it had to be firmly established. To get the NRC going, the SI provided funding, for it could do as it desired with its private money. However, the Smithsonian was about as well off financially as the National Academy. Therefore, with the support of the Ex Comm, President Woodward of the CIW gave a grant to the Smithsonian, which in turn passed it on to NRC. Actually, the CIW itself had little money to spare, money that was not committed to its research programs. Fortunately, when asked for financial assistance, the Carnegie Corporation in New York City provided a significant sum to CIW. Secretary Walcott was officially the final link in the chain, but one could safely bet that it was he who had forged the other links.

There is even a bit more to the beginning of the NRC story. When diplomatic relations with Germany were severed, Hale telegraphed President Wilson from California officially offering the NRC's services. There was no reply. In 1916, Wilson had established a council on national defense headed by the secretary of war and consisting of three other cabinet officers. On March 1, the Council for National Defense finally replied to Hale, and the NRC was really in business. Pres. William Welch is given credit for intercession with the council, and indeed, he did labor to that end (Cochrane 1978, 222). On the other hand, Welch was based in Baltimore, whereas Walcott was on the scene in Washington.

According to some sources, Walcott would call on a person, chat about a subject, and steer the conversation until the person agreed with Walcott's view. Just before leaving, Walcott would pull out a paper and mention that he had taken the liberty of jotting down some points that might be put into the forthcoming memorandum. Without trying to take any credit away from Foreign Secretary George Ellery Hale or President Welch, the NAS vice president probably played a major role in steering the NRC toward its war work. There is no documentation that it was Walcott who had the NRC acknowledged formally, but Walcott almost never wrote in his diary the subject of discussion with the people he met. So much for a revised, speculative history of the NRC from April 1916 to March 1917.

In mid-February, while the Council for National Defense still had the fate of NRC in its hands, Walcott testified before a Senate committee on aeronautical appropriations and left Washington on the midnight train. (He might have saved money in the long run by having a permanent berth on the train.) Walcott took care of CIW Ex Comm business, for the affairs of the Carnegie still required just as much attention as in the past. He met with Freer for an hour and no doubt told him of efforts to recover the tax money. The millionaire was continuing to buy objects for his collection and wanted to show his latest treasures. Business of the RC and discussions with chemists in New York took another day. Walcott returned to Washington to spend the day at, first, a meeting of the NRC Military Committee, and second, a meeting of the NRC Executive Committee. Crisis or no crisis, this is a poor way to spend a Saturday. To end the week of meetings, or perhaps start a new one, after church there was a long session of the Carnegie Board of Trustees.

Fortunately, the following week was a little better. "A quiet, busy day at the Smithsonian. Worked on *Albertella* fauna paper at intervals. Hope to complete paper this week" (February 1917). Then came the annual meeting of the GWMA, still trying to raise money to build on the site given them by Congress in 1913. In 1916, thanks to their Washington connections, the deadline for raising funds had been extended to 1917. Fortunately, the Congress this session had been persuaded to extend the deadline for two more years and had halved the money to be raised for the building fund to $500,000. Even with this extra boost, however, the GWMA could not meet its goal.

The Washington Monument Society met on Washington's birthday, and again this was a quiet day for Walcott. The pace picked up with a visit from J. J. Carty. After that came an informal NACA gathering to worry over the patent situation; even with this morning meeting, Walcott made it to church services. "Resumed duties at the Smithsonian. Mail, routine & a little investigative work on Ptarmigan formation paper. Latter about ready for press" (February 26, 1917). Unfortunately for the progress of the sciences of geology, paleontology and stratigraphy were once more shouldered aside. One result of the NACA involvement was a host of callers on diverse subjects. He ended the month listening politely to a man who had invented the perfect ignition system, ultimately sending him off to the Bureau of Standards; this inventor was only one noted by Walcott, but there were many others.

Walcott began March conversing with an authentic scientist, a chemist from the DuPont Corporation, to discuss the problem of producing smokeless powder. He went to Capitol Hill to listen to the debate about arming merchant ships and two days later attended the inauguration of President Wilson for his second term; the man who had been elected because he had kept America out of war was about to lead America into conflict. Speaking of switching from one subject to another, the day after the inauguration, Walcott attended the Church of the Covenant trustees' meeting, followed by a meeting of the NRC Military Committee. The next day brought the annual meeting for the directors of the Ontario Apartment House, followed by his taking physics professor Michael Pupin to the office of Secretary of the Navy Daniels. Then the NACA met again.

It was a busy week, but one without focus, as Walcott phrased it. On Sunday, aeronautical matters kept him from church.

"Routine matters & a little research work on the Mount Whyte fauna kept me busy during the day. A few callers. The wet chilly weather keeps me stiff & achey [*sic*] but Mary & I get a walk morning & evening despite snow & wind" (March 12, 1917). Two days later, Walcott was again devoting his time to the problem of aeronautical patents. Then came the problem of the nitrate shortage. "Last evening Dr. Cottrell spent with me talking over the general situation in relation to chemical preparedness. They [apparently Walcott meant the military] are still lame, halting, and blind in many things, though making some fairly rapid progress. The chemical industry is outside my field, but as chairman of the Military Committee of the National Research Council many matters of general interest come to me. I am giving more time to the work of the National Advisory Committee for Aeronautics."[15]

It is curious how Walcott's involvement with Telluride Power and his general knowledge of electricity, combined with his respect for Cottrell, came together to provide that scientist the basic information he needed. Understandably, no one would associate the later activity of building a nitrate-extraction plant at Muscle Shoals, Alabama, with Cambrian trilobites. The random arrangement of events plays a bigger part in human affairs than most people care to acknowledge. Even with the Military Committee on his shoulders, Walcott was both trying to arrange a field season and reporting on the status of an unusual duty he had undertaken as secretary, indicated in the last paragraph of a letter.

If we do not take the northern trip we will be puttering about very much as last summer, but giving more time to the region very near Field.

Do you think it possible to get two good horses, broken to ride and pack, that would correspond to Mrs. Walcott's horse "Buck" and to my gray mare "Cricket" as to size and weight? They should be from 4 to 6 years old and cost $125, more or less, if good for the purpose.

We have had a rather strenuous time here. I am Chairman of two Committees interested in getting our national defense into shape, and also have the routine work of the Institution to look after. We made an arrangement with the Park authorities so that we have five mountain sheep that came down from Banff, at our Zoological Park here, and Mr. Karkin writes me that two carloads of elk from Yellowstone National Park have reached Banff.[16]

In the midst of these matters so far removed from geology, Walcott received word that he was to receive the Prix Gaudry. This medal, awarded by the Societé Géologique de France (Geological Society of France), represents a major achievement. The outcrop of Cambrian rocks in France is relatively small and has never been of prime interest to French geologists, yet Walcott's scientific accomplishments had been so outstanding that the French geologic community recognized its merits. The medal was actually awarded in late April; the citation, after a review of Walcott's life and accomplishments, ended on a personal note, acknowledging the service of Helen Walcott in a hospital (Margerie 1917).

The honor was hardly noted before George Ellery Hale and J. J. Carty were in town wrestling with the problem of closer cooperation between the scientific and engineering communities. Various aeronautical matters kept Walcott moving for four days. Then came the culmination, perhaps Walcott's single most significant contribution to the war effort. "Meeting of Aircraft Association and Nat. Ad. Com. Aeronautics 10 A.M. to 1 [and] 2:30 to 6:20 P.M. A very successful and important meeting" (March 22, 1917).

The complex story of aircraft patents has been nicely summarized in the official NACA history (Roland 1985, 38–39). In brief, in January the army and navy turned to the NACA for help in resolving the patent difficulty. Walcott acquired leverage by asking President Wilson to support an appropriation of a million dollars to acquire the patents. Wilson approved, and this was why Walcott appeared before the naval appropriations committee. From the beginning of the request for funds to their authorization took little more than a month.

At a meeting on March 22, Walcott assured industry representatives that the NACA viewed condemnation proceedings to obtain the patents for the government as a last resort, but he left no doubt that the NACA had the power and the will to take that route, if necessary. With that, Walcott finally caught the attention of the warring parties, and this led to serious discussion of a cross-licensing agreement, such as had been worked out by the automobile industry. Two days later, he reported success to the secretary of war. Since no one had the slightest idea how much the agreement would cost, Walcott suggested the funds appropriated be used to buy the patents. Before the government could act, however, war would be declared.

The day after this closed-door meeting, the *New York Times* ran a long article in which Walcott talked about the need to build two thousand planes a year, and how unsatisfactory the support the government had given the aircraft industry had been in the past. There was not a word about the possibility of patents being taken over by the government.

The prospect of great profits in royalties raised itself, and the NACA Subcommittee on Patents, whose chairman happened to be Charles D. Walcott, was called in again. The various parties were soothed, cajoled, threatened, or whatever it took to bring accord and place a ceiling on the amount to be received in royalty payments. While Walcott was away in the field, final agreement was reached. "It is expected that this agreement will bring about harmony and cooperation in the industry, and that it will aid materially in the progress of the art and the quantity production of aircraft" (Roland 1985, 41). That is exactly what happened. The one nasty postscript is that the Aeronautical Society of America objected, and nothing that was said or done would mollify the organization. Nonetheless, Walcott and his subcommittee had satisfied the main parties and ensured that airplanes would be manufactured in record numbers.

Sunday saw Walcott at breakfast and dinner meetings at his house, with church service sandwiched between. The NACA met again; its meetings were taking on the character of weekly events. "At my office nearly all day. Correspondence, interviews & a *very* little time for Cambrian work. Aeronautic Committee matters take more time each week" (March 30, 1917). His next day was taken up by a meeting under Chairman Hale of the chairmen of all the NRC committees. Late in the afternoon, he squeezed in a meeting with Glenn Curtiss and, still later, the recently promoted Gen. George O. Squier. At home finally, he found that Mary had arranged a surprise birthday party; no doubt about it, she was a good partner.

Breakfast meetings now became more or less routine as the foreign situation worsened. "A mixed up day. At my office & aeronautic committee office & office of Council of National Defense" (April 4, 1917). After that, the next day was hardly any better, some of it being spent with the secretary of war and Howard Coffin; Coffin had been the driving force behind the Liberty engine.

"War declared with Germany" (April 6, 1917).

The NACA changed from a group concerned with preparedness to a wartime agency. At its suggestion the Aircraft Production Board was established. Meanwhile, during the winter and spring, Stuart had been wrestling with his future; he wanted to be involved in the conflict. His father suggested he join the ambulance corps, but Stuart decided that that was not for him. Although Walcott wanted Stuart to stay in college, more than a hundred of his classmates had left, and Princeton University decided that seniors who went to serve their country would be guaranteed their degrees. "Stuart entered service as volunteer asst. Signal Service" (April 10, 1917). Stuart began his wartime efforts by helping to inspect aircraft engines.

In Washington, Walcott became involved with uniforms; airplanes were going to fly at ever-higher altitudes, and the cold would become a serious matter. Glenn Curtiss came to dinner, and they discussed sundry matters concerning aircraft production. There followed a shifting of gears at the NAS council. When the spring meeting opened the next day, he "gave paper on Ptarmigan & Mt. Whyte formations" (April 16, 1917). There was other business besides science to transact at the annual meeting, for during the past fall, President Welch had served notice that he intended to resign.

Consider the following: "Welch was on the boards of half a dozen institutions calling on his energies, including the Carnegie Institution of Washington and the Rockefeller Institute for Medical Research, as well as the Medical Advisory Board of the President's Council for National Defense. As he neared his sixty-seventh birthday, he was also contemplating resigning his professorship of pathology at Johns Hopkins in order to give more time to the School of Hygiene and Public Health that was under construction there" (Cochrane 1978, 217). No doubt about it, Dr. Welch was a busy man.

Under such a load, few could fault Welch for stepping down from the last two years of his term as president. At the last day of the annual meeting, "Council Nat. Acad. Scie. 9–9:45. I was elected president of the Academy for six years" (April 18, 1917). Whereas Welch was "nearly his sixty-seventh birthday," Walcott had already passed that milestone. A comparison of Dr. Welch's administrative load with that which Walcott carried would be in poor taste; a comparison of the research efforts of Walcott compared to those of Welch would be in equally poor taste. Just as the issue of how the Council for National Defense came to approve the NRC is left for others to evaluate, so should this subject also be left open. One can state with reasonably certainty that Walcott did not seek this office to bolster his ego.

From his new presidency of the NAS, Walcott went on to the semiannual meeting of the NACA. After that, it was a meeting of the CIW Ex Comm, which thankfully this time was in Washington, for he had then to go to the NRC executive committee meeting. Incredibly, despite this schedule, that Saturday Walcott found the time and the will to study some trilobites from the Mount Whyte Formation. Church was a welcome relief, even with a Sunday business meeting following.

The NACA had plans for a laboratory building at Langley Field, and it was Walcott who roughed out the first sketches. An important chemical colleague from the Research Corporation, Elan Hooker—the Hooker Chemical Company had been in business for years—came to Washington with a scheme to organize an army troop in honor of Roosevelt, much as Roosevelt had organized his "Rough Riders" for the Spanish-American War; Walcott disarmed Hooker without hurting his feelings.

On the immediate home front, Sidney was in the Reserve Officers Corps and was off to camp at Plattsburgh, New York. Walcott's youngest had decided what direction to take. "Stuart went to Newport News [Virginia] to begin aviation training" (April 30, 1917). After his first flight, Stuart signed up for a hundred minutes of instruction. This hardly qualified him to fly, but at least he learned the rudiments.

As more or less a counterpart to NRC activities in Europe, French and English scientists came to Washington, and Walcott helped them get settled. If there was one theme of those hectic days, it was meetings. "Presided at joint meeting of EX Com NRC, United Engineering societies, & Military Comm of NRC" (May 3, 1917). He gave a dinner for Arthur Balfour and the British Scientific Mission. He conducted innumerable interviews and formally introduced the French foreign mission to the NACA. Near the end of the week, he slipped off to New York, where the CIW Ex Comm continued to function. He saw Sidney briefly, talked to shipping people to get a special pass, and that Saturday escorted Helen off her ship and home to Washington.

While Walcott was in New York, his fourth SMC volume started with two papers. The first is relatively short, but in it he established the Ptarmigan Peak Formation between the underlying Mount Whyte and the overlying Cathedral. This provided a framework for the large work that dealt with the *Albertella* fauna in British Columbia and Montana. A major geologic loose end had been tied up.

Back in Washington, the NACA began hunting for a building and site so that airplanes and engines could be displayed to the foreign missions. It was Walcott's chore to find such a place, not an easy task in the booming capital city. Eventually, the SI secretary offered space behind the Castle, and an aircraft hanger due to be erected at Bolling Field in southeast Washington was diverted to the space.

Throughout this part of May, Walcott was sitting for a portrait. Trying to keep up with his subject must have driven the artist, Ossip Perlma, a bit frantic. On the middle day of May, Walcott posed, cleared up his mail, and had hours to devote to Cambrian trilobites before he said goodbye to his youngest, who was leaving for New York. Benjamin Stuart Walcott, born July 8, 1896, and not quite twenty-one, was off to war. On May 24 he boarded a ship and sailed off to become a French army aviator.

Decoration Day was quiet; Walcott had a full day in his laboratory, while Mary painted flowers. Then it was back to business as usual, and after a full day of meetings to start the month of June, Walcott was on the midnight train to New York. He had his usual round of meetings to attend and people to meet. An extra incentive was that Helen had enrolled in a training program for nurses at New York Presbyterian Hospital; France had changed her. Walcott and Mary met en route and attended the Friends meeting at Haverford, Pennsylvania.

Walcott wrote to the vice president of the Canadian Pacific Railway. "I am hesitating about going west this year, as there are so many matters to be attended to in connection with preparation for our part in the war. However, all of them that come in my jurisdiction will be left in the hands of capable men, and I shall return in the fall with renewed energy to take them up."[17]

One June day in Washington brought a crush of activities greater than any to date. A meeting involving the Aircraft Production Board was followed by a welcome to 2,300 Confederate Civil War veterans. A little time could still be stolen for research, and before going to the field, Walcott was "endeavoring at odd moments to get notes on Lower Cambrian Ptychoparia" (June 11, 1917).

Legislation was pending to increase the role of the Signal Corps, and Walcott had to keep his finger on that pulse. For those who do not know their aviation history, it was the Signal Corps that controlled the army's airplanes at that time. Two days later, the NAS president held a reception in the Smithsonian Castle for members of the French Scientific Mission. Both French and English scientists spoke, and the event was considered significant enough to be mentioned in the *Annual Report*.

Stuart arrived safely in France, relieving one anxiety. Fred Walcott, now more or less permanently in Washington, attended church with his cousin. Helen came down from New York, ill. Walcott decided that she should go west with them; indeed, it may have been her generally worn-down state that had been the deciding factor in his going out that summer. There was the standard frantic rush to wind up affairs. On the last full day in Washington, Walcott had to accept a statue of Robert Emmett for the National Gallery of Art; war or no war, President Wilson was in the audience.

Mary and Walcott went to New York City and stayed at his favorite Hotel Belmont. "We took breakfast with Sidney & Helen. Attended wedding of Sidney & Helen Louise Davis at 12 o'clock. 437 Clinton Ave. Brooklyn N.Y. We are very happy in the event as she is a fine woman. Left N—Y— at 7:45 P.M. with Mary & Helen for Montreal thus bringing to an end [an] eventful day" (June 30, 1917). It was also the end of an eventful fiscal year.

After checking into the Windsor Hotel, they spent the day in Montreal, and naturally Walcott took Mary to the Redpath Museum. Friends called in the afternoon, but they got a bit of rest before boarding the evening sleeper. Walcott talked to permanently disabled Canadian soldiers and was further incensed at the war. After three and a half days on the train, they arrived in Banff.

"Alex Mitton met us & we went to camp at the Buffalo ranch of the Banff Park" (July 5, 1917). The weather was fine. Walcott bought four horses and picked up two more that had been pastured since last season. They visited friends in Banff. The three days in camp getting organized seemed to lift all burdens. It was like old times, and for a while at least, the war could be ignored.

5

The Frantic Years (1917–1919): The Notion of Giving a Job to a Busy Man to Ensure That It Is Done May Be a Good Idea, but It Can Be Carried to Excess

> A society that spends many billions of dollars on a varied cornucopia of deleterious trivia, to say nothing of untold billions on military outlays and mind-numbing diversions, assumes an uncomfortable moral position in deciding that science—even big and expensive science—is a game that's not worth the candle.
>
> —N. Rescher

"After many vicissitudes we got out of town at 12:30 P.M. Paul the new horse bucked his pack off twice[,] Pat & Jack wished to return home etc. Camp about 1 mi east of Massive [railroad siding] side track of C.[anadian] P.[acific] R[ailwa]y. A hot tedious day & all dead tired at night" (July 9, 1917). It had been a difficult first twelve miles. (Railway men give names to sidings, water towers, and other points of interest only to them, hence names like "Massive," which do not appear on maps.)

Three more camps in four days, forty-three miles by horse, and they were at Lake O'Hara, near the foot of McArthur Pass. "A beautiful camp with fine water wood & pasture for horses. The log house & surroundings for tourists are in most disgraceful condition" (July 13, 1917). Even in the rare places where accommodations were present, Walcott preferred to be under canvas. Helen had tarried in Banff but caught up with them, bringing mail and fresh fruit; as a counterpoint, Alex went to Field and packed in ten pounds of dynamite.

The fossil collecting began, Walcott concentrating on beds above the Albertella zone. He then gradually worked down through the underlying rocks and measured another geologic section of the Mount Whyte Formation. Before leaving Washington, Walcott had completed yet another manuscript, this one on the Mount Whyte fossils; it was published in September while he was still in British Columbia. "One of the striking features of the 28 genera and 60 species of the Mount Whyte fauna is the presence of several species common to it and to the Lower Cambrian fauna of Newfoundland and the Champlain Valley of Vermont" (Walcott 1917f, 65).

The rationale for additional collecting from the Lower Cambrian during this field season is given in a footnote. "It must be recalled that all the collections were obtained incidental to stratigraphic work and are necessarily a very imperfect representation of the entire fauna at each locality and horizon; future thorough collections should yield much additional data" (Walcott 1917f, 63). Walcott probably had as many fossils from the Mount Whyte Formation as would be collected by the next generation of field men, or more, but he knew that more collecting eventually yields better specimens and occasionally a rare form.

For this paper, Walcott also gave due credit for assistance. He acknowledged an artist, Miss Frances Weiser, who for years had been touching up details that were not clear on the photographs. "The drafts of the description of species of *Ptychoparia* for this and other papers to follow were drawn up by Dr. Julia Gardner, who studied the material with great care" (Walcott 1917f, 67). This was high praise and as good as any he ever heaped on Mr. Burling.

Having spelled out the need for more fieldwork, Walcott did it. "With Mary went up to McArthur Pass & up on the N.W. shoulder of Mt. Shaffer. Measured section of Mt. Whyte & Ptarmigan formations. A strong hot west wind made the day most uncomfortable & tedious" (July 18, 1917). Although his field methods are not spelled out, commonly Walcott would measure a section, sampling bits of rock as he went up from the base. He would indicate the promising horizons, and the assistant, if there was one, would then devote time to hammering rock at those places to break out fossils. Many sedimentary rocks are unfossiliferous or poorly fossiliferous, so one simply collects from selected intervals.

They moved camp to Hector, stopping en route at the Alpine Club camp. A day was wasted trying to get up the north side of Mount Stephen on a washed-out trail. The next day they were at Popes Peak, but the Mount Whyte Formation was poorly exposed. It was time to take a day's rest. "Moved camp from Hector to our old Burgess Pass camp 3000 feet above Field B.C. Helen & I went to Field by train. Found the old camp site dirty & littered with tin cans old bough beds etc. Cleaned up & settled by 6 P.M." (July 23, 1917). They would stay here for almost two months. It was Walcott's last major season of quarrying the Burgess Shale.

"Went up to Burgess fossil quarry & worked on rocks left out in 1913. Mary & I collected two pkgs about 150 specimens" (July 24, 1917). A great deal of rock had been left in camp in 1913 to weather, which make the shale easier to split.

However, tourists had broken some pieces and dragged off others, so that only a few good *Marrella* were obtained. William Stevenson came to camp, but he was now a fire warden and was not available for quarrying work. A William Oke from Field was employed. On his first day in camp it snowed, so it back to Field for Oke for several days. To fill in the time, Walcott read proofs of the Mount Whyte fauna paper and wrote letters, including one to Chief Clerk Dorsey. "Will you not have the old Kubki tent that should be in the store room on table rolled tightly put in mail sack & sent as you send mail bags of paper. Also get from Mollie at house 2 thermos bottles & send by mail securely packed. Hailing this morning so we will need a cup of hot tea or coffee up at the quarry wh[ich] is 800 feet above camp. Have decided to take a section out at quarry. It will be the last probably for all time."[1]

Punctuation and spelling out were not for Walcott when he was in a hurry. His concluding prediction was not correct, but it stood for half a century.

Walcott wrote to Washington again two days later. Twine to tie the bundles of fossils had been accidentally left in Banff, so Mr. Dorsey was asked to forward several balls. The ten inches of new snow was melting, but he and Alex would have to shovel out a six-foot drift in the quarry. Walcott proposed to take out a small section in the center of the quarry. If that yielded good fossils, the center would be quarried deeper into the mountainside. "I do not think anyone else will try it as it involves blasting down for 24 feet. Only the center of the quarry has given any good things."[2] He concluded by noting that Mrs. Walcott was busy painting her ninth species of wildflower for the season.

A day after the serious work began, Walcott hired another hand, a Mr. Mc-Connell. They kept at it fairly steadily, and at the end of four days, including a Sunday in camp, McConnell had had enough of fossil collecting. "Raining during night. Cleared up 9 A.M. & Alex, Oke, & I went up to quarry. Mary came up at luncheon time. We found a few good fossils & a lot of average—service for exchange" (August 10, 1917). Because the Museum had no money to purchase collections, the more common Burgess Shale fossils were exchanged with Ward's Natural Science Establishment, which then gave the museum other fossil material. Today, the thought of giving away any of the Burgess Shale fossils boggles the mind, but at the time it was one way the Museum had to increase its collections.

The work went on and on, commonly during ten-hour days. For evening relaxation, Mary painted while Helen did embroidery; any friction was long past. Commonly the ladies took turns riding up to the quarry with lunch and staying to wrap fossils. "Mary went down to Field & bro't up mail etc. Helen came up at lunch time to get photo of 'Granny' the mountain squirrel" (August 13, 1917).

The N.Y. Times is coming thru quite regulary now but often much worn on edges. At the quarry we will finish take out a small section marked

(d). If that is good may take a section (a) wh will be very difficult. I do not think any one else will try it as it involves blasting down for 24 feet. Only the center of the, quarry has given any good things this. Walcott is painting on her ninth species of wild flower for this reason. Before the man great banks & slopes of wild flowers were all about us. Will write Mr. Rathbun Monday. Yrs—
W. D. Walcott.

Part of a July 29, 1917, letter from Walcott to Chief Clerk Harry Dorsey, sketching his plans for a new excavation at the Burgess Shale quarry. Smithsonian Institution Archives (SIA), Record Unit 45, box 61, folder 7.

This is the appropriate introduction to Walcott's only paper on biology, a couple of pages in the *Journal of Animal Behavior* (Walcott 1917g). During the 1913 season, Walcott would commonly blast with dynamite just before lunch, and then the group would stop to eat. The ground squirrels came for the sandwich crumbs. One, "Granny," had a broken tail and was easily recognized among the other squirrels. When the blasting began again in 1917, Granny showed up for her meals. It was a Pavlovian reaction but a remarkable one, in that such a small animal should remember after so a long time. On the other hand, the mountains of British Columbia can be harsh, and there are not many free lunches.

Though Washington was far away, news of the impact of the war kept coming: "The aviation shed back of the s.i. has been finished and painted and glassed, and they have commenced to move machinery in. We all heartily hope that the results there will very materially aid in smashing the Germans. The Smithsonian Red Cross ambulance is an assured fact. Miss Munroe tells me that the $1000.00 is practically in hand, and she hopes for more, the excess to be used to provide litters &c. Quite a number of our boys have left to enter one service or another."[3] Among the boys who went off to war was Miss Julia Gardner, who, as noted, left to drive an ambulance in France.

The shed deserves a few words, even though it is long gone. This was a sheet-metal airplane hangar; according to some authorities, the hangar was of a new type and the first of its kind to be prefabricated. In later times, this tin shack behind the Castle might have received historic-preservation status. As it was, it served for many years as an aircraft museum before it was bulldozed down to be superceded by the National Air and Space Museum, which opened in 1976.

Still, that summer the war was far distant, and the collecting continued unabated. Mary left for Glacier to study the movement of the glaciers. "We worked at quarry all day as weather is unsettled. A blast at 3 P.M. loosened up the last rock that I shall try for this season" (August 19, 1917). Even that last rock turned up a unique specimen.

Mr. Oke left with Alex, who took three more packloads of fossils to Field. Helen and Walcott had earned a busman's holiday and went to join Mary at Glacier. "Out with Mary on the Asulkan glacier during the day. We measured the recession of the toe 386 feet since 1909 and photographed the lower portion of the glacier. A beautiful day. Helen climbed to top of Mount Avalanche" (August 22, 1917). The western trip was precisely what Helen had needed; her health was back, and the horrors seen in France were receding into the distance. They spent another day and a half measuring and photographing ice.

Back at Burgess Pass, there were five uninterrupted days in the quarry, despite cloudy and chilly weather. Snow squalls came, so Walcott and Alex put up the tent at the south end of the quarry and continued collecting. "Mary came up & we worked all day 7:30 to 5 P.M. Cold & rain but well sheltered in the tent" (August 30, 1917). "At 11 A.M. snow squalls began on the President range and a fine one struck us at noon. Worked in tent, but at 2:30 P.M. we gave up & returned to camp" (September 1, 1917). That is devotion to collecting. Several pictures of the quarrying are in "Explorations" (Walcott 1918). One photo has an incorrect date of 1914, which was to lead a local Canadian museum into an exhibit error as to when Walcott was at the Burgess Pass quarry.

They switched tents with Helen and took her white tent to the quarry, for it was sturdier. "Continued work at quarry with Mary & Alex. We found many Marella's [sic] and a few good things. As a whole the rock is playing out as far as large good fossils are concerned" (September 4, 1917). They kept at it for a few days longer; no matter how interesting the collecting may be, sustaining interest day after day is difficult. In some ways, this requires the kind of inner drive needed to complete a marathon. "With Mary, Alex & Helen completed work at the quarry for 1917. We have packed up 126 pkgs of fossils & a number of slabs. A good collection but the quarry is played out" (September 10, 1917).

In rain and sleet, they packed the fossils and rocks to Field and then moved the camp back to Hector. "Helen & Alex went to Field & packed up collections etc. Shipped 18 boxes, I blb. 3950#. Mary & I work on south slope of Mt. Bosworth. A fine day" (September 15, 1917). A fine day in the field is never to be wasted. Walcott's poundage recorded was the total shipped; the barrel mentioned was simply a convenient container he had acquired.

Walcott's use of "packages" is an unknown measurement. A guess is that "seventy to eighty small pieces were wrapped and combined as a single parcel. Each package probably contained five to six kilograms of rock, and if so, the number of packages on a pack horse, gleaned from his diary, is in accord with the amount of weight one might reasonably expect to be carried by an animal" (Yochelson 1996, 579).

Despite the long rides and hard climbs of other seasons, the day-after-day drudgery in the quarry may have been the most arduous field season Walcott spent in Canada. They rested on Sunday and took two days to move camp to Vermillion Pass, thirty-five miles by horse. "All tired—I look at rocks in pass & after 2 P.M. went fishing" (September 19, 1917). "Out on Mt. Whymper all day with all hands. Found section very sandy & few traces of Mt. Whyte formations" (September 20, 1917). The change in the rock suggested that this area had been near a shoreline.

They moved camp again. Fortunately, one of the rangers had come out a few days earlier to assist them, and the geology party soon turned to hunting and fishing. Mary painted. They moved again to Moose Creek, where Alex and Walcott bagged a mountain goat. Walcott planned to look at the rocks at the Continental Divide, but bad weather turned him back. With no prospect of hunting because of the storm, they saw eighteen goats on one mountain. "Moved camp to Tokeem Creek ¼ mile above its mouth on Vermillion river. A tedious day owing to cold wind, heavy clouds & mist" (September 28, 1917). This was camp number thirteen of the season.

That turned out to be a lucky number for hunting. After two days of searching, the party bagged a bull moose, a cow, and a calf; these were specimens for scientific purposes. "Rain[.] Alex & Wood went to skin cow moose & bring in meat. Mary & Helen working on skulls & skin at camp. Wrote Sidney & Stuart. S—— is at Spartanburg S.C. & Stuart at Arvod Aviation school France" (October 3, 1917). A wagon took the skins, horns, and meat to Castle, and Ranger "Tex" Wood bid farewell. Camp fourteen was on the Bow River, a mile west of Castle. The weather was good, and Walcott again photographed photogenic Castle Mountain.

The skins required preparation that took another day, and the next was devoted to taking panorama views along the Bow River. "Mary, Helen & I went into Banff from Castle by train. Alex & Arthur took pack train in. Camped in moose pasture" (October 8, 1917). This season Arthur Brown got this one mention in Walcott's diary, better than some years. Walcott and the ladies spent a day taking photographs around Banff. "The season of 1917 has given unusually dry weather. We have had fair success but nothing unusual. Left Banff & camp 10:45 P.M. with Mary & Helen via C.P. Ry." (October 10, 1917). As usual, Arthur, with the help of Alex, put away the camp equipment and made arrangements for pasturing the horses. The trip east was fast, and less than three days later the Walcotts were in Chicago, where Helen left for Cleveland. They got to Washington on a pleasant Sunday autumn day. "At home found Mollie, Annie & Elizabeth & house in fine order" (October 14, 1917).

That Monday at the office, the war came back. Walcott and other Smithsonian officials met in the office of an assistant secretary of the treasury; "Arranged to give 15000 sq ft space in New Museum building for use of Soldiers & Sailors Insurance Division" (October 15, 1917). Office space was at a premium; before the war was over, the population of Washington had more than doubled. The mammals were pushed aside, and the clerks came in; it was the nose of the camel, but Walcott could hardly refuse the request to dedicate part of the building to such a good cause.

One day in Washington—after months away—and it was off to New York for Secretary Walcott; Helen met him there. The RC took some of his time, but mostly Walcott was concerned with the CIW Ex Comm; he got back to Washington that night. Life would have been so much simpler if all meetings had been in Washington. However, Elihu Root in New York was head of the CIW trustees, in addition to his many other activities, and it was no easier for him to travel than for Walcott.

Helen had a beau, who stayed at the house for a few days. Walcott had meetings with the National Research Council, with future chief of the Army Air Corps Maj. Benjamin D. Foulois, interviews, and piles of mail. In three days, three months away vanished into the far distance. By dint of hard work, on the following Monday, after various meetings, Walcott "dictated a lot of letters & nearly caught up with office work" (October 22, 1917). After that, it was the Military Committee and informal NACA discussions. A day later, after more war work, Walcott actually had all business in hand and could devote a bit of time to laboratory work.

Life was more or less into its normal pattern: "Callers, interviews & routine used up most of the day" (October 29, 1917). The Military Committee met again; Col. Harry Binghamton, in charge of aviation training, called; a Colonel Filley of the British aviation service visited the office. Howard Coffin, Dr. William F. Durand, and Dr. Samuel W. Stratton of the NACA accompanied him to the National Research Council headquarters. As October gave way to November, trilobites moved farther and farther from the scene.

That Sunday, the Walcotts drove to Baltimore. Walcott spoke at a memorial service for William Bullock Clark, head of the geology department at Johns Hopkins, founder of the Maryland Geological Survey, and chairman of the NRC committee on geology and geography. "A very interesting day as the meeting was a dignified tribute to a fine man & my friend" (November 4, 1917). Clark's obituary was reprinted in the SI *Annual Report*.

"Routine & a little work on Neolenus" (November 5, 1917). This is the first mention of a Middle Cambrian trilobite that would dominate Walcott's next research activity. The next day the secretary of the treasury was pushing for more space for his clerks. Walcott pointed out how readily temporary buildings could be constructed on the Mall, and he roughed out the costs. (No one was listening at that time, but before the war was over, the Mall would be covered with temporary buildings, some of which would still be around in the 1950s. Say what you will about the Wilson administration, it knew how to build a temporary building that would last.)

Durand, Stratton, Joseph Ames, and Walcott went off on a major inspection trip. They had a very full day in Dayton, Ohio, examining Wilbur Wright Field, seeing a flight of a De Havilland using a new Liberty engine, going to the Delco plant, and a host of other activities. The next day they saw more laboratories and factories and then caught the night train for Detroit. They looked into engine construction and airplane frames until dark, when the group caught the evening train to Buffalo. There the four studied a new, well-planned aircraft factory. Walcott stuck an extra paper in his diary, noting that a contract to build Spads (the ubiquitous French pursuit plane) had been canceled. The group got back to Washington the next morning; Mary took him immediately to the office, and the Washington routine continued.

"At my office all day. Mary unpacking Burgess Shale sp[e]c[i]m[en]s, & Helen working at stenography & typing" (November 13, 1917). Walcott had written Alex Mitton, the packer, that Helen was going to learn shorthand and typing so that she could assist with Walcott's office work. Evenings were hardly Walcott's own, as the pace of Washington business continued to increase. Generally three or four people were at dinner, and war-related business followed. Aviation took a full day, with General Squier at breakfast, the NACA until lunch, and the Aircraft Production Board in the afternoon. Major Foulois and his party, accompanied by Helen's beau, arrived safely in France; the submarine menace was receding.

After church, it was back to New York again. The Carnegie Ex Comm was polished off in time for a luncheon meeting concerning a possible manager for the Research Corporation. Walcott caught an afternoon train to Philadelphia and that evening presided at an NAS council meeting. In addition to vigorous walks with Mary, Walcott must have gotten considerable exercise running to catch trains. It was a pleasant enough two days. Walcott took the night train back to Washington, while Mary stayed in Philadelphia. Helen went up to join her; the field season had been a good one from many aspects, and the breach between the two was completely healed.

Temporary bachelor Walcott spent two hard days at the office and had all the loose ends tied up before the ladies returned. The Treasury was pushing for more space in the Museum, and Walcott could hardly fend it off. It was a relief when Sidney and his new wife came into town for a few weeks, to be joined later by Mary's family at Thanksgiving. Before that happy event, Walcott had to spend two more days worrying about airplanes and their production.

Saturday, Walcott met with George Ellery Hale and two members of the Council for National Defense to smooth the way for the National Research Council. The two groups kept bumping heads, and Hale had a generally short fuse. Walcott kept NRC on the right track and that particular council out of Hale's hair. The aircraft board and the NRC council met, but between the two meetings, as was his custom, Walcott snatched a few minutes to look at appendages of trilobites, his perennial interest.

Two more days were given almost entirely to the aircraft board before Walcott could get another two hours with his trilobites. The administrative load was worse than usual, for Mr. Rathbun, short of stature but strong of spirit, was quite ill. In addition, daughter Helen became ill as well.

Life did not get easier as December wore on. "Meetings Nat. Ad. Comm Aeronautics 10–11 A.M. 2:30–4:30 P.M. Aircraft Board 11–1 P.M. Attended to mail at my office between times" (December 11, 1917). Walcott sent Helen and Mary to Spartanburg, South Carolina, in the hope that Helen's cold would clear up. He skated through the annual meeting of the SI Board of Regents, the CIW Ex Comm, and the annual Carnegie lecture and reception.

"At office 9–9:50 A.M. 1:30–2:45 P.M. Meeting of the Trustees Carnegie Institution 10–12 A.M. & Ex Comm 12:10–12:50 pm. Meeting of Regents Committee on use of New Nat. Museum Building 3–4:45 P.M.—at Sen. Stone[']s Committee. At home with Sidney & Helen Louise in evening. Stuart reported to have been brot down in aircraft [illegible] France" (December 14, 1917). Just when life seems dark, cruel fate makes its darker. Helena had been killed abruptly, a terrible shock. Charlie had lingered for months before dying. Now here was something even worse—uncertainty!

Young Stuart had trained in France, commenting in a letter to his father that generally three planes crashed in the training of one flyer. Despite problems with a French instructor who seemingly hated Americans, Stuart graduated and joined a French air group quartered adjacent to the Lafayette Escadrille, the famous French unit of volunteer American airmen. He got there at the tail end of its happy days. The mascot, a lion cub known as Whiskey, had not yet been sent off to a zoo, and despite occasional losses there was a core of camaraderie into which Benjamin Stuart could fit. It was unfortunate that he could not spend all his time with the Escadrille. For several months he flew observation missions; he shot down no German planes. One day he did not return. Meanwhile life in Washington had to go on.

"With Hon. Henry White fixing up letter etc. to Sec'y Treasury *en re* use of Museum building. We called on Sen's Lodge and Stone & left letter at Treasury at noon. At my office P.M looking after mail etc. Cousin Fred & Mary Walcott called in evening & Mrs. Sherlock Davis. No word about reported accident to Stuart" (December 15, 1917). The next day was Sunday, but Walcott was too upset for church; he went to his office and puttered. It was fortunate that Sidney and his wife were in town; "We are all feeling the suspense as to what may have happened to Stuart" (December 16, 1917).

Also fortunately, Mary came back the next day and reported Helen well settled in South Carolina. The following day, she unpacked Burgess fossils, while

Walcott attended to his mail and the aircraft board; no doubt her presence helped soothe him—surely a trite phrase, but an accurate one. The NRC met, followed by the NAS council. No word came from France.

"Gen. [John J.] Pershing [commander of the American Expeditionary Force in France] cables that Stuart was killed over German lines in France Dec. 11*th*. God alone knows why the Huns are permitted to continue their career of the murder of men of all nations. At my office all day except for a call on Charles Moore with Dr Geo. E. Hale" (December 20, 1917). His youngest son dead, war committees overwhelming him, and Hale took him off to meet with the chairman of the Fine Arts Commission about a possible NAS building! They met with Mr. Moore again the following day; perhaps it was just as well to think of something in the future.

Walcott spent his day at the office replying to letters of condolence; he referred to Stuart's "accident," perhaps in his own mind with that phrase seeking to ease the horror of his son's falling to his death. Sidney and Helen spent Christmas in their new home. Church did not help. "A quiet day at my office. Could not work or think or play so flattened with many things. Mind & body out of tune. A blue, rainy tiresome day. At home in evening fixing up Christmas packages with Mary" (December 24, 1917). Christmas was subdued, and Walcott grasped at straws. "Stuart may be a prisoner in Germany or with his mother and brother Charlie" (December 25, 1917). At his office he could not concentrate, so he went to examine the Burgess Shale fossils, seeking escape.

He was interrupted by a conference concerning a wind tunnel at Langley Field. A cable announced that Stuart had been shot down on 12th, not the 11th, and to make things still worse, two letters arrived that had been mailed by Stuart before his death. Walcott was ill, but he tried to catch up with his mail. Sidney and Helen-Louise returned, enthusiastic about their new house. "Cable from Genl. Pershing that Stuart may have escaped serious injury & be a prisoner in Germany" (December 29, 1917).

"No good, the influenza bacilli have a good hold on me. This has been a year of trial to millions of men & women. War Conditions. Food shortage & unsettling of old traditions & practices. We may have lost Stuart in aircraft battle in France. If so he died fighting for human liberty. We will wait patiently until his fate is made known to us from within the German battle lines" (December 31, 1917).

It was one of the coldest winters on record in Washington, nine degrees Fahrenheit on January 1; it was the winter that more people died of influenza than were killed in battle in Europe. "Confined to house by influenza cold. Mary well. Helen recuperating at Summerville, S.C. Lieut. Sidney S. Walcott and Helen-Louise in Washington. Stuart possibly somewhere in Germany as a prisoner of war." There is a parenthetical note, written in months later: "In June [1918] learned that Stuart was killed Dec. 12 in aircraft fight near St. Sauplet, France, and buried at Leffincourt" (January 1, 1918). Walcott was confined to bed, but Miss Brigham came up from the Castle and for two days, he alternately dictated letters and napped. "Cold better but still no good. Unofficial word from Germany that Stuart was killed Dec. 12 1917 in aircraft battle. It is a crime that Germany must account for, the killing of men, women, and children" (January 5, 1918). At least the uncertainty was more or less over. The term "cold comfort" surely applies here.

The comment added in June was based on an official announcement; Walcott wrote it in as a matter of record keeping. No matter what, he kept his records straight, and each sum he spent or received was recorded in the diary, along with whom he met and what he did. Possibly it was keeping the record straight that impelled him to his next action. The February 1918 issue of the *National Geographic Magazine* is devoted to wartime aviation. Included in it is "The life story of an American airman in France." No author is given, but this item is included in Walcott's bibliography, and the introduction is in Walcott's style.

> Stuart Walcott was a senior at Princeton University in the winter of 1916–17. In view of his approaching graduation in the spring, his father wrote to him that he had best begin to think about what he was to do after graduation, in order that he might get on an independent basis as soon as practicable. In response, under date of January 7, he wrote:

> > You spoke of my being independent after I graduated in the spring. If I go to Europe, as I want to, to drive an ambulance, or in the air service, I will be doing a man's work and shall be doing enough to support myself. If the work is unpaid, it is merely because it is charitable work and as such is given freely. If you want to pay my way, I will consider it not as dependence on you, father, but as a partnership that may help the Allies and their cause. I will furnish my services and you the funds to make my services available (Walcott 1918a, 86).

This was followed by some letters that Stuart wrote home and a final, short section on his death.

Shortly thereafter, Princeton University Press published a book in which much of this material and more letters to relatives and friends were assembled. The letters portray a fun-loving youth, a bit of a daredevil. Walcott added three pages of personal data at the end: "I find in my notebook under an entry of July 6, 1905, a few days before Stuart's ninth birthday, that with him and his brother Sidney I had measured a section of over 10,000 feet in thickness of rock with dip compass and rod in northern Montana, and that night we slept out on the Continental Divide after a sandwich apiece for supper" (Walcott 1918b, 80).

Deciding to publish Stuart's letters helped ease the loss, and perhaps coincidentally, Walcott's sickness eased. He was finally able to return to the office and its problems. Mr. F. W. Hodge, chief of the Bureau of American Ethnology, Major Powell's old bureau, notified the secretary that he was leaving, presenting another administrative difficulty. Dr. Elan Hooker came into town, spent the night, and discussed the Research Corporation. The next day the two met with Cottrell. The RC would not run itself, and no one wanted to spend time with a business so determined to be unprofitable for anyone or anything against science; eventually Hooker came to the rescue as corporation president. Various other meetings and complaints in the aviation field came Walcott's way, but it was generally a quiet week, permitting some recovery from his grief.

In mid-January, Walcott was on Capitol Hill; the deficiency appropriation bill to cover budget overruns included items for the Museum. The next day brought more complaints, followed by a full day of meetings—the NAS council, the NRC, and the aircraft board—ending with a dinner meeting with Stratton to talk over the NACA. The dinner kept him occupied until it was time for the 11:00 P.M. sleeper to New York. The board of the Research Corporation met, the CIW Ex Comm was reorganized, and Walcott caught the night train back to Washington.

Two days of conferences with various people were not made easier by Walcott developing a head cold. The cold became slightly better, but the interviews continued. "At my office—Dr Goddard and Dr Stratton came *en re* aviation & new rocket for high altitudes—Mary came for Luncheon. After 4 P.M. went to Bureau [of] Standards & Dr [apparently both men] came for dinner. A very busy day" (January 21, 1918). Walcott occasionally used the phrase "promising young man"; he had applied it to Stratton, who eventually went from head of the Bureau of Standards to head of the Massachusetts Institute of Technology.

Goddard requires a bit more introduction, although those who have visited Goddard Space Flight Center near Washington know of him. During the Sputnik era and subsequent lunar race, he was well known as America's pioneer rocketeer. The Smithsonian can take credit for supporting his accomplishments. In September 1916, Goddard wrote to the SI asking for support. Receiving a reply asking for amplification, he sent in a manuscript entitled "A Method of Reaching Extreme Altitudes." Walcott had this reviewed by Charles Greeley Abbot, who in turn solicited another opinion from a colleague at the Bureau of Standards. Both were impressed (Lehman 1963).

The Smithsonian has an account known as the Hodgkins Fund to support studies of air, and in January 1917 Walcott determined that Goddard could have five thousand dollars. This was the first step toward the moon. As an indication of how little money the institution had to spend, when Goddard asked if his manuscript could be published, Abbot deducted the cost of printing from the grant. In 1924, and again in 1926, Goddard received $2,500 from the RC—that is, indirectly from Walcott; these sums sound almost laughable, but in those days they constituted major funding. Meanwhile, there was a war on, and the next day Walcott introduced Goddard to various army officers to discuss rockets.

One saving grace of the war was that formal dinners in Washington practically vanished; however, meetings, especially those dealing with immediate crisis situations, more than ate up that gain. "At my office during the afternoon. At capital A.M. Talked with Chairman Dent of Military Committee. Secty of Commerce Redfield & wife & Fred C. Walcott dined with us. Left letter *en re* aviation developments at White House 5 P.M." (January 26, 1918).

A bit of explanation concerning aviation development may help here. The NACA had recommended formation of the Aircraft Production Board. It is clear from diary entries that Walcott was active on the board, yet he was not an original member of that group; just when and how he became involved is not clear, but obviously he was now involved nearly to the point of being mired in this board's business. The group was headed by Howard E. Coffin; after a meeting or two, Coffin may have decided to insist on the presence of Walcott, who had the knack of keeping meetings calm. Warring parties would be obliged to work together, yet there was never a heavy hand, and in retrospect no one could ever quite figure out how the great difficulties had been smoothed over.

The particular letter mentioned above has vanished. It may be somewhere in the myriad rolls of Woodrow Wilson's microfilmed papers, or somewhere in the National Archives and Records Center. All that is known today is that two days earlier, Walcott had telephoned the White House and left a message for the president. The NACA had been investigating the status of aircraft production program and "found a condition very satisfactory" (Baker 1939, 420).

Fortunately, a quiet day thereafter offered an opportunity for research and escape from the reality of airplanes. A major snowstorm in Washington essentially stopped the government and allowed more time for fossils. "Snowing. Quiet at office. Worked on structure of the Trilobite paper at odd times all day. Secty & Mrs. Redfield dined with us" (January 30, 1918). In all, it was a quiet week as Washington slowly dug out. The outside cold and Walcott's bad cold or influenza or grippe persisted, which in his words kept him "50% efficient."

Surprisingly enough, quiet times persisted for another two weeks. There was only a single meeting of the NACA and one of the Aircraft Production Board. The Burgess Shale collections were being unpacked by Mary and examined by Walcott. It was almost as though there was no war. Walcott fell, injuring his shoulder, but otherwise there was little to record in his diary. "Attended to routine & cleared up all of the Burgess Pass quarry fossils cut out to date. This leaves me free to take up trilobite paper next week" (February 16, 1918). The "cut out" refers to trimming away of the excess rock, leaving the fossil on a squared-off piece of rock; shale is relatively soft and sawing it is easier than sawing limestone. "At my office & laboratory all day. Completed work of examining Marrella 7000 specimens" (February 18, 1918).

A later count indicated that by the end of the 1919 season, Walcott had collected as many as fifteen thousand individuals of this form, plus an unknown number distributed or exchanged by the Museum. In terms of volume, his efforts at the Burgess quarry can only be compared to some of the major dinosaur digs. He worked week after week, totally perhaps half a year of daily activity in the quarry from 1910 through 1917 and recovered an average of about two hundred specimens a day (Yochelson 1996). It was a legacy to be mined by many paleontologists two generations later,

Still the unnatural quiet persisted. The NACA did not meet again until after George Washington's Birthday and the Washington Monument Society gathering. Apparently, the mechanism for the NACA and the NRC having been finally established, they could run along for weeks with minimum advice from Walcott. Of course, such relatively good times could not last, and near the end of February aviation problems arose. Walcott resolved them and rushed around to finish his odds and ends.

The first of March, he and Mary left for the south to visit Helen, now in Beaufort, South Carolina, and perhaps to rest a little themselves. Helen was somewhat improved in her health. For Walcott, it was a vacation with no geology. He napped, talked to the town folk, visited Parris Island naval station, walked with Mary, saw a school for "colored boys & girls," as he put it, and went crabbing with Helen. "Beaufort, S.C. is a sleepy old town of Colonial days—Nothing to do but walk about—go crabbing & sleep. . . . My arm is about the same. Suspect that a muscle has been slipped out of place. The average doctor is helpless in such cases—It is the 'Charley Horse' of the base ball player. Will remain here this week unless something happens. We are simply resting now."[4]

Indeed, a full week went by before Walcott did any work; it was almost a record for him. "Worked over ms of trilobite paper A.M. Out crabbing with Mary P.M. I do not see much of Helen as she is not interested in active work or play & is not strong. A quiet evening & early off to slumberland" (March 9, 1918). Walcott was regaining his equilibrium from the loss of Stuart. His arm was giving trouble, but at least the cold had finally vanished. He continued to vacation, except for the last day, which Walcott devoted entirely to the trilobite manuscript.

After two weeks in Beaufort, they said adieu to Helen and headed north. "Arrived in Washington 10:30 A.M. Went to meeting of Ad. Comm. Aeronautics 10:45–1:15 P.M. Left for my office & cleared up accumulated mail before 4 P.M.

Called at Signal Corps office & went home for a walk with Mary" (March 15, 1918). Walcott was back. "Attending to mail & administrative matters most of the day. Talked with Genl Squires *en re* P[ost] O[ffice] aerial mail service 5 P.M." (March 16, 1918).

After a day of quiet, more or less, dictating letters, and the aircraft board met again. "A broken up busy day. Called on Asst Secty Crowell of War Dept & Genl. [Peyton] March Chief of Staff with Dr S. W. Stratton *en re* aviation matters" (March 18, 1918). The next day was peaceful, but then the aircraft board met again; it is curious that Walcott's deep involvement with this wartime agency was never to be mentioned in any of his memorials. The NACA met again; this was far less troublesome than the aircraft board. In a sense, the difference between the two groups is comparable to that between of science and technology. Invariably, applying what has been discovered is more difficult and more expensive than discovering it in the first place.

On Sunday after church, Walcott went to Rock Creek Cemetery for his first visit in a very long time; later the family went to an aircraft demonstration. Aviation had come a long way in a short time. The Iowa Apartment House meeting took less than an hour this year, and the NAS council meeting took only half a day. Until just before Walcott was elected president, the council had not gathered between the spring and fall meetings, as there was never any business to discuss. Both the formation of the NRC and Walcott personally had stirred the NAS to more activity.

Difficulty appeared when the Military Committee on Capitol Hill decided to investigate aircraft production. "At my office 9–10:15 A.M. 12:30–2:15 P.M. At Hearing on aircraft situation in Senate Comm—on Military Affairs 10:30–12 [and] 2:45–5 P.M." (March 29, 1918). The hearings could not have been too worrisome, for the next day Walcott was back to work on trilobites. A recovered Helen finally came home, to Walcott's delight; Sidney and wife, in town frequently, dined or had breakfast at the house, but it had not been the same as having his daughter home. That Sunday at church "Stuart's name was read as having given his life for the cause of liberty" (March 31, 1918); a birthday celebration was inappropriate, and Walcott did not note his age in his diary.

April began with three full days of quiet. "Hearings on S.I. appropriations before house Appr. Comm. 10 A.M.–1 P.M. Advisory Comm. on Aeronautics 3–5:30 P.M. with Dr Stratton" (April 4, 1918). This was followed by hearings on Aeronautics; Walcott found them "interesting." Sidney finally left Washington, transferred to Langley Field. Several days later, Walcott was in to see General March again. Once more the Aircraft Production Board met. Evenings, Walcott considered the reconstruction of trilobites that Mary had drawn; streamlining of flying machines make an interesting contrast with legs of extinct creatures.

Walcott dropped in on the War Department to discuss aviation matters and conferred with General Squier, but there seemed to be no serious problems that Walcott could not resolve.

Unfortunately, not all was well at home, for Helen became ill again with influenza. Two sons were dead, and Sidney was in aviation, which carried a high degree of risk even without combat; Walcott wrote little more, but he must have fretted over Helen. "At my office most of the day. Called on Secty Daniels *en re* aviation situation & at 12:30 left memoranda at White House for President Wilson on aircraft production" (April 15, 1918). This must be an interesting document outlining what was being done to produce airplanes. A copy probably still is in Washington somewhere, and one can only hope that an earnest historian of aviation will uncover it some day; like Walcott's earlier letter, it is not in the obvious places one might look.

This may be a good place for a summary of aircraft-related actions, both private and general, that Walcott wrote about to W. F. Durand, who was away in France (Durand was NACA chairman from 1917 until Walcott took over).

> Yesterday a cablegram was received. . . . Red Cross advises Stuart hit in head Leffingcourt Ardennes which means he was killed before going down. I have often said that I thought he was shot or else he would have recovered from the nose dive before striking the ground.
>
> If Stuart's commission can be issued I should like very much to have it done, as it would complete his record and be in conformity with the understanding that if he made good he would be transferred to the American Army. His only object in going to France before the others was to obtain the training that would enable him to be of greater service in the development of the American Air Service in France.
>
> Everything is going along here as rapidly as possible in connection with the development of the bombing machine. The twelve cylinder Liberty motor is making good every day and is now an assured success. 108 were delivered last week from Packard and Leland plants in Detroit. Next week Ford begins production. . . . The double geared 500 horse power Liberty is advancing rapidly and should be in production in June. . . .
>
> Dr. Millikan attended the meeting and I think the friction that existed between his organization and the [NACA] Committee has been removed, and that it arose from misunderstanding.
>
> Wish you could be here with us at the meeting of the National Academy of Sciences next week, as it promised to be of interest. As you probably know, we are housing about two thousand workers in connection with the War Risk Insurance Bureau in the new National Museum building, which makes us very short for meeting rooms. This has led to utilizing the Smithsonian Hall and the adjoining exhibition rooms.
>
> I should be very glad to get any suggestions that you may have to make either for the Committee or the Aviation Service.[5]

There were other organizational stirrings in Washington. Almost from its inception, George Ellery Hale had wanted the NRC to be on a permanent footing. Late in March he wrote to President Wilson about it, and on May 11, 1918, the president requested the NAS "to perpetuate" the NRC. This was indeed another triumph for Chairman Hale.

There is a bit more to the official story. Hale's letter and a draft of an executive order were somehow sent to the Council for National Defense, where the request was turned down flat (Wright 1966, 296–97). On May 10, Hale was finally able to meet with the president, and the executive order was issued the following day. Ultimately, the NAS acted as directed, and the NRC was perpetuated.

There is, however, even more yet to the story. From time to time, Walcott would write Wilson and formally request that certain persons in the military or civilian branches of government be allowed to serve on the NRC in order to facilitate its work. On April 14, he wrote requesting this for Walter Gifford.[6] It so happened that Gifford was a key member of the Council for National Defense. If bureaucratic scores were kept, and in baseball terms, Walcott would at a minimum be credited with an assist. Finding the letter *en re* Gifford's connection was luck. It may have been Gifford Pinchot who first referred to Walcott as "snowshoe Charlie," because he left such a faint trail when he moved that it was hard to tell what snowshoe Charlie accomplished.

"A quiet day at office & laboratory, working on diagrammatic restoration of Neolenus. Completed drawing in evening & Mary inked it" (April 15, 1918). Quiet ensued for a couple of more days until "Committee Day" (April 18, 1918); Walcott had quote marks in the original. The NACA met for two hours; ten minutes later, the Aircraft Production Board assembled. After a hurried lunch, it was time for NRC meeting, and then, for the finale, the CIW Ex Comm gathered. This was an endurance contest.

Fortunately, two days of relative quiet intervened before the NAS annual meeting. Walcott was busy presiding at the business meetings, the evening lecture, the council, the scientific sessions, and the dinner. There he told the academicians about the state of the country's aircraft program, but he found time for a little science: "I gave a short talk on structure of the trilobite Neolenus" (April 23, 1918). When the NAS members left town, the Walcotts had a small dinner party in honor of the British ambassador. It was the first really formal evening affair for them that year.

The NAS talk was the trigger needed to put finishing touches on the trilobite paper. Then the meetings started again. "At my office most of the day. Routine & a little research work. Aeronautic situation takes up much time" (May 1, 1918). If there were not meetings during the day, guests came to dinner or to breakfast to discuss airplane production or future aeronautical research. "An hour with Secty of War Baker A.M. *en re* aircraft situation" (May 5, 1918). What makes this unusual is not that there were problems with the "aircraft situation" but the meeting was another on a Sunday. Washington and Walcott were on a 100 percent wartime footing.

The next week was devoted entirely to aircraft matters. The Aircraft Production Board was accused of mismanagement, excessive costs, and a host of other sins. Conferences were held with military officers, cabinet officers, members of the board, manufacturers, representatives, senators, and the vice president. As a result of the November 1917 inspection trip, whereas Walcott, Stratton, and Durand were pleased, Ames thought there was little prospect of American industry being able to produce the needed planes. He wrote of his discouragement, the words leaked out, and concerns escalated. There would be no investigations of trilobite limbs this week. By Friday, the newspapers had gotten wind of charges against the board and it was a full-blown story. Despite the flurry, Walcott did get to church that Sunday, and then he was off to New York City once more.

After a quick meeting of the CIW Ex Comm and a few telephone calls to conduct RC business, Walcott returned to Washington for a meeting with the Signal Corps, preparatory to a major event. "At my office 9–10:30, 1–5. P.M. Went to see first U.S. mail airplane leave Washn for N-Y 11:50 A.M. A great event in aeronautics. Several interviews *en re* aircraft matters & a half hour at meeting of aircraft board. Dined with Mr & Mrs Jenning. Mary in Philid." (May 15, 1918). For a man grounded in the geologic past, Walcott had a grasp of the future. That airmail flight marked the start of American commercial aviation.

Thereafter, Walcott had a few quiet days to catch up on matters and go back to the trilobites. That Saturday, Mary and Helen accompanied him for a weekend away in Greenwich, Connecticut. Elan Hooker, founder of Hooker Chemical Corporation and a RC stalwart, and his wife welcomed them to their home. One full day of vacation was enough. "Motored to New York with Mr. Hooker, Mary, Helen & the two children—With Hale & Millikan talked to Carnegie Corporation Board *en re* grant for National Academy. At meeting of Ex. Comm. Research Corporation 2:50–5 P.M. Returned to Greenwich 7:20 P.M. and went to Mr. Hookers" (May 20, 1918).

They bid farewell to the Hooker family and went off to Mineola, New York. Walcott spoke to Glenn L. Curtiss, inspected the airfield, and left the ladies in New York, while he took the midnight train south. General Squier had retired, but otherwise the military aircraft front was relatively stable, and Walcott could get back to the mail, and even to the trilobites. The good spell, however, could not last.

"At conference Ad. Comm. Aeronautics 9:30–1 P.M. Office P.M. Dr Goddard turned up in trouble *en re* his rocket work" (May 28, 1918). The next day was a meeting of the aircraft board, mercifully short. "Decoration day—Went to my office 9 A.M. Geo. H. Maxwell called & then genl [*sic*] Squires [*sic*] After 11:30 I worked until 5. P.M. on trilobite paper" (May 30, 1918). During his years with the USGS, Walcott had learned that there is nothing like a government holiday to provide uninterrupted research time for a government scientist.

Once more, the interlude did not last. The next day began with a NRC committee meeting, followed by a visit from Stratton, followed in turn by further reports of Goddard's problems. When June began the next day, Walcott went to see General Squier to discuss the mutual difficulties of Goddard and the Ordnance Department of the army; the problems were resolved. To make sure that no one interfered with Goddard's investigations, Hale offered Goddard facilities at his California observatory. The result was that Goddard invented the bazooka, which was to be famous in the Second World War as an antitank weapon; he demonstrated it to high-level brass four days before the first war ended (Lehman 1963, 85–86).

With Goddard happy, it was off to the train station and the Hotel Belmont in New York for Walcott. There was no church attendance that Sunday. "Conference with Charles L. Freer *en re* care of his collections in the Museum. Met Miss K. Rhoads his asst" (June 2, 1918). That all went so smoothly Walcott was able to catch the afternoon train and have a walk with Mary before dinner. There ensued four days with only one meeting of the aircraft board and relatively few interruptions. "At meeting of Ad. Comm. Aeronautics 9:30–1 P.M. Genl. [W. L.] Kenly came to meeting. Aviation situation not very good. At my office P.M. & at home getting camp things in order" (June 8, 1918).

War or no war, Walcott was going to the field. War or no war, Walcott was determined to finish his manuscript. "At my office all day attending to routine, interviews, etc. A little work in research. Questions *en re* aeronautics came up almost hourly in some form" (June 10, 1918).

"The outlook for a victory of the Allies over Germany is very depressing at the present time. The U.S. is slowly coming in to help & we hope it not be too late" (June 12, 1918). Although students of the First World War know that the end was to come in six months, the fighting in the late spring was fierce and at the time seemed inconclusive. Gloom or no gloom, that Saturday Walcott's trilobites received his attention for half a day. He kept plugging away. "At my office during the day—Routine correspondence—interviews & a little time with my own research work" (June 17, 1918).

Another day and a half of odds and ends, plus research, went by before aviation flew in again. This time the aircraft board had movies of the big new Handley Page machine to show to its members. The next day, Walcott picnicked in the Zoological Park, compliments of Mary and the wife of the secretary of war; a little break in routine does marvelous things for morale.

"At my office A.M. Meeting of advisory comm. aeronautics 3–6 P.M. Col. Waldan came in for breakfast. Whitman Cross & Dr Merrill came 8–9:45 P.M. *en re* Research Council work" (June 23, 1918). Merrill, the geologist/mineralogist, must have been one of the first people that Walcott met in the Museum when he moved back from New York City in 1882, yet almost four decades later formality still prevailed in Walcott's private jottings.

Helen wanted to return to France, and Walcott spent a Saturday unsuccessfully trying to obtain a passport for her. Sunday after church was quiet; "At my office all day except for a brief call on Secty of War Baker & Secty of Navy [Josephus] Daniels" (June 24, 1918). This may have been social, simply to let the powers in Washington know that Walcott would be away for the summer.

"At Smithsonian all day. Routine & finishing up paper on structure of trilobite" (June 25, 1918). Part of one day thereafter went to the aircraft board. Also, and although he was desperate to leave, Walcott now started another venture. Some background helps explain this additional diversion from research.

Steven Mather is both the hero and the founding father of the National Park Service (NPS); the two are not always the same. An extremely able young California lawyer, Horace Albright, aided him (Albright 1985). Essentially the only other part of the NPS administration in Washington was Robert Sterling Yard. Yard was a newspaperman and had been the best man at Mather's wedding. Mather brought him to Washington in 1915, but since there was no parks organization yet, he became a USGS employee and was immediately detailed to the office of the secretary of the interior, with office space provided by the Bureau of Mines. Actually, Mather paid his salary directly from his own pocket.

Yard launched a publicity campaign, and the NPS came into being in 1916, though there was no funding until 1917. Mather collapsed after the January 1917 NPS conference (Shankland 1951, 110), leaving the twenty-seven-year-old Albright in charge. Albright and Yard had difficulties with each other while Mather was in charge, and these became worse during 1917 when Albright took over for Mather (Miles 1995). In addition, there was the legal question of a publicist for a government agency being paid privately. The brand-new NPS needed all the help it could get, and Yard needed a different job. "On June 26, 1918, at a meeting held at the Smithsonian Institution, there was organized the National Parks Educational Committee. Dr. Charles D. Walcott, Secretary of the Smithsonian Institution was chosen chairman. . . . The committee will support a plan for systematic selection and development to secure for American national parks the recognized first place in world scenery, thus realizing their value as a national economic asset. Its educational plans are based upon views of national parks as popular classrooms and museums of nature" (Walcott 1920, 13–14).

In eleven months, this committee metamorphosed into the National Parks Association, and Yard joined, serving the organization until late in 1933.

Mr. Yard recognized the need, thought of the organization, and deserves credit for developing it as a way to assist the Park Service. Still, Yard had absolutely no "clout" and could not have started such an organization, particularly with the stress of wartime. There is no logical reason whatsoever why Walcott should have joined him in this endeavor. Walcott did not have to chair yet another group. Setting aside his position as secretary of the Smithsonian Institution, if the various government boards plus the CIW were not enough to fill his days, and his NAS and NRC activities left him with time, he was still promoting the GWMA. The only logical thought that comes to mind is Walcott judged that it was his responsibility to protect the parks and enhance their use. This was a small investment of his time, but all of it was taken from his research. Duty had called once more, and once more Walcott had answered.

Part of another day went to the NACA, and then he was finished with business. "Cleaning up all things possible at office so to get away tomorrow" (June 28, 1918). The two did get away as planned to Philadelphia and then out to Bryn Mawr. They went to the Friends meeting that Sunday. "Mary & I have had 4 years of happy married & this is our anniversary" (June 30, 1918). The grammar may have been weak, but the sentiment was strong. They did a bit of shopping and caught the train to New York, then transferred to the Montreal train. They called on railroad magnates in that city, bought a few more supplies, and took the Imperial Limited west. "Am glad to be off as we are both tired and a strenuous rest will stock up energy for next fall & winter" (July 3, 1918). "Strenuous rest" may sound like an oxymoron, but Walcott meant a switch from office to field, from car to horse, and from daily cares to interest in long-dead creatures and their entombing rocks. During the next two days as they rolled westward, Walcott put finishing touches on his trilobite manuscript.

"Arrived at Banff 7:50[.] Alex Mitton met us with buckboard pulled by Cricket & Dolly. We were soon in camp at Buffalo Park and unpacking" (July 6, 1918). The presence of Arthur Brown is such a given that his name does not appear in the diary that summer. They spent a couple of days at the Buffalo Park getting organized and resting up. "I worked on trilobite mss nearly all day. Altho not in A-No. 1 shape I sent it in or rather sealed it up to go" (July 8, 1918). "Packed up & got off at 11 A.M. A broken cinch in Banff delayed [us] but finally we jogged along & despite many automobiles camped on Johnson creek 3 mi from Castle at 5 P.M. A pretty camp but mosquitoes by the hundreds" (July 11, 1918). They made fifteen miles that day. They moved on to Lake Louise, "one of our favorite camps," and the next day converted Saturday into Sunday; Walcott was tired and needed a day of rest.

Two more camps, and the party was far up the Bow River valley. "With Mary & Alex went up to foot of Bow glacier & after lunch collected a few fossils from limestone at the base of the Mt. Whyte formation. Out 7½ hours. Can get a section of Mt. Whyte etc. west of camp on north side of head of Bow Lake" (July 17, 1918). Walcott was metamorphosing, and the geologist was emerging from the administrative cocoon; in fact, the enclosing trap of administration with its manifold trivia makes this an almost respectable metaphor.

They spent two weeks in camp, much of it in frustration because of bad trails, hazy sky preventing photography, snow squalls, rain, and trout not biting most of the time. Eventually, Walcott (1919) got his pictures—as good as any he had published—measured a section of the Mount Whyte Formation, and caught twenty-five trout in one day.

Walcott was told of telegrams at Lake Louise, and Alex headed in to fetch the mail. "Packed up cameras etc in our tent and made ready to move tomorrow if necessary. Alex brot in mail & telegrams. My dear friend Asst. Secty Rathbun died July 16*th*. Mr. W*m* de C. Ravenel succeeds him as acting Secty of Smithsonian" (July 31, 1918). Rathbun had been ill off and on for years, but fighting with the Treasury Department during the last year may have been the final straw in his weakened condition. Once the Bureau of War Risk Insurance had moved into some of the space on the ground floor, it had been insatiable in its need for more. Rathbun protested the disruption, but Secretary Walcott and the Regents could hardly ignore a request from President Wilson, especially one to ensure lives of the servicemen fighting for their country. More clerks poured in, and the building was closed to the public. It is one of the ironies of fate that the formal closing of the Museum and Rathbun's death occurred the same day (Yochelson 1985, 66–67).

With several thousand young ladies jammed into the exhibit halls, working conditions must have been intolerable. The displays were simply pushed aside to make room for desks. Seventy years later, a sprightly lady who had come to Washington in those years could remember looking from her desk on the second floor rotunda down to the dinosaurs and living in a dormitory erected near Union Station.

Walcott immediately telegraphed Ravenel in Washington telling him to consult with the appropriate members of the staff. "We have lost our greatest museum thinker but work will go as planned & successfully."[7] A few days later, in connection with another urgent matter, he expanded that thought. "Richard

Rathbun was a worthy successor of Goode and cannot be replaced as conditions have changed. Will outline plan on my return."[8]

Walcott considered returning to Washington, but by the time he got the telegram, news of Mr. Rathbun's death was two weeks old. He made arrangements by telegram to be notified if he was needed. With the Museum closed for the duration and a reduced staff, there really was little in the way of SI business that summer. In addition to other assistance that Mary provided her husband, she occasionally helped Walcott plow through his mail. There is no difficulty in differentiating her neat script from Walcott's scribblings. From time to time she acted as amanuensis, an old-fashioned word for stenographer, because in that long-past generation, dictating was still in style.

> I was very much shocked by the news of Mr. Rathbun's death, altho I had anticipated that it might come suddenly at any time. With large museum closed and plans approved for the summer, I do not see that it is essential for me to return, unless some emergency. . . . I found on getting away on the trail that I was more tired than usual. It took about two weeks for me to get back to steady nerves and sound sleep. . . . After the first week the weather was fine. When the change came we had ice on the water bucket. . . . The fishing is fair in the lake about 100 yards from camp. Have taken out about 100 trout averaging 10 in. in length. Large ones occur, but they can only be caught by trolling with live bait. We leave here in the morning for the Saskatchewan area, where we will be from four to five days travel from Lake Louise. I hope to find some very interesting & valuable geologic data from a camp on Glacier Lake which is just below the Continental Divide. Thus far the sections have a repetition of those obtained near Hector & Field.[9]

Walcott guessed wrong on his expectations for the area, though it is understandable, for one has to be an optimist to be a field geologist. The scenery was beautiful near Pinnacle Peak, but "sections do not appear sufficiently different from Bow Lake to work them" (August 6, 1918). Next, the weather turned against them. Walcott was able to take a few photographs now and then; however, several attempts to use the large panorama camera were defeated by mist. Mary at least was enjoying herself painting the wildflowers. "Measured Ptarmigan formation & part of Mt. Whyte formation 750+ feet of beds. A tedious bit of work owing to bad talus slopes. Located Ross Lake shale in the section. Half clear day & cold wind" (August 13, 1918). Throughout the season, Alex Mitton was invaluable as collector and geologic field assistant; he was far more than just a skilled packer.

Mary took the train west to Glacier to measure the retreat of the glaciers, and Walcott and Alex tried to carry on the geology. "Steady rain up to 1 A.M. Cleaned up—wrote letters & read—after 3 P.M. tried for a few trout in the Bow River. Only small ones caught. Am getting tired of this damp, uncertain weather" (August 21, 1918). Then there was a telegram from Mary, who was not well. Walcott met her at the train and took her into Banff. A doctor diagnosed neuritis in her arm. A day or two later, she was better and back in camp. Once more the war intruded into the peace of the mountains by way of a chatty letter from Chief Clerk Dorsey in Washington.

> The Signal Office has made an additional grant of $5,000 for Dr. Goddard. . . . I am enclosing a copy of the Senate report on aircraft production. . . . I understand there was a confidential report made at the same time. . . . Our big company of Engineers is still located here in front of the building. They keep their guns in racks in the entrance to the main hall, which looks quite like an arsenal sometimes. . . . Every day or two some member of our force comes in to say that have enlisted or gone into Red Cross or some other kind of service. . . . [O]ur family is becoming smaller and smaller each day, and when the new draft law goes into effect it will include even some of us old ones who are left.[10]

It was a factual report, not a complaint.

War or no war, the fieldwork proceeded. "Moved camp to Tokuman Creek on Vermillion river. A cldy, threatening day with a little mist now & then" (August 28, 1918). This was the thirteenth camp of the season, and not much more was accomplished here than at the earlier ones. Lots of game was seen; the hunting season would open in three days, and Walcott cleaned the guns, for the Museum wanted a bull moose and other big game. "Wood & Alex went out to spot a bull moose. None showed up" (September 2, 1918). They moved the camp to near Wolverine Pass. Walcott took a few photographs and collected Upper Cambrian fossils, while the hunt went on for something to shoot. "Cloudy threatening day. With Alex rode over to head of s.w. head of Ochre creek & thence across to west branch. A long ride but without special result. All Upper Cambrian calcareous & clay shales. Mary in camp painting on a yellow Arnica flower" (September 8, 1918).

That day was a reasonable summary of the geologic results of the entire season. Walcott finally did obtain some fine panoramas of the high peaks to the south of the Bow River, but not nearly as many as he had hoped for. Tex Wood came back to camp empty handed. "Moose (bull) & goat appear to have skipped out for the time being" (September 11, 1918). Walcott had been trying to obtain a pair of moose for the Museum collection. They looked at the geology near Vermillion Pass and near Booma Lake, but there were no dramatic discoveries. They moved back along the railroad where Wood got a black bear and Alex a sheep. They moved back into the mountains near Sawback Lake. "After lunch Alex &

I went up above head of Sawback Lake and Alex skinned out 'Ram,' that Wood had shot while I caught a few fine trout in Lake—Returned to camp 6 P.M. Fine mist falling" (September 22, 1918). Fog prevented more photography. They moved to Banff, the twenty-first and final camp of the season. It took a couple of days to collect another skull and skin from Tex Wood, pay bills, finally take a bath, and pack up the outfit. At 11:00 P.M. on September 20, the season was finally over. The Walcotts left by train, but Alex and Arthur moved south with the horses and gear.

Earlier Walcott had written to the superintendent of the Blackfoot Reservation, after first checking with headquarters in Washington, for permission to leave the outfit on the reservation. "As an active member of the U.S. Geol. Survey 1879–1907 I could not carry on work in Canada. In 1907 I was appointed in chg of the Smithsonian Institution under which the U.S. National Museum is placed. I soon planned to carry the Montana work north. . . . Have 12 fine horses—pack outfit, baggage wagon & a buckboard, tents, blankets, etc. I wish if practical to place the camp equipment, wagons & harnesses in govt. building. . . . The horses (12) could be placed in chg. of reliable Indian if pasturage is available. It has cost me one dollar per month per head near Calgary which included salting & herding & and hay if heavy snow came".[11]

Friday, the Walcotts were in Ottawa. They called at the Geological Survey of Canada to see Director McConnell, the paleontologist Dr. Edward M. Kindle, and Mr. Burling. In Toronto the following day, they paid their respects to Sir Edmund Walker at McGill University. The bad weather followed them to Buffalo. Walcott and Mary arrived home on Sunday morning and had only the rest of that day to recover from their long ride. "At my office during day. Interviews & looking over mail took up time. Went over museum matters with Mr. Ravenel" (October 7, 1918).

The next day it was the NACA Executive Committee that met; Walcott was still the chairman. "At my office & over museum buildings during day. Dr. R. S. Millikan (Col[onel]) came in P.M. for long talk en re Science & Research Division" (October 9, 1918). This was followed by the annual meeting of the NACA and more NRC business. "Columbus day. At home as offices are closed. Worked on proof & mail a little but my cold makes me feel useless. Helen doing Red Cross work among influenza patients" (October 12, 1918). "On acct influenza all churches & schools closed. Helen & Sidney out looking up sick—Helen out all night" (October 13, 1918).

Monday, Walcott read proof on one of the many annual reports he had to prepare, dictated to Miss Brigham (who again came up to the house from the Castle), and talked to Bassler of the Museum staff about the poor reproduction of illustrations in his trilobite manuscript—just odds and ends for a half-sick man. He woke up with a fever, but fortunately after two days in bed the fever passed; it was not the dreaded influenza. Still, a week ensued before Walcott was back at the office. Outside of finishing the reading of the trilobite paper proofs, matters were mostly routine.

Sunday at church was not that restful, as finances for the Church of the Covenant enmeshed Walcott in yet another meeting. "Conference at Ad. Comm. Aeronautics 12–2 P.M. Dr. Ames, Dr. Sabin, & Col. Millikan *en re* correlation of research work" (October 28, 1918). The next day, the NACA Executive Committee met, and two days later Walcott presented Colonel Millikan with a copy of a resolution that the NACA had just passed. It was classic Walcott organization to decide in advance what the Army Air Service wanted the NACA to do and then have the action formalized by the NACA and moved forward.

Mary escorted Helen to New York; the young lady was shipping off to Italy to help with war work. "Meeting of Trustees of Church of Covenant 9 A.M.—At my office 10–4:30 P.M. Appointed W*m* de C Ravenel Director Arts & Industries Museum & Administrative Asst to the Secty of Smithsonian. Conferences with head curators & others during day" (November 1, 1918). Rathbun's death had left a major administrative gap, and this appointment helped close it. Ravenel worked long and hard, especially with the Museum, but he was never given the status of assistant secretary.

A couple of days more of routine, lightened by an automobile ride on a fine autumn afternoon, and then Walcott was in New York at the Hotel Belmont. He met Mary and Helen and the next day spent four hours with Mr. Freer, who was understandably concerned about his building; construction had stopped because of the war. Walcott smoothed over the situation as well as he could. Later, he and Mary made several social calls that afternoon and then dined with friends.

"Slept late. Called on Jacob H. Schiff, Mr. Child, & lunched with Elan H. Hooker. With Mary went to Brooklyn with Helen-Louise and called on our granddaughter Evelyn Breese Walcott 5 weeks old. Met Mrs. Davis. E—is a fine child" (November 8, 1918). The next day, Helen boarded the *Lorraine* and sailed to Bordeaux, her final destination Rome, where she was to enter Red Cross civilian relief efforts; the giddy debutante had become a caring woman. The Walcotts returned home, and one cannot help but wonder what thoughts might have gone through Walcott's mind that Sunday at church—a baby girl of a new generation to cherish, but his own girl returning to the war zone.

"At my office A.M.—Official report of signing of armistice with Germany & the Allies received 2 A.M. We thank God that the end has come & that Germany is defeated. Now she will be regenerated & become a republic. Kaiser Wilham the head criminal has fled to Holland" (November 11, 1918). Suddenly, the horror in Europe was over. The next day was quiet at the office; Walcott noted, with satisfaction, the internal turmoil in Germany.

"Research men & military men waiting for orders to demobilize in Washington" (November 13, 1918). The armed forces were to demobilize rapidly after the Second World War, but slowly compared to the rate at which the nation went back to a peacetime footing in 1918 and 1919. Walcott called at the NACA headquarters en route to New York. The CIW Ex Comm meeting there was over by noon, and he was back home that night. "A quiet busy day at my office—attending to correspondence and at odd moments, sorting fossils from the Burgess Shale of B.C. Canada" (November 15, 1918).

After church, Walcott welcomed a French scientific commission and then moved to Baltimore for the NAS fall meeting. An unused feature of the meeting was a petition circulated by William Morris Davis, a geologist from Columbia University, urging Congress to join a league of nations; NAS members seldom mix in politics, but a number of those present signed the petition. Walcott went back Washington and to aviation matters. The abrupt armistice caught both the aircraft manufactures and the Army Air Service off guard; it would be a bad pun to state they were up in the air as to what would come next. "At my office during day. A cold kept me guessing all day as to whether I was in for a grippe attack" (November 21, 1918). For Walcott's diary entries, it was a very rare bit of humor.

"Called on Secty of War at noon *en re* aircraft etc. Talked with Mr. Potter & Col. Waldron *en re* war museum aeronautical exhibit" (November 22, 1918). "At my office all day. Wish to get things cleaned up so that I can push along research work as much as possible. The development of the museum & other Smithsonian activities progresses steadily considering war time conditions" (November 23, 1918).

"We gave our first large dinner since 1916–1917 in honor of Secty & Mrs. Daniels" (November 25, 1918). After dinner, they adjourned to a French victory party, which may have been just as well for the guests, considering that no alcohol was served by Mary. That event out of the way, Walcott polished off the annual NACA report. "At my office all day. Cleaning up odds & ends and sorting algal fossils from Burgess Pass quarry" (November 27, 1918). Walcott was starting a new research project.

Mary's brother, his wife, and their two boys, George and Henry came in town for Thanksgiving. It must have been a happy but restrained occasion. All were glad that the war was over, but surely thoughts of Stuart must have crossed the minds of the adults. The Vauxes stayed to see the sights in Washington for another day, while Walcott sorted his mail and sorted his Burgess Shale algae.

The Vauxes left, and the Hookers came to town; they visited on Saturday and after church on Sunday.

"At my office A.M. Meeting of Nat. Advisory Board for Aeronautics 2:30–4 P.M. A small meeting as members are out of town" (December 2, 1918). Library work and routine kept Walcott occupied for a few days. "Meeting of Committee on subject of legislation for government of aeronautic navigation 10–12:30 A.M." (December 5, 1918). The airmail flights had shown the need for a navigation system, and Walcott gave this need his attention.

"Working in laboratory nearly all day. A few callers & a little mail. Mary developing the film we exposed last summer & getting fine things. Dr H. Foster Bain, geologist, came in after dinner for a talk *en re* mining experimental stations in all states of the U.S." (December 7, 1918). Among other callers was "Dr George Otis Smith"; Walcott had approved of this much younger man for position as director of the USGS, but he still was formal in this reference to him, as indeed to virtually everyone. Walcott actually had a few days to work on Middle Cambrian fossils before major meetings in December began. "Meeting of Ex-Comm. S.I. Regents 9:15–10 A.M. & meeting of Board 10–12 A.M. Dr Abbot appointed Asst. Secy. S.I. At 4 P.M. meeting Ex-Comm Carnegie Institution of Washington" (December 12, 1918). Abbot had first come to the SI in 1895 as an assistant to Secretary Langley; in 1928, he would succeed Walcott as the fifth SI secretary.

The regents' meeting was followed the next day by that of the CIW board and the Ex Comm. The NACA Executive Committee met on Saturday, and Walcott polished off the week with a dinner in honor of Vice President Marshall. After church, Walcott was back at his office to look at photographs as a prelude to yet another research project.

Before going on to the next research project, the one just completed deserves comment. "Appendages of Trilobites" came out during December. No day was given, and Walcott did not bother to note its publication. For any scientist, once proofs are read, it is the next manuscript that is the prime concern. This paper, however, was dear to Walcott's heart, as shown in part by his concern about the poor quality of some of the illustrations. The work warranted a separate paragraph and separate heading in the *Annual Report*: "In my laboratory work for the past 45 years I have been on the watch for evidence bearing on the structure and organization of fossil trilobites. The study of a small and unique series of specimens secured at Burgess Pass since 1910 has so greatly increased our knowledge of these interesting animals that a special paper, accompanied by 28 plates of illustrations, is now in press to appear in the Smithsonian Miscellaneous Collections" (Walcott 1920, 7).

Walcott referred back to his 1881 paper and noted changes and corrections as a result of these new specimens. He summarized the work the late C. E. Beecher of Yale had published on the Middle Ordovician *Triarthrus becki* and revised some of his findings. New data from the Burgess Shale trilobites with preserved appendages was incorporated. Even so, in all there were less than a dozen Burgess of trilobite specimens that had appendages preserved.

Walcott (1894) had earlier concluded that the trilobites constituted a group distinct from the Crustacea. In 1913, P. E. Raymond of Harvard University contributed to a revision of the classic textbook by the German paleontologist Karl von Zittel. In it, he placed the the trilobites as a subclass of the Crustacea, not as a separate class. Raymond and the zoological community did not share Walcott's view of such great distinctiveness of the trilobites. Walcott did not press his case and in this work modified his views, concluding that the trilobites had diverged very early from a primitive crustacean stock. A reviewer commented, "Some conclusions drawn are that the trilobite's appendages show it to have been a marine crustacean far more highly developed than would have seemed possible in a period so infinitely remote" (Brigham 1919, 231).

Zoological classification, especially above the species and genus level, is an uncertain business. Walcott did touch briefly on *Marrella* again, suggesting that this fossil was a primitive form "possibly ranking in development between *Apus* and the trilobite" (Walcott 1918c, 171). He did not comment on the other genera of arthropods from the Burgess Shale that Walcott had described half a decade earlier. Inasmuch as no high-level rankings in Linnean nomenclature are used by Walcott in this paper, one cannot speculate at what level of classification Walcott judged the trilobites to fit within the Arthropoda.

In addition to morphology of the trilobite limbs directly, Walcott went back to the evidence of tracks and burrows and expanded on material he had presented earlier. Walcott concluded that most had trilobites lived by hunting worms shallowly buried in the sea bottom. This seems to be the consensus of the present generation of investigators. Walcott's view of evolution included the concept of race vitality, and presumably the trilobites were in decline after the Ordovician because their vitality was being exhausted. This seems to be an idea whose time has long since passed. In his words, "Never having penetrated into fresh or other nonmarine waters, or into the deep sea, those havens of refuge where the relics of many ancient types may still be found, the trilobite, unable to cope with the new world in which it found itself was consumed as food by its new enemies, both internal and external, and at the same time subjected to overwhelming competition, so that the individuals died off more rapidly than they could reproduce, and the race disappeared with the close of Paleozoic time. It persisted for many million years and left its remains more or less abundantly through about 75,000 feet of stratified rocks" (Walcott 1918c, 179).

The trilobites were given their due, and that particular drawer was closed for a while. "Began draft of algae from Burgess Shale" (December 18, 1918). If one follows a division of more complex lifeforms into plant and animal, algae are plants. These markings on the shale were quite unlike the Precambrian stromatolite buildups Walcott had studied earlier, but they were a part of the biota and had to be described to provide a clearer notion of life during the Cambrian.

Cottrell and fellow Californian John C. Merriam dropped in to talk about the RC and other matters. Planning of NRC reorganization, now that peace was at hand, took two full days. "The sudden collapse of the central powers, and the consequent swift transition from war to peace conditions, fortunately did not take the National Research Council wholly unaware. From the time of its initiation in 1916, the Council always recognized that the chief service could be best formed in times of peace" (Abbott 1919, 39). The NRC had proved worthwhile during the war, but obviously it now had to have a different role. Putting into effect President Wilson's official request that the NRC be made permanent would require a great deal of planning. Merriam, who had been elected to the NAS that spring, was now running the NRC, in fact if not in title, replacing Hale, who was anxious to return to his telescope on Mount Wilson.

Walcott also spent some time with Col. O. Deeds of the Equipment Division of the Air Service. The army suddenly had a large number of planes, and no one was quite clear how the surplus should be handled. Even with these distractions, Walcott managed to obtain a little research time for the Middle Cambrian algae. He was not neglecting the social aspect of his position; he gave a dinner in honor of Chief Justice White. (The chief justice is by statute a regent and almost always holds the office of SI chancellor.)

The day before Christmas, the Walcotts went to Bryn Mawr to spend the holiday with Mary's brother and family. It was home on the 26th for another rather somber house Christmas with Annie and Mollie. Walcott read a letter from Helen, who had visited Stuart's grave.

"Routine at office most of the day. Selecting material for micro-slides at odd times. A few callers. Dr Geo. E. Hale and Prof. Noyes dined & spent the evening with us talking over Research Council work" (December 28, 1918). After church, he called on Cousin Fred, while Mary went off to the training school for girls. This restful Sunday was followed by a "meeting of Council of National Academy 10–1 P.M. Considered peace organization of Research Council" (December 30, 1918). On the last day of the year, Walcott "spent the morning in considering aeronautical matters especially at meeting of committee on aeronautical navigation" (December 31, 1918).

To sum up the year 1918, for the first time in his summaries Walcott needed more than one page in his diary. He recounted Stuart's death, the end of the war, and gave vent to his feelings about Germany and the Germans, who had taken his son. "Whipped, they acting like cringing brutes to be forgiven and taken back into family of nations without atoning for their many crimes" (December 31, 1918). He listed birthdays, adding daughter-in-law Helen-Louise and Evelyn Breese Walcott to the list; Stuart, Charlie, and Helena were no longer on that list.

Walcott began 1919 by writing in his diary where the remnants of his scattered family was, with Sidney still in the army and Helen in Europe. He and Mary spent the day at the SI looking at photographs. They dined with Dr. A. A. Michaelson of Chicago, the first American to win a Nobel Prize and vice president of the National Academy. It was a quiet time. Seemingly, one of the casualties of the war was the tradition of formal calls on New Year's Day to the White House and the homes of cabinet officers.

The first workday, after the odds and ends were disposed of, was devoted to a staff memorial meeting for A. Howard Clark, the late editor. Such gatherings when important members died were an SI tradition; the funeral was the next day. Walcott attended the Archaeological Society meeting, went to church, joined Mary at a tea held at the Marine Corps Barracks, discussed legislation for the aerial navigation scheme, and considered routine matters.

Walcott's longtime associate ex-President Theodore Roosevelt died on January 6, yet curiously this was not noted by Walcott; perhaps it was such general news that the death seemed not to need recording. Two days later was a major day on Capitol Hill, with the SI appropriations hearings immediately followed by the NACA appropriations hearings. These hearings did not discomfit the secretary, and on January 9, the Walcotts hosted a dinner party for retired General Squier.

"A quiet day. Only two callers[,] so worked on Cambrian algae part of the day. The Smithsonian staff met at 3:45 for a family talk" (January 11, 1919). The year was developing a pattern of administration and research, with relatively few meetings; research was receiving more time than in the past two years. The Iowa apartment house annual meeting was a mere formality, and a NRC council meeting took only two hours.

The algal study was progressing nicely. Walcott needed thin-sections, and since the USGS had a specialist who could grind the rock slices thin enough to be examined at one thousand times magnification, Walcott asked Director Smith for assistance. As just a touch of the imperial secretary, he ended his brief request with: "In order to save time and in anticipation of favorable action I am sending herewith material for possibly 75 to 100 slices."[12] It was a large order, but by the end of April the sections were delivered.

Just as the research was starting to move forward, Walcott came down with a cold; it was so bad that he actually skipped a meeting of the CIW Ex Comm in New York. He recovered enough so that Mary could leave for a day to see friends and Friends in Philadelphia. "At my office all day. Obtained a few hours work for Cambrian algae & Mary colored lantern slides" (January 17, 1919). "A busy day at office. At 4:40–5:25 gave a talk on photographing in the Canadian Rockies in Auditorium of National Museum" (January 18, 1919).

Even though Congress was in session, with the war over the pace in Washington slowed dramatically. Walcott could enjoy church on Sunday and then go to his office to look at photographs; there were no more emergency meetings. "Routine & a little study of recent algae kept me busy during the day at the office" (January 20, 1919). As another change, the social scene blossomed in Washington, and the Walcotts were dining out frequently. The Ex Comm met, Mary and Walcott went for a long walk, and it was time for church again.

The last part of January was mainly involved with callers, most of whom were concerned about the future of aeronautics, and with Congress, about a Roosevelt memorial. It was to be another three decades before serious consideration of such a memorial was renewed. Today Roosevelt Island in the Potomac River hosts a statue of Theodore, but Congress during Walcott's time was not interested.

February began with another conference with George Ellery Hale; there is no doubt that Hale was a sparkplug, but once he proposed ideas, others had to fill in the details. Cottrell called again, this time about helium, the lighter-than-air gas; he and Walcott got on quite well, regardless of which particular concerns "Cott" brought with him. Walcott's cold must have lingered on, for he wrote, "Feeling stupid so jogged along in my office all day clearing up mail etc" (February 3, 1919); even if the brain was not up to research, there was plenty to do. Walcott improved, went to hear the Philadelphia Symphony, which was in Washington on tour, and pursued his manifold interests at the Capitol building.

"Quiet day at the Smithsonian—worked several hours on Middle Cambrian algae. At home in evening. Mary & I are enjoying long walks morning & evening as the roads & walks are dry" (February 6, 1919). Washington weather has a reputation for changeability, and the next day brought snow squalls; this did not deter Walcott from a meeting with the CIW staff, for he was no stranger to snow squalls.

"At church A.M. and Memorial meeting to Theodore Roosevelt 2:30–5 P.M. Senator Lodge delivered a fine address" (February 9, 1919). The Walcotts hosted a dinner for fourteen in honor of the ambassador from the Netherlands; social life had indeed returned to Washington. He spent a day at the office, and then it was off to New York once more.

There Walcott dropped in at the American Museum. Professor Robert P. Whitfield had died, but his successor showed Walcott the fossils he wanted to see. Whitfield had been the assistant to James Hall in Albany, and his leaving, actually firing by Hall, had made the place for Walcott in 1876. From 1880 to 1882, Whitfield had provided office space at the American Museum in New York when the USGS had no place in Washington. Whitfield's death broke Walcott's last connection to his youth.

Walcott lunched with Elan Hooker, discussing the RC, and then made the rounds of the money/art crowd—Otto Kahn, Jacob H. Schiff, S. C. Childes— and ended with baby granddaughter Evelyn. The next day the CIW Ex Comm met, but Walcott polished off the meeting in good order and was back in Washington in time for dinner with the vice president. Saturday night, Secretary of War and Mrs. Newton D. Baker were greeted by a dozen guests at a Walcott dinner; peace had returned to Washington.

After church on Sunday, the Walcotts called on Mrs. Dimock, and on Monday the accounts of the GWMA were audited. A new scheme was hatched to have the inside of the proposed dome covered with stars, each representing a fallen service man, and each sold by donation. Walcott gave five hundred dollars to the now-renamed National Victory Memorial Building. Although this attempt to raise money also eventually failed, the plans continued to move forward, and a model of the building was made for display in Washington.

The week began with a meeting of the NACA Executive Committee. The war may have been over, but research in aeronautics was bound to continue. "Mary left for Phila 10 A.M. At my office all day attending to routine & a little research work. Meeting of Geo. Washgn. Memorial Ass. 4–5:30 P.M." (February 19, 1919). Walcott had three days alone, and he made the most of them in research. Naturally the NACA, having problems before it of how to pursue aerial navigation, intruded a bit, and the Washington Monument Society had to gather and certify that the obelisk was still standing, or whatever the organization did. Just to show he was still a handy man with tools, Walcott repaired the porch curtain at home, rather than ask William or Arthur to do it.

Following church, Walcott had a long talk with Secretary Baker; the wartime habit of business on Sunday was not easy to break. Afterward he and Mary went to the Smithsonian to select photographs for that year's "Explorations" pamphlet. Dr. and Mrs. Hale joined them for dinner.

Monday, February 24, 1919, is the first mention in Walcott's diary of a new research project. He had decided to describe the sponges that had been collected from the Burgess Shale. Some sponges, though not all, have an internal support of spicules that are mineralized; others have a support of organic material. Unless these pieces are fused into a solid skeleton, the sponge disintegrates rapidly after death. Sponges have few characters, relative to, say, brachiopods, and more often than not they are best described as blobs in a rock. During its life, many of a sponge's characters are changed, depending in part on the speed of water flow where the sponge lived so a group of specimens of the same species may show considerable variation in shape. A further complication is that all specimens from the Burgess Shale were flattened. To be frank, sponges do not appeal to many paleontologists. It was more of a duty to record them as part of the biota than an excitement, as had been the case for the holothurians and worms. The descriptions of the algae must also have been difficult, for Walcott had no experience with describing marine plants, but by working on both alternately, Walcott kept both manuscripts moving along.

To provide some larger historical perspective, this was the time when debate on the League of Nations began at the Capitol; it was to be a nasty fight with the White House. Meanwhile, the Japanese ambassador was formally entertained by Secretary and Mrs. Walcott; perhaps it was Freer who had interested Walcott so much in the Japanese. As early as 1908, Walcott had sent Freer a photograph of a tree on the SI grounds in a snowstorm and commented on the similarity to a Japanese print.

"A few callers so turned in early to work on Middle Cambrian sponges from Burgess Pass" (February 26, 1919). "A quiet day at the S.I. At 11:30 went up to Capitol with Dr Stratton. Some prospect but not much of its passing [legislation on aerial navigation]. Mary & I went to church meeting in evening to hear Training School girls sing" (February 27, 1919). It was to be half a decade before the Kelly Act passed, putting the Federal Aviation Authority, with its regulated, marked routes, into place. Once again, Walcott covered a large stretch of country, between airplane beacons and ancient sponges.

"Mrs. St. Gunard came to work & asst. in examination of microscopic sections of Cambrian rocks" (March 1, 1919). This lady appears only once and disappears without any further clues as to what she did or for how long. "At my office 9–11 A.M. 1:20–4:15 P.M. At closing session of Congress 12:15–12:45. Spoke to President Wilson and many Senators. The session terminated in a deadlock on many important bills" (March 4, 1919). There would be worse in Congress before the Wilson presidency ended.

"A long quiet day in my office. Worked on Cambrian & fussed with various odds & ends of things" (March 5, 1919). The house was particularly quiet, for Mary was off to Philadelphia once more. She came back in time to supervise a dinner for the Japanese ambassador. The NRC met again, and again Walcott had dinner with Merriam to organize matters.

Mary played her part as the secretary's wife. In 1917, the elephant that had been donated when the National Zoological Park opened died. Two years later, a pair of baby elephants from Sumatra came onto the market. "Hitam" (black) and "Kechil" (small) were purchased, and it was Mary who went out and raised five thousand dollars to pay for them. For several years these animals were favorites with the local school children, and although one died, the other enjoyed life in Rock Creek Park. Meanwhile, the Burgess Shale sponges were keeping Walcott fully occupied. As soon as Mary discharged her official duties with the elephants, she was back at Walcott's office, touching up photographs of the Middle Cambrian algae.

"Spent an hour looking over recent sponges & E. O. Ulrich's diagrams of undulations of old surface in Cambrian & later ages" (March 26, 1919). Dr. Ulrich held the view that different kinds of rocks meant deposition from different seaways. Whereas many geologists would suggest that a sand to the east graded to a shale in the west as one moved from shallow to deeper water, Ulrich would have it that the sand had been deposited by a sea that encroached from the east, while the shale was deposited by a sea that came in from the west. It was a strange idea.

Ulrich did not suffer from excessive modesty. A few years earlier he had written to a colleague on the New York State Geological Survey about his interactions in 1913 with Walcott.

> First I took up the Cambrian section in the upper Mississippi valley. That meant ten days of comparing of notes and specimens collected during my recent field investigations; followed by two weeks with Walcott during which we tested my classification by comparison of a hundred or more drawers of prepared old collections and notes on local stratigraphy. Finally, Dr. Walcott being in a hurry to use my classification, I presented a digest of results and names of formations to our Survey for consideration and adoption by the Committee on Formation Names. But that Committee is a very painstaking and conservative institution, so that it was only day before yesterday when the real and fancied difficulties were finally adjusted.[13]

On the other hand, Ulrich knew fossils and was a pioneer in the study of major groups. The general view of those who followed Ulrich was that he was a master paleobiologist and a dreadful biostratigrapher. Dr. Ulrich, the title a result of six months in a medical college, must have had great charm, for Walcott used his new terminology in western Canada. Despite the sometimes vitriolic encounters Ulrich had with other geologists, his colleagues nicknamed him "Uncle Happy."

Near the end of March there is a rare glimpse into Walcott's concern for his subordinates: the Walcotts were to go to a concert, but they did not take the car; William's wife was seriously ill, and Walcott insisted he stay with her. "Making headway slowly on Cambrian fossil sponges. Notified that C.I. Corporation of

New York had voted a large grant to the National Academy and National Research Council" (March 29 1919). That was news worth celebrating in church.

"Resumed duties at Smithsonian 9 A.M. Routine & research work kept me busy all day. Papers state that a grant of $5,000,000 has been made to Nat. Research. Council by Rockefeller Foundation. A quiet evening at home. I am 69 years old today" (March 31, 1919). Walcott had something of a birthday present in April with three quiet days that he could devote almost completely to the Middle Cambrian sponges. Whitman Cross, the NAS treasurer, dined with him, and they conferred about NRC business; Walcott wanted no surprises at the coming NAS meeting.

"Meeting Ex. Comm. Nat. Parks Comm." (April 5, 1919). What was to be the National Parks Association was evolving out of last year's National Parks Education Association. This was another distraction for a man who already had too many distractions. On Sunday after church, he and Mary went to his office. On Monday, Walcott again got a few hours' work in on his sponges.

The research effort was broken by a meeting of the NACA Executive Committee; this was the third year that Walcott was chairman of that committee. That night Mary gave a lecture on the Canadian Rockies at the Congressional Church, and afterward they caught the midnight sleeper to New York. "Attended meeting of Ex—Comm. Carnegie Institution 10–12. Conference with Elihu Root & Henry S. Pritchett *en re* to Nat. Acad. & Research Council foundation" (April 11, 1919).

Again, it is important to recall who knew whom and for how long. Root, among other jobs, was chairman of the CIW Board of Trustees, and Prichett was president of the Carnegie Corporation. Walcott and Root went back a long way; their early contacts in New York had been cemented at the CIW founding in 1902. Ever since 1913, when Root became chairman and Walcott vice chairman, the organization had run as smoothly as glass. Association with Dr. Pritchett did not go all the way back to New York State, but it did date from Walcott's early days in Washington, when the two had both been federal scientists.

In Root's papers there are only a few letters to Walcott, and most of those are concerned with topographic maps of New York. Those who want proof in writing before they accept an interpretation will ignore or diminish Walcott's importance in obtaining this little meeting on NAS-NRC funding. Hale was a persuasive visionary, but those who controlled the purse strings knew Walcott intimately, and that was equally important, if not more so, in the high-stakes game of applying for grants from foundations.

The New York afternoon was more relaxing, for after luncheon he and Mary saw his granddaughter. The next day was equally busy at the Board of Directors of the Hooker Electrochemical Company, another new diversion for Walcott.

On the social side, they called on Mrs. Carnegie. William met them at Union Station when they returned home the next day.

"A broken up quiet day at the Smithsonian. Mail, interview, routine & a little research in the way of making up plates of B[urgess] S[hale–fossil algae. Mary & I dined with Mr. & Mrs. Gilbert Grosvenor & friends" (April 14, 1919); Grosvenor was the one who built the National Geographical Society into a world-wide cultural institution. In mid-April, the NRC met. The following day, Walcott worked on plates of fossils and talked over matters with Dr. Hale to make certain that Academy-Council relationships would be properly worked out.

"At my office A.M. Luncheon with Elihu Root & Geo. E. Hale & went over Nat. Acad. matters & then looked about for a suitable site for a future home of the Academy" (April 17, 1919). Walcott revised his two manuscripts in progress, and with that out of the way, he celebrated Easter service. The evening was most pleasant, what with Dr. and Mrs. Hale, and Dr. and Mrs. Abbot for dinner; the conversation must have been about life on Mount Wilson and the latest advances in astrophysics. Unfortunately, not all of April was fun; "Dr Geo. F. Becker my old friend & colleague for many years died this afternoon" (April 20, 1919). This was nearly the last tie with the USGS of old.

There was no doubt that spring was in full force in Washington, for Mary was out painting watercolors of wildflowers. She had a delicate technique and almost never used white, allowing the paper to add that color. Wildflowers and flowering trees in Washington generally graced the time of the NAS annual meeting. The NRC council met to review the plans for its peacetime organization. To offer some perspective, there is an anecdote that in 1916 when the American Chemical Society offered its services to the U.S. Army, a letter of reply thanked the group but informed it that the army already had a chemist. Once the NRC was well established and the war had started, the scientists became more important.

In wartime arrangements, when there was both pressing need and lots of money, arrangements could be facilitated, provided one had the ears of those at high levels. Consider, for example, the Research Information Service, first suggested in a different form by the British. A letter of interest went to General Squier, who directed it to the Military Committee. Discussion there indicated that a more comprehensive plan was desirable. "It accordingly appointed a committee consisting of Dr. Walcott, Mr. Howard Coffin, Dr. Stratton, and Mr. Millikan to formulate recommendations. The committee formulated a plan which was approved by the Military Committee and then by the Secretaries of War and of the Navy and finally by the President, who appropriated $150,000 from his war emergency fund for the establishment of four new offices" (Millikan 1920, 35).

No one has ever counted to see if the statement of Walcott's being on thirty-five major committees during the war is accurate, but it must have been close to the truth; the information item was one major effort, discussed in the NAS *Annual Report* for 1918, but subsequently little noted by others and hardly mentioned in Walcott's diary.

Peacetime was different, yet Hale was enthusiastic about the future. "Educational institutions are also likely to recognize that science should play a greater part in their curriculum and that men skilled in research should be developed in greatly increased numbers. The enlarged appreciation of science by the public, the demand for investigators in the industries, and the attitude of industrial leaders of wide vision toward fundamental science, should facilitate attempts to secure the added endowments and equipment required" (Hale 1920, 394).

Hale emphasized that the horizons were unlimited in science, if cooperation came to the fore. This was a point Walcott had argued privately with Carnegie in 1903, when the future course of the Carnegie Institution of Washington had been uncertain (Yochelson 1994).

With NAS president Walcott as the NRC's first vice president, most in the inner circle of NRC agreed that the new organizational plan was carefully constructed, and this hurdle was crossed with ease. In these plans there were two grand NRC divisions: general relations, and science and technology. Within general relations, "Government Relations" was chaired by Walcott, and "Foreign Relations" was headed by Hale.

To consider the second of these, two wartime conferences in Europe that Hale had attended decided to scrap virtually all earlier high-level international groupings in science and start fresh; too many had been dominated by German scientists. When the armistice finally came, Hale drafted a plan for an International Research Council and gained NAS approval. He asked Walcott to head the American delegation, but Walcott sensibly demurred, one of the few times he declined to do something. In July 1919, Hale went off to Belgium and arranged the components of international cooperation in science.

So far as domestic general relations were concerned, the Division of Government Relations was as close as the United States has ever come to a cabinet-level Department of Science. On several occasions, the NAS had proposed such an office; in 1903, Walcott and others had suggested that the Department of Agriculture serve as the home for all scientific bureaus, as a step in that direction. A federal Department of Science never happened, nor is it likely to. Rather than concentrating on "pure" science, various agencies practice applied science, with a bit of research hidden here and there. Walcott could not bring off a cabinet department, and if he could not, no single individual could. This division of 1919 was the next best thing. "The constituency of this Division at the present moment is made up of forty-one members. It will serve as a liaison agency to keep the several Divisions of the Council in touch with the scientific work which is being done by the Government. It will also afford opportunity in bringing constantly before notice of representatives of the Government scientific projects both in this country and abroad. Finally, it is believed that the Division may serve to perpetuate and develop a full and frank coöperation among the scientific forces of the Government, such as were successfully initiated by the Council during the war, but which prior to that time had not generally existed" (Angell 1920, 420).

The statement went on to suggest that this division would be a channel for cooperation among government agencies, or between them and outside groups. The last sentence is particularly striking; it harks back in particular to the 1890s and the troubles of the Coast and Geodetic Survey, when the U.S. Navy desired to take over its functions, but was a recurring theme for federal scientists. "Incidentally, it seems not to much to hope that a fuller knowledge among representatives of the scientific bureaus of the Government, each regarding the work of the others, may exercise a highly beneficial influence in discouraging radical and inexpedient legislative action such as has been more than once threatened in the ill-informed attempt to avoid duplication of government where only the appearance and not the fact of such duplication is involved" (Angell 1920, 422). Neither Hale, Millikan, Noyes, Cary, Merriam, nor any of the other academic and industrial researchers swept into the wartime NRC would have thought of this angle.

Even while Walcott was struggling with the NRC, there were other irons to be kept warm in the fire. Not the least of these was the Freer Gallery. This had been a long struggle; it antedated Walcott as secretary. Freer first made the offer of his art collection to the SI late in December 1904. Freer's mansion in Detroit was stuffed with art, and he had recently completed a sixty-foot picture gallery. "Freer's regimen was to show his other artworks only during daylight hours, one or two at a time. In order to ascertain the merit of the proposed gift, the Washington quartet (Langley, secretary of the Smithsonian Institution, plus a university president, a former senator and the president of the National Geographic Society—all three Smithsonian regents) sat still for four days as the art treasures were hauled into view and then taken away. The host's opinion was not too flattering. The four Regents are men of broad education, wide experience and of unquestioned judgement," Freer wrote to a friend, "but what they do not know about art would fill many volumes."[14]

Thereafter the regents and Secretary Langley had dithered—though, in fairness, part of the problem had been the restrictions Freer placed on the proposed donation. At the annual meeting in January 1906, President Roosevelt had taken a hand in the affair, and he had waved a very big stick in a four-page letter. "I hope that the Regents of the Smithsonian will feel warranted to close with the offer, for they are the national guardians of such a collection. If in their wisdom, they do not see their way to accept the gift I shall then be obliged to take some other method of endeavoring to prevent the loss to the United States Government, and therefore to the people of the United States, of one of the most valuable collections which any private individual has ever given to any people."[15]

This message was read by the regents and was understood. Unfortunately, Langley's death further complicated relationships with the donor. One of Walcott's first actions as secretary was to visit Freer, taking along William Henry Holmes, an authentic artist. They soothed him, and by June of 1908 the si was acting as receiving agent for material Freer was shipping from Egypt. Freer received kid-glove treatment and generally prompt answers to his letters. The exception proves the rule: "Owing to the illness and death of my sister at our home I have neglected this and several other matters during the past month."[16] Walcott went on to write that he was trying to convince Congress to fund a building for the collection. Congress was not interested; the next year Walcott wanted to convert the Castle into an art museum, but someone scuttled that idea, because the Smithsonian headquarters was not a government building. Art was not a priority of the Taft administration.

The si continued to act as Freer's receiving agent, and Walcott obtained a letter from the secretary of state to facilitate Freer's travels. Walcott continued to charm and accommodate Freer, which eventually led to the temporary exhibit in the Museum in the spring of 1912. Walcott knew exactly how to exploit that. "The taste that you gave them last spring has aroused an interest that will not be satisfied until the collections are placed permanently on view."[17] The next year Walcott was involved in Freer's plan for an archeological school in China, and he had interested Freer in a grant of money to the point where Walcott was looking at potential building sites in Washington. Freer had indicated from the beginning that he would leave money in his will for a building, but had not really moved beyond that. It was a chicken-and-egg situation, in that Freer would not commit to a building unless there was a site, and no site could be found until it was clear a building was forthcoming.

The following year, the prospects changed dramatically. The distinguished astronomer F. H. Seares recalled that

> during a day in 1915, while in Dr. Walcott's office, I asked him what lay behind the change in plans. "It really was a very simple matter" he replied. Continuing, he said in substance, we had only to point out to Mr. Freer that if the collections could be transferred to Washington in the near future, it would be of immense value to us during the construction and installation. We

would be able to draw upon his intimate knowledge of the history of the objects and their significance and to have his advice as to the most effective method of the presentation to the public. We thought, too, that he might find satisfaction if the collection could be displayed during his lifetime in a manner that had his approval.[18]

This was quite an accomplishment, particularly as Freer was now a sick man. "He intimated that there was in his family a history of what could only have been congenital syphilis."[19] As Freer grew older, he became increasingly nervous and irritable (Meyer 1970). Fortunately, Walcott had convinced him in time to act rationally. "Concerning Freer's financial situation, in October, 1915, it appeared that construction of the museum, then estimated at $1,250,000, would have to be delayed because there was no market for Freer's Parke, Davis Drug Company stock. Eugene Meyer, New York financier, knew Freer through his wife Agnes Meyer, also a collector of Oriental art, and he offered to buy this stock, which forced the Parke, Davis partners to acquire what Freer wanted to sell to avoid any 'Wall Street' involvement" (Morgan 1985, 165).

Early in 1913, Freer had consulted Charles Platt, and some preliminary plans had been made. As mentioned earlier, on November 29, 1915, Freer had written Walcott that he had a million dollars in the bank, that he would consult the architect as soon as his strength permitted him to look at the plans, and finally that he wanted construction started in the spring of 1916. Walcott was ready and immediately made arrangements to have the money invested. Freer suggested Berea stone for the exterior, which Walcott rejected as not being durable. Freer then suggested Bedford oolite. Walcott returned a resounding no, pointing out that the building was to endure. This, of course, delighted Freer, and that is why the building is made of granite.

Not all was rosy. Almost immediately thereafter, as noted, Freer had difficulties with the Internal Revenue Service. Walcott had to go to Capitol Hill, see his friends, and have a bill introduced. He even enlisted the support of the president. Eventually, through an act of Congress, the money that the Internal Revenue Service had taken was restored to the endowment. The incident reveals Freer's elitist views.

Postponement until next winter of formal action on the bill providing for the cancellation of the assessment on the sale of the Parke, Davis & Co. stock was to be expected in view of the rush of many things forced upon the House. I think that you know my personal feeling concerning this bill and realize how unjust the taxation. Whether or not Congress chooses to refund the money, is a matter of indifference to me and will always remain so. If the money is ever refunded to me, I shall refuse to make personal use of it, but if the Smithsonian cares to add it to the appropriation for the building, it may do so at its own pleasure. I consider both the assessment and collection of the tax an action on the part of the Treasury Department characteristic of the present administration.[20]

Late in 1915 Freer was suddenly in a rush to build, but Walcott was several steps ahead. Early in the year, he had written Freer pointing out that if a building was situated on Smithsonian property it would not require permission from Congress. Having planted a seed, Walcott left it to grow. "I shall write you rarely in the next few months, as I think it exceedingly desirable that you take an absolute rest if possible."[21] When the Freer money was announced, the press release touched on the issue of a site. "At the December (1914) meeting of the board of regents a committee was appointed upon the question of a site for the Freer art building."[22] It should come as no surprise that Walcott was a member of this committee. That is why "adjacent to the structural monstrosity called the Smithsonian Institution, [is] a perfect example of Florentine Renaissance architecture" (Meyer 1970, 3).

This site led to a turf war, in the literal sense of the expression, for it was fought over whether the original Smithsonian reservation granted by Congress was still valid. The argument went all the way to the Judge Advocate General of the U.S. Army, for in 1912 the chief of engineers had been given authority over public buildings in Washington. The headlines read, "Smithsonian Regents in Control of Grounds" and "Secretary of War Approves Judge Advocate's Ruling in Jurisdictional Dispute."[23]

Construction did not start until September. As the ultimate twist, Walcott, after all his years of effort, was away in the field at that time. Assistant Secretary Rathbun wrote to Freer suggesting that he preside at the opening ceremony, but Freer declined for health reasons. It was Rathbun who presided at the groundbreaking; he wrote Freer a humorous account of the event.

Three months later Walcott added a handwritten note to a brief Christmas letter. "The dirt is nearly all out of the foundation site & with good weather will go ahead rapidly. I expected to be in New York today but a grippy cold say[s] *nay!* Keep well & come see us in the spring if not earlier."[24] Walcott having fixed the income tax problems resulting from the bond sale, Freer continued on a buying spree. Freer originally gave about two thousand objects to the nation, but by the time of his death this had grown to more than nine thousand. When the war came, construction on the art building nearly stopped, but a little momentum was maintained, and Freer was mollified. Finally, the war ended, and construction could proceed more rapidly. "We are still suffering from the demoralization following the war, but it now looks as though matters would get back to normal before summer. We expect that the 3,000 war workers in our big

Natural History Museum will all have moved to their new quarters in March. The collections have not suffered at all, and will speedily be restored to their former positions and condition. Every case in that building is on caster-rollers, so it a very simple matter to move them back. Your building is beginning to show what it really is, and if [we] can only get back to normal labor conditions it will advance rapidly during the spring and summer."[25]

To break the sequence just a little, there were some problems in getting the government to pay for repairs and repainting in the Museum, but Ravenel and Walcott were able to resolve them. A net gain from the wartime use of the Museum was a large building in the east courtyard. This toilet for the thousands of lady clerks became a taxidermy shop, in use for about the next forty years. The government also turned over a pile of coal, left in the coalyard; it was small enough pay for the housing of clerks in the Museum. Another postwar gain was the hangar south of the Castle donated by the army; this tin shack housed the growing aircraft collection. Now, back to Mr. Freer.

> Mrs. Walcott and I made a pretty thorough inspection of your building yesterday and were very much pleased with the progress being made. Owing to the thoroughness with which it is being built, and the great amount of care necessary, the work appears to move slowly, but as I said to Mrs. Walcott yesterday, this building is for the centuries, and a few months spent in careful work in construction will be repaid many times in the future. I well recall how, when I insisted that certain things should be done in the large Natural History Museum, I was told that it would hold up the final completion from three to six months. I said "All right, I will stand for it, so go ahead," with the result that what might have been a very dangerous fire condition was entirely obviated.
>
> All the war workers are now out of the Natural History Museum and most of it has been cleaned and opened to the public. It is a real pleasure to have the collections accessible, and the public shows its appreciation by a large daily attendance.[26]

Presumably, Mr. Freer was as pleased with progress as were the members of the National Research Council; now other interests had to be pursued. "At meeting Nat. Advisory Committee for Aeronautics A.M. Genl. Geo. O. Squire [sic] called 2:30 P.M. & told me of his wireless system using trees for antennae" (April 24, 1919); Walcott went to a meeting of the Physical Society to hear Squier's formal lecture the following day; attending that talk is yet another indication of Walcott's loyalty to friends.

"At my office all day. Used odd moments to examine thin sections of Burgess Shale for microscopic evidences of life" (April 26, 1919). These were the thin-sections he had requested the USGS to make in January. After church, Walcott was off to a GWMA meeting; it was one thing to have a new idea for fund-raising, but quite another to institute it. A war memorial just might succeed, where other attempts to gather funds for a building always fell short. Walcott donated five hundred in memory of Stuart. The same philosophy of a new approach held with the NRC meeting that afternoon and carried over to the NAS dinner. Keeping the NRC in the postwar world was a good idea, but making certain this happened had taken much planning.

Walcott was ready. "Business & public meeting of National Academy of Sciences during the day & evening. Presided at 4 meetings. Dr Brasted of University of Chicago gave lecture in the evening & we had a reception later" (April 28, 1919). That was a warm-up to the Tuesday business meeting. "Constitution of Nat. Research Council approved by Academy A.M. A most important step in advance of science in America" (April 29, 1919). The NAS met for one more day, and by the time the academicians left town, Walcott was dead tired.

Steering the NRC to a safe haven under the wings of the NAS was a triumph. In some ways, the arrangement followed the model he had insisted on for the NACA. A few academicians in charge had the right to bring non-NAS members to various committees and panels; this was a feasible and proven scheme. Among the various problems that had to be worked out was making sure the NRC was subservient to the NAS, even though the NRC was far larger, far more active, and far better financed. On the other side of the coin, with peace in the wind, some academicians could not see the need for support of and cooperation with much younger near-colleagues who had strange ideas, let alone with pseudo-colleagues who engaged in more practical than esoteric problems. Keeping everyone more or less satisfied meant walking a fine line.

With the NRC settled for the future, at least for the moment, Walcott went to an Interdepartmental Committee on aircraft photography. After all, he had a working knowledge of aircraft, knew the fine points of mapmaking, and was a superb photographer. This must have been one committee he enjoyed, though how active he was and how much he contributed is another loose end for others to pursue. Later, he had a conference with Merriam in regard to possible future relationships between the CIW and the NRC; that was a harbinger of developments the following year. Walcott wanted to ensure harmony, cooperation, and lack of duplication. For relaxation that weekend, he and Mary went to visit friends in central Maryland, a round trip of 120 miles; the automobile was here to stay.

After church, it was to the Castle for the afternoon. Pursuing research on Sunday afternoon was becoming a tradition. Monday, Walcott looked at photographs of thin-sections of his algae and tried to develop a better notion of their shapes in three dimensions. Going from a slice to a reconstruction is not simple, but Walcott had been doing this since he first found trilobite limbs in the 1870s. Breaking away from science, Walcott "Called on Acting Sec'y [Franklin D.] Roosevelt 10 A.M. with Mr. Ravenel *en re* Naval Exhibit of War Material. Meeting of Ex. Comm. Nat. Parks Association" (May 6, 1919). This mention of an exhibit is the place for an anecdote concerning Secretary Walcott.

A contractor had installed several display cases in the foyer of the Museum, and a marine lieutenant was directing the arrangement of uniforms on dummies. The glass front was finally put on a case, with considerable difficulty; apparently the size was not quite right. Immediately, the lieutenant wanted to make a minor change, but the contractor expressed concern that if moved the huge piece of plate glass might break. The lieutenant insisted, and, as predicted, the glass broke. The officer was berating the contractor and ordering him to pay for another glass when Walcott, who had been nearby watching, stepped in. Very shortly thereafter, the lieutenant apologized for his remarks and agreed that the contractor would not have to buy another plate glass. The contractor later joined the SI staff; he would praise Walcott till the day he retired, decades after Walcott had been mostly forgotten. He made a point of describing Walcott's presence and bearing. When that man walked through the halls, especially with an overcoat draped over his shoulders, there was never any doubt as to who was in charge. Walcott looked and acted like the secretary.

So much for trivia; meanwhile, a more significant change was taking place in the Washington scientific scene. James B. Angell, on leave from the University of Chicago, was to be appointed chairman of the NRC, to take office in July. This was important in a game of musical chairs, for it meant that Merriam was free to go elsewhere; during the war, Merriam had been chairman of the committee on geology and geography, of which Walcott was a member; he had taken over when W. B. Clark died. Then Merriam had moved up to acting chairman and finally NRC chairman. He was now able to return to California, but Walcott saw Merriam as a promising young man and had his eye on him for future activities.

With the NRC in hand, Walcott left for New York. "At meeting Ex. Comm. C.I. Washington 10–11:30 A.M. Ex. Comm. Carnegie Corporation approved of site in Washn. of Nat. Acad. building" (May 9, 1919). Even if this was a rubber-stamp type of proceeding, it was monumental news, for if any organization needed a building of its own, that organization was the National Academy of Sciences. Picking the building site was another unrecorded Walcott coup. Hale is conventionally given full credit for obtaining funds for the building, yet in his biography there is a long account of a fiasco in 1914 when he asked Andrew Carnegie to finance this project (Wright 1966, 308–10). Both Walcott and Hale would have been far more interested that the battle for a building had been won than in who received credit for the victory. Science won.

On Walcott's return to Washington, the day was quiet, notable only for a dinner at the Japanese embassy, a tit-for-tat for the Walcotts' earlier dinner. The Walcotts ventured out again by car, over Maryland's Blue Ridge to Burkettsville once more, a fine drive at a fine time of year.

"At my office all day. The settling of questions raised by the European war is proceeding slowly but surely. Germany as the criminal nation will be placed in durance for many years as she deserved" (May 12, 1919). It is hard to say what brought on this particular comment; it may have been a plan by Mrs. E. W. Harriman to have paintings made of the delegates to the peace conference. For years, these pictures hung indiscriminately around the Museum, as there was no space for a proper display.

In mid-May, Walcott was off to New York once more. He spent the train ride working on his sponge manuscript. The prime reason for the trip was to present a paper on the National Gallery of Art to the American Federation of Arts. This, however, gave him another opportunity to call on Freer. For the last half-dozen years, Freer had spent more time in New York City than in Detroit; he had even bought a country place in the East. That spring Walcott wrote him, "I am delighted to learn that you were feeling somewhat better, and trust that you will be able to get into the hills the latter part of this month. I am a great believer in the psychological effects of coming in contact with the great Out-of-doors, and I cannot imagine myself really getting well in a large city where there is so little of genuine Nature."[27]

Freer had been in ill health for years, but he was increasingly fragile and seemed to sense that he was near his end. Several years earlier, Freer had thought that George Draper would make an ideal curator. Major Draper went off to France, seeing Freer before he left but not mentioning his coming trip so as not to disturb the sickly collector. Three months after the war ended, Walcott wrote Freer, "We had a very nice visit with Dr. Draper, Sunday, as he and Mrs. Draper accepted our invitation to take dinner with us. I like them both and hope that they will make their home in Washington."[28]

At some time between that February dinner and the May meeting in New York, either Freer or Draper changed his mind. The issue of who was to head the new gallery was of great concern to Freer. One consequence of this May meeting was that Freer settled on John E. Lodge, son of Senator Lodge and curator of Chinese and Japanese art at the Boston Museum of Fine Arts. Thus, it was the donor who contacted the secretary.

"You were so entirely sympathetic and in harmony with my ideas concerning the fitness of Mr. Lodge to undertake that work at the Washington Museum, that I trust that at the next meeting between yourself and the Regents of the Smithsonian Institution, you will take up the question with them and will, with them, give the matter your earnest consideration."[29] Like Andrew Carnegie, Freer had a whim of iron.

Walcott's response was properly circumspect. "Yours of June 4th, with copy of letter sent to Mr. John E. Lodge, received yesterday. In the afternoon I had a talk with Senator Lodge and showed him the letter that you had written to his son. He was greatly interested and somewhat surprised, as he had not heard anything of it. I thought it best not to speak to him about it on account of his being on the Board of Regents, in order to avoid any appearance of his having used any personal influence to have his son considered. He said he had no idea whether his son would accept the offer or not, as he had a very independent character and makes his own decisions."[30]

Walcott went on to discuss money. Before he died, Assistant Secretary Rathbun had given the impression that Freer intended to leave a sufficient endowment to pay the salary of the curator and assistant, yet Walcott could find no clear mention of this point in the copy of the will that he, as one of Freer's executors, had received. "I think that your original thought was a very wise one, as it is exceedingly desirable that the director and such technical staff as may be needed should be independent of Congressional appropriations. There are no Smithsonian funds available for the payment of additional salaries. In fact, I am planning next fall to make an effort to increase our endowment in order to meet the increased expenses of our various activities. We have an income of a little over sixty thousand dollars a year from the Smithsonian, and we should have at least five hundred thousand in order to properly handle the opportunities for research and other work that come to us.[31]

Sixty-nine-year-old Walcott, worn thin by the war, could still look to the future and make great plans. Meanwhile, before their May meeting, Freer had added a codicil to his will such that four persons could add material to the Freer collection. Additionally, in the near future, John Lodge would come to the Freer. The collective views of Freer's four designates and Lodge were to cause management problems for the secretary.

6

The "Normalcy" Years (May 1919–May 1921): Time Flies Like an Arrow, but Fruit Flies Like a Banana—One Contribution to the Silly Season

> To begin with, a good tent is required, plenty of warm blankets, and a canvas sheet to spread under and over the blankets on a bough-bed, to prevent dampness from above and below; then a small pillow is a great luxury, and takes but little room in the pack. Of course, it is pre-supposed that women of the party wear rational clothes.
>
> —Mary Morris Vaux

ART IS ART, and science is science, and about the only thing the two fields have in common is that occasionally a comment or an object provokes controversy. This may be concerned with the authenticity of a painting or the authenticity of an observation. The arguments are important to the combatants but seldom reach beyond the interests of a limited number of people. Thus it was with a visit by Rudolph Ruedemann on May 19; it was one act of a minor scientific controversy concerned with the nature of trilobite appendages.

More than four decades earlier, Walcott (1876) had been the first person to demonstrate conclusively that trilobites had limbs. By this time, the argument on trilobite limbs had become so advanced that the finer details of structure of the legs could be interpreted in several different ways. Concern about the legs of long-dead creatures may seem scant reason for a long discussion, but it often happens in life that matters that some view as trivial are of vital concern to those involved.

Rudolph Ruedemann deserves a brief introduction. As might be expected from his name, he was a German emigré; he had came to New York State just about the time James Hall died. Ruedemann was a talented paleontologist and was soon John M. Clarke's right-hand man. Eventually, he also became New York state paleontologist and an NAS member. Ruedemann was skilled in the study of a variety of fossils, but his major contributions were with investigations of graptolites, which he used to help unravel some of the geology on the west side of the Taconic Mountains. Walcott had a great deal of respect for his ability, as witness a letter three years earlier.

> I was glad you worked up the median eye in Trilobites. It was something that needed the careful attention that you could give it.
>
> I have just sent to press another contribution on the Cambrian trilobites, illustrated by twenty-two plates. Two or three more such will put the preliminary study of Cambrian Trilobites in such shape that a monograph may be attempted.
>
> I expect to leave by the middle of June for the Canadian Rockies, with special reference to studying the faunas and lower part of the Cambrian section, and incidentally looking over some of the rock that I left up on the mountain side two years ago for frost action.[1]

As a clarification, for some years it had been thought by a few paleontologists that several kinds of trilobites had a third eye. A few more years ensued before this was determined to be an error in interpretation.

Another person needs to be introduced here—P. E. Raymond, a Harvard professor. Raymond also was a pretty good paleontologist, and although he worked on many groups, increasingly his forte was trilobites. As mentioned in 1913, he prepared the classification of the Trilobita for the *Zittel-Eastman Treatise*. In its time, this was the standard reference for classification of all fossils. Walcott's copy is heavily annotated in the section dealing with descriptions of these fossil arthropods.

Charles E. Beecher, a Yale professor whose job Charles Schuchert now held, near the turn of the century had written the trilobite section in the first English edition of this work, and Raymond had become in a sense his literary heir. Beecher had devoted a great deal of effort to the Ordovician trilobite *Triarthrus* from near Rome, New York; on some specimens, the preserved appendages are replaced by pyrite, and with considerable care, these tiny delicate structures can be prepared for study. Beecher had died before writing up much of his findings, and Raymond was in the process of completing a monographic effort on that material. Between Raymond's borrowing specimens and Walcott's wanting to examine some of the same specimens, Schuchert could have had difficulties, yet he managed to keep both parties more or less satisfied.

After Raymond's work on the *Treatise*, but before he got deeply into the finer points of Beecher's material, he reviewed Beecher's classification of trilobites, plus those proposed by others, and ended with an interesting thought. "The samples which Dr. Walcott has recently been giving us of his wonderful store of Cambrian trilobites indicate clearly the futility of preceding in the refinement of classification until that fauna is quite fully described" (Raymond 1917, 210). Four years later, he commented: "It cannot be said that an ideal and complete classification has yet been reached, and only when a fuller understanding of the structure and ancestry of the whole group is attained will there come full realization of the relative importance of the various parts of the anatomy. We are, in our descriptions, still struggling somewhat blindly toward the goal" (Raymond 1921, 352). That is a fair statement, for generalizing before all the information is available may lead to new ideas. It is also wise in scientific writing to leave an "out" for oneself, as Raymond clearly did.

Now we may skip back to 1919 and the great trilobite limb committee. Dr. Ruedemann wrote Dr. Walcott:

> Dr. Clarke on his return from Washington tells me that in view of Dr. Raymond's announced intention to dispute the correctness of your observations of the appendages in trilobites, you would like to have me make an unbiased study of your specimens to see whether I can corroborate your observations.
>
> I do not know whether I can be unbiased in this matter since Raymond has also announced his intention of challenging my median eyes and facial sutures [of] Trinucleus, in short everything that disagrees with Beecher's conclusions. Nevertheless, I shall be glad to go to Washington to see your material with a mind as unbiased as possible under the circumstances. I expect to be able to come toward the end of next week, if that is suitable to you. I am being held here just now since I expect a happy event in my daughter's family.[2]

It was two years before the committee report appeared, as a preface to one of Walcott's papers; Raymond was never mentioned in it. "When, however, my old friend, Dr. Charles Schuchert, questioned the presence of epipodites on the limbs of *Neolenus*, I decided to ask three well-known invertebrate paleontologists to make a detailed examination of the material and render their opinion as to whether there was sufficient evidence to warrant the conclusion that in addition to the endopodite and exopodite of the limb of *Neolenus* there was present another element which was clearly an epipodite" (Walcott 1921, 366).

In January, Schuchert had written:

> On Sunday, Professor Raymond came to see me to talk over his and your trilobite papers and his conclusions in regard to your interpretations of the ventral anatomy of trilobites. . . . We see in *Neolenus* only crawling and breathing legs, i.e., endopodites and exopodites. Your epipodites are, to our thinking only the exopodites. . . . The further reason for writing is this: Raymond does not want to make a mistake any more than you do, and therefore it is necessary that he see some of your specimens. I told him that I would pay his expenses if he would visit you and study the specimens in your laboratory, but unfortunately he says he cannot do this until next summer,

and I do not want to hold up publication until then. Therefore to advance this matter I want to ask you to loan Raymond. . . .

I am sorry that we must differ with you in your interpretation, but then you differ not only with Raymond and Schuchert, but as well with Beecher. There should be no personal feeling in regard to these differences, since that is a matter of science, and of all our observations paleontologists keep that which best stands the test of time.

Your Burgess fossils are the most wonderful ones ever collected, and therefore we are all very deeply interested in them. So far, all of us have kept off your ground, but the gold mine is so rich that sooner or later some one will storm the citadel and get some of these things. If science is to advance rapidly, this is as it should be, for the gold of science belongs to all. This is socialism, of course, but in science we are all socialists.[3]

Act two followed: "We sent all the specimens that Raymond asked for of *Neolenus*, and will send the *Triarthrus* this week. I wished to see if there was other material in the collections that might be of service to him. In this connection have you any *Triarthrus* which you think could be rubbed down from the dorsal surface in the hopes of finding further evidence of the character of the appendages. If so, I will be very glad to have the work done here if you wish. I think we should obtain all the evidence we can before Raymond publishes his paper."[4]

There is considerable information in these few sentences. One of the posthumous charges against Walcott, as we have noted, was to be that he built fences around his interests and prevented others from studying the Cambrian—not true. He did follow the accepted scientific course and let a rival investigator see his unique material. Further, as for *Triarthrus*, Walcott had visited the locality in 1893 and published (Walcott 1894). Walcott could have sent only a few specimens, yet he was going out of his way to search through the nonfigured specimens to see if there were others of potential utility. This is not the least bit unexpected, yet for decades, the rumor persisted that Walcott had been possessive of his fossils. By the same token, Walcott had invested a great deal of his career in trilobite limbs and was not leaving the field to Raymond uncontested, as indicated by his eagerness to prepare additional specimens.

Two other sentences in the same letter are of interest in regard to Walcott's personal conflict between administration and research. "I should be happy with the Burgess fossils if I could get time to work on them. At this season there are almost constant interruptions, which as you know is not conducive to good work."[5]

There was a long entr'acte while specimens traveled back and forth, but in late spring, act three began. Ulrich of the USGS, Ruedemann of the New York State Museum, and Bassler of the Museum looked at the specimens. They rendered the opinion that Walcott had been correct. Perhaps the committee was biased from its very selection, perhaps not. Apart from the fulminations of Jules Marcou concerning the "Taconic system" in the 1880s (Yochelson 1998), this was one of the few instances in which Walcott's scientific findings were called into question during his lifetime. Walcott seems to have gone out of his way to justify the correctness of his interpretation. The incident could have represented a hardening of his views, but equally it could have been a valid effort to have his observations checked and either confirmed or refuted.

In a way, two years later, Schuchert made a correct judgement of the affair. "No one has the interpretation all to himself and the truth is only won through friction, some heat, and suffering."[6] There are some differences in the legs of these few trilobite genera that preserve the limbs. On a different level, there seems to be consensus that the trilobite limb is more generalized and that the limbs of other arthropods could be derived from it. On the precise point of whether an epipodite is present in *Neolenus*, the interested person can consult the nearest specialist in Middle Cambrian trilobite legs. Raymond may well have suspected this committee had been handpicked to come out with the desired answer; the median eye of trilobites, which Ruedemann wanted to defend, did not exist, nor did the epipodite.

While the great trilobite limb committee was in session, Walcott was in his office meeting with ladies of the GWMA. The books of the organization had been examined and were in good order; the basic problem, however, of too little money in the treasury remained. Hope springs eternal, and if the organization was to be revitalized, a memorial building to casualties of the First World War just might be the key to funding.

On the same day, Walcott picked up another distraction. On May 19, 1919, the National Parks Association was formally incorporated, the papers being signed in the Cosmos Club. This association, like its predecessor, was a lobbying group for the Park Service, though in later years, it was not always in agreement with NPS policies. The association was "to study our national parks, their origins and meanings, their wild animals, their wealth of vegetation, in order that we may better understand and enjoy Nature and better appreciate Our Country" (Yard 1919, 1). Walcott certainly could not say no to such noble sentiments and so important a duty, and accordingly more time was taken from paleontology.

The final week in May began with a purely administrative matter; whether the SI clerkships be classified as Civil Service positions. This may sound simple, but it came back to the basic issue of whether the Smithsonian was (and is) part of the federal government or whether it was (and is) a private organization, advised and partially controlled by the government. The salary rate of the clerks was not sorted out in 1919; SI employees are still paid from SI funds, which are private, whereas Museum employees are public officials, and like those of any other government agency are paid from a federal appropriation. Nevertheless, today institution employees receive almost the same benefits as federal employees. This sounds obtuse, for the simple reason that it *is* obtuse. In the 1980s the distinctions became painfully clear when some SI employees were fired because of Smithsonian budgetary problems, but the federal employees were untouched.

Having made a decision to delay a decision on the clerks, Walcott could go back to science and organize the photographs of Burgess Shale sponges. On Sunday, Merriam came to dinner so that they could discuss NRC matters. On Monday, at a joint meeting of the councils of the NAS and the NRC, harmony prevailed. For decades Walcott had practiced the old maxim that the proper kind of spontaneity requires considerable advance planning.

The first meeting of the new National Parks Association occurred on May 29. Walcott was a member of the Executive Committee and chaired the meeting. Bylaws were read and approved, and officers were elected to provide a wide geographic spread and support from other groups; this fledgling made the GWMA look like a rock-solid, going concern, yet before the year was out, the executive secretary, Robert Sterling Yard, had produced a pamphlet on Grand Canyon National Park; the park had finally been authorized in February.

On Decoration Day, Walcott went to the cemetery to place flowers in remembrance of Stuart. Happy as he was with Mary, he also remembered Stuart, Charlie, and Helena. The last day in May brought exceptionally good news; both Helen and Cousin Fred had landed in New York. "We met Helen at the railroad station 8:20 P.M. Am glad to have her back. She left for France November 1918" (June 2, 1919). In writing to Freer a few days later, Walcott included, along with the weighty matters of a potential curator, his joy at the return of his daughter.

With Helen home, Walcott continued jogging along with a variety of chores. His use in his diary of "odds & ends" and "jogging along" seem to refer to times when minor items of routine prevailed. Among other events, he participated in revision of the GWMA's bylaws; perhaps this time would be the charm. Spring must have been gorgeous that year, for the Walcotts actually played hooky from church and were driven across the Blue Ridge once more to see Mary's friend Amanda Horse in Burkittsville, Maryland.

In keeping with his pattern of mixing up jobs, Walcott added a little to the sponge manuscript before going off to the Capitol to see about the appropriation. A day or so later he was in the final stages of touching up the photographs of the sponges. A government half-holiday allowed Walcott to organize some of his pictures of the Rockies for the next "Explorations" pamphlet (Walcott 1919). "Helen left 7 P.M. for Squaw Lake, N.H. She needs quiet & a rest for summer as a result of work in France" (June 15, 1919). Not counting household help, Dr. and Mrs. Walcott were alone once more.

Dr. Merriam dropped in to clear up last details with Walcott before he handed over the NRC to Dr. Angell. Dull administration closed in for a day. "Many events are occurring *in Paris en re* 'Peace Treaty' but all is quiet with us in Washington. Debate in Senate of Treaty very strong" (June 18, 1919). There is a wisp of a rumor that President Wilson asked Walcott to speak to Senator Lodge and persuade him to modify his stand on the League of Nations. This is not the sort of mission that ever leaves a paper trail, but it is quite possible that Walcott did play the role of messenger.

Two days later, the NACA intruded into Walcott's quiet with many pressing matters. They were resolved forthwith, and Walcott went back to his fossils. "A long, strenuous day at my office—endeavoring to clear up odds & ends & finish up paper on Middle Cambrian algae" (June 22, 1919). "Meeting of Nat. Acad Council [at] 1 & Research Council A.M. Finished up at my office P.M. turned in paper on M.[iddle] C.[ambrian] algae. Mary & I went to train for New York & our trip to the Canadian Rockies. Our sixth trip together" (June 24, 1919).

In New York, Walcott saw Freer for what was to be the last time. It was a less than jolly visit, for Mr. Freer produced a four-page memorandum, apparently now gone, listing various complaints and future plans. One complaint had to do with nonpublication of a paper by Miss N. K. Rhoades, Freer's assistant; she was one of the quartet authorized to add material to the Freer collection.

Several years earlier, when Freer had prepared another appendix to his list of art objects, Walcott had asked permission to send out a press release, noting Freer's additional gift to the nation. Freer had given his permission, and Walcott had then asked if he might have a photo or two of some of the more striking pieces included with the press release. Some months later, about a dozen photographs and an equal amount of text had arrived on Walcott's desk. He turned the material over to Assistant Secretary Rathbun, and at the latter's suggestion Walcott had asked Freer's permission to send the material to an art journal, which could do better justice to the illustrations. Permission was granted by Freer, and the material was turned over to the SI editor to forward. Rathbun had then died, and so had the editor, Clark, and somehow in the midst of wartime confusion the material had never been sent off to a journal.

This suddenly loomed as a major slight, but it was only one facet of the larger problem of what was to become of Miss Rhoades when the gallery opened. Another issue of concern was whether Freer's gallery was to be part of the National Gallery of Art; a newspaper story had intimated that. Still other concerns were Freer's desire to see the grounds kept up and the curator paid handsomely; in the provisions of his will, Freer sprinkled money around freely.

To skip ahead a bit, almost as soon as he was settled in camp, Walcott dictated to Mary an eight-page, handwritten letter addressing Freer's complaints and plans. The original is undated, but in his diary Walcott noted writing it on July 13. "After talking with you on June 25th I wrote to Washington to have the entire correspondence in relation to the article prepared by Miss Rhoades forwarded to me in the west. It arrived at our camp today." Walcott spent three pages recounting the tale of that manuscript and another two pages pointing out that the Smithsonian could not read every story a reporter wrote, especially before it was published. Walcott explained the circumstances to Freer; he did not apologize, for he had done no wrong. Then he got down to serious business.

> Some years ago when we were talking over the administration and care of your great collection you spoke of providing for the payment of a suitable salary to the head curator, and possibly of his chief assistant, who you thought might be Miss Rhoades. I replied that that would be a splendid arrangement as it removed any possible danger of any uncertainty as to the salary of the curator, in event of Congress failing to provide adequate salaries. . . . The largest salary paid to curators is $3500 & assistant curators $2000[,] the latter receiving $20 per month additional on account of increased cost of living. . . .
>
> Conditions have changed in the past two years owing to war expenditures & there is a natural desire on the part of Congress now that will undoubtedly continue for years to decrease rather than increase expenditures of all kinds, and in this connection objections may be raised to persons in government employ receiving a larger salary from any source than that provided for by the government. In fact such a proposition has already been under discussion in Congress.
>
> In view of all considerations now & prospective, I would, if in your place, provide what I considered to be a suitable income for the salary of a curator & assistant curator of the Freer gallery (museum) & omit, if necessary, other items such as care of grounds, or would omit altogether any provision for the salary of curator and assistant curator. I fear complications will arise if it is planned to pay the two salaries under the plan of paying part by the government & part by a grant by you.
>
> I am thinking, not of my administration of the s.i., but of the long run of years.
>
> You were very frank with me and I wish to be equally frank with you in making suggestions as it is in the interests of the Freer collections & the generations of art lovers to come that we both have in mind.[7]

To take a little of the sting out of the last paragraph, Walcott scribbled at the bottom, "May you soon get off for the Berkshires. Freer prepared a reply in September, but because of his death, it was never mailed.

With Freer and New York City behind them, the Walcotts moved north to Montreal, where they stopped at the Redpath Museum to see the collection of sponges from Little Metis, Quebec. These bore some similarity to the Burgess

Shale forms and warranted several paragraphs in his paper. They paid a social call on the president of the Canadian Pacific Railway and caught the train heading toward the north shore of Lake Superior. The trip west was noted as very comfortable.

"Banff 7:50 A.M. went direct to camp & found Arthur as usual. Alex met us at the station with buckboard. Unpacking and fixing up belongings and tents during the day" (June 30, 1919). It took a couple of days to get the camp outfit organized, fix saddles, and so forth. They moved out to Lake Minniewanka on July 4. "Decided to observe this day as Sunday. Fussed about camp & edge of lake. All tired from first day on trail for 1919. Mary & Wyckoff went out after wild flowers brot in some rare orchids" (July 5, 1919). A young man, N. C. Wyckoff, was serving as field assistant; it is not clear how Walcott had found him, nor are any personal details known.

"All our party rode to head of lake and to Devils Gap. Located next camp & place to try for Upper Cambrian fossils. A strong gale made everything difficult. Mary bro't in a number of wild flowers & some new to her" (July 6, 1919). High wind the next day kept them in camp. "Moved camp to head of lake and settled down on south side of N.W. slope of Saddle Peak. High wind & heat made life tedious. Scotty Wright Forest & Game Warden came to camp 5 P.M. Caught a few trout in the evening" (July 8, 1919).

The air was full of smoke from the burning trees of a forest fire, and the heat continued. "Broke camp early & moved back to Banff. The spreading forest fire & dense smoke render further work impracticable. May get back in September if all is well" (July 10, 1919). Early indications were that this was not to be a good field season, but that is the luck of the draw. Camp four was back at Banff, and camp eight was at the old site on the north side of Burgess Pass. "Began work at the fossil quarry—with Alex—Mary came up after luncheon. We found a few good fossils including a cup-shaped sponge & a large annelid tube" (July 16, 1919).

The afternoon of the next day the weather suddenly changed to fog and snow squalls; Walcott put a stove in his tent and prepared to wait things out. Despite three inches of snow by evening, in the afternoon Walcott and assistant were at the quarry. The pain of a raw, cold wind was tempered by the pleasure of seeing Granny, the mountain squirrel with the broken tail. "Up at the quarry all day. Alex & Wyckoff cleaning off dirt & loose rock. Mary & I breaking up shale—found a few good & a number of poor specimens. Dry, smoky & warm" (July 13, 1919).

On Sunday everyone slept late. Mary and Walcott rode over to Yoho lake to see the Alpine Club campsite. Wyckoff came down with a cold. "Alex & I at quarry all day & Mary P.M. We found a small lot of fossils. The quarry is about played out & we now have the dump to overhaul. Wyckoff ill in camp" (July 21,

1919). Mary went for the mail while Alex and Walcott worked at the quarry; on another day all three worked. "Alex took Wyckoff (N.C.) to Field with his belongings. W is half sick but he has been of little service & should not have come west. Mary & I worked at quarry" (July 24, 1919). Ever since Burling left, Walcott had not fared well with field assistants; thank goodness for packer Alex Mitton, who did double duty.

They collected parts of two days before Sunday, when they all went to the Alpine Club camp. "Ate luncheon at camp where Stuart & I stopped also Sidney & Helen on another occasion years ago" (July 27, 1919)—bittersweet memories. "Went up to quarry with Alex about 9 A.M. Mary came up at noon with luncheon. L. D. Burling dropped in about 1 P.M. for a few minutes & several others came up from Alpine Club Camp. At 3:30 went to camp on acc't of fine rain" (July 28, 1919). Another Walcottian myth is that Burling resented being exploited by Walcott—again, not true. His visit dates an undated communication to Washington.

"So Washington is at war—Bootlegging & excessive war wages may have something to do with it. . . . We have had light rains but the fires still fill the air with smoke. . . . Burling turned up in camp today. He looks well & is hard at work for the Canadian Geol. Survey. Arthur rec'd his canvas shoulder bag & is greatly pleased with it."[8]

The Walcott party—that is, Walcott and Alex, with part-time help from Mary—scrounged the quarry dump for almost a week. A few good fossils turned up. On Sunday they went again to the Alpine Club, and Walcott engaged an assistant, though two days later the man decided not to come; the season was not improving. Despite rain and fog, Walcott continued to search the rocks and smaller shales, which had been thrown down-slope from the quarry. Another full day at the quarry brought the end of Burgess Shale collecting for Walcott. Walcott reported to the chief clerk on his activities: "We parked 8 boxes fossils yesterday at Field & shipped—Bill of lading enclosed. Perhaps you had best notify U.S. Customs as there is no way of making a declaration at Field. Will go over Soo Line via Portal, Minn. Mrs. Walcott & I have been getting our thick clothing, guns, etc. from trunks here today. Alex & Arthur are on way to Lake Louise station with outfit. We go up in the morning & start north Monday for a four week trip away from Ry & P.O. Engaged a stout young Swede today to help Alex & Arthur. With good weather we should get some good results. Cool & fine today. All well & happy. Greater tourist travel this season."[9]

The second day on the trail, the best packhorse, Pat, was stuck in the groin by a branch and died two days later. They moved camp to the middle fork of the Saskatchewan River, only to find the water too high to cross, causing a further delay. Finally, they made it to their fourteenth camp, on the north side of

Glacial Lake. "With Mary & Alex went up slope of Sunny Mt above camp. Found shales & limestones of Upper Cambrian age. Collected a few fossils. Air thick with smoke from Columbia river forest fire" (August 21, 1919).

The party cut logs and brush to clear the trail and camped at the head of the lake; Walcott ended up with a blinding headache. "About camp all day as result of upset yesterday. Fixed up tent cut out brush etc. Alex & William [the young Swede] went out to locate game but found only tracks. Flies are abundant & worry man & beast" (August 26, 1919). "Out looking up section of rocks at head of Glacier Lake canyon valley with Mary & Alex. Upper Cambrian in cliffs at front of East Lyell Glacier. Abundant corals etc of Devonian age on glacier derived from cliffs high up" (August 27, 1919). "With Mary collected fossils all day from Upper Cambrian. They are small & rare" (August 28, 1919).

The party had a tedious day cutting a trail and a couple of nasty days alternating between smoky haze and cold winds. Finally, after several days of frustration, Walcott found a good place to measure and collect a geologic section. "Measured section up canyon 1 *mi* east of foot of East Lyell Glacier. Worked up through 2700 feet of beds & located 3 horizons of Upper Cambrian fossils" (September 3, 1919). "Measured 1300 feet of beds & collected a few fossils. Mary collected A.M. from Upper Cambrian rocks. A wet nasty day. The weather is still too warm for the season" (September 4, 1919).

A hunting party was leaving for civilization, and Walcott took the occasion to send a four-page letter to Assistant Secretary Abbot: "After four yrs search I have found at Glacier Lake canyon a well preserved section of the Upper Cambrian & have measured over 4000 feet in thickness of it and found fossils at several horizons. Still have 2000 feet or more to study and measure to collect from. With good weather will get through in ten days. We have done what you spoke of wishing to do. Left all worldly news & arrived ourselves in a quiet spot 60 miles from P.O. & houses."[10]

Ten days turned out to be a high estimate. They spent four more days, only one of which had fine weather, measuring and collecting. After that, the fossils were packed, the tents were struck, and they moved to Mazda Creek for the night. "Moved camp to Bow Pass—Trail bad & wet. Rain most of day. Put up tents & had dinner 9 P.M. Alex with a severe attack of grouch & temper from many causes" (September 19, 1919). It was five more moves of the camp before they were settled at camp twenty-one, Hillsdale. "An easy day for man & beast. Read proof of algal paper 3 hours in morning" (September 17, 1919).

The young Swede went back to Banff with Alex, while the Walcotts went on a fishing trip—no fish. "Mary and I rode up to the devide [*sic*] between head of Hillsdale Gulch & Thompson Creek. A rain & sleet squall drove us in before we could do any work. Fussing about camp, reading and resting P.M." (September 19, 1919). (The writing is so cramped that this is the first diary entry where one might argue that Walcott spelled "divide" correctly.) "Cloudy and threatening A.M. Walked up on s.w. side of Sawback Range" (September 20, 1919). Of course, when writing home, one accentuates the positive.

> We had a great Hillsdale camp trip in the glacier, 12 m. from Banff Lake region and returned to the R.R. pretty well tired out, picked up the mail at Lake Louise, and took two days to come down to this beautiful camp, where there is abundant pasture, wood, and water. . . . Your letter of August 19th I enclose herewith, with comments on the margin. [Ravenel had written about proposed budget cuts and the steps he had taken to enlist the help of the congressional regents; Walcott scribbled on the letter, "Senate Committee must be working hard to reduce expenses"].
>
> We will probably leave this camp the 22nd, and go directly thro to the Ghost River, which we tried to reach, but were prevented by forest fires in July. It is quite important that I should see the Cambrian rocks there, and make some collections and comparisons with the Glacier Lake section, which is the finest of the Upper Cambrian that I know of in America. We also hope to get a few skins and heads for the Museum. . . . I will return the proof of the algal paper to Mr. True as soon as I can get up enough energy to read it. Camp life, proof reading, and letter writing do not seem to harmonize. Just now I had much rather be out, mousing around on the hill sides than dictating this letter to Mrs. Walcott. . . . Arthur and Mrs. Walcott are trying to feed me up so to restore some of the 20# worn off in the Glacial Lake area. A mountain sheep will help out.[11]

Between the dictation, the transcribing, and retyping in Washington, punctuation may not be all that one might expect. What is particularly interesting about this communication is a footnote: "Am glad to be far away from Treaty debate, etc .—for a reason." This hardly qualifies as a "smoking gun" to prove that Walcott was an intermediary between Wilson and Lodge, but the comment certainly does not refute that rumor.

The trip to Ghost River was not to be. Walcott spent another five days collecting in the Sawback Range. "We now have fossils from 4 distinct zones in the Cambrian" (September 25, 1919). Most of the time the weather was poor. They moved to Banff. "Cold & snow on mountain makes work too difficult" (September 28, 1919). "Endeavoring to obtain some photographs but smoke & mist interfered" (September 30, 1919). "Snow fell on the mountains all about & a raw cold wind made out of doors work very unpleasant" (October 1, 1919).

This was definitely the end of the season. Walcott sent Alex Mitton back to Montana the following day, while he and Arthur began putting away the camp gear at the Buffalo Park. "A busy day storing away tents etc.[,] cleaning up. Left Banff 6:37 P.M. on the TransCanadian express. A beautiful ride down the Bow valley until darkness came. Wish I could stay out for a month longer" (October 3, 1919). That sentiment is the mark of a real field man. His assistant had been unsatisfactory, forest fires had chased him from a section, streams had been too high to ford, placid Alex Mitton had been driven to distraction, the weather had been either too hot, too cold, too rainy, or too windy, yet a tent was better than their house in Washington, and there had been a great section, at Glacier Lake. Fieldwork is similar to childbirth, in that one recalls the pleasure as the pain recedes.

While Walcott was en route home, he crossed a letter from Washington. "I know you will be grieved to learn, as we all were, of the death of Mr. Freer, which occurred in New York on Thursday night. . . . We telegraphed Colonel Hecker that you were out of reach in the mountains. Mr. Abbot left last night to attend the funeral."[12] Despite years of ill health, Freer had assembled an incredible art collection. His American material, particularly strong on James Abbott McNeill Whistler, is frozen in time; the Freer is better known for Oriental art, and from time to time the collection has been increased, thanks to the codicil in the will. It reflects one of the idiosyncrasies of Charles Langdon Freer that nothing but Freer material can be displayed in the gallery and no object can be lent to other museums (Lawton and Merrill 1993).

The Walcotts left British Columbia on Saturday evening, and by Tuesday morning they were home, a dramatic increase in the speed of train travel. After lunch, Walcott went to his office and noted that all had gone well with the Smithsonian during his absence. He spent several days on SI paperwork and then presided at the NACA meeting, where "many matters needed attention" (October 9, 1919). They got the attention they deserved, as the NACA went from wartime to peace; research at Langley Field became a major theme. Two days later, all other chores had been settled, and Walcott was working up his field notes on the Upper Cambrian rocks of Mount Bosworth.

"After a walk with Mary in Potomac Park went to Smithsonian & attended to mail and began examining collections of Upper Cambrian rocks & fossils from Glacier Lake section" (October 13, 1919); there was no sense starting another new project. The National Resource Council (NRC) board met, and the Iowa Apartment House group met, and the Commission on Fine Arts met, but in between Walcott unpacked his collections.

Another bittersweet occasion came when the local American Legion group was named the Stuart Walcott Post. Walcott administered part of that day and did research the other part. In later years, Walcott's orders were to be that short of dire emergency, he was not to be disturbed before 10:00 A.M. or after 4:00 P.M.

Research was vital, not only to satisfy his own intellectual needs but to set the tone for the institution.

After Walcott's long field season, he had nearly three weeks in Washington before going off to a CIW Ex Comm meeting in New York City. The next day, Sunday, was the occasion of the christening of his granddaughter. "Fine child & a happy day" (October 9, 1919); she was to be the only child of Sidney and Helen-Louise. Back in Washington, Walcott heard the king of Belgium, whom he admired, speak to the Senate. The week was one of routine and research, followed by research and routine. Helen stopped by for the weekend. Walcott was present when Gen. "Black Jack" Pershing spoke to the Red Cross, and then another week was over.

Monday, Walcott took Mary to Detroit for the reading of Freer's will. While in the automobile capital of the world, they were toured around the Ford motor plant by Henry Ford himself. They saw the Packard plant and, just to complete their education, they ended with a trip through the Lincoln plant. It was a thorough grounding in u.s. autos.

"With Col. Hecker, Mr. Stone & Judge Averell attended to probating of Mr. Chas. L. Freer's will A.M. Lunched with Col. Hecker & then went with him to Parke Davis & Cos—plant. Also to Pewabic Battery [Company]. Conference with Miss Rhoades in evening" (November 8, 1919). Fortunately there were no surprises in the will; the codicil of May 1919 was the last change Freer had made. The evening conference must have been interesting, for Miss Rhodes presented the posthumous communication from Freer already referred to, dictated in response to Walcott's letter but not signed before his death later in September. In this letter Freer had accepted Walcott's explanation for the nonpublication of Miss Rhoades manuscript; if there was any breech between the two, it had been healed before Freer died.

Walcott discussed with Miss Rhoades the packing of the art collection, and then he and Mary headed east. They paused in Cleveland, in part to see the Art Museum, but mainly to see the Garfield family. Next President Walcott presided at the fall NAS meeting in New Haven. If there was any discussion with Schuchert about trilobites, it must have been brief, for Walcott was fully occupied running this meeting and keeping the council organized. From New Haven, it was an easy train ride to New York to carry on a bit of CIW business at the botanical garden, and finally on to Philadelphia to see Mary's family for the evening.

"With George & Mary called on Langdon Warner at Phila. Museum. Also Dr. Gorden at Univ. Penn. Museum—to enquire about men of suitable training for director of art museum under s.i. No one in sight" (November 13, 1919). In light of Freer's letter to John Ellerton Lodge that spring, this is a most interesting observation. Walcott was conducting his own inquiry and was asking the right people. Walcott and Freer had considerable correspondence concerning Langdon Warner, who traveled extensively in the Orient under the auspices of the Archaeological School that was contemplated for Peking.

After lunch, the Walcotts returned to New York City. The Carnegie Ex Comm met, and later Walcott had a great deal to discuss with architect Charles Platt concerning the still-unfinished Freer Gallery. They arrived home tired, but they rested up by hunting for mushrooms and dandelions; to find dandelions around Washington at almost any season hardly requires much hunting.

Walcott saw a few senators and spoke to a CIW botanist concerning work in the Southwest. "Quiet Day. Spent most of my time on review of Middle Cambrian sponge paper which should go to the press in Jany—1920" (November 20, 1919). He took an evening for the Archaeological Society meeting; whether it was Cyrus Adler, D. C. Gilman, or Charles Freer who had first interested him, Walcott maintained this minor involvement in ancient civilizations for years.

The Executive Committee of the NACA met. The Walcotts sent out 315 invitations to tea. Walcott approved the algal paper for printing and, just before Thanksgiving, reviewed the sponge manuscript for the editor. Once more Mr. and Mrs. George Vaux and their two sons came in for Thanksgiving; before turkey, Walcott took them to the zoo. There was a slight shadow, in that J. J. McChesney, who as the first chief clerk had held the old USGS together, was seriously ill. The Vaux family left, and any shadows lifted when daughter Helen came into town for a week.

December began with a flourish. "At my office during the day until 3:30 P.M. Mary & Helen receiving at home to our friends of whom some 200 showed up, many of whom we had not seen for two or three years" (December 1, 1919). Various odds and ends took time, including talking to a few senators and the vice president. The Walcotts had a dinner for Lord Godfrey, the British ambassador. All in all, the holiday season was starting early and developing well.

Although Walcott did not know it at this time, the holiday spirit prevailed in Europe, so far as the secretary was involved. December 5, 1919, the Royal Swedish Academy of Sciences wrote Walcott that he had been elected a foreign member. As a step in this process, Walcott had been asked to prepare a brief biography. (In this, he had listed his marriages to Helena and to Mary but not Lura Rust. His private life at Trenton Falls and her long illness remained a closed book.) This news from Europe circulated slowly, but two months later, half a dozen lines in a local paper noted the election and made the point that only a dozen Americans had been so honored.

There was more. On December 6, 1919, the Académie des Sciences de l'Institute de France wrote to Walcott. He was no longer a corresponding member but had been elected as a foreign member. Foreign memberships were for life and were limited in number, so that very few people received this honor. Relative to the French académie, the American NAS brought in foreign associates in far larger numbers even though it only elected them at the rate of one or two a year.

It was a pity that Walcott did not have the small benefit of whatever comfort these honors might bring at this time so as to help him face a difficult moment. After church, Walcott "with Mary spent the afternoon at the Smithsonian looking over Stuart's old letters, papers, etc. Mary busy with retouching photographs" (December 7, 1919). If there were memories of Stuart, they were private, for inside of a few days Walcott was dining out as the guest of George Ellery Hale and the NRC Foreign Relations Committee. The SI regents met, followed by the CIW Ex Comm, in one of those double-meeting days that Walcott seemed to handle with ease. The day after, the CIW board met and again all went smoothly. On Sunday, the Walcotts picked out their Christmas card photograph; they had begun sending out greetings with nice prints from the field. Prof. A. Mayer of Princeton came for dinner; for years, Mayer had worked in the Florida Keys, with support of the CIW, studying the growth of corals, among other marine biological activities. The Dry Tortugas laboratory, at the end of the Florida Keys, was a mecca for tropical marine biologists.

A new week unfolded. "Began study of fossils collected from Upper Cambrian rocks of Glacier Lake section last summer" (December 18, 1919). The following evening he spoke with Dr. Angell, the new head of NRC, and to make sure that no wires were crossed, the next day he conferred with Angell and Hale. Between a new building and the relationships of the NRC to government agencies, there were enough sensitive issues and sensitive people to make it worth ensuring that their leaders were informed and knew their roles.

"Meeting of Council Nat. Acad. Sciences 9:30–12:30 A.M. at Smithsonian. Nat. Research Council 1–4:15 P.M. Reception to employees Smithsonian Institution 4:30–6 P.M. At home in evening. The govt section N.R.C. is a most interesting grab [? bag] of men, Army, Navy, & Civil Depts." (December 20, 1919). All one can say is that Walcott must have been made of iron to withstand such a day and still make a comment that his second meeting was interesting.

The next day was almost as difficult. The NRC met in the morning, and in the afternoon he had a conference concerning the coming NAS building; presumably, there was time for lunch. Walcott was a member of the NAS building committee, and it was certainly was not an honorific appointment. That night, John C. Merriam, A. A. Noyes, and G. E. Hale, "all of California[,] dined with us" (December 21, 1919). NAS-NRC matters were pursued farther.

During the next couple of days, Walcott was able to work a little on Upper Cambrian fossils. At one evening dinner he noted meeting the Belgian ambassador. "Edwin S. Hewitt of Santa Fe called & spoke of Franz Boas" (December 4, 1919). Professor Boas will appear again in what was to be an unpleasant matter, but the day before Christmas is not the time to describe unhappy events.

Walcott and Mary joined Helen at Mary's brother's house in Bryn Mawr to celebrate Christmas, but they were home the next day. Despite having to deal with finances for the Church of the Covenant, Walcott got his Christmas present in "Middle Cambrian Algae," the fifth paper in Walcott's fourth *smc* volume on Cambrian geology and paleontology, which has the date of December 26, 1919. The *si* issued a two-page press release.

> That many of the algae or seaweeds of the middle Cambrian epoch of geo-
> logic time, some 25 or 30 millions of years ago, closely resemble the algae
> growing in the sea at the present time is the statement made by Charles D.
> Walcott.... This is the first authentic proof that this form of plant existed in
> that far-off past although many primitive forerunners of animal life have
> been brought to light in the form of fossils.... Several new genera and nine-
> teen new species of fossil algae were determined and are described in the
> Smithsonian publication. The fossil remains from which these algae forms
> were identified occur as shiny black films on the surface of the hard siliceous
> shale.[13]

The sixteen plates in this paper include a few pictures of living forms for comparison.

"All comparisons of the fossil Cambrian algae with living algae, with the exception of *Morania* are based on similarity of outward macroscopic characters and forms of growth. Anyone possessing a slight acquaintance with living algae, knows that this is a very uncertain standard as essentially the same outward form may occur in different genera and orders" (Walcott 1919a, 222). Walcott knew his limitations as well as his strengths. "During the forty years in which I have been collecting and examining other collections except those from the Burgess shale, I have seen a few fragments that indicated the existence of algae in the Cambrian strata, but none of the specimens have satisfactory evidence of their undoubted algal origin. Many annelid trails, tidal water markings, trails of crustaceans and drifting medusae had been referred to as of algal origin but all were susceptible of some other interpretation" (Walcott 1919a, 224–25).

Even so, Walcott did not describe one interesting microfossil. Between May when the thin sections arrived and late June when he left for the field, there could not have been much time to examine these sections. They contain *Obru-schevella*, a tiny form coiled like a screen-door spring (Makiewicz 1992). Once seen, this organism is hard to confuse with any other fossil, and it is relatively abundant in the Burgess Shale.

Between Christmas and New Year's, the height of the social season, the Walcotts dined with the British ambassador. However, they spent the penultimate day of the year quietly. On December 31 they attended a social gathering at the Church of the Covenant. In his usual fashion, Walcott summed up the year in his diary, noting that Sidney and his family were settled in Brooklyn and Helen was living in New York City. "The world's unrest following the war still continues & the outlook for 1920 is not a rosy one but I think conditions will slowly and surely improve during the coming year" (December 31, 1919).

New Year's morning, Walcott and Mary were at his office. He was describing species of *Agnostus*, an atypical trilobite with few segments and a tail similar to its head; these were probably pelagic forms that had floated in the water. After a noon breakfast with friends, the couple called on four or five cabinet members to wish them the best for the new year. Work began for 1920. "Continued routine in laboratory & office during the day. Mary worked on retouching a lot of photographs for sending away" (January 3, 1920). Walcott was determined not to be misunderstood on his interpretations of trilobite limbs, and he was in the process of preparing duplicate prints of his illustrations for distribution to colleagues.

Sunday after church, it was back to the Castle. The weather was cold and bracing, just what both Walcotts liked. They went to a formal dinner for eight and the next evening gave a much smaller dinner party, for the French ambassador. Postwar social life began to resemble that of prewar Washington. Commonly, when the Walcotts held a dinner, the maximum number was sixteen. Guests knew not to expect any wine or other alcohol, for Mary was a strict teetotaler, as were many of the Society of Friends of her generation.

Walcott had a few mixed-up days early in January, but overall the month began well, and he waxed philosophical. "The weeks come & go and a little research work, administrative work, and correspondence is cleaned up each week. Reading & resting at home in evening" (January 10, 1920).

General Squier told him of experiments with high-frequency transmission of telephone messages; the Walcotts dined out frequently and attended the Philadelphia Symphony on tour in Washington. The month moved on. "Routine & preparing note of S.I. Expl. Rept. for 1919. A broken up busy day. Mary coloring lantern slides & attending to errands & household matters. We were tired at night & turned out on porch beds at 9:30" (January 16, 1920).

Events necessitated a shift of emphasis. "At my office during the day which was given to routine, interviews & a little cogitating on a bill for organization of an Air Service" (January 20, 1920). This may the place for a little history lesson on legislation. As early as 1918, the NACA concluded, "Federal legislation should be enacted governing the navigation of aircraft in the United States" (Komons 1977, 36). The NACA had then organized an interdepartmental committee, but this had foundered as military personnel were transferred and civilians shuffled papers. "In haste, Walcott (with the approval of the secretaries of war, navy, and commerce) recommended to the president new emergency legislation empowering the secretary of commerce to license and regulate interstate civilian flying in the United States. Though President Wilson endorsed this recommendation and forwarded it to Congress on 26 February [1919], it was lost in the crush of legislation in the last weeks of the 65th Congress" (Roland 1985, 55).

Walcott appointed a subcommittee in the fall of 1919 to study the regulation of air traffic, and it was against this background that Walcott was cogitating. "Left draft of Air Service Bill with Rep. Hicks of New York A.M." (January 22, 1920). "On 19 May, 1920, Congressman F. C. Hicks introduced a bill 'To Create a Bureau of Aeronautics in the Department of Commerce.' . . . Modeled on the draft NACA legislation, the bill was the joint product of Hicks on one hand and Dr. Walcott and two military members of the NACA on the other" (Roland 1985, 54). Walcott had been cogitating seriously, but unfortunately the issue of a separate air force, as propounded by General "Billy" Mitchell began to cloud the issue, and nothing came of the draft legislation.

Research on rocks and fossils was now getting short shrift. Miss Rhoades came in to see the Freer Gallery, the CIW Ex Comm met, and the French embassy had a reception. "Meeting of trustees of Carnegie Inst. 10–12:15 & Ex. Comm. 1 P.M. Trustees decided to offer presidency to D r Angel [*sic*] first, John C. Merriam second choice" (January 24, 1920). The process of selecting a president is not simple. Walcott and Woodward had had a dust-up the previous year when the latter wrote that he was omitting the appointment of a search committee from the minutes, to which Walcott had replied that matters of business should be recorded; it was a minor tiff. Both thought highly of Merriam.

By now, Sunday afternoon at the office was a family tradition, but Walcott had more to do on his research than ever. "Talking with E. O. Ulrich A.M. *en re* Ozarkian fauna & rocks" (January 26, 1920). Between receptions and routine, the month was wearing down. "Quiet day. Worked a little on mss—Also talked with E. O. Ulrich *en re* Ozarkian System of strata & sent letter to Director of Geological Survey recommending adoption of name. At home writing in evening" (January 31, 1920).

February was February, a time of dreary weather. Still, there were evening lectures, receptions, dinners, and there was a display by the NRC of "wireless" and a visit from Helen. The draft of the Air Service bill went to members of the NACA for their comment. "At my office & laboratory during the day. Correspondence and work on oral appendages of Marrella" (February 11, 1920).

"Went to see Pageant of American History 10–12 P.M. Helen represented 'America'" (February 12, 1920). That is all to this diary entry for the day, except for ditto marks referring to the previous day, yet somehow one is tempted to read a father's pride into the handwriting. Considering what she had done so far during her life, Helen was a good choice for the role.

"A busy but quiet day at the Smithsonian. After dinner put in an hour on structure of trilobite paper" (February 16, 1920). Two days later the GWMA had its annual meeting. It, and the appropriations hearings which followed, were perennial events. Art matters took some of the time, but Walcott was also working on a reconstruction of *Marrella*. Good scientific illustration is art, not just drafting, and Walcott had the sense to give his sketches to an artist for polishing. It would be nice to know whether it were Mary who did the final drawings, but that information is gone.

They dined out three nights in a row, but fortunately all were small gatherings, not mob scenes. "Meeting of Executive Committee Government Div. Nat. Research Council at our home 8–11 P.M." (February 27, 1920). Walcott kept moving from one subject to another to make sure that all pots were properly stirred; research occurred when he had time to lay down the spoon. February ended.

Walcott slimmed down his personal library by donating some books to the SI library. A few of these were duplicates and years later were scattered to the wind. It would be nice to know what kind of a scientific library Walcott maintained at home, but that information is gone.

The weather improved as March began. "Attending to routine at office & preparation of a short paper on *Marrella splendens* a small crustacean from the Middle Cambrian" (March 1, 1920). The Joseph A. Holmes Safety First Association met, and that pot was properly stirred, but Walcott then recorded the death of Henning Jennings, a longtime Washington friend. Even that could not cause persistent gloom, for spring was in the air.

The Walcotts went off to New York and that Sunday saw a fine family gathering with Helen, and the Sidney Walcotts (little Evelyn included) visited their hotel. Between lunch with Helen and dinner with Sidney, they also saw Cousin Fred. Monday and Tuesday were devoted to business, talking to stockbrokers, to Elihu Root, and to representatives of General Electric. It was a nice break from the paperwork in Washington. Mary took a day in Philadelphia, but they both attended the Annual Meeting of the Church of the Covenant, and the following evening had a small dinner for the Peruvian ambassador and a few cabinet members.

"Busy all day with routine & a little research work" (March 20, 1920). Life was fairly placid, and after the Sunday trip to the Smithsonian, Walcott tried out a new camp cot. He weeded through his reprints and donated 5,800 to the Museum;

for several generation of paleontologists, this reprint collection was to be a valuable source for older literature. A bad cold held him at home, but he still managed to preside at the board of trustees of the church; not unexpectedly, the issue was the church's debt and how to pay it.

The weather improved, health returned, and Walcott visited the zoo on business. "Administrative matters kept me occupied most of the day" (March 29, 1920). Mary went to Philadelphia, and while she was away, Walcott talked to Secretary of the Navy Daniels and Adm. David W. Taylor concerning aeronautics.

"At my office during the day working on scheme for developing the Nat. Gallery of Art. After dinner called on Whitman Cross. Telegram from Helen & telephone from Mary *en re* my 70th birthday. May I have ten active years in which to finish up my Cambrian work" (March 31, 1920). The war had changed a great many things. In 1916, the seventieth birthday of William Henry Holmes was celebrated with a formal dinner and the presentation of a thick festschrift of articles written by his friends and colleagues. If Walcott even got a cake at the office on his seventieth birthday, he did not record it.

April Fool's Day: "Ugh! A chill at the office 10 A.M. & home & to bed. A grippy condition mixed with a chronic catarrhal condition" (April 1, 1920). Fortunately, the condition passed almost as rapidly as it developed, and a couple of days later, Walcott was up. He had a morning at the office, and then he and Mary left for a short vacation in New Jersey. Visiting the shore in April is pushing the season; the weather could have been better. They took an overnight trip to New York City to meet Mrs. Harriman and see some of the portraits of war leaders that she had commissioned; it was a brief interlude before they were back at the shore. "Walking, reading, resting, & visiting with Mary & Helen. N.W. cold winds all the week—no rain" (April 11, 1920). Despite poor weather, they stayed a couple more days before going home.

It may be an awkward time—while Walcott is en route to Washington—to mention the Burgess Shale sponge paper (Walcott 1920a). On the other hand, sponges themselves are awkward, with respect to how they are related to other animals. Presumably they developed early, but they are off to one side of the main activity of animal evolution. Although the editors of the *Smithsonian Miscellaneous Collections* were characteristically meticulous in indicating the date of publication, on the cover of volume eighty-seven, number six, one finds only the year 1920. This was one of the minor effects of the disruption caused by the war—trivial in a sense, but symbolic of great change in the American way of life.

The publication date can be approximated on the basis of a letter Walcott wrote in the latter part of March to a colleague in Sweden. "The paper on the

Sponges from the Burgess shale is now to press, and should reach you some time in May."[14] Late March–early April is a reasonable estimate for publication, although if there were a question of priority concerning any of the new names, one should look for more evidence.

There were plenty of new names in this paper, with more than thirty new species, a dozen new genera, and two new families. This was the most diverse fossil assemblage of sponges. The material from Little Metis, Quebec, which Walcott had examined at the Redpath Museum, was the only described fauna that was even generally similar to the Burgess Shale sponges. A restudy of Walcott's collections, supplemented by later-collected material (Rigby 1986) added six new species. Of the six new genera added to the faunule, four are based on Walcott species; other two are based on material collected in the 1960s from Mount Stephen and are geographically close, but not strictly part of the Burgess Shale fauna.

This study was almost as groundbreaking as the arthropod-assemblage paper. Nevertheless, one is treading on dangerous ground comparing humble sponges to more complex arthropods. It may be enough to mention that Walcott did a workmanlike job of description and illustration, and then get back to Washington and on to other items.

"At my office all day—Many matters came up as a result of absence" (April 14, 1920). "Routine & looking over mss of my note on *Marrella* etc." (April 15, 1920). "At my office during the day. Gave thought and time to consideration of the *National Gallery of Art*" (April 16, 1920). The next day Walcott called on Senator Lodge to see what could be done to move the National Gallery from a paper concept to a real entity.

To jump ahead of the story, Walcott would accomplished this goal: "In June, 1920, a small congressional appropriation made possible the establishment of the National Gallery of Art as an independent bureau under the administration of the Smithsonian Institution, instead of being as previously a part of the Museum, the change to take effect on July 1, 1920" (Walcott 1922, 29). With the world war over, this was not a bad time to start a new enterprise, but for this collection of art to become significant, a new building was needed. That there was a need was absolutely clear: "The Natural History Building was designed exclusively and is needed entirely for natural history collections. It has been necessary, however, to make provisions in this building for the National Gallery of Art, one large hall in the first story being devoted to that purpose. Further crowding has resulted from the utilization of the west and northwest ranges and foyer with adjoining rooms on the ground story and in the rotunda in the first story in the assembling of the war collections" (Walcott 1922, 120).

As an aside, the war collections themselves make quite a story. For years the Museum was crowded with artifacts of that struggle, taking up valuable space from natural history displays (Yochelson 1985).

The original SI building itself was not in very good shape. The Castle walls were covered with ivy, which looked quite poetic but was hard on the stone. The ivy was just starting to be pulled down when that action caught the eye of a reporter and a storm of protest arose. Walcott called an immediate halt to the activity; next, he told the gardener quietly to cut the vines at root level. When the ivy died it was taken down without any fuss. When Walcott was out to skin a cat, he was able to use more than one method.

Sunday afternoon, Walcott enjoyed a picnic luncheon with wife and daughter. Monday brought Glenn Curtiss's attorneys, perhaps concerned with his place in aviation history. "At Smithsonian all day. Routine and a little research work. Dr. Geo. E. Hale dined with us" (April 24, 1920). "Presided at semi-annual meeting of Nat. Advisory Committee for Aeronautics A.M. At my office P.M." (April 22, 1920). Walcott did not bother to note that he had been elected chairman of the NACA. He would continue in that position until his death.

"A quiet busy day at Smithsonian most of which was given to study of *Waptia fieldensis* & *Hymenocaris perfecta*" (April 22, 1920). The arthropods of the Burgess Shale were much on his mind, though he could hardly get to look at them. That Sunday there was no church for Walcott. The executive committee of the NRC met during the day, and the NAS council met in the evening; the NAS annual meeting was an indication that spring was in full bloom.

"Session Nat. Academy Sciences 9:30 A.M. to 1 P.M. Luncheon & Council Nat. Acad. 3 P.M. Smithsonian matters until 5 P.M. Hale lecture & reception at National Museum 8–11 P.M. A few minutes at Pan-American Reception & home—at midnight" (April 26, 1920). The next day involved the annual business meeting and the annual dinner. Wednesday morning was devoted to the election of new members. "Luncheon & Academy meeting dispersed. Am glad as my duties as president have been rather strenuous. Cleared up mail P.M. & went home for a walk & rest. Mary tired too as she has been of great assistance all thru [the] meeting" (April 28, 1920). Walcott at seventy kept up the pace, but he was no longer an iron man, and he felt the strain.

Life got back to normal rapidly, and Walcott stopped by to see Alexander Graham Bell's latest hydroplane model. Like Walcott, Bell kept active and did not retire quietly into old age. Walcott cleared up his letters and had a meeting on the NAS building. May Day saw him on Capitol Hill to see what might be done for the cause of art.

After church, Helen and Walcott went to Rock Creek Cemetery, where Stuart's name was to be engraved on the family marker; afterward, Merriam was invited

An undated rough pencil sketch of *Waptia,* drawn and labeled by Walcott. Associated with it are two sketches of *Naraoia compacta* drawn in pencil by a skilled artist, possibly Mary Vaux Walcott, with minor annotations in ink by Walcott, dated May 12 and 14, 1920, respectively. They demonstrate that Walcott was pursuing a more detailed investigation of selected Burgess Shale fossils after World War I.

for a family dinner. "At the Smithsonian during the day. Took up work on crustaceans from the Burgess Shale" (May 2, 1920). "Meeting of the Ex. Comm. Carnegie Institution 4–6:30 P.M. John C. Merriam offered Presidency of Carnegie Institution of Washington" (May 4, 1920).

The executive committee of the Government Relations Division of the NRC met, but otherwise life was fairly quiet. Walcott moved on with the Burgess Shale fossils, now concentrating on *Naraoia*, seemingly a trilobite, or nearly a trilobite, but lacking a hard covering and having two main parts, not three. There were a few minor evening distractions, but no major dinners; several evenings when Mary and Helen went out, and Walcott was able to work on his manuscript. The sequence of quiet evenings was broken by a dinner for the British ambassador.

"Spoke of Nat. Art Gallery['s] need to Senate Committee 10:30 A.M. At Smithsonian remainder of day" (May 15, 1920). Requests for money are submitted to the House of Representatives, and budgets are prepared a year in advance. One way for Walcott to speed the process was to ask the Senate to amend the civil appropriations bill. His aim was to add a provision for more money, and, far more significantly, to establish clearly a new organizational entity within the Smithsonian fold. Once the National Gallery was distinct from the National Museum, it would appear as a separate budget item.

"The Chairman: We have here a proposed amendment for $15,000 for the National Gallery of Art. Do you wish to be heard upon that?" Walcott read the amendment and then proceeded to the history that had led to the 1906 court decision that the Smithsonian was, legally, the National Gallery of Art. He then presented the history of Freer's bequest, the building, and the various funds to pay for gardens, maintenance of the gardens, additions to the collection, and salary of a curator.

> Mr. Freer's will does not provide for the administration of his collection . . . and in addition we have great collections that have come from various sources . . . now in the Natural History Museum Building. They have been taken care of very largely by Mr. William H. Holmes . . . in his evenings and Sundays and at odd times. . . . I realized when, during the past winter, I came to take up the consideration of the administration and proper care of these collections, that we must have some kind of organization to do it. There is nobody directly responsible for the art collection as such.
> Senator [Reed] Smoot: The Freer collection?
> Dr. Walcott: He does not provide for the physical care of the collection.
> Senator Smoot: He did provide for that by allowing the income from $200,000.
> Dr. Walcott: That is for one man, solely for one man, the curator.

The Chairman: Have you a list of the employees you expect to employ? . . .

Dr. Walcott: They are: Director; 1 stenographer and file clerk, 1 picture hanger, who should be expert in handling objects of art, also in packing and unpacking pictures, etc; 4 watchman [*sic*], at $750 per annum (these are necessary as a watchman is kept night and day in the gallery); 2 laborers, at $660 per annum (these are needed to assist the picture hanger and to clean cases and glass); 2 charwomen, at $240 per annum; 1 messenger boy. . . .

Senator [Wesley L.] Jones of Washington: Is there no appropriation carried now for the administration of the National Gallery of Art?

Dr. Walcott: Nothing.[15]

Any federal funding that Walcott could obtain would be a plus. Having pictures and statues donated by wealthy individuals was one thing, but maintaining them was quite another. It is curious that with all the provisions in Freer's will, building maintenance had not been included. The Museum had coal-fired boilers and a direct-current generator. A steam tunnel had been constructed under the Mall to carry heat and electricity to the Castle and the Arts and Industries Building; a tunnel was run from the Castle to the Freer to carry steam pipes and electic cables. Unfortunately, there was no one officially even to clean the floor in this new building. Security for the material on display in the National Gallery within the Museum was even more of a concern.

By the end of the session, Walcott had funds and a distinct National Gallery of Art in the budget. On August 1, 1920, William Henry Holmes became head of the new organization. There may have been just a little more behind the action. The Freer collection had been given to the nation and was under the aegis of the Smithsonian. It was housed in its own building that was supported by its own funding, with a curator also funded independently. By having the National Gallery of Art provide for maintenance of the building, the Freer could be placed under a modicum of control. Freer may have personally desired a totally independent gallery, but Freer was no longer around, and the realities of administration indicated the Freer Gallery should be subordinate to something. The Freer was a very big tail on the pitifully small dog of the National Gallery of Art, but it was another step in the SI art initiative.

Having presented his case for the gallery to the Senate committee, there was little more that Walcott could do publicly. Mary went to Philadelphia for a couple of days. During her absence, Helen and Walcott did not go wild, but they did attend the circus one evening and a horse show on another. Mary returned, and "we had a quiet dinner and evening at home" (May 20, 1920). Thereafter Walcott was back on the straight-and-narrow path of more seemly events, such as dinner with the surgeon general.

"An unusually quiet day at the Smithsonian in which I did considerable work on Burgess shale fossil crustacea" (May 22, 1920). The pastor, Dr. Charles Wood, was away, and the Walcotts played hooky once again from church. "A very busy day at the office. Prof. Chas. Richards of Cooper Union New York called *en re* Freer Art Gallery. Dr. Herbert of Santa Fe N.M. came in *en re* work in Chaco canyon. At home in evening reading & writing with Helen & Mary" (May 24, 1820). "Meeting of Board of Trustees Carnegie Institution 10–12 A.M. Dr. John C. Merriam was elected president by unanimous vote for which I am greatly pleased" (May 25, 1920).

This was a case of mutual admiration, for Walcott had written formally to Merriam inquiring as to whether he would take the position, if offered. Merriam had been delighted, doubly so because the offer had come from Walcott. Dr. Merriam went officially on the payroll on July 1 but did not become president until 1921; he was given six months to serve as understudy to Woodward. That ensured a smooth transition; wise though it might be, this approach to administration seldom happens today in scientific, let alone commercial, establishments. For nearly two decades, Merriam would faithfully steer the Carnegie Institution of Washington.

Life continued to be rather quiet except for dinner invitations. On the Sunday preceding Memorial Day, the Church of the Covenant had a service for the church members killed during the war. Afterward, Helen and Walcott went to Rock Creek Cemetery to place flowers and a flag. Perhaps it was just as well to do this the day before the actual holiday. "At home attending to odds & ends—working on *Waptia fieldensis* from the Burgess shale" (May 30, 1920). During the spring of 1920, Walcott probably had more time to devote to the Burgess Shale arthropods than in any other period since 1909.

"Mrs. Eugene Meyer and Miss Catherine Rhoades dined with us. We conferred over Curatorship of Freer Gallery of Art, etc. I wrote Ex. Comm. S.I. rec[ommending] Mr. Lodge of Boston Art Museum for Curatorship" (June 3, 1920). The next day Walcott spoke with Mr. Lodge's father, the distinguished senator and longtime SI regent. To carry this through: Mr. Lodge would decline the appointment but agree to oversee the Freer Gallery on a temporary basis. Subsequently he would accept a permanent position, although it was to be on a part-time basis, the remainder of his time being spent at the Boston Museum of Fine Arts. This dual arrangement was to continue into the 1930s.

In regard to the Freer Gallery building itself, the regents had been advised the previous year that "steady progress has been made on the building, and it is hoped that the gallery will be ready for the collections in March 1920. The secretary added that the formal opening was expected to take place by the date of the next annual meeting of the board, in December, 1920" (Walcott 1922, 137).

The Freer was more or less on schedule, and interest was so high that the place was closed to all visitors so that installation of the collections could proceed without interruption. Walcott's estimate on the time of opening was not to be met, however, in large part because of Mr. Lodge.

Two days after recommending the younger Lodge for curator, Walcott was on his way to Detroit in connection with the Freer estate. A day and a half of meetings was spent with the other executors of Freer's estate, and then he was on his way home. The executors were anxious to close out the estate, yet the cost of installation of the exhibit, which included salaries, was to be paid from the estate; it was not a simple matter. "Mary met me at Union Station 9:30 A.M. Went to my office for the day. Many letters & matters waiting for me" (June 9, 1920). Once these were out of the way, routine and research took over. "A busy day clearing up various administrative matters for the fiscal year beginning July 1" and in getting ready to leave on Saturday for the Canadian Rockies" (June 17, 1920).

Before we allow Walcott to leave for the field, two young men have to be mentioned. World War I aviator Paul Garber had given a temporary position, after the expiration of which he stayed on for the summer to make a model of da Vinci's ornithopter.

> I made that model and then went downstairs to put it on display, made a label and put my name on it.
>
> Along came a nice old bald-headed gentleman. Looking up at me on the ladder, and he says "What's that?" "Oh," I said "this is a model of Leonardo da Vinci's idea for an aircraft." . . . Gave him about half an hour on who da Vince was. He asked who I was and [did] I work there. I said I had a temporary appointment but that was several weeks ago but I wanted to finish this. So he was nice to me and off he went.
>
> Up came the chief clerk of the institution. Said "Your name's Garber? You built this thing without permission, I understand?" I said "Yes, but I'm leaving right now, sir." He said "Can you take a civil service examination?" I thought I was going to get fired or put in jail. He said "Secretary's orders."[16]

At least, that is the way Paul Garber remembered it sixty-five years later. One cannot speak of the National Air Museum or the National Air and Space Museum building, which opened in 1976, without speaking of Garber.

Not much later, Frank Taylor also came to the Arts and Industries Building as a temporary employee. He was rearranging a lighting display that included some classical early Edison light bulbs. He was well into the work when one slipped. For several desperate seconds he grasped at it, trying to keep it from breaking. He managed just barely to save it and then heard a great exhalation of breath behind him. Walcott had observed the juggling act and approved. If any one single person was to be responsible for the National Museum of History and Technology, now the National Museum of American History, which opened in 1964, it was Frank Taylor.

Walcott could not have known it, but with these two he had sown the seeds for the future of the institution.

"Closed up the last of plans etc. at the office A.M. Packing up P.M. Mary & I left Washington for Buffalo. Found train crowded with discharged government war workers" (June 19, 1920). Sidney, Helen-Louise, and baby Evelyn had moved to Buffalo, and the Walcotts spent a full day with their family. On the first day of summer, the Walcotts were in Toronto in good time for dinner with Sir Edmund and Lady Walker; then they boarded the westbound train.

The "Explorations" pamphlet for 1919 (Walcott 1920b) was very short on text; apart from the photographs, it essentially contained only a chart listing new names for geologic formations. It was, however, the first in which Walcott had his part produced as a separate publication for distribution. Not only did his sponge monograph receive a favorable short review, but this pamphlet engendered some nice words: "The photograph of the environs of the Mount Lyell Glacier makes a folding plate nearly 3 ft. long, and includes the superb stratigraphic sections of the Mount Forbes and Mona Peak region" (Anonymous 1920, 158).

For the 1920 field season that pamphlet listed two main objectives "(1) the determination of the character and extent of the great interval of non-deposition of sedimentary rock-forming material along the Front Range of the Rockies, west of Calgary, Alberta; (2) the clearing up of the relations of the summit and base of the great Glacier Lake section of 1919 to the geological formations above and below" (Walcott 1921a, 1). Both objectives were accomplished, and in some respects the field season was better than that of 1919.

"Calgary 10:05 A.M. Banff 1:05. Joe Earle our new packer from Missoula, Mont. met us & we were soon in camp where Arthur had luncheon waiting for us." (June 24, 1920). Walcott had tried to hire the packer Flaherty again, but he was not available. Earle had been employed by the U.S. Forest Service and had recommended by Orrin Bradeen, a forest ranger Walcott knew well. Walcott had described ways and means to the prospective employee.

We have 11 good horse at pasture in the foot hills of the Red Deer River. These will be brought down to Banff by one of the Park Wardens in June. We are planning to buy one or two more, as one of our best horses was accidentally killed on the trail last summer.

The party will consist of Mrs. Walcott and myself, and Arthur Brown, who has worked with me as cook all the way from Nevada to the Yellowhead Pass in British Columbia. Mrs. Walcott has been accustomed to camp life and the trail for many years, and thoroughly enjoys it.

Mr. Braden has probably told you that we will pay $125 per month and expenses. Now expect that you had best be in Banff about June 15th where you will meet Arthur Brown, who knows all about the camp outfit, camping place, and getting the things ready for the summer's work. There will be a number of things to do, such as having the horses shod, and getting the outfit ready for the trail. We wish to remain out until October 1st, and probably a week or two longer if there is any chance of getting some big game.[17]

In later letters, Walcott laid out fairly precisely what he expected Earle to do in Banff to get the outfit ready. He also mentioned in passing that Arthur Brown was five feet, ten inches, tall and a light-colored man. When the Walcotts left Banff, Walcott summarized Mr. Earle. "He is an excellent packer but an unpleasant man to have in camp. Grouchy" (October 5, 1920). Apart from Earle's disposition, physical conditions ensured that 1920 was not the best field season. "The work was considerably handicapped by forest fires in July and August and by unusually stormy weather in September" (Walcott 1922a, 8).

The Walcotts were out early from Washington, and they spent five days around camp; all field seasons start out well. "Mary looking well & happy. Joe & Arthur ditto" (June 7, 1920). "About ready for the trail but decided to try out our new horses. We have 14 horses & 3 colts" (June 29, 1920). "After various incidents, such as Breese bucking her pack off etc. we got away at 11 A.M." (June 30, 1920). Camp two was at Lake Minniewanka, sixteen miles distant. They spent several days near Devils Gap, time partly devoted to finding Ginger, who managed to wander off thirty-five miles, but mostly to take photographs. On American Independence Day, the trout fishing was excellent.

The party moved twelve miles to Ghost River, where Walcott recorded being "sore and not much good" (July 9, 1920). "We went up the Ghost River about 2 miles & then went up on an outlying mountain about 5 miles east of Devil's Head, which I name Marsh Mountain on acct large Marsh East of it. Found Middle Cambrian Albertella fauna on south side about 1000 feet from summit" (July 9, 1920). Walcott traced that fauna back to Devil's Gap and then concentrated on collecting nearer to camp. "Measured section on ridge at south side of mouth of Ghost River Canyon. Owing to heat pretty well played out at night. Mary photographing wild flowers" (July 15, 1920). They moved back to the lake and investigated the Cambrian at Devil's Gap for a week before moving back to Banff.

Walcott described the first part of the trip:

The Rocky Mountain front is formed of masses of evenly bedded limestone that has been pushed eastward over the softer rocks of the Cretaceous plains-forming rocks. This overthrust is many miles in extent and occurred long before the Devils Gap, Ghost River Gap, and other openings were cut though the cliffs by running water and rivers of ice. Great headlands and high buttes have been formed by the silent forces of water and frost, many of which stand out against the western sky as seen from the distant foothills and plains. It was among these cliffs that we found that the first great cliff was of lower Middle Cambrian age, and that resting on its upper surface there was 285 feet (86 meters) of a yellowish weathering magnesian limestone, named the Ghost River formation, which represents the great interval between the Cambrian below and the Devonian above. Sixty miles to the west, over 4 miles in thickness of limestone, shales, and sandstones occur in the break in sedimentation of Ghost River cliffs. (Walcott 1922a, 7–8)

Through the years Mary had frequently assisted Walcott with collecting, but just as she seems to have inspired him, he likewise reinforced her interests. Mary was painting, seemingly, more flowers this season than ever before and appeared to be more interested in finding rare forms she had not considered during her many earlier years in the Rockies. Perhaps living with a taxonomist made her conscious of subtle differences that she had previously overlooked among the flowers.

Fossils were packed, supplies purchased, gear mended, and the party moved out. "Breakfast 5 A.M. Packed up & went up Bow Valley to the motor road bridge 1 *mi* above Castle & camped on the shore of the Bow River which is in flood from melting snows" (July 24, 1920). They made twenty-one miles after breakfast. The next day the horses strayed; when they got to the corral campground, the new road for automobiles had taken all the grass, and the horse had to graze near the railway tracks.

Three more camps in four days and they were on the south side of Pipestone Peak. "Mosquitoes were numerous but unduly a nuisance. Firewood scarce as we are at timber line 7500'" (July 29, 1920). Walcott looked at the folded and faulted strata and the cliffs along the river on the other side of the pass. After a Sunday of rest in camp, the pack train moved on. "In the northwest facing cliffs, 25 miles (40 kilometers) east of the Glacier Lake section of 1919, and 40 miles (64 kilometers) north of Lake Louise, a geologic section was studied that tied the base of the Glacier Lakes section with the Middle and Lower Cambrian formations. Returning up the canyon valley of the Siffleur River to the wide upper valley of the Clearwater River, a most perfectly exposed series of limestones, shales, and sandstones of Upper Cambrian and later formations were found which cleared up the relations of the upper part of the Glacier Lake section to the Ordovician above (Walcott 1922a, 8).

Summaries do not record any days lost because rivers could not be forded, or fatigue from more than eight hours in the saddle, or camps being hot and smoky from nearby fires, or fallen trees on the trail. Walcott measured his section of older rocks and found *Olenellus* where it should be, in the Lower Cambrian rocks. He went higher in the geologic section. "It is difficult to measure formations on acct of cliffs and the heat after 9 A.M." (August 12, 1920). "With Joe went up on top of cliff of Cathedral limestone & found the Murchison, Arctomys & Sullivan formations on top & cliffing back. A long hard day" (August 13, 1920). Walcott finished the section, collected trilobites from the Albertella zone, and, as indicated above, moved to the Clearwater valley, scouting the rocks en route.

Joe went to Lake Louise for four weeks' accumulated mail, while Walcott collected Devonian fossils; it was almost going back to the days of the Eureka district for him to look at these younger rocks. The weather was poor for three days, but there was more than sufficient mail to keep the secretary busy dictating to Mary. The weather cleared, and the Walcotts were able to take photographs. "I measured about 300 feet of section, but it was too cold to go higher" (August 23, 1920). So much for a summer Sunday in the Rockies.

Bad weather kept them in camp, though Mary stayed busy painting flowers. Walcott finally got in a fine day on the upper part of the section, and though the weather continued good, tooth trouble returned to complicate life. The toothache passed, and the good weather held. "Measured 1400 feet in thickness as everything was favorable. Mary & Joe met me at brook on North side of ridge north of camp. Footsore & weary on return to camp" (September 1, 1920).

They moved camp, fished, cut firewood, and moved again. "Found we could do nothing worthwhile so after looking about camp was moved down to a point on the Pipestone river about 10 mi. from Lake Louise" (September 6, 1920). Cold rain fell in the afternoon. They moved twice more to get to the old Hillsdale campsite. Mostly they experienced rain every day. When the weather finally improved, the group put in two hard days clearing the trail to Ranger Canyon. "Cricket dropped my collecting bag etc. in creek wh[ich] Mary rescued along with saddle. Cricket acts like an hysterical old fool if tied up away from other horses" (September, 17, 1920). Every kind of field transportation, whether mule, Model T Ford, horse, or jeep, has its own problems of temperament.

Joe and a helper, Lewis, continued trail work, while Mary and Walcott tried unsuccessfully to take pictures, defeated by deteriorating weather. "With Mary & Lewis went up to head of Ranger Canyon but could not do any collecting as snow squalls & cold wind rendered it impracticable" (September 26, 1920). So much, now, for a September Sunday in the Rockies.

"It is nearly three weeks since the Autumn bad weather began & only two all clear days. Now for 'Indian Summer'" (September 28, 1920). Walcott's optimism worked this time. "Went up Ranger Creek Canyon with Lewis and found that the Devonian rested on Cambrian with possibly a little Ghost River or Sarbach between. Mons Formation present. Collected a lot of brachiopods from the

Mons. Will have to measure one section in north branch of canyon" (September 29, 1920). This is not gibberish but the almost equally strange language of geology; Walcott was recounted the names of formations. The locality was another example of the great unconformity at the front of the Rockies, which a few miles west is represented by a thickness of miles of Ordovician and Silurian rocks.

Bad weather moved in, and snow prevented Walcott from measuring that section. It was time to end fieldwork. They moved to Banff in disagreeable weather and packed up in even more disagreeable weather; it was arranged for the chief game warden to take the horses to pasture the following day. Walcott shipped four boxes of fossils on October 4. Year after year he had had delays in receiving his samples, but 1920 was almost to set a record: after numerous letters, the harried si chief clerk was finally able to determine that the shipment crossed the border on December 6! Fortunately, fossils do not need to be fed and watered, for otherwise they certainly would have died while the customs officials or railroads dallied.

On the morning of October 6, the Walcotts were on their way home, leaving Arthur to store the camp equipment for next season. They stopped in Toronto and had a good bath at the hotel after a monotonous trip east. The next morning, in Buffalo, the Sidney Walcotts met them, and again there ensued a most pleasant overnight stay and family visit; Helen-Louise was pregnant. "Wash'n 9:20 A.M. Helen met us at station & I went to my office for the day at the Smithsonian. Found all going well & at home[;] house in order with Mollie, Annie & Katherine at work as usual" (October 11, 1920). In the midst of Walcott's papers, the names of Mrs. Molly Scoggins and Miss Annie Hager appear. They had been around for years, which says something about the quality of life for the servants in the Walcott household; Katherine's last name remains an enigma.

Two full days in Washington, and Walcott was off to New York City. Merriam and Helen came along; the secretary's daughter was moving back to New York. Walcott had a busy time, first with the CIW Ex Comm, then looking at portraits of those who had attended the Versailles peace conference, and another meeting with architect Charles Platt. He also had lunch with James B. Angell, who was now briefly at Yale University and soon would be heading the Carnegie Corporation. The next morning there was a business trip to the Metropolitan Museum of Art, and then he was off for home. The following evening, the Walcotts had Dr. and Mrs. H. A. Bumstead for dinner; he had taken over the NRC from James Angell.

"A quiet busy day at the office. Began to get my notes of last summer[']s work in order" (October 21, 1920). This was a fairly placid time, with ideal Indian summer weather. The finance committee of the GWMA met, and few friends were in for dinner, but there were no elaborate dinners or major committees to interrupt life. "Dr. Chas. Kelly of Columbus Ohio came 10 A.M. as prospective oriental art curator" (October 30, 1920).

"General indications point to election of Senator Harding of Ohio as President of U.S. next Tuesday. I wish I could vote for him" (October 31, 1920). This appears an ambiguous remark, but considering Walcott's later comments about Harding, it is not. To explain: for years on the USGS, so far as civil service was concerned, Walcott had been a citizen of New York. He may have become a citizen of the District of Columbia when he was elected secretary; citizens of Washington could not vote. The only way he could vote would be to go back to New York, and even then he might not have been allowed to cast a ballot.

"Charles Moore chairman Fine Arts Commission dined with us & we talked over matters pertaining to the Nat. Gallery of Art" (November 1, 1920). This was the man who had played the fundamental role in the Freer Gallery, next to Freer himself, of course. "The idea of presenting his collections to the Smithsonian Institution came in 1902 from Charles Moore, a historian who had recently returned to Detroit after serving in Washington as Senator James McMillan's administrative assistant" (Lawton and Merrill 1993, 183). Union Station was built, taking the trains off the Mall, and the Natural History building is where it is, due to the McMillan plan. In some areas, Mr. Moore, as chairman of the Fine Arts Commission, was the most powerful man in Washington. He was a logical ally in Walcott's quest for a building for a national gallery of art in Washington.

"Senator Harding elected President of the U.S. by a great popular majority. The Congress is also Republican by good working majority. We are well satisfied as the country & our city have suffered by the incompetence of the Wilson administration" (November 3, 1920). A paleontologist at Princeton University, who had known Wilson for years, summed up the principal failure of Wilson's administration: "His intense partisanship made it impossible for him to give the Republicans a fair representation [at the peace conference], thus inviting the disaster which eventually wrecked his plans. I am convinced that, had the commission contained Mr. Root or Senator Lodge, we should have entered the League of Nations" (Scott 1939, 310).

"Miss Catherine Rhoades and Miss Guest came in at 4 P.M. They will be occupied with the unpacking & installation of the Freer art collection" (November 8, 1920). This was a bit later than the March date Walcott had predicted, but still well within reason. If Freer had lived a year longer, he would have had the satisfaction of knowing that his wishes for a permanent, dignified home for his collection had been carried out.

Apart from this progress in art, the past week recorded only trivial events. Walcott sorted photographs for part of a day and then came down with a cold, lingered at the office for another day, and finally gave up and took to his bed. "I am disgusted with myself for getting this cold" (November 12, 1920). "Am exceedingly sorry not to be able to attend the meeting of the Nat. Acad. Sciences at Princeton" (November 15, 1920). Had Walcott gone to Princeton, he and Professor William Berryman Scott might have discussed the passing Wilson administration and their expectations for the future.

Instead of getting better Walcott became worse, developing chills and fever. "Mary takes splendid care of me but I am selfish & obstinate. Not sick enough to give up entirely" (November 20, 1920). "Mary read to me from Pollyanna" (November 23, 1920). Possibly that was the right medicine, for the next day he was a bit better.

"Thanksgiving Day—We are thankful for many things. That the American people had the common sense and judgment shown by election returns Nov. 2d. That the human race is gradually finding itself & forging ahead—Personally we are glad to be alive, able to think & do things worth while—that none of us are seriously ill" (November 25, 1920).

Walcott was still not well enough to go to the office. He answered mail at home, saw visitors, had a meeting of the NAS council in the house, and fretted that he could not go out to enjoy the good weather. "I am gaining strength & vitality but am only about 50% good. November has been a bad month for me so am glad it is at end" (November 30, 1920).

Walcott was still at home as December moved along. Miss Rhoades came for dinner, Merriam stopped by, and he dictated and sent off letters. "Mr. John E. Lodge of the Boston dined with us & we talked over the new art gallery situation" (December 7, 1920).

Walcott was back on his feet in time to make a satisfactory presentation of past activities and plans for 1922 to the SI Board of Regents. He went to the Carnegie Ex Comm that afternoon. The following day, the CIW board met, and that evening Dr. Woodward gave a lecture, essentially his valedictory address as past president. "At my office & the museum except for two trips to the capitol to explain S.I. estimates for printing. Conferences with Mr. Lodge & Miss Rhoades *en re* Freer Art Gallery. Tired at night & turned in for a long sleep" (December 11, 1920). One of the minor reasons that Walcott was able to accomplish so much during his lifetime was that in those days Saturday was a working day. Even with that, most people would consider one trip to the Capitol a full day's effort.

"At my office most of the day. Explained estimates for printing S.I. publications to Committee on Appropriations 2 P.M. Meeting of Nat. Gallery of Art

Commission 3 P.M. Meeting Board Trustees Church of Covenant 5 P.M. At home in evening" (December 13, 1920). "At my office most of the day. Conference with John E. Lodge—*en re* to his taking curatorship [of the] Freer Gallery of Art in which agreed to accept it if appointed" (December 14, 1920).

"Mary left for Philadelphia 9:30 A.M. Interview with Secty of War Baker 11 A.M. *en re* getting money for History & Art building. Meeting of Ontario Apt. House Board at noon. Routine & interviews P.M." (December 15, 1920). It is a little hard to reconcile the Department of War and another Smithsonian building, but Walcott was seeking support within the cabinet as well as in the legislature.

Apart from a meeting of the NRC Division of Federal Relations, life was fairly quiet again for a few days. Helen came in from New York for the holiday season, and Sidney passed through Washington; Walcott took him to the Museum to show him the war exhibit. "Christmas. A beautiful day. Our family held Christmas at 10:30. Helen—Mary—C.D.W.[,] William Dahlman, Arthur Brown, Annie, Mollie & Katherine" (December 25, 1920). At least the chauffeur finally had a last name; Katherine remains a shadow.

Walcott and Mary made up New Year's calendars for friends. Helen left, and the George Vaux family came in from Philadelphia. Walcott spoke to the Stuart Walcott Post of the American Legion both about Stuart and his own work in the Canadian Rockies. It was all in all a satisfactory time, save for one administrative matter: "Notified Miss Brigham my Secy & stenographer that she had best plan to leave for other work on or before Apl. 1st on account of her having outgrown her position" (December 31, 1920). Walcott put it gently here, but in a later memorandum to Miss Brigham he outlined a series of shortcomings.

For 1920, Walcott delivered one of the longest summaries in his many years of diary keeping.

Nothing of special importance has happened to Mary or myself. Sidney our boy is now 27½ yrs old & living with his wife & 2 year old girl in Buffalo, N.Y. He is with the Dunlop Tire & Rubber Co., and doing well as office manager. Helen our daughter is living in New York & studying portrait and landscape painting.

Mary (60) & I (70) are well, vigorous for our age & engaged in active work. I am now Secty of Smithsonian Institution, President Nat. Acad. Sciences—Vice Chairman Nat. Research Council—Chairman Ex. Comm. Carnegie Institution of Washington—Chairman of Nat. Advisory Committee for Aeronautics & member of Ex. Comm—Prest. of 2 Apt. House Co.'s of Washington. Too much but it is difficult to get out when once thoroughly immersed in the work of any line organization.

My personal research work moves slowly but a little has been accomplished the past year.

May 1921 deal as kindly with us all & may our country & the nations of the world be far along toward greater moral & material soundness than at present. The aftermath of the "Great War" has been worse than the actual conflict. (December 31, 1920)

An item not recorded was that on December 31, the physicist H. A. Bumstead, chairman of the NRC, died unexpectedly. Walcott as first vice president had to take over additional administrative chores, just about at a time when he was considering how to relieve himself of some of the burdens imposed by other organizations.

January 1 was recorded as a very pleasant day. It began with several hours at the office, followed by a noon breakfast. The Walcotts saw the Vaux family off, attended four receptions, and polished off the day by having dinner with Miss Rhoades and her brother. Fortunately, the next day was Sunday, and after church they made only a couple of calls before relaxing.

"At my office in the Smithsonian building during the day. Routine administrative duties, correspondence & interviews occupied my time & attention" (January 3, 1921). After several such days, a formal dinner for sixteen in honor of Vice President Marshall was almost a relief. "Put in three hours in search for Algonkian bacteria in slides of rock from Montana" (January 5, 1921).

In 1921 Sunday visits to the office remained a family tradition. The Walcotts also had three formal dinners in a row. "At odd times endeavoring to locate Pre-Cambrian bacteria in rock sections" (January 11, 1921). They packed up for a trip to New York. Walcott's first day in New York was typical Walcott. The CIW Ex Comm met early, followed by a meeting of the building committee of the National Academy with the architect; after a business luncheon, a scientific conference ended the day.

On Saturday he accumulated a bust of Gen. Joseph Wheeler for the national collections, saw Elan Hooker and Cousin Fred, and then went back a long way to have dinner with a schoolmate of half a century earlier at the Utica Free Academy. Three full days were devoted to the art initiative and to seeing committees, museum displays, private collections, and people with money who might be donors. The Walcotts were back in Washington in time to change clothes and attend another dinner in honor of the vice president. On Friday, Walcott and Dr. Stratton saw the secretary of war about funds for Langley Field, and then Walcott went home, tired. "Too much New York activity" (January 21, 1921). Notwithstanding, the next day he had meetings with John Lodge concerning the Freer Gallery and with William Henry Holmes concerning the National Gallery of Art.

After church, it was the season to work on the "Explorations" pamphlet for the past field season (Walcott 1921a). That out of the way, a new minor distraction came to the office. "Miss Marian Becket began to paint my portrait" (January 25, 1921). The Executive Committee of the NACA met, and the Walcotts gave a dinner for sixteen in honor of the ambassador of Peru, but otherwise the rest of January rushed by.

February was a bit better for research. "I had a little time *en re* trilobite structure" (February 1, 1921). The Walcotts were invited out almost every night until the 10th, when they gave a dinner for the French ambassador. It was over in time for Walcott to catch the midnight train and attend the Ex Comm of the Carnegie in New York; had Elihu Root remained in Washington, some of the New York travel might not have been necessary. Walcott spent Saturday and part of Sunday with Helen; she started to paint his portrait. It was back to Washington on Sunday evening.

"A mixed up busy day at the office with routine, callers, etc. Mrs. Henry F. Dimock, Collins of Philad. etc. Sent in my resignation as president Nat. Acad. Sci." (February 14, 1921). At the fall meeting in 1917, the Academy had approved a change in its constitution reducing the term of president from six to four years. He began his letter by quoting this chapter and verse: "At the time of my election as President of the Academy, the annual meeting in 1917, I stated informally that I proposed to terminate my term at the end of four years, although when elected, the Constitution provided that the term would be six years. I think that this would be in accordance with the spirit of the present Constitution and I therefore present my resignation as the President of the Academy to you, in order that you may notify the membership in sending out notices for the annual meeting in April, 1921" (Abbot 1922, 12–13).

In one of those curious twists of a chain of command, Charles Greeley Abbot was the Academy's home secretary. Thus it was Walcott's subordinate, as assistant secretary of the Smithsonian Institution, who received the letter of resignation. On such matters as setting up the Carnegie Institution of Washington or the National Advisory Committee for Aeronautics, Walcott could move like greased lightening, but where others were involved, he always provided a long lead time for discussion.

Life moved on. The Philadelphia Orchestra came to town, and after its concert Mary took one of her periodic short trips to the Friends meeting in Philadelphia. She returned, and February wore on with dinners out; the position of cook in the Walcott household must have been relatively easy during this part of the social season. "This has been a quiet week at the office & I have done quite a little research work" (February 26, 1921). Walcott ended February on the same cheery note. "Routine & work on my trilobite paper occupied most of my time during the day" (February 28, 1921).

Walcott began March by actually skipping a meeting of the Ex Comm in New York; apparently the CIW was being run well by new President Merriam. "Mr. & Mrs. Herbert Hoover & Dr Stratton dined with us" (March 3, 1921). The Hoovers lived just down the street from the Walcotts, and they were good neighbors. Walcott attended the inauguration of President Warren G. Harding and saw a number of old friends at the Senate.

"At my office all day attending to routine, cutting a few sections of trilobites, and seeing callers" (March 5, 1921)—now, that is an interesting mix for a day's activities. At church the following day, Walcott accepted a tablet inscribed with the names of those who had died during the war. (When the church was torn down, the memorial vanished.)

"At museum laboratory much of the day, cutting slides of trilobites" (March 7, 1921). A technician might have done the work while Walcott stood by, but much more likely he did it all himself. The making of thin-sections had improved dramatically since his days on the Rust farm. There he had used a foot-powered spring pole lathe to cut the rock and had laboriously ground slices down by pushing the rock back and forth on a glass plate covered with an abrasive. Now there were grinding wheels powered by electric motors, so rapid that unless one checked frequently under a microscope, one could grind away critical details.

Meetings became more prominent. A new secretary of war had to be instructed as to aviation matters; the executive committees of both the NACA and CIW met later that same day. Several meetings in one day are hard on the constitution, but by scheduling them closely, Walcott could ensure that they began promptly and ended at finite times; that may well have been his strategy. It would have been particularly effective, since Walcott was presiding.

Spring came to Washington before mid-March; sometimes it is early. Mary and Walcott derived more enjoyment from their nearly daily walks. Once more they gathered dandelions, certainly not for dandelion wine. Helen came in for a brief visit before sailing off to France and Spain. Mary left for Philadelphia; upon her return she organized a dinner in honor of the secretaries of war and the navy; there was no sense wasting time in breaking in new cabinet members. A couple of days later, the secretary of agriculture came to the house for a family dinner.

Trilobite specimens that Walcott had requested from the Museum of Comparative Zoology arrived. "Routine & study of slides of trilobites I made from 1873–1879" (March 22, 1921). This is an important comment, for it is the only indication that Walcott had started his study of trilobite limbs that early. "Picking up odds & ends correspondence etc. preparatory to moving off tomorrow with Mary for a weeks holiday" (March 24, 1921).

The next day they were off again to Spring Lake in New Jersey. Obviously, the poor weather of last year had not dampened Walcott's notion of the place; this year the weather was kinder. Walcott walked along the shore, napped, collected flowers, napped, looked at pictures of trilobite sections, napped, and received a telegram that all was well with Helen in France. "This is my 71*st* birthday. Am in fair condition but not as strong as ten years ago. Enjoy work & play as usual" (March 31, 1921). The Vaux family came by for a day and took the Walcotts for a motor ride. "Our visit has been a pleasant & enjoyable one altho I have a rheumatic arm most of the time" (April 13, 1921).

Walcott got to back Washington that afternoon and wasted no time. "Meeting of Ad. Com. for Aeronautics 2:15–3:30 P.M. to consider President Harding's request for recommendations on an aviation policy" (April 4, 1921). From what is known of Harding, one might wager that the request did not begin with him—and one would win. "On the initiative of the NACA, a meeting was held in the War Department 31, March 1921. A subcommittee was appointed to draft a letter for the signature of President Harding" (Roland 1985, 58). Harding signed, asking the NACA to advise him, and on April 4 the deliberations began.

The NACA met the following day and again the day after, after which there was a meeting of the NRC Government Relations Division. The request for aeronautical policy was being taken seriously. Two days later the NACA met once more, and Walcott had a completed report. "Rept on Federal Regulation of Air Navigation sent to President Harding 10 A.M. via [John] Victory. Cleared up mail & worked over trilobite sections etc" (April 8, 1921).

The situation was more complex than these comments indicate. General Mitchell was still agitating, and four members of the NACA submitted a memorandum asking that the issue of a department of air, a unified military air service, or the current division of air activities in the army and navy be considered. "Walcott, however, considered this issue a dangerous diversion from the main point, the need to establish in the Department of Commerce a bureau to regulate and encourage civil aviation. Although he advised the president of the sentiment of the four members who had petitioned him, he did not forward their memo; instead, he recommended that the president accept the position of the majority of the subcommittee" (Roland 1985, 59).

The incident reveals another facet of Walcott's administrative style. Once he had determined what the proper course of action should be, he pushed it vigorously. He reported the concern of others, but to have given Harding an extra piece of paper would have weakened his own position, and almost nothing deflected him from a chosen course. As it turned out, all this effort was for nothing, for no legislation on civil aeronautics was to pass for years. Still, having done his share, Walcott could return to other efforts, particularly those involving his beloved trilobites.

There were a few days of routine, including photography of the trilobite sections. The Walcotts formally met the Coolidges at a dinner and the following night had a dinner for twelve in their honor. Mr. Hoover was now secretary of commerce, but Walcott and he could still chat about mineral and coal deposits. Hoover is the only president of the United States to have worked for the USGS and the only one to be a member of the National Academy of Sciences, to which he was elected in 1922; he was a key member of Walcott's postwar network. "Warm, summer-like day. Tired & sleepy at night" (April 15, 1921). "Routine mail etc—& grinding slides of Trenton limestone trilobites" (April 15, 1921). Not the best way to spend a sunny Saturday, but Walcott kept at it.

On Monday church finances came up again, and Walcott was requested to write and send a letter to members of the congregation. This is just one of those extra duties that could not be avoided. "Routine & photographing sections of trilobites. Semi—Annual meeting of Nat. Advisory Comm. for Aeronautics 2:15–4:15. Committee was received by President Harding 1 P.M. in a very pleasing manner" (April 21, 1921).

Three days later, Walcott was still in a mellow mood, presiding at the NRC Executive Committee and then at the NAS council. "A fine summer day. Meeting Nat. Acad. Sci 9–12 A.M. Presented Acad to Prest Harding 1:15 who was most courteous" (April 24, 1921). That evening the NAS heard a lecture by Prince Albert of Monaco—he really was a scientist, interested in oceanography—followed by a reception.

"Meeting of the Academy A.M. & P.M. gave a talk on trilobite structure P.M. Academy dinner in evening at wh[ich] I presided. Medal presented to Prince Albert etc. I rec'd the Mary Clark Thompson medal" (April 26, 1921). John M. Clarke, the state geologist and paleontologist of New York, was acquainted with a lady who performed many good works. She had started a hospital, given a state park to the citizens, and had aided various charities. Lectures by Clarke had interested her in the earth, and when he pointed out there was no great prize for work in this field, she was persuaded to part with a ten-thousand-dollar Liberty Loan bond to endow a medal: "I know from conversations etc. that Dr. Clarke primarily intended the Mary Clark Thompson medal for paleontologists and only later added "geology" to give the medal a broader scope and make the offer of the gift more palatable to Mrs. Thompson. I made the first sketches for the medal at Clarke's request and they represented a fairy, more or less good looking, holding a fossil (ammonite). Later [John] Marchand made another design in plaster, a lady partly emerging from the rock, that meant coming out of the rock (ie evolution)."[18]

Clarke, the one who started all this action, had a more enthusiastic view of symbolic awards than did Walcott.

> Regarding this medal Mrs. Thompson says she wishes to do the right thing and she wants design and medal to be of first order of merit. That was my thought—I believe the award should be superlative in the value it carries and should also be as artistic as possible in its rendering—in other words, should be the finest expression of the Academy's appreciation of service. Mrs. Thompson has entered this agreement and obligation in her book of "liens & promises" so that we are quite secure in regard to the gift as in hand.
> I understand your feeling regarding less gold and more money, but I wanted this to be the maximum award—I think the fund for grants for work in Geology and Paleontology can be provided for a little later.[19]

In organizing for a medal, there are artistic considerations along with scholarly and monetary ones. "The concept of life struggling to the light, eyes upward to the sun, is probably a better expression than afforded by the young woman who is backing into the light with her face still concealed in the rock. I really think that Mr. Henry Fairfield Osborn would prefer a bust of the Honorable Pithecanthropus Murphy to the figure of the little maid, but here it is and I hope we shall have money to pay for it."[20] Vertebrate paleontologist Osborn had now moved into the study of early man, and Clarke was trying to be humorous.

When the design is finally finished and the medal struck, it was the artist who had the final word on what was portrayed on the obverse. "The idea pictured is that the rays of the sun warm the ooze formed from water and powdered rock until a favorable condition for life arise[s]. Life then starts and is laid away in the strata like a book until eventually man, the highest form, is reached and is shown attempting to exteriorize himself still higher, matter into spirit."[21] Just to make sure the honor did not go to the head of the recipient and cause him to stop his efforts, the edge of the medal was engraved "VIRTUTE ET CONSTANTIA."

Between the time the offer was first made and its final acceptance by the Academy, months elapsed. The donor was nervous, and Walcott wrote a friendly letter in the interim to Mrs. Thompson of Canandaigua, New York. He added a homey postscript: "As a schoolboy boy in Utica I tramped over much of western New York and am very found of the 'Finger Lakes' and the towns on them. I often wish I could go all over them again."[22] It was old age recalling youth.

Clarke had in hand the funds, acceptance of the idea by the NAS, and finally an actual medal. The next question was what to do with it. The committee—Clarke, the engineer Gano Dunn, and Henry Fairfield Osborn—decided with a minimum of difficulty that Walcott was the logical candidate for his "distinguished and unsurpassed contributions to geology and paleontology"; it seems a bit strange that after Clarke's efforts to make this an award for paleontology, that geology should be mentioned first—no matter. The committee asked the council when voting on its decision to keep the news secret. The members were happy to do so, but it is an indication of the general tenor of the NAS that one member questioned "unsurpassed" as being controversial.

At the Powhatan Hotel, now long gone from Seventeenth Street and Pennsylvania Avenue, N.W., the annual dinner was held, and the various awards and medals were distributed. The choice for the first Mary Clark Thompson medal was an appropriate one, and the awardee was aware of the honor bestowed on him by his colleagues. One cannot help but wonder, however, if Walcott was not more interested in whether his colleagues were awake when he spoke about trilobite appendages. It is a pity that no abstract of that talk was published.

Despite a fine dinner and a full evening, there was no time to relax. "Business meeting of Academy A.M. Fifteen new members elected. Dr Geo. E. Hale resigned as foreign secretary—The Academy refused to accept my resignation as President so I remain until 1923" (April 27, 1921). Hale was elected to the council for three years, a post he had held before the war.

Walcott presented his resignation once again, pointing out that in addition to the constitutional change of term, he had held various Academy offices for twenty-three years. He suggested Hale for the presidency and, having made his case for resigning, left the room. "Remarks from the floor were made by a number of members of the Academy, expressing the desire and wish that President Walcott remain in office and the feeling of appreciation of the sacrifice in his scientific work which this entailed."[23] At least some NAS members were aware of what the position cost a scientist. "Upon motion of Mr. Hale, which was promptly seconded and adopted, the Academy voted that Mr. Walcott's resignation not be accepted, and that he be informed that it was the earnest desire of the Academy that he remain as president throughout the full term of six years to which he was elected. After much persuasion Mr. Walcott was finally prevailed upon to continue in office throughout the remainder of this term" (Abbot 1922, 13). As a bonus, President Walcott was sentenced to more time on the standing committees on publication and on finance.

It is interesting that NAS members were willing to accept the resignation of Hale, the visionary and grand planner, but declined to let Walcott leave. A new building was in the offing, and one may speculate that having a man on hand in Washington who knew what he was doing, a real "nuts and bolts" type, seemed critical to ensuring that the building actually materialized. There is no question that Walcott was tired, that he had done more than his fair share, and that he had earned the right to resign. When Dr. Welch, "nearing 67," had resigned in 1917 to be replaced by sixty-seven-year-old Walcott, there had been no fuss from the members; Walcott was now seventy-one and feeling his age.

The Academy had given Walcott a most impressive vote of confidence. Whether it was a celebration, a commiseration, or just a gathering of friends, the following evening the Walcotts had a small dinner for the Hales, the Merriams, and the Crosses, a last fling of the annual meeting. "We are a bit weary & will be glad to rest a little the remainder of the week" (April 28, 1921). Walcott's rest included entertaining the prince and his entourage at lunch the following day. Walcott ended the month with the "usual routine during day. Put in some time on trilobite paper" (April 30, 1921).

7

The Fretful Years (1921–1922): Major Problems, Serious Concerns, Minor Aggravations, Plus Little Upsets

> The describer of trilobites has an advantage over the student of Brachiopoda, Mollusca, and various other invertebrates in that the animals with which he deals has more parts, and hence present more combinations of characteristics which may be used in the discrimination of species. On the other hand, he suffers from the disadvantage that his specimens are apt to be dismembered, and very many species are known from fragments only. Due, perhaps to this latter contingency, trilobitists have, as a rule, been rather conservative, and it is only within the last few years that an era of nice distinctions has been inaugurated.
>
> —Percy E. Raymond, 1921

THE ACADEMY had given Walcott a rousing vote of confidence, but the membership had also saddled him with responsibility for two more long years. The presidency was a duty, and duty had called. Walcott was seventy-one and had a massive research program he wished to complete, but once again research time was sacrificed. Unfortunately for him, Walcott was by now a little too old to learn the new trick of saying no. When duty calls and one answers the call, the result is at best a mixed blessing.

As an illumination of the concept of mixed blessings, it may be appropriate to consider a few less-than-satisfactory items of the last few years that had resulted from answering the call of duty. They either do not loom large in his diary or are not mentioned at all, but collectively these serve as a prelude to a major problem of the fall, which resulted from Walcott responding to a call from duty when he should not have. Fortunately, his major problem came after the 1921 field season.

First on this list of mixed blessings may be the Aircraft Production Board, and with it the military's approach to aviation. Despite all the effort Walcott had poured into the cross-licensing agreement, almost nothing came out the other end. None of the problems were his fault, but as a spokesman for aviation, he must have been somewhat embarrassed.

By April 1918, after a full year of war and expenditures in excess of $600 million, the United States had produced a grand total of 15 aircraft. The following month, Wilson overhauled the program. By the end of the war, 32,000 aircraft engines and 12,000 aircraft had been produced. The trouble was that most of this came too late. . . . Fewer than 200 aircraft were actually produced in time to reach the front.

There was plenty in this mixed bag of failure and achievement for the critically disposed to seize upon. . . . Some of the men in charge of the production program . . . were accused of deliberately funneling Government contracts to favored firms—firms in which they had a financial interest. Wilson . . . persuaded Charles Evans Hughes to conduct an investigation. . . . A subcommittee of the Senate Military Committee, headed by Charles S. Thomas (D-Colo), initiated its own probe. (Komons 1977, 38–39)

Between scandal and the dumping by the army of surplus planes at rock-bottom prices after the war, the aircraft industry was in a mess.

Walcott had seen it coming, as a 1919 letter indicates.

You state that the new Chief of Training never had any experience in the Training Department. I am surprised that you consider this as any possible objection. Joking aside, I am no longer making suggestions or discussing such matters with the secretary of war or officials of that Department, as I consider it a waste of time under the present organization. I should be very glad to talk with Major Phillip Roosevelt, as you suggest.

It is probable from the general current of opinion and expression both here in Washington and elsewhere that in due time a number of questions will be asked pertaining to the administration and conduct of the Air Service and other military activities both in this country and France.[1]

The situation must have been exceedingly convoluted for Walcott to forego giving advice.

A second concern was the matter of Mr. Freer during his last few months. He was in failing health, and the relationship, if any, of the coming Freer Gallery to the National Gallery of Art was troublesome. Though there was administrative good sense in combining them, it was fairly evident that Freer wanted his gallery to stand alone, with his collection intact for eternity. Then he had suddenly changed his mind, to allow more Oriental art to be added by a few select persons. Who could predict what these select people might do to complicate matters?

After seeing Freer in June 1918, Walcott had written a letter to the *New York Times* to soothe one of the art patron's upsets, but the newspaper had not published it. At the least, this was for Walcott an annoyance. Though Freer had died in the fall of 1919, the estate was still not settled, for the installation of the collections was to be paid for by the estate. Likewise, the matter of a permanent head for the Freer was still dangling. Walcott was trying to establish the National Gallery of Arts as a clear-cut entity; the Freer Gallery was in effect a very large loose cannon on a very tiny boat.

Third, there was the unfortunate matter of Franz Boas, the first anthropologist to be appointed to Columbia University (Kardiner and Preble 1963). In October 1919, he wrote a letter to *The Nation*. In this communication, which was not published until late December, Boas indicated that several persons had spied for the government outside the United States under the guise of being anthropologists. Leading up to that accusation, Boas made several comments about the discrepancy between what President Wilson had said concerning the evil of using secret agents and the actual events, at least as they had been relayed to him.

Walcott's reaction was immediate, and it was extreme. Boas was known to have strong pro-German sentiments, despite his having been on the NRC during the war. As were shown by various diary entries, Walcott considered the Germans savages for having started the protracted war; he had expressed this view long before he lost his youngest son. During wartime one supported one's country. Walcott considered Wilson ineffectual by the end of his term of office, but he must have viewed the League of Nations as a grand idea. For anyone, let alone a foreign-born, naturalized citizen, to impugn the patriotism and honesty of the president was unthinkable.

Secretary Langley had established an advisory position in the Bureau of American Ethnology for Boas. Four days after the Boas letter appeared, Walcott canceled it. He immediately wrote to NAS council members asking whether the contents of the letter constituted grounds for expulsion from the Academy; Boas had been a member since 1900. Walcott also wrote Nicholas Murray Butler, now president of Columbia University, directing his attention to the letter—as if he had not heard about it already. Butler and Walcott had been reasonably close since the early days of the GWMA and had in common the loss of sons in Europe. Walcott was quite consciously adding his full weight to those who would fire Boas.

Fortunately, F. L. Ransome, a USGS geologist who had succeeded Whitman Cross as the National Academy's treasurer, tried to cool things down. George Ellery Hale added his comments: "I heartily agree with your opinion of Dr. Boas, and wish that he were not a member of the Academy or of the Research Council. However, I doubt very much whether his letter to the Nation [the magazine], objectionable though it may be, affords sufficient grounds for action."[2] Abbot also acted to calm the situation: "Referring to your letter of Dec 29 perhaps I am too easy going, but I should rather shrink from trying to force Boas out of the Academy or of Columbia. He is not really but 61 years old, yet he gives the impression of a doddering old man, and actually having suffered a stroke of paralysis has a foot already in the grave. I should fear that the effort of acting against him would make a martyr of him. I am inclined to think people are too sensible and too much to do to be poisoned by anything he can write."[3]

Boas resigned from the NRC council before a vote could be held as to whether he should be expelled. The Anthropological Society of Washington had already condemned him, and the majority of those attending a meeting of the American Anthropological Society voted in favor of a similar resolution. His condemnation by this society has been the subject of several studies (Pinsky 1992). In contrast, nothing about the possible expulsion of this member appears in the official NAS history, and he remained a member for years after Walcott died. Whether he attended any meetings while Walcott was NAS president hardly seems worth pursuing; his presence on the Academy membership rolls must have been a source of aggravation. It's important to note that Walcott's reaction was to Boas as an individual. He had nothing against anthropologists, nor did he comment on others who might have had pro-German sentiments.

One should make an allowance for the temper of the times. The specter of worldwide Bolshevism frightened many in the United States; in fact, American troops had been fighting in Russia. Soon the country would be in the midst of a scare over the red menace. Not only did this foreign-born scientist have bizarre ideas in his field of anthropology, he had cast aspersions on other scientists and on the government. Complex though the matter may be in terms of freedom of expression, it is best interpreted as straightforward hatred of a pro-German attitude. Walcott considered Boas to be unpatriotic, a cardinal sin in Walcott's moral code. In December of 1921, for instance, Walcott wrote to new President Harding quoting a letter he had received from a German scientist and commenting most unfavorably on it.

The violent reaction to Boas was part of the rending of the old social fabric; the terrible disruption in Europe also had major consequences in America. The issue of whether it was the First World War or the Second that caused the greater changes in life has filled numerous books. In any event, 1914 was a watershed, and little of the postwar society bore any relation to the prewar, whether with respect to morality or technology.

Fourth on the list of problems was the perennial subject of funds. On the last day of 1919, in the midst of the self-inflicted turmoil over Boas, Walcott wrote to an associate in Sweden about the grim situation for science in America.

> I can readily understand your description of the financial conditions in Sweden, for although we are quite prosperous we are suffering from a burden of high taxation and high cost for everything that comes into living and research. The Smithsonian Institution with its limited foundation is now unable to take advantage of many opportunities offered to it to conduct very interesting and valuable lines of research. Even the Carnegie Institution of Washington, of which I am chairman of its Executive Committee, [sic] is unable to expand although additional income to the extent of $250,000 a year will soon be available. It will take all this and more to keep up with the increased cost of the work that had under way at the beginning of 1918.[4]

Fifth was the National Advisory Committee for Aeronautics. Between the two world wars, the NACA "stood pre-eminent in the field of fundamental research" (Holley 1964). This had not happened without annual battles with Congress for funding and an occasional inspection by Walcott of increasingly technical people, machines, and reports, ever more distant from good, solid field geology.

Another battle in the same field, but far less successful, had to do with general legislation dealing with aircraft. As early as 1919, when the first attempt at a statute was made, the *New York Times* quoted Walcott's letter of transmittal. "Mr. Walcott, pointing out that absence of any federal authority for establishing rules and regulations governing civilian operation, said if the War Department sold its surplus machines many amateurs would attempt flying, which would result in many accidents."[5] The War Department sold its equipment anyway, and the barnstormers proved Walcott correct.

Two years later, a different aspect of the same theme was mentioned. "The problem of developing the uses of aircraft requires the Federal regulation of air navigation and the establishment and regulation of transcontinental airways, including the necessary airdromes and weather report stations" (Walcott 1922b, 3). That may have been the view of Chairman Walcott and other members of the NACA, but Congress was not receptive; it would be some years before any positive steps were taken. Meanwhile, General "Billy" Mitchell kept promoting controversy, to the point that John Victory, NACA employee number one, finally told him that he was no longer welcome at the NACA office.

In December of 1921, the NACA annual report and its recommendations were featured in the *Times*. This elicited at least one reply from an interested party.

"I believe, from my observations and acquaintances with the companies who are active in the development of commercial aviation, that no move which has been made since the War will do more to advance this method of transportation. I congratulate you and your committee on the very thorough way this has been investigated and the complete recommendation you have made to Congress. I hope that the bill will be promptly passed and that the Department of Commerce may get behind the recommendation in every way possible."[6]

The bill did not pass, and chaos continued in the aviation industry; chaos is particularly unsettling to one who has a scientific mind. The NACA, which had so important during the war, was continuing to use up far too much of Walcott's time, and there seemed to be no way to halt this squandering.

Sixth on this list was Percy E. Raymond, the paleontologist at Harvard. As a general rule, it is good to have a fellow worker in one's field, but it was not at all clear just how closely Raymond's interpretations of trilobites would coincide with Walcott's. If Walcott had not been concerned, he would never have bothered to assemble the "Great Trilobite Limb Committee" in the spring of 1919.

Everyone in science espouses the free exchange of opinion, but notwithstanding the public lip service about the dispassionate inquiry after truth, scientists are more human than most other humans. Their subjects are their passions, and not even less passionate people like to have their views challenged. Add to this the general factor that older people prefer to have younger people listen to them than argue with them. Walcott was in the role of the true objective scientist in sending his specimens for Raymond to examine, but whatever he recorded, or did not record, in his diary, the anticipation of what Raymond might be writing was less than joyful.

One of the famous comments concerning classification of animals is, "There is something about writing on arthropod phylogeny that brings out the worst in people."[7] Fortunately, as it turned out, the differences between the interpretations of the two people concerned with trilobite limbs were not as great as they might have been.

One might add, as seventh on the list, a general concern about support for art. In the spring of 1919, when Walcott spoke before the American Federation of Arts, he noted that galleries of art had been mentioned by Congress when it set up the Smithsonian Institution in 1846. "The progress that has been made since that time has not been creditable to the nation. We should have in Washington great collections housed in a building which should hold a worthy position among art museums of the world."[8]

As has been said, a journey of a thousand miles begins with a single step, but it was a long step from the fifteen thousand dollars Walcott obtained from Congress in 1920 to formalize a National Gallery of Art to a true art museum building. Up until 1920 the only assistance Dr. Holmes had in art matters was an advisory committee, one of the five members of which was Holmes, to decide on whether gifts offered should be accepted.[9] Now Walcott was in the process of setting up a fifteen-member National Gallery of Art Commission to push toward a building.

Art was not necessarily a new field for Walcott, but it was not one of his strong points. Once again, he was cajoling friends and friends of friends to take on an extra burden. Recruiting volunteers is never easy, and the longer the cause has been around, the more difficult it is to find people willing to serve. Art had been more or less in the forefront for two decades, yet the Smithsonian Institution had little to show.

Eighth on this list was an inclination in the country to return to the good old days and solid family values. Prohibition of alcohol beverages was abroad, and essentially the same group that had stamped out the evils of drink was now expounding the horrors of the theory of evolution. Fundamentalists who interpreted the Bible literally were unsettling, and they were becoming more vocal. President Walcott had appointed a small NAS committee to consider the matter, but so far Chairman John M. Clarke had been unable to stir the members into any formal action.

Although it came later in the year, yet another aggravation in 1921 was the Senate's withdrawal of the Smithsonian secretary's privilege of the floor, a privilege going back to Secretary Baird. Walcott had used it six times a session at most. It was another straw in the wind, indicating how much the federal government had changed. The days when Walcott could walk in at a critical moment, discuss his concerns, and gain support for his cause had gone.

There is one good account of Walcott's style on Capitol Hill:

> One day he took me [C. G. Abbott] for a conference with some of the members of the House Committee on Appropriations. As we were waiting, Representative Burleson of Texas expressed a deprecatory view of scientific research. He said it was not properly a Government function to promote it except for directly visible utilities. I was combating his view when Dr. Walcott took the conversation out of my hands and apparently turned to quite another subject. He asked Mr. Burleson if he had followed the work of Dr. Cottrell on the electric precipitation of dusts. He went on to describe it interestingly. In a couple of minutes he had the fact staring Mr. Burleson in the face that a research, begun with no practical end in view, was now on the road to be worth millions to the Government and Nation.
>
> As we rode back to the Smithsonian, I complimented Dr. Walcott on the neat way he had countered Mr. Burleson's proposition. "Oh!" said he, "never argue with those men. They are all lawyers and will beat you. Just show them the facts that cannot be beaten." On another occasion Dr Walcott said to me:

"When you have something in charge act quickly as best you can. You may make mistakes, but if you are right seventy-five percent it will be a good batting average." (Abbot 1958, 97)

One can probably add that there was no one left to talk about "the good old days." Describing fossils is a solitary business, but occasionally one needs a break in routine, and it is nice to chat with colleagues. Arnold Hague had died in 1917, G. K. Gilbert in 1918, G. F. Becker in 1919, and Joe Iddings, his tentmate from Eureka, Nevada, days in 1920. Dr. Merrill and William Henry Holmes could still recall the original USGS, but Merrill was never part of the organization, and Holmes was not in Washington at the beginning.

There were also minor issues around. One small aggravation was the annual report of the Daughters of the American Revolution. Back in the early days of the Langley regime, arrangements had been made that their annual report was to be transmitted to Congress through the Smithsonian, and so it was. Walcott pointed out to the Regents that there was no legitimate connection between SI and DAR. Nevertheless, it would require a special act of Congress to rectify the situation and though the congressional regents mentioned it several times in their other capacity, Congress did not act for years. Each time Walcott had to write a letter of transmittal of the DAR annual report, it was like a small infected hair that itches from time to time and defies all attempts at a cure.

There were a few in-house matters that caused mild upset. Junior curators had protested a civil service action by Walcott. He had considered the matter and finally agreed that as secretary he was not the proper person to judge their scientific ability and had transferred this responsibility to the head curators.

Then there was the matter of a replacement for his secretary, who had been told she had outgrown her position. It was Walcott's practice to tour the museum about once a month, chatting with people and asking about their work. Generally, after a few minutes, Walcott would say, "I commend you" and proceed along the way. A frequent stop was to see Paul Bartsch in the Division of Mollusks. Bartsch had a secretary who was so skilled after seven years that he could dictate descriptions of snail shells to her. Walcott offered her a position, and when she took it Bartsch did not speak to Walcott for a year. Finally, Walcott said, in effect, that Bartsch was young and Walcott was old and therefore needed all the help he could get. That mended the riff.

The Sunday that began May was a cool, March-like day. Monday and Tuesday were harried and broken up as Walcott raced to get away from Beecher's trilobites until it was time for a reception in honor of Dr. Angell. Schuchert was away, so Walcott left a note to document his efforts: "Sorry to miss you. I have looked over the type of material of Dr Beecher & Dr Raymond & if agreeable to you would like to try photographing of details of specimens. . . . These all have details not well bro't out by Raymond. We may not succeed but it is worth trying."[10]

Walcott went on to write that he had heard Schuchert was using his Canadian panorama pictures for teaching. "As they were taken for educational proposes as well [*sic*] scenic beauty I will send you a few for inspiring the boys with a love for the mountains & nature."[11] Walcott then suggested an exchange of some of this trilobite material for Burgess Shale fossils. It was a mutually agreeable trade.

The next morning the Walcotts caught an early train to New York City so Walcott could see various associates. Scurrying from office to office continued the following day, winding up with a visit to Mrs. Harriman and a conference with Dr. Angell. There is no mention of subject, but a reasonable surmise is that this activity was devoted to seeking money for art. They moved to Philadelphia, called at several art museums, and settled for the night at Bryn Mawr for a family visit. After the Friends meeting the following day, they caught the train south. "Found all well at home" (May 8, 1921).

"A Quiet very busy day at the office catching up with mail etc. Also working on a statement with relation to the Smithsonian endowment" (May 9, 1921). Money, that is, the lack of it, was even more of a concern than when he had written in 1919. Each year the Institution received sixty thousand dollars as the interest on one million dollars in the U.S. Treasury. Various funds and bequests contributed a few dollars more, but these added little. The tiny government agencies administered by the Smithsonian each received an appropriation at the pleasure of Congress. Costs had escalated during and since the war, and while the bureaus were strapped, the Smithsonian was in distress; at each annual meeting Walcott reminded the regents of the ever worsening financial situation.

The secretary and Mrs. Walcott dined out three evenings in a row and then Walcott was knocked out of action by a cold. Fortunately, in one day it was gone and he could get back to the office on Saturday to sign the mail. The family skipped church and rested up. Monday morning Walcott stayed at home to work on the trilobite manuscript in his study but got to the Castle that afternoon. He snuck in another morning for research before a reception for the American Federation of Art. Thereafter Walcott was busy with various arts people, "working the crowd."

A major scientific-social event came that May. "At home A.M. & office until 3:30. Received with party in hon of Madame Curie at the White House where President Harding presented the gram of radium to her. Presided at reception to Madame Curie at the National Museum in evening[.] 780 present" (May 20, 1921). The Nobel Prize winner had outdrawn the arts federation by 285 people. Sunday morning Walcott called on her, and later that day she returned the call.

When Madame Curie left town, Walcott went back to research, "Revising mss of trilobite paper at home & attending to correspondence etc. P.M." (May 23, 1921). He took the time to write Schuchert, asking for the partially prepared specimens he had set aside. "If you will send down three or four barrels of the virgin material by freight, Mr. Mirguet can go to work on it under Bassler's direction while I am absent during the summer."[12] Mirguet was a preparator in the Division of Mollusks; it was just as well Walcott and Bartsch were cordial. The preparator worked on the fossils after regular hours and was paid separately for his trouble. One of the longtime employees recalled that originally Mirguet walked to the Castle to pick up material, but after Walcott realized how much time this wasted, Arthur Brown brought over the specimens.

Research was moving along, so it was time to poke up a different fire. Walcott met with Charles Moore of the Fine Arts Commission and they discussed membership of the group to support the National Gallery. In Senator Lodge's office, a special "Meeting of Smithsonian Regent 10 A.M.—vice-President Coolidge elected Chancellor. Commission of Nat. Gallery of Art appointed by Regents" (May 23, 1921). The chief justice, who had served as chancellor for a decade, had died, necessitating the special meeting.

"The secretary brought to the board's attention the needs of the institution in the way of endowments to permit the carrying on of large projects in scientific research. He stated that the fund was small and inadequate, and among the methods adopted to bring these needs before public spirited citizens a small pamphlet had been prepared which he brought to the board's consideration in the hope that should opportunities arise they would direct attention of prospective donors to the usefulness of the institution" (Walcott 1922a, 34). It had been less than three weeks since Walcott contemplated the wording for this pamphlet, not bad time for such a document to be produced; seemingly no copies of it exist today.

As was customary with him, Walcott wasted no time once a course was set. The day after the regents' meeting, he sent out a call for the Arts Commission appointees to assemble. Decoration Day began with a quick visit to the cemetery, followed by seven hours on the *Neolenus* manuscript. This was not an easy paper to write, and though it is about the same size as the sponge paper that preceded it, far more intellectual effort went into the text, and far more sweat by photographers went into the illustrations.

He dictated a quick letter to Schuchert informing him of the safe arrival of material. "I will send you some Burgess Pass fossils before I go on June 18th. Will also return Beecher types. I [do] not think that we know all about the structure of the limbs of *Triarthrus*, but I will not make any conjectures until after the new material has been carefully worked over and all promising specimens studied."[13] Walcott had a quick pen, but on this study he spent month after month.

"Afternoon garden party at the White House by President & Mrs. Harding which we greatly enjoyed" (June 1, 1921). "Routine and mss" (June 2, 1921). "Am trying to get matters cleaned up so as to get away for a visit to New York next week" (June 3, 1921). Try as he would, matters would not clean up, and this was one trip that Walcott was unable to bring off.

The Walcotts had several informal dinners over the weekend, possibly in lieu of the trip. Walcott settled down to work on his manuscript, but then a toothache struck, getting worse the next day. "Meeting of Nat. Advisory Art Commission 10 A.M.–1 P.M. Luncheon given by Mary at S.I. & a glance at Freer building. The Commission was organized & put in running order. Had my aching tooth extracted 8:30. At home except for a walk with Mary in the evening" (June 8, 1921). Smithsonian business was more important than an extraction. It may be coincidence, but in December 1901 the Carnegie Institution of Washington was started when Walcott also had an toothache; perhaps this commission would be as successful as the Carnegie.

Besides the new commission, June brought another piece of good news. "Mrs. Henry F. Dimock called to tell me that she expected to start on the Geo. Washtn. Memorial building Nov. 11th 1921 by laying corner stone" (June 10, 1921). Caution dampened the enthusiasm a bit. "Meeting of G.W.M.A. at C. J. Bell's office and decided we could not approve of starting building until money was all in to limit set by Congress" (June 12, 1921). In designating the site on federal land, Congress had stipulated when construction should start, and this deadline had been extended several times. The reason was that the minimum amount of money to be raised for this building had also been stipulated, and funds had been insufficient for two decades.

It was terribly hot that Sunday. Not only was there no attending church, but Walcott's teeth were so bad that he spent the day in the dentist's chair. He was back in the chair on Monday and again on Tuesday. "Am having much trouble with three old teeth" (June 14, 1921). One might be tempted to moralize that some of the problem with his teeth came from biting off too much for too many years.

Between visits to his dentist, Walcott was trying to wind up affairs and leave for his field season. Though Walcott needed the time for other matters, Mr. Nunn came to town after a long absence and for two days occupied a fair number of his hours. The finance committee of the GWMA held yet another meeting. A meeting of the NRC ate up an entire afternoon. A visitor from Detroit dropped in. Almost everything was conspiring to keep Walcott from his chores.

"Finished up long siege at dentist. Turned in paper on trilobite structure A.M. Meeting Ex. Comm. N.[ational] G.[allery of] A.[rt] Commission 10–12 A.M. Cleaned up my office P.M. sending fossils back to Cambridge & Yale. At home in evening" (June 17, 1921). "At meeting of Nat. Research Council 10–11:30 A.M. & closing up matters at the Smithsonian until 3 P.M.—Packing up at home & at 6 P.M. Mary and I left Washington en route to the Canadian Rocky Mountains" (June 18, 1921). Finally! That Sunday in Buffalo they enjoyed a delightful June day visiting with their granddaughter. The next day Sidney drove them all to Niagara Falls for a picnic; "Little Evelyn is a splendid little traveler" (June 20, 1921).

The following day they were on the train to Toronto, and at 9 P.M. the Walcotts headed west; summer had begun both by the calendar and psychologically. "We are slipping along over the prairie, which is green & beautiful with the spring week. Last evening we watched the sunset on the bays & islands of Lake Superior. . . . Last year we got down to actual field work on July 8*th* owing to the cold rainy weather. We hope to be on the trail July 1st this season."[14]

It was just as well that Walcott did not know of the summer's weather ahead of time. Hard on the heels of the first joy of heading west, Walcott was feeling "pretty well played out" (June 22, 1921). After they passed Winnipeg, however, on the second day in the West, he recovered and spent the day "resting & checking index of vol. 67 S.M. Coll" (June 23, 1921). Since Walcott had not finished volume sixty-seven, this must have been the index to the trilobite manuscript. Anyone who has ever prepared an index will recognize the oxymononic use of "resting," but then, what can one expect from a man who so rarely rested?

The importance of Arthur Brown in his role of camp manager, as well as cook, cannot be overstated. Walcott sent him ahead to western Canada to make arrangements; a 1921 letter is representative. "I received notice this morning that our new tent is now at Banff. Enclosed find an order on the Express Company for it. I would not put it up until June 23, as we are not due in Banff until the morning of the 24th. . . . In case Lewis has not turned up tell Wallensteen to take charge of the horses and carry out the instructions which I have written to Lewis and of which you have a copy."[15]

Walcott later reported that he went to the field that year to "secure data on the pre-Devonian strata of the Sawback Range in Ranger Brook Canyon and to conduct a reconnaissance of the pre-Devonian formations to the Northwest as far as the headwaters of the North Fork of the Saskatchewan River, Alberta" (Walcott 1923, 7). The season began traditionally. "Billy Lewis met us at the station & we drove out to camp in the Buffalo park where Arthur had lunch for us" (June 24, 1921). The grumpy Joe Earle was no longer around. Walcott had written to Lewis, whom he knew from earlier seasons, and receiving no reply had written to another packer. Naturally Billy Lewis then responded, and there ensued a long correspondence. At the last minute, the assistant packer withdrew, and Walcott had to hire a local, Cecil Smith, to clear trails, pack the horses, and so forth. The group made thirty camps that season.

"Measured section of Sawback formation beneath Devonian 1182 feet & found fossils at horizons. Out nine hours on foot. Mary came up for luncheon" (July 9, 1921). "Out all day working on sections of Upper Cambrian Mons formations. Measured 1535 feet of strata" (July 10, 1921)—not a bad day's work for a Sunday.

This was one field season in which Washington would not stay away. "Since you went to the field, the administration has gotten busy to try and reduce expenses, and has employed General Dawes to be Budget Officer. Not content with controlling the matter for the fiscal year 1923, they are endeavoring to induce the departments to make savings out of the funds already appropriated for the fiscal year 1922."[16] This news, which went on in greater detail, provoked a long reply.

> I do not think we can reduce expenses with discharging needed employees or accumulating routine work that should be kept up to date. The appropriations for the government work placed in charge of the Smithsonian Institution were inadequate in 1914 & with slight additions that could not be avoided they have not been increased up to date. The Smithsonian persued [*sic*] a business-like economic, patriotic course during the war and after and it has sacrificed men & opportunities in taking such a conservative position. Any reduction in available funds either for 1921 or 1922 would mean a curtailment of work & results that would be a waste of available plant & highly trained men.
>
> The Smithsonian wishes to continue its patriotic, useful, public service and I cannot see any more effective way of doing it that by maintaining and increasing the present standards for the government activities entrusted to it for administration. The matter should be placed before the Director of the Budget in a clear cut business statement. Then whatever the government supplies will be used to carry on the work as far it will go. The Smithsonian will seek funds from private sources for research work but it cannot consistently do so for maintenance of enterprises that the Government should support the activities of the S—— are educational in the broadest sense and the results cannot be estimated in terms of business.[17]

The news from Washington had certainly struck a nerve. There was no question in Walcott's mind that funds were short. He was equally clear in his thinking as to the line between the Smithsonian and the various governmental bureaus that it administered.

"Packed up camp & moved to Lake Louise station on C.P. Ry. A long trying trip in buckboard on account heat & dust" (July 18, 1921). Thirty-four miles in a buckboard would be trying in pleasant weather. The next two days brought the chore of proofreading the galley on the structure of trilobites.

Washington, this time in the form of Special Assistant Ravenel, reported again on the fun-filled developments there.

> The Bureau of the Budget on July 1, instead of taking up the estimates for 1923, by order of the President took up the question . . . of reducing expenditures. I was appointed Budget Officer by Dr. Abbot for all of the bureaus under the Institution and submitted on the 15th of July the statement required. . . . Notwithstanding the fact that our Museum is broader in its scope than any museum in the world and with as able a staff as any, it received exactly half of what the staff in the American Museum received in 1920. They will take up the estimates for 1923 in August.
>
> The Freer matter is still hanging fire, due to the fact that Judge Gray, though he highly approves of the plan suggested by you, of borrowing $250,000, states that before further action is taken he would like to use the opinion of an attorney. . . . Mr. Lodge left for Boston the first of the month and will not return until autumn. Miss Rhodes leaves tomorrow for an indefinite stay and Miss Guest later on.[18]

The executors wanted to settle Freer's estate, but by the terms of his will they could not until the obligation that the exhibits be installed had been met. Rather than sell some of the stock to provide cash, Walcott suggested turning all assets over to the SI and then using the stock as collateral. It was clever, though complex. To add a little spice to the matter, the state of Michigan wanted to collect estate taxes.

As to the Freer Gallery itself, in June the building had been turned over by the architect. "The plan of installation is first to catalogue and arrange the collections in the storage rooms so that they will be accessible for study, then to select the objects for exhibition, and finally to arrange the public exhibits" (Walcott 1922a, 18). This was not the type of plan that Walcott would have devised, for thousands of people wanted to see the treasures. Until the exhibits were installed, Walcott was bound by Freer's will. Even if this outline was the plan of Mr. Lodge, if no one worked on the collections the Freer would never open. Between the will and John Lodge, Walcott was stymied. Being between a rock and a hard place with respect to that situation, Walcott concentrated on the rocks at hand.

"Out on east slope of Fossil mt. until 11 A.M.. Heat knocked me out so rested, read, wrapped up fossils P.M. Mary painting wildflowers. Bill & Cecil cutting out trail down Baker Creek. Cooled rapidly at night 20° in thirty minutes" (July 25, 1921). Five days later they moved to the famous wildflower camp, the sixth campsite of the season. "Mary has recognized & counted 50 varieties of wild flowers in bloom within 200 feet of our tent" (July 30, 1921). By the time this was written up for an "Explorations" pamphlet (Walcott 1922c), the total had risen to eighty-two forms near the tents. Although Walcott had problems in 1921, this may have been the most productive season for Mary's paintings.

"Mary & I went up on Johnson Creek devide [*sic*] for photographing. Bill & Cecil brot up camera later. Found Lower Cambrian quartzites of Castle Mt. overthrust on Sarback (Ordovician) limestone at the devide" (August 1, 1921). After another day in the area, it was time to move camp again and time to write a few comments to Washington.

> Mr. Ravenel is the right man in the right place in the budget matter. I fear that Mr. Holmes cutting off $500 on this year[']s appropriation will cause him to run short before the end of the year, as the expenses of the Commission may amount to more than he anticipates.
>
> As far as the Freer Gallery is concerned, there is no doubt about the extravagance connected with it from the beginning. This was necessarily the case under the direction of Mr. Freer & the provisions of his will & as the estate is still unsettled it will be difficult to plan intelligently until that is done. . . . We arrived at camp yesterday & just after getting everything in order for the night a storm swept over the high mountain ridges s.w. of us bringing rain & hail throughout the night & today. . . . We are in a region where mountain goat sheep & deer abound. Only two grizzly bears have been seen thus far.[19]

"Out all day with Mary & Bill taking photographs up on west side of Badger Pass. Fine exhibit of upturned Devonian, Cambrian & Ordovician strata" (August 7, 1921). Lest anyone comment on Walcott's incorrect listing of the geologic periods, recall that a few days earlier that he had commented on a thrust fault; the Cambrian is below the Devonian, except where it has been thrust up and over the younger rocks. "About camp A.M. After lunch went up on slope of Castle Mt. to see section of Mt. Whyte formation. Ran across a mule deer (buck) & brot it back to camp during a heavy shower" (August 8, 1921). Apparently a rifle was standard equipment when Walcott was using a horse for fieldwork.

They moved again and took more photographs, though several days were smoky. The responsibilities of a geologist's wife as helpmate are summarized in one diary entry for a Sunday. "Mary left 8 A.M. for Lake Louise to get supplies, mail, etc. Cecil & two pack horses went with her. Packing up, fixing notes etc. A very warm disagreeable day. Bull dog flies & mosquitoes in swarms all day" (August 14, 1921). Tuesday afternoon Mary returned to camp ten. There is no question that if Cecil had not been around, Mary would have taken the pack string and brought the groceries. She was one tough lady.

They moved along toward the North Fork of the Saskatchewan River. "Taking photographs A.M. of trails on river mud and of quartzite cliffs beneath Devonian on end of Mt. Wilson cliffs. Mending various things P.M. The valley is broad & flat at the point with broad anticlinal structure" (August 28, 1921). In simple terms, first the rocks had been curved and bowed up in the middle, and second, the crest of the bow had been cut down by the river, producing a broad, flat area.

Two camps and twenty-nine miles later, they were at 6,800 feet, and bad weather gave Walcott time to write to his children the longest letter he ever composed in the field; it provides considerable detail on the problems of fieldwork. The reason for using "and" rather than an ampersand is not more time on Walcott's part—old habits seldom change—but because the letters were eventually sent to the SI, typed, and probably returned. Walcott may have had more periods, which the typist mistook for commas; over the years, his handwriting had gotten a bit worse, especially when he hurried.

After a most strenuous week on the trail we arrived here last eve after eight hours on the trail in a cold rain. 48° at camp 3 P.M., and snowing on mountains and glaciers all about us. We forded the Saskatchewan river without mishap and went up the North Fork camping on the edge of the river flats over Sunday. On Monday Mary and I went on ahead working our way up the gravel bars crossing and recrossing the river which was cream color from the glacial mud—It is a curious feeling one has when urging the horse to step in a rapid flowing stream that may be a foot or six feet deep. The width and rapidity of the stream is the only guide—quiet water is usually deep. About 7 miles up we turned up the Alexandra river where marshes, bogs, and sand bars furnish the pathway. At 4:30 we came to a dry, well wooded flat and camped—there was very little feed for the horses and after looking it over the entire 15 started on a trot on the back trail, fortunately, Tom, one of the new young horses was in the lead—he missed the trail on a gravel bar and started across the main stream and soon all were swimming, for the channel was deep. They landed on a gravel bar next to thick forest and there they were marooned. Bill tried to ford the river but it was too swift and too deep and as it was nearly dark, he had to return to camp. We could see the horses, with our glasses, try to find a way out but there was nothing to do but swim back and it was miles to any feed down the river. Some one of them, probably old Cricket, decided that half a meal was better than none so at midnight, they all marched back to camp to nibble and browse until morning. The men caught two of them and tied them up to make sure of having means to go after the others.

The next morning, Mary and I went on ahead, about six miles, up the river and found where the trail turned up the Castleguard river. I made a fine sight, as one of my shoes filled with water in crossing the river. About two hours later, we forded the Castleguard and one of my rubber boots was filled, Mary also wet her feet. The rain pattered on our rubber coats but did not get inside. We came to a canyon and the trail was blazed in the woods. We soon began to go up and for an hour climbed through the brush, over logs and slippery turf. At last the forest began to thin out and soon we went up a steep slope and this large Alpine valley was spread out before us. It is surrounded by high ridges and glaciers and a fine stream flows through it. Clumps of spruce trees occur and near one of these we found a relatively level spot. The rain ceased for a time and by dark tents were up and Arthur had a fine dinner. We later put up our camp stove in the tent and were dry and warm when turning in for the night.

Today it is raining—Mary is sketching some new wild flowers on the trail. I have fixed up the inside and outside of the tent. The men have cut a supply of wood and now we are waiting for an Indian summer day in which to take photographs of the superb scenery all about us. No game up here so we will cross over to Thompsons Pass to see the rocks and then back toward the Saskatchewan if all goes well.

I will add to this and sent it out later if we meet any hunting parties below. After Sidney reads, he will please forward to his sister Helen.

We came up Castleguard river and followed a zigzag trail to about 1200 feet above the river.[20]

This was dated August 31; Walcott wrote more later: "Out between snow squalls & found a few Upper Cambrian fossils in the Sullivan formation. There is more limestone & less shale than in the Glacier Lake section to the s.e. We rode up to the head of valley & returned in a driving snow storm. Visited cave below camp 5 p.m." (September 1, 1921). The comment about limestone and shale is just the sort of generalization that geologists strive for in trying to interpret the history of an area. It means that this area had been in shallower water, which in turn indicated that the region had probably been closer to the shoreline during the Cambrian.

The weather did not improve, so Walcott added to his letter:

Great masses of fog and mist are rolling up through Thompsons Pass and trailing over the ridges and peaks and glaciers. When the clouds grow dark a driving snow squall comes drifting over our broad Alpine valley and we skip for the tents or a thick spruce thicket if there is one at hand. Geologic work under such conditions is a bit difficult.

Yesterday, I managed to find a few fossils in a small canyon below camp that served to identify the limestones and shales as belonging to the Sullivan formation of the Upper Cambrian of the Glacier Lake section studied in 1919. Glacier Lake is 30 miles s.e. This clears up this side of the canyon of the Castleguard river. As soon as we can take photographs of the fine peaks and glaciers we will move across to the s.w. side where I expect to find the Lyell, Mons, and Sarbach formations in Mount Bryce and Mt. Rice (named after the British ambassadors). We can see the little lake Cinema where the next camp is located. It is just below the Continental Divide, which is low in the Pass (6511'). This camp is about 7000' and very little timber is growing above it, scrub and dwarfed trees pressed almost flat by the prevailing westerly winds.

Bill has just brought the horses to camp, they had wandered several miles until stopped by the glaciers at the head of the valley. Mary, Cecil and I rode up there yesterday and were caught in a cold snow squall. We were above timber line so we faced the gale for an hour. I had on a woolen wrapper, army shirt, buckskin vest, heavy sweater, and until I put on a rubber coat the cold wind went thru to the skin; the squall passed just as we reached camp so we went on a half mile below to see a cave Cecil found while hunting the horses. We found a deserted stream channel that came down through the limestone from the floor of the valley below. When the snow melts in the spring great floods of water must run thru the cave as boulders several feet in diameter have been rolled along in the channel in front of the cave.

Cecil is ill—acute indigestion. He permits his stomach to run away with his mind and judgement.[21]

Three days later the letter had not yet been mailed.

Walcott was a dab hand when it came to describing the scenery. What holds even more interest is his laconic account in his diary of the weather, compared to the information he sent on to his children. Walcott got in a couple of hours for picture taking before the clouds came down again. The party moved camp, and another page was added to the growing letter.

This is the twelfth more or less stormy day. This morning snow covered the ground and squalls passed over the mountains and canyons all day. There were high points all about us but the clouds cover them. Yesterday as we were nearing this camp, there was a climb of over 1000' feet of a forested ridge— now and then we caught a glimpse of Athabaska glacier but the Peak was in the clouds. By reputation it is a beautiful mountain country and I hope we may see it on a fine day. Almost no good photographs this season so we deserve a few good days.

This is supposed to be a good goat and sheep area and Bill will try for them higher up. Our camp is near a fine tumbling brook, abundant spruce trees with grassy glades all about and firewood in a few standing dead trees. With sunshine the camp would be extra fine. It is on the trail between Jasper and Lake Louise and as the trail is worn deep where it passes through the forest the Indians must have camped along the brook long ago. In places the slender tepee poles are half buried in the moss and grass while the long strong poles of the white man are leaning on the trees or grouped ready for the canvas.

About two miles below a fine falls (called Panther) occurs. A sunny day will give us a photo of it.

We were all dead tired on arrival here last eve and the horses looked it as they browsed about. The younger ones promptly laid down for a time. The trail was a hard one—several miles over river gravels, a mile of down timber and the long climb up the ridge—the forest trail is usually good.

We are very comfortable in our tent as the little camp stove is a good one altho getting the worse for wear (six seasons). Now it is asking for wood. I will feed it and go out for a stroll before dinner.[22]

They moved camp twice more and Walcott added more paragraphs.

This is our sixteenth stormy day. Woke up at 6 A.M. and found the ground covered with snow and fine flakes sifting down like powdered sugar. About noon the sun began to peer through the fog. Now (5 P.M.) except above timber line the light snow has melted or evaporated. Mist hangs in clouds on the west side of the peaks as the wind is east.

Yesterday we took a few photographs in the morning before the snow began to whiten the mountains above 7000.

Tomorrow, we start down the river for two days march and then turn south up the Whiterabbit which is a famous sheep country. Expect to cross the Clearwater river about September eighteenth-twentieth and over to the Red deer and out via Pipestone to Lake Louise. If we get any sheep, goat or deer, we may reach the railroad about September twenty-sixth, twenty-eighth, provided Dame Nature will be good and give us fine weather.

We are all well but feel sore and rheumatic from exposure to cold winds and wet. It was 22° yesterday 7 A.M. and 34° 5 P.M. We speak of the weather as getting warm at 40°.

Cecil is to take mail in and bring out supplies. He will have five (5) days ride so we will get mail for the first time in four weeks. It will be of interest both personal and public.

I have some notes to write and packing to do so will send love to all my dear ones and best wishes until we see them.[23]

The weather cleared for photographs, and Cecil left for the post office. Walcott scribbled a note to Mr. Dorsey telling him of the letter to Sidney, reporting the bad weather, and promising to report on his future whereabouts. "We are 4 days march from railway but Cecil will go light & make it in 52 hours."[24]

They moved on, making five camps in six days and suffering from the cold, which had returned. The snow also returned, and Walcott stayed in camp while the younger men shot a few goats, partly for the Museum collection and partly for the pot. One of the letters Cecil brought reported all well but gave some more information on the dramatic change in the way money was now to be handled.

There has been nothing particularly startling happening, a large part of our time being taken up with compiling figures and answering questions for the Budget Bureau. They asked for information and figures about appropriations and expenditures which filled a sheet almost half as big as the desk. Some of the questions were almost impossible to guess at, for instance "What amount of the appropriation for 1922 [which we now sending in estimates] will remain unexpended on June 30, 1923." I will tell you when you get back what Mr. Holmes' reply was when I asked him this about the Gallery appropriation, but I can not write it in a letter. We have been getting an average of one circular request for information a day from the Budget Bureau and it has required a great deal of time to get the information together, but of course they have a big new job and it is necessary for them to ask a lot of questions, but I believe they are disposed to treat the Institution very fairly.[25]

The paperwork described by Dorsey was a harbinger, and if he had had an inkling what the new budgetary bureau would bring, he would not have been so charitable. Since the old days of going to Capitol and making a strong case for the appropriation were gone, an intermediary had to be persuaded to present all requests. A problem was that an intermediary asking for funding all at one time for several groups allowed the Congress to make larger cuts. Secretary Walcott would have to be more agile than ever in gaining support for the government bureaus under his wing.

While Mr. Dorsey's reply was in transit, Walcott wrote to the assistant secretary, summarizing much of what he had written in his long letter.

This has been the coldest & most disagreeable field season we have known. . . . The search for fossils was greatly hindered by the presence of snow on the exposed slopes above timberline. If health & conditions permit we will get many next season as we now know of a new & very good section for them about 100 miles to the southwest. It was discovered by a railroad engineer when looking for rock ballast. So here is hoping. We have been well but the exposure to cold & wet has stiffened me up at times. . . . Mrs. Walcott has sketched 24 flowers & fruits new to her collection. . . . We are warm & snug in our big tent. It has been put up in 28 camps this season wh means packing up and unpacking our belongings 28 times & it will require 4 more before we close up.[26]

"We packed up & moved to Lake Louise in face of a cold wind & snow" (September 27, 1921). The outfit arrived in Banff the last day of September. Cecil Smith left, and Walcott, Billy, and Arthur spent three days packing and getting the gear organized. The Walcotts finally left October 4 on the Toronto Express; Arthur would follow after the tents had been stored.

"Woke up to find cold rainstorm. Arrived at Toronto 4 P.M. & went on to Buffalo" (October 7, 1921). The next morning Sidney breakfasted with them, and they walked out to the house to see his wife and daughter. They had a good family visit before they caught the night train. "William met us at the station 10:20 A.M. Went home—found Mollie and Annie with house clean & ready for us. Unpacked trunks, cleaned up & rested. Not going out all day. It is delightful to be at home again" (October 9, 1921). Perhaps for the first time, the years were beginning to weigh on field geologist Walcott.

Walcott summarized the western season for Schuchert: "We returned last week from the Canadian Rockies, after a long and unusually severe season. Snow fell on 27 days, and while it was so hot in the east, the temperature was running from 20° in the early morning to 45° at noon where we camped. We made thirty camps and covered a large area of country in making a reconnaissance of the Upper Cambrian formations. We collected only a few Upper Cambrian fossils for stratigraphic purposes. The Burgess Pass quarry was filled with snow all summer and the storms swept over it two-thirds of the time from June to October. It was the worst summer for field work that I have known in the Canadian Rockies."27

Walcott's weather summary for the season had given forty clear days, twenty-eight when it was cloudy and cold, and thirty-five stormy days. This really had been a poor season to be out. In a earlier letter to Schuchert, Walcott had mentioned that he was contemplating opening the quarry again; perhaps he wanted one more trilobite with the appendages perfectly preserved. That was not to be, and the quarry would remain quiescent for four decades. At any rate, the 1921 field season was over; despite the hardships, there had been some accomplishments in unraveling the geology.

A small note appeared in one of the local papers: "Miss Helen B. Walcott, daughter of Dr. Charles D. Walcott, who has been continuing her art studies this summer in Brittany, France, is now in Paris, where she will remain until December, going from there to Spain. There she will take advantage of the special opportunities for art work and study. Dr. and Mrs. Walcott have returned to Washington after a successful season of geological field work in the Canadian Rocky Mountains."28

The first full day in Washington began with Mary and Walcott taking a morning walk in Potomac Park. The Walcotts had put in a "war garden," and Mary was still tending it. Then it was off to a large accumulation of mail and conferences with his staff. Mrs. Eugene Meyer dropped in to see when the Freer Gallery would be open; that event was nearly two years away. The next day was just as crowded; it included a meeting of the NRC Executive Board, an eye examination, and an evening meeting of the NAS building committee. Walcott was still suffering from a cold but carried on with his conferences; the building stone for the Academy was an immediate concern.

The following day, enough of the pressing problems had been resolved to allow Walcott to relax and examine fossils from the Kootenay Valley in British Columbia sent to him by the Geological Survey of Canada. Two days later, all the mail was in hand, and identification of the fossils, etc., was complete. That was not bad for an old man, but then, as often happens to older people, Walcott was out sick for two days.

During the time Walcott was confined to his bed, another honor came his way. At their meeting of October 16, the members of the Societé Géologique de Belgique (Belgian Geological Society) elected him an honorary member. Without taking anything away from his accomplishments, one should note that nineteen other geologists were also so honored. It was a way of reestablishing scientific relations disrupted by the war. To be honest, there are no outcrops of Cambrian rocks in Belgium, or even close to Belgium, and none of his close correspondents were from that country. Still, recognition of merit always is nice.

Walcott eased back into his office routine, spending the afternoons working at home for a couple of days. He and Dr. Merriam spent a good portion of his first full day at the Castle wrestling with the CIW budget. Next, he was "at my office during the day. Began work on Upper Cambrian of Alberta & B.C. Meeting of Iowa Apartment House Board at noon" (October 20, 1921). Once again, there was no sense wasting time in starting a new project. The study of trilobite appendages was out of the way, and the data on Upper Cambrian stratigraphy had to be organized.

On October 20 a most unexpected event occurred in England. We must set aside fossils, rocks, and other daily events of Walcott's life to consider a most unfortunate aspect of the history of the Smithsonian Institution. On the day in the question, Griffith Brewer, a British aviator and aviation historian, spoke before the Royal Society of Arts. His lecture, "Aviation's Greatest Controversy," was highly critical of the test flights made in 1914 by Curtiss (Crouch 1989, 491).

Thanks to the wonders of the cable and the radiogram, accounts of this speech reached America almost immediately. The following day Walcott responded. As has been shown earlier, not all of Walcott's activities are mentioned in his diary. Some items that he considered minor, such as honorary memberships, were not recorded. Some items that he considered sensitive, such as his extreme reaction to Franz Boas, are also not recorded. Which category of non-entry Walcott might have assigned to this matter cannot be known. It is possible that he considered the lecture a relatively minor irritant. Unfortunately, this was the start of the infamous public argument between the Smithsonian and the Wright brothers.

More specifically, it was an argument between Orville Wright and Walcott, and argument that continued for years after Walcott's death. Sadly, during his lifetime the controversy was virtually the only thing that a significant portion of the general public had ever heard concerning Secretary Walcott's activities. The controversy is a feature of the Smithsonian's history that, like all historical events, will never quite disappear. It has been the subject of so many articles, books, and monographs that one can hardly justify writing still more about it. Nevertheless, the evidence on some aspects of events leading up to this controversy is slim, so much is based on interpretation. The interpretations given by any writer vary with background, prejudices, and other intangibles, and each account thus varies a bit in emphasis. Thus, indulgence is asked here for one more review of this matter.

Everyone agrees that shortly before Samuel Pierpont Langley was appointed si secretary, he became interested in the problems surrounding mechanical flight, using a whirling table at the Allegheny Observatory to obtain some data on lift and drag. Everyone agrees he conducted tests with rubber-band-powered models and then he moved on to larger models powered by steam. What may be most unbiased account of the controversy is quite flattering as to this accomplishment. "These flights of May and November, 1896, not only silenced the skeptics but turned the Secretary into something of a popular hero" (Crouch 1987, 36).

Langley was an unlikely hero, being an extreme autocrat, as well as an aristocrat. A great deal of the Smithsonian's very limited funds had be spent to support these experiments, at a time when he was letting aspects of the institution other than his own scientific pursuits steadily slide downhill. When Walcott became acting assistant secretary in 1897, he revitalized the National Museum and, to a limited extent, the entire institution.

Now, we may speculate that Walcott, who traveled extensively and had a certain amount of mechanical ability, was aware of the need for good transportation and would have felt that if a man-carrying machine could be built on this basis, as seemed feasible, it would be a boon to the country. Such an event would also be dramatic and could not help but have a significant, positive effect on the future course of the Smithsonian Institution. In 1897, the problems with Spain, which appeared to be leading to a war, brought out the extra factor of patriotism as a reason to develop a flying machine. From what is known of Langley's mode of operation and of his character, it seems almost certain that he would never have gone out seeking funds to continue his efforts. Walcott, however, put considerable effort into obtaining the money for Langley's renewed experiments. It follows that Walcott was interested in seeing a successful conclusion.

Langley, with his inability to delegate, his frequent changes of orders, his long summer absences from Washington, and his obsessive concern for secrecy, made many of his own difficulties, all the while using up government dollars. Several times Walcott discreetly intervened to prevent the funds from being cut off. Despite Langley, the engine eventually developed by Charles Manly was a technological achievement, and there was hope of success. The failure of October 7, 1903, followed by the dramatic failure of December 8, 1903, ended this hope. "Langley was reviled on the floor of Congress and in the nation's newspapers. For the last three years of his life the failure of the Aerodrome was to hang over his head like a cloud" (Crouch 1987, 37).

Adding to Langley's misery was that shortly after Manly nearly drowned in the Potomac River in December, when Langley's aerodrome collapsed, the SI treasurer was caught embezzling. The scorn of the newspapers was directed not only at Langley but at the SI itself. As a culminating indignity, after Langley's death the regents selected a successor who promptly turned down the honor.

When Walcott was elected secretary in January 1907, the situation in the Smithsonian Institution was not dissimilar from what he had faced when he became USGS director in 1894. The organization had been attacked and ridiculed, funding was inadequate, and employee morale was about as low as a snake's belly. Within a year or so Walcott had blunted all the negatives and was in the process of building, not simply repairing past damage.

Awarding a medal has several effects; to be candid, it is a method of gaining favorable publicity for an organization. Walcott could see the growing interest in aviation and may have moved to utilize this to the advantage of the Smithsonian. Today, so far removed from the events, it is difficult to say whether Walcott or some other party initiated the Langley Medal or the Langley Memorial Tablet, or which came first in concept. Both, but particularly the medal, would help mark Langley's contribution and thereby reduce the impact of his failure. In December 1908, both were authorized by the regents at their annual meeting. At least in part they were acts of loyalty to Langley. Walcott had been loyal to Hall, to King, and to Powell, and it was characteristic of him to be equally loyal to yet another man who had nominally supervised him. Walcott had had difficulties with all three, but if his actions record his feelings, he rose above any grudges.

There was no question but that the first Langley Medal should go the Wright brothers. There is also little question, however, that the awarding of that first medal, in February 1910, was not done with the grace and dignity that the Wrights' achievement deserved. For this, the responsibility falls on Smithsonian regents Bell and Lodge, whose principal speeches extolled Langley and his contributions to aeronautics. So far as the Wright brothers were concerned, Langley's contribution had been giving them some data that had turned out to be incorrect; the achievement of flight was their own.

Nearly twenty years later, Orville gave his interpretation of the published account of the event: "It [the Smithsonian Institution] misrepresented in the Annual Report for the year 1910 (page 23) the statement made by my brother Wilbur at the time of the presentation of the Langley Medal to us by inserting a quotation not used by him on that occasion. The improper use of this quotation created a false impression over the world that we had acknowledged indebtedness to Langley's scientific work; that it was Langley's scientific work and our mechanical ingenuity that produced the first flying machine. This is not true" (McCormick 1928, 30).

About fifteen years after that comment, Orville was still concerned about the ceremony. "The medal was established to honor Dr. Langley, not the Wright Brothers. Neither in the award nor in the presentation of the medal to the Wright Brothers was there any suggestion that the Wrights were the first to fly."[29] That is a fair analysis of the event. As a minor added complication, because the Wrights were otherwise engaged, the medal was not awarded in 1909, as anticipated. Events were moving swiftly in the early days of aviation, and an extra year dimmed the significance of their first flight by just a bit.

The next event of this prickly drama was a request for display material by the Smithsonian. As with any history, the sources used influence the spirit of the final product. One ought to try to balance the presentation by quoting from both sides involved in a dispute, but that would make a long, drawn-out story even longer. A supporter of the Wright cause (no pun quite intended) detailed this episode, years after the fact.

On two different occasions requests for a machine for exhibition purposes were made to the Wrights by the secretary of the Institution, the late Dr. Charles D. Walcott. [On] March 7, 1910, Doctor Walcott wrote to Wilbur Wright that "it has been suggested that you might be willing to deposit one of your machines, or a model thereof for exhibition purposes." To this Wilbur Wright replied, asking what was wanted and stating that as most of the parts were still in existence, the original machine could be reconstructed. Doctor Walcott answered that a quarter-size model of the 1908 machine would be most desirable, and if there was any radical difference between the 1908 machine and the Kitty Hawk machine—which there was not—a quarter-size model of the latter would be appropriate. For a full-size airplane the 1908 plane was declared the "most suitable." "If however," it was added—and this is the only reference on the definite offer of the original plane—"the Wright brothers think that the Kitty Hawk machine would serve the purpose better, their judgement might decide the matter." The letter farther [*sic*] stated that the original full-size Langley machine and three Langley quarter-size models were to be exhibited.

The Wrights took this letter to mean that Doctor Walcott's preference was to place in the Museum a quarter-size model of the man-carrying 1908 or 1903 machine alongside Langley models of an earlier date, never built to full size or flown with a man, and to hang the original full-size Langley plane of 1903, which had never flown, with the Wright full-size machine of 1908. They were so convinced of the unfairness of the proposed exhibit, and the intention to create the impression that Langley had preceded them by five years, that Doctor Walcott's second letter was never answered. (McCormick 1928, 33)

One may guess that Wilbur and Orville were smarting from the ceremony in February of that year and were willing and eager to take offence at any perceived slight.

During the late summer of 1909, curators of natural history collections began to move out of the old United States National Museum building. Finally there was some space for new displays, and aviation was a topic of great interest to the public. Exhibit space is not infinite, and from what can be surmised from this letter, a display documenting the steps in aviation and the latest developments was being contemplated. The most modern airplane was to be shown to the public. In essence, the Wrights could have that displayed or the 1903 original. What was not made clear to them was space limitations, a point so obvious to a museum person that it was overlooked in Walcott's second letter.

Perhaps Wilbur was truly so upset that he did not reply. On the other hand, it is likely that he had more on his mind. In the summer of 1909, while the Wrights were demonstrating their airplane to the U.S. Army, Glenn Curtiss made an actual sale. Wilbur filed suit to prevent the airplane from being flown; he also sued the Herring-Curtiss Company, which manufactured it. Early in January 1911 the Wrights won the suit, but Curtiss appealed and had the injunction withdrawn in June.

In the face of this, the SI request for display material could not have loomed large for the Wrights. On yet another hand, this is a curious neglect, for having one of their aircraft, even if not the first one, in the SI, where Curtiss did not have one, might have strengthened the case for the Wright lawyers. This aspect of the problem is hard to understand, but a moderately safe conclusion is that if the quoted material is correct, the Wrights could certainly find an insult where none was intended.

The next development in the saga was in Washington. "Langley Day," May 6, the date of the first successful flight of a steam-powered model in 1896, became an event. By 1911, there was an increasing number of airplane enthusiasts and aviation boosters. Nothing indicates that Walcott ever had a hand in promoting or encouraging a Langley Day celebration; by the fall of 1910, the secretary had a large number of Burgess Shale fossils to occupy him, he was deeply involved with Mr. Freer, and was supervising, at least nominally, the opening of halls in the new Museum. Langley Day celebrations in the second decade of the new century may have been fine publicity for the Smithsonian, but this publicity was a gift from others.

Interwoven with the increase in interest, as indicated by the growing size of the annual Langley Day celebration, was the development of a research facility for aviation. It would seem that everyone and his brother had ideas on how to design and fly aircraft, but all of it used the old method of "by guess and by gosh"; combined with stunt flying and dramatic deaths, aviation was not living up to its potential. Attempts to found a research laboratory for national investigations of flying, however, collided with politics and bureaucratic infighting. As a way of getting started after several years of delay, in 1913, with the support of the regents, Walcott reopened Langley's shed as the Langley Aerodynamical Laboratory and formed an advisory committee on aeronautics.

After that came the suggestion by Curtiss, in March 1914, that the Langley aerodrome be rebuilt, tested, and flown for the next Langley Day. An earlier request, which was denied, is fully documented (Crouch 1989, 484), but the comment is also made that "without informing Bell or any of the Smithsonian regents, he [Walcott] authorized A. F. Zahm . . . to turn over . . . the old machine to Curtiss. In addition, Walcott provided $2,000 to underwrite rebuilding and testing" (Crouch 1989, 486).

That seems not to be quite the way it really happened, for as mentioned earlier when discussing Walcott's activities in 1914, he and Bell did discuss the matter. As documented above, the two even considered putting up their own money for a test to see if Langley could be vindicated by getting the aerodrome to fly. The matter was certainly not a matter of a straightforward request by Curtiss and an immediate agreement by Walcott. Among others that the secretary might have consulted informally was Zahm. Zahm was now in charge in the Langley Laboratory, and it was appropriate that the laboratory do something more than compile literature. To repeat, an important piece of background is that several years earlier, Zahm had been a witness for Curtiss when the Wrights sued him for patent infringement.

Without any question, Curtiss had a vested interest in testing the Langley aerodrome, because a flight might, just possibly, provide ammunition for a further court battle. Curtiss had lost the suit on patent infringement, and in January 1914 he had lost his appeal. In the interim, Wilbur Wright had died; the Wright family would always think that the fight with Curtiss had weakened him and that therefore "that man" Curtiss was the proximate cause of Wilbur's death. By dealing with Curtiss, the SI was aiding Orville Wright's enemy.

Professor Zahm may have been high-minded in wanting to test a tandem-wing type of airplane, but a better and more economical way to do this would be simply to build a new plane. There seems to be good evidence that the planes Curtiss were building were superior to those coming out of the Wright factory; the Wright patent would inhibit further improvements by Curtiss. Perhaps Zahm wanted to ensure that progress in aviation would continue by allowing the fertile mind of Glenn Curtiss to continue to come up with new developments. After all the noble motivations one can possibly conjure up are considered, one cannot help but feel that if there was anyone who had a hidden agenda in this affair, it was Zahm.

Zahm was not alone in wanting a test; Bell was also enthusiastic. If there was anyone who should at the very beginning have said no to a test, it was Alexander Graham Bell, a regent. Bell had been deeply involved in aeronautics, with the Aerial Experiment Association in 1907 and 1908, which had included Curtiss as a member. Bell also had been a principal in a major patent suit concerning his rights to the telephone and knew what was involved in patent infringement. To balance that, Bell had known Langley for longer and more intimately than he knew Walcott; they had close scientific interests in common. Many interpretations are possible. A reasonable one is that because Bell was so eager to refurbish Langley's memory, he forgot or ignored the possible pitfalls of a test of the aerodrome.

If this interpretation is followed, the worst one can say is that Walcott was misled and given poor advice by his friends and associates. Pulling quotes from articles scattered here and there does not prove much, but sometimes—when writers do not make them up—the quotes are based on interviews. "Prior to [the tests] the Wrights had sued Curtiss for infringement . . . of patents, but Dr. Walcott ever maintained that this legal action in no wise concerned his selection" (Hall 1928, 69).

As to the charge of risking a priceless relic, the aerodrome was a pile of junk. At this time it was in about as poor shape as the original Wright plane of 1903. If nothing else, restoration of the plane would allow the object to be placed on display. From several aspects, authorizing and financing the test was a reasonable action by Secretary Walcott.

There also seems to be general agreement—now—that in the reconstruction by Curtiss significant alterations were made, quite apart from the attachment of pontoons and, later, the replacement of the original motor. How many alterations were made at the time of the first flight with the Manly motor depends on whom one consults. There are the remarks of Capt. William Johnson, which have been lost sight of in most of the later claims and counterclaims. "Johnson was one of three men who ever flew the Langley plane. The other two were

Glenn Curtiss and W. Ellwood ("Gink") Doherty. . . . Captain Johnson, in describing the plane tests said: "The pitch of the wings was not altered, but they were strengthened and repaired. The aerodrome would not fly with its original motor. It would hop, that is barely clear the surface of the lake, but that was all" (Hall 1928, 69–70).

In a slight defense of Curtiss, he received the machine in early May, restored it, and flew by late May, so there was no time for alterations as significant as those made later. Charles Manly was on the scene, and after his dramatic bath in the Potomac River in 1903, he would have encouraged the strengthening of the wings.

Whatever was done, and whenever it was done, apart from the obvious pontoons and the motor change, Walcott did not have the technical knowledge to evaluate the extent to which the machine had been altered. He had to depend on what he was told by Curtiss and Zahm. He was told that there were essentially no alterations.

At the annual meeting that year, Walcott reported to the regents. "The machine was shipped from the Langley Laboratory to the Curtiss Aeroplane Factory to have the plane recanvassed [*sic*] and hydroaeroplane floats attached. . . . Dr. Bell felt that the Institution and the board also should be congratulated at the verification of Langley's work. He thought that the Langley type of machine was a correct one" (*Proceedings* 1916, 121–22).

One can thus add to the mix Bell's pride in his own judgment. Of course, the actions of the secretary are enmeshed with those of the institution, and in vindicating Langley the regents were vindicating their own good sense in selecting him and in supporting his aerial investigations. Every step added more subtle complications.

Zahm published a glowing account of the 1914 tests in the Smithsonian *Annual Report* for that year. There is a mention of modifications made later by Curtiss, but the article ended with the conclusion that Langley had "developed and built the first man-carrying aeroplane capable of sustained flight" (Zahm 1915, 222). This claim was no secret to Orville Wright, for a small point neglected by Wright partisans is that the article immediately preceding Zahm's in that volume is by Orville Wright (1914), the reprint of a speech he gave in March 1914 upon receipt of a medal from the Franklin Institute. Papers for the *Annual Report* were either original works or, as in this case, reprints of items judged to be of general interest. Reprinting his speech in the series was hardly a hostile act on the part of the Smithsonian, and many would even consider it a mark of prestige. Partisans of Wright seem to have neglected this point.

Of course, as might have been anticipated, Curtiss went to court once more. This was no great surprise to at least one newspaper reporter: "That Dr. Langley's invention would appear in the litigation was foreshadowed when the Smithsonian Institution, of which he was secretary, last spring resurrected the wreck of the famous flying machine, smashed more than ten years previously."[30] The court battle went on and on till the war came along and the cross-licensing agreement made it moot.

In 1915 more tests were made of the aerodrome; they were reported in the press, and by Zahm in a more technical style. Meanwhile, Orville sold his business in 1915, and in a way retired from the field of aviation. The next step on the slippery slope belonged to the Wright plane.

> Nothing more was heard of the matter [the display material requested by the SI] until 1916, when the original Wright machine was exhibited at the opening of the new building at the Massachusetts Institute of Technology. Dr. Alexander Graham Bell, a regent of the Smithsonian, expressed astonishment that the Kitty Hawk plane was still in existence and asked Orville Wright why it was not in the Smithsonian. "Because the Smithsonian does not want it," was the reply. "Indeed the Smithsonian does want it," exclaimed Dr. Bell, and on December 23, 1916, Doctor Walcott wrote to Mr. Wright that "the importance of securing for the National Museum the Wright aeroplane which was exhibited at the opening of the new buildings of the Massachusetts Institute of Technology has been suggested to me." Mr. Wright answered that the machine was available and that he would be glad to take up the matter with Doctor Walcott in a personal interview. From a conversation on the subject with Doctor Walcott in Washington a few days later, he came away convinced that the secretary's attitude had not changed.
>
> By this time, also, the Hammondsport tests of the Langley plane had taken place and Mr. Wright had made up his mind that the Smithsonian was not a trustworthy or impartial repository of aeronautical relics. He says that he could not with any confidence or self-respect turn over his machine to an institution which had already allowed Doctor Langley's to be tampered with and lent itself to a systematic perversion of the facts. (McCormick 1928, 33–34)

That conversation between Wright and Walcott must have been interesting. It was not viewed by Orville as an olive branch but as another brandishing of a club. The 1910 exchange of letters is often quoted by those who judge that Wright was greatly wronged, but this later encounter seldom appears in those histories.

In December 1917, Walcott reported to the regents: "The original Langley man-carrying flying machine . . . soon will be placed on exhibition in the old National Museum building. . . . It is also an important historical relic as it confirms the claim that Secretary Langley was the first to design and construct a heavier-than-air machine capable of carrying a man in flight. There has never been any question that he was the first to successfully fly a heavier than air machine propelled by its own power" (*Proceedings* 1920, 114).

Now, this really is a curious set of affairs, in that Wright was concerned about Langley's aerodrome as a priceless relic, whereas Walcott was defending a claim that Langley had never made and supporting it by a fact no one ever disputed. That *Annual Report* was delayed because of the war, and Orville may not have seen it. Even a Walcott partisan would have to admit that "capable" is not the same as "accomplished." The si was prepared to admit to that extent that Langley's plane had been a failure in 1903, but that was all that it conceded to aviation history in America.

The war came, and Walcott was caught up in the NACA activities and the Aircraft Production Board. The later part of the war brought a great many military objects to the museum to document, at least in part, that conflict. "The Museum is particularly fortunate in having a very excellent series of objects showing the development of the airplane, beginning with the Langley models, which have been in its possession for a number of years, and the first government-owned aeroplane of the world purchased by the United States from the Wright Brothers in 1909" (Ravenel 1921, 28). By now—that is, 1919—the army had turned over the hangar behind the Castle to the Smithsonian, and the si was busy stuffing it with examples of planes and engines.

The annual reports do not mention when the Langley aerodrome was displayed. Probably it was not exhibited in the Arts and Industries Building until after the war, because of the numerous problems in 1917 and 1918. The display in that building was intended to be a history of flight, whereas the hangar behind the Castle recorded current events. A discharged army flyer, Paul Garber, was hired on a temporary basis to help with displays; among other efforts, he put his uniform on a mannequin in the Wright army plane. As mentioned, his lecture to Walcott about a model made from da Vinci's drawings resulted in a permanent staff position.

For Orville Wright, the objectionable part of this aircraft display was the label on front of the Langley aerodrome. It read: "The original Langley flying machine of 1903 restored. In the opinion of many competent to judge, this was the first heavier-than-air craft in the history of the world capable of free sustained flight under its own power, carrying a man. This aircraft slightly antedated the machine designed and built by Wilbur and Orville Wright, which on December 17, 1903 was the first in the history of the world to accomplish sustained free flight under its own power, carrying a man." Quite apart from being far too long for the average tourist to read, this text was legalistic hair splitting. If the machine had not been significantly altered by Curtiss in May 1914, the wording might have been technically correct, but if the machine had been substantially changed before the first flight, the claim was false. Orville Wright objected.

Another minor point in this affair that no one seems to have touched upon is why the fuss became public in 1921. Why not raise an objection when the tests were being done? Why not object to the statements in Zahm's first article? Why not object when the aerodrome was first displayed? If there is an answer, it lies in another Wright-Walcott interaction. On January 29, 1920, Orville Wright became a member of the NACA. The Wright partisans have not explored this connection, but if the chairman—that is, Walcott—was harboring any ill will toward Orville, he would not have arranged for a presidential appointment; after all, the NACA successfully carried on for a number of years without Orville Wright as a member.

From the views Orville Wright expressed after his 1916 conversation, he might never have set foot inside the SI again. It is a reasonable surmise that on some occasion when the NACA meetings brought Orville Wright to Washington, he saw the display with its objectionable label. At some time afterward, he made contact with Griffith Brewer concerning his irritation; Brewer looked into the matter and delivered his talk in 1921. There is no indication that Orville Wright ever discussed the issue with Walcott before Brewster virtually accused the SI of perpetuating a hoax. In the great game of what-if, had Orville not been appointed to the NACA, he might never have come to Washington and seen the aerodrome on display, and then the whole public controversy might never have happened.

Both Manly and Walcott prepared statements and sent them to the *New York Times* on October 21. Walcott prefaced his with: "I take pleasure in saying at the start that the Smithsonian Institution recognizes the well deserved success of the Wright Brothers in being the first to make actual flights in heavier than air power-propelled machines. This recognition the Institution was among the earliest to make in a formal manner by an award of merit. This being so, I am not prepared to concede that the Wrights were the first to construct such a machine capable of such a flight."[31]

At the annual meeting of the regents in December, Walcott gave a history of Langley's investigations, the authorization for Curtiss to test, and the two-thousand-dollar appropriation.

The secretary went on to say that recently an attack had been made by Mr. Griffith Brewster, an Englishman, on the credibility of the tests and the claim that they had proved the Langley machine to be a success. These charges were answered by the secretary, by Mr. Charles M. Manly, who designed the engine of the machine, by Dr. A. F. Zahm, an aeronautical expert, and by Mr. Curtiss who tested the machine. He was bringing it to the Board's attention because one of the criticisms was aimed at the Institution for giving its approval to the results of the Curtiss tests.

In reply to an inquiry as to whether any formal action was desired from the Board, the secretary said he did not think it was necessary; that a suggestion had been made by a disinterested person that the machine be studied by expert aeronautical engineers so as to settle the question for all time, and that the proposition should be prompted outside of the Institution, and that he would wait for such action from some reputable organization.[32]

After one volley back and forth, the affair should have ended; Walcott seemed not to have viewed it as a major matter. Unfortunately, the accusation gathered steam that the Smithsonian was cheating the Wright brothers of credit. It was a popular item in the press, a David-and-Goliath story. The full resources of the Washington government had been pitted against two small-town inventors. They had won the contest, but now the rules were being changed to deny them the victory.

Eventually the fight was to be settled, though not in Walcott's lifetime. It has been analyzed and dissected time after time. Perhaps the best thumbnail summary was given by Secretary Alexander Wetmore after he retired. He suggested that both parties were defending the reputations of dead men and that once the issue was raised, neither could retreat. As an aside, one of the two flyers who assisted Curtiss in the tests was Wetmore's cousin. It is a small world.

Now that a not-so-brief history of one of the feuds marking early aviation in America has been given, the strand of October 1921 may be picked up where it was dropped. Nothing about Wright, Brewster, or the *Times* appears in Walcott's diary for October 20 or 21. In fact, one wonders when there was time to prepare a statement for the newspaper.

"Col. F. J. Hecker & Mr. Spicer came 10 A.M. & spent the day. Conferred with Charles Bell" (October 21, 1921). The colonel was the longtime business partner of Freer, and Spicer represented the bank; the third of the group, Bell, was the local Washington banker. They hammered out the agreement for the executors to close the Freer estate and for the Smithsonian to borrow money against the stock in the estate until such time as the Freer Gallery opened. Mary ensured that all three enjoyed their dinner at the Walcott home. Charles Moore of the Fine Arts Commission, who had planted the notion of a gallery in Washington, joined them for what must have been a pleasant evening.

"Col. Hecker and Mr. Spicer called in morning & left for New York P.M. Robert S. Yard & Mrs. Mechlin of the Nat'l Parks Association called 1:30 P.M. and we had a meeting of the Ex. Committee at which I was elected Vice Prest to help out on acct death of Henry B. F. MacFarland. At home with Mary after 6 P.M." (October 23, 1921).

Robert Yard was the executive director and essentially the only employee of the National Parks Association. The association had a president who with four other people constituted an executive committee. When Yard and Leila Mechlin, secretary of the American Federation of Arts, met with Walcott, this constituted a quorum. "Stepping in as acting president was Charles Walcott, but he was very busy, quite elderly, and not really interested in being president" (Miles 1995, 53) is how the official history records this arrangement. Walcott was busy, and he was elderly; the third point was an error, for if nothing else, Walcott served for more than two years and kept the organization alive.

The National Parks Association could hardly meet its payroll, let alone print any pamphlets and lobby of the parks, yet this was a worthy cause. Walcott gave it time and money. It is hard to figure out the cost of this extra commitment, for it would have to be reckoned in trilobite species not described, a peculiar and highly specialized currency.

On Sunday, in the office after church, Walcott looked at the season's photographs and was exceedingly pleased with the results. The NAS geologists met to consider potential new members, Walcott read proofs of his trilobite paper, the Chemical Society presented a portrait of Joseph Priestley, and the Italian embassy had a reception—and that was only the first two days of the week. "Continued work on the photographs & mss of Upper Cambrian paper between interviews & routine duties" (October 27, 1921). Several more receptions, church, more work on photographs, more interviews, and October was over.

Somewhere in this late October and early November dullness, "the director of the Smithson institution [sic] and Mrs. Charles D. Walcott entertained a company of sixteen at dinner last evening in compliment to the Secretary of War, John W. Weeks and Mrs. Weeks, and the Secretary of the Navy, Edwin Denby, and Mrs. Denby."[33]

On November 1, final details of the Freer estate were settled, everyone hoped. Walcott went up on Capitol Hill to begin spadework for the appropriation, and he and his wife dined with the Herbert Hoovers. "Called at H.R. building (office) to see regent Frank L. Green & talked with him about s.i. matters. Very busy at office with mail, interviews, etc." (November 3, 1921). Thereafter things quieted down and in the evening, Walcott, with Mary, called to leave his card at several embassies. Protocol in Washington had not changed much, despite the war.

In addition to regular activities, a few unexpected visitors came through. "Robt. S. Brookings called for talk with me en re Capital & Labor. Read his dialog in evening & wrote him" (November 4, 1921). For those who are not familiar with the Washington scene, the Brookings Institution is what is whimsically known as a "think tank." Think tanks come in all sizes, shapes, and persuasions; Brookings is generally considered to be liberal in the views that its writers espouse. Mr. Brookings had been appointed an SI regent several years earlier, but this was the first private meeting with him that Walcott reported.

"The inventor of a rapid motion picture machine came & showed a few films with extremely slow movement of figures" (November 9, 1921). Yet another example of a broad sweep of activity is that when the unknown soldier lay in state in the Capitol rotunda, Walcott placed a gold star on the bier; that was the action of a father, not a secretary. On Armistice Day at Arlington National Cemetery, "President Harding spoke. A most impressive service" (November 11, 1921).

"Attended opening of Conference on limitation of armament 10–10:30 A.M. Secy Hughes presided & President Harding gave a strong opening address, as did Mr. Hughes—Christian principle, [*sic*] force & ideals will be necessary if the conference functions successfully" (November 12, 1921). Anyone with a smattering of world history knows that less than two decades later the world was rent asunder; the ideals of Walcott did not apply here. Whatever remnants of pre–World War I society and mores had been left after November 11, 1918, vanished forever in the cauldron of World War II.

"At my office A.M. & laying of cornerstone of G.W.M.A. building P.M. by President Harding. Genl. Pershing, and Admiral Kook also spoke for army & Navy. We went to reception of Secy of State & Mrs. Hughes to conference delegates in evening" (November 14, 1921). If any example of persistence by Walcott is needed, the GWMA supplies it. The twentieth century had not dawned when Walcott became involved with that group, and a quarter of a century later the GWMA still had not accomplished its goal. Nevertheless, one word that was never used by others to describe Walcott was "tenacious," perhaps because Walcott always camouflaged his campaigns toward a particular objective. Apart from the matter of the Langley aerodrome, he always presented a manner of being willing to compromise. Still, he almost always ended up getting what he wanted, no matter how long he took. "Persistent" is apt, but "tenacious" may be a closer word in describing his character.

Tuesday was another one of those days devoted mainly to meetings. Chairman Walcott and the members of the NACA hosted a luncheon for Gen. Mason M. Patrick, head of the Army Air Service. The committee then held a two-hour meeting. Most unusually for him, Walcott noted in his diary, "Great Expectations." Langley Field finally was becoming increasingly important, but the army had developed its own facility for research. The quotation marks may have been used for Patrick's expectations rather than those of the NACA.

November ambled onward; some months have a slower pace than others. "Getting photographs ready for illustrating Upper Cambrian paper in afternoon" (November 16, 1921). Whatever this paper might have been, it was incorporated into a larger work and never appeared under an Upper Cambrian title. The next day was "a repetition of yesterday at my office" (November 17, 1921).

Walcott might have issued a small sigh of relief, for though the trustees of the Church of the Covenant had to meet, they did not meet in his office or during working hours; the little time he had for research was preserved. Naturally, one cannot forever live by research alone, and Walcott treated himself to a meeting of the Archaeological Society. That might have been to balance off a half-hour conference with Mr. Lodge, who had finally come back to Washington. It is a safe bet that in one form or another Walcott asked the question of when the Freer Gallery might be expected to open.

The next week, routine paperwork was alleviated by a little time for research, stolen here and there. On the social scene, the British embassy held a reception for the disarmament conference delegates. On the family scene, Helen-Louise had been pregnant, but Sidney wrote she had lost the child, a sad event to be reported on the day before Thanksgiving. The Vaux family came down from Philadelphia; the two boys went to museum to look at the guns, tanks, and other items of war in the military collection while their seniors went to church.

The day after Thanksgiving, Walcott entertained a covey of British visitors, one of whom was particularly noteworthy. "Mrs. Herbert Ward of Paris & London came to look after and assist in installation of her husband's African collection" (November 29, 1921). Ward had gone with Stanley to help explore the Congo, not that the river was not already well known to the natives; he subsequently had made some remarkable sculptures of the natives and collected many artifacts. Four months after Mrs. Ward arrived, the Museum opened a replica of his studio. As recorded in the Board of Regents minutes, "Some years ago during a lecture tour of the United States, Mr. Herbert Ward visited the Smithsonian Institution and was favorably impressed by the work which was being carried on in scientific research and museum installation and education. This impression remained . . . and he expressed his desire that his unique collection of African Ethnology, including sculptures, should be ultimately deposited in the Institution. . . . It is not excessive to say that no collection regarded by science as ethnological was ever illustrated by sculptures of comparative merit."[34] Art and science had melded. Unfortunately, by late in the twentieth century a collection of knives, spears, and nearly naked people—unclothed because where they lived was hot—was not politically correct, however artistically and scientifically correct, and Mr. Ward's material vanished from display.

Walcott shuffled his papers in preparation for the annual meeting of the regents. The Walcotts gave a dinner in honor of William Howard Taft. It never hurts to have one's longtime friends in control of a meeting at which one reports, not that Walcott need ever have worried about the regents. About the only request of his that they ever turned down was to take the Cottrell patents, and probably in the long run this had saved him a great deal of effort; if the patents had come to the Smithsonian, all the growing pains of the Research Corporation would have been in Walcott's lap, rather than only some of them.

"This has been a broken up week as far as any research work is concerned. Routine—mail, interviews, last summer[']s photographs & getting data for Regents meeting & settlement of Freer estate" (December 3, 1921). Church was a relief from at least the routine; Sunday afternoon was devoted to research at the Castle, as usual.

"Spent the day at my office engaged in usual duties & in getting ready for meeting of National Gallery of Art Commission" (December 5, 1921). The executive committee of the commission, of which Walcott was naturally a member, met that afternoon. At the full meeting the sculptor Daniel Charles French—*The Minuteman, Abraham Lincoln,* and other noteworthy pieces—took charge. A number of subcommittees were organized, and it was apparent that this group was determined to see the federal government move into the arts field; Walcott finally had some strong support.

Walcott could report this highly successful gathering to the Executive Committee of the regents and discuss it further the next day at the regents' annual gathering. The regents' meeting in the morning led into the CIW Ex Comm in the afternoon. Neither was noteworthy, which is perhaps the best possible outcome for an annual meeting. That night at the Carnegie reception, President Merriam was the host, the third person to be at the helm of the Carnegie; clearly, presidents of Carnegie were not to have the same longevity in office as Smithsonian secretaries.

"At meeting of Board of Trustees of Carnegie Institution 10–12:30 & Ex. Comm. 12:45–1:10. I was reelected Vice Ch. of Board & Ch. Ex. Comm. At my office 8:45–9:45 A.M. 2–5:30 P.M. Working over minutes of s.i. regents meeting in evening" (December 9, 1921). Walcott just could not say no. Following his reelection, Walcott had "a busy day at office catching up with administrative and correspondence" (December 10, 1921).

After church, the Walcotts went to the office to prepare the "Explorations" pamphlet for 1921. As one goes over these pamphlets, a subtle detail emerges, in that some photographs are credited to C. D. Walcott, some to Mary Vaux Walcott, and some to both; the latter must be the ones taken after both had struggled to bring camera equipment to a good vantage point.

Even before winter officially started, Washington had a snow squall, but it did not prevent a meeting of the NRC Executive Committee. That out of the way, Walcott went to call on the Speaker of the House. Since three of the regents came from the House of Representatives, there was more turnover from that group than for the other groups appointed. As expected, the meeting was a formality, leaving plenty of time to get home, where Secretary and Mrs. Walcott held a dinner for twenty in honor of the visiting Lord Balfour; it brought back memories of responding to Britain's call for help in the Great War. "Mr. Balfour dined with us May 4, 1917" (December 14, 1921). "At my office all day sleepy—lazy despite bracing air" (December 15, 1921). It must have been a fine dinner, but at seventy-one burning the candle at both ends is not recommended. Walcott continued feeling "dumpy" and worked on papers for the Church of the Covenant at home.

The dumpiness vanished when, four days before Christmas, Walcott's "Notes on the Structure of *Neolenus*" was delivered by the printer. The official date of publication is given as December 26, 1921, but Walcott immediately sent out copies to colleagues. Almost never did Walcott record receipt of a paper, for once the proofs had been read, it was done with. This paper, however, was different, and dear to his heart: it was his final word on the interpretation of trilobite limbs.

Although the title suggested that the work was confined to the Burgess Shale trilobite, in it his work of 1918 was reviewed and in large measure reaffirmed. Both the geologic history of a large part of North America and the most esoteric details of the morphology of fossils were within Walcott's scope of interest.

"On my return from the field in October, 1920, I learned that a memoir on the structure of the trilobite by Dr. Percy E. Raymond, was in press. This caused me still further delay in publication, in the hope that some new evidence might be presented by Raymond. A copy of the memoir was received in January, 1921" (Walcott 1921, 378). A minor piece of information for those interested in the Burgess Shale is that out of the thousands of specimens collected, Walcott had fourteen specimens of *Neolenus* that had the appendages preserved. A lot of paper was used, and continues to be used, in discussing these specimens.

In addition to arranging for publication, Schuchert wrote a foreword for Raymond:

> Trilobites are among the most interesting of invertebrate fossils and have long attracted the attention of amateur collectors and men of science.... Students of trilobites have always wanted specimens to be delivered to them weathered out of the rock by nature and revealing the ventral anatomy without further work than the collecting, but the wish has never been fulfilled.... No surgeon was needed, but a worker knowing the great scientific value of what was hidden, and with endless patience and marked skill in preparation of fossils.... No man loved a knotty problem more than C. E. Beecher.... The final cleaning work was done by hand.... Finally Beecher became so expert with these fossils that after one side was developed he would embed the specimen in Canada balsam and fix it to a glass slide thus enabling him to cut down from the opposite side.... Then came illustrations

... [Schuchert] expected to find considerable manuscript relating to the ventral anatomy of the trilobites, but there was only one page. It was Beecher's method first to prepare and thoroughly study the material in hand, then to make the necessary illustrations. (Raymond 1920, 5–7)

A minor point that is not clear is just when Raymond received Beecher's prepared material; he noted that the monograph had been first completed in 1917 and then expanded. Walcott's comment that in effect he became aware of the monograph in 1921 is so much blowing smoke, for the paleontological community was minuscule, yet several different sources could have told Walcott that Raymond was engaged in a major study of Beecher's specimens. Raymond must have delayed publication when he became aware that Walcott had a large work on trilobite limbs in the works.

One may properly ask why Beecher's material not sent to Walcott to complete. Schuchert owed a great deal to Walcott, first for having been given a job in 1893, despite the horrendous budget problems of the USGS, and second for having supported him for the position at Yale University that opened after Beecher's death. A logical explanation is that until 1907 Walcott was swamped by administration of the USGS and would not have had the time for a detailed study. After 1909, with both the discovery of the Burgess Shale fossil and a taste for fieldwork in the Canadian Rockies, he probably would have turned down any offer to complete the investigation. It is a reasonable surmise that Schuchert and Walcott privately discussed Raymond's abilities one of the times that they met. If Walcott was not available, Raymond's part in the 1913 textbook made him the most logical candidate.

That is all well and good, but if one wants speculation at a deeper level, Walcott may have been just a tiny bit resentful, because the presence of the eighteen-year-old Beecher, who would work for essentially no pay, had been one of the factors that had caused James Hall not to renew Walcott's contract in 1878. Moving ahead in time to the monograph, Raymond not only considered all that was known of trilobite limbs, not just Beecher's material, but produced a classification of the Burgess Shale arthropods and arthropod-like fossils. Inasmuch as these had been published, they were in a sense fair game, yet in a way they were still Walcott's intellectual property. Judging from the Schuchert-Walcott letters, Raymond did not look at the material in Washington. This is all legitimate and ethical, but it would be nice to find a letter in which Raymond indicated to Walcott what he was doing.

To go one step farther, about the time that Raymond's monograph was published, Schuchert was nominated for president of the Geological Society of America. An opposition slate was proposed, most unusual for any scientific society. This turned out to have been masterminded by E. O. Ulrich, jealous of his one-time protegé Schuchert, but for a time there was suspicion that Walcott may have supported the move. Science may be straightforward, but scientists are not always equally straightforward. Fortunately, this matter was worked out; Walcott's hands were clean, and there was no breach between Walcott and Schuchert.

Walcott began his paper with an explanation of methodology, if not exactly an apology.

> During the past few twenty-five years I have published from time to time preliminary results of investigations, even though I realized that a few months' additional work might give data for more reliable conclusions and protect me from reasonable criticism. I thought it better to present the data with tentative conclusions and stimulate others to investigate rather than wait for a time of relief from administrative duties. A recent contribution on "Appendages of trilobites," [1918] is an example of hurried investigation under pressure of many duties, also of indifferent illustration brought about by conditions incident to the great world war and my absence during publication, while engaged in field-work. (Walcott 1921, 365–66)

Walcott gave Raymond's monograph considerable praise. "This is a fine contribution and gives evidence of prolonged, thorough study, keen observation, and a comprehensive grasp of detail and the broader aspects of the subject" (Walcott 1921, 373). There were basically two areas of disagreement between the two men. Living Crustacea have biramous—that is, two-part—appendages under their bodies, consisting of a gill and a walking leg. Raymond saw the trilobites as having similar appendages of a generalized form, from which all other crustacean legs could be derived. On *Neolenus*, Walcott interpreted a walking leg (endopodite), a gill-bearing appendage (exopodite), and a third, smaller structure (epipodite). He applied the same threefold division to the limbs of three Middle Ordovician trilobites. The right and the wrong of this interpretation concern few people, but in effect the epipodite has disappeared under restudy. Raymond was more correct in his interpretation.

The second main difference between the two investigators concerns the structure of the exopodite. Fringed structures were presumably gill filaments hanging from a bar. In earlier works, Walcott had interpreted the structure as a spiral. Raymond, however, assembled

> a formidable array of arguments against the presence of spiral exopodites, but after reading them I [Walcott] was still unconvinced but realized that the presence of a spiral-like structure in *Calymene* and *Ceraurus* was rendered exceedingly doubtful to the general student and that it was relegated to the class of disproved theories. As a last resort I decided to make thin sections of

a number of specimens of *Calymene* collected by William F. Rust for the National Museum many years ago, and a few of *Ceraurus,* all of which came from the locality and layer of rock worked by Walcott prior to 1876. . . . [I]t was not until the next to the last slide of *Calymene* was rubbed down thin that a series of undoubted spirals was seen in shadowy outline. . . . I had in my hands the evidence that I had searched for from 1873 to 1879 and at intervals since. (Walcott 1921, 408–9)

Walcott's sections made in the 1870s do show what looks like a spiral structure, and he never changed his mind. It is a classic example of the old saw that the eye beholds what the mind perceives.

Walcott went on to reinforce his case by discussing and illustrating coils of wire he had imbedded in plaster and sectioned. One of the few persons to study trilobite limbs between the two world wars was to mention seeing these plaster blocks. Strange things occasionally happen with museums collections, and these plaster blocks are now with paleobotanical specimens from the Burgess Shale. Walcott was wrong in his interpretation, and Raymond was right; the gill filaments did not come off a spiral structure. The issue was resolved by making a series of sections through the gills (Størmer 1939).

"I did not discuss the affinities of the trilobites at length as I wish to consider them in connection with other crustaceans from the Burgess Shale" (Walcott 1921, 376). So much for the larger picture, and unfortunately Walcott never wrote the work alluded to in that sentence. About all Walcott said further was that not all students of crustaceans would necessarily agree that the trilobites were the most primitive of crustaceans, as Raymond had written. "Already in his first description, Walcott (1912) abandons his earlier view of the trilobites approaching the merostomes. . . . Walcott (1918, 1921) presents new and valuable material toward the elucidations of the trilobite appendages. . . . Concerning the zoological position of the trilobites Walcott concludes very defiantly they were primitive crustacean. . . . Practically all the modern paleontologists follow in general the American authors in their conception of the trilobites as a subclass of the crustaceans" (Størmer 1939, 149).

Today, there is general agreement among paleoarthropodologists that the trilobites are a class separate and distinct from the crustaceans. In that sense, Walcott's proposal in 1894 has finally been accepted, and Raymond's treatment of the trilobites as a subclass of Crustacea has only historic interest. Among the other Arthropoda in the Burgess Shale, several workers recognize Crustacea, but there is still no consensus on that issue.

Walcott ended this, his last work of paleobiology, on a happy note. "My interest in the organization of the trilobite has been revivified by this study and I hope to add a little more to what is known in the course of two or three years" (Walcott 1921, 432).

Truly, Walcott was satisfied, as indicated by a note he wrote to himself early in January 1922: "49 years ago I told Louis Agassiz that I would make the structure of the trilobite a special bit of research work. My last paper on it appeared Dec. 20th 1921. Nothing like sticking to a job. It keeps one young."[35]

Just to reinforce this work, Walcott had the long-suffering photographer prepare nearly two dozen sets of prints from the original negatives, and he made up, or had made up, sets of the seventeen plates. This was both a time-consuming and expensive effort. As soon as the paper was published, these sets were distributed worldwide to leading institutions. One is led to the belief that a few paleontologists were muttering that Walcott retouched his photographs to bring out details that were not present, and that the Burgess Shale fossils really did not show what Walcott thought. With original photographs to study, no one, Raymond, Schuchert, or anyone else, would have grounds for claiming to misunderstand him.

Upon receipt of the publication and a set of prints, an eminent specialist on living marine arthropods at the British Museum (Natural History) wrote to Walcott. "It is impossible to appreciate fully the evidence for your conclusions without seeing the untouched photographs. Some of them—notably No. 1 on Plate 10—are astonishing and, although I am very unwilling to admit the 'spiral brachinae' such as you have described, I must confess that these photographs do, for the moment, somewhat shake my faith!"[36]

To make certain that his colleagues knew he was very much alive, some of Walcott's current research was delivered at the thirty-first annual meeting of the Geological Society of America. "The Secretary [of the Paleontological Society] then presented for the author, in his absence, an account of the wonderful anatomical structures preserved in the Middle Cambrian Burgess Shale branchiopod crustaceans found near Field, British Columbia. Illustrated by lantern slides and specimens." Only a short abstract is given. "A presentation of the appendages and internal anatomy of the three Middle Cambrian branchiopod genera *Waptia*, *Naroia*, and *Burgessia*, preliminary to a more detailed work to be issued in the near future by the Smithsonian Institution" (Bassler 1921, 127). Walcott was telling the profession that he was doing more with the Burgess Shale arthropods and that the trilobite limb paper just published was only the beginning.

The paper mentioned never appeared, and this abstract was atypical, for Walcott characteristically gave his findings publicly only after a paper was in press. (For those who are reading closely, brachiopod and branchiopod are not the same; branchiopods are a group of crustaceans.)

Before leaving this esoteric subject, there is one trivial matter to mention. At one of the Geological Society of America banquets, a songbook was prepared; possibly the occasion was the 1910 twenty-second meeting in Cambridge, Massachusetts, for there are some Harvard-like aspects to some of the lyrics. Included in the collection is "Triarthrus becki," to the tune of "Crambambuli."

1. Triarthrus Becki is the title
   Of the trilobite we love the best,
For it alone has organs vital
   That fail the heads of all the rest.
Good Charles Walcott keen of sight,
Tried hard for years, by day, by night,
But never found one that was right.
   Triarthrus Beck.
2. Should Charles D. Walcott change his trade,
   'Twould be a shame, 'twould be a shame,
   Since Fortune still, the fickle jade,
   May send him fame, may send him fame.
Just mind the angler's rule so trite,
   And change the bait, when 'tisn't right,
   And thus you'll make a trilo-bite.
Triarthrus Beck.

The pun in the last line is atrocious, but the serious paleontologists have rendered it moot. Restudy indicates that the *Triarthrus* prepared by Beecher is a different species and should be called *T. eatoni*, a much harder rhyme. The latest study of its limbs (Whittington and Almond 1987) has provided more detail on the paleobiology of this long-dead creatures.

Any reader may legitimately wonder why trilobite limbs, a subject of interest to only a handful of people, should occupy about as much space as the Wright controversy, which brought the si bad publicity for years. One justification is that trilobites were Walcott's job, whereas aviation was, in a sense, only his avocation. To put this in more forceful terms, defending Langley was Secretary Walcott's duty, but understanding trilobites was his passion. Enough. It is past time to return to Walcott's daily activities.

"A quiet day with Mt. Robson Ozarkian fauna & a little routine" (December 22, 1921). The next day, Walcott published a letter in *Science* concerning pending legislation on the metric system. This did not amount to much, but it is just one more example of an action that took away his time both from research and running the Smithsonian.

That evening, the Walcotts dined at the Willard Hotel with the British ambassador, Lord Lee, and an intimate gathering of seventy-five guests. They celebrated Christmas a day early, giving cards and gifts to the household staff. Then it was off to Bryn Mawr for a family Christmas with the Vaux family. When the Walcotts returned home the following day, Walcott received an unexpected present in the form of a radiogram from Helen, who was returning from Europe. "Helen came in 9:25 P.M. having landed in New York in the morning. She is looking well. We are glad to have her back in America" (December 27, 1921).

The penultimate day of the year, *Science* included a small article by a Canadian geologist reporting the Early Cambrian trilobite *Olenellus* from the Cranbrook area of British Columbia; this was the material Walcott had examined earlier (Schofield 1921). His identifications are acknowledged, and a few words are quoted, for paleontologists do more than write their own papers; they examine and report on fossils for others. Identifications by Walcott are scattered throughout the literature, and it would be almost impossible to find them all. Fortunately, he lived in a time when the be-all, do-all, and end-all of promotion was not solely the number of titles published—or the citation of one's work by others.

"Continued office & laboratory work at the Smithsonian. Went before D.C. subcommittee on appropriations for zool. park with Ned Hollister 4–5:30. Mary & I attended reception given by Senator & Mrs. King to Vice-President & Mrs. Coolidge 10–12 P.M." (December 30, 1921). A little clarification might help here. In setting up the zoo, Congress had decided that the citizens of Washington would derive most benefit from it, and therefore half the cost should come out of the budget for the District of Columbia. It was treated as a local facility, not a national institution. Congress never gave the district sufficient money to repair all the city streets, let alone take proper care of such frills as a zoo. The consequence was that the zoo became more and more dilapidated, especially in the post-Walcott era when the SI secretary had less personal influence with congressmen.

The day was clear and cool, a good way to end the year. "At my laboratory most of the day working over Ozarkian fossils from Alberta Can. collected over the past four field seasons. Mary writing letters. Helen & I had a long talk *en re* her art work & future. The year closes with those of our family at home. Sidney & his family at Buffalo. May all be as well & happy a year from now. The world of humanity is slowly recovering from the 'Great War.' We are further along than Dec. 31 1920 & should be getting far on the way to normal peace conditions by the close of 1922" (December 31, 1921).

Helen never did become a great artist, but she was listed in a directory of Washington artists, so she was certainly more than just a Sunday painter. As to science, 1922 would be a barren year for publication, with nothing except the official reports and the "Explorations" pamphlet, and 1923 would be almost as barren. This happens in a career; after switching from one subject to another, it takes time to build up sufficient information for publication.

Though he had described all the obvious fossils from the Burgess Shale, it would not be correct to judge Walcott as having completed his investigations, as the abstract to the Geological Society of America demonstrates. Nevertheless, so long as he could still get out in the field, the overall stratigraphy and, by extension, the geologic history of the Cambrian in western Canada were now his main interests. With all due respect to stratigraphers, once one goes out and measures a section, the main work is done; when fossils are collected from a section, the work has just started—they then have to be described. Walcott could determine the age of strata within the Cambrian readily, and therefore his work on the stratigraphy would go fairly rapidly. It was a good scientific strategy to concentrate now on the rocks themselves, while the fossils accumulated slowly.

In addition, the administration of his manifold organizations was now pressing on him as much as in the later years of his USGS directorship, when he had had equally lean patches in his publication record. Several junior people who knew him after the First World War commented that he always kept a few fossils in his desk drawer. When staff members or visitors came in, he would close the drawer and concentrate on the issue they raised; as soon as they left, he would open the drawer to look at the fossils again.

Able assistant Arthur Brown was also no young man. He was reduced to five teeth, none of which matched top and bottom. The joke was that he could cash his salary check anywhere in Washington, because his smile was so well known. The sawing of the Burgess Shale into little blocks, which had taken place in his tiny space on the third floor was finished, and Arthur now spent more time near the secretary's office. Many years later, at least three staff members in the Castle referred to him as the "majordomo"; he was liked and respected throughout the institution.

Walcott may have been showing all his years at the end of 1921, and Arthur was getting along, but they both had a few more good field seasons in them.

8

The Stasis Years (1922–1923): Sometimes a March Is Two Steps Forward and Three Steps Back

> British Columbia is a marvelous place for anyone
> who is curious about nature.
>
> —R. Cummings and S. Cummings, 1996

IF WALCOTT'S LIFE were set to music, 1922 would be a section "marking time," for there were no obvious indications that any events were transpiring. His publication list for the year is uninspiring, consisting of the "Explorations" pamphlet and two Smithsonian annual reports, as the last effects of the war's delay were finally shaken out of that publication. Several bibliographies list two 1922 papers by Walcott published in the *Pan-American Geologist*.

Its editor, Charles Rollins Keyes, had wanted to use the title of the *American Geologist*, a journal defunct since 1906, and when he could not, he simply continued the volume numbers. Like many editors, Keyes faced the problem of finding sufficient material for each issue, a problem he resolved by writing much of the journal's contents; Keyes has more publications than any other American geologist. For variety, from time to time he would put another person's name on an article he had written. More often, he indicated the source of material by putting a name, though not a reference, at the bottom. One memoir on Walcott (Yochelson 1967) does not list two short 1922 papers that have his name at the end; whether this was bibliographic skill or dumb luck is no longer certain.

As for the virtual absence of publications, it is as though the *Neolenus* paper had used up all his strength and he had to rest. Actually, Walcott kept working just as diligently on science and on administration, even though no dramatic developments were to be seen.

The year 1922 began with a quiet New Year's Day; the Walcotts made only one informal call. "The New Year opens with world still in turmoil, but not as much as a year ago" (January 1, 1922). On Monday, Walcott started on the fossils from the Mons Formation, for if he had any mottos, one must have been "Never put off till tomorrow." The Smithsonian was quiet, and the research continued apace. Eight days into the new year, Walcott wrote his remaining son:

> The past week has been a mixed one for us. . . . The dinner on Thursday went well & I was glad to have Helen home to be with us and our friends. She is gaining strength and flesh and will soon be in fine condition. Just now she has no plans altho talking about several places to go for study etc—She is to remain at home for a time. Lunches, quiet dinners and out-of-doors exercise are the limit of present activities.
>
> Mary has been active in connection with "Girls Training School" matters—political influence threatened to upset the administration of the school so she took the matter up and will probably come out on top—Mary is a good fighter when aroused—as most Quakers are.
>
> The conference outlook is good. The "Irreconcilables" will kick but the nations will go on a higher plan than in 1914.
>
> The passing of Senators [Boise] Penrose and [Philander Chase] Knox will have a strong influence on constructive legislation as they were standpatters of the "Old Guard"—Lodge, Nelson & others will soon follow & a later generation will control the Senate.
>
> I have heard nothing from Fred (Walcott) about business matters. I may be in New York on Friday and see him if he is in town. I have a "nasty cold" in my head and one ear is discharging freely so it is a little uncertain what can be done. We have a dinner in honor of Secty of War—Wed eve—a reception at White House Thursday and two dinners with friends but I hope to be in New York Friday & Saturday.
>
> The weather has been very variable [but overall too] . . . mild for the season. Tex Wood writes that it was 40° below zero at Banff Xmas week. At the govt ranch Cricket, Baldy and the bunch are digging down through the snow for their daily feed—hard work but it keeps them warm.
>
> Love to Helen-Louise[,] Evelyn and my big boy Sidney.[1]

Those who desire deep psychological insight into biographical subjects may ponder this letter. Was Walcott simply conveying news, or was he sending a message that he was slowing down? One curious source of information is the collection of accession cards recording donations of objects to the SI and various museums. From Walcott there was a steady stream of natural history objects, mostly fossils but with the occasional biological specimen sprinkled in. Walcott donated artifacts of Stuart's life as a flyer. Beginning in the 1920 one sees an increasing number of personal and family items given to the collections. One might infer that Walcott was getting some of his affairs in order. One might also take the alternative view that with children gone, it was time to move heirlooms of no family interest to museum collections, where they might have some future utility. Inquiry along deep psychological lines does not always lead to insight.

Research continued, but as Walcott commented, he was not worth much because of a cold, and the trip to New York mentioned to Sidney never materialized. He called at the White House and called on Mr. Hoover. "A nasty day. Attended meeting of Appropriations Committee *en re* publications" (January 11, 1922). Almost certainly the comment was about the weather, but with a congressional committee one never really knows what will happen. With January more than half over, Walcott commented, "I have much to do with the fossils from the Upper Cambrian & Ozarkian of the Cordillera Paleozoic trough of Alberta & B.C." (January 17, 1922). Notwithstanding Walcott's wish to be moving along, the cold laid him out for days. "My cold is improving but right ear is troublesome" (January 21, 1922). No matter how tough older people may be, winter can be hard on them.

His cold cleared up finally, and Walcott went back to the office. The Vauxes came in from Philadelphia in time for a small dinner in honor of the ambassador of Peru and to be taken to a White House reception.

On the same day as President Harding's reception, the NACA held its first meeting of the year. The NACA had put a great deal of effort into trying to obtain legislation for a civilian body to regulate civilian aviation. Late in December 1921, aircraft manufacturers had met with the NACA, and presumably all difficulties had been worked out. By mid-February, a bill had passed the Senate, but it died in the House (Roland 1985, 62). Arguments and infighting would continue for another three years, but fortunately, most of the effort was carried on by the Commerce Department. How much Secretary Walcott might have chatted with Secretary of Commerce Hoover is not recorded. After 1921, the NACA concentrated more on aviation research and less on aviation politics.

Congressional testimony was a constant in Washington year in and year out. Despite the Bureau of the Budget being interposed between the SI and the Congress, Walcott still knew how to play the game. A nice example (even though not in 1922) is provided by NACA hearings before the Senate. Walcott began by lecturing on what the NACA was and how it was constituted. He then went into his troubles with the House of Representatives. The appropriation for the NACA had been killed on a point of order: an item for construction of buildings was included, whereas there was no specific authority in the original act for the NACA to have buildings. Walcott wanted the Senate to grant that authority.

"Senator Jones: What need is there for the construction of buildings now? Is there any?" John Victory told of the engine dynamometer laboratory in a hangar at Langley Field, which leaked when it rained and was cold in the winter and hot in the summer. Senator Jones then suggested that another building might become vacant; when Victory called that unlikely, the senator suggested relocation somewhere else for a while. Walcott got the discussion back on track. "The rest of the plant is right there. We would have to have this building with it. There is the difficulty" (Walcott 1921b, 59–60). Authority to have buildings was granted; positions of the forty-five men at Langley Field and the future of the NACA in aeronautical research were saved.

With that aside, it is appropriate to return to late January 1922. After President Harding's reception, the snow began. It snowed, and it snowed, and it snowed. A theater roof collapsed from the weight, causing the greatest naturally induced disaster in the history of Washington; even though ninety-eight people were killed, Walcott made no comment in his diary. The traffic tie-up was such that Walcott missed the funeral of Mrs. Arnold Hague, wife of his old boss from the Eureka district.

Walcott fretted about Helen's health and his own, but Mary and he went to the British embassy for dinner and later a reception for President Harding. Social life went on, bad weather or no. Helen began work again on his portrait, Cousin Fred came into town, the executive committee of the NRC met, the NAS building committee met, the GWMA held its annual meeting, and the Walcotts began to go to the Smithsonian office on Sunday after church. In terms of a perennial problem and a sort of man-bites-dog approach, Walcott was asked to help collect funds in Washington for the GWMA. "I regret that owing to the many commitments I now have, it will not be practicable for me to give attention to this matter. The members of the committee should be young, vigorous men, who can make a through canvass."[2] In other words, life was normal for mid-February. "Attended to routine and worked on post Cambrian fossils in laboratory as time permitted" (February 21, 1922). The Walcotts dined out a few times and reciprocated, in a sense, with a dinner for the French ambassador.

March began with a reception opening the Herbert Ward collection, formally accepted by SI regent Calvin Coolidge. This was a great increase in the Museum's holdings of African material, and it was exhibited as though it were in the sculptor's studio, with artifacts on the wall and completed statues adjacent. "The dramatic style of the installation, the inclusion of a brief biography of the collector, and the fact that the Ward sculptures mediated between the viewer and the African objects, and between the authoritative voice of the Museum and its lay audience represented a significant departure from the Museum's standard practice" (Bourgoin 1996, 61). Years after the original installation, through somewhat complex maneuvering, the Smithsonian was able to have the terms of the donation modified and the studio dismantled (Yochelson 1985). More years later, the sculptures of African natives were deemed politically incorrect and banished from the Museum (Arnoldi 1997). Times change, and exhibits change, sometimes for the better and sometimes not.

Walcott was getting in a bit more time to study the Cambrian faunas, and the social whirl slackened. Unfortunately, ptomaine poisoning struck him down for a day, and that in turn may have weakened him, for cold germs again attacked. He sniffled along through the annual church meeting and then started pursuing an endowment for the National Gallery of Art. Still, his paleontology continued: "Completed first review of fauna of Mons Formation for making up lists" (March 23, 1922). A faunal list gives the name of fossils found in a particular formation and, for those who can read it properly, provides the relative age of the rock. For the nonpaleontologist, it is about as informative as a Mayan calendar.

Mary went back and forth to Philadelphia on a regular basis but was able to handle her social duties with ease. A dinner for twelve in honor of the vice president came off without a hitch. The next evening, she gave an illustrated lecture to the Wild Flower Preservation Society at the Museum auditorium. Few details are known of Mary as a public speaker, nor is it known how many times she appeared before an audience, but, like her husband, when she lectured she was a professional.

Helen had left weeks earlier for the better climate at Beaufort, South Carolina, and had written about its pleasures. That might have inspired Walcott to a vacation; in any case, on April 11 he and Mary left for Letchworth Cottage at Spring Lake Beach, New Jersey. "We are both tired, so slept, read & walked A.M." (April 2, 1922). It was very much a working vacation, or rather a time away from interruptions, for Walcott hauled out his growing manuscript on fossils from Canada and began to assemble the plates. "A walk to the post office A.M. & P.M. was about all the exercise we had during the day. Making out lists of fossils from the St. Charles formation of Utah and Idaho kept me occupied" (April 4, 1922).

Despite leaving Washington, Walcott could never find uninterrupted research time. A permanent home for the NAS was coming along at a fast pace, and it moved to near the top of the agenda. As mentioned earlier, Hale had campaigned for a building as part of his grand scheme for the Academy he had brought forth at the time of the fiftieth anniversary celebration in 1913. The Academy charter had been amended in 1870 to remove a limitation on members and again in 1884 to allow it to hold trust funds. In 1914, the charter had been amended a third time, to allow the NAS to hold real estate. The historian of the NAS would refer to the change as Walcott's amendment (Cochrane 1978, 271).

Hale had gone looking for building money, but first the formation of the NRC had occupied him, and then the war had come along. Again as noted, after the war Hale and Walcott visited the Carnegie Corporation in February 1919. On March 28, the money was granted, subject to a few provisions, one of which was that the Academy procure a satisfactory building site. Hale was chairman of the building committee. "Now he set about raising the money with a simplicity and directness that amounted to genius" (Wright 1966, 312).

Shortly thereafter, Gano Dunn became chairman of the building committee, and Hale was not quite so conspicuous, leaving most of the details to other members, which included Walcott. Least anyone read too much into this, Hale and Walcott had worked closely together for years and held each other in high regard. Hale had been considered for president of the Carnegie to replace Woodward. When Merriam obtained the position, Walcott wanted to make certain that there was no misunderstanding from the new president regarding Dr. Hale. "Hale is an exceptional man & the Mt. Wilson Observatory & its staff reflect his character and ability. I should be very glad indeed to talk with you over each and every one of the projects now being carried on under the direction of the Carnegie Institution, as I am intensely interested to see it one of the great and active forces in the development of scientific thought in America."[3]

If Hale was the star of the Academy production, Paul Brockett was one of the spear carriers, but he had a monumental bit part to play. In the Smithsonian Castle was a library equipped with a rolling ladder to reach the upper shelves. One day Walcott slipped and tangled his tall frame in the ladder. The new librarian became tongue-tied; he kept waving his hands but was not able to speak. Finally, Walcott said, "Well, young man, are you going to help me up or not?" That may or may not have been Brockett, who had started as a Smithsonian librarian and was then eased over by Walcott into NAS and NRC affairs. At Walcott's suggestion, Brockett was made secretary of the building committee, with his principal duty to keep an eye on things and report on construction. His reports make interesting reading.

Hale wanted to put the Academy building on Sixteenth Street in what is now Meridian Hill Park. That did not work out, and Walcott found a site in the former swamp near the Lincoln Memorial, then under construction. For the site to be properly squared up, Upper Water Street had to be closed. This required an act of Congress, and the bill had to originate with the District of Columbia Committee. To put it mildly, the governing of Washington was not a high priority for Congress. Walcott went off to the field in 1921, leaving Brockett to get a bill passed. He did engineer the necessary bill, just barely in time, and his saga would make a wonderful paper on how legislation proceeds.

Walcott was not an ex officio member of the building committee simply because he was NAS president; he took an active role. After all, considering his involvement with the University Club, a couple of apartment houses, the new Museum, the CIW headquarters, and the Freer Gallery, he had some notion of what was involved in major construction. For instance, when bids came in higher than expected by the committee—which almost always happens—the

rest of the committee came up with a money-saving idea, namely, constructing the building of Indiana limestone rather than marble or granite. Although
Walcott was away, he was as effective as if he had been in his Washington office.
Dr. Abbot, NAS home secretary as well as Smithsonian assistant secretary, wrote
him: "Upon receiving your letter I got Mr. Charles Moore on the phone, and he
had not received your telegram but promised to get in touch with the Fine Arts
Commission and wire you later today about the matter. He is also inclined to
feel with you that either granite or marble should be used and not Indiana limestone."[4] The same day, Walcott fired off a telegram to J. C. Merriam, a member
of the committee. "After consulting architect members of the Comm of Fine
Arts find they cannot approve chg. to Indiana Limestone for building facing
Lincoln Memorial ground."[5] The next day he sent another telegram: "Committee appears to have overlooked that grant of funds by Carnegie Corporation was
on basis of approval of plan by Fine Arts Commission. The latter approved with
understanding building was to be made of granite or marble. This matter must
be cleared up before I can sign contract."[6]

To make certain that the issue was thoroughly resolved, Walcott scribbled a
note to Dr. Abbot. "Telegram to members of Academy should be so detailed that
they can vote intelligently on authorizing President to sign contract for Academy
building. Mail me copy of it."[7] Thus the NAS building is located where it is and
built of what it is because of Walcott, just as in the case of the Freer Gallery of Art.

The good news that a new home was coming was revealed to members at the
Academy annual meeting. "The outstanding feature of the opening session . . .
was the announcement . . . that a magnificent building, costing $1,300,000[,]
will be erected."[8] This particular newspaper account had Walcott as secretary of
the Academy rather president, but that did no harm.

As he often did to record ongoing events, he indicated with ditto marks that
he was still working on his manuscript. None of this activity over the Academy
building made it into Walcott's diary. The Vauxes came down from Philadelphia
to Spring Lake Beach for a day and a half, and they drove the Walcotts around
the countryside. "I worked on Nevada list of Ozarkian in evening" (April 8,
1922). In other words, Walcott reexamined his list of collections from the Eureka Mining District in Nevada—his first major publication—do decide which
ones characterized Mr. Ulrich's proposed Ozarkian system shoehorned in above
the Cambrian. They had another day at the beach, nominally in his case, most
of it was spent on his manuscript. Then it was off for home.

"With John C. Merriam signed contract for National Academy building"
(April 11, 1922). That was a little more than just marking time. "Stopped at
dentist & Mary's Potomac Park garden. At the office 9 A.M. to 5 P.M. Cleaned up
routine and resumed work on Lower Ozarkian fauna of Texas, etc. Tired after

dinner so napped & turned in early" (April 13, 1922). Mary planted her garden, Walcott went to the annual meeting of the Iowa Apartment House, and cousin Amandah Bartlett came from Utica. All might have been well with the world, except that "Helen at home & feeling spring fever & weakness" (April 17, 1922). Under the heading of "no surprise," the next day the NAS building committee voted to use marble.

Walcott presided at the semiannual meeting of the NACA and attended the CIW Ex Comm, a busy afternoon following a morning of research. Fortunately, the frequency of Ex Comm meetings had dropped dramatically. "At organization meeting of Institute of Economics. Dr. Henry S. Pritchett presented statement from Carnegie Corporation in presenting endowment. Robt S. Brookings elected president" (April 21, 1922). In the study of the history of organizations, there might be some utility in tracing the route from the Brookings manuscript that Walcott had read some years earlier to the opening of what became the Brookings Institution. Walcott was on the board of this new institute. Unfortunately, the archives of the Brookings are scanty concerning its early days.

Ancient geologic history, in two senses, appeared. Arthur Keith of the USGS stopped by to tell Walcott of his work in western Vermont. Keith had investigated thrust faults in the southern Appalachians and had taken this knowledge north. His mapping had demonstrated that some rocks in the Taconic Mountains had been pushed miles westward. It was an observation that Walcott had not known of or could not have guessed at when he was in that area four decades earlier.

The NAS council took place on Sunday afternoon, and the annual meeting began. The various lectures, receptions, and dinners occupied three full days. "Resumed my work on the Cordillera Cambrian & Ozarkian Formations report" (April 22, 1922). The merry month of May began. Time was passing, and as a indication of it, Walcott attended a luncheon to mark the fifteenth anniversary of George Otis Smith as USGS director; it was difficult to imagine Walcott had been gone so long from that organization.

John Merriam and Walcott put their heads together on NAS-NRC relations. Walcott went to Capitol Hill to discuss vacancies on the Board of Regents, and this lead to an informal regents' meeting at the Smithsonian to resolve the appointments. That done, Walcott was driven to southern Maryland to meet Mary. This year was the two hundredth anniversary of the coming of Friends to Maryland. The celebration ended at one of the old Quaker meeting houses, and it was a pleasant way to conclude the week.

To start the new week, Arthur Keith came in for further discussion about the geology of northern Vermont. Another quiet day at the Smithsonian followed; "Routine & a little work on Cordillera stratigraphic sections occupied the time"

(May 9, 1922). "Talked with Smithsonian staff & employees at noon. Owing to trouble with teeth am feeling badly when not in action" (May 10, 1922). "Am not getting much done owing to teeth aching. Old & worn out after long service" (May 12, 1922). Walcott may have been referring to his teeth, but it could just as well have been a more comprehensive remark—and a reflection on life.

Bad teeth or no, Walcott did not really slow down. "At my office & museum during the day. Mary sketching a new wildflower in afternoon. I am working on a scheme to get small foundations in the Smithsonian" (May 13, 1922). On Sunday the teeth were so bad that Walcott was at the dentist, and again on Monday. They improved enough so that he could escort some Detroit men to call on President Harding; this was a group that Walcott hoped to interest in increasing the Smithsonian endowment: life was never quiet. "A day of interviews routine & very little review of mss. Meeting of Ex. Comm. Natl. Gal. Art. Commission 9:45 A.M. [A]t dentists 8–8:45, 10:45–11:20 A.M. Spoke to Asso. Office Managers 11:30 A.M." (May 20, 1922). There were times when Walcott was still a man of iron. Few people attend a meeting between visits to the dentist. Fortunately, the next day was Sunday, a day of rest. Walcott skipped church and went neither to the office nor to the dentist.

"A broken up more or less ineffective day. Routine, callers, odds & ends" (May 22, 1922). It was back to the dentist the next morning and then to the office. Walcott met with students who were at the Smithsonian; he gave them two hours of his time. The next afternoon he was off to New York. Considering all the trips he had made in past years, it was novel that this was his first for 1922. Walcott saw Helen briefly; she was off to Nova Scotia for the summer.

Walcott had a busy day. He met with Dr. Pritchett of the Carnegie Corporation and the NAS architect before going to a meeting of the building committee and ending up with Mr. Hooker. The next day was the CIW Ex Comm gathering; after a late lunch, Mary and Walcott left to meet Mrs. Harriman at her country place, Arden House. On Saturday they motored to West Point to see a polo match, and Sunday afternoon they were home. "Glad to find all well in our modest home & to be able to sleep out in the open air" (May 28, 1922). That Walcott considered his home modest gives some glimmering of how the New York millionaires were living.

The Sulgrave Institution presented a painting of the signing of the Treaty of Ghent to the Smithsonian as a prelude to Decoration Day. That day began with an hour at the dentist and a half-hour at the White House, where a flag was presented by France. Walcott took flowers to Rock Creek Cemetery. From there he went to the dedication of the Lincoln Memorial, probably the finest public building in Washington, and back to the White House "*en re* presentation of painting to Prest & Mrs. Harding by Sulgrave Institution" (May 30, 1922).

June arrived. "Spent the day at my office working up financial plan for Freer Endowment & for a personal gift to the Smithsonian" (June 1, 1922). Occasionally close attention to the fine print can yield interesting details. The Smithsonian finances are complicated. The basic fund, consisting of Smithson's money and some accumulated interest, is held by the Treasury. Various other small funds had been donated over the years, and eventually Walcott was able to get them into a consolidated fund, easier to administer. Two new line items were in this fund at the end of the 1922 fiscal year. The report of the executive committee lists one of them as "Charles D. and Mary Vaux Walcott research fund," at $11,500.00. There are no further details.

On June 6, 1922, Walcott signed an indenture donating $11,300 worth of securities to the Smithsonian Institution; this rated a note in his diary. He gave a hundred shares of preferred stock in the California Electric Generating Company and twenty shares, preferred, in the Electric Bond and Share Company; there were no buggy-whip manufacturers in Walcott's portfolio. The fund was for geological and paleontological investigations and for publishing the results of these studies. Walcott also added a couple of interesting provisions, with an eye to the future. For the first hundred years after his death, half the net income was to be added to the principal, together with the income from any additions to the fund. He left a loophole that the provisions could be changed by a two-thirds vote of the Board of Regents. This is vintage canny Walcott! Walcott's scheme for increasing the fund has not since been modified by the regents.

Financial arrangements out of the way, Walcott could get on with other affairs. The trustees of the National Parks Association met, and they dined with the Merriams. "Mary & I went down river with Mrs. Tho's Walsh's picnic steamboat party. Full moon & cool air. Left wharf 5:30 P.M. returned 1:15 A.M. Dancing by old & young. Senators & clerks. A curious & instructive sign of the times" (June 9, 1922). Now, there is social commentary.

The June rush began. Walcott went to the dentist again early and spent a full Saturday cleaning up odds & ends at the office. "Hot and humid weather. After dinner we cut off rosebuds for an hour & then turned out on the sleeping porch to cool off" (June 11, 1922). Fortunately, the weather broke; "Last night's storm cooled the air and revivified all nature" (June 12, 1922)—what an elegant word. Dr. Hale came in for a meeting of the NRC executive committee and dined with it. A lot of business was transacted, and Walcott felt justified in relaxing and taking a motor trip for the day to Gunston Hall, a colonial plantation along the Potomac River. "The old colonial house & hedges are most attractive" (June 13, 1922).

"Clearing up last things at the office & house including mss of short paper on new formation names. Packing at home in evening" (June 16, 1922). Walcott was in his office Saturday morning, but that evening he and Mary caught the 6:20 sleeper for Buffalo. They spent Sunday with Helen-Louise and Evelyn, no longer baby Evelyn, before leaving Monday morning for Toronto. That evening, they were on the familiar track west.

They stopped off in Medicine Hat, Alberta, for half a day so that Mary could collect flowering cacti; her painting of flowers was growing more serious each season. On Friday morning they were in camp on Tunnel Mountain near Banff; thirteen of the horses had arrived from the government ranch, and they (people not horses) were properly fed by Arthur. It was a promising start. Two days later, the Walcott party camped at Buffalo Park. Walcott fussed around getting supplies while the men had the horses shod and put out to pasture. Two days later, however, it was evident that not all was well: "Owing to delay in getting to camp we have lost nearly a week of good weather and opportunity" (June 27, 1922).

Walcott procured the necessary permits and purchased a few more supplies while the men initiated the horses into the concept of pulling a wagon. "Owing to new men & difficulties with new horses we are moving slowly in getting ready for the trail. Happily we are well altho tired as result of long winter in town" (June 29, 1922). "This is our ninth wedding day—We have had eight happy years together & hope for more if such is in the book of life for us" (June 30, 1922).

This year Walcott had come west earlier than usual, but the party was still in camp. Horse trouble ensued, although not from the new animals. A horse named Eagle was injured in an accident and had to be left to heal; it ended up permanently out of service. "Ginger & Spike have struck out [escaped] so here we are for a day or two longer" (July 1, 1922).

They spent two more days in Buffalo Park, with vague reports of the missing horses' having been spotted twenty-three miles down the Bow River Valley, and with Morley Indians in pursuit. "Moved camp to Hillsdale. Mary & I went out on buckboard & men on horses with 7 pack animals" (July 4, 1922). They spent a day settling in that camp.

"I went up Ranger canyon with Jesse to repair trail & make a campsite for work on the Mons formation. Had a tumble and bruised myself up a bit" (July 6, 1922). It was more serious than that, though Walcott made light of the matter in a letter: "Today I am in camp as a result of not watching my footsteps in a rocky canyon. It was a combination of smooth quartz boulder & hob nailed shoes—Result bruised knee—elbow and hand and a lump on top of head—Not at all serious but inconvenient. The mountains are shrouded in mist this morning and temperature 45°. A thunder storm last eve cooled & cleaned the air of forest fire smoke. A fresh layer of snow covers the old snow above 2000 feet. Mrs. Walcott has gone to a Ranger cabin to telephone to Banff in the hopes of getting our mail sent out."[9]

Walcott wrote further of the injury in his journal: "A quiet wet day in camp. Read & fumed over my knee as the open skinned spots are infected & much irritated" (July 9, 1922). This was a seventy-two-year-old, out among horses, long before penicillin was even thought about, let alone any of the later antibiotics. "Spent most of day trying to burn out 'proud flesh' in abrasion on knee. Am unable to do any work or walk freely" (July 10, 1922). One can almost see the old gentleman grimacing from the pain.

While Jesse Anderson went to recover the two missing horses, which had been finally tracked down, Walcott and Mary tried a buckboard ride to a ranger's cabin. It was painful for him; the knee was a long way from healed, and matters otherwise were not getting better. "Horse stepped on Ray's toe & crippled him for the day. Cricket got mixed up in fence wire & cut hind leg under fetlock. My knee improving" (July 13, 1922). Cricket was what one would call a mixed blessing, like the faithful family retainer who always broke pieces of the best china. Walcott hoped to get out in a day or two; "Jesse brot in the horses but it was too late to ride" (July 14, 1922). Two more days were spent in camp; by now nearly a month had gone by with no results whatsoever. So far as known, Walcott never cursed, but he must have muttered.

"With Mary & Jesse went up Ranger Canyon to examine contact of Devonian & Ozarkian on south side. No trace of Sarbach (Ordovician). We collected a few fossils & returned early in afternoon to rest as the trail is a hard one. Mary & I walked to Ranger station after dinner" (July 18, 1922). Finally, there was a bit of fieldwork.

A few words of explanation might be appropriate. First, is "Ozarkian," a concept of E. O. Ulrich, for an interval between the Cambrian, the upper part of which he had restricted, and the Ordovician, the lower boundary of which Ulrich had also wanted to change. Walcott was one of the few to accept Ulrich's notions. The majority of the professional geologists never used "Ozarkian," and today most geologists have never heard of this proposed period of time. The path of the history of science is littered with discarded ideas. Second is the matter of the missing Sarbach Formation. At an unconformity, some rocks are missing; this is the essence of the term. Either they were never deposited originally or they were eroded away before the overlying rocks were deposited. If the surface of an unconformity is irregular, rocks of a formation that has otherwise been eroded away may be preserved locally in low places on the surface of the unconformity. Walcott may have been searching for such a remnant.

After that one day in the field, two days passed in looking for a new campsite and going to Banff in the buckboard for supplies. "Unable to find man that we wish for a trip north" (July 20, 1922). This was definitely not a good season. Smoke from forest fires made it worse, but following a rain there was finally a good day. "Packed up & moved camp to Lake Louise station on C.[anadian] P.[acific] R.[ailroad,] a tedious ride as the motor road is rough in places. Camped near the Park Wardens station opposite depot. Found warden Chas Phillips & family well & as courteous as in 1921. We dined with them" (July 24, 1922). Sidney Phillips, born in 1917, would write an account of his growing up at Lake Louise for his children. For the period when he was a young boy his dates are understandably a little hazy, but he would recall the Walcotts coming to dinner, and that might have been the meal mentioned above. He would describe the arrivals of the Walcotts from Washington.

> The first that happened was that Arthur would arrive with all his paraphernalia for camping. Arthur was the Walcott's hired man who ran the camp for them. He was baker, cook, waiter, and jack of all trades. Arthur was black and in fact he was the first black man that I had ever seen who was not a porter on the railroad. Arthur had short white curly hair, wasn't too tall as I remember, and it had been said that he was quite influential in Washington, D.C., where he was the unofficial mayor of black Washington. Arthur would proceed to erect the tents: one was the Walcotts' private quarters, a second was the cook house and dining room and sort of lounge area, and the third was where the supplies, equipment, and food were stored, and it was also Arthur's bedroom. . . .
>
> The tents were set up fairly close to our log cabin because, in the summer, we were able to run a water pipe from the [railroad] roundhouse to a spot quite close to our house. Arthur and the Walcott's took advantage of our running water, and also our large two-holer privy. Arthur baked regularly and we were the recipients of pies, cookies, and other goodies that he cooked. You can imagine how a couple of small boys enjoyed running to Arthur's several times each day to get cookies. He always seemed glad to see us.
>
> When the Walcott's left they generally gave Mother and Dad most of the food items that were left over. . . . One thing that used to intrigue me was the hominy grits they used. . . . [T]hey used to bring up a big sack which weighed about 50 lbs, or more and I think there was generally more than half of it left to give us. . . . Other things that were left over included such things as baking powder, flour, canned goods, and some things that we had never seen in Canada back at that time. It was much like Christmas.[10]

There is both written and oral evidence of Arthur Brown as superb cook; one rumor is that he was a crack shot and when the camp was low on meat, he was both hunter and butcher.

Walcott added a bit of color in his diary: "Sent Ray Bell home & Jesse V. Anderson quit and left on evening train. In all my 40 years of life on the trail I have never had two more inefficient useless men in service. Engaged Paul Stevens who began work in the morning." That fall Walcott immortalized his efforts in print. "The first half of the season was unfavorable owing to dense fire smoke and inefficient trail men, but the latter part of August and all of September fine weather and capable field men enabled the party to push the work vigorously" (Walcott 1923, 1).

Walcott also hired William H. Shea to assist, and by the following day it was "Paul & Bill," unexpected informality for Walcott, but a sign that matters were improving in camp. The party moved to the Pipestone River and continued upstream to the upper meadow. "I went fishing p.m. & caught 20 fine brook trout" (July 29, 1922). No doubt, things were improving.

The Walcotts moved over Pipestone Pass to the head of the Clearwater River. "Found tent site & poles as we left them Sept 23d 1921 when the ground was covered with snow" (July 30, 1922). Walcott had sent some fossils from the 1920 season to Edwin Kirk, one of the USGS paleontologists office in the Museum, and later had written him. "I am very glad to get the identifications of the various lots, especially those of the lower Banff limestone. In the event of my going over Pipestone Pass next summer would you care to have a larger collection made? There are quantities of material, but the difficulty of getting at it is considerable, owing to its being above timber line and quite a distance from any feasible camp site."[11]

"At camp until 3 P.M. when Mary & I went over to base of long south cliff & found a mass of broken up Mons limestone (upper) that appeared to have come from beneath the Sarbach" (July 31, 1922). "Out all day on ridge N&S–facing upper Clearwater Canyon, it is across the south branch of the Clearwater. We collected a few lower Mons fossils but the fauna is poorly preserved. The warm, smoky weather is very trying as no photographs can be taken" (August 1, 1922). "Out on the Devonian rocks with Mary. We failed to find any good fossils. Returned to camp early, as the heat & mosquitoes made it difficult to work" (August 2, 1922). "Mary & I searched for Devonian fossils but without success. Another disagreeable August day" (August 3, 1922). Perhaps the able field men and the twenty brook trout were snares and delusions.

"All out after fossils in lower part of Sarbach formation. By using dynamite we brot in quite a collection of the Receptaculitidae. Rain came at dinner time & continued during night" (August 4, 1922). Using dynamite is not a generally accepted field procedure. When one is dealing with a massive limestone, however, this may be the only means of breaking it up. As to receptaculitids, picture a fossil vaguely like the head of a sunflower and then argue whether it is an animal or a plant. Some of the critical information about these forms comes from the study of thin-sections, so dynamite did no major harm in breaking them. In the final analysis, broken fossils are better than no fossils, if the aim is to give a geologic date to a formation at a particular place.

Walcott slept in on the following day; it had not been easy collecting. Mary and Bill went off riding, and the following day they moved back across Pipestone Pass, getting the tents up just before a storm. "All slept late. Mary painting on sketches of wildflowers all day. Went fishing & caught a fine mess of brook trout. Paul also brot in a lot in afternoon. Cool at night & a camp fire was in order" (August 7, 1922). Perhaps Mother Nature was not so bad after all.

They moved to the camp on Red Deer River that had been occupied in 1921. "The forest fire smoke is dense—blowing in from southwest" (August 8, 1922). "A most exasperating day on acct of heat flies & mosquitoes. About camp as my interior was on a strike" (August 9, 1922). "Out all day with Mary & Bill on Fossil Mtn. Found a new fossil zone in upper Mons. Raw cold wind and rain began to fall 6:30 P.M. Paul returned [from Lake Louise] with a quantity of mail" (August 10, 1922). Despite the rain, finding a new fossil zone made life very much better. Bill went to get a new horse, Paul was cutting a trail to Lake Douglas, and Walcott was reading proofs for the last part of SMC volume sixty-seven.

This is a relatively small paper formally describing features of formations that Walcott had mentioned in one of the "Explorations" pamphlets without giving the necessary details, such as thicknesses and lithologic composition of the rock in the formation. The work was simple and straightforward, short and without illustrations, yet it did not come out until March 5, 1923. That kind of delay, especially for the secretary, was most unusual.

There was snow one night in this camp, which made for interesting photographs. "Out on Fossil Mountain all day with Mary. Measured upper part of Mons formation & we collected fossils from three zones. This is the first really fine day for work since we came to the mountains" (August 14, 1922). There is nothing like a good day to drive away previous gloom. Rain started early the next morning, but Walcott took the day to catch up on correspondence. Regent Alexander Graham Bell had died, and the secretary penned a few lines to his widow. He also wrote CIW President Merriam.

The rain is gently pattering on our tent as it has been doing for the past 48 hours. We are thankful as the forest fire menace has been a very real one. Not only in B.C. to the west but in the Clearwater forest on the north and the scrub on the foothills to the east.

An extensive burn north of Golden has put an end to the work I had hoped to do on that side of the Cordillera trough. We have met with much success in this area. A section exposed just above the camp [illegible] has yielded many fossils and given us a firm base for the Ordovician, Sarbach formation. We passed along its base last September in a fine snowstorm.

We hope to secure 4 mountain sheep for the National Museum after Sept 1st. The big rams begin to seek lower levels & their mates by Sept 15th and they have a fine coat of hair. They are not troubled by theories of evolution & theology, so we will relegate the latter to the future and be happy & content in our 12x14 cotton cloth home. We are well and having a fine season. Mrs. Walcott has made 15 wildflowers sketches and we are both free of that "tired feeling" of last June.[12]

"Mary sketching flower of yarrow (moonshine). I read, worked up geologic notes & slept" (August 16, 1922). Camp life surely has its good days. "Mary & I went out on slope of Fossil Mt. in search of graptolites, poor success. Returned to camp for cameras & went up on slope north of camp & photographed Mt. Douglass & ridge east & west" (August 17, 1922). Despite what was generally a poor season for photography, Walcott took advantage of the few opportunities and once again brought back some superb panoramas; Mary's photographic eye was as good or better than her husband's. As to graptolites, as may have been remarked before, most look like pencil marks on shale, but are not as interesting. However, there were some pretty ones illustrated in the "Explorations" pamphlet for 1922.

Mary and Walcott rode to the ridge at the head of the north side of the Red Deer River. The rocks were Devonian in age—no surprise here. They went back to Fossil Mountain to collect from the Mons Formation, but the pickings were slim. "Camp moved to upper end of Lake Douglass canyon valley. A rather rough slow trail. All settled in spruce grove about 400 feet below timberline by 8 P.M." (August 20, 1922). It was a hard Sunday but a good campsite. "This beautiful valley is only 12 to 15 miles (19.3 to 24 km) in a direct line east and northeast of Lake Louise Station. . . . This superb canyon valley with its forests, lakes, glaciers, and mountain walls and peaks should be opened up to the mountain tourist who has the energy to ride along a fine Rocky Mountain trail from Lake Louise" (Walcott 1923, 8). Thus, in the fall, back in Washington, the rough trail was to smooth quite a bit.

Walcott had a chance to take more photographs and collect from the Mons Formation; he spent several days, but with limited success. "A fine day. Completed section [of Mons] down to Lyell formation. We found the Hungia fauna in lower part of Mons formation. Out all day with Mary" (August 26, 1922). That trilobite told Walcott where he was, in a time sense. Walcott summarized his work for the general public. "The measured geologic section was from the base of the Devonian, above Lake Gwendolyn, across the canyon to the deep cirque below Halstead Pass, where the great Lyell limestone forms the rest of the ridge. The section includes the Ozarkian Mons formation down to the Lyell formation of the upper Cambrian" (Walcott 1925, 7). The party had two more days in the area after the section was completed.

This portrait of Walcott, age thirty-eight, was taken in 1888 during the International Congress of Geologists, which Walcott attended on his honeymoon with Helena and ten years after he joined the U.S. Geological Survey. Photograph by Maull and Polyblank, Picadilly, London. Reproduced by permission of the Geological Society of London, Number P51/46.

Portrait photograph of Smithsonian Institution Secretary Walcott,
late September or early October 1908, by Bach Brothers, New York.
SIA, no. 2000-2032.

The only known picture of the Walcott family, taken at Olmstead, Utah, in 1909. *Left to right:* Sidney Stevens Walcott (age seventeen); Charles Doolittle Walcott, Jr. (age nineteen); Charles Doolittle Walcott (age fifty-nine); Helena Stevens Walcott, "our mother" (age fifty-one); Benjamin Stuart Walcott (age thirteen). *Seated,* Helen Breese Walcott (age fifteen). SIA, no. 83-14107.

Lunch at Burgess pass, 1910. *Left to right:* Mrs. Burling; Lancaster D. Burling, Walcott's assistant; unidentified child; Sidney; Helen, partially hidden; and Helena Walcott. SIA, no. 85-11428.

Camp at the fork of Moose River (Mount Robson area), July 22, 1912. Preparing marmots for the taxidermists, Clausen Otto, one of the guides, is sharpening an axe next to Sidney Walcott; Walcott, wearing a disreputable field hat (a redundancy), is standing. Harry Blagden, a friend of Sidney, who replaced the ill Charlie Walcott, is seated facing Sidney. Doc Burgan, another guide/hunter is to the right. SIA, no. 82-3134.

Leaving the Smithsonian building after a meeting of the Board of Regents at which the first Langley Medal was awarded, February 10, 1910. *Left to right,* Walcott, Wilbur Wright, Alexander Graham Bell, and Orville Wright. Taken on the east side of the Castle, this photograph shows the new museum across the Mall, behind Walcott but obscured by trees. SIA, no. 82-3350.

Walcott and Glenn H. Curtiss on Lake Keuka, New York, in the pusher seaplane *America*. Presumably this was taken during the first trials of the Langley aerodrome in May 1914, but it is not mentioned in Walcott's diary. SIA, no. 82-3219.

Walcott in the Grand Canyon down the trail from Indian Garden, 1915. He is standing on the Cambrian sandstone and looking north into the Precambrian rocks of the Granite Gorge. In his hand is either a compass or, less likely, binoculars. Note his leggings. At that time Indian Garden was a commercially run campground on what has been renamed the Bright Angel Trail. SIA, no. 30166.

Arthur Brown, "an assistant for all seasons," in an undated photograph taken in a camp in the southern Canadian Rockies. SIA, no. 31656.

Annelida-Polychaete Worm *Canadia spinosa* Walcott (approximately four times its natural size). USNM, no. 83929c. Photograph by Chip Clark, National Museum of Natural History.

Walcott in his anteroom laboratory in the Castle, between the secretary's office and the reception area, ca. early 1920s. Behind him are two cases holding drawers of fossils. The size of this tiny space is indicated approximately by the door frame and person to the right. Library of Congress.

The aircraft building south of the Castle, forerunner of the National Air and Space Museum. This prefabricated hanger was to be erected at Bolling Field in Washington, D.C., but was diverted to the Smithsonian grounds for easy access by the foreign purchasing commissions during World War I. The artillery piece and the tank are part of the "war collection." This area is now part of the Haupt Garden, with two museums below the surface. SIA, no. A33465.

Mary Vaux Walcott in camp. Walcott, a citizen of the United States, flew the American flag (then with 48 stars); and because he was working in British territory, he flew the Union Jack, as Canada did not yet have its own flag. As a token of his career from 1879–1907, he also flew the flag of the U.S. Geological Survey. Other pictures show that he also flew the Geological Survey of Canada flag, as he was affiliated with that organization during most of his years in Canada. SIA, no. 89-6346.

Tenth annual meeting of the National Advisory Committee for Aeronautics, 1925. Orville Wright is near the rear of the room to the left of the standing John Victory. Walcott is seated to the extreme right. National Archives and Records Service, Archives II, College Park, Maryland.

Walcott in tails during the dedication
of the National Academy of Sciences
building, April 1924. Members File,
National Academy of Sciences;
reproduced by permission.

Walcott on the Burgess Shale trail with Mount Burgess in the background, 1924.
SIA, no. 83-11112.

Walcott stands with the marble bust of him sculpted by Morris Dykaar (*left*).
SIA, no. 99-3029.

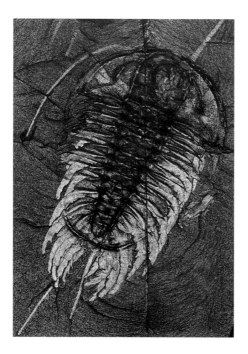

A Burgess Shale trilobite with legs and antennae preserved. *Olenoides serratus* (Rominger) was formerly placed in *Neolenus* (USNM, no. 58589), approximately 0.8 times natural size. Photograph by Chip Clark, National Museum of Natural History.

"Camp moved back to head of Red Deer River. No special incident. W*m* H. Shea left camp on foot 7 P.M. for Lake Louise. He was mad because he could not use cowboy camp manners at dinner table. A capable packer but heedless, egotistic & unreliable" (August 29, 1922). There must have been more of a story, though Walcott was not telling it. His words are a strong judgment against Mr. Shea, but Walcott was the boss, and there were limits to behavior when a lady is present.

Paul went into Lake Louise and came back two days later with mail and M. S. Baptie, who stayed until nearly the end of September. Mr. Baptie not only watched his manners but was interested in the work. More than a year later, Walcott sent to the head curator of geology a very large chuck of rock received from Baptie. "He wrote me he had found some unusual specimens, and said that he would send one on. I think the concretion weathered out of the carboniferous Banff shale. Please acknowledge the specimen to Baptie and tell him something about it. He had a hard job carrying it several miles in a rucksack on his back."[13] Concretions are common and generally of little interest, but it was nice of Walcott to reply with more than a simple thank-you.

Camp twelve was at Lake Louise Station. Walcott and Mary spent a day repacking and then "went to Glacier House B.C. for a few days rest & to measure recession of Illaccilewat [*sic*] glacier" (September 5, 1922). "Mary measured the recession of the Illaccilewat glacier. It has retreated 1510 feet since 1910 & is a very dead glacier" (September 7, 1922). Those who suggest the globe is warming assemble evidence of this sort. It rained for a day but relented the next, so the couple could engage in blackberry picking before they returned to Lake Louise. All was well in camp.

"Packed & moved camp along motor road to one mile west of Castle. . . . All tired at night as it is our first day out with wagons" (September 10, 1922). There is no question that though Walcott's enthusiasm for fieldwork remained, his stamina was waning. They crossed Vermillion Pass, moved down the river, and camped again. It rained the next day and was thoroughly disagreeable; one should not try to move wagons in the rain on a dirt road. They moved camp downstream to where the river turns west and joined the engineers in charge of constructing a new motor road.

Geologists view the countryside from a different perspective than does than the average tourist. "Rode up Simpson river A.M. Found nothing of interest. The Vermillion river canyon is eroded in Chancellor formation shales from Tacoma Creek to Simpson river (16 *mi*). It then crosses west thru the Ottertail formation" (September 14, 1922). If one knows the sequence of formation names in the area, the jargon makes sense.

Walcott puttered around the camp for a day waiting to talk to the chief engineer of the new road. The next day the party crossed the Kootenay using the new bridge instead of the traditional crossing. They rested a day at camp sixteen of the season before Walcott began local observations in the Mitchell Range. "Found a thick series of thin bedded limestone but not any fossils" (September 18, 1922); at least there were trout waiting to be caught. "Mary & I went to the canyon of yesterday but did not find any fossils. The limestone may belong to the Goodsir formation" (September 13, 1922). In the absence of fossils, Walcott did what any other field geologist would do; he took his best guess, based on the general structure of the area and the way the rock itself looked.

The wagons were packed, and the party moved over Sinclair Pass into the Columbia River drainage and camped about two miles south of Radium Hot Springs. "Out all day with Mary. We collected Devonian fossils above a white quartzite (Ghost River) and the Symphisurina fauna of the Ozarkian 5 & 4 mi up the canyon" (September 21, 1922). On the first day of fall, Walcott was busy packing the fossils while Mary was out sketching plants. "Mary & I went up the Sinclair canyon. I measured the sub-Wilson quartzite & we drove up to the pass. Took a number of photographs" (September 23, 1922). "We found Billings *Ella coloradoensis* along with Symphisurina in locality at bridge No. 3" (September 24, 1922). To translate, Elkanah Billings had been the first full-time paleontologist employed by the Geological Survey of Canada; Walcott found specimens of one of the species that Billings had described. (Walcott probably should have emphasized the name of the other fossil, but he was writing for his own use and he knew what he meant.)

"Fine day. We went up Sinclair canyon & while Mary collected Devonian fossils, I went after Ordovician fossils beneath the Mt. Wilson quartzite and found a few. Out all day" (September 25, 1922). A few years earlier, Walcott had reported a major unconformity on the front of the range. This area gave details on some of the rocks eroded at the unconformity. "Collected a lot of lower Mons fossils at third bridge & graptolites ½ *mi* below fifth bridge on motor road" (September 26, 1922). The new road was a blessing, and the time Walcott had spent with the engineers to ensure he could use it and also find out what they had seen during construction had been time well spent. They collected a few more fossils the next day and finished up just as the weather began to turn bad.

The group spent a couple more days in camp—Walcott walking, Mary sketching, and both taking a few local photographs—but the fieldwork was over. The goat hunt mentioned in the letter to Merriam never materialized. They packed up, found another locality for Mons fossils, and moved on to Lake Windermere for a few days with friends. Arthur joined them en route to Banff; they said goodbye to Paul and his wife and spent two days packing up. That evening

Arthur left for Washington, and the following morning Walcott and Mary were on the Toronto Express. They saw granddaughter Evelyn, who had broken a collarbone but was otherwise flourishing. Two days in Buffalo meant two trips to the dentist before they headed for home.

Helen met them at the station. All was in order at home and at the Smithsonian, but after one day in Washington, they left for a quick trip to Bryn Mawr to attend a funeral. Upon their return, Walcott "went to Potomac Park garden & then to my office. Attending to mail & callers until 4:30 P.M. Under the able direction of . . . Ravenel, Dorsey & heads of departments the administrative work has gone along well since I left in June" (October 14, 1922). Walcott could go to church with an extra-clear conscience, not that he had trouble in that department.

Getting back into the Washington routine, Walcott "discussed with the Secretary of the Navy the use of the Presidential yacht 'Mayflower' to take NACA members to Langley Field" (October 16, 1922). The secretary agreed, and a fine time was had by all committee members. Life went on, with Mary coming very much into her own. She escorted members of the Garden Club of America to Mount Vernon. That evening, after a few brief talks, 180 people went to see her flower sketches, which were displayed in the Castle.

During the first half of the year, Mary traveled alone to Philadelphia fairly frequently, and this time, by contrast, Walcott took a solitary trip to New York. He visited with Helen and spent the night in her apartment rather than a hotel. The Carnegie Ex Comm and the Research Corporation occupied him, but Saturday he was back in Washington and on Sunday was at church services.

The month ended on a high, but quiet, note. Ground had been broken for the NAS building the first week in July, just about the time that Walcott had managed to wreck himself in Ranger Canyon. The groundbreaking had been done with a minimum of fuss, setting a pattern. The cornerstone was laid in the southwest corner on October 30, 1922, with simple ceremonies. Charles Doolittle Walcott, as president of the Academy, was the first to place cement under the stone, followed by members of the Academy and research council (Michaelson 1925, 3). A copper box containing documents was placed within the cornerstone; there were no speeches.

Until the time Joseph Henry became president, the Academy had wandered from pillar to post. In 1872, Henry obtained a legal determination, or perhaps he established it by force of character, that the permanent home of the Academy was in Washington, D.C. Thereafter the Smithsonian Institution had become the official address, and virtually all the annual meetings had been held in the various Smithsonian buildings. This was to change, finally.

"Routine, mail, interviews & labeling photographs took up the day" (November 3, 1922). "Routine etc.—Studying methods of work for s.i. Tired and sleepy in evening" (November 4, 1922). Walcott had been trying to raise money for the Smithsonian for years. In 1920, he had written to a few of the rich and powerful, along with several foundations, but he had been generally refused. After all, everyone knew that the Smithsonian was wealthy and that furthermore it was lavishly supported by the government. What everyone knew and the truth were far apart in this case. Clearly, another approach was needed to increase the endowment.

It was difficult to think what a new approach should be. "Have cold in head & neck for ten days so keep close to office" (November 10, 1922); there is no question but that his health was worse than in earlier years. Despite the cold, Walcott was a pallbearer at the funeral of the ambassador from Honduras; President Harding attended, and Walcott could hardly refuse. "At my office. Cold in head annoying. Not fit to go to New York to Nat. Acad. Meeting much to my regret" (November 13, 1922). An interesting matter was on the agenda, and grist for the "what if" game is whether Walcott would have changed matters if he had presided at the NAS council meeting.

Anti-evolution sentiments were on the rise in America. Prior to the fall meeting, John M. Clarke had been constituted as the chairman and sole member of the Committee on Organic Evolution. He rendered to the council his report, which included this assessment: "The leaders in this outbreak are busied with lampooning the best thought and foundations of the highest philosophy which the human understanding has attained. They are casting obloquy on the highest endowments of human reason. They are putting ignorance on a pedestal and bowing down before it in worship. They even go further and in the fancied strength of number, are entering upon a campaign of mendacity, menace and contumely."[14]

Clarke—who had a way with words—urged the Academy to speak out in support of evolution. The council moved, however, that it was inexpedient to take any action. Slightly more than half a century later, the NAS distributed a pamphlet supporting the concept of evolution. Some tasks take more time than others.

Walcott recognized the importance of evolution and more significantly the importance of fighting anti-intellectualism, as one might see from his written remark to Merriam about evolution and theology. Walcott, however, was generally otherwise engaged. "Looking after odds & ends & arranging about my personal research" (November 14, 1922). An informal NACA meeting convened in his office, and "at 4:30, attended informal conference of committees *en re* union of N.Y. Ave. Ch. & Church of Covenant" (November 15, 1922). The following evening Walcott presided when the matter was discussed by the congregation.

Though Walcott did not make it to the fall NAS meeting, the organization was clearly on his mind, as is evident in this letter to the president of Johns Hopkins

University. "The old days of the Academy have passed largely as the result of the development and activities during the war. We hope that the April meeting of the Academy will be held in its new home, or at least the building will be so far advanced that the members of the Academy will obtain a full realization of what it is to be when completed and equipped. You must certainly endeavor to come over to that meeting. My term as President will expire at that time, for which I am duly thankful, as I wish to withdraw as far as possible from all outside activities in order to concentrate on certain research work and the interests of the Smithsonian."[15]

One difference between religion and construction is that in the latter, man proposes and the contractor disposes; there was to be no new home for the NAS in 1923. Once more Academy members met in the Museum.

Sunday afternoon at the office had again become standard. "Routine & getting illustrations out for Exploration paper" (November 16, 1922). These pamphlets were a fine means of explaining the work, and they constitute one of the many hidden monuments to Walcott scattered within the SI structure. The year after Walcott's death, they were issued separately from the *Smithsonian Miscellaneous Contributions*, and the series continued until World War II.

"A quiet day at the office & laboratory. Our collections from Sinclair canyon arrived & when opened were found to be in good order. This has been a rather monotonous week at the office" (November 25, 1922). Church was nice, but the next few days were monotonous, each of them, as Walcott put it, "a typical November day." The Vaux family arrived the night before Thanksgiving. "Helen came in time for dinner—so we had a fine party" (November 30, 1922). December began with "a broken up quiet day at the office" (December 1, 1922), while Mary visited with her family. The next day they toured a radio station, and then the Vaux family left for Philadelphia. Another cold kept Walcott home from the office for a day.

"At my office during the day working on plans for development of Smithsonian. Lunched with Henry White to meet the great Frenchman [Georges] Clemenceau, Genl. [Tasker H.] Bliss & Secretaries [Charles Evans] Hughes, [Andrew] Mellon, [John W.] Weeks & [Edwin] Denby" (December 4, 1922). Walcott went to a couple of evening lectures, decided on several administrative changes, and moved along the process of getting ready for the Commission on the National Gallery. The commission had two meetings with no problems, and there were no problems either when the Board of Regents met two days later. This led into the CIW committee meeting, which preceded yet another meeting.

"Meeting of Trustees Carnegie Inst. Wash'n 10–12:30[.] I resigned from Executive Committee after 20 years service. I need the time for other things & my work for C.I. is done with Merriam as President. Attending the Smithsonian matters P.M." (December 15, 1922). Saturday there were no meetings, just appearances before the Appropriations Committee in the morning for the NACA and the afternoon for the Smithsonian. For a December, it was a routine week.

The next week was quieter. The last points of the Freer estate were settled. Administration was down to odds and ends, but Walcott was feeling tired and chilly. The NACA met and drafted a letter to President Harding concerning the airmail service of the Post Office Department. Two more days of routine, and then the clerks were given Saturday afternoon off as a Christmas bonus. The Buffalo branch of the family came in, and Helen arrived that evening. That Sunday they all went to church. The Christmas celebration on Monday was the best in years.

On Tuesday Walcott was back in the office, and on Wednesday he had a small, informal meeting to consider the best way to raise money for the institution. "At my office during day engaged in routine & study of Freer Art Gallery matters. Conference with John Lodge [and] Miss Rhoades at Freer Building" (December 29, 1922).

The end of December brought another honor to Secretary Walcott.

> Your telegram congratulating the A.A.A.S. [American Association for Advancement of Science] upon my election as President, came shortly before that from Dr. Livingston notifying me of the election. I have rarely been more surprised, as no suggestion or intimation had come to me that there was a possibility of such a happening. I have long been a believer in the American Association and its influence and power for good constructive work in connection with science in America, and I will do what I can to assist in its work. It is a great honor for any man to be elected President of the Association, and I thoroughly appreciate it; but at the same time I wish you had selected a man in the prime of life who has the vitality, energy, and time that should be given to the duties of office. The council is a strong one, and Dr. Livingston has the affairs of the association well in hand, but in the present shifting conditions of the scientific, economic and educational activities of our country and the world it is exceedingly desirable to have as strong leadership as possible for so great an organization as the Association.[16]

The AAAS was even more of an orphan than the NAS. There was a tiny staff, which ever since the days of Secretary Baird had hidden out in the Smithsonian Castle. Between Jacques Cattell's editing *Science* in New York and the secretaryship's moving from place to place, apart from an annual meeting there was little that the organization could do. At the funeral of the ambassador of Honduras, Walcott had mentioned to Dr. Livingston a permanent home for AAAS. That might have been the reason that Walcott was nominated, or it may have been coincidence.

Sunday, after a fine sermon by Dr. Wood, Mary and Walcott walked to the Smithsonian for their normal Sunday picnic lunch. "New Years eve finds us well and happy & our children the same. Helen in New York, Sidney in Buffalo at his home. No special event in our life in 1922. My research work has moved slowly but some results should appear in 1923 if I remain well" (December 31, 1922).

A late breakfast on Monday started the New Year, followed by a run to the office and calls on half a dozen members of the cabinet; a visit to President Harding was bypassed. "Occupied with duties as Secty of Smithsonian Institution 9 A.M. to 4:30. Considering many matters connected with the Freer Gallery of Art & general research at the problem of research funds. My personal research is moving very slowly at present. At home in evening reading mss" (January 2, 1923). Walcott seldom used such weighty words as "duties of the Secretary" in connection with administration, so these must have been serious cogitations.

Congratulations poured in on Walcott's election to the presidency of the AAAS. *Science* published a biographical sketch (Livingston 1923). The positive was balanced by a negative: "John B. Henderson Jr. died last night. A good friend gone" (January 4, 1923). The Hendersons, father and son, had been stalwart members of the Board of Regents for decades. For almost that long, "Henderson's Castle" had been a landmark on the west side of Sixteenth Street. (When Prohibition was passed, Mrs. Henderson was to empty the cellar, and according to local legend, the wine was to flow down Meridian Hill for hours.) After the death of Alexander Graham Bell the previous summer, Mr. Henderson had been elected to the Executive Committee but served less than a year. Just at a time when Walcott needed support and help in an endowment drive, the most experienced people were lost.

To add an extra twist of the knife, Mrs. Alexander Graham Bell died. Fortunately, Mary had been scheduled to give an illustrated lecture at the church, and attending that kept meditating on the past to a minimum. Walcott went back to office routine and commented that the unsettled state of the world and other general problems had left him "only an hour for revising mss of Mons formation" (January 8, 1923). Another trip to the dentist did not help; on the other hand, both the Iowa and Ontario Apartment House meetings went well, the NACA meeting went well, and a Baird Memorial Committee was getting into action. After a reception at the British embassy, a visit from a geologist who had worked in China, plus several dinners out, the funerals faded.

All was not sweetness and roses, however. John Marr, the namesake of *Marrella*, sent Walcott a clipping from the *Times* commenting most unfavorably on Harding's Bureau of Efficiency, especially as it concerned museums. The article quoted Walcott as declaring that the system "added considerably to the duties of the officials." Marr wrote, "You must have had a hard time in meeting the necessary arrangement to accord with the scheme."[17] In his reply Walcott commented, "We have had a lot of reformers at work on Governmental problems the past two years, some of whom are doing good work, but most of them are impractical doctrinaires and their 'reforms' soon fall by the wayside."[18]

"A quiet day at my office & laboratory working a little over the Mons formation. Next thing to do is to get correct list of fossils" (January 11, 1923). A slight cold slowed his work. "Mary went to the McCormick supper & party. I felt tired stupid so remained at home to read & rest" (January 13, 1923). He was in Senator Lodge's office on Monday, for the issue of vacancies on the board of regents had not been resolved. The next day he was back at the Capitol. "Called to see Senator Smoot & [Francis E.] Warren 8:30 A.M. & 9 A.M. *en re* authority for building on S.I. grounds" (January 16, 1923). This was for a proposed National Gallery of Art.

With an informal assurance of a building site for a new art gallery, Walcott could get back to the manuscript on the Mons Formation. He spent two and a half hours with Charles Resser. This is one of the few indications in his diary of any direct assistance since Burling left, but everyone knew that Resser was Walcott's assistant, apart from his curatorial duties in the Museum's Department of Geology. Thereafter it was back to routine, except that Walcott skipped church. "As my teeth are all off in from upper jaw we went to S.I. about 11 A.M. to read look over papers etc." (January 21, 1923). Walcott must have developed quite a love/hate relationship with his dentist.

Walcott was able to put in another two hours work on the Mons manuscript before a distinguished French geologist, who was to be the next person to receive the NAS Mary Clark Thompson medal, came to town, and then the grippe hit. "We cancelled all dinner engagements" (January 25, 1923). Bed rest for more than a week was a necessity. "At my office 8:45–12:30 P.M. Dentist 12:45 to 1:30 P.M. to have new front upper teeth fastened to the old roots. A nap at home & 2 hours work on proof before dinner" (February 2, 1923). All must have gone fairly well with the dentist, for the next few days record only routine and preparation for the regents' meeting.

That meeting went as planned. Text for a pamphlet explaining the aims and needs of the institution was approved. The regents agreed with Walcott's concern as to the necessity for a new building devoted to art and history; he had been talking about this since 1919. Walcott mentioned that at his request the congressional regents had tacked onto the appropriations bill an amendment setting aside the northeast corner of the Smithsonian grounds. Walcott had not felt the need for such legislation in finding a site for the Freer Gallery; this was a more ambitious project, for it was both larger and, unfortunately, did not have a private philanthropist to fund construction.

The next day, ever hopeful, Walcott attended a meeting of the GWMA Finance Committee. He was well enough for a dinner planned earlier for the ambassador of Belgium. Two days later, the Walcotts had another formal dinner for the secretary of the navy. Mary had gone out for a few evenings, but Walcott was conserving his strength, and social activity outside his home was at a low ebb. "All dinners away from home cancelled as the grip cold still hangs about me & takes strength & pep out so that I am used up by evening each day" (February 16, 1923). He did not even attend a dinner in honor of the director of the British Museum. At times, without any question, Walcott was an old man.

On Sunday Walcott was still coughing, but he recovered rapidly. "A quiet effective day at Smithsonian. A few hours work on the Mons paper illustrations. At home 5–7 to meet some of Mary's friends" (February 13, 1923). The day before George Washington's birthday, the annual meeting of GWMA ensued, but no obvious dramatic improvements in that organization ensued; there simply was not enough money to build. Walcott went on to other things and accepted a bust of Jeanne d'Arc on behalf of the regents. Walcott attended a dinner at the Gridiron Club for "Uncle Joe" Cannon, who after many a year was losing his power at the House of Representatives (from Ste. Joan to "foul-mouth Joe" in twenty-four hours). After years on the Appropriations Committee, Cannon had been Speaker of the House from 1903 to 1911, and he was still enough of a power in politics to be on the cover of the first issue of *Time* magazine. Walcott finally got to church after the several Sundays wherein he was either ill or toothless. Unfortunately, the net result was the return of a cold.

Walcott struggled through another couple of days of routine, with a bit of time stolen for his manuscript. Then the Walcotts left for Beaufort, South Carolina. "My cold hangs about me & we are both more or less tired as the winter has been a rather trying one owing to changeableness of the weather" (February 28, 1923). They began March in the bright sunshine of the South.

Two days later Helen joined the couple. The most strenuous activity was crabbing, as a break from watching Mary sketch wildflowers. Of course, inside of a week Walcott was involved with the mail; he could not stand to be idle for long. "Working on Cambrian[-]Ozarkian paper A.M. & Mary painting flower of white pine. After dinner we went crabbing & caught a fine lot. Reading in evening" (March 12, 1923). To be honest, Walcott did not do all that much work. The third Sunday in Beaufort, the Walcotts had to miss church to catch the train. "We have a very pleasant visit & would like to remain another week" (March 18, 1923). The months in western Canada did not count as vacation, and Walcott judged the institution did not need him then.

When they arrived in Washington, Walcott went immediately to the office and his mass of mail. Inside of a few days administrative matters were under control, and Walcott was revitalized for research. The faunal lists and the resulting correlation of formations throughout North America were put aside for a more restricted topic: "I began working on brachiopods of Mons & other Ozarkian formations" (March 22, 1923). This was, geologically speaking, a slight upward extension though time of the fossils Walcott had described in U.S. Geological Survey monograph fifty-one. Under the heading of minor events, Walcott saw a movie at the Smithsonian about the excavations by Earle Douglass at what is now Dinosaur National Monument in Utah. Walcott's teeth went out of commission again, and so he and Mary gave church a miss.

Walcott started getting his camp outfit ready, for spring had clearly arrived in Washington, and summer would soon follow. The Smithsonian research committee met, the church trustees met, and to make a full day, Walcott conferred about the National Gallery of Art. On Friday, Walcott was back to his own research. "A quiet day at the Institution. This is my 73d birthday. I am fairly well and full of the joy of living & of interest in our home and my work. In evening over 60 geologists came to the house & we had a very enjoyable evening" (March 31, 1923).

April 1 was Easter Sunday; it was a cold, bright day in Washington, setting the tone for the beginning of the month. "This has been a quiet week: & I have done some work on the Cambrian brachiopods of the Ozarkian & Upper Cambrian of Alberta, Canada. Dr Resser is working on the trilobites for me" (April 7, 1923). Life was so much back to normal that Sunday afternoons were again spent at the office.

There were a few discussions concerning the NRC with Drs. Kellogg and Merriam, but nothing exciting transpired. Mary, now quite the polished lecturer, spoke to the Biological Society of Washington on wildflowers; Walcott must have taken some pride in her performance before a group that had been one of his own audiences four decades earlier. The National Parks Association council met, there were one or two more days of routine, and then the NAS came to town.

As a warm-up for his duties later in the year, the council of the AAAS met for a few hours, followed by the NAS council. Walcott spent three full days presiding at the Academy, handing out awards, and running elections. After a final dinner four long days later, he turned in early. "Correspondence, interviews, routine and a little work in my laboratory kept me occupied all day. At home in evening.—Am glad be out of office in Nat. Acad. after 25 years of service" (April 27, 1923). Walcott may have been out of office, but he was still deeply involved with the building committee. Despite Mr. Brockett's efforts, the building was still behind schedule.

The new NAS president was A. A. Michaelson, the first American to win a Nobel Prize. He wasted no time in writing Walcott: "I have received your resignation from a number of committees of the NA and wish to express my great re-gret, and hope that this action may be reconsidered. I would certainly appreciate the sacrifice as I am sure would every member of the Academy. Could you therefore be persuaded to continue? And if not on all the committees, at least on that on finance?"[19]

Walcott gave in and rejoined the Finance Committee. Even though he had loosened a few of the ties that bound him to the NAS, he continued with the NRC as second vice president and as chairman of the Division of Federal Relations.

Even with the Academy meeting over, there was hardly time for Walcott to catch his breath. Helen came in for a few day to attend a big event in the art world. "A broken up day on account of special view of Freer Gallery by Cabinet, Supreme Court & Regents" (May 1, 1923). As curator Lodge later wrote, "The autumn, winter, and early spring were largely devoted to the installation of exhibits and to other preparations for the opening of the gallery to the public on May 2" (Lodge 1925, 59).

The opening of the Freer stretched over several days, and when that concluded, Charles Moore and the Fine Arts Commission gave a dinner for Walcott. He had earned it. In the late spring of 1921, the contractor turned the building over to the Smithsonian. When Lodge was asked by reporters when the Freer would be ready for visitors, his reply was that it would be ready when finished and finished when ready—not the sort of response to engender warmth. Incidentally, Miss Rhoades received a permanent appointment after the exhibits were finally installed.

The Freer building is an architectural jewel. Charles A. Platt changed the plans several times to bring Mr. Freer's notion to hard reality, and the final result was a delight to the eye, as well as excellent exhibit space (Lawton and Merrill 1993). Quite understandably, architect Platt was appointed to the National Commission, but after a year he resigned, for a practical reason: if there was to be a National Gallery building, he wanted to submit a design for it.

Life moved on, and two days later Mary was again lecturing on wildflowers, this time to the Arts Club. The Walcotts were tired, so Sunday church gave way to an outing at Great Falls on the Potomac River. Except for a couple of meetings and a formal dinner or two, once the Freer was open the first half of May was fairly quiet. Helen left for the Pocono Mountains. "Took up administrative matters & routine during day. Sent plan of operations of Freer Gallery to Ex. Comm Members" (May 21, 1923). (Just for clarity, this was the executive committee of the Board of Regents, not of the Carnegie Institution of Washington.) At that meeting Secretary Walcott had his plan, and Curator Lodge had his plan, and later they were not to coincide.

Walcott attempted to extricate himself from the NACA, without success. Stratton had left the Bureau of Standards to become head of the Massachusetts

Institute of Technology and therefore no longer had a statutory seat on the NACA. Walcott wanted him to stay on and wrote another member about it:

> I have written Dr. Stratton that I would gladly withdraw from the Committee and have him appointed as the Smithsonian representative, but this has met with a strong protest from the membership of the Committee, as they feel I could be of service to the Committee in connection with its governmental relations, which includes the Congress and the departments. Thus far, Dr. Stratton and I have looked after these relations together, but with his removal from the city I shall have to call in the assistance probably of Admiral Taylor.
>
> If I remain on the committee, it has been suggested to me that your active interest in the Committee is not as great as it was during the war, and that possibly you would be willing to resign if you knew Dr. Stratton was to be appointed in your place. If I had known what was going to happen when you were here, we might have talked it over, as a letter is a very difficult and clumsy method of discussing such a matter. I think, however, you will understand and not hesitate to write me very freely about your feeling about it. If you wish to continue as a member, everyone will respect that feeling and have always felt that you were one of the valuable members and that you would be still more valuable if it practicable for you to attend the monthly meetings and take a more active part. Personally, I should like very much to drop out and would do so were not for the earnest desire that I remain, at least for the present.[20]

Stratton was reappointed to the NACA.

Less substantial commitments of time were also being reevaluated by Walcott. "I have been withdrawing from active participation in a number of organizations and feel that I must withdraw from all official connection with the National Parks Association. This is in order that I may give more time and energy to matters connected with the Smithsonian Institution and to the research work the data for which has been accumulating the past thirty years. What the organization needs is a group of young, vigorous men and women who will take hold and back you [that is, R. S. Yard] up as vigorously as you have worked for the Association in the past. Will you not present my resignation as Vice President at the annual meeting in June, and oblige."[21] At the June meeting no young, vigorous man or woman stepped forward. Walcott continued on with the financially struggling association and aided Yard's efforts to advertise the parks and garner public support for them.

The days were getting longer, and each evening Walcott put in an hour in the garden; that and walks with Mary were his training for the coming field season. Most of the middle of May rated only ditto marks in Walcott's diary. On the last

Sunday in May, Walcott was presented with the French Military Medal in honor of Stuart.

"At my office during day & clearing up odds & ends so as to leave tomorrow. Packing up last items in evening. We dislike to leave roses & fine days but there is work to be done in the Rockies & the call of the 'Wild' is strong" (May 28, 1923). On Tuesday, Walcott had a full day at the office, plus a quick trip to the cemetery to leave flowers, before he and Mary caught the 6:50 evening train to Buffalo. After a scant twenty-four hours with the Sidney Walcotts, they were off to Toronto and the West.

Walcott slept, commenting that it was too hot to do much else on the train. At 8:45 on June 4 they were in Banff, the earliest Walcott had ever come west. They spent the night with friends. The next day it was a quick trip to Lake Louise, a transfer, and up the Columbia River valley to Radium, the site of the hot springs, from which point he reported back to Washington.

> We arrived on schedule & found tents up & dinner ready. Soon our 18 boxes and rolls came up from the station & by 10 P.M. we were in our blankets en route to Slumberland wh we visited for 9 hours. Yesterday morning we all worked unpacking & getting things in order. At 3 P.M. a friend bro't his motor & we had a beautiful ride out along the foot of the Stanford Range & overlooking the Columbia river valley & beyond the many peaks & ridges of the Selkirk Mountains. A cup of tea with Mr. R. F. Bruce at his fine home on Lake Windermere & a surprise party in front of the Inveremere Hotel where we met Capt & Mrs. McCarthy & Mrs. Stone widow of Dr Stone who was killed two years ago. Also the manager of ranch K2 & the head game warden of the Windermere district. Capt. McCarthy leaves today for Geneva Switz.
>
> Please send R. R. Bruce Lake Windermere B.C. Can. Expl. pamphlets for 1919–20–21 if in stock. I gave him ours for 1922. He is a Scott [*sic*] that winters in London & summers on Lake Windermere. Send Mr. ?R. N. Stranach Supt R.M.P. Banff 20 copies of 1922 Expl. pamphlet of C.D.W. -------------
>
> Tell Mr. Hill that some one rolled 3 bottles of Wizard oil together in a bit of newspaper & outside a lot of manila paper. Two of the bottles were broken up, a small bottle escaped. Get a $10.00 bottle of Wizard Oil at Gilmans & send out. We use it on horse & humans.
>
> Will check up pky labels tomorrow. The last . . . on list is no.? Have some bring it up to date & send me copy. Tomorrow's mail may bring missing sack of mail. Mail comes twice a week. All well.[22]

Walcott's scribbles from the field had not improved with age, and if anything he was abbreviating more. If anyone could figure them out and if anyone could sit in Washington and discover the initials of the head of the Royal Mounted Police in Banff, it would be Chief Clerk Harry Dorsey. Despite the scribble,

Walcott clearly differentiated between the entire "Explorations" pamphlet and the separate printing of his part. The letter also indicates that Walcott applied the same methods in southern Canada that he used in Washington, namely, meet everyone of consequence in an area and tell them of one's research. As to the last loose end, there are still a few old-timers in Washington who remember Gilman's drugstore on Pennsylvania Avenue. The last paragraph is enigmatic. It is possible that mailing labels were printed or typed and numbered in sequence for the packages sent to Walcott. If one were lost, at least its general content would be known. He was a man who left little to chance if it could be avoided

The real test of an authentic old-timer in Washington is whether a person knows of the existence of the *Washington Herald*, later the *Times-Herald*, briefly the *Post* & *Times-Herald*, and now totally vanished. In its day this was a most respectable newspaper. The Sunday edition devoted a full page to a story on Walcott's coming season, his past work in the Canadian Rockies, and an accurate account of his life and career. A few of Walcott's postcards and letters from the field are mentioned. "A[rthur] is bringing up the horses up after their night on the mountain side, and rain is pattering on the tent."[23] The article noted the panorama photographs and Mary's paintings of flowers.

After one day in camp, the weather interfered. "High water in Sinclair creek compelled us to move camp to dry ground back of Capt. McCallangh house" (June 7, 1923), but it did not cause a setback. They found a few poorly preseved fossils in the Mons the following day, and that evening "Dr Edwin Kirk" arrived. Kirk was a USGS paleontologist who specialized in Silurian and Devonian but had a reputation of being able to determine the age of almost any group of fossils. (Kirk had joined the USGS in 1909 and was to die at his desk in the Museum in 1955. His career as an active field palaeontologist would abruptly end in 1935, when his leg was pinned under a slab of rock and part of it had to be amputated. Thereafter when Kirk walked, the squeak of his artificial leg echoed through the Museum corridors.)

Mary and Walcott collected from the Mons, and Kirk found an Upper Ordovician fauna at the mouth of Sinclair Canyon. "Mary & I out on 'Mons' all day collecting fossils from 'Saukia' zone & one above it with *Eoorthis* strongly ribbed & striated. Dr Kirk out on Silurian in Sinclair Canyon" (June 11, 1923). Translation: *Eoorthis* was a brachiopod, and since this shell was a new species, Walcott noted it to jog his memory.

Camp life settled down. Wet items from the previous night's rain were dried. Fossils were labeled and packed. A broken camera shutter was finally repaired. "With Kirk & Paul went up Sinclair Canyon & then up on a west spur of Cabin Mt. We found the *Ophileta* fauna of the Upper Mons about 5 to 700 feet beneath the Cabin Mt. quartzite. I now have 4 faunules in the Mons here which correspond to the Clearwater canyon section. Driven home early by rain" (June 15, 1923). When Walcott first began in geology, there had been an argument as to the validity of the Cambrian as a system; then had come a phase of argument about the sequence of Early, Middle, and Late Cambrian fossils; and now work was so detailed that he was correlating four different levels of fossils from one section to another. That is remarkable progress in geological precision during his lifetime.

A motor road up the canyon made life easier and work faster; it was the start of a technological revolution in fieldwork. The backcountry and the high mountains would still be physically difficult for geologists until the advent of helicopters, but the automobile made a dramatic difference. Prospecting for young fossil vertebrates in northwest Nebraska was still not like fieldwork in the Canadian Rockies, but there were some similarities. "The coming of the automobile has revolutionized the fossil hunting business. For one thing, it has greatly widened the range of practical field work. The old conditions limited it to a radius of five or ten miles from water and feed" (Colbert 1992, 162).

Late in life Walcott was starting the use of roads and automobiles, but they never displaced the horse for him. In the Canadian Rockies, feed and water were seldom difficulties. Instead, Dr. Kirk had trouble with a grizzly on one outcrop, and Walcott came down with neuralgia in his face and neck. Notwithstanding these setbacks, "We are making headway slowly on the section of the Brisco Range, but gaining a little each day" (June 17, 1923). Meanwhile, if any of the group was making dramatic progress, it was Mary with her flower sketches. "With Mary, Kirk, Paul & Billy went up to the graptolite beds & collected until 3 P.M. when the heat in the canyon became to [*sic*] severe. Mary & I also collected a lot of Mons fossils from locality 16*a*" (June 19, 1923).

The sequence of faunas established elsewhere worked well in this area, and summer began on a happy note. "The geology of Sinclair Canyon is most interesting & weather permitting we will have a fair concept of it by June 30" (June 21, 1923). "With Kirk & Paul went up canyon 5½ miles to work on section beneath quartzite. We found Glenogle graptolite fauna & and relations of quartzite to Richmond fauna to be as I had worked it out in Sept/22. Mary rode up 4 P.M." (June 25, 1923). There is a special satisfaction in showing a colleague, particularly a younger one, a sequence and having him confirm the correctness of one's earlier conclusions.

Sunday was on Saturday this week; "Our wedding day. Ninth anniversary. With Mary, Dr. Kirk & Paul motored to Kootenay Crossing to celebrate the opening of the Banff & Windemere motor road. Met many of our Canadian friends. A hot day. Billy drove his car well & we had a fine day" (June 30, 1923). Sunday they were on the cliffs east of camp and found a few fragments of the trilobite *Saukia* in the Mons Formation. It was another hot day, but the evenings were cool.

"Out with D*r* Kirk on area 5–6 miles south of camp. Found a section of the Mons that appeared to be underlain by the massive limestone of the Lyell Upper Cambrian formation. Mary at camp sketching wildflower" (July 2, 1923). The geologic section of the Brisco Range, a sequence of rocks comparable to the pages of a book, was being unraveled.

They moved to Windemere Creek. "Am glad to be off on new work as we are tired of Sinclair Canyon" (July 4, 1923). This is nearly the epitome of the distinction between the pursuit of paleontology and the pursuit of stratigraphy: Walcott the paleontologist could sit day after day in the Burgess quarry breaking rock, but Walcott the geologist, like all field men, wanted to keep moving and trace the formations laterally. Nonetheless, the next day brought an interesting note. "All went up Windemere Canyon. D*r* Kirk & Billy to Tagger Pass. Mary, Paul & 15½ *mi*. Geology uninteresting so we went to the upper lake & fished for trout—bro't in 10. Kirk found nothing of special interest up the canyon" (July 5, 1923). The rocks of particular concern to Kirk were younger than those of interest to Walcott, so unless there had been dramatic upheavals, Kirk naturally had to go farther up the mountain to work.

They moved camp, and it was a hot and dusty trip with the flies and "skeets" starting up for the season. The next day it rained, and Saturday again was Sunday. There was little of interest here either, and after Dutch Creek camp four was established at the south end of the Kootenay Bridge. "This is a section I have wished to see for several years (18) as the Lower Cambrian is well developed" (July 8, 1923).

Kirk and Walcott went up the Kootenay River to Whitehorse Creek to get a general idea of the structure of Granger Mountain. "Out with Mary on west slope of Mt. Sabine searching for the Upper Cambrian locality of Schofield. We found it after lunch & collected a few identifiable specimens" (July 11, 1923). Geologists were still fairly sparse in the southern Canadian Rockies, but there were more than before the war, and when they turned up fossils, as Schofield had, Walcott either saw the fossils or at least was aware of it.

Walcott and Paul fooled away one day on some very elusive trout, but the next day was serious business. "With Mary worked on west slope of Mt. Sabine. We found the *Saukia* fauna near base of lower Mons (Sabine of Schofield). Kirk collecting Richmond horizon fossils. We left camp 6:30 A.M. & returned 5:30 P.M." (July 13, 1923). Translation: geologist Schofield had established the sequence and supplied new names to some units; Walcott found that the lithology, and especially the fossils in the Sabine Formation, to be the same as to the north; therefore he correlated the Sabine Formation with the lower part of the Mons

Formation. Richmond is a name applied to part of late Ordovician strata in the Cincinnati, Ohio, area and, hence, another correlation of strata.

Walcott measured a section of the upper part of the Mons and then was visited by a Colonel Pollen. After spending the night, Colonel Pollen drove the couple to Cranbrook to meet his family and inspect his collection of Early Cambrian trilobites. During the next several days, Walcott and the colonel were out in the field at his localities. Despite rain every afternoon, Walcott obtained some fair specimens. Colonel Pollen drove them back fifty miles to camp. The automobile indeed had its impact on fossil hunting.

Walcott was rained out the next day, but it was just as well, for he was tired and needed a rest in camp. "Hot. Out all day with Mary, Kirk & Paul in search of Lower Cambrian fossils. We found them on south west side of Granger Mt. but not well preserved. Sun very hot but nights cool" (July 20, 1923). "All tired as it was difficult to sleep on acct of mosquitoes & flies. About camp resting & reading. Mary sketched one wild flower" (July 22, 1923).

"Up 5 A.M. Left camp 6.15 A.M. with Paul & went up on s.w. angle of Mt. Sabine. Completed section of Mons down to the Lyell? limestone and returned to camp 3 P.M. to find Dr Kindle, M. L. Bancroft & John L. Walker of the Geol. Sur.[vey of] Canada. They left at 6 P.M." (July 22, 1923). The camp was moved back to Dutch Creek; Walcott commented that the weather was beastly because of the heat, but in the "Explorations" pamphlet he was to remark that the hot days and cool nights made it a fine season.

Kirk left to join the Geological Survey of Canada field party, while the Walcotts and Paul searched for fossils in the rocks along the shore of Columbia Lake; these rocks might have been Upper Cambrian, but there were no fossils to be found. They moved camp again, and Paul took a short break to visit his wife. They spent a day looking unsuccessfully for fossils in the Precambrian Belt–age rocks and a more successful day photographing the Stanford Range.

Paul returned, and they moved from Welmer to Horse Thief Creek. That Sunday in camp, Mary read to Walcott while he repaired the panorama camera. They left the wagon and moved the camp up to the head of the canyon; the horses had a difficult time on the bad trail. "A wet day so we remained in camp to rest & sleep most of the time. Much cooler 42° at night. This is Mary's birthday[,] 63 with it. Wish it were 23 & I was 33 but as that cannot be we will do what we can" (July 31, 1923).

The Walcotts began August with a ride to the Lake of the Hanging Glaciers. It was a difficult trip, but they obtained some nice pictures. The next day Walcott was tired again, so Mary & Billy went off to photograph the glacier at the head of Horse Thief Canyon. The party moved back down the canyon; the return trip was easier, and the mosquitoes were not so numerous.

"Taking chances of a clear day we drove in buckboard up to the Ptarmigan Mine 13 miles & 2500 feet up. A late start & showers kept us 4½ hrs on road. A fine bit of scenery. Returned 2½ hrs in rain. Wet & disgusted with thing[s] generally" (August 4, 1923). Walcott hung around camp, except for wrestling with a bull trout; that helped his headache. They moved the camp back to Welmer, hoping that the heat wave had been broken by the rains. Mary sketched a maidenhair fern, Walcott took a panorama photograph, and they moved on to near Radium Hot Springs.

"Began examination of Mons section between Dry & Stoddard Creek. Located *Ophileta* & *Hungia* zones which with *Saukia* zone give a fine start on the section. Mary writing letters and sketching flowers. Dr E. Kirk returned to camp" (August 9, 1923). "With Mary worked on Mons above camp. A portion of the formation dropped in against Silurian on a N&S strike. We found *Hungia* zone & collected a few fossils" (August 10, 1923). Translation: a break in the rocks, a fault, had moved the Mons Formation up or the Silurian down. Only part of the Mons Formation was present in the area—Walcott found only the one fossil zone—but this was enough to tell him how much vertical movement had taken place.

"Left camp at 7 A.M. with Billy. Rode over to Stoddard Creek and measured section of *Mons* up to *Hungia* zone. Over 2300 feet in thickness. The sun heat was intense after noon & we returned at 3:30 P.M. Mary sketching cones of Tamarack" (August 11, 1923). "At camp, resting writing & fussing over self. Have not been very well for a week on acct stomach grouchy" (August 12, 1923). The field season was taking its toll, to use an old chestnut. When Walcott was not well, Arthur boiled rice and made it into a loaf, which was then sliced and the slices toasted to nearly charcoal over the fire. Walcott thought it helped his stomach.

Still, old Walcott kept going. "Mary & I left camp 7 A.M., & worked on upper part of section of Mons. I measured from *Hungia* zone up to *Ophileta* zone. We collected quite a lot of fossils. Men shoeing horses and fixing up buckboard" (August 13, 1923). "Mary & I left camp at 6:50 A.M. I completed remainder of section to [the] fault [displacement] between Richmond & Mons. At 10 A.M. was obliged to return to camp on acct severe pains in bowels etc. Much better at night. Mary took fine care of me" (August 14, 1923). Everyone has a sick day or so in the field, but Walcott had never had a season quite like this; the old machine was wearing out. Walcott was in pain the next day as well and concluded he was passing a kidney stone.

"Dictated letters A.M. Sore & aching in muscles. Very hot in afternoon, but I broke up & packed in box a quantity of fossils from the Hungia zone that Dr Kirk & men bro't in large pieces of limestone" (August 16, 1923). When one is a Walcott, one simply does not give in. "Mary & I drove to Radium Hot Springs P.O.

in morning & up Sinclair Canyon. Returned 1 P.M. Read mail & papers and wrote President Coolidge" (August 17, 1923). That was a curious way to refer to the news of the death of President Harding. The next day Walcott was out with Mary collecting from the Mons; he was better.

"Mary & I went up on ridge north of Dry Creek & collected a small [*sic*] of fossils from the *Hungia* zone of Mons. Returned after lunch to write out field notes & get ready to move camp tomorrow. Mary sketching a small *aster*" (August 19, 1923). When it was necessary, Mary also modified the position of the Sabbath within the week; during the time Walcott had been ill there were too many Sundays. They moved to camp twelve, four miles south of Brisco.

"Went up Vermillion Creek to Canyon & found Mons limestones & shales very much altered & twisted & altered" (August 21, 1923). They took the buckboard to Brisco for supplies, read the mail that Paul's wife brought to camp, and caught up on miscellaneous matters. "Mary took me up to the Red Wall Cliff [presumably by buckboard] above Radium Hot Springs. Work[ed] on section from Red Wall Cliff to canyon at mouth of canyon. Measured section of Mons formation from base to *Hungia* zone" (August 17, 1923). The next day Walcott and the men collected in Sinclair Canyon from the Hungia zone and another zone was found and reported to be 168 feet lower.

"Up at 5 A.M. Taking Paul[,] rode up Sinclair Canyon 5½ miles & then went up Cabin Mt & measured section of Mons & superjacent Ordovician to base of Cabin Mt Quartzite. A long hard day & hot p.m. Returned to camp 6:30 P.M. Delighted to complete pre-Silurian section" (August 29, 1923). They packed up fossils and camp gear. Paul was to take the pack train east to Lake Louise while the Walcotts went west to Glacier House. Billy Harrison left to be replaced by Clay Robbins; Walcott could keep household help better than he could assistant packers, but then again, they have different duties and temperaments.

Mary went out to measure and photograph Illecillewaet Glacier once more; Walcott was in Glacier House, sick. They left the next day for Golden. Walcott talked to a local mining geologist about the Purcell Range, while Mary sketched. "We went by motor to high terrace N.E. of Golden & then to the south to examine limestones 10 miles up the valley. Found nothing to help decide age of bluish gray, mottled limestones" (September 4, 1923). The next day, on another motor trip, Walcott found fragments of the *Saukia* fauna at another spot to the south, but it is not clear that this helped with the problem of the age of the mottled limestones.

"Mary & I walked up Kicking Horse Canyon about 4 miles. We found two horizons of *Mons* fossils & a few graptolites in the Glenogle shales" (September 6, 1923). When fossils were present, Walcott found them; his stomach might act up, but there was nothing wrong with his eyes. They left Golden early and joined the camp at Lake Louise. They spent a day reorganizing and resupplying before heading north. "The plan to move the camp today was defeated by rain in early morning followed by mist & clouds all about on the mountain" (September 9, 1923).

Despite snow squalls, the following day they set up camp seventeen near Baker Lake. "Collected a few Syntrophisura faunule fossils before lunch from limestone ledges at camp. Middle Mons" (September 11, 1923). Inasmuch as Walcott knew the zonal arrangement of fossils in the Mons, it was as though the individual outcrops had their positions in the section written on them. "Out with Mary & Paul taking photographs. Large panoramic camera acted like a balky mule & ruined several 8 foot films & made me half crazy as it ruined the opportunity I have been hoping [for] for 3 years" (September 12, 1923). It was not always apparent, but like other humans Walcott could lose his temper.

One result was that Walcott was laid up again for three days, but then the camera was fixed and his stomach returned to working order, or so it seemed. "I had a bad night & day. Severe pain in lower bowels. Mary nursing me all day. This kind of thing is most trying. Fine weather & unable to get out & do my work" (September 16, 1923). Walcott was laid up for two more days, and then the party raced back to Lake Louise.

The horses and the rest of the outfit were taken back to Radium Hot Springs for the winter, while Walcott hung around Lake Louise for a few days. Whether Walcott liked it or not, his field season was over. He took a few photographs but otherwise slowly recovered. Almost without fail, each year there was a problem with his shipments, and 1923 was to be no exception. "Agent at Golden notifies me that Baltimore and Ohio refuses to accept our freight shipments at Chicago. Get it straightened out."[24] As in past years, Mr. Dorsey got it straightened out.

The train ride east was a bit quicker than in past years. The fall foliage along Lake Superior was nicer this year than in previous years. The Sidney Walcotts met them at the train station for a pleasant day-and-a-half visit. Walcott telegraphed Mr. Dorsey: "We expect to arrive in Washin at 1:50 P.M. *via* B&O Thursday. Superb weather here after two warm days. We have seen many things & I learned much that may be of service if we live to use it. Dead tired tonight."[25]

For the *Annual Report*, Walcott summed up his fieldwork and added a few comments to edify the general public.

It was found that the Mons formation which was discovered on the headwaters of the Saskatchewan River at Glacier Lake, extended southwesterly on the western side of the Continental Divide in British Columbia to the southern end of the Stanford Range between the Kootenay River and Columbia Lake, which is at the head of the Great Columbia River, which here flows northwesterly in what is known as the Rocky Mountain Trench. The valley of this latter river was found to be largely underlain by the limestones and shales of the Mons formation of the Ozarkian system and the strata have been upturned, faulted, and folded prior to the great pre-Glacial period of erosion that cut out the Rocky Mountain trench. On the eastern side of this valley, the Mons formation is more than 3,800 feet in thickness in the Beaver-foot-Briscoe-Stanford Range, and contains four well-developed fossil faunas which show it to lie between the Upper Cambrian and the Ordovician systems of this and other parts of the continent. Near the head of Sinclair Canyon there was discovered a great development of the Lower Ordovician, and at several localities cliffs of massive Upper Cambrian limestone were recognized beneath the Mons formation. (Walcott 1925a, 6–7)

Years earlier, Walcott had measured many sections in northern Vermont. This had helped him understand the rocks and ended use of the "Taconic system" for the complicated rocks to the south, but the data he had assembled was never published. Fortunately the work on the Mons was not in the same category of problem, but there were similarities. The various sections measured all helped in a general understanding of the history of the southern Canadian Rockies. In this instance Walcott had the opportunity to publish the measured sections and discuss them.

The Walcotts arrived on schedule Sunday at Union Station, where William met them. On Monday, Walcott was in his office. "All well & matters moving along smoothly at the Smithsonian & its branches" (October 1, 1923). First on Walcott's agenda was to meet with retired general Herbert W. Lord, the director of the Bureau of the Budget, for there was no sense wasting time with intermediaries. That still left sufficient time the same day to take care of the Iowa Apartment house and chat with Bailey Willis. Walcott had not lost his edge. By Friday Walcott could recorded, "A quiet day at my office. Am getting matters well in hand & will soon be able to take up the summer field notes. Mary is getting the house in order for the winter" (October 5, 1923).

"Called on Mr. Resser Mr. Merguet [*sic*] & Miss Julia Gardner at the Nat. Hist. Building all of whom are working more or less in connection with my work. The outlook for illustrations is slow as Miss Wieser has too much to do" (October 7, 1923). Scattered notes in a museum drawer show that Miss Julia was writing descriptions of some gastropods from the Mons Formation, but these were never published. On Sunday, Walcott and Mary heard a fine sermon from Dr. Wood and hung Indian baskets on the wall in the library of their house. "Attended to usual routine & began putting field notes on Sinclair section in order for publication. Talked with several members of the s.i. staff in relation to their work. Read draft of Annual Report in evening" (October 3, 1923).

The NAS building committee met, followed by a meeting of the Research Council, followed by office work, and the day—a representative one—concluded with a visit to Mary's garden at the Anacostia flats; seemingly the Potomac Park plot had been taken over by the Park Service. "Routine & work on Sinclair section notes & preparation of memorandum on Smithsonian *en re* Dept of Education kept me occupied at my office" (October 11, 1923). "Called on President Coolidge 11 A.M. *en re* Smithsonian matters. Found him favorably disposed toward independence of Smithsonian under Board of Regents. Dr. Percy E. Raymond of Harvard called 10 A.M. Occupied with routine & research work at odd hours all day" (October 12, 1923). "A quiet day that enabled me to work for several hours at report on field work of the past summer. It is a bit difficult at my age to plan for 10 years['] office & laboratory work with the tho't that all will be finished before I pass on. At home in evening" (October 13, 1923). All paleontologists collect more material than they can possibly describe during their lifetimes, and Walcott was facing that dilemma, along with the desire to visit new sections in the Rockies.

Mary was off on one of her visits to Philadelphia when Walcott had Robert Sterling Yard to dinner. The National Parks Association and Yard were virtually synonymous, and both were almost always in difficulty, the former because of serious lack of funds. Walcott had written to Mrs. Harriman for help, and for one of the few times in her life she turned him down. Part of the problem was that Yard was a zealot for the national parks, and it is the essence of being a zealot to take an extreme position. Even with Walcott's backing, Mr. Yard's future was most uncertain, though fortunately for the National Parks he remained active for another decade.

On Sunday after church, Walcott held a meeting of the AAAS council at the Cosmos Club. Although the position of president is largely honorific, Walcott did not treat it that way. By the end of the year, the unwieldy council was reorganized, and an executive committee was in operation. Quite apart from this major change, a donor gave a prize of a thousand dollars to be awarded for the best paper. Walcott was one of a committee of three to set up the rules, and he awarded the prize for the first time in the winter of 1923, at the seventy-fifth-anniversary meeting of the association.

While that meeting was going on, a new major project was starting. "Mary had Dr Paul Bartsch at dinner. They consulted on wild flower publication" (October 14, 1923); more will follow on this subject. "Routine & research work at the office during the day" (October 15, 1923). "We dined with Secty Mellon and Sir Robert & Lady With of London. Miss Helen Frick of New York. Mr. & Mrs. Charles Glover" (October 16, 1923).

At the semiannual meeting of the NACA, Walcott was reelected chairman, just as year after year he had been reelected president of the Washington Academy of Sciences. The next day he was at the meeting of the board of the new Institute of Economics. Church began another week. The main agenda item now was Mr. Yard; Walcott spoke to Secretary of Commerce Hoover, who was active in the National Parks Association, and to one or two others. Mr. Yard stayed on.

"Am getting paper on last summers['] field work well advanced" (October 23, 1923). "Continued work during day at my office & laboratory. Talked with Edwin Kirk *en re* Silurian-Ordovician boundary in America. Hit by 'blind' headache at noon & went home to sleep it off" (October 24, 1923). Several days later, Walcott began sitting at the Corcoran Art Gallery for a portrait by Edwin W. Dickinson of New York. After one sitting and Sunday morning at church, Mary and Walcott were off to the artist's hometown.

"I called on President Keppel of Carnegie Corporation & Mr. Jas. Rogerson in morning" (October 29, 1923). In the afternoon Walcott joined Mary at the Metropolitan Museum of Art. He spent the next morning at Columbia University, in conversations with President Nicholas Murray Butler and with a few geologist friends on the faculty, and looking over the Heil Indian Museum and the Hispanic American Society Museum. Walcott next called at the American Museum of Natural History and on Mrs. Jacob Schiff, and he had dinner with the Rogersons. Even by Walcott's standards, this was a busy day.

"Called on Dr Hammerschlag, Dr Geo. F Kuntz, Elan H. Hooker A.M. Lunched with Mr. Hooker & talked over Muscle Shoals, Nitro, etc. Mary & I dined with Mr. & Mrs. Hammerschlag. I have started several prospects for s.i. on this trip" (November 1, 1923). This kind of statement was unusual for Walcott, so he must have had remarkable success in his discussions. Satisfied, the Walcotts went back to Washington, to be followed a few hours later by Elan Hooker. Hooker spent the night, and Walcott took him to the Freer Gallery before getting back to the office. The last of the collections from the summer finally came in. On Sunday after church, Walcott and Mary were at the Smithsonian "for luncheon & to look over photographs of 1923, some of which are very good" (November 4, 1923). Walcott never did believe in false modesty.

"At museum & Smithsonian until 3 P.M. Talked with Resser *en re* Hungia fauna" (November 5, 1923). The next day he went to sit for his portrait, but it was too dark for the artist; half a dozen sittings would occur during the rest of the month and early December.

Minor administrative issues with the NACA arose. The Walcotts attended a few receptions and gave a small dinner for the secretary of state; this would rate a note in both the *Washington Star* and the *Washington Times*. How much of the high-level social life in the capital appeared in print was partly a function of what other news occurred, yet almost every time Walcott noted in his diary the giving of a formal dinner or an invitation to one, the affair became part of the public record.

No great events transpired as November wore on. "A very quiet day at office & laboratory. Began study of collections of Mons formation of Brisco-Stanford Range. Mary & I had a fine evening at home" (November 15, 1923). "We went to description of Naval Air Service before Nat. Geographic by Admiral [William A.] Moffat. Occupied with business paper in evening at home." "Business" meant Walcott's private dealings, which he did not mix with official duties.

Weariness had prevented attendance at church the Sunday before, and a cold now conspired against it a second Sunday, yet Walcott struggled to the office both afternoons to keep up his research momentum. Despite the cold, there were conferences concerning a new museum building as the prospects for art improved. Mary went off to Philadelphia, and Walcott went to New York. "Went up to Helen's apt. for the night. Found her well & enthusiastic about a trip to South America" (November 22, 1923).

Walcott spent the next day on money matters. That morning, he run into Julius Rosenwald of Chicago on the street and mildly twisted his arm for funds. Elan Hooker introduced him to a few men at lunch, and that evening he was guest of the Hookers at the International Federation of Collegiate Women. The next morning, it was off to see Mrs. Harriman, who was always a potential source of support, to examine pictures painted by Lincoln Ellsworth, and to call on an architect; then home. With both weather and health improved, Walcott attended church and then worked on the annual Christmas card. Some years, Walcott's section of the "Explorations" pamphlets was produced as an offprint, and when a picture appeared on the cover, it was often the same as that on the annual card.

"A very much broken up day at the office by interviews etc. Began a paper for the Belgian Geol. Soc. 50 year book. We gave a dinner in honor Secty & Mrs. Weeks & 12 other friends. A very pleasant party & evening" (November 27, 1923). Because Mary was a strict teetotaler and for a decade Walcott dinner guests had known not to expect anything more exciting than grape juice, the secretary was spared a major social problem of the Prohibition era, as to whether one served a bootleg cocktail to a government official.

The Vauxes came down for their traditional Thanksgiving visit and stayed for a couple of days. The manuscript for Belgium must have been developing rapidly as December began; translation of his manuscript into French was completed before 1923 ended. In this short work (1925b), within a few pages Walcott gave the essence of the great unconformity within the Paleozoic rocks on the eastern edge of the Canadian Rockies, adding several large format photographs to document his words.

The old year was slipping away. "Routine & a little research during the day" (December 3, 1923). The Walcotts had a small dinner for the ambassador from Italy. "Routine letters and study lower Mons fauna brachiopods etc. Sent letter to Mr. Heckscher & Mr. Longyear *en re* s.i. endowment" (December 6, 1923). At Walcott's direction the Smithsonian had issued a pamphlet noting its accomplishments and asking for support. A few contributions in the one-to-ten-dollar range had come in, some with fascinating letters attached about how much the Smithsonian had meant to a particular individual.

As meaningful as these letters were, the money itself was trivial, and it was the millionaires that Walcott tried to contact. This was by no means an either pleasant or easy activity. Walcott commented a few years earlier that "one man who was able to give twenty million without missing it said to me 'Why should I give my money to perpetuate the name of Smith?'"[26] Increasingly, the endowment would become more and more of an issue over the next few years.

December weather was fine, the couple had a pleasant dinner or two out, and Walcott became a movie critic; "The Covered Wagon," a tale of pioneer days, was "a fine film." Church, lantern slides for his coming talk, and inviting the Merriams for dinner so that he and the president could talk over Carnegie matters, made for a full Sunday.

The National Gallery Commission met, in what was a highly successful gathering. Walcott reported that he had obtained congressional approval for a building site. The next step was an architectural plan, which would cost about eleven thousand dollars, for which the Smithsonian had no funds. Half was offered on the spot, and the rest was raised easily. Not unexpectedly, Charles A. Platt was recommended as the architect, and in February the regents rubber-stamped his appointment. In 1924, Regent Lodge tried to include an amendment to the deficiency appropriation bill to provide construction money, but, not unexpectedly, this was defeated; gathering support for buildings take time and several attempts.

That evening the Walcotts formally entertained Chief Justice and Mrs. Taft, and Walcott must have been in a good mood. "Meeting of Board of Regents. Smithsonian Institution 10–12 A.M. I explained work of Institution etc. Cleaned up odds & ends in afternoon & stopped on way home to see Mrs. E. H. Harriman & Mrs. Read. Mary & I received at the Carnegie Institution reception 9–10:15 & then went to White House reception" (December 13, 1923). Because Calvin Coolidge, who had been chancellor, was now president rather than vice president and therefore no longer a statutory regent, Chief Justice Taft, another statutory member of the board, was elected to that office.

There was other business before the regents. A scheme was afoot to establish a Department of Education, into which the Smithsonian would be placed. Naturally, Walcott was against this, and he raised three points. First, the Smithsonian was apolitical; second, it had a worldwide reputation, which would be lost if it were subordinated to a cabinet department; and third, by being independent the institution had freedom of action. The regents, metaphorically at least, nodded in agreement.

"Presided at board meeting of Carnegie Institution trustees 10–12:30 as vice Chairman. Mary & I lunched with Trustees and then went to Smithsonian. We dined with D*r* & Mrs. Charles Wood & friends" (December 14, 1923). If there were any inward doubts about Walcott losing his steam, these two days would seem to have resolved them.

Walcott completed work on the "Explorations" pamphlet, and the workweek ended, only to begin again. "Mary & I wrote letters in early morning & attended Church of Covenant. We lunched at Smithsonian. She colored lantern slides & I wrote memorandum on Smithsonian relation to gov't. branches & to research" (December 16, 1923). In 1925, a five-page pamphlet, "Relations of the Smithsonian Institution to the National Government," was distributed, but all copies seem to have vanished. "Routine & general work at s.i. Late in afternoon began making up plates of brachiopod illustrations" (December 171, 1923).

Ever since Mr. True had died, long before the war, the Smithsonian had had one assistant secretary, but Walcott now moved to correct this, starting at the top. "Sent communication *en re* secty. s.i. to President Collidge [*sic*] A.M." (December 18, 1923). Like most of Walcott's enterprises, it did not fall on deaf ears. "A very quiet day at my office & workroom. Making up plates of brachiopods. Prest. Coolidge wrote that he had for's [forwarded] my letter etc. [to] the Budget Bureau" (December 19, 1923). The Smithsonian received authorization for a second assistant secretary.

An architect called concerning the proposed new art building, and when he left, Mary and Walcott began getting Christmas candy and presents ready. "A very busy day at my office 9–5 P.M. We put up the last of the Christmas pkgs. & had our Christmas eve gifts for household in evening. Arthur, Mollie, Annie, Delia" (December 24, 1923). The same household help stayed for year after year.

On Christmas Day, the Walcotts left for Cincinnati and the seventy-fifth annual meeting of the American Association for the Advancement of Science. Once they left the train, the fun began. As both the president and a leading geologist, Walcott was interviewed concerning fundamentalism.

Religion and science are not in conflict, said Dr. Walcott. They are both seeking after truth, but in different fields. Science is trying to discover the truth about the physical phenomena of life, of nature, while religion is interested in the spiritual development of man.

We have had these furious controversies between the theologians and advocates of evolution for a long time. There has been an eternal conflict between the theologians and the scientists. It has gone on since the days when they threatened to execute Galileo and it will always go on.

Dr. Walcott pointed out that it was not necessary for a churchman to be a theologian any more than it was for a scientist to be an atheist. He said he was a churchman himself, but not a theologian. He is an active worker in the Presbyterian Church of the Covenant.

It would be surprising if you knew the number of scientific men who are connected with church activity. . . . Despite claims of some fundamentalists in the churches that the evolutionary theory is being abandoned, Dr. Walcott said the scientists were becoming more and more impressed with the facts of evolution as time goes on.[27]

The following day, Walcott's comments figured prominently in an editorial in the *New York Times* that concluded with the suggestion that the various religious groups should talk to one another, in an American Association for the Advancement of Religion.

The questions from the reporters were minor, and Walcott did not bother to jot down the incident. Still, they might have been responsible for a shift in Walcott's views as to the significance of the meeting, for he telegraphed Washington: "Get off on 4:35 train today special delivery my Cambridge cap red gown and hood. In box upper shelf of closet bookcase room Arthur and Annie know. Telegram if sent."[28] That scarlet gown on the podium would certainly make a statement that AAAS and evolution were not to be taken lightly.

Walcott had been in Cincinnati when he was collecting fossils for Professor Hall in the 1870s, but it was not one of his regular stops. The Walcotts enjoyed the city, and they were treated royally by their hosts. "Meeting of Ex. Comm AAAS A.M. & of Council p.m. At. 4 P.M. I spoke to geologists on my work in Canadian Rockies. Presided at meeting of AAAS In evening" (December 27, 1923). They visited the art museum and were entertained at the University Club.

"Presiding at meeting of Council 9–11 A.M. Talking with members & after lunch with Preset. Hicks of University went to hear Mary talk to Garden Club. It was fine. Presiding at meeting of Association 8:15–10 P.M. Drs Fairchild, Mendenhall, Chambering & Howard spoke on history of A.A.A.S. since 1898" (December 29, 1923). The annual meeting ended, but Walcott and Mary had another fine day and a half in the city. "The Cincinnati people have been most kind

& thotful [*sic*] & we enjoyed our visit & the meeting of the A.A.A.S." (December 31, 1923).

The awarding of the thousand-dollar prize was big news in *Science*. The anonymous donor continued on a year-by-year basis until his death, when his award ended; it is now the Newcómb Cleveland award, named in his honor. The AAAS seldom had much to report other than the scientific content of the annual meeting, but this year the secretary filled nearly a page with council activities; Walcott had not been idle.

Walcott and Mary spent New Year's Eve on the train returning home. He wrote of the ending year: "The year 1923 has not been of unusual interest to us to Mary and me but it has had much joy & agreeable work. Helen is well & in South America. Sidney, Helen-Louise & Evelyn our grandchild are well & very happy in their home life in Buffalo N.Y. May 1924 be a good to us all. The U.S. is gradually recovering from the effects of the war of 1914–18. The death of President Harding was a great shock to our people but he had done his work & Calvin Collidge [*sic*] will serve the country as well if not better as he is a sane, well-trained type of American & with more mentality & courage than Harding" (December 31, 1923).

9

Up and Down Years (1924–1925): Two Wrongs Do Not Make a Right, but Two Wrights Did Make a Plane

> There is no science whose value can be adequately estimated by economists and utilitarians of the lower order. Its true quantities cannot be represented by arithmetical figures or monetary tables; for its effect on the mind must surely be taken into account as its operations on matter, and what it has accomplished for the intellect, as certainly as what it had done for the comforts of society or the interests of commerce.
>
> —G. Y. Craig and E. J. Jones, quoting H. Miller, 1982

THE WALCOTTS arrived in Washington from Cincinnati at 6:50—not simply early in the morning, but as recorded. Times for trains in his diary were precise, so it is a reasonable assumption that all other minutes Walcott emphasized in his diary were precise. He had been noting the minutes for years, and it was apparent that the stock of them was dwindling, though Walcott never dwelled on that aspect of time. He jumped into the accumulated pile of mail, like a child jumping into a pile of leaves. Since it was New Year's Day, that afternoon the Walcotts called on the chief justice and three cabinet members to wish them well for 1924.

"Resumed work at my office 9 A.M. Cleaned up mail & various odds & ends. A few interviews & at 3 P.M. went to my laboratory to study brachiopods from Ozarkian of Sweden. Mary occupied with errands, paying bills & household matters & coloring lantern slides after 3 P.M. At home in evening settling up accounts" (January 2, 1924). The habit that Walcott developed early of listing expenditures and income in his diary remained throughout his life.

The following day, Walcott noted examining fossils from Novaya Zemlya; presumably, the Swedish material had been examined for comparison. Mary's book had progressed to the point of preparing a list of those who might be induced to subscribe to copies. It is hard to say which of the couple first seriously mentioned publishing Mary's flower watercolors, or when, but the project was maturing, yet from its first mention in Walcott's diary it proceeded rapidly. As a result, four hundred prints of Mary's color drawings in five volumes would be published.

The couple had several dinners out, at one of which Walcott agreed to sit for the Russian emigré sculptor Moses Dykaar; he was given a space in the Museum and for several years made busts of eminent folk in Washington. A display of Russian art was opening, and this was an opportunity for the artist. The Walcotts entertained the French ambassador and were entertained at the White House and at a brace of embassies. Social life in Washington was normal under the new president.

The middle of January saw a pleasant event at the Museum: a patron donated a colonial room. This was installed in the foyer and remained absolutely unchanged for nearly four decades. Each year Mrs. Ritter would send her chauffeur to examine the display; the man kept coming for years after she died and would gaze at the room for hours. The entire room was moved out and it became one of the first displays to be installed in the adjacent American history museum when that building was constructed.

Walcott took a quick trip to New York and saw a few potential art patrons. The next day, he attended a Research Corporation meeting; that organization awarded five thousand dollars to the Smithsonian to further research. This was a productive two days, but the trip also produced a cold. Saturday, Walcott remained home as a result; "Attended to mail, slept, sneezed[,] growled" (January 19, 1924). He was confined to the house for several days more but dictated letters and hosted a dinner for the Belgian ambassador.

Walcott completed a location map of the sections that he had studied in the Canadian Rockies and sent it off to Brussels. The text of this paper for the fiftieth-anniversary volume of the Geological Society of Belgium had been sent a month earlier. Other good news was that the last of the funds needed for drawing plans for the projected National Gallery of Art building were in hand; Mr. Platt could get started as soon as Walcott arranged the formalities of having him selected as architect. Notwithstanding, Walcott skipped church, though he and Mary walked the three miles to the Smithsonian for their Sunday office lunch and work routine.

They attended a formal dinner at the home of the secretary of the navy; it became another of those little social items that filled the Washington papers. A cable from Helen reported that all was well and that she was crossing the Andes from Argentina to Chile. "The month has passed very rapidly. Each day is filled full of interesting matters. Mary is busy with her Wild Flower book & I have my research work to fill in all available time. The sculptor Dykar [*sic*] takes an hour each day. Charles Moore came to talk over Art Building in evening" (January 31, 1924).

Art having been mentioned, quoting a letter Walcott received is appropriate. It sheds light, on one hand, on the Washington class / race structure of the times and, on the other, on the importance of the si in helping a little to change that structure. Unlike so many places in the southern city of Washington, the Smithsonian buildings were open to all. Had Mr. Freer known, it would have outraged his aesthetic sensibilities.

I suppose that in handling administrative matters for the Freer gallery of Art you sometimes wonder just how wide its influence is. I was much amazed one evening in going home on the street car to find that two colored men in the seat next to mine were discussing the gallery. They did not look like any extraordinary individuals; I should judge they were workmen or certainly not more than small tradesmen. One was a visitor from out of town and the other was recommending the gallery to him strongly as one of the things it was important for him to see. It pleased me very much, and I think perhaps you will also be pleased to know that so fine a thing as the Freer collection makes a definite appeal to people even of this class.[1]

It is best to make no comment and move on.

February began with the viewing of a film on the development of aviation, but that evening neuralgia hit. The next day Walcott was once again confined to bed. "Intercostal neuralgia developed finely & made me miserable. Trying to be comfortable and cheerful. Coiled up & slept and wiggled most of the day. Woodrow Wilson passed away. An able, dominating self centered spirit by chance given the opportunity to be the world's leader but he could not hold the place he had aspired to" (February 4, 1924). One may ponder a moment or two on the point that Walcott's evaluations of Wilson and of Harding are almost the antitheses of those rendered by history three-quarters of a century later.

Though neuralgia began to fade, Walcott was still confined to the house. "Reading, attending to mail etc. but not much good. I had much to attend to this week & I am sorry to lose [*sic*] the time and opportunity for it. Woodrow Wilson buried physically—where is his spirit[?]" (February 4, 1924). It was a full week more before Walcott got back to the office. First on the agenda was a meeting of the Arts Commission to discuss who should be the architect. No surprises there.

Walcott was able to work on his manuscripts, and the couple began going out to dinner again. Walcott had a quiet day when Mary went to New York on business with her book. By now Mary, who could move as fast as her husband when opportunity knocked, had lined up thirty-four subscribers for the deluxe, five-hundred-dollar edition. The printing was almost prohibitively expensive, and the special edition had to have buyers before printing could even be contemplated; the standard edition cost $125, a little more than a quarter a picture. Walcott finally made it to church, where he enjoyed the sermon. Sunday was becoming more and more a business day, especially when the Walcotts did not walk to the office. Steven Mather, head of the National Park Service, and his family came to dinner, and the evening was devoted to talk about the parks.

Mary went off to New York once again. It began to snow. "A quiet peaceful day at the office as there were no callers & few telephone messages. Working up some odds & ends of brachiopods P.M. Wrote Mary & read in the evening" (February 19, 1924). The GWMA met, but there was nothing new to report. Mr. Platt came to town, and he and Walcott discussed plans for the building plans; it was not until April that an art journal announced his appointment as architect. Mr. Yard called in with a different kind of plan for the National Parks Association. Mary came back with a few additional subscribers to her credit. The Washington Monument Association met on President Washington's birthday. "Usual day at the Smithsonian. Am getting along slowly with research work. We are now having the midwinter quiet except at the Capitol where there is great activity" (February 25, 1924).

"At my office A.M. & P.M. Presided at meeting of Nat. Parks Also. 3–4:30 P.M. Herbert Hoover elected President for which I am glad on acct of Ass.[ociation] work and because I must be relieved of so many outside duties. A quiet evening. Mary went to Archaeological Soc. at Mrs. Dimock[']s" (February 26, 1924). His resignation to the National Parks Association (NPA), tendered in May 1923, was finally accepted. Because Henry McFarland had died and no one else had come forward, Walcott felt honor bound—what a quaint, old-fashioned word—to serve as acting president. Had he not filled in and kept this infant alive, who is to say what fossils he might have described in that tiny bit of extra time? How can one evaluate the support for the national parks and National Park Service during this first decade of the existence of the service and the boom in vacations by automobile travel?

Hoover served as president for about eighteen months. "Why would Hoover accept the NPA presidency? A man of his prestige and rising political influence would have been in high demand at the time, and there is no evidence he had been active in NPA" (Miles 1995, 53). The history of the National Parks Association quotes his letter of acceptance as evidence that Hoover cared about the parks, and indeed he must have, to have taken on this chore. The real reason he agreed is probably much simpler. In addition to all the professional contacts between Walcott and Hoover, they were neighbors on S Street Northwest; Walcott persuaded him.

About a month letter, Walcott shed another small obligation. He had been a "collaborator" in the Forest Service, which entitled him to a per diem of twelve dollars if he ever did any official work for that agency. The chief forester wrote him: "It is greatly regretted that in view of the demands of your geological work you deem it best to withdraw from the service, and I wish to take this occasion to express to you in behalf of the Forest Service the appreciation which we all feel for your valuable cooperation and interest during the past ten years."[2]

"A quiet day for work. Rounded up paper on brachiopods so as to send it to printer this week. Mary canvassing for her book. Making duty calls etc. At home in evening" (February 27, 1924). The next day, the secretary made an appearance on Capitol Hill about the Smithsonian appropriation, and the following day he spent hours with other members of the NACA explaining those estimates to the same subcommittee. Then February finally was over.

The Walcotts took a minivacation, going to New York, on Saturday afternoon. They visited a few friends but dined alone. Mary was having a show of her wildflower sketches in the Anderson Gallery, and while she saw to the hanging, Walcott read his manuscript. Afterward, Walcott talked to Mr. Platt, met some members of Tambly and Brown (a firm Walcott hoped could raise endowment money), and went to a couple of operettas. One was judged "a foolish little play without reason for existence" (March 6, 1924). The next afternoon they left for home. "New York trip was a diversion but I do not like being there" (March 7, 1924).

Walcott met in his office with Mr. Lockwood, whom Walcott hoped would be the prime money raiser. For a change, it was Mary who developed a cold, while he carried on. A small blizzard quieted the town and gave some uninterrupted research time. Walcott arranged to use the presidential yacht *Mayflower* when the members of the NACA visited Langley Field. "Routine & half a day picking up odds & ends in connection with paper on last seasons field work" (March 14, 1924). Mary's cold lingered, and Walcott was not quite well, but he decided he would be better off at the office than moping at home. On Sunday they rested, and then he worked on. "At my office & laboratory during the day. Routine & working on lower Mons fauna—'Briscoia fauna'" (March 17, 1924). Three days of ditto marks in his diary followed. More snow was dumped on Washington, but Walcott got to his office, and research proceeded.

"A quiet day at the s.i. working on genera Saukia & Briscoia several hours. Mary lunched with me. A quiet evening with Dr Geo. E. Hale as our dinner guest. He is one of the unusual men & most delightful" (March 22, 1924). On Sunday both Walcotts nursed their colds. "A routine day at the Smithsonian &

working up odds & ends of last seasons collections. Met Helen at the Union Station in evening. She has been in South America Dec.–March. She is well. Mary well but not able to walk as usual" (March 23, 1924).

Walcott considered the next few days quiet ones. The National Parks Association meeting and the Church of the Covenant trustees were the only items to interfere with routine and research. "Writing report to Canadian Survey of field work 1916–1923" (March 28, 1924). Another two days of routine were broken by Walcott's appearance before the House Ways and Means Committee in connection with the rebate of taxes on the Freer estate. It would seem that Freer matters would never be resolved.

"Broken up day & my 74 birthday. Am fairly well & fully occupied with administration & research work. At my office 9 A.M. Went up to capitol 11–12 to see Senator Lodge. Dykar [*sic*] completed my bust. At museum 2–3:30 Mary & I went to musical given by Mrs. Coolidge 4–5:30[.] Met the President. At home in evening" (March 31, 1924). All in all, it does not sound like such a bad way to spend a birthday.

April 1 brought six inches of snow but also the opportunity to finish reviewing his manuscript; snow days in Washington are marvelous for concentration. The next day Helen left for New York; it had been a most enjoyable visit. "Meeting of Board of Trustees Ch. of Covenant 5–6 P.M. I was elected President of Board" (April 1, 1924). Walcott just never said no to a good cause.

"A quiet day at my office. Studied & described at trilobites from Mt. Robson B.C. collected by Sidney in 1913. Am getting along fairly well with my personal work but many interruptions make it discouraging. At home with Mary in evening" (April 13, 1924). Mary was recovering, though she was still was not up to par. Walcott discussed Ozarkian fossils with Ulrich and Resser, and read proofs of his brachiopod paper. Three days later, the proof was returned to the printer.

Walcott did a little private lobbying at the Capitol for the Museum. As usual, the appropriation for printing was inadequate; that was one roadblock Walcott could not remove. He saw a film on Alaska, and April rolled along. "Mary & I went to Philadelphia & thence to Spring Lake N.J.[,] putting up at the Letchworth Cottage. We need a change of pasture & rest from the friction of life in Washington. This is a quiet restful spot & the Letchworth sisters are fine women & excellent homekeepers" (April 12, 1924).

Three days of resting and then Walcott was writing a manuscript from his 1913 field notes on the Mount Robson fossils. The *New York Times* reported that Senator Lodge had asked for an appropriation of $2,500,000 to start construction on the gallery building; Walcott pasted the clipping in his diary. "A stupid

Easter Sunday as I had a cold in my neck & head. Mary much better than when we came down here" (April 20, 1924).

They returned to Washington, and Walcott discussed his manuscript on stratigraphy with Ulrich. Walcott was totally committed to Ulrich's Ozarkian Period; as noted, he was one of a handful who accepted the concept. The NACA semiannual meeting featured a luncheon, organized by Mary, for the secretary of the navy. A few days of quiet ensued before a great event.

"Dedication of National Academy building. Prest. Coolidge made a fine address. Also J. C. Merriam, Vernon Kellogg & Gano Dunn. Mary & I received at reception in the evening" (April 28, 1924). Regular business of the Academy, if such there could be on such an occasion, took up the next two days. "A day broken up by interviews, routine & a committee meeting *en re* Forestry Reserves at Secty Herbert Hoovers office. Com. Jones, Merriam, Hoover, & Walcott present" (May 1, 1924).

Dedication of the new building should not be passed over so lightly. A joint committee of the NAS and RC organized the event; it should come as no surprise that Walcott was chairman of the committee. For the occasion, many temporary displays graced the building. The Smithsonian produced all six in the north exhibit hall. These included paintings of wildflowers by Mary and a geologic section across the Cordilleran Trough, plus a display of Burgess Shale fossils, prepared by Walcott.

The building itself should not be passed over lightly either. It is an excellent piece of neoclassic architecture. The Greek inscription carved in the marble across the main facade, the window panels showing eminent figures of science, the ornate bronze doors, and the alternating figures of the owl (for wisdom) and the lynx (for alert observation) along the roof line all give it the aura of a temple to science. One decorative touch of interest is tucked away on the ceiling of the Great Hall: a painting of a trilobite. Next door to the east is the Federal Reserve building, and next to it is a building that once housed the Public Health Service; for years the tourist guides mentioned the three as "healthy, wealthy, and wise."

The NAS had good manners and passed a resolution thanking the SI for housing the group for more than half a century and for hosting the annual meeting almost every year during that interval. The second paragraph of the resolution would have approached hyperbole had it not been factual: "[Resolved:] That the academy expressly acknowledges its high esteem and thanks to the Secretary of the Smithsonian Institution, Charles Doolittle Walcott, for his personal interest in the work of the academy in the advancement of science, and his distinguished services as treasurer, vice president, acting president, president, and member of the council and committees, both official and unofficial, in its behalf" (Michaelson 1925, 23).

It was all true.

Of course, Walcott carried on as second vice president of the NRC and as chairman of the committee on federal relations. That also meant he was still on the NRC executive committee. Just to keep his hand in, he also was on the committees on policies, the building, the exhibits, and the Mary Clark Thompson Medal. Besides that, he was appointed a member of the forestry commission, a special NAS group.

It was time to return to business. Walcott and Merriam called on Secretary of Agriculture Henry C. Wallace, to discuss concerns about hoof-and-mouth disease. A formal request from the secretary then went to the White House, and the president duly requested the NAS to make a study. (This was the general route for NRC studies, though today such requests come from much lower levels of the executive branch.) In a note to Merriam, Walcott commented that the White House staff did not know the difference between the American Academy and the National Academy: "Such is fame," were the words Walcott used.

Life became quiet when this bit of NAS business had finally been started. Mary went off the Philadelphia for an extended visit, leaving Walcott very much at loose ends. The SI publications committee met to consider policies. Walcott attended the National Press Club, where a portrait of the late President Harding was presented. "A quiet day at the office. Moving my laboratory study downstairs from 3rd floor to back room of office" (May 9, 1924). That was one less flight of stairs for the secretary to climb. On Sunday, Walcott was at his new laboratory getting things in order and generally moping.

Mary came back, the American Association of Museums came to town, and life was better. This meeting overlapped with one held by the American Federation of Arts. Walcott was at the board meeting, having been elected a vice president of the federation in 1923. From there he went to a zoning commission meeting, to discuss some building lots in Washington confiscated from the German government, making this yet another day of diverse interests. By Saturday, Walcott was worn out. Church was skipped. "As we are both tired & sore we walked out into the woods in morning & enjoyed the wildflowers & sunshine" (May 18, 1924).

That walk helped, as did some yard work. "Talked with Dr. Gerrit Miller, Dr. Schram [sic], Dr. Abbot. Am looking for an exceptional man for S.I." (May 20, 1924). All this had to do with another assistant secretary, and just possibly with a successor to Secretary Walcott. Miller was a mammal specialist at the Museum, and Schramm taught botany at Cornell.

The National Parks Association board met in Secretary Hoover's office, in part to prepare for a major event that potentially could help the organization (Miles 1995). "Prest. Coolidge addressed meeting of outdoor recreation gathering 10 A.M. T[heodore] R[oosevelt] Jr. presided after president left meeting in Nat. Museum" (May 22, 1924). Mary came home from Philadelphia in time to help receive at the evening reception. Walcott met a number of friends the next day and had a quiet evening at home with a Cole Younger of New York; Mr. Younger was to appear repeatedly. "Routine at office and attending meetings of Conference. The results of the conference are promising for future development of public interest in the out-of-door life & recreation" (May 24, 1924).

The week following the conference on outdoor recreation began with a meeting with representatives of a publishing firm. During the day, Abbot and Walcott discussed a twenty-volume series, and over dinner Mary discussed her wildflower book. Galley proofs of one of his manuscripts came next. Walcott talked informally to several of the regents and invited Dr. Schramm to become assistant secretary. There were a few more informal discussions around the SI, as the shortfall of funds for printing was becoming a critical matter. At the end of May, the Walcotts picked dandelions, not a difficult job in Washington. He also commented on receiving edited manuscripts for parts 1 and 2 of SMC volume seventy-five.

On the 3d of June, part 9, which completed Walcott's fourth volume in the SMC, was published. "The field reconnaissance of the pre-Devonian formations of Alberta and British Columbia, Canada, that I have been conducting the past six seasons has resulted in the accumulation of collections that have received preliminary study and are now being prepared for illustration and description" (Walcott 1924, 479). In it, after a few general remarks Walcott got right to the description and illustration of the brachiopods—twenty from the Cambrian, twenty-six from what he called the Ozarkian, and two from the Ordovician. He threw in two specimens of cephalopods and also a peculiar crustacean he had turned up. There was a bit more description at the end of the work.

"Through the courtesy of Dr. Olaf Holtedahl, I have had the opportunity of studying a small collection of brachiopods from Novaya Zemlya, Russia, which he discovered there. The brachiopods are described and illustrated in this paper, and they will also be published later in Norway with the associated trilobites. The fauna is essentially a lower Mons facies and belongs as Dr. Holtedahl states, with the Pacific province and not the Atlantic" (Walcott 1924, 480–81).

This means that the fauna looked like the fossils from the massive limestone in Canada, not like the brachiopods from the shales and shaly limestones of similar age that occur in Europe and in eastern North America. It was an interesting point. These descriptions were republished (Walcott 1924a) as part of the results of Professor Holtedahl's expedition report. As in the earlier material from India (Walcott 1905), there is no known correspondence that explains how or when the specimens were sent to Walcott. The Holtedahl report is one of the few instances where Walcott repeated earlier work nearly word for word.

As promised in the brachiopod work, the Novaya Zemlya trilobites were later described in a collaborative effort with Resser (Walcott and Resser 1924). Unlike the reprinting of brachiopod illustrations and descriptions, this was a paper in its right, with two plates and eleven pages of text. It includes six new genera, plus one taken by permission from a manuscript of Ulrich. The paper is typical descriptive paleontology, boring in itself but providing basic documentation. What is interesting is that this is the only joint paper that Walcott ever published.

What is also interesting is that Resser did not publish again until after Walcott died. During the 1930s and early 1940s he turned out a flood of papers. The judgement of the profession is that each was worse than the preceding one; Resser was an amiable fellow but proved to be not much of a scientist. One gathers that Walcott suspected Resser's limitations and gave him this one chance to prove himself.

It is time to return to day-to-day life. June 1 being a Sunday, Walcott enjoyed an excellent sermon by Dr. Wood, whom he characterized as a clear thinker and a good speaker. Monday was routine except for a trip to the White House, where medals from the Theodore Roosevelt Foundation were presented to Elihu Root and Oliver Wendell Holmes. The next day saw him at an informal meeting of congressional regents at the Capitol. Walcott fixed up some odds & ends and left for New York; Mary had preceded him by a couple of days. They visited with Helen and Cousin Fred. Helen left for Boston that night, and Walcott commented that Cole Younger escorted her to the station. Something was going on.

The next two days were devoted to Mary's book. The Walcotts called on William E. Rudge, who was directly involved in producing it. Most time was devoted, however, to meeting potential subscribers; three additional deluxe, five-hundred-dollars copies were sold. Mary and Walcott spent a morning looking at a private art collection and then left for Tarrytown and a weekend with the W. R. Warners, neighbors of the Rockefellers.

The country rest was just what both needed. Back in New York City, they discussed art collections and sold books; "Mary now has 90 subscriptions of wildflower book" (June 11, 1924). They tried a few more prospects and then went back home, tired but satisfied. "Attending to mail & administrative matters all day. Conference with Mr. Lodge. He would like to continue permanently as Curator of Freer Gallery" (June 13, 1924). Saturday was a half-holiday for the Smithsonian people, so Walcott spent the afternoon at the Museum with

Resser. "I worked on genera of trilobite paper. At home found page proof of Beaverfoot-Brisco-Stanford Range paper no. 1 of vol. 75. Read proof 8–11 P.M." (June 14, 1924).

Three weeks after the brachiopod paper was published, the first part of Walcott's fifth SMC volume was released, "Geological Formations of the Beaverfoot-Brisco-Stanford Range, British Columbia, Canada" (Walcott 1924b). This was a work by Walcott the geologist, not Walcott the paleontologist. If the 1923 season had been physically hard on Walcott, no indication of that shows up in the writing. There are appropriate acknowledgments of assistance, lots of details of measured sections, and especially faunal lists. Walcott even included some structure sections and photographs to make the paper a little clearer. A map showed the sections measured by Walcott over the years, the same map used in his Belgian paper.

The church service that Sunday was fine, and a motor trip to the Bell estate in the country helped dispel some of the muggy air, but the typical Washington summer weather persisted. "The warm damp weather is most debilitating & causes all things to go slow. Mary getting home & other matters ready for the annual summer work in the mountains" (June 16, 1924).

Mary went to Philadelphia to say goodbye for the summer to family and friends. Walcott and Assistant Secretary Abbot spoke to a publisher concerning a Smithsonian junior science-book series. Several days of routine and of hot weather ensued. "At organizational meeting of Robert Brookings School of Government & Economics" (June 20, 1924).

Summer began on a Saturday. "Office closed at 1 P.M. so I worked on genera of trilobites P.M." (June 21, 1924). After services, Walcott attended a meeting of the church board, followed by another drive to try to cool off. "Clearing up many matters at the office. At odd times working on genera of trilobites. Mary still occupied with matters pertaining to her flower book" (June 23, 1924). Heat and humidity continued. "Mr. Rudge came 8 P.M. to talk over printing of Mary's Wild Flower book" (June 26, 1924).

"At my office 8:45 to 4 P.M. Completed paper no. 2, vol. 75 to go to press. Cleaned up papers and matters of office. Packed up odds & ends & we left at 6:50 P.M. for Buffalo" (June 27, 1924). (There was more to come on this particular manuscript.) Sidney and Helen-Louise had a new house, which the Walcotts admired on the very day that part 1 of volume seventy-five was issued. Sunday afternoon they were on the train to Toronto, and that evening they left for the West.

The prairies were green, for the growing season had started late. "Lake Louise 9 A.M. Found Arthur & our tent waiting for us. Also Paul V. Stevens & Dan Derrick. Horses nearly ready for the trail. Unpacked trunks etc. We are both tired as result of travels & bad weather. Greater part of Lake Louise chalet burned during day" (July 3, 1924). That sensational fire is still part of the local lore of Lake Louise.

After a couple of days getting organized and a day of bad weather, Walcott decided that his first move would be by train westward to Field. A motorcar took the couple to Takkakaw Falls, where they stayed in a bungalow; times had changed. The camp outfit came in the next evening. The Walcotts stayed around camp, collected wildflowers, and visited with Jack Giddie, who had been their guide in 1909 and 1910 when the Burgess Shale fauna was found and first excavated. "Left Yoho Camp (Takkakaw) with outfit & went up to Burgess Pass camp ground & put up our tents in the same spot as in 1919. Collected a lot of *Marrella* from fragments left about camp. Camp 3" (July 9, 1924). Walcott was "not good for any work" the next day, though later they took a short ride, and Mary sketched a snow lily.

"We went up to my old fossil quarry & collected 2 pkgs of fossil from rock quarried in 1919. Nothing new but all good for exchange" (July 11, 1924). The next day Walcott was "tired & lazy." In contrast, Mary rode down to Emerald Lake, garnered a white wild lily, and sketched it in camp, while they watched the goats on Mount Field. The next day, a Sunday, they did little, although Jack Giddie came to the camp with his new wife. It seems pretty clear that Walcott was not in the pink of health. "Mary & I went up to the fossil quarry in the morning and collected about 50 specimens, but nothing new. Mary sketching in afternoon & I fussed over notes for A.A.A.S. address" (July 14, 1924). This was the last time Walcott would see his Burgess Shale quarry. The next day they went down the trail and back to the Yoho Valley, where the "Trail Riders" were holding their first gathering.

This organization was a creation of the Canadian Pacific Railway. One qualified for membership by riding a minimum number of miles in western Canada; there were several categories, and Walcott was in the highest. "I have traced on the map the principal trails over which I have ridden in connection with geological work. . . . [W]e made from 18 to 30 base camps each season . . . averaging 100 days each season . . . [w]hich would give 780 days at a minimum average of five miles per day. This is in addition to the riding in connection with moving from camp to camp."[3] Walcott mentioned that Mary had not yet received a map to record her travels, which had begun twenty years before his first trip in 1907. The Trail Riders prepared guides to local trails and put out a bulletin; for a few years Walcott contributed photographs to it.

The Walcotts met many old friends at the gathering. He was the honorary president of the organization, but like every office in which Walcott was involved, it was more than honorific. "Occupied with Trail Riders matters. In the evening presided at the 'Pow-Wow.' Many interesting events, stories, music, etc. etc. Rain prevents the outdoor camp fire" (July 17, 1924). Walcott skipped a trail ride the next day because of indisposition. After another day of visiting, Walcott sent the pack train back to Lake Louise; they moved to a bungalow, where Walcott was wiped out by bowel trouble.

Washington reported. "We received today the final allocations from the Personnel Classification Board which they have been working on for months, and am glad to report that twenty-six Museum employees were re-allocated with increased salaries; . . . The large majority, however, remain as originally allocated by the Board, so there is considerable dissatisfaction. . . . [I]t [the pay increase] will undoubtedly necessitate our asking for deficiency appropriations for several of the Bureaus."[4] In this era of change at every increasing rates, it is good to know that some things in the federal government remain constant—for instance, Civil Service regulations mandate pay raises but Congress does not provide the money to cover them. The situation for bureaus is even worse when Congress gives all government employees a raise, but gives the government no additional funding.

The Walcotts went back to Lake Louise by train and to their familiar tent. The horses scattered; Dan Derrick, one of the packers, found some of them fifteen miles away. "Attended to a few letters etc. Copy of No. 2, Vol. 75 S.M.Coll rec'd. Cambrian & Ozarkian trilobites" (July 23, 1924). The story of this particular publication is recounted in a memorandum from Resser to James G. Traylor, for the manuscript that Walcott had left in Washington became number three in this volume. If nothing else, the memorandum provides information on what printing really involved in the primitive, precomputer days.

Last Thursday morning (July 17) a telegram was received by you from Dr. Walcott asking that I secure a copy of a paper by Prof. P. E. Raymond dealing with Cambrian and Ozarkian trilobites and compare it with Dr. Walcott's manuscript about to be sent to the press. This request was telegraphed to Prof. Schuchert, who informed Dr. Walcott of Prof. Raymond's paper, and he in turn asked the Boston Society of Natural History to send me a copy. I received a copy of the proof on Sunday (July 20).

At noon Thursday (July 17) a second telegram arrived from Dr. Walcott requesting the Editor and myself to get out a brief summary incorporating the new genera of Dr. Walcott's paper as no. 2 of vol. 75 (s.m.c.). Dr. Walcott gave very brief instructions as to the nature of the presentation and asked that the paper be off the press by July 22.

Mr. True [the editor] came over to the museum shortly after the receipt of the telegram and we arranged the make up of the paper. He then made arrangements with the engravers and printers for turning out this work as rapidly as possible. Dr. Merrill [head curator of geology] kindly lent his stenographer for the latter part of Thursday afternoon and Friday forenoon. Miss Visal also assisted Friday forenoon.

I reached the office 7 A.M. Friday (18th) and had the figures which had been assembled the evening previously, mounted before 9 and by 9:30 Mr. True was able to take them to the engravers. By dictating alternately to two stenographers the manuscript was completed by 12:30, and taken at once to Baltimore by the Editor.

Shortly after his departure the idea was advanced that the article could possibly be printed by Saturday (19th). I called up Mr. True at the Lord Baltimore Press in Baltimore and proposed the matter of printing by Saturday. He immediately held a conference with the officials of the printing company and they agreed to print the paper Saturday. I arranged with the engraver to call for the plates and deliver them personally, but because someone telephoned from the Smithsonian after I had made these arrangements, when I called they had been mailed.

I went to Baltimore, reaching the plant at 8 A.M. (19th). We had to wait until 10:15 for the delivery of the plates. In the meantime I read the proof and reduced the paper by a half of [a] page so that it might be set on one press form (16 pages) thus saving printing time. Within one hour after the arrival of the plates the final page proof was delivered from the plant and the 30 copies of the completed paper were delivered by 1 P.M.

The officials of the Lord Baltimore Press are to be highly commended for the courteous aid and willingness to assist in everything. Nothing was too much trouble.

I mailed twenty copies at 1:30 in Baltimore (19) thus insuring distribution on the date the paper was issued.

Considerable improvement would have been possible in the text and in the mounting of the figures if more time had been taken and I very much regret overlooking a typographical error in the description of the genus *Bellfontia*.[5]

Walcott marked his copy "received at Lake Louise 7-23-24."

If one assumes that Resser acted as secretary rather than author, *Bellfontia* should be cited as "Ulrich *in* Walcott 1924"; Ulrich had a manuscript in preparation, and this name had been taken from it. Otherwise, there are thirty-two new generic names by Walcott of trilobites in this short paper. Raymond's 1924 paper, which had started the rush to publish, was on trilobites of approximately the same age from Vermont. This seems to be a clear-cut case of Walcott's trying to obtain priority for his names, just in case Dr. Raymond had found the same undescribed forms and was about to bestow his own set of new names. Thus 1924 marked not only Walcott's only joint publication but the only time Walcott engaged in a rush for priority.

As it turned out, there was essentially no overlap between Raymond's material and that of Walcott. Nothing of this rush to publish is mentioned in Walcott's diary. What is even more curious is that Raymond was in western Canada that summer and Walcott did not note a visit to him. T. H. Clark, still working at McGill University when he was in his nineties, would recall this meeting.

"During the 1924 trip we were visited by Dr. Walcott and his wife who spent all afternoon with us. Walcott and Raymond stayed together while Mrs. Walcott cruised around camp criticizing everything down to the tent pegs" (Clark *in* Gould 1990, 16). Personal recollection of Mary by a few others suggests that this is an extremely accurate observation. Apparently Walcott and Raymond were on cordial terms. Allowing for that, perhaps Walcott was building a fence around the western trilobites. Another way to look at this matter is that he had invested a great deal of time and effort in assembling his collection and was now protecting his investment.

While Resser was running up, down, and sideways to get the short manuscript out quickly, Walcott sat in camp. "Paul Stevens our packer has not returned" (July 24, 1924). "A warm day. Engaged Tex Wood as packer to replace Paul Stevens who apparently is off on a spree" (July 25, 1924). Tex, a displaced Englishman, had packed for Walcott in earlier seasons, and with his help they moved to camp six, along Baker Creek to the base of what had been dubbed Brachiopod Mountain. "I hope to find a good exposure of the upper Mons & lower Sarbach near here so that their contact may be seen" (July 27, 1924). Man proposes, nature disposes, and the following day fog, mist and rain kept them in camp.

The Walcotts next were on a section east of the mountain, only to be driven in by rain. The following day was a bit better on Fossil Mountain, where they collected fossils from the upper part of the Mons. Meanwhile, Dan had found a missing mare and her colt. The end of July was Mary's birthday, celebrated by a horseback ride; the Walcotts had similar, simple tastes.

"The boundary between the Mons and Sarbach appears to pass just west of camp" (August 1, 1924). A day of rain prevented Walcott from examining this boundary, and it was followed by a day of snow. Walcott fussed around camp for still another day waiting for better weather; meanwhile Mary was sketching flowers almost every waking minute. "A fine cool day. Out taking photographs A.M. & going over Sarbach section at east base of Brachiopod Mt. It is glorious to have a fine day. Sun warm, wind cool" (August 5, 1924).

Another fine day came, and they collected nine packages of fossils from the Mons on Fossil Mountain. The party scattered, Dan taking the fossils to Lake Louise, Mary to find a green gentian, and Tex and Walcott up the valley to collect from the Lyell Limestone and scout prospects for big game. They collected

more fossils the next day, Mary doing double duty by both collecting and keeping up her sketching of flowers. "We packed up and moved to our 'Wild Flower'
camp of 1921. A warm day in the sunshine. The trail was not bad. By 4:00 P.M.
our tent was in order & Arthur had a good dinner at 6:30" (August 10, 1924). Life
has its good moments.

Mary and Tex accompanied Walcott up the trail to Johnson Pass. They collected fossils from the upper part of the Mons and photographed the overthrust.
Good and bad were intermixed, for Walcott had neuralgia that afternoon. The
next day he collected Middle and Upper Cambrian fossils closer to camp and
continued to break fossils out of the limestone of the Mons Formation. Neuralgia in the afternoon, when he was tired, now seemed a daily occurrence. The
weather was intermittently fair and wet, the fossil collecting intermittently good
and poor. During the rainy times Walcott completed his presidential address for
the AAAS December meeting.

The weather did not improve, and Walcott was unable to work under such
conditions: "Am not able to climb so I have to make old Cricket take [me] up as
high as the going will permit" (August 19, 1924). Walcott never named a species
after Cricket, but he did put the horse's picture in "Explorations" (Walcott
1925c). Cricket had earned it, and in the photograph the animal looks as tired
as Walcott felt.

They moved down below Baker Lake, but the wind and mist persisted. At this
eighth camp of the season, the weather was no better. They collected a few fossils from the Mons close to the tent. Walcott hung around camp hoping for
better weather, while Mary rode to Lake Louise for the mail: all was well with
the SI and with the family. There was news that Calvin Coolidge's son had died.
Walcott wrote a touching personal letter, to which he received a reply from the
family: "He [Coolidge] realizes how much more than most people you could
understand, and how genuine is the sympathy you extend to him. He asks me
to send his best wishes and profoundest appreciations to both you and Mrs.
Walcott."[6]

"A very disagreeable day with gale of wind from s.w. wh[ich] continued
through the night" (August 24, 1924). The gale persisted another day. When the
wind relented, Walcott and Mary rode out to the section, only to be driven back
in by wind and rain. "Weather cleared during the night. Mary & I crossed to
Cotton Grass Cirque in Oyster Mtn. ridge & worked on section all day. All upper
Cambrian. I measured over 2500' in thickness. Returned at 5:30 P.M. Charles E.
Phillips took Tex Woods place today" (August 26, 1924). Good help in the Rockies was even harder to keep than it was to find; Tex could make more money
guiding a hunting party. Phillips was probably the ranger at Yoho Park, or at
least a namesake.

Mary and Walcott went back through the cirque (a steep-walled basin, which was the head of a former glacier and was carved out by ice action) and to Tilted Falls for another day of collecting. The fossils were Late Cambrian in age, in the Lyell Limestone. One more day with Mr. Phillips increased the collections and provided the extra muscle needed to bring up the cameras. After three hard days, it was just as well for Walcott that a snow kept them in camp.

"Snow melted rapidly & after lunch Mary & I rode over to Tilted Mt. Brook to collect a few upper Cambrian fossils & locate them in the section i.e. upper Saukia faunule" (August 30, 1924). Some translation is required. Just as Walcott could differentiate four different zones within the Mons Formation, he could distinguish several zones in the older rocks. The trilobite *Saukia* has a fairly long range within Upper Cambrian beds, but there were subtle differences. Walcott had seen certain kinds of *Saukia* elsewhere, hence the use of "upper." He wanted to confirm the position and range of this form within a measured section. A faunule, by the way, is a collection of a fauna from a very limited area.

The last day of August brought excellent weather, and they moved camp to the Red Deer River. "A mixed up wasted day owing to 'Pinto' & her gang of horses losing themselves in the forest. Camp finally made 6 mi down Red Deer river to Snow Creek trail. All settled 9 P.M." (September 1, 1924). A fairly safe rule of pack trains is that the more horses, the slower the movement. If one drives loose horses, there is always a potential for trouble.

"The men went out for sheep & brot in a fine ewe at 5 P.M. The horses Cricket, Ginger, Pinto & Roany ran off to the ranch 14 *mi.* Dan brought them back at 2 A.M. Mary sketch [*sic*] wild flowers & I puttered about" (September 2, 1924). Clearly this was a summer in which only a limited amount would be accomplished. The next day the Walcotts were still in camp, he with neuralgia, she with her sketchbook, and Phillips with his skinning knife. "Camp moved down the Red Deer River to Eagle Pass. East of Government Ranch house 5 miles. 18 mi from Dutch Creek" (September 4, 1924). Not much country was being covered this season.

Mary and Walcott spent the night at a ranch house, coming to camp the next day to spend that next night in the tent, soaked by rain, but thereafter life did improve. "With Mary & Phillips spent the day in examining Eagle Pass section. It is much like that at Devils Gate–Ghost River, the Devonian having been pushed out eastward over the Cretaceous. We caught 3 fine trout in James Brook, one 18 *in* long" (September 6, 1924). Field geologists think in several dimensions. They may think vertically—that is, about underlying and overlying rocks— or they think laterally, as Walcott was doing here with his comparison; they simultaneously think about the structural complications that confuse the rock sequence either vertically or laterally. Some also think about fishing.

The next morning it rained, but in the afternoon Walcott and Dan rode down the canyon a few miles to observe the strata on the canyon walls. The rocks were not worth noting, but several sixteen-inch trout were. The next day Mary went up the canyon to photograph, while Dan & Walcott went fishing. This time they had six trout over twenty-two inches. Walcott says nothing in his diary about health, but one senses that he had run out of steam for pounding on the rocks to collect fossils.

They moved camp again, lost the trail in a swamp and had to put up the tents without reaching their goal. They continued up the Panther River for fourteen miles and reached campsite thirteen on Wigmore Creek. "All settled at 5 P.M. & Arthur had a good dinner for us at 6:30" (September 10, 1924). Walcott knew to give credit where credit was due. Arthur was a gem.

"Mary & I remained in & about camp all day. We are both tired and I have intercostal neuralgia when walking or riding" (September 11, 1924). This was not good news at all. Phillips went looking for an old ram to use in a museum exhibit in Washington; with the perversity so characteristic of animals, twelve rams allowed themselves to be seen, but all young ones. "With Mary went up Harrison Lake 6 *mi* to see contact between Devonian & Cretaceous by overthrust fault" (September 12, 1924). "Mary & I were lame & tired so we remained in camp" (September 13, 1924). Phillips and Dan went out and got an old ram, as specified. The next day was devoted to taking panoramic views and with packing skins and skulls for another move.

"Owing to Pinto & her bunch straying off into the woods Dan did not get home until 1:30 P.M. too late to move camp. We packed up & waited & then went for a horse ride down the Panther River. Mary read me to sleep. A restless, useless sort of a day" (September 15, 1924). If it was not the weather, it was horses.

The party moved over Snow Creek Pass to McConnell Creek, and finally had a beautiful day and a good ride. "Moved camp up the Red Deer Valley to the Uppley game warden cabin where we camped in 1920 & 1922" (September 17, 1924). Walcott wanted some photographs in the canyon, but the next day brought more snow; this season seemed to have an inordinate number of "Sundays." Dan took in a load of fossils and brought back a large haul of mail. That was just as well, for they were stuck in camp for two more days before they gave up and retreated to Lake Louise station; camp sixteen was the last of the season.

The Walcotts spent a day packing and admiring the snow high on the mountains. That night, another three inches of snow was dumped on the tents. Charlie Phillips left, and Tex Wood took the horses. "We finished packing & left Lake Louise for Banff" (September 25, 1924). Walcott settled various bills, arranged with customs officials about his thirteen pieces of baggage, and looked at the local museum. "It is good to have a clear day after 8 days of cold, snow squalls & high winds" (September 26, 1924). At 11:10 on Saturday, they headed east to Buffalo, where more mail caught up with them.

Chief Clerk Dorsey reported on the Bureau of the Budget. "We had the Budget hearings on Saturday, were with them from two o'clock until after five. They went into things very thoroughly, asked lots of questions, but were not unfair or unduly critical about anything. As hearings go, it was quite satisfactory, although this, of course, does not necessarily mean anything when it come to making appropriations."[7] Again, despite other changes, concern about appropriations remains perpetual in Washington.

Sidney and family met the Walcotts at the train station and took them home. "Found letter from Helen stating that she was leaving for France" (September 30, 1924). They spent a full day with Evelyn, who was about to start school. The next day there was a daylight train ride to Washington rather than the normal Pullman sleeper of past years. All was well at home, and at the office "nothing serious has occurred since we left in June" (October 3, 1924). Walcott read proofs for the index to volume sixty-seven, a thankless job. Relaxation was listening to World Series baseball game on the radio; Washington lost to the New York Giants, 4–3.

Walcott skipped church and fussed around the house. He was at the office Monday. During the trip across Canada his cold and neuralgic pains had reappeared; as he wrote, they kept him from being very happy. New York won again, 6–4. "Our field collections are in & unpacked. Work will begin on them at once" (October 7, 1924). Washington won the next game, finally, 7–2.

The next day Washington won, 7–5. Walcott, with Mr. Dorsey and Mr. Ravenel, looked over the Budget Bureau estimates. "Began getting papers in order for work on pre-Devonian formations of Cordilleran trough in Alberta" (October 3, 1924). Washington won, 2–1. "Was'n club won ball game from N.Y. Giants & thus won the all world championship for 1924. The city celebrated until midnight" (October 10, 1924). Walter Johnson, "The Big Train," had begun pitching for Washington the year Walcott became si secretary and would continue through the year of Walcott's death; this was his finest moment. There are now several generations of Washingtonians who have never seen a ball game in their hometown, let alone World Series play.

The city was quiet the next day, and Walcott worked on his field notes. On Sunday, Mr. Rudge stopped by for breakfast and spent the day discussing the printing of Mary's book. Monday evening, Mr. William T. De Van and his wife had dinner. The arrangements for selling the wildflower books and the Smithsonian scientific series were smoothed out.

"Mary left for Philadelphia 9:15 A.M. I attended meeting of Board of Research Council 10–12. At my office P.M. Called at Museum to see Ulrich, Bassler, Resser, Merguet [*sic*] & Miss Gardner 3:30–5 P.M. Wrote Mary & Helen in evening" (October 14, 1924). "A quiet day at office & work room. Looking over notes on Robson Peak section. Looking over mss of trilobite paper in evening" (October 15, 1924). "Had three teeth taken out of upper jaw as they were no longer of service" (October 16, 1924).

Walcott held a couple of interviews, still trying to get the position of assistant secretary filled by the right person. That was not his only vacancy problem. "W*m* Dalman who had been my motor car driver during the last 12 years [was] dropped today" (October 20, 1924). Dalman wanted a raise and was not going to get it. Notwithstanding these problems, Walcott worked a little on the geology of Mount Robson and saw Yard about the struggling National Parks Association. Life was in fact so quiet that Walcott was able to spend several nearly uninterrupted days on his field notes. The biggest problem was the prospect of frost, threatening Mary's "war garden" planted along the Anacostia River in southeast Washington. They drove down to harvest flowers and vegetables.

Mary was busy. "A series of water-color sketches of the striking wild flowers of the Canadian Rockies and Glacier National Park . . . is now on exhibition in the main hall of the Smithsonian Building. . . . Many of the sketches have been shown to the public previously, but there are also a number of new ones. . . . Altogether the exhibition contains 160 water-color sketches."[8]

Walcott attended a few embassy functions, came down with a cold, saw the dentist, and went to the funeral of Secretary of Agriculture Wallace—another friend gone. Plans for the National Art Gallery building were reviewed. "Political battle for President of U.S. is quite intense on the part of speakers but the people are rather quiet. Looks like Coolidge now" (October 29, 1924). Walcott looked over drawings of geologic sections made by a draftsman and arranged with Mary for three formal dinners. They also decided to buy a radio set; there was nothing quite like keeping up with the times. The coming election had people a little on edge.

"*Election Day.* As we cannot vote in D.C. I spent the day in my office & laboratory. In the evening D*r* & Mrs. Chas Wood came & we listened to election returns" (November 4, 1924). "Election yesterday resulted in a Republican victory which will mean much to the people of the U.S. & the world. A reliable steady government controlled by principles of a high order. At my office except for a call at the Geological Survey. We attended the funeral of Ned Hollister 7 P.M." (November 5, 1924).

"A quiet but broken up day at my office. Talked with Alex Wetmore *en re* Supt. Zoological Park to take the place of Ned Hollister[,] deceased. At home in evening.

Bachrach showing Mary how to operate radio receiver" (November 7, 1924). Hollister had taken Charlie to Mount Robson in 1911, the year Helena was killed, and Hollister's death must have brought back memories. He had been head of the zoo since 1916. Even by the standards of the time, Hollister, born in 1876, was a young man, and his death before fifty must have had some effect on Walcott.

Vacancies on the CIW Board of Trustees had to be considered, and the photograph for the annual Christmas card had to be selected; November dragged on. A prospect for assistant secretary was discussed but rejected when it was found that he already had a salary substantially more than the Washington position paid. "Henry Cabot Lodge, United States Senator since 1893 and Regent of the Smithsonian Institution for 22 years, died November 9, 1922" (Walcott 1926, 25). Regent Lodge was not mentioned in Walcott's pocket diary.

Overall, Walcott was not doing well physically. "My cold has resulted in considerable deafness which may be permanent" (November 11, 1924). Charles Darwin was the greatest worrier about his health in the history of biology; Walcott might have a similar title in paleontology. "Am feeling the reaction incident to life in office & home after camp life during summer" (November 13, 1924). Still, Walcott kept the routine going and was well enough to drop by the White House to discuss SI matters with President Coolidge.

Walcott's gums were healing from his last ride in the dentist's chair. "Considering questions connected with publication of a series of scientific books by Smithsonian and of increasing endowment by asking gifts from private sources" (November 14, 1924). The Executive Committee met and looked favorably on Walcott's plan to publish as a means of raising funds; gray November was getting brighter.

"A quiet day at the Smithsonian. Routine & looking up data *en re* my report on geologic sections in Canadian Cordillera. Meeting of Board of Inst of Economics & Government. Playing with radio in evening" (November 19, 1924). The next day was a mixed-up one, what with introducing Dr. Alexander Wetmore to the employees of the National Zoological Park and hearing a talk at the Museum auditorium by President Coolidge on lumber conservation. "Silent Cal" Coolidge is known to many, but gentle, tall, storklike Alex Wetmore is not a household name. He was already a most creditable ornithologist with the U.S. Biological Survey, Department of Agriculture when Walcott recruited him.

"Usual odds & ends at my office & a little work on the subjects of publications & endowment two very vital & important matters at the present time" (November 20, 1924). The next day he met with Secretary of the Treasury Mellon concerning the new art building. Walcott was not in contact with Mellon as frequently as with other cabinet members, particularly the war and army, but he had had him to dinner at least once, and Mellon had known for years that

Walcott wanted an art gallery. After all, Mr. Mellon did have a few pictures in his home in Pittsburgh.

Art at the SI was still causing perturbations. The physical anthropologist Aleš Hrdlička was presenting a series of Friday lectures, but one Friday the Museum auditorium was unavailable; he wrote Walcott as the only person who could make a decision on use of the auditorium in the Freer Gallery. "Sorry but the use of the Freer Gallery lecture hall is limited to matter connected with Mr. Freer[']s plan."[9] Walcott felt honor bound, again, an old-fashioned word, by Mr. Freer's will.

Walcott looked up some papers relative to the Smithson endowment but otherwise was not doing much because of another cold. He did attend a meeting and sign the charter of the Brookings Institution. He also witnessed an event unlikely to occur again, Mrs. Coolidge christening a dirigible. After that high excitement, the Walcotts dined with the Italian ambassador. Walcott observed the Thanksgiving tradition of attending church service, and he started a new tradition by listening to a football game on the radio.

On November 29, the *Washington Post* reported that Secretary Walcott was to receive a doctorate from the Sorbonne, his eleventh honorary degree. Secretary Walcott expressed his regrets at not being able to attend. The French ambassador, who was on a trip to New York wrote a note: "I am very glad to think that this is one more case in which the learning, the conscientious work and the success of one of the leaders of the American scientific world will have been recognized in France."[10] The month ended with a small dinner in honor of Secretary of State Hughes.

December began clear and cold. "Administrative matters, routine & interviews took all my time during the day. At home in the evening calking doors & sash to keep out cold wind" (December 1, 1924). The Walcotts gave a dinner for the British ambassador. Senator Smoot was added to the SI Board of Regents to replace the deceased Senator Lodge. This helped, but then another regent resigned. Sunday was busy. Senator Smoot was given a tour of the exhibits. The John Lodges dined, and later Mather and Albright came to see him in regard to the National Parks; no surprises on that topic.

Art was very much to the fore. Walcott spent Monday considering development of the Freer Gallery and talking to John Lodge about the National Gallery of Art. The National Commission met the following day. The annual meeting of the regents was adjourned until January, for discussion of the SI in relation to the federal government was the principal matter, and more data on various proposals was needed.

The Carnegie Institution of Washington trustees met. Walcott wrote President Coolidge asking him to make a few remarks at the opening of the AAAS, but this did not fit into the schedule of the White House. He wrote a letter to the attorney general, and the week ended. After church he and Mary had a short walk in the sunshine, a nice break for mid-December.

Monday Walcott corralled Secretary of State Hughes to do the honors at the opening of the AAAS and during the week got the details worked out. He took Mr. Ravenel up to Capitol Hill and had an informal meeting with the House of Representatives regents to ease the way for the appropriation hearings. "A day of administrative and routine matters. Sent letter to House Regents *en re* appropriations. At 9 A.M. held brief talk with Atty. Genl. *en re* authority of Regents to contract for service in soliciting funds for endowment" (December 17, 1925). Agreement on a contract for what was to be the Smithsonian Scientific Series of books was reached on December 19, and the following day the contract was sent to New York. The Vaux family came to visit on Saturday, and as had been the pattern in earlier jaunts, on Sunday the seniors went to a Friends meeting, and the two boys, George and Henry, went to the zoo.

Monday was busy. Walcott worked on his talk and prepared notes for the appropriations hearing. In the midst of this came a meeting concerning the Brookings Institution. He returned to his earlier chores, completed them, and had another meeting about the Brookings. "Routine & writing out note for talk Dec. 31st on geol. work in Canadian Rockies. Gave Christmas gifts to some of the people at office. All left at 1 o clock. Went home 3 P.M. to assist Mary. We had our Christmas gifts in evening with Arthur, Mollie, Annie & Delia" (December 24, 1924).

Christmas Day itself was quiet, with Walcott in his office working on his lecture and later visiting a few friends. To clarify matters: this talk and his AAAS presidential address were two quite distinct items. Work on the talk continued the next day. December 27 was significant as the day a contract was signed for Mary's wildflower book. On Sunday the Walcotts skipped church, and Mary hand-colored lantern slides for his geologic talk; later that Sunday they telegramed Mr. Rudge with some details on the book contract.

The first work day was spent "on routine & a large mail. Talk in evening" (December 29, 1924). Thus, did Walcott mention his presidential address to the American Association for the Advancement of Science, which was published the following week (Walcott 1925d). It had been just as well to give the president a year to rest up after his term in office. The late Waldo Schmidt from the Museum, Division of Crustacea, had taken an out-of-town friend to the session at Constitution Hall. The friend was shocked at how old and frail Walcott looked at the podium.

Nevertheless, there was still vigor in Walcott's writing. Revisionist historians might pick at a few of his sentences: "The story of the onward march of scientific research in quest of truth is not unlike that of the white race in the conquest of America"; "I believe a good scientist should be a good Christian, and a good Christian should be a scientist in his method and work, as both are seeking the truth and the fundamental principles underlying their respective fields of endeavor"; and, "Why not provide for a junior section of the American Association, and last and in some respects the most important, a woman's section and sessions, at which all the scientific problems of peculiar interest to women could be considered?"

To those who want to look for slights, Walcott was a racist, a religious bigot, and a sexist. However, historians who take the time to read the piece in full will note that it is an attack on "the 'sociosophists' defined by David Starr Jordan as 'apostles of systematized ignorance'" (Walcott 1925d, 1). "The scientist need not enter into controversies with [the] theologian, or the sociosophist. He may make mistakes and interpret nature incorrectly, and he will never become so infallible or omniscient as to be sure that he has the entire or exact truth" (Walcott 1925d, 2).

Walcott then used a paragraph to summarize his investigations into the past, pointing out that in 1876 nothing had been of life known below the Potsdam Sandstone. He noted the three series of the Cambrian and mentioned that apart from cephalopods and vertebrates, almost all organisms known then were present in the Burgess Shale. His next paragraph mentioned the presence of bacteria and algal growth in older rocks, and the absence of intermediate forms. "This leaves the field open for the research student of the future to discover the earlier forms of life that in a slow evolution through millions of years finally developed into the high organized invertebrates of early Cambrian life" (Walcott 1925d, 2). This is not the only place Walcott uses the word "evolution," and in the context of 1924 it was most important that he do so. Walcott used a shotgun, not a rifle, to shoot at the nemesis. "The sociosophists will rail at and denounce the scientific method, as they cannot or will not comprehend it, but it is clearly the only method by which the errors of the present and the truth of the future may with certainty be known."

He chided the association for doing too little to counteract extreme specialization and promote understanding of science. "More attention must be paid to the unity of nature in order to counteract the artificial divisions which are the natural result of specialization in research. . . . There is something wrong when ten minutes is the limit for presentation of a valuable paper, with practically no time available for discussion" (Walcott 1925d, 3). If Walcott could attend a current meeting, he would be heartsick at how much worse oral communication has become.

Walcott discussed natural resources and their waste in the United States as the result of lack of knowledge or interest in the underlying scientific principles. He urged that more be done to promote conservation. He also, as was his nature, offered positive suggestions. One was a closer liaison with industry. He also suggested a news service and other positive steps to increase public awareness of science. He ended with a challenge: "The Pilgrim fathers knew little of science, but they brought the great principals [*sic*] of law, truth, freedom and faith in God to America. Are we doing all in our power to perpetuate and develop them in connection with the multiplex activities of the world of to-day?" (Walcott 1925d, 5).

That ought to have been enough for the year, but more was to come. "Routine and getting lantern slides in order for talk tomorrow afternoon. Cleaning up odds & ends of 1924 matters. At home in evening writing etc. & listening to addresses by radio" (December 30, 1924). "At meeting of A.A.A.S. council A.M. & my office. Spoke on my geological work in Canadian Rockies 4:15–5:30 in Auditorium of Nat. Museum. A quiet evening at home cleaning up odds & ends & reading" (December 31, 1924). "Dr. Charles D. Walcott, retiring president of the association, gave a lecture on 'Geological explorations in the Canadian Rockies,' beautifully illustrated by ninety colored lantern slides. This session proved very popular and the large auditorium was filled to overflowing" (Livingston 1925, 129). If there is ever any question as to whether Mary was more than just a helpmate, consider the lantern slides. Hand coloring one or two would be tedious, but ninety is a major effort.

> This year has passed quickly & pleasantly and without notable events in our home life. Helen is at her studio in Paris, France—Sidney with his wife & child Evelyn is at his home in Buffalo, N.Y. Mary & I are well but a year older & a little less vigorous. We had a hard summer season in the Canadian Rockies & much to attend to since returning home. The coming year will undoubtedly bring change in and to us as I am in my 75*th* yr & Mary her 65*th* yr.
>
> The preparation of Mary's American Wild Flower book for publication & the making possible [of] its publication is the most important event to us in our work. No unusual event has occurred at the Smithsonian.
>
> The election of Calvin Coolidge as President from March 4th 1925 to Mch 4th 1929 is the most important event in our national life & only so to all nations as he stands for orderly constitutional government & high ideals of duty & life. (December 31, 1924)

Walcott could not have known it on New Year's Day, but 1925 was destined to be his worse year so far as administrative aggravations were concerned. That day, however, the Walcotts called on the Tafts, the Weeks, the Hoovers, and the

Mellons—that is, the secretary of the treasury and his daughter. "We are glad to be alive & able to carry on our work & play" (January 1, 1925). It was a nice sentiment to start a fresh year.

"Attending to administrative and other matters at my office as Secty of Smithsonian Institution. Hope to go ahead with research work next week" (January 2, 1925). That evening the Walcotts gave a small dinner for the AAAS officers and officials. It was an appropriate gesture by the past president. The next day was routine, though Walcott looked up data on the Roosevelt African Expedition, just in case any of the regents asked him about past policy on donations to the institution. Eliot Blackwelder, who had accompanied Bailey Willis to China and had collected all the fossils, and Lancaster Burling called. Both visits were good geologic breaks from administrative routine. On Sunday, Walcott stayed home except for a walk; the weather was not entirely satisfactory. Once inside, the working of his new toy, the radio, was excellent; he heard church services and an organ recital from New York. This was an interval of calm before the storm.

"Meeting of Board Regents S.I. 9:30–11 A.M. Several items of great interest to the Smithsonian were considered & approved by the Board. Saul S. Wyer came at noon to discuss his paper on 'Niagara Falls its Power Possibilities & Preservation.' At 4:30 P.M. we called on Secty Hoover in relation to it & its publication. Mr. Wyer dined with us. A quiet evening as he left 7:45 P.M." (January 5, 1925).

There are two different themes here, and whereas the first was long-range and quiet, and the second was immediate and turned out to be explosive. For the first, Walcott had decided that outside help was needed to run a proper endowment drive. That is, a committee of regents had been appointed, and Walcott had led it to this conclusion, which was reported at the December meeting. There was some concern among the regents as to the legality of hiring fundraisers; Walcott had written to President Coolidge in December asking if the attorney general could give an opinion as to whether there was any prohibition against consultants—and could an answer be forthcoming in a few weeks, so that regents could act in January? Not unexpectedly, Walcott was assured in two days that the attorney general had no objection to the SI hiring consultants. Walcott, of course, had laid the groundwork by visiting the attourney general a few weeks earlier. Later in December, Walcott tried to convince Coolidge to send out a press release supporting the SI endowment drive, but the president declined, for the money in his view would be for a private rather than a public purpose.

The Wyer matter moved along faster. "A mixed-up day at my office. Settled on publication of Wyers paper at once. Attended to routine mail etc. Feeling tired & lazy in afternoon. Had 2 teeth taken out 5 P.M. At home with Mary in evening" (January 6, 1925). Walcott wrote an introduction to Wyer's twenty-eight-page publication, which was part of a new Smithsonian venture, published

under the general rubric of "Study of Natural Resources." Wyer had earlier published a study on energy resources of Pennsylvania. Events of January stemming
from this publication were later chronicled from the viewpoint of a biographer
of Senator George Norris:

> In January, 1925, in the midst of the fight on the Underwood bill, it [the
> Smithsonian Institution] issued a handsomely printed pamphlet. . . . It was
> written by Samuel S. Wyer, whose title was given as "Associate in Mineral
> Technology, United States National Museum" [footnote: Investigations re-
> vealed that Samuel S. Wyer was not an employee of the Smithsonian Insti-
> tution and not on its payroll. He was a private consulting engineer, a resident
> of Columbus, Ohio, who was very actively opposed to public power pro-
> grams. Most of his statements Norris felt were fallacious, misleading, and
> unfounded.] Seemingly it was a report by a reputed government scientist.
> . . . But the greatest part of this pseudoscientific pamphlet was a diatribe
> against the publically owned and operated Ontario hydroelectric system. . . .
> Walcott had written an introduction in which he called special attention to
> Wyer's assertions of the superiority of private over public ownership. (Lowitt
> 1971, 260)

What Walcott wrote was, "Enough data are given in Part III to permit the
reader to make an evaluation of these two methods" (Walcott *in* Wyer 1925, iii).
Norris's biographer remarks how widely the pamphlet was distributed and notes
that later in the month, Sir Adam Beck in Canada prepared a rejoinder:

> Appearing when it did, the pamphlet served as a propaganda weapon in favor
> of private operation of Muscle Shoals [Alabama], the view supporters of
> public ownership imputed to it.
>   That the importation [*sic*] contained more than an element of truth is evi-
> dent from a January 1925 letter from Charles Walcott in his capacity as sec-
> retary of the Smithsonian Institution to Calvin Coolidge. Walcott suggested
> that "in continuation of the Smithsonian's study of natural resources" there
> had been no thorough study nor "a concise statement of the outstanding fea-
> tures of the Muscle Shoals power situation." Writing while the controversy
> over the Underwood bill was at its height, Walcott proposed a "concisely
> summarized" statement "so that the average intelligent American citizen"
> could readily "comprehend the energy possibilities and what has been and is
> now involved in their development and utilization." Within the context and
> coming after the Wyer report, Walcott's letter indicated that the secretary of
> the Smithsonian Institution was prepared to print more propaganda to help
> the hard-pressed Coolidge administration get rid of Muscle Shoals. (Lower
> 1971, 261)

That is one way to analyze events and letters, for if one is looking for a hidden agenda, lack of conclusive evidence to the contrary is strong proof itself

of a thorough and deep cover-up. Muscle Shoals, which was originally named "Mussel," for the freshwater clams that had been abundant locally in the riffles, had had more than its name modified. During the war, when nitrates were in critical supply, the government built a power-generating dam and produced this necessary ingredient of fertilizer and explosives. For several years in the postwar period, Walcott had discussions with Cottrell and others concerning the nitrate project. Since the days of the Reclamation Service, the coal-testing laboratory, the Cottrell Precipitator, and his association with L. L. Nunn and the Telluride Association, Walcott had been interested in electric power. Walcott did write at least one private response in a letter on the question of private or public ownership.

> If you are interested in "public ownership," I wish you would, as a clear-headed businessman, go to Toronto and made a thorough investigation of the statements made by Wyer in his pamphlet. To my mind, the most dangerous enemies to public ownership are those who mismanage public ownership enterprises. Like all things under human direction, some are good and some are bad. Personally, I have never entered into any controversy on the subject. My interest is to present all of the natural and economic facts available in connection with the energy resources of America, and leave it to the persons interested to form their own opinion, not from previous preconception or prejudice, but, if in doubt, upon a thorough investigation and study of the original sources of information.[11]

Norris wrote Walcott, and Walcott wrote Norris, defending Wyer as an engineer of fine character. Walcott later released a four-page statement.

> Niagara power is in part distributed by Canadian publically owned agencies, and in part by private corporations regulated by the state of New York, but in the final analysis economic conditions control the utilization of all energy resources. . . . As for my own responsibility for the publication: It is, as Sir Adam Beck supposed, complete. Neither this paper nor others which the Smithsonian Institution publishes are passed upon by the Board of Regents before printing. Judgement upon the manuscripts is among the duties entrusted by the Regents to their Secretary. . . . However, if there be statements in the pamphlet which in courtesy to a friendly power ought to have been omitted, or statements which it shall finally appear do not square with the truth, I here state my regret.[12]

Walcott here both supported his subordinates and accepted responsibility, but did not back down.

The issue of selling off publicly built facilities to private corporations would not have been affected one iota by another study under the auspices of the Smithsonian. Scientific investigations seldom result in political decisions, though some scientists still delude themselves that rational presentation of information is the basis for policy. Finally, anyone who suggests that in 1925 Silent Cal had trouble in proposing legislation that was good for business is rewriting history.

No other group was seriously studying power usage and power production in the United States; this was several years before the Federal Power Commission was established. Walcott saw such studies as an appropriate job for the SI to perform, nothing more. Walcott was a staunch Republican, but as evidenced above, he never expressed an opinion as to whether the government or private enterprise should produce electricity. The Reclamation Service produced electricity for sale, and L. L. Nunn did likewise, so Walcott had experience with both public and private power production. So far as the rest of year was to go, this Niagara power controversy was, in boxing parlance, a preliminary to the main event.

While Mr. Wyer's bombshell was still being printed, Walcott was occupied in his office. "Looking over Cambrian fossils from the Columbia River valley sent by Geol. Surv. Canada" (January 7, 1925); the field work around Radium Hot Springs in 1923 had given him a "feel" for the rocks and the fossils in southern British Columbia. Walcott was still a collaborator with the Geological Survey of Canada, and examination of collections were part of his "duties." He was also making plans for his future, as he wrote a colleague in France:

> I received a report from the officers of the National Museum a short time since stating that I had turned over to the National Museum over 50,000 specimens of fossils from the pre-Devonian, in addition to 15,000 from the Burgess shale quarry; also a considerable number of wild animal skins, skulls, and horns. I doubt if more than one-half of the material has yet been worked up and published. I have a paper that will appear in the early summer on genera of trilobites, illustrated by twelve plates. After that I hope to take up a considerable group of Burgess shale fossils of great interest which have not yet been published. Over 100 drawings and photographs have been prepared. They would have been published before this if it had not been for the time given to administrative duties and matters concerned with our scientific organizations. I am now about through with the latter, as I gave my address as retiring president of the American Association for the Advancement of Science on December 29, and am also out of the Council of the National Academy, but still connected with the National Research Council Executive Board, and two or three committees of the Academy. I am planning to resign as a member of the Board of three organizations that are carrying on most interesting and valuable work, but I think my duty to them has been done.[13]

It is a reasonable assumption that the fifteen thousand Burgess Shale specimens mentioned were those quarried in 1917. Information on the number of trips the pack horses made from the quarry to Field that year, and an estimate of the weight of the fossils that Walcott shipped back in 1917, give two independent "data points" to support this interpretation.

The Smithsonian Institution is a public trust dedicated to the "increase and diffusion of knowledge among men." The U.S. National Museum, a federal agency, has as one of its missions the preservation of the nation's treasures. Thus it was proper for Walcott to transfer his collections to the National Museum. He would have done this periodically, as space in the Castle became crowded, but he would not have transferred material until he had examined it and retained critical specimens for his research.

The same day Walcott was writing about his removing himself from organizations, he was becoming involved in yet another project. "Signed contract with De van [*sic*] Cor[poration] for publication & sale of 20 books of S.I. Scientific Series" (January 8, 1925). One of the notions for increasing the endowment was an encyclopedia-like product that the si would sell to the public. This scheme was approved by the regents in June 1924. Thereafter, a member of the De Van firm went on a money hunt seeking $250,000 to underwrite publication; he collected $20,000. Just as with the results of the little brochure directly appealing for funds, however, this figure amounted to failure.

The company then proposed that it produce and market the series; the si would receive a fixed royalty from sales. This idea reversed the original concept, but it turned out to be practical. The series eventually had a dozen volumes, written by si members and associates from affiliated agencies. Sales brought money into the endowment. Series on various aspects of science are relatively common today in libraries, but for its time this was a novel approach to the "diffusion of knowledge," as well as to fund-raising.

Routine administration, church matters, a major dinner in honor of the retiring French ambassador, and church services on the radio brought Walcott to the start of another workweek. "Meeting of Trustees of Nat. Park Ass at Secty Hoovers office 4–5:30 P.M. for discussion of combining with other organizations of a similar subject" (January 12, 1925). This proposal was rejected; the present title, "National Parks and Conservation Association," stems from concerns for conservation half a century later (Miles 1995).

The annual meetings of the Iowa and Ontario Apartment Houses came next; Walcott would continue for another year in his position as president of each. "Mary began to write draft of wild flowers for her book" (January 14, 1925). When the books were published, each wildflower portrait was accompanied by about half a page of text. The book was to absorb most of Mary's time for the coming years. She was active on several fronts. "A lecture on 'My Wild Garden' was given by Mrs. Walcott. . . . [It was] illustrated by lantern slides of the Alpine flora of the Canadian Rockies, hand-colored by Mrs. Walcott."[14]

"A long day at my desk in connection with correspondence administrative matters. Slowly getting ready for financial campaign to increase endowment of s.i." (January 15, 1925). Just as the book was to occupy Mary, the endowment campaign would occupy Walcott and cut farther into his research time. However, as a good sign of immediate progress, Walcott began reading proofs of his latest trilobite manuscript. As a further good sign, the snows melted, and that Sunday Walcott got to church for the first time since the new year began.

"Attending meeting of Nat. Acad. Comm. on Forest Research." Walcott had finally gotten off the Finance Committee of the Academy and had finally turned the collection of instruments, manuscripts, and portraits over to George Ellery Hale, but here he was, still on this Academy committee. The group soon decided that the prime need was for funds to investigate what was being taught to budding foresters. By 1926, the General Education Board had accommodated this need, and there was little more for Walcott to do in this arena.

Walcott was feeling in a chatty mood when he wrote some advice to George F. Kunz, the eminent gemologist at Tiffany's and member of the Research Corporation board:

> Last evening I stopped at the drug store and purchased four ounces of *syrup iodine of iron*, as we always keep a supply in the house. The moment anyone shows up with an eruption of any kind on the skin, a dose of ten drops stirred in half a glass of tepid water is administered three time a day before meals. The results of this has been that no one in our household has had boils, carbuncles or similar skin trouble in the past twenty-five years.
>
> The iodide of iron is also a splendid tonic and I often take it in the spring time when I feel played out and unfit for work. I have never known any ill effects from taking it, but everyone must try out such things before knowing what the effect will be.[15]

What with the various diagnoses and cures he tried, one has the sense that Walcott might have been a fine medical doctor had he not collected his first fossil.

The Wyer issue hit. "A broken up day. S. Wyer came 9:45 & we went to Capitol to confer with Senator Smoot & at 3. P.M. to confer with Senator Wadsworth *en re* Niagara Falls pamphlet of Wyers. Usual routine & study of papers while at the Smithsonian" (January 21, 1925). Walcott did not write as though he were perturbed; minutes of the regents meeting for 1925 make no mention of this event, and it seems not to have been a problem. "A quiet day at my office consulting with members of staff about increasing the Smithsonian endowment" (January 22, 1925).

Two days more were much the same, except for an eclipse of the sun, which the Walcotts watched from the plaza of the Lincoln Memorial. Sunday was spent fussing at home, walking in the afternoon, and entertaining an English couple. "At my office during the day. Routine & future endowment campaign occupied my time. Mr. Tamblyn of N.Y. came in 3 P.M. to talk over endowment campaign" (January 26, 1925). "Mulling over endowment papers & conferences" (January 27, 1925).

A happy note: "Helen came at 8:45 P.M.—having left Paris 10 days ago. She is well & glad to be at home again" (January 28, 1925). Walcott and Mr. Tamblyn conferred further and spoke to the staff concerning the endowment campaign. The conferences on the campaign continued into the next day. "Routine & administrative matters. Had short interview with President Coolidge at noon *en re* study of utilization of resources of Muscle Shoals" (January 31, 1925). (In the interests of full disclosure, one should mention that in Walcott's diary the words "study of" were written in later. Those who favor the conspiracy theory of government have here evidence of a cover-up of the real reason for the meeting.)

February began on a Sunday, but Walcott again missed church. In the afternoon he made a few calls and at dinner entertained someone Helen had picked up on the ship. "At my office during the day except for a call on Secty of War Weeks at noon *en re* Energy Resources of Muscle Shoals. Nothing material has come from our endowment agitation" (February 2, 1925). Two more days were routine, except for a church meeting, another call on the secretary of war, and Mary's assisting at a reception given by the Hoovers.

It was time for the first trip of the year to New York; the Walcotts stayed with Mrs. [Alfred D.] Pell and dined with mutual friends. "At 10:06 A.M. went out to Wm. E. Rudge Printery to see about Mary's American Wild Flower Book. Very much pleased with plates already printed" (February 6, 1925). They returned to the city and Mrs. Pell, as it was possible that the Pell art collection would come to Washington. Cousin Fred called just before they left for Washington. "At the home found Helen was happy as Carl Younger her best young man was in town. He came for dinner & the evening" (February 7, 1925). By the next day, he had the first name correct: "Helen & Cole decided to be married next spring" (February 8, 1925). It is perhaps symptomatic that Walcott had this as the last entry for the day, preceded by a business call from John C. Merriam, for Cole Younger was indeed Helen's best young man. "Dr. Charles D. Walcott, Secretary of the Smithsonian Institution, and Mrs. Walcott announce the engagement of their daughter, Helen Breese, to Cole Younger of the city [New York]. Miss Walcott recently returned from Paris. Mr. Younger was in the Ambulance Service in France prior to the entry of the United States in the World War, when he joined the American Air Force as an aviator, serving in France and Italy. The wedding will take place in the early spring."[16]

Someone in the Castle made a mistake and mailed out the announcement in government envelopes. In response to a letter from the Third Assistant Postmaster General, Walcott apologized and sent $3.08 to cover the cost of stamps.

"At my office A.M. cleaning up mail. Saul Wyer called P.M. *en re* Niagara Fall power discussion" (February 9, 1925). Apparently Senator Norris's outrage was not troubling Walcott. "Routine & matters pertaining to Niagara Fall power paper & Sir Adam Beck's pamphlet. Have not had a chance in two months to work on my scientific papers" (February 10, 1925). In the midst of countercharges from Canada and general upset, Walcott knew what was important—his research was lagging.

Walcott went to a large dinner put on by Theodore Noyes, owner of the *Washington Star* and fellow member of the Washington Monument Society. Mary spoke to the Wild Flower Club, and Helen made wedding plans. "A quiet day with Mr. Wyer & matters pertaining to the Niagara Falls paper. Helen left for New York 4:30 P.M. At home in evening looking over mss of trilobite paper" (February 13, 1925). Though this was a Friday the 13th, any day Walcott was able to find a little time for research was a good day. The week ended with dinner at the home of the attorney general. After church and some visiting, the Walcotts had the secretary of interior for a family dinner. Washington government was still relatively small and friendly.

The new week began with routine, and the quiet continued. "Conference with Chauncey Hamlin & John C. Merriam in evening *en re* union of societies interested in outdoor recreation" (February 17, 1925). Walcott always liked the outdoors, Merriam wanted more research to be done in national parks, the automobile was changing the fabric of America by providing mobility, and it was natural (at least to some) that outdoor recreation be promoted as a national goal. Apart from a meeting with Mr. Yard on National Parks Association business, the week ended quietly.

Washington's Birthday was equally relaxed, and Walcott took a long nap after church. Mr. Wyer called that evening. "Called to see Senator Smoot 9 A.M. at his office. Talked with Wyer. D*rs* Hamerschlag & Cottrell called at the office. Mr. Rudge came with proofs of sketches of wild flowers. Attended meeting of Wash'n Monument Society 4 P.M. & at 5:30 Mary & I went to G.W.M.A. tea at Mrs. Dimocks. Rudge & Hamerschlag came in for family dinner" (February 23, 1925). If nothing else, the GWMA was tenacious.

Rudge and Walcott signed a contract for sale of the first edition of the wildflower book. Wyer called concerning his proposed study of Muscle Shoals, and

Helen returned from New York; all in all, it was a busy day. "At my office attending to routine etc—In evening talked to Geol. Soc. Wash'n about Robson Peak section B.C. Can." (February 25, 1925). It had been years since Walcott last spoke to the GSW, and this requires a bit of explanation.

Walcott had been in the Robson Peak area in 1912 and had been, as he pointed out, the first to do a stratigraphic study of the rocks. He had published his geologic findings, as well as a popular article, in the *National Geographic Magazine* and had returned for some additional investigations in 1913. While working for the Geological Survey of Canada, L. D. Burling had later visited the area and collected during several seasons. The explanation for this sudden reawakening of interest lies in an earlier letter and a posthumous publication (Walcott 1928).

In the spring of 1920, Walcott had written to the director of the Geological Survey of Canada:

> Just before leaving for England Mr. Burling wrote me . . . that he saw no reason why the fossils he had collected in the Sawback Range and from Cambrian localities should not be sent here for working up and identification. . . . I doubt very much if anything practical would come of this, as I do not know how thoroughly Burling did his work or what preconceived notions he may have had as to the stratigraphic formations. You know how difficult it is to take another man's field notes and make out anything from them except in the field unless they have been carefully written up in the office by the author. . . . I am keenly disappointed that Burling did not round up his work as he went along from year to year and publish a preliminary report. He might have made a few mistakes, but that would have been better than to have left five or six field seasons' work unstudied, undigested and unwritten up.[17]

When the GSC moved to a new building in Ottawa, Burling's crates of fossils were sent to Washington. Resser unpacked them and matched collections with field notes. "A number of the most essential lots from a stratigraphic standpoint were found to be merely comminuted fragments of no diagnostic value while others were evidently rough pieces that might afford something of service when broken up and the fragments identified."

"Burling did not publish his detailed field sections or list the fossils occurring in them. He made many generalizations, but did not present the evidence on which they were based" (Walcott 1928, 357). That last statement was damning, so far as Walcott was concerned. When Burling's collections were sent to Washington, the original notion was to write a short paper for the GSC, but that was not feasible. The data from these fossils were incorporated into Walcott's major stratigraphic work, and it was a taste of this that was presented to his geologic colleagues in February 1925.

To be honest, the Mount Robson study was not one of Walcott's better efforts. In 1912, he had duplicated some formations. Because of the long distances and great heights, he had used field glasses and had incorrectly correlated across the glaciers. The terrible weather that year had compounded the problem. His 1913 geologic investigations were not published until 1928. Even with Burling's collections and a much better grasp of the succession of trilobite faunas a decade later, he could not straighten out the fundamental errors in the sequence of formations. Further, some of the formations had somewhat different physical characteristics from those at the Lake Louise area, and Walcott did not have sufficient information on the outcrops between there and the Robson massif to grasp that these lateral changes were gradual. Still, it was a pioneer work, and if viewed against the background of what he had written in 1912, rather than what he would write in 1928, the investigation was not too bad.

Geology was put out of the way for a bit while Walcott worked on the address list for Helen's wedding. "Spent the morning at the Natural History building. Routine & conference at my office P.M." (February 27, 1925). "Getting odds & ends in order at my desk. Wrote Prof. Kindle *en re* Walker Windemere collections. Overhauled illustrations for Robson District section of my report" (February 28, 1925). Dr. Kindle was in charge of paleontology for the Geological Survey of Canada. It was he who referred fossils to Walcott. He was quite an able paleontologist, but Cambrian trilobites were not his strongest suite. The Windemere district was to the west of where Walcott had worked in 1923.

March began with church and, afterward, the customary office visit. Monday was quiet, and Walcott was able to work on the Mount Robson text of his big report. Mary was "at home" that afternoon, and the house was crowded with her friends. Tuesday was equally placid at the office and far quieter at the house. "Inauguration of Calvin Coolidge as President of U.S. With Mary & Helen went to capitol to witness ceremony of inauguration. Listened to address of Vice Prest. Dawes & later Prest. Coolidge. The President's address was fine in spirit & character. We went to my office 3–5:30 to work over mss" (March 4, 1925). Never waste a minute.

"A dull quiet day at my office routine and conference with Austin Clark & Mr. Mitman *en re* future development of work in Nat. Museum etc." (March 5, 1925). Austin Clark was an eminent invertebrate zoologist, whereas Mr. Mitman held forth in the Arts and Industries building; that was a part of the museum more in need of building up than natural history. The rest of the week continued to be routine.

Sunday brought church, and Monday brought routine. Two hours work on manuscripts were squeezed in before Walcott took care of the reappointment of an admiral to the NACA. "Talked with Mr. Hoover Secty Commerce *en re*

Muscle Shoals and Amer. Parks asso." (March 11, 1925). Now, there is an interesting combination of interests; like Mr. Walcott, Secretary Hoover was a man of many parts. Despite problems, Mr. Yard was surviving, and seemingly Mr. Wyer was surviving.

Helen came back from New York and of course deeply involved herself in the coming festivities. Walcott skipped church to serve the Smithsonian Institution that Sunday. "Met Senator Woodbridge N. Ferris our new Regent & showed him about the museum & talked with him about the Smithsonian. Mary & I had lunch at my laboratory & looked up odds & ends until 5 P.M." (March 15, 1925). The weather was nice, and they walked home. Not only was this three miles, but it was slightly uphill. The first two days of the workweek were routine.

"Mary left for Philad'a 9:15 A.M. Called on Mr. Robert Brookings A.M. and Mr. Theo. W. Noyes P.M. with me[sse]rs Gilbert, Dorsey & True. Mr. S. S. Wyer called A.M. Senator Norris spoke *en re* Wyer's Niagara Falls paper in the Senate. At home with Helen in the evening" (March 18, 1925).

> On his part Norris intended to discuss the Wyer pamphlet to help avoid a final vote on the Underwood bill if it came to the floor again at the end of the Sixty-Ninth Congress. Instead, he waited until the brief special session of the Senate in the new Congress in March, 1925. Then he denounced the pamphlet as propaganda "pure and simple," and called for the removal of Walcott by the trustees of the Smithsonian Institution. The pamphlet, besides being an indefensible attack on the business methods of a friendly nation, contained facts and figures differing from those found in official sources. While Norris felt Samuel Wyer was acting within his rights as a "professional propagandist," the role of Walcott in printing the pamphlet as a scientific document under government auspices seemingly called for his expulsion. Norris suspected that he was acting in accordance with administrative wishes, supporting it in the Muscle Shoals controversy. The incident served only to lower the standards of the Smithsonian Institution by using its name on behalf of private interests. (Lowitt 1971, 262)

The call of Senator Norris for the expulsion of Walcott was a story for the newspapers, but in his diary, Walcott ignored the matter. "A quiet day at my office occupied with correspondence, routine, & studying over mss for Can. Rockies paper. Mary returned 6:20 P.M. & we spent the evening considering matters connected with Helen's wedding on the 31st. Many friends have been most kind to her" (March 19, 1925). "Mrs. Walcott is leading a rather strenuous existence, owing to the home affairs and necessity of getting eighty descriptions for the first volume of the wildflower book written by April. The reproduction of the plates is progressing favorably and subscriptions for the edition de luxe are coming in so that we are beginning to think that the five volumes will be published in due course."[18]

A letter from a younger cousin who had moved from Baltimore to Albany brought back to Walcott thoughts of the 1870s: "I have not been at Trenton Falls for the past ten years. The locality where I collected most of my trilobites is now deeply buried and I do not think it would pay to work it. I found more specimens between the upper High Falls and the lower High Falls, on the east side of the stream. . . . I rather enjoyed my three years' residence in Albany, as it was then a most conservative, clean town, despite its political conditions."[19]

Petty feuds, overwork, conflicting orders from James Hall, and concerns about funding from the state legislature had faded with the years.

So far as Walcott was personally concerned, the quiet times prevailed. Key items were a visit from a member of the Rockefeller Foundation, a possible source of endowment funds, and Mary's starting another season in her "war garden." Senator Norris and Niagara Falls vanished.

For the next week, one item of interest was the showing of films by Byron Harmon of the scenery along the Lake Louise–Jasper trail; Walcott knew the route only to near the head of the Bow River Valley. The Walcotts had camped on the Harmon place during the 1922 field season. A far more significant event also marked this week. "Talked with Dr Alex. Wetmore & Mr. Ravenel *en re* Asst. Secty of S.I. in charge of Gov't branches of s.i." (March 28, 1925). Wetmore had a short tenure at the National Zoological Park, for Walcott had finally found a man to meet his specifications for the important position of assistant secretary. With all due respect to Assistant Secretary Abbott, the governmental agencies under the Smithsonian were a more complex matter than all the rest of the institution's business combined.

Sunday evening Sidney and Helen-Louise arrived from Buffalo; Monday Cousin Fred and family came to Washington. Tuesday was cloudy, but no matter: "Helen married to Cole Younger of New York 4 P.M. Reception 4:15 to 6 P.M. All well & happy. We are delighted. My *75th* birthday. Had a luncheon for 31 family & special friends of Helen's 1–3 P.M. I am fairly well & carrying on my work & play as usual. Mary the same. This has been an eventful day" (March 31, 1925). "The young bride was unattended and entered the drawing room with her father."[20] For Walcott to state that the day had been eventful was a rare show of emotion, but many thoughts must have swirled through his mind as he escorted his only daughter.

Walcott's birthday was deliberately played down so as not to take anything away from Helen's day, yet she must have picked that occasion. If so, good for Helen, the wild teenager who loved her father and now gave him a present he would cherish. About all that needs to be added is that the Rev. Charles Wood of the Church of the Covenant presided, but that too is no great surprise.

One letter of congratulations on Walcott's birthday, from F. H. Newell, should be mentioned. Back in the summer of 1902, Walcott had taken the time to send him a personal letter:

> In the general haste connected with pushing through the plans, etc. for the reclamation service, I neglected to say anything to you personally of the good work you had done since our talk in 1894.
>
> My general opinion of it you are of course able to judge from the fact that you have been placed in entire charge of the reclamation service. I have full confidence that you will do all in your power to make it a success, also that the men who have been associated with you for so long a time will support you in every way. The only suggestions I have to make are—keep cool, do not worry, and do not be swerved from your course without the best reason for doing so.[21]

Newell had been appointed number-two man in the new Reclamation Service, and when Walcott resigned in 1907, Newell moved up to chief; when he left, the organization was renamed the Bureau of Reclamation.

Newell responded twenty-three years later to Walcott's letter: "I want to add my congratulations to those of your other friends on your birthday. It is not possible—nor is it necessary—for me to write or try to express my appreciation of your lifelong friendship and the inspiration you have been to the younger men. We have all benefited by your example and join in wishing you all good things. With highest regards."[22]

April 1, following Walcott's eventful day, included a brief conversation with President Coolidge in regard to budget matters. He also formally introduced the new assistant secretary to the staff of the National Museum. In the evening, everyone pitched in to pack away wedding presents. Thursday was a full day getting the Smithsonian office in shape. Friday was almost as bad, what with Saul Wyer stopping by for a minute—Senator Norris seemed not to have wounded him—and Reverend Wood inquiring about a new church building, but that afternoon Mary and Walcott made it to the 3:45 P.M. Atlantic Coast Line train to their southern haunt at Beaufort, South Carolina.

There was one complete day of resting and napping. Then Walcott cleaned up the mail, paid the bills, and sent back the proofs of his next SMC paper. He sent off another manuscript a few days later, but the part of the team who was really working was Mary, busily sketching the few flowers she did not have in her portfolio and searching for new ones to draw. By the 18th they were back in Washington from what had clearly been a working vacation. An eye doctor examined Walcott and reported no change in his vision. Years later, Dr. Edwin Kirk would mention that he noticed Walcott had trouble with one eye; if so, this visit to an eye doctor was the first indication of it in his diary.

On Sunday, the Walcotts were out hunting wildflowers at the zoo. Walcott had the practical sense to have the weather dictate which day was Sunday when they were in the field, and Mary knew that flowers bloomed for only a limited time; neither view affected their deep religious convictions. It was just as well that they collected the flowers when they did, as Walcott reported to the deputy director of mines in Ottawa:

> We have been having an usually mild April, but yesterday a furious storm from the northwest swept over the city, with the result that the thermometer has taken a drop of 20 degrees, but I do not think that it will go low enough to affect the foliage and the Japanese cherry blossoms, which are most beautiful in the parks today.
>
> Last [field] season we had 43 stormy days, on 23 of which more or less snow fell. This greatly interferred [sic] with the work, so I am now planning to return the latter part of June, with two objects in view; one is to go over the ground if possible, between Golden and the headwaters of the Saskatchewan, also to endeavor to obtain further paleontological data south of Golden and the Kicking Horse Canyon. I shall soon be wishing to send material out for the fixing up of our outfit, so I am enclosing my usual request for a customs permit.
>
> I received this morning page proof of a paper on Cambrian and Ozarkian genera of trilobites, with 9 plates. This with the paper on the Brachiopoda will be of great assistance in determining the horizons in the pre-Ordovician formations, as they are nearly all from the Canadian Rockies. The more extended paper on the pre-Devonian formations is fairly well advanced but its publication will probably be deferred until next winter.[23]

The study of trilobites was published June 1 (Walcott 1925e). It contains the detailed species descriptions and illustrations omitted from the rushed publication a year earlier. This paper treats occurrences throughout Canada and the United States. Walcott did not prepare any range charts for genera or summarize geographic distribution, but all the details needed for correlation of formations were presented for future workers to assemble.

The manuscript that was to be deferred until next winter finally became a posthumous paper. Its earlier stages are worth recording. A year previous, Walcott had written to the Canadian deputy director of mines, "I have ready a paper of about 100 pages, with quite a lot of illustrations, on some of the pre-Devonian sectors, especially those I studied last season [1923]. As your publication fund is so limited, I have not offered it to you, but if you wish a synopsis of it I will be very glad to prepare it."[24] The reply to that particular sentence was: "I note that you propose publishing your paper on the Pre-Devonian sections, on account of the limitations of our own publication vote [appropriation by Parliament]. If, however, you have an abstract or a synopsis of this paper already prepared, we will be very glad indeed to have a copy of it."[25]

The manuscript on stratigraphy kept changing and growing, so Walcott never got around to sending a summary to Canada. This exchange does speak to one issue, however. Walcott published material on Canadian geology for the simple reason that the Geological Survey of Canada could not afford to publish it. As impoverished as the si was, the gsc was poorer.

With the first steps taken for the coming field season, Walcott returned to routine. Page proofs went back to the printer, William Mann was appointed to head the zoo, the Iowa Apartment House board had its annual gathering, and the naca met; when all these odds and ends were in order, Walcott went off to join Mary at Bryn Mawr. The next day Walcott and Mary went into the big city to attend the meeting of the American Philosophical Society. Walcott neglected to mention in his diary that he had been elected president of that august group, the oldest philosophical society in America.

After the meeting, they were off to the bigger city of New York. The Walcotts spent the next morning with Mrs. Pell and her art collection and then were driven to Long Island to see the wonder Mr. Rudge had wrought with his color printing presses. The Hookers drove them to Greenwich, and the Walcotts spent the evening with the new Mr. and Mrs. Younger. They visited until train time and arrived home safe and sound.

Since it was spring in Washington, the nas was holding its annual meeting. Walcott saw many of his old friends. He took Mary to the dinner Tuesday night, and he visited with his old friend John M. Clarke from Albany. Walcott had become chairman of the Thompson Medal committee and had the pleasure of presenting it to Clarke before he retired from that committee. It was just as well, for a month later Clarke died. On Wednesday Walcott attended the business meeting, squeezing in time for needed si business in his office.

One significant piece of nas business was the report of the Forestry Commission (Jones *in* Michaelson 1926). A national conference had been held the previous November, and among the concerns expressed had been lack of proper training for those interested in forestry research. The committee was able to gather funds to support several nrc fellowships.

The nas members decamped until next year. "At my office during the day. With Mary dined at the house of Chief Justice & Mrs. Taft to meet D*r* & Mrs. Judson" (April 30, 1925). So ended the peaceful month, and with it the last of peace for a while.

On May 1, the Walcotts dined with the minister of China, again to meet the Judsons. The other comment of the day is "Orville Wright explodes and proposes to send the original Wright biplane to England" (May 1, 1925). An explanation to readers before proceeding is important. In general one can develop a biography thematically or chronologically; though Walcott had many irons in the fire, the latter approach seemed most liquid. The Wright affair was so complex, however, that to understand it one must proceed step by step, and even then some aspects cannot be comprehended. To develop the views of those involved, material presented in early chapters has been summarized or even repeated.

The *New York Times* on April 30 had a small story on page 10: "First Wright Plane for British Museum." On May 1, the follow-up story moved forward to page 4 and consisted of quotes from Wright that certainly could be construed as an explosion.

For twenty years I have kept possession of the machine in the hope that a suitable home could be found for it in America. Several American museums have asked for it, but the one institution among these which seemed of national enough character was one to which I did not care to entrust the machine.

This lack of confidence was the result of the way the officers of this institution allowed the priceless relics of the Langley machine of 1903 to be taken out of the museum in 1914 and the original materials of its structure be mutilated for the purpose of private parties to a patent litigation.

The machine now hanging in the museum is not the original machine, but is mostly a new machine with many of its restored parts of different construction from the original.

The label hanging on it is true neither of the restored nor of the original machine.[26]

Wright went on to express grave fears that his plane therefore also might be mutilated or mislabeled. He indicated that the machine had been restored to its original condition. His prime concern was that it would not be secure from fire in Dayton, Ohio, whereas the Science Museum in South Kensington, London, could house it safely.

Much has been written about this episode, almost all of it from the standpoint of Orville Wright. Without getting into any special pleading for Walcott, some remarks ought to be added to the other side for balance. One place to begin is the condition of the 1903 Wright machine.

"The engine broke loose as the disintegrating machine rolled over backwards [in 1903]. . . . When the dust settled, the world's first airplane lay transformed into a twisted mass of wreckage" (Crouch 1989, 269). "Of all the surviving reminders of their early work, the world's first airplane was probably least important to Orville. He and his brother had never given much thought to their old machines" (Crouch 1989, 454).

The great Dayton flood of 1913 further damaged the machine. "The 1903 airplane was the only one they had saved, stowing the shipping crates behind the bike shop when unpacking them. Now it survived the great flood. Orville cleaned the mud off the top of the cases as best he could, and put them back in the shed" (Crouch, 1989, 454).

> Most Americans were not aware that the 1903 Wright airplane was still in existence. Orville himself had scarcely given it any thought until 1916, when Massachusetts Institute of Technology officials asked to exhibit the historic craft as part of the ceremonies marking the opening of two new institute buildings. He and Jim Jacobs of the Dayton-Wright Company pulled the parts out of the crate and began the job of reconstruction, adding new material only when absolutely necessary to repair the damage that had occurred in 1903. . . . Walcott requested the loan of the machine that December, but Orville would no longer consider such an arrangement with the organization that had sponsored the Hammondsport tests [Curtiss testing of Langley aerodrome]. (Crouch 1987, 491–92)

When Wright represented himself as having been the guardian of a priceless relic for decades, he was shading the truth just a wee bit.

In the midst of the thousands of words dissecting the Wright-Walcott problem into ever finer pieces, no one seems to have inquired as to what prompted Orville to make the statements he did when he did. Griffith Brewer had seen the tests of the modified Langley machine in the summer of 1914, yet it was not until the fall of 1921 that he attacked them dramatically. At least two articles had appeared during June and July of 1914 in prominent aviation journals on the flight of the aerodrome. Wright did write a letter to the *New York Times* on June 14, 1914, which was reprinted a month later in an aeronautical magazine. In it he had pointed to weaknesses in Langley's work and questioned the need for the test. Still, if a great fraud was being committed by Curtiss, and indirectly by the si, more detailed follow-up articles could have been written at that time. The delay of seven years in presenting his charges makes little sense.

A summary of the NACA written to note its tenth anniversary includes a picture of the April 25, 1925, meeting, at which both parties in the dispute are present (Walcott 1925f). The offending restoration and the offending label had been on exhibit in the Arts and Industries Building since 1918. Certainly April 1925 could not have been the first time that Orville Wright saw the new label. There appears to have been no public trigger to Wright's explosion.

One may speculate, but even that leads nowhere. The Air Mail Act had been signed in early February of the year, and for the first time since the end of the war aviation seemed to have a future. Meanwhile, Orville Wright was sitting on the sidelines. "With the sale of the company in 1915, Orville walked away from the entire business. . . . The patent suit was no longer his problem. Orville accepted the appellate court decision of January, 1914, as his final vindication" (Crouch 1989, 466).

Despite that decision, Orville had a grudge against the institution, and especially against Walcott as its leader, for giving what he considered undue credit to Langley. The Langley Day celebration on May 8, 1913, had extolled the professor, unveiled a tablet to him, and presented medals to Gustav Eiffel and the hated Glenn L. Curtiss (McCurdy 1913). Nothing on that occasion indicated that it was the Wrights who had actually flown, shortly after Langley's failure. Following the death of Wilbur in 1914, Orville had plenty of time to dwell on real or imagined injustices and fan these sparks into flame. Perhaps there was no external event that caused him to decide to send his plane to England, though a biographer of Curtiss suggests the Englishman Brewer had planted the idea with Orville on an earlier trip to America and had fanned the ember into a flame when he returned to Dayton in 1925. There may be a germ of truth in that view, for in theory Orville might equally well decided to send the machine to France. Whatever triggered Wright's action, if his aim was to embarrass Walcott, it was a brilliant strategy.

The fight was on, and Walcott did not sit by idly. "Sent article to Outlook on Langley Plane & Orvil [sic] Wright" (May 2, 1925); that weekly was more or less the *Time* or *Newsweek* of its day. Walcott gave an account of Langley's work and the history leading up to the Hammondsport tests, but though it was printed in eleven days, by the time the piece appeared it was ancient history (Walcott 1925g). The same day the article was mailed, the *Times* had an editorial generally sympathetic to Orville Wright; it mentioned Langley but not Walcott. The argument had moved forward both in the paper and in the length of letters and articles; Walcott in his reply denied that Langley's plane had been mutilated. Dr. Walcott commented,

> Mr. Wright does not like the card on the Langley plane in the museum here, which says, "This is the first airplane capable of flight."
> While the lawsuits were in progress, I had the Langley plane taken to Hammondsport, Lake Keuka, N.Y. to make tests. Langley never really had a chance to try his invention and I, out of sheer interest in aviation, wanted to see whether the plane would fly. I was present at the tests and I saw the plane rise from the water. The test was successful.
> Then I decided upon further tests. I gave orders for a heavier and more powerful engine to be installed and then I left. The plane flew under these conditions.
> An English attorney, representing the Wright Aeronautic company of London, witnessed these second flights and made the statement that the plane could never fly in its original condition. This statement is evidently the one on which Mr. Wright bases his assertions.[27]

Walcott ended with three paragraphs on restoration of the plane to its original condition, pointedly commenting that this was no different than what Wright had written the day before regarding replacements of parts as a result of the 1903 crash and the 1913 flood damage. In contrast to the description by Crouch of the 1903 plane, Wright mentioned "a few replacements."

There are several items that Walcott could have added to shed more light on the Hammondsport test. One is a letter, mentioned earlier, that had been written six years prior to the tests and two years before the legal battles began. In reply to an inquiry from Walcott as to whether it would be wise to attempt to fly the Langley aerodrome, Octave Chanute, the most widely respected engineer in America in the field of aeronautics, had had some interesting words. "My judgement is that it would probably be broken when alighting on hard ground and possibly when alighting on water, although the operator might not be hurt in either case. If the institution does not mind taking this risk and suitable arrangements can be made about the expense, I believe that it would be desirable to make the test, in order to demonstrate that the Langley machine was competent to fly and might have put our government in possession of a type of flying machine, which, however, inferior to that of the Wrights, might have evolved into an effective scouting instrument."[28]

There were major differences between the biplane arrangement of the Wrights and the tandem wings of Langley, quite apart from differences in size (Crouch 1987).

Chanute was on the committee to award the first Langley Medal. His opinion of the Wrights was given earlier but deserves repeating, for it is less than flattering. "Now the results obtained by the Wright brothers are far superior to any others, but the resolution mentions 'meritorious investigations' not achievements, and this seems to imply that those investigations should be given to the world, a thing which the Wrights have hitherto declined to do."[29]

The issue of the first machine that actually flew carrying a person took up even more space in the New York Times the following day. The head of an engineering museum in New York tried to make peace. Orville Wright repeated his charges of mutilation and gave a list of the changes made by Curtiss. "No one can possibly regret more than I that our machine must go into a foreign museum. It is not safe where it is. It suffered in one flood and has always been liable to fire. Excepting the National Museum of the Smithsonian, I know of none in this country so suitable for such an exhibit as the Science Museum at South Kensington, London."[30]

Orville Wright neglected to mention that in 1916 Alexander Graham Bell had personally asked for the original Wright plane and that Walcott had later written asking for it. "'I asked Mr. Wright in 1916 if he cared to present his plane to us,' said Dr. Charles D. Walcott, director of the Smithsonian Institution. 'He replied that he was not prepared to consider it. That's the last I heard from him on subject.'"[31] Granted, this was after the Hammondsport tests, but it was before the Langley aerodrome had been restored—or transmogrified, depending on one's viewpoint—and it was several years was before the machine was hung with the offending label. Had Orville Wright really regretted the lack of a suitable home for the 1903 machine, in December 1916 he could have placed it in the Smithsonian.

May 3 was a Sunday, but Mr. Wright took precedence. "On account of article by Wright in morning papers, I asked Mr. H. W. Dorsey, Dr Albert Zahm & Miss Visal [secretary] to meet me at the Smithsonian where a reply to Wright[']s attack on my good faith in the ability of the Langley airplane of 1903 to fly. The mss went to the Ass. Press 5 P.M." (May 3, 1925). The incomplete sentence is unusual for Walcott; perhaps it indicates how deep was the upset.

The *Times* had two full columns on the 4th on this matter, further inflaming it; the story sold newspapers. An Ohio congressman called for an investigation and was quoted as stating that tampering with the Langley machine, and its label, had been deliberate frauds. Walcott tried to set the record straight on several points. He cited a few letters to and from the Wrights in 1910 when the question of a display of the 1903 machine first came up, and then he went into the history of tests of the Langley machine.

> After the final tests of 1903, the War Department turned the Langley plane over to the Smithsonian. . . . It was left in Dr. Langley's possession and available for any future work that he (Langley) might be able to carry on. . . . I talked the matter over with Dr. Albert F. Zahm, who was then not in the employ of the Curtiss Aeroplane Company. . . . Dr. Zahm agreeing, I then talked with Dr. Alexander Graham Bell who was most enthusiastic, . . . I asked Mr. Glenn Cutiss[sic] if he would not undertake the tests and submit an estimate of the approximate cost of restoring and testing. . . . It was not an historical relic belonging to the National Museum, but an airplane left . . . for experimental purposes. Mr. Wright is mistaken with reference to my having told him that the Institution bore no expense of these tests except the transportation charges.[32]

This is only a smattering of what was printed, and the paper itself cut part of Walcott's statement.

Walcott left no doubt that it was he, and he alone, who had authorized the test of the Langley aerodrome. If there was blame he would shoulder it, but what he would not accept was imputation of bad faith. Again, just as comments on Orville Wright's concern for his historic object provide background, some of Walcott's statements may be amplified. The "precious relic" aspect of the charges was treated by Walcott. The aerodrome had not been an object for display but had been available for experiment. Had it been taken off exhibit rather than from the recesses of the carpenter shop, there might have been more substance to Wright's apparent concern.

A bit more may be added to the issue of the timing of the original test. One biographer of Curtiss considers a letter from him to Bell germane: "There has been some talk of reproducing the old Langley machine and having it flown. I should like to know what you think of this plan as it would be an easy thing to do, provided it is worthwhile" (Roseberry 1972, 383).

If this is correct, Curtiss's hands are a bit cleaner, for any lawyer could argue that a replica is not the same as the original. Just because a replica might fly does not mean that the original would have flown. It is a narrow argument but a valid one. (Incidentally, in recent years the National Museum of American History did take a relic off exhibit for use. The steam engine *John Bull* was taken for a run on its 150th birthday; everyone at the event cheered—but then again, there were no patent suits of one railroad against another in the background.)

The next three pertinent dates are jotted in Walcott's handwriting in a sheet headed "Aeronautics." "MCh. [March] 10/1914. Suggested organization aeronautical research laboratory to appropriations committee of Congress—at hearing on S.I. Appropriations." "Mch. 13/14. Talked with Manly [Langley's assistant] & Glen Curtice [*sic*] en re testing of Langley aerodrome." "Mch. 30/14 Talked with Glen Curtice en re Langley aerodrome."[33] An associated sheet notes Walcott speaking to President Wilson about aeronautics, on March 2d, and suggesting an aeronautical laboratory to the Appropriations Committee eight days later. Walcott had been trying to organize research in aeronautics before any theoretical effort to fly Langley's folly to add spice to the Langley Day celebration of 1914 had materialized.

A reasonable surmise is that Curtiss conducted the tests because he had both most experience with landing on water and owned the largest aircraft factory at the time. As to the rest, another reasonable surmise is that once Walcott proposed the concept of an aeronautical research laboratory, it was appropriate to begin research as soon as possible. Seeing whether the Langley aerodrome would fly with its wing configuration, which was different from that of airplanes in service, was research. In contrast, trying to get it into the air as part of Langley Day festivities was a useful propaganda gesture for aviation, but hardly a valid reason to undertake the effort.

As mentioned earlier, prior to the March 30 meeting with Curtiss, Walcott telephoned Alexander Graham Bell. In his notes, Bell wrote that Walcott had stated that Curtiss was anxious to make a copy of the Langley machine. Curtiss could have it ready to try out by May 6, Langley Day, and the cost would not exceed two thousand dollars. He then inquired whether Regent Bell would approve the use of Smithsonian funds. Bell responded warmly but questioned the wisdom of using Smithsonian money. Secretary Walcott responded to this with: "I was thinking that I might chip in myself personally to the extent of $1,000." Bell responded that he would also and concluded the conversation with the view that it would be better to have the test financed by outside parties than by institutional funds.[34] More detail of earlier and later phone conversations is available but need not be repeated here (Roseberry 1972 384). In the newspapers Wright made the claim that it was Walcott who wanted the original aerodrome to be flown; earlier discussion of a replica never was mentioned by Walcott.

There is a fair amount to mull over from these notes. Curtiss did (as we saw in an earlier chapter) receive two thousand dollars from the Smithsonian. Money is hard to trace, and just possibly, somewhere in the reams of old records, is an indication that Bell and Walcott each gave the SI one thousand dollars. Some future historian can spend his time on what might be a fruitless paper chance. If Bell and Walcott funded the test but wished to keep this private, that would in part explain why Walcott used the words "attack on my good faith" in his diary.

A final morsel to add to 1914 is a short letter from Bell. "I have not yet heard what has been decided upon in relation to Glenn H. Curtiss's proposed attempt to fly a machine built upon the Langley machine. I sincerely hope that the attempt will be made with a duplicate and not with the original machine."

"I do not wish to express an opinion upon the propriety of aiding this experiment by an appropriation of Smithsonian funds, as I am in a measure, associated personally with Mr. Curtiss, as a member of the Aerial Experiment Association."[35]

Those not up on aviation history should be aware of a small group between 1907 and 1909, financed by Mrs. Bell, whose aim was to build and fly one or more planes. The AEA existed for several years with Curtiss as a member, and it made the first flights in Canada. The group dissolved shortly after Curtiss went into the aircraft business for himself. If, as the letter indicates, the aim at the time was still to build a replica, then Bell is also free of a charge that he had a hand in assisting Curtiss in a deliberate attempt to break the Wright patents. When it was decided to test the original rather than a model is not known, nor is it known who first suggested this course. Walcott assumed full responsibility in 1925 and did not muddy the waters by mentioning any earlier plans to build and test a replica.

Much has been written herein concerning Walcott and Wright, but any reader who has gotten to this point should be forewarned that more is to come. With its plot of sturdy, hometown boys succeeding by native ingenuity where distinguished men of science had failed and then battling the massive forces in

Washington to obtain due credit for their accomplishments, the story is great drama. Great drama and total accuracy are not incompatible, but once a drama begins to unfold, what appear to be minor details fall to the wayside as the forces of good battle against those of evil. For many the feud became a black-and-white issue, no matter how complex it really was, and Walcott was often given the black hat.

The Wright-Langley affair, or the Wright-Smithsonian feud, therefore, continued. Orville Wright later was careful to emphasize that his disagreement was with Secretary Walcott, not the late Professor Langley or the Smithsonian Institution. The appropriate designation depends on one's viewpoint, as witness the "War for Southern Independence" or the "War against the Southern Rebellion." Whatever the name eventually bestowed by history, it might have been a bit more of a contest had Walcott's statement been published in full by the *Times*—though as it was, his printed remarks were fairly extensive.

Unfortunately, his words lost their impact, preceded as they were by the call for a congressional investigation, and followed by a statement from Grover Loening. Loening was well known as a designer of amphibian aircraft. He had graduated from Columbia University and in 1913, after a couple of years with a small aircraft manufacturer in New York, he had taken a position as Wright's assistant. This was a year before the second round in the Wright-Curtiss patent suit began. Loening had become discouraged with prospects in Dayton and in the fall of 1914 had left for a position with the army. "For years thereafter he was convinced that Orville regarded him as disloyal and ungrateful" (Crouch 1989, 464).

Loening had no hesitation in coming out in the *New York Times* totally for Wright's views. "Many of the old failures which antedated Langley's failure could be resurrected, made over and caused to fly with the knowledge that we have of airplanes today. . . . The one mistake the authorities of the Smithsonian Institution did commit was that of turning the Langley machine over to Mr. Curtiss while he was in the midst of an intricate patent litigation which might be affected by the success or failure of the flight. They should at least have turned the Langley plane over to disinterested men to give it a test, and they should have held it publically, with plenty of disinterested witnesses."[36]

These comments were preceded by advice to the SI that all it needed to do to resolve the controversy was change the label on the Langley plane. The piece concluded that the Wright plane should be in the center of the Smithsonian. "I believe that the country will demand this and will force such corrections of labeling and other conditions as will justify Mr. Wright's reconsidering his intention of giving the plane to England."[37]

Loening was holding out an olive branch to Wright, but he was surely pouring gasoline on the fire so far as the SI is concerned. The National Museum was—and is—obliged by law to house the collections made by other government agencies. There is nothing in the rules and regulations of the SI that require it to take objects offered by private individuals. One may have the greatest collection of paper clips in the world, but if that collection is not wanted by SI or one of the government agencies administered by it, the collection will not be accepted. Granted, the first man-carrying flying machine and a paper clip may be worlds apart in significance, but the principle holds. In 1925, even if Wright changed his mind and desired to donate his machine, at least in theory, the SI might not have wanted to take it—though admittedly that is stretching credibility. Actually, when Curtiss wanted to donate the *June Bug* a few years before the Langley brouhaha at Hammondsport, the SI declined, because there was no space to display it; thereafter that historic plane aged, then decayed, and finally was junked. The other side of this particular coin is that no matter how much the SI may desire an article owned by a private individual, if that individual does not wish to donate or sell, the SI cannot confiscate. The country might demand that the Smithsonian take the Wright plane, but if Mr. Wright did not want to present the object, the matter ended.

It was the issue of the patent suit and the timing of the initial test that brought Walcott's good faith into question. On February 27, 1913, Curtiss had lost the patent suit, but he had appealed and was permitted to continue in operation until the appeal was decided. On January 13, 1914, the appeals court had spoken, and Curtiss lost. Curtiss sent a telegraph "Congratulations Curtiss" to Orville (Roseberry 1972, 350). It is entirely possible, and perhaps probable, that Curtiss had in mind flying the Langley aerodrome to provide grounds for taking this matter to the Supreme Court, though that legal tactic is difficult. On the other hand, in February he had suggested to Bell building and flying a replica, which is not the same as flying the original. Still further, by the spring of 1914 he had seized on the notion of having the ailerons operate independently rather than in tandem. "Curtiss had found his loophole. The Wright Company would have to bring suit all over again" (Crouch 1989, 462).

To recast these dates from Secretary Walcott's view, the Wright Company had sued the Curtiss Company and won. The Curtiss Company had appealed and lost. By mid-January 1914, the issue had been legally settled. For Wright to state that the flight was made in the midst of litigation is not true, though he could have been speaking in anger, without thinking of the dates. For Loening, who had been in Dayton when the appeal decision was announced, to repeat the charge seems a shade dishonorable.

While waiting for the Monday papers to appear with his statement, Walcott spent his morning "working on Canadian pre-Devonian geology at home"; he did the same for an hour that night. "Wright keeps up his attack. Sounds as tho

Brewer wrote his mss" (May 4, 1925). Wright issued another statement: "Does Dr. Walcott dare affirm that the location of the trussing [trusses, stiffeners] of the wings in the Hammondsport machine in 1914 was the same as the location of the trussing of the wings in the Langley machine of 1903?"

"This controversy can never be settled while one side is talking about one thing and the other side answers by talking about something else. It can be settled by an investigation of impartial experts."[38] Apart from the point that persons impartial to the argument, experts or no, were becoming scarce, Wright had shifted from a complaint about the label to emphasizing the changes Curtiss had made after the initial test. Pontoons had been added by Curtiss because there seemed to be a better chance of landing without killing oneself on water than on land. Their weight must have resulted in some changes being required elsewhere in the aerodrome, but how significant they were is open to argument and conjecture.

The *New York Times* waded in with an editorial discussing Loening's suggestion that the si change the label and concluding that a panel of experts was needed. The following day, President Coolidge was heard from, not for one side or the other but urging that the Wright plane stay in America. The si pulled out a check for five thousand dollars, paid to Curtiss in 1917, and a group in Chicago offered to house the Wright plane. The *Times* produced yet another editorial.

"Dr. WALCOTT and Mr. WRIGHT are men alike reputable, and neither is intentionally making false representation about the Langley plane and what was done to it, yet they disagree as to vital facts, and both simply cannot be telling the whole truth and nothing else."[39] The newspaper called for disinterested arbiters, but no one was listening.

Although the newspapers were boosting their circulation as one person or another commented, nothing more was immediately recorded in Walcott's diary. For the rest of the week, all appeared quiet, and the only note of significance was a meeting of the Smithsonian Executive Committee.

"Attended church service 11–12:30 A.M. Called on Mr. Justice Lamar on way to Smithsonian. We had our picnic luncheon & then Mary sketched a wild flower & I overhauled cameras for field season of 1925. At home in evening" (May 10, 1925). What could be more peaceful? That Sunday, the *Times* gave its readers a full page, including pictures of both the Langley aerodrome and the Wright airplane in flight.

Monday geologist Walcott spent mostly working on his manuscript, but he commented, "The discussion *en re* Langley aeroplane is taking much space in the newspapers" (May 11, 1925). They went out to dinner, Walcott presided at a church meeting on the issue of a new building, and he attended the White House ceremony at which Roosevelt Association medals were presented. "This has been a quiet week & we have made some progress with our work" (May 16, 1925).

Two days before the end of this quiet week, Walcott had been mentioned in still another *New York Times* editorial, which tried to smooth the issue. "It is not necessary to assume that anybody involved is a villain. . . . That the WRIGHTS claimed priority over Professor LANGLEY, that the surviving brother still claims it and resents the inscription that has been attached to the Langley plane is more than comprehensible—it is inevitable. It is another case where to the disinterested there seems to be glory enough for all, or at least for three."[40]

Orville Wright also wrote a letter to Chief Justice Taft, in his capacity as chancellor of the Board of Regents. Wright wanted to meet him to present his facts, namely, that since 1921, when Walcott had replied to Brewer's charges, the secretary had known of fundamental changes to the Langley aerodrome and had deliberately ignored their significance. Dr. Walcott could also be present to present his views. Taft declined to be involved, insisting his position was purely nominal; so much for supporting the secretary. What is of interest is that Wright indirectly contended here that it was the reply Walcott had written in 1921 to Brewer that had begun the problem, not the label that had been on display since 1919.

As a further addition to the quiet week, the piece Walcott had written May 2 for *The Outlook* was published. It too contains a few choice quotes. "These tests [Hammondsport] were no more initiated for the purpose of influencing patent litigation than were Langley's original experiments. . . . The label on the Langley machine . . . is based on the results of the early 1914 tests at Hammondsport, made with the machine as nearly as practicable in the original form, and driven by the original engine. . . . There are other great American Museums in New York, Chicago, St. Louis, and other cities that would be glad to give the Wright plane an honored place and great publicity" (Walcott 1925g, 54–56). Placing the airplane in another American museum would not have soothed Wright. Walcott's aim was not to soothe but to present his side of the story and perhaps call Wright to task about his threat to send the plane to England.

The new week started with another nearly full page in the Sunday *New York Times*. This had a sketch of Orville's life, but it also included three 1910 letters in which the issue of placing the Wright plane in the museum had first come up. They make for interesting reading, in view of the interpretation given them by Orville. In them Walcott transmitted to the Wrights the request of the curator in charge of the display, who wanted an engine and a quarter-size model; these were not Walcott's specifications. Orville's interpretation was that the placing of a model beside the Langley machine was a deliberate attempt to downplay the Wright accomplishment. He did not mention that a later-model Wright machine was already on display at the time. He also neglected to mention the 1916 request for his machine and Regent Bell's comment that the SI dearly wanted it.

The *Times* article characterized Wright in a way that was at variance with most of his competitors in the aircraft business and several of his biographers. "He manifests not the slightest personal heat nor rancor. . . ; There is no pique in Mr. Wright's decision to send out of the country the most interesting single exhibit in the history of aeronautics."[41] That may have been true, but Wright had accused Walcott of mutilation and attempts to suborn the law, as well as of deceiving the public. What might he have said if he had felt heat or rancor?

Whatever effect this article had on Walcott, he made no mention of it. On Sunday Walcott was in church, and after the service he wrestled with the issue of an addition to the church building. At the Castle that afternoon, he discussed lending the Fort McHenry flag, the "star-spangled banner," to a New York exhibit, and in the evening he and Mary walked through "Lover's Lane" in Georgetown. Mr. Wright vanished temporarily from the news.

"Up at 6:30. Shave and saltrub bath. Breakfast 7:30[.] Away at 8:10 to downtown. At Nat. Museum 8:40" (May 18, 1925). Anyone who has driven in present-day Washington traffic would be astounded at the speed of this journey; perhaps he walked. On Tuesday, it was work on the manuscript at home in the morning and at the office answering letters in the afternoon. On Wednesday Walcott accompanied Mary to Philadelphia; while she went to a Friends meeting, he visited with her brother George. Walcott went back to Washington the next morning. "Meeting of Nat. Parks Ass. 3:45 P.M. A complete reorganization was made. Geo. Bird Grinell was elected president & the board strengthened by adding new members & dropping useless members" (May 21, 1925). Unlike so many small Washington-based groups devoted to good causes, the association was to survive (Miles 1995).

By Friday, Walcott was still in good form. He walked in Potomac Park right after breakfast, worked at home in the morning, polished off a mountain of business at the SI in the afternoon, called on Senator Smoot, and then tackled the home mail. To add to his satisfaction of a full day, "The roses are in full bloom in front of the house" (May 23, 1925). Despite the eighty-five-degree heat, Walcott spent a full Saturday at his office. "Mary brot back favorable reports of work on the N.A. Wild Flower book" (May 23, 1925). As sharp-tongued as Mary could be, to receive praise from her the printer must have been performing miracles.

Summer heat was bearing down on Washington, so the Walcotts skipped church and stayed close to home most of the day. "A fine shower after 4 P.M. cooled the air and made all nature rejoice" (May 24, 1925). Some of the colorful writing and wonder at nature that Walcott displayed on his first trip west in 1879 still remained.

Because of the heat, Walcott's routine was now to work at home on his stratigraphy manuscript in the mornings and go to the Castle in the afternoons. It was another quiet week, but it included a formal dinner at the home of the secretary of the navy and a reception in honor of President Coolidge at the Pan-American Union Building. "*Decoration Day*. We went to Cemetery in early morning to place flowers beside Helena, Charlie & Stuart" (May 30, 1925). Walcott's loyalty to those close to him was never in doubt, and this was certainly one of the factors that prolonged the Wright-Walcott dispute.

There suddenly seemed to be a prospect of resolution, for Loening had conferred with Wright and had some terms to offer. "They are that Dr. Walcott agree to label the Wright airplane . . . as the first successful man-carrying airplane in history, make the label now hanging above the Langley machine in the institution a 'truthful statement' and publish the entire argument in the yearly record of the institution."[42]

To assist with resolution of the difficulty, Wright had a condition or two more to add. "In changing the label on the Langley plan Mr. Wright declared he wanted the new label to note that the machine had been wrecked twice while it was being launched and had been altered."[43]

Mr. Loening diplomatically commented that thousands of citizens were now streaming into the Smithsonian Institution to see the Langley aerodrome and that "it is an insult to the intelligence of the American public to permit the Langley to remain in the museum falsely labelled as the first aircraft to make a successful flight."[44] So much for the word "capable." As a further attempt to "soothe" matters, he offered as proof that Langley machine had been greatly restored that many of the prominent families in Washington boasted of having pieces of it as souvenirs. Langley was so secretive that he would not talk to reporters and would hardly even let his assistants near the machine. If nothing else, Mr. Loening was a creative writer. Walcott declined to speculate for the *Times* until after he spoke with Loening.

A meeting with Walcott then took place, and Grover Loening issued his statement to the newspapers: "'Director Walcott is a broad-minded man and is anxious to do justice to the Wrights.' said Mr. Loening. 'He is in a receptive frame of mind relative to the technical tests made with the Langley plane in 1914, and I have no doubt that the matter will be handled in such a way as to satisfy Mr. Wright and result in the Wright plane being placed in the custody of the Smithsonian Institution where it belongs. It would be a sad thing, indeed, if this plane, which occupies such a unique place in the development of aviation in America, should be sent abroad.'"[45] Another source claims that Loening found Walcott "pretty bitter and equally fighting mad" (Roseberry 1972, 438).

The *Times* added to its growing pile of editorials. A new one, entitled "They Must Come to Terms," applauded Loening's efforts and noted what a fine display the Wright and Langley machines together would make. "DR. WALCOTT is no more likely to inflict intentional injustice on anybody than MR. WRIGHT is to claim more honor than he and his brother deserve."[46] Presumably all was to be peace and harmony.

While Loening was preparing his statement, Mary and Walcott were off to Philadelphia again. As president of the American Philosophical Society, he was now on the building committee of that organization. No matter how he tried, Walcott seemed to be unable to avoid new commitments. Duty always called, and unlike Odysseus, Walcott had no crewmembers to tie him to the mast when the siren called.

Back in Washington, Walcott had lunch at home with John C. Merriam. "We talked on fundamental forestry research" (June 4, 1925). This was Walcott's methodology boiled down to its essence. One need not write elaborate reports in an effort to affect policy; rather, be on good terms with the key people and convince the person in charge of the sincerity and importance of one's request. This approached worked with almost everyone except Orville Wright.

The Washington heat aggravated everyone, yet plans for the next fiscal year had to be approved and go forward to the Bureau of the Budget. "Owing to heat the employees of the s.i. & branches went home at one o'clock. . . . Temperature 102° outside my office window" (June 6, 1925). A free Saturday afternoon for the employees—so much for those who think that the federal bureaucracy does not have a heart! Sunday was "too warm & sultry to read anything but the newspapers" (June 7, 1925).

During some interval in May or June, Walcott dashed off a page to an aeronautical journal: "Smithsonian—A Pioneer in Aeronautics." This short piece mentioned support of the balloonist Thadeus Lowe and his efforts, a bibliography of aeronautics, and the growing aircraft collection. "As Professor Langley conducted the most important of his aeronautical experiments when Secretary of the Smithsonian Institution, the important work of this pioneer is very nearly completely shown. The original first government-owned machine of the Wright brothers attracts much attention" (Walcott 1925h). This little piece was neither here nor there in the midst of the newspaper articles. Some Wright biographers paint a picture of Walcott cowering under the righteous wrath of that wronged man, and this simply is not so. Walcott did not hesitate to reply to charges and mount his own campaign to set the record straight, as he saw it. As a matter unrelated to the controversy, 1925 was the tenth anniversary of the NACA, and a short summary of its work was published (Walcott 1925i).

The second workweek in June began with another chapter in the Wright drama, a development overlooked by most historians of this incident. Walcott examined a report prepared by Joseph Ames, of Johns Hopkins University, and Admiral David W. Taylor. They were members of the NACA, along with Walcott and Wright. As Secretary Abbot would noted in 1928, after Walcott's death, they became the NACA's chairman and vice chairman, respectively.[47] They examined the Langley aerodrome and various papers including some unpublished material. According to Walcott, the two men had volunteered; according to Abbot, they were appointed by the secretary. They could have volunteered and then been officially appointed, but that is a minor point.

The two men constituted a panel of aircraft experts, as requested by Wright. Since, however, Walcott had appointed them or was associated with them, it would seem to follow from Wright's viewpoint that they must be suspect. Their report was issued to the press on June 9 and the following year was reprinted in the SI *Annual Report*. Meanwhile, fortunately for his disposition, Walcott was in his early-summer mode of rapidly polishing off his odds and ends, packing his field clothes, and making preparations to leave. This was to be a good summer, and Walcott had ordered a new tent with plenty of space for his worktable. A rain moderated the Washington climate to only 90 degrees.

"Loening left a memorandum *en re* Orville Wrights idea of label for Langley airplane" (June 11, 1925). Through various writing by many people over the years, Professor Langley's machine had evolved from "aerodrome" through "aero plane" to "airplane"—good progress. One more incident was recorded in the *Times*. "Orville Wright welcomed in a correspondence made public here yesterday the suggestion that the National Academy of Sciences, or any other disinterested national body should investigate his charges of misrepresentation, and complicity in fraud against the Smithsonian Institution, but disapproved the suggestion that the Langley craft should be taken out for another attempted flight."[48]

Wright may have read the Ames-Taylor statement and decided that it was not disinterested enough for his purpose. Actually, it would have been excellent if the NAS had become involved, for the odds are overwhelming that the same general conclusions that those two men reported would have been reached. "Dr. Walcott said: . . . the idea of having the controversy investigated by the National Academy sustains his contentions. Asked who had appointed these two investigations, Dr. Walcott said: 'They volunteered.'"[49]

There are other items. Curtiss wrote privately to Wright suggesting they jointly build a replica and jointly test it, the loser in the dispute to pay all costs;

Wright did not reply (Roseberry 1972, 438). Charles Manly, who had been the erstwhile pilot in both of Langley's failed attempts, offered to put up ten thousand dollars, if Wright would do the same, and have additional tests made of the old machine. Mr. Wright wrote Manley to decline: "The issues of this controversy do not relate to events of the future, but to events of the past."[50] He also used this letter as another occasion to repeat his charges.

Over the summer Walcott considered several drafts of a new label for the aerodrome. When the machine had been first displayed in 1918, the label had been quite simple. It had been changed in 1919 to the one that so offended Wright. Insofar as the captain has ultimate responsibility for a ship, Secretary Walcott had ultimate responsibility for the label. In a time of preoccupation with the presidency of the NAS, various war activities, the transition of the NRC to peacetime, and the chairmanship of the NACA in 1919, he was too busy to read labels, and in any event he would not have been concerned with that level of exhibits. If one wants to penetrate far into the fields of surmise and speculation, someone knew of Walcott's efforts to obtain money for Langley in 1896, and when Walcott became chairman of the NACA in 1919, that someone changed the label as an indirect compliment to the secretary. This is, at best, wild and totally unsupported speculation. Regardless, the text for a new label was sent to Walcott in the field in 1925; he changed one word, in the hope of avoiding future confusion.

At the regents' annual meeting in December: "The Secretary reminded the board that Mr. Orville Wright had opened controversy within the last year in regard to the label on the Langley aerodrome on exhibition in the Museum, claiming that it was inaccurate. The question has been investigated by experts who reported that while the language of the label in question was essentially correct, it might be extended somewhat; without detriment to its historical accuracy, and at the same time meet possible objections. He exhibited a copy of the label as emended."[51] If, at this point, anyone cares, the text of the new label is given below.

LANGLEY AËRODROME

THE ORIGINAL LANGLEY FLYING MACHINE OF 1903, RESTORED

IN THE OPINION OF MANY COMPETENT TO JUDGE, THIS WAS THE FIRST HEAVIER-THAN-AIR CRAFT IN THE HISTORY OF THE WORLD CAPABLE OF SUSTAINED FREE FLIGHT UNDER ITS OWN POWER, CARRYING A MAN.

THIS AIRCRAFT SLIGHTLY ANTEDATED THE MACHINE DESIGNED AND BUILT BY WILBUR AND ORVILLE WRIGHT, WHICH ON DECEMBER 17, 1903, WAS THE FIRST IN THE HISTORY OF THE WORLD TO ACCOMPLISH SUSTAINED FREE FLIGHT UNDER ITS OWN POWER, CARRYING A MAN.

The large print was followed by a great amount of detail on Langley's investigations, in a type face too small to be read except by the most ardent museumgoer. This is surely more than enough detail about an unpleasant six weeks.

The emphasis has been on flying, but that was not the only aggravation. Those who were opposed to even the word "evolution" were in full cry. To provide a historical context, in July 1925 the young high school teacher John T. Scopes was brought to trial in Dayton, Tennessee, for teaching about evolution. In June, Walcott was quoted in a local paper as mentioning the "facts of evolution." That brought a strong letter from the proprietor of the Christian Life Book Room in Washington. Walcott presumably personally prepared the response, for the letter was forwarded west for his signature.

> Acknowledging receipt of your letter of June 11, it does not appear to me more necessary to reconcile the statements of Genesis with astronomy than it does to reconcile the statements of First Samuel, Chapter 21; or Second Samuel, Chapter 24, with the character of God as revealed in Psalm 103, or in the Gospel of John. There is evolution in Biblical testimony, quite as much as in species.
>
> The views of scientific men as to the age of the earth, the evolution of species, and the origin of man, are based on so many and convincing kinds of evidence, which appear to devout Christians among them as so manifestly the witness of God, that it is impossible for them not to be substantially agreed on the general facts.[52]

The reply to this was that Walcott had not answered the original question as to whether the original length of the day had changed, and by whose order. There is no follow-up letter in the SI to that one.

During July of 1925, Assistant Secretaries Abbot and Wetmore discussed evolution. As a result, Abbot wrote a three-page statement, which was then slightly modified by Wetmore. This was mimeographed and used as a standard reply to those who wrote in inquiring about evolution. Walcott was far away in Canada, but such action would not have been taken without his blessing and probably was at his suggestion. In the face of Walcott's AAAS remarks, a law court was actually determining whether teaching evolution was a crime. At least a few copies of the statement were mailed out under the signature of Acting Secretary Abbott. Considering the passion generated by the Scopes "monkey trial," this was a remarkable thing for the Smithsonian authorities to have done. A year later, Abbot sent Walcott a copy of a "lay sermon" he had written, concerned with evolution.

A few months earlier, shortly before his death, Clarke, still fulminating about evolution, had written a letter indicating that he was going to test the soil at several places in New York State where Walcott had lived. "There is a suspicion in the back of my mind that *soul* and *soil* are derived from the same root word. Was not man made out of dust of the ground?"

"You have done as much as anyone can do to rid the world diabolism, even though you always insisted on making your lovely fossils a personal diversion."[53] Just as more than enough has been written about Wright, so a few quotations from Clarke go a long way.

It was time to leave Washington for the West. On Saturday, Walcott was at his Smithsonian office. "Clearing off desk, approving plans & estimates for 1925–26 & conferences 9–11:30. Completed packing up at home. At 7:25 P.M. we left Washington on B&O train for Chicago & San Diego. Mary packed up wild flower sketches for 3 volumes of her book & left them at Smithsonian & sent 40 to Mr. Rudge" (June 13, 1925). Tradition was broken, for instead of going to Buffalo, Toronto, and then west, as had been the route to western Canada since 1907, they went to Chicago. This trip was being made to pursue Mary's interests.

10

The Last Years (1925–1927): There Is An Old Saying That All Good Things Must Come to an End

> We felt ourselves necessarily carried back to the time when the schistus on which we stood was yet at the bottom of the seas, and when the sandstone before us was only beginning to be deposited, in the shape of sand or mud, from the waters of a superincumbent ocean. An epoca still more remote presented itself, when even the most ancient of these rocks, instead of standing upright in vertical beds, lay in horizontal planes at the bottom of the sea, and was not yet disturbed by the immeasurable force which has burst asunder the solid pavement of the globe. Revolutions still more remote appeared in the distance of this extraordinary perspective. The mind seemed to grow giddy by looking so far into the abyss of time; and while we listened with earnestness and admiration to the philosopher who was now enfolding to us the order and series of these wonderful events, we became sensible how much further reason may sometimes go than imagination can venture to follow.
>
> —J. Playfair, 1805

"JOGGED ALONG ALL DAY across Kansas. We read a little & rested as the heat in the cars was too great for extension of mind or body" (June 15, 1925). The description of Kansas weather is as accurate today as it was when the twentieth century was only a quarter completed. "Crossing northern New Mexico & Arizona quite warm, but not as bad as yesterday. We are weary from the heat & dust" (June 16, 1925). The railroad was better than the stagecoach Walcott had used in this country four decades earlier, but not all that much better. One more day and they were finally settled in San Diego. Walcott wrote to Washington:

> Please wire me at Vancouver Glencoe Lodge if Arthur got thru Toronto with baggage & if all is well at the office. We had a strenuous 3 days here & learned much.

The wildflower sketches here were painted by contract & naturally their spirit & much of their grace & fine characters have gone with the fading flowers in oblivion—Miss Scripps [owner of the sketches] is a most interesting woman & doing much good for her fellow humans. We met D*r* Vaughan yesterday. Mr. Harper & Mrs. Crandell have been most courteous. We visited the naval air station yesterday & have seen something of San Diego & vicinity. . . . Mrs. Walcott still has about 500 sketches to look at. The artist painted aliens, hybrids & very common weeds. All were fish that came his way.[1]

Another day, another letter to Washington: "Have had 4 very full days. D*r* & Mrs Vaughan bro't us to the station. He has a fine piece of work laid out here. The carpenter had my surveying rod to make a new one from. Mr. Crosmen may have the ferrule point & brass strips to hold the compass. I should like a new ferrule about ⅛ in large in diameter. If a rod can be made duplicating the old one & cut diagonally midway, it can be sent by mail. This must be a hurry up job if it is to be of service. Possibly the rod may have been made as it (old one) was turned over last Oct—(cut in two parts)."[2] Ever concerned with detail, Walcott had a little sketch of the angle at which he wanted the rod cut.

For those interested in people, Dr. T. Wayland Vaughan had worked for the USGS for some years before moving to his present position on the West Coast. He was the expert on Tertiary fossil corals and large microfossils; the latter sounds like an oxymoron, but some single-cells organisms grew to the size of silver dollars and occasionally larger. The establishment Vaughan headed eventually became the Scripps Institute of Oceanography, thanks to Miss Scripps.

In San Francisco, Mary sketched a wildflower; she was under pressure to complete the material for all five volumes of her book. Mr. Rudge had sent her proofs, and the project was moving ahead. After a short stay in San Francisco, they headed farther north, to Mount Rainier National Park. It was hot in the lower reaches of the park, so the next day they went up Paradise Valley. "Mary secured several species of flowers new to her collection & sketched the Avalanche Lilly [sic]" (June 26, 1925). Mary was busy all day sketching and at night lecturing about her work; Walcott was suffering from the heat.

The weather cooled. "After lunch we walked up on the Ramparts 1100 feet up & 2 miles. Our first walk of the season for 1925" (June 28, 1925). It was not a bad first field walk for an old man. Most of the following day Mary was busy sketching, but they did get to Seattle in time to catch the steamer to Vancouver and hear news of the Santa Barbara earthquake.

"Our wedding day. Eleven very happy years together" (June 30, 1925). While they were in Vancouver, Mary stayed busy sketching most of the time, but in the four days they tarried, they did see the Dominion Day parade and shop for a camp stove. Lots of old friends greeted them; they were royally entertained—which is the best way to put it, for the expression "wined and dined" would have provoked Mary's wrath as a teetotaler and plain-living Friend.

On Saturday morning, the Walcotts were on the train east. "Woke up near Golden. At Field found air smoky. Arthur was waiting for us at Lake Louise station & we walked across to our tent. Tex Wood & Bill Lewis came in with the horses about 7 P.M." (July 5, 1925). The ever-resourceful Arthur had arrived with the baggage, and if there had been any problem en route, it was never recorded. They spent two days resting and getting their gear organized, and a third day in their tent while Tex and Bill moved most of the camp outfit to Ptarmigan Pass. The weather was fine. "At noon the men came with horses. Camp was then moved up to below Ptarmigan Pass where Mary & I camped in 1916. Our tent faces ssw towards Mt. Temple 9.4 *mi* distant. Camp 7200'" (July 3, 1925).

"Headache kept me quiet all day. A combination of elevation & upset stomach. Mary well & sketching a 'Buckbean' wild flower. Men resting & cleaning up. We have fine scenery, good water, grass & wood. An ideal camp" (July 10, 1925). Despite the headache, Walcott was enjoying life. Walcott was well enough the next day to take four photographs from camp while Mary went off looking for a Cathay (a local name for a flower) to sketch. Next, Walcott went out to photograph away from the tents, but a cold mist drove him back. "Mary & the men went up on pass for grass, rocks, etc for *Goat Group*" (July 12, 1925). (Translation: for a number of years there had been a stuffed family of mountain goats in the Smithsonian's mammal hall, as part of the exhibit backdrop. During the 1930s the goats and another group of mountain sheep were to be refurbished and moved into a fine hall of North American mammals. In 1998 they disappeared.)

"Spent the day about camp waiting for the clouds to break away so that we could take photographs. Mary sketching P.M. We should get away from here by Thursday if one good day for photography shows up" (July 13, 1925). The next day was also disagreeable, but finally the weather came up to specifications. "We went up on north ridge of Mt. Richardson & photographed the Ptarmigan massif, Redoubt Mt. etc. Looked over quartzites of Fort Mt. formation & returned to camp 4 P.M. This is our first *work* at over 8000 feet elevation" (July 15, 1925)—again, not bad for an old man. One has the sense that after years in the area, Walcott wanted quite specific views to illustrate particular points of the geologic history that he had interpreted. More was involved than an artistic urge to have the right composition and lighting.

Next morning, the entire party was out on a successful search for a yellow columbine. Mary sketched it, while Walcott wrote letters and the men went to make ready the next campsite. "Horses strayed away so wrote letters until 11 A.M. We then went over the pass into Skoki Lake Canyon. A small glacier occurs on the north slope of Ptarmigan Peak. A strong s.w. gale met us on the pass along with dense forest fire smoke" (July 17, 1925). The smoke made it impossible for Walcott to take his photographs.

He fussed around camp for two days; indeed, he did not number this as a camp in his diary, another break with tradition. "Camp moved to near small lake above Tilted Mountain Falls. We found a pleasant spot & were settled before dark. Flies & mosquitoes abundant but not troublesome. The camp is close to the upper Cambrian Lyell fossil locality we found last summer" (July 20 1925). "With Mary & Bill I went after fossils A.M. & brot in material for five (5) pkgs which I wrapped in strong manilla paper in afternoon" (July 21, 1925). That was more like it, and to add a bit more to the day, Tex and his little daughter, Ruth, caught six trout for dinner.

The ever-helpful Mr. Dorsey sent in a long letter with a few tidbits of news. He listed a dozen packages sent to Walcott between July 10 and July 17; the secretary was not out of communication.

> Your telegram called for 30 lbs. of rice. As they did not have but about 20 lbs. at the house, I got Mr. Hill to send 10 additional pounds.
> This week we have been busy putting the preliminary estimates in shape. . . . Webb sent the page proof of the 1924 [Annual] Report back to the printer last week, so we ought to have this out before you get back—the first time that we will have been so nearly up to date almost within the memory of man. . . . Nick [Dorsey] and John Poole are still working for funds for the endowment campaign. I believe that things are definitely shaping up for us to get at least a material part of the necessary amount to start the campaign, even if we do not get it all.[3]

All was normal in Washington.

"Mary, Tex, Bill & I collected fossils from Upper Cambrian (Lyell) on Tilted Mountain Brook. Material very fragmentary but very desirable. Put up fossils in packages P.M. Hail & rain more or less after 1 P.M." (July 22, 1925). It rained that night and part of the next day, but by afternoon Walcott was out with Mary looking at the upper part of the Lyell Formation; while Walcott had sat out the rain, Mary had added another flower sketch to her collection.

"All out collecting on Tilted Mountain Brook P.M. I measured more in detail [the] section in which fauna occurs. Packed up 5 pkgs fossils P.M." (July 24, 1925). This was the old-time Walcott, not the old Walcott, refining the biostratigraphy with each new fossil horizon discovered. "With Tex & Mary went up to Tilted Mt cirque to collect U.[upper] C.[ambrian] fossils beneath the Lyell limestone. Cold raw wind drove us in 2 P.M. Packed up fossils & wrote out notes. Cleaned up & we had dinner 7 P.M. Cricket & 3 horses strayed off & not found" (July 25, 1925). Collecting fossils from limestone requires a great deal of patience in breaking up rock; if any example is needed of Walcott's patience, it is that he put up with Cricket for season after season.

"Mary & I went over to the west side of Baker Creek and endeavored to find a contact between the Mons & Sarbach but all such places were covered by debris" (July 27, 1925). The contact between two units formations is an important point for geologists, as it is the place to see whether the underlying unit had been inclined or folded before the overlying unit was deposited. "We looked for fossils in upper beds of Lyell limestones along the ridge north and south of camp. A.M. Returned to tent 2 P.M. as I had an attack of intercostal neuralgia" (July 7, 1925). That was not good. Walcott sat around camp the next day recovering; fortunately, Tex brought in a large mail to keep him occupied. Mist and squalls extended the stay in camp.

"Camp moved to Skoki Brook between Fossil & Skoki Mts" (July 30, 1925). The camp stove was unpacked, for the nights were cool, and Walcott commented on the good dinner Arthur prepared. "Began working on N.E. shoulder of Fossil Mt. by locating & collecting a lot of fossil from the Sarbach graptolite zone" (July 31, 1925). So far it had been a profitable summer in terms of new data for refining the biostratigraphy.

August began on the same high note, but an electrical storm drove them in. The lightning was severe enough to start a blaze in the forest, which Bill put out. Sunday was a lazy day, broken by a four-hour ride into Skibob Valley. Apparently the horses did not always enjoy a Sunday off, but then again, they were not ridden every day. Life for a Walcott horse was not bad, even with being ridden on an occasional Sunday.

The horses were collected Monday in time to do some riding along the east side of Fossil Mountain, looking for a good place to measure a section. "Collecting from Xenostegium zone of Sarbach formation Bill & Mary assisting. Put up six pkgs in evening. Cold winds, clds & forest fire smoke made us seek shelter under a cliff" (August 4, 1925). As noted earlier, collecting is not always fun. "Measuring section of N.E. shoulder of Fossil Mt. up to the Devonian. Located 3 fossil zones. About 4 P.M. Mary, Bill & I went for a ride along east slope of Skoki Mt. Rough going & nothing of interest" (August 5, 1925).

"Strong west wind. Worked on section & collected fossils from two zones in Sarbach. Mary & Bill assisted. The raw cold wind was very trying" (August 6, 1925). This was a far cry from the sweltering heat of Washington. They spent another day completing the section and collecting a few more fossils. A day in camp was needed to label and pack the fossils and write up the field notes.

"Mary left camp 9:30 A.M. for Lake Louise & Wapta Lake Camp to attend meeting of Trail Riders. I had too much intercostal neuralgia to undertake the ride. . . . Am getting along much better than I anticipated a month ago"

(August 9, 1925). "Collecting from 69*a* Lower Sarbach A.M. but returned to camp as both Bill & I were cold & the work was above timber line. Went out after 2 P.M. for photographs but clouds closed down" (August 10, 1925). The number and letter refer to a fossil locality previously collected. When the fossils were identified in Washington, a locality number would be assigned, and a little green sticker with the number written on it would be glued to each specimen. This curatorial effort was labor intensive, but it ensured that fossils from different localities would not be inadvertently intermixed.

"Out collecting from Receptaculties zone until 4 P.M." (August 11, 1925). "With Mary & Bill collected a lot of fossils from the Phyllograptus zone of the Sarbach. Returned at 5 P.M. to clean up for dinner. Turned in at 8:30 as we were tired from pounding away on a very hard, tough limestone" (August 13, 1925). No translation is necessary. If any comment should be made it is that even the worst of Southern chain gangs in the bad old days did not have seventy-five-year-old men breaking up rock.

"I wrote out a copy of the Sarbach Formation section to send in for copying" (August 13, 1925). In this sentence is the solution of a minor mystery. Except for a few scattered pages from earlier years, few documents anywhere within the SI can be classified as field notes. For example, apart from the diary, no manuscript or draft material records the field investigations of 1909, when the Burgess Shale fauna was discovered. Evidently Walcott wrote up his stratigraphic material in the field and mailed it back to Washington to be typed by the time he returned. (G. K. Gilbert, noted American geologist, operated by writing his field notes more or less as pages of a future paper, and Walcott used a modification of his technique.) The diary entries obviously are not scientific notes, yet in the absence of those notes they are the only detailed source of the where and when of Walcott's field investigations.

Rain—"All in camp reading, sleeping except Arthur who is busy early & late The horses are inclined to wander but Bill keeps a watch over them" (August 14, 1925). More rain. "Bill brot in the horses but no one desired to ride" (August 15, 1925). "A repetition of yesterday" (August 16, 1925). Walcott wrote letters, including one to John Merriam:

> The rain is gently pattering on the tent as it has been doing for the past 48 hours. We are thankful as the forest fire menace has been a real one—not only in B.C.—to the west but in the Clearwater forest to the north & in the scrub on the foothills to the south. An extensive burn north of Golden has put an end to the work: I had hoped to do on that side of the Cordilleran Trough. We have met with some success in this area. A section exposed just above this camp (Skoki) has yielded many fossils & gave me a fine base for the Ordovician Sarbach formation.

We passed along its base last September in a fine snowstorm. We hope to secure 4 mountain sheep for the National Museum after Sept 1st. The big rams begin to seek lower levels & their mates by Sept. 15th and they then have a fine coat of hair. They are not troubled by theories of Evolution & theology so we will relegate the latter to the future and be happy and content in 12 x 14 cotton cloth home.

We are well and having a fine season. Mrs. Walcott has made 15 wild flower sketches and we are both free from the "tired feeling" of last June.[4]

The next afternoon, life improved briefly. "With Mary & Bill went out on Fossil Mt & collected a fine lot of lower Sarbach fossils" (August 17, 1925). "Out with Mary & Bill all day endeavoring to secure some good photographs but the cl[ou]ds shadowed the sections we wished & the day was lost & a lot of tedious work with camera" (August 18, 1925).

Walcott, Mary, and Tex went down the Red Deer River and made a "spike camp," wherein one takes the minimum needed for an overnight stay. The afternoon light was not to Walcott's liking, so the next morning they worked with the cameras before returning to the Skoki Mountain camp. They packed exposed film, deer horns in velvet, fossils, and miscellaneous items to be to be taken by the pack horses to Lake Louise and shipped to Washington. It was a disagreeable day, and that evening the snow began. By next morning the snow lay ten inches thick on the ground. "Remained in tent & reviewed section on Ranger Creek etc. This section recalls one of Aug. 24th 1911 at Burgess Pass B.C." (August 22, 1925).

"Read & wrote letters. Enjoying more or less neuralgia in muscles of back" (August 23, 1925). "A little snow melted but not enough to clear even the steep slopes" (August 24, 1925). "With Mary & Bill went up on Skoki Pass to take photographs. High wind & cold drove us out & down to timber line at noon. Returned to camp disgusted with the weather" (August, 25, 1925). "Another November day. About camp until 2 P.M. & then went up on Fossil Mt. Cleared away the snow & brot in about 250# of the 69a fossil layer. A good haul of lower Sarbach fauna" (August 26, 1925). Obviously, it is better to break up rock and trim fossils on the outcrop, but if one cannot get to the outcrop, one brings the outcrop to camp to recover the fossils. This was the method used in the early days of collecting the Burgess Shale.

Walcott packed up the collections and that afternoon looked at the upper part of the underlying Mons Formation. It was cold work, but the next day was worse; he stayed in camp while Mary and Tex took three packloads to Lake Louise. He spent another day fussing about in camp, as the snow squalls and high winds prevented any other activity. "Packed up and moved camp down Baker Creek & up Wild Flower Canyon to an old campsite beside Wild Flower Pond. All snug by 6 P.M. & Arthur had a warm dinner for us" (August 30, 1925). Walcott did not number this campsite, another lapse on his part. Walcott and Mary went up to the pass between Johnson and Wild Flower Canyons, and just below a fault they found a fine lot of fossils, a good way to end the trying month of August.

The mail came in, including another chatty epistle from Chief Clerk Dorsey: "Your letters of August 8 and 3 were received, and Mr. Hill has ordered the pair of saddle bags, which are to be delivered today, and will be promptly mailed. He could not get the russet leather sooner. About the three boxes of 30-30 Winchester shells, Mr. Hill tells me that he bought these for you before you left. He got first the steel nosed bullets, and these were returned, as you wanted the soft nosed.... I know that Arthur's hot cakes and corn muffins must be a joy to you. I am living in the hope of some day getting Arthur to cook me a batch somewhere out in the woods."[5] The suggested budget had been cut, and the painting in Walcott's house had been completed. All was normal in Washington.

A letter from Dr. Abbot, back from vacation, noted receipt of Walcott's letters of August 4 and 8, plus the change in the draft of the Langley aerodrome label; Walcott had added one word, in order "to avoid future controversy." "Mr. Poole has been successful in raising $22,300 which, in addition to that which was subscribed and which has no strings upon it, meets the authorization you gave me just before leaving, so that we are signing the contract with Tamblyn and Brown for the drive, their work to begin during September and the whole campaign for the million dollars to be finished by July, 1926."[6] Abbot was conservative in the use of periods but liberal in his optimism about raising money.

The field party packed up and moved to Johnson Creek Canyon; this Walcott designed as camp six. They spent a day in camp fixing a workstand in the tent while Tex shot a ram for the Museum display. "Mary & I went up on Johnson— Wild Flower Canyon Pass & collected a lot of fossils from the *Sarbach* (loc. 69g)" (September 3, 1925). It was a repetition of earlier work, but sometimes information in another locality necessitates backtracking.

> Camp near head of Johnson Canyon Sept 4. [19]25, 7:30 A.M. Dear Mr. Dorsey[:] Park Warden Galvin dropped into camp last eve & goes out in 30 minutes & will mail this at Castle tomorrow. All going well. A fine "Ram" came to camp at 6:30, yesterday just after Mrs. Walcott and I came in from a days work up on the pass. We found a new fossil zone in the "Sarbach." Tex goes out again today for a "Big" ram & 2 ewes—The "Big" fellows are shy & rare & we may not get one. Small ones are abundant. The men saw 23 yesterday. No goat about here but many deer. We met a large black bear & a grizzly was digging out gopher holes up on the pass.
>
> The 30-30 *shells* came & the skinning knives—the latter are fine. Due at Lake Louise by the 14th. Cool nights—Day's 45° to 60. Now for breakfast. Remembrance to all. C.D.W. fingers cold.[7]

Walcott packed up the fossils collected the day before and helped a little in cleaning the ram's head, although, he wrote, Mary did nine-tenths of this messy job. Tex and Bill hunted for larger sheep specimens, without success. Snow squalls kept geologist Walcott in, and the poor visibility prevented the hunters from going out. The next morning they awoke to see three inches of snow, which fortunately melted by late afternoon.

"A perfect fall day. Mary & I went up on devide [*sic*] & photographed Johnson Cirque etc. I found contact between Sarbach & Mons. We collected three faunules. Tex & Bill out all day & located 3 large rams above Badger Pass. We counted 25 ewes & lambs in Johnson Cirque. This has been the first fine day all for a long time" (September 7, 1925). The good weather did not last; the next day was cold, made worse by a raw wind. "Mary & I went up Badger Pass Canyon. Collected a few lower Bosworth formation fossils & rocks. The section is fine from the Sawbach down thru Mons, Lyell & Bosworth. Tex shot an ewe on devide [*sic*] at head of Johnson Creek" (September 8, 1925).

"Ridge pole of tent broke at 3 A.M. from weight of 6 in wet snow. Snow squalls all day. Reading & writing at tent. Horses browsing 2 *mi* down Johnson Creek. This storm terminates our work in this area for 1925" (September 9, 1925). They spent another day in mist and rain squalls; "A long tedious day as [I] wish to be out on the section up near Badger Pass" (September 10, 1925). "Nothing to do but read & work on field notes" (September 11, 1925).

They broke camp at 10 A.M. and by 6 P.M. were settled in their old campground below Baker Lake. "Fine day. Made a late start as horses strayed away. We rode *via* Ptarmigan Pass & Corral Creek to Lake Louise Station on the C.P.R.R. and camped opposite the depot. All very tired at night. Found a large mail" (September 14, 1925).

Walcott worked on the mail while Bill took six of the horses to Hillsdale for winter pasture. After that Bill left for home, and Tex went off with another party, taking four horses. The logistics of a pack train are complex, but the numbers suggest five saddle horses—even though Arthur is hardly mentioned, he was very much a presence—plus ten horses for the pack string. Walcott was sick again, but Arthur was on hand to crate up the fossils. Another day passed; "The rainy damp, chilly weather makes it difficult to do anything" (September 17, 1925). Conditions did not improve. "A cold, raw, disagreeable day. Looked after packing, accts etc. Intercostal neuralgia kept me from doing any writing except scraps of letters" (September 18, 1925).

Arthur and Walcott finished the packing the following day and sent the crates and trunks off to Washington. On Sunday the snow finally melted, and they spent the last afternoon with friends at the Lake Louise Chateau. "We went to Banff 9:35 A.M. Glad to leave camp for home" (September 21, 1925). That may have been first time Walcott ever expressed such a sentiment about western Canada, and he probably would not have written it had he known this was his last field season. Still the "Explorations" pamphlet summed matters up: "The field season was even more unsatisfactory than that of 1924" (Walcott 1926a, 13–15). There is a fine panorama, but most of the other pictures are camp scenes or flowers, with a dearth of text on geologic accomplishments. In what might be another example of aggravation that summer, the separate printing of Walcott's part of this pamphlet does not have a picture on the cover, as had been Walcott's custom for a number of years.

It took a day to straighten up accounts and visit in Banff. When it came to keeping accounts straight, Mary was as good as her husband. She replied to a bill sent to Washington, "No doubt your records are incomplete. I have the bill for the molasses and certain other things that we bought after August, and in addition I came into your store the day we were leaving for the east and purchased fruit and other odds and ends. Your man who usually waits on me when you are not in the store, arranged the purchases for me, made up the bill, and I paid him the cash for it. I think if you will look in your cash register about the 22d or 23d of September you will find the cash paid at that time."[8] So there.

The Walcotts headed east. "A beautiful ride north of Lake Superior. Autumn colors fine. Wrote letter & memorandum on John M. Clarke" (September 24, 1925). As had been expected, in view of his illness, Clarke had died during the summer; he had been a kid, just starting out, when twenty-eight-year-old Walcott was working for James Hall in Albany. They arrived in Toronto and immediately left for Buffalo and family. There is a story, though whether or not it relates to this trip is unknown. The Walcotts had purchased some Alaskan Indian baskets in Canada. Because they were staying in a cramped roomette, they stacked them on the toilet in the closet. They had also purchased a wheel of monastery cheese, and because there was no room they had cut it and stacked it with the baskets. A u.s. customs agent disputed the origin of the baskets, wanted to collect duty, and insisted on seeing them. He undid the package, got a whiff of the cheese, and fled without arguing about the baskets.

"We are delighted to be back in 'Gods [*sic*] Country' an old name for western New York" (September 25, 1925). A rough ride from Banff had been added to the terrible weather. The Walcotts spent almost two full days with their granddaughter. "Arrived Wash'n 10:20 A.M. Alfonso [Jones] met us with our new Pierce-Arrow car. At home found Mollie, Annie & Delia. Arthur came in train with us. At my office 1:30 to 5 P.M. All well at the Smithsonian. All our baggage came through safely including skins, horns, etc. At home in evening" (September 29, 1925).

Walcott jumped into administrative chores and the accumulated mail. "At odd moments looking up data for a paper on Joseph Henry. We are delighted to be at work in a clean, peaceful & contented home. September has been a trying month on account of bad weather & travel" (September 30, 1925). A few days later Walcott wrote the president of Stanford.

Mrs. Walcott and I returned from our fieldwork in the Canadian Rockies, full of the joy of living and ready to take up the duties of the winter. They are many and will call for all the energy we have to given them. The Institution is fortunate in having two very capable Assistant Secretaries: Dr. Charles G. Abbot, who carries on his research work and looks after the interest of the Library, Exchanges and the Astrophysical Laboratory; the other is Dr. Alexander Wetmore, who has supervisory charge of the National Museum and Zoological Park. He came to us last June from the Agriculture Department. Mr. Ravenel is Administrative Assistant in charge of the Arts & Industries Museum and overlooks the physical welfare of all of the buildings. If Dr. G. Brown Goode or Professor Baird could return they would find many changes since their day. The next building should be an art building, corresponding in size to the Natural History Museum. This will relieve congestion in all of the other buildings and give our research workers more comfortable quarters.[9]

Thoughts of bad weather in Canada faded rapidly.

Despite his enthusiasm on paper, Walcott was quite concerned with the lack of funding. The research facilities were poor, and the older staff members were in financial hardships. He turned to the New York General Education Board for help; like so many of his efforts to raise the endowment, this was not productive.

Routine administration settled in, and on, Walcott; his eyes were definitely giving difficulty. Helen came down for a few days' visit. He enjoyed going to church with the two ladies and then moped around the following day when they left for a short visit to Baltimore. "Feeling tired & dull. Messrs. Rudge & Grant came to talk over N.A. Wild Flower book with Mary & me. At meeting of Roosevelt Memorial Committee 3:30–5:30 P.M." Somehow, Walcott was not getting less involved in projects, no matter how much he intended to cut down. Helen left to go to her own home.

The Walcotts now gave the Pierce-Arrow a thorough tryout. They left Washington at noon, Alphonso Jones driving, and spent the evening at Bryn Mawr with Mary's brother. They left at 9:00 A.M. and were in Newburgh, New York, by 5:00 P.M.

Walcott, in good humor, scribbled a note to Mr. Dorsey the next morning: "All well. We had a beautiful ride & restful too.—A shower last night purified the air & now 8 A.M. the sun is out & all nature in a cheerful mood.—It is 90 miles to Albany up along the Hudson."[10]

The party left Newburgh at 9 A.M. as soon as the note was mailed to Washington, and by 2 P.M. they were in Albany—not bad time for that course. That evening Walcott spoke at the John M. Clarke Memorial meeting. "Dr. Clarke was so delightfully human, so broad in his culture and interests, that we always looked forward to a visit from him with keen anticipation of enjoyment and to the strengthening of the spirit of friendship and good fellowship" (Walcott 1925j, 538).

"Visited in N.Y. state museum A.M. Met Ruedemann, Miss Goldring, etc. After luncheon visited with Mr. Rice & friends. Met. D*r Wm*. L. Magi of Princeton. In evening spoke on Joseph Henry. Magi told of Henry's scientific work. Received degree of L.L.D. of University of State of New York" (October 16, 1925). So it was that the man who never went to college was honored by his native state with his final honorary degree, making the total an even dozen.

As to his predecessor, Walcott was unstinting in his praise: "Joseph Henry was an international figure. . . . Joseph Henry's great success as a scientific administrator came in large measure from his versatility and his broad viewpoint regarding matters of science. . . . Henry insisted that all researches which had for their purpose the increase of existing knowledge should receive due consideration. This broad-minded policy resulted in keeping the activities of the institution well diversified, practically all branches of science sharing its attention, and this ideal has been followed to the present time" (Walcott 1925k, 405–8). For Walcott, as for Henry, science, that is, the "increase" of knowledge to quote James Smithson's will, was the prime business of the Smithsonian Institution.

The trip south was more leisurely, the first leg being to Norwalk, Connecticut, the summer home of cousin Fred. There they spent the following day; there was no sense driving on Sunday when it was unnecessary. Monday evening they were in Mount Vernon, New York, having stopped on the way to confer with Mr. Rudge about Mary's book. The next day they paused to see Mrs. Harriman for an hour on their way to Pennsylvania. On Wednesday Mary left the men in Philadelphia, and Walcott arrived home at 5:15 P.M.. "Feeling very tired at night owing to catching cold & improper diet" (October 21, 1925).

A large accumulation of mail did not sit well with the cold, and for three afternoons Walcott gave up early and went home to nap. "The trip to Albany etc. used up my digestive track so that I am not much good" (October 24, 1925). It is a pity that Walcott could not hold up as well as the new car. He rested at home on Sunday morning and was braced up by a car ride in the afternoon.

Monday was a better day, with Walcott answering letters while Mary worked on her flower book. On Tuesday they labeled and admired the photographs from the past field season. "At my office 9–12:30 A.M. Conference *en re* s.i. endowment 10:30–12. At home—in afternoon studying proposals for endowment campaign & mss of paper on geology of Alberta & B.C." (October 28, 1925). This schedule was to his liking, and he pursued it for three more days. "Snow began falling about 2 P.M. A genuine Skokie mountain day" (October 30, 1925). Walcott seldom showed a sense of wry humor, but it crept out occasionally. The weather and the time he had for his manuscript put him in a mood to write to the chief paleontologist of the Geological Survey of Canada. "I have been looking over with interest your brochure on 'The Bottom Deposits of Lake Ontario.' It is most suggestive, and should be carefully read by all geologists who are engaged in active fieldwork. I spent a month during the summer of 1876 and another in 1877 studying the bottom deposits in the bays and inlets as well as on the open shore of portions of the coast of Maine, and I owe much of the success met with in discovering fossils (where they were not supposed to occur) to the information obtained in relation of sediments to the animal and plant life. It would be a fine thing if all paleontologists and geologists could have the same experience."[11]

The Walcotts observed November 1, after a fashion, by spending a full day at the office. They finally finished labeling the field photographs, and they celebrated by attending a lecture on Arctic exploration. On Sunday, a trip to Gunston Hall with a Supreme Court justice and his wife substituted for church. For most of the week, there was little office routine; Mary went off to Philadelphia, and Walcott stayed mostly at home, wrestling with the geology manuscript. Friday he joined her. "Presided at meeting of Amer. Phil. Soc. 8:15–10 P.M. Prof. gave a fine talk on Evolution. Met a number of old friends. Returned to Bryn Mawr 11 P.M." (November 6, 1925). Inasmuch as Walcott had agreed to serve as president, he served, regardless of his other responsibilities. What is curious is the lapse in the diary of the name of the lecturer. It may have been haste, but it may have been just another of those little slips associated with aging.

Sidney was with them on the train when they went home, and the three attended church together, for the first time in many years. Sidney was now trying to start his own business in New York, and it was his affairs that brought him to the capital. That was a pleasant interlude in an otherwise wearisome week. Walcott met with the executive committee of the regents to try to move the endowment drive forward, and other chores ate into his research time as well. "Attended Meeting Inst. of Economics 10–12:30 A.M. Called on Chief Justice Taft 6 P.M. *en re* s.i. endowment increase" (November 11, 1925). "At my office during day except for a call at the White House to leave a memorandum *en re* status of the N.A.C.A. Chief Justice sent letter to Mr. Herbert Hoover *en re* s.i. endowment" (November 12, 1925).

Because there are two different thoughts in this last entry, clarification is in order. As an example of how to pull the levers of power in Washington, consider Walcott's desire to have Herbert Hoover assist with the endowment campaign. Secretary of Commerce Hoover might have argued with Secretary Walcott that he was just too busy to undertake another duty, but it is exceedingly difficult to say no to the chief justice of the Supreme Court.

As to the other matter, aviation affairs were finally coming to a head in Congress after years of acrimony. It was increasingly evident that the Department of Commerce would control civilian aviation. To some it seemed logical that the NACA should become a part of the new bureaucracy. To Walcott, it was obvious that the strength of the committee lay in its not being affiliated with any one part of the government. There was no sense fooling around with lower levels; Walcott gave his opinion directly to President Coolidge (Roland 1985). Groundwork had been laid earlier, as reported by John Victory: "Following your instructions to see Mr. Foster at the White House during the summer and acquaint him with the story of the Committee's position on the general plan of government reorganization. . . . I think I got across to him practically all of the major points I wished to leave with him, and also received from him some very good advice with a view to killing the plan to transfer our Committee to the Department of Commerce."[12] One wonders how Walcott away in Canada could direct Victory to just the right person, but then Walcott almost never left tracks; this is just an example of the appropriateness of his nickname.

The issue of independence for the NACA was part of a larger concern for Walcott. At some time during 1925, the SI released a small brochure entitled "Relations of the Smithsonian Institution to the National Government." (Despite the best efforts of nearly a dozen people, no copies have been found, though a draft has been discovered.) "I have failed to find anything to justify even the presumption that the Accounting Officers of the Government have any authority to require an accounting by the Board of Regents. . . . In contradistinction to the trust—duties imposed by the Smithson will, there are a number of activities which are the Government's own enterprise (National Museum, Bureau of Ethnology, etc) the administration of which has been confided to the Regents as the mere agents of the United States."[13] For Walcott, the line between private and public functions and funding was clear, and that line was inviolate.

"At my office during day. Correspondence[,] interviews[,] routine matters. Am not making much headway on my personal work owing to having a lot of detailed work in connection with raising money for the s.i." (November 13, 1925). This is the lament of a scientist prevented from pursuing his own interests. "Called on Secty. Herbert Hoover with Mr. Delano & Rep. Walton Moore *en re* s.i. endowment. Learned that he was at the head of a drive for funds for the Nat. Acad. Sci. & Nat. Res. Council" (November 14, 1925). That was a most unfortunate circumstance for Walcott, as Hoover might have been able to take some burden from his shoulders. On the other hand, the NAS endowment drive turned out to be something of a failure (Cochrane 1978); there is no certainty that Hoover could have done any better for the SI. In a different sense, this item shows how thoroughly Walcott had severed his connections with NAS management once he had retired from the Finance Committee.

Sunday evening the Merriams came to dinner, and Walcott discussed SI endowment hopes with the CIW president. The endowment drive was still in the hope stage. "Usual routine and matters connected with s.i. future" (November 16, 1925). "Called on Senator Smoot *en re* art building A.M. Talked with Messers Clark & Mitman & Dr. Cottrell *en re* s.i. endowment. A broken up day" (November 18, 1925). What is perhaps even more interesting is that while Walcott was pursuing outside money for the Smithsonian, he was actively seeking federal funds to build an art gallery. Never overlook an opportunity to raise money from private sources, but likewise make absolutely sure that Congress knows of the line between federal funding and private endowment and of the importance of the annual appropriation. After all, the National Gallery of Art was a federal agency, just like the National Museum and the National Zoological Park.

Two more days were "fully occupied with routine & s.i. endowment matters" (November 20, 1925), and the week was over. "Mary & I walked to s.i. in morning. Wrote letters & looked over photographs until 4 P.M.—A nap, dinner & at 10 P.M. pulled flannel blankets over me out on the porch & went off to slumberland" (November 23, 1925). (The notion of sleeping in such an unheated space in November likely would strike the present younger generation as erratic behavior.) Walcott was content, and with just a little more time for research he would have been delighted.

Rested up, Walcott attended a meeting of the SI Executive Committee and the New York fund-raisers. Walcott also had Gilbert Grosvenor of the National Geographic Society, Dr. Merriam, Dr. Wetmore, and Mr. Ravenel present to help set up a local executive committee for the endowment drive; it was a good gathering. "Arrangements for the s.i endowment are coming along very well" (November 23, 1925). Unfortunately, things got immediately out of hand, for the newspapers announced a drive for ten million dollars, not one million; the smaller goal was realistic and might have been reached. Meanwhile, Walcott had a full but quiet day at the office, apparently without endowment concerns. The Vaux family came in for the traditional Thanksgiving dinner.

468 Charles Doolittle Walcott

On Friday Walcott was back at the office. "The s.i. drive is now marking time, owing to the absence of men we wish to lead the work" (November 27, 1925). Mary entertained her relatives while Walcott stayed at the office. They went to church, but that afternoon Walcott was talking to Mr. Delano and Senator Smoot concerning the endowment. The workweek began. "Endowment matters & routine took up the time. Busy with papers at home in evening" (November 30, 1925). Walcott had year after year become involved in projects that cut into his research, but with the endowment drive he had created a Frankenstein monster that seemed intent on destroying both him and his research.

An inquiry from a professor of biology in Ohio made Walcott recall the past. "I do not think it would be practicable for you to have the Burgess shale shipped to you with the hope that you would find something in it worthwhile. I have sometimes split up to a thousand pounds or more of the shale and have not found a good specimen. At other times a single split of a piece eighteen inches square might afford half a dozen or more specimens of crustaceans, annelids, etc. The best specimens, however, have been found separate."[14]

November oozed into December. "Busy with routine & s.i. endowment matters" (December 1, 1925). It was all in all a routine week; even a formal dinner for Justice and Mrs. Sanford was more or less routine. On Saturday, Cousin Mary Williams came in from Baltimore for a couple of days. There was no church attendance that Sunday. "Messrs Cottrell & Wetmore came to the house 10 A.M. & we talked over research problems until 1 o'clock" (December 6, 1925). Apart from wartime, Walcott had rarely conducted business on Sunday; the problems of the declining si budget and facilities must have weighed heavily on him.

Monday was devoted to routine. On Tuesday, the National Gallery of Art Commission met in the morning; "Routine & Endowment matters P.M." (December 8, 1925). Wednesday, Walcott, Senator Smoot, and Mr. Delano called on Vice President Dawes, the reason not given but perhaps to remind Dawes to attend the regents' meeting. (Chancellor Taft had decided to step down from this position, and traditionally either the chief justice or the vice president served as chancellor. Fortunately, Mr. Taft later changed his mind.) There was also another vacancy to fill on the board. After thirty years of service as a regent, Judge Gray had died in August.

The annual meeting of the regents the following morning went well, and that night Walcott relaxed at a White House diplomatic reception. Mr. Root was unavailable, so the next day Walcott presided at the CIW board meeting and that night helped the Merriams in the receiving line of the reception. Mary left on the midnight train. "Cleaning up accumulation of past 4 days. Eight years ago today Stuart gave his life in the protection of France & human dignity" (December 13, 1925); the past had intruded.

What thoughts Walcott might have had of the past were quickly replaced by prospects for the future. "Met Mary at station 6:20 P.M. She brought my copy of Vol. 1 North American Wild Flowers. It is fine & we are very happy as it has cost much time energy & money to bring it out" (December 13, 1925). One does not have to be a flower lover to appreciate this book (M. V. Walcott 1925). The comments about time and energy were true enough, and *Wild Flowers* would cost considerably more money before the final volume was published. "This work, which is being published by the Smithsonian Institution, is to consist of five volumes, each volume containing eighty plates in color with a page of descriptive text for each."[15]

"Usual routine & s.i. 'Drive' matters all day. Called to see President Coolidge *en re* Chairman of s.i. drive" (December 14, 1925). If there is one conspicuous absence from Walcott's diary, it is comments about his manuscript; the endowment drive was absorbing all his time. The next evening they entertained the Italian ambassador at a small dinner. "Mary & I left for Philad. 9 A.M.. I met Dr R. A. L. Penrose 12:30 & we had luncheon together & talked over candidates for Hayden medal etc. Meeting of committee on site & sesquicentennial of Amer. Phil. Soc. 3 P.M. and 4 P.M. Talked with Dr Cyrus Adler *en re* s.i. 'drive' P.M. Went out to Bryn Mawr 6 P.M. to G. V. Jr. Mary came out later" (December 16, 1925). To introduce a new person, Penrose was a mining geologist. From the standpoint of money, he was perhaps the most successful mining geologist in the country. When he died, he left half his fortune to the Geological Society of America and half to the American Philosophical Society. What if Walcott had been able to persuade him of the merits of the Smithsonian? To reintroduce a name, Dr. Adler had been assistant secretary under Langley and for a few years under Walcott. This scholarly man left Washington to head Dropsie College in Philadelphia, a place that lived on donations.

Walcott met a couple of Philadelphians to tell them of the research conducted by the si, dropped in again at the American Philosophical Society, and moved on. "Went to Mrs. Pell's [at] 22 w 53d New York City. She met me most cordially & we visited & talked over her gift to the s.i. etc." (December 17, 1925). Ever since Walcott obtained the Frederick Church painting *Aurora*, whenever the opportunity appeared he had assiduously gleaned art for the nation.

"Conference with Dwight B. Morrow 12–1" (December 18, 1925). Here was the essence of this trip. Mr. Morrow was prominent on Wall Street. That September, President Coolidge had taken the initiative on aviation matters away from a congressional investigation, by appointing the "Morrow Board," which conducted hearings and issued a report in short order. Walcott had his eye on Morrow as the ideal man to raise money and must have approached Coolidge to lay groundwork for him. Both before and after the conference with Morrow,

Walcott met with his old friend Elan Hooker. The next day, Hooker took him to lunch at the Republican Club; if there was endowment money to be found anywhere, it was here.

The Walcotts left for home satisfied by the trip. "We woke up feeling tired & as the day was unpleasant remained at home to look over a large amount of mail & to rest" (December 20, 1925). Once the children were grown, Walcott did not feel quite so compelled to attend church every Sunday, rain or shine. "Attending to routine & correspondence at the Smithsonian all day. Occupied with Christmas gifts in evening" (December 21, 1925). The end of a long, long year was finally approaching. Christmas day was spent writing letters to the scattered family members, cleaning odds and ends, napping, and inviting the Merriam family for a family dinner. As a diversion the following day, the Walcotts motored to Baltimore for the morning; "Endeavored to review mss. but was heavy headed & took a nap. Took up names for Nat. Committee of S.I. drive in evening & read for an hour" (December 26, 1925). A national committee was working wonders for art at the SI, and perhaps a comparable committee would dramatically increase the endowment.

Sunday was too cold to attend church; besides, Walcott had tired nerves and muscles. On Monday morning, tired or not, he was at the office until noon. Work on mail and manuscript continued at home, stopping only for a dinner at Mrs. Dimock's, a small affair with only thirty-one of her friends present.

Morrow had finally agreed to serve as a regent, and a joint resolution appointing him was making its way through Congress. "I wish very much to discuss some important matters with you, so if it is not practicable for you to come here and look over matters on the ground, I will run over to New York to talk with you when it is convenient for you to see me."[16] Walcott so badly wanted Morrow to head his endowment drive that he was prepared to do almost anything to snare him.

To give a notion of the complications of running the SI, consider the regents. These begin with the chief justice and the vice president. Well and good, though each is busy with other duties. They are followed by three senators, appointed by the president of the Senate, and three representatives appointed by the Speaker of the House. Because of elections, those regents may be displaced overnight; a one-term vice president is ineligible to continue as a statutory regent once he has left office. Finally, six private citizens are appointed for terms of six years. Two are to reside in Washington and four in various states, but no two may come from the same state.

Morrow was appointed by a joint resolution of Congress as a regent from New York. Unfortunately, he lived in New Jersey. Walcott wrote the appropriate letter to obtain the unanimous consent of Senate and House that was required to change the joint resolution. Then it could be signed by the vice president and sent on to the president for his signature. Finding new regents was a perpetual process. Getting a quorum of members to meetings was nearly as complex as getting a board. Morrow was away and did not attend the January meeting of the regents.

Never mind, with Mr. Morrow in the bag, other steps could be taken. "Consultation with Wetmore & Ellingston *en re* s.i. 'drive'" (December 29, 1925). Walcott expected this endowment campaign to be organized soon, but it moved at a slow pace. The penultimate day of the year was occupied with a photographer who had dramatic photographs of the great falls in Labrador, and with Mrs. Pell, down from New York. Walcott found time for a letter to L. L. Nunn's brother, showing some of his sentimentality for old friends and giving a hint of the future; unfortunately, in 1926 he would not take his own advice.

I have been just looking through the pamphlet "Telluride Association and Deep Springs Work." It is most interesting, and indicates that some of the boys have been taught to think and to express their thoughts in well chosen language. The tribute to the spirit of L. L. Nunn on page 36 is a beautiful one and all through there is a fine idealism.

I am glad to have the picture of Deep Springs. It does not look much like it did when I camped under the cottonwood trees about 1895. I think that Mrs. Walcott and I will have to pack up our mountain outfit and camp there again during the spring or summer of 1926. It will be a great change for us, as we have been working for the past ten summers in the Canadian Rockies, where rain, snow and high winds do all that is possible to prevent field work, but they toughen one's physical organization and supply energy to sustain one during the enervating life of a Washington winter. We are fond of the high mountains, snow and ice, but now I think a season or two in the warmth and dry air of the sagebrush country will not only give us vigor and health but also many things of interest and beauty.[17]

The long, long year ended with routine correspondence. The Walcotts dined out, Mary being escorted to the table by the distinguished senator from Kentucky. "This has been a year of ups & downs for us. Helen was happily married Mch. 31*st* to Cole J. Younger. Mary & I had a tiresome field season in Alberta Canada owing to inclement weather from Aug. 20th on to Sept 22d when we left Banff for home. Movement for increase of Smithsonian endowment began by Dr. Abbot in September by signing contract with Tambyn & Brown of New York. Very little done up to Dec. 31 'owing to lack of organization'" (December 31, 1925). How very curious that it was still "Dr. Abbott"—a man he had known since 1896 and had worked with on a daily basis for more than a decade. Formality toward others was a constant in Walcott's diary.

Another constant was a daily comment on the weather; 1926 began with what Walcott labeled a "fine day." New Year's Day was a quiet time, with only a few calls—Secretary Mellon, the Tafts, and Secretary and Mrs. Davis. Today, federal offices are closed on Saturday, but January 2 found Walcott and his employees at their desks; how hard they each worked, apart from Walcott, probably depended on how active had been his New Year's celebration.

Sunday was for church services and a visit to the Whitman Crosses; apart from Walcott, Dr. Cross was virtually the only old-timer from the USGS left. Dr. Dall, two years older than Walcott, and also USGS, was in the process of retiring from the Museum. The old guard was going rapidly. The workweek began. "Dictating letters *en re* Wild Flower Book A.M. Mail & routine P.M. Looked over papers *en re* S.I. endowment plan in evening" (January 4, 1926).

Walcot was tired and all was not well. "Review mss. at home in morning. Matters move slowly with me as I have no force to drive ahead" (January 5, 1926). This must have been a difficult admission for him. What Walcott wrote to Regent White was that he had "a wee cold." As another concern, the SI continued to be plagued by the Freer will. By now, the regents had virtually given up trying to recover any of the state inheritance tax paid to Michigan; that futile effort had taken an enormous amount of time. Current events at the Freer were equally time consuming. As Walcott writes, "I had a long talk with John Lodge. We looked over the Thayer-Dewing and other American paintings of exhibition and in storage and I think he is right in keeping the inferior ones in storage. I wish Mr. Freer had not provided in his will that no objects were to be taken out of the Freer building. . . . Mr. Freer did a wonderful work and made a magnificent gift, and had he retained his health from 1900 to 1925 he would have grown in knowledge, experience, and vision to an extent that would have led him to trust the people of the future and not attempt to make them conform to his point of view indefinitely. Ill health had much to do with certain peculiarities developed in the latter part of his life."[18]

Ah well, there was nothing to be done. Walcott ended his letter by wishing that Mr. Freer was still around to consult, but that was not possible. The Freer is a classic case of the myriad of problems that may arise when a major gift has too many strings attached to it.

The secretary got to his office for a conference on the endowment drive, and he caught up on the mail and routine. "A grippy headache in evening made me brace up but it was no good so I turned into my blankets for a long nights sleep" (January 6, 1926). Seemingly in all but the worst weather, Walcott was on the sleeping porch, as close to tent living as he could get in the city. The ill feeling persisted, and Walcott stayed home. "Many telephone calls kept me in touch with matters at the s.i." (January 8, 1926). Walcott never seemed to have any difficulty keeping up with technology, despite his nineteenth-century roots. The secretary improved enough to attend a dinner given by Secretary of State and Mrs. Kellogg.

Walcott skipped church for a motor ride to see friends and then got into serious business, especially for a Sunday. "Dr Wetmore called to speak of Na[tional] Committee of S.I. endowment drive. At home in evening. Wrote Dwight W. Morrow *en re* his election as a Regent of s.i." (January 10, 1926). Walcott had his eye on Mr. Morrow. This was to be a week devoted to serious matters. Regent Delano and Secretary Walcott called on Vice President Dawes, perhaps to remind him that in his position as a regent he was needed to help with the endowment drive. Mr. William T. De Van called to talk about the Smithsonian Scientific Series, which was slowly beginning to make its way through authors, editors, and press. The executive committee met with Assistant Secretary Wetmore and Chief Clerk Dorsey in attendance, an unusual occurrence, but trying to raise money was an unusual event. A representative of the New York fund raisers called the following day, and the Walcotts gave a small dinner for Secretary of War and Mrs. Davis. Quite apart from the social obligations of Washington official society, the Walcotts seemed to be on friendly terms with most members of the cabinet and occasionally had small informal dinners for the secretaries.

The week ended. "I have not been able to do much of my own work since my returning from the west owing to s.i. duties & various insistent demands on my time" (January 16, 1925). Once more, Walcott gave the lament of a scientist kept from his science. Another week began. "Mary rather tired owing to her persistent work on her book. The sale of the Edition de Luxe is slow but continuous. It should be all out by June" (January 17, 1926). The five-hundred-dollar payments for the deluxe edition provided a significant part of the financing. The worry of funding the wildflower publication was separate from the worry about trying to increase the si endowment, which is analogous to whipped cream on top of the ice cream; this may be a poor analogy, for worry about lack of money is not at all enjoyable.

Mary left that evening to pursue potential out-of-town patrons for her book, leaving Walcott to rattle around in the house that night. "A day full of detailed administrative matters at the Smithsonian" (January 19, 1926). He wrote a regent: "Mrs. Walcott is in Boston today in connection with the question of the publication of a library edition of the Wild Flower book. She will be in New York for two days in connection with that matter and the securing of a few more subscriptions for the work. We are getting many fine letters of commendation from the subscribers, some of which are most enthusiastic. It is a big undertaking for her, and I sincerely hope that she will preserve her usual good health until the last volume is delivered to the subscribers."[19]

On Thursday evening Walcott met Mary in New York, and Friday he conferred again with Mr. Morrow. He also saw Sidney's new office, and the Walcotts dined at the apartment of the Youngers. Walcott summed up the trip: "Mary has done much for her book this week. The s.i. drive is lingering" (January 23, 1926). Mary went off to the Friends' meeting, and Walcott wrote letters. Office routine took another day, but finally Walcott had a chance to spend a few hours on research. Walcott then talked to the staff for an hour and a half about the drive for funds. It was a worthwhile investment of time. "A small committee of our younger men was formed to consider interesting prospective subscribers to [the] research endowment" (January 19, 1926). During Walcott's time there seemed to be ready and easy communication between staff and secretary.

There was another conference with the fund raisers. "Dr Wetmore lunched with me at home & we talked over conference with T[ambyn] & B[rown]. Mary is tired as she is working on the Wild Flower Book, running our house & and keeping some social activities" (January 30, 1926). The marriage was a happy partnership, and they were a well matched pair. Sunday was a rainy day. "Slept late—Resting & fussing about the house. Dr Stearns called to see me at noon. Said that I used up energy faster than my machinery generated it" (January 31, 1926). Notwithstanding the doctor's pronouncement, Mr. Delano and Dr. Wetmore called in the afternoon, no doubt to discuss the endowment drive. Walcott simply would not quit.

Walcott stayed home. On Monday, John Victory brought over papers from the NACA office. On Tuesday Dr. Wetmore was in attendance to discuss the appropriations hearing. Wednesday was occupied with more NACA business. Thursday it was mail from the office, and Friday Walcott finally admitted he was sick. "Still puttering around the house. Hope to be out next week & resume work at my office & laboratory" (February 6, 1926). Sick or well, Walcott's level of nervous energy would never permit him to be idle. Sunday was worse, and he was back in bed; pleurisy added to his misery,

The next week was marked by a foot of snow on Wednesday. Walcott was slowly rallying; he had been so sick that he did not attend a meeting of the SI Executive Committee. By Saturday, he was mending and was up to one meeting at home and a glance at his manuscript. Sunday Walcott wrote that he was "going slow," but he was finally going. "Called at dentist 8:25 A.M. Conference with Resser & & Ulrich 9–11 A.M. *en re* Alberta & B.C. geol[ogical] sections. At my office 11:10–12:45 & then went home" (February 15, 1926). "I find that I am not much good in the afternoons" (February 16, 1926). Nevertheless, Walcott was well enough so that Mary could leave him for a quick trip north. "Met Mary at 6:20 P.M. She reports Sidney & Helen & their families well & getting settled to the life in a great city" (February 18, 1926). Life was getting back to normal on Sundays. After church, Walcott and Mary gathered up papers at his Castle office. "Working at home all day on illustration for report on Can. Rockies work" (February 22, 1926). Walcott's conference with Resser and Ulrich and his bout of ill health may have convinced him to prepare a summary of his opus on the stratigraphy of the southern Canadian Rockies, just in case the more detailed work was never completed. If so, it was a realistic decision. Walcott noted that he was not much good after 3:00 P.M.; still, this was an improvement. While he was slowly regaining his strength, Mary was pushing ahead on the text for the second volume of her work. Mr. Delano called to say goodbye before leaving for Persia. Mr. Samuel Insull, who had been mentioned to head the endowment drive (and who was to become notorious in a few years, when the stock market crash and Great Depression rocked this match king), called in regard to a scheme for a national engineering museum, of which he was president. Walcott approached the end of the miserable month of February. "I am still feeling results of cold & am much below par" (February 28, 1926). Withal, he still took on a small chore: "Dr. Walcott has accepted membership on the Council of the Princeton University summer school of geology and natural resources."[20] It was a little nothing, but even little nothings take a little time.

The past came back again with a letter from Elliot Blackwelder, who had collected fossils in China for Walcott. Blackwelder sent some photographs of structures from Precambrian rocks that superficially resembled cabbage heads.

Your photographs suggest the forms that I have referred to [as] Collenia.... Of course we do not know the genera and species of algae that made the deposits, as we have found nothing of their microscopic structure preserved, and there is not much prospect of finding it in the material you have photographed....

I have completed my field work in the Canadian Rockies of Alberta, and British Columbia, in 1925. I have only made a reconnaissance of a portion of that vast field, but if it stimulates others to go on, it will have repaid me well for the time and energy expended. The work should now be taken up and followed through to the Arctic Ocean. There is a wonderful opportunity for a few well trained, enthusiastic, vigorous young geologists.[21]

Walcott had no illusions concerning the progress of the endowment drive and wrote the firm in New York in a bleak vein:

It now looks as though the general campaign on the lines which you have suggested would drag along for some time to come, unless a strong leader turns up. From the experience we have had it now appears that it would have been wiser to have secured the chairman before any work was undertaken. . . .

The publicity work has been fine, and I think it should be vigorously continued; also, that where we know of individuals that may be brought to take an interest in the endowment or in special research funds, they should be approached by some of our best qualified workers. My past experience is that the personal approach is the most effective. . . .

I caught cold when in New York in January, and have been laid up more or less as a result for the past month. It may be that I shall be obliged to go South in order to get rid of it.[22]

Dreary, miserable February had come to an end. The shortest month crawls by so slowly that each day seems like three days of spring, but it was over. "At my office cleaning up odds & ends & mail. Getting things in order to go south tomorrow P.M. & evening" (March 1, 1926). They left on the 3:15 P.M. for Beaufort, South Carolina. This still gave Walcott plenty of time for a long conference with Dwight Morrow on the endowment campaign.

The next few weeks at Beaufort were better than Washington, but because of bad weather in the South, they were a long way from heaven. "We took a walk around town & unpacked our trunks. Enjoyed a nap. Visited with the people at Miss Emmy's & turned in at 9:30 P.M." (March 3, 1926). Walcott reported his activities to the SI chief clerk:

We came through to find that the cold snap had also come through on time & was waiting with a skin of ice at Charleston & 40° here with a strong wind. We have a fine large room in an old colonial house—outlook over the water—good "Franklin grate" stove & plenty of cannel coal—so our physical wants are provided for. Miss Emmy's house is 2 doors away & ex Secy Denby & family are next door in their own house.

The pkg of twine & tape came & Miss Munro's pkg but the 2 pkgs of stationary [sic] are not yet in evidence, but may turn up tomorrow. I am all fixed up to go to work but haven't the slightest impulse to do it as the sunshine & crisp air are too attractive. Mrs. Walcott is also *conservative* on getting under way, Tell Mr. Ravenel it is the S.C. influence & the D.C. bugs. Regards to all—Feel 50% better.[23]

Mr. Ravenel was of the South Carolina Ravenels. How the bugs in Washington enter into this is not clear, unless this means flu bugs. Humor does not always translate well.

"Pkgs came today badly crushed. Even wrapping paper inside was cut & torn. MSS from Resser also rec.'d & pkg of letters & all is well. Cool east wind today. . . . We have walked more today than any day since last September & our faces are red from sun & wind. Nothing like it."[24] Four days later came a scribbled note telling of more cold weather, and a need for paper clips. "Have been working on photos all morning for No. 4 vol. 75—Am lazy & sore footed from walking."[25] Work was the exception, not the rule. "My cold is wearing away slowly but I am no good mentally or physically at present" (March 12, 1926).

A storm broke, followed by a cold snap, and Mother Nature may have invigorated the old man a bit. High wind kept Walcott indoors most of the time. "A stupid kind of day. Read a little & fussed about our room & a short walk in afternoon. Wrote for an hour on description of photographs" (March 15, 1926). An hour was not a lot of time for Walcott, but at least he was thinking and working again on his beloved research. "A repetition of yesterday. We are thoraly [*sic*] tired of this cold, windy March weather & long for a few days of warmth & sunshine" (March 16, 1926). Mother Nature must have heard and approved, for she smiled on the weather. The Walcotts walked again, and he even wrote captions for illustrations. Mr. Dorsey was kept fully informed.

"At last a mild pleasant warm 'spell' has arrived. We saw crabs at the old crabbing hole yesterday & will go after them tomorrow morning if a blizzard does not show up. Except for the 'Drive' & W.F.B. [wildflower book] I would remain the rest of this week & try to leave the cold germs to flow out to sea, which by the way is 12 to 15 miles away."[26] This was followed by another scribbled note, changing the arrival date in Washington. "Letter mail had better be sent to house—as I shall stop to take a bath. Have had two since coming. Cold bathroom & little warm water. We caught ½ bushel of fine crabs today. Thermometer 65° with a light breeze off the water. This is what they usually have all through March. Sorry I cannot remain a week longer & get a few sea trout & a good tanning."[27] Mother Nature frowned Monday morning; "Cold N.E. gale—straight from the ocean via Greenland[,] Cape Cod & Hatteras."[28] Nevertheless, it was their last full day in Beaufort and not to be wasted. The Walcotts caught nearly two bushels of prime crabs.

They arrived home safely. "Nothing unusual was [*sic*] occurred while we were away" (March 24, 1926). Walcott worked on his mail but had time to prepare captions for more of his photographs; the delight at having time for research was enhanced by a visit from Helen. Two days later Helen and Mary were planting Mary's garden; it is amazing what a few years can do to change a relationship. Walcott kept steadily at office routine, and his manuscript illustrations for the weakness of the winter seemed to have vanished. "This is the last day of my 75*th* year. Helen's marriage the most important event. As a whole the year has been a trying one to me on account of bad weather" (March 31, 1926).

His reply to a letter of congratulations casts a little light on the inner man: "I would derive the greatest happiness from being able to go on with my research work up to the point of placing on record the data which I have been gathering for the past fifteen years in the West. Many of my contemporaries have passed on, leaving a large amount of material undigested, and in such condition [it] could be of very little service to anyone interested in the subject which they are studying. Administrative duties have not been unpleasant or disappointing, but I regard them as a passing incident, and not serious work, although of course at times one is called upon to put his best efforts into the solution of the questions that arise."[29]

"My 76th birthday. Am fairly well but not as strong as in 1925. All the family in good form" (March 31, 1926). At seventy-six Walcott was a bit more realistic than at seventy-five, for his troubles were greater than just bad weather. Still, he was able to keep going. A few days later, Cole Younger came in for a few days, and he and Helen had a belated first-anniversary celebration. The Walcotts and the Youngers attended Easter Sunday services together, and he generally enjoyed the visit of his son-in-law. Money concerns for the SI, however, did not dissipate.

> Matters here are progressing slowly in connection with the attempt to increase our endowment. The publicity campaign is going on and will be continued until next September, when a determined effort will be made to build up the endowment. The Congressional appropriations for the maintenance of the Government activities are fairly satisfactory. We hoped that some action would be taken toward providing an additional building for the art and historical collections, but in this era of practical economy it does not seem wise in the judgement of our representatives in Congress to push the matter. It would relieve the present rather serious congestion in the Natural History building, and also make available to the public a large amount of material that is now inaccessible.[30]

There are some constants within the ever-increasing rate of change that marked the twentieth century. Probably since the sixteenth century, those who manage museums have complained about lack of space.

Walcott was recovered enough to be back in the social whirl. Secretary and Mrs. Walcott gave a small dinner for Vice President and Mrs. Dawes, taking advantage of the point that the Youngers were still in town to attend the gathering. Mary and Walcott dined with the Merriams and the next night with Justice and Mrs. Stone. It was to be the last evening Walcott and Mary were to be together for some time. Characteristically, Mary was in Philadelphia for a day or two at least once a month, but she was embarking on a major trip. "It is hard to have her leave me but it seems best for her work [on the] N.A.W.F." (April 8, 1926). Duty frequently called Walcott, but equally it called Mary. Walcott wrote to David Starr Jordan, the former president of Stanford, that he had hoped to come west with Mary but that it was impossible.

Her special mission is in connection with her work on "North American Wild Flowers," the first volume of which has recently appeared. It is not a systematic contribution to botanical literature, but it will give to both botanists and amateurs a clearer conception of the beauty and character of many of our North American wildflowers. It is a large undertaking, as the cost of the five projected volumes will be about $250,000. As we have no funds available, the work was put on a subscription basis, a De Luxe edition being issued to meet the cost of the experimental work, preparation of the plates, etc.

You were a wise man to free yourself from administrative duties. I hope to do so in due time and be free to do some of the things that I have been dreaming of for the past fifty years. It has been a pleasure to dream of them in the past, and every hour that I can get in my laboratory for work is a delight.[31]

Mary gone, Walcott puttered around the house, puttered around the office, attended at church trustees meeting, wrote Mary, and wrote to the assistant curator of the Freer, who was engaged in fieldwork in China.

You have probably learned of Dr. William H. Holmes['s] mishap. Blood poisoning in his foot necessitated the removal of the leg so he is now just beginning to go about with the aid of a cane and a crutch. It is wonderful that at his age (seventy-nine) he has recovered so as to be about. This incident brings up very forcibly the fact that he has no understudy, and that there is no one on hand here to take charge of the National Gallery of Art. It is unfortunate, as there is a great deal of favorable sentiment in the country toward the Gallery, which if taken advantage of, would be very effective, both in securing a new building and fine material for the gallery. I wish you were here so that I could talk the matter over with you. It needs a person who has enthusiasm, vision, and appreciation of his fellow man, and a willingness to meet the public and attempt to interact and educate it so that the Gallery will be given strong moral and financial support. A gallery situated as the Freer Gallery is can perhaps afford to carry on research work and leave the public out of account, but a national gallery must operate with the public in mind, as well as the scholar and research student.[32]

Walcott may have lost some of the vigor of his body, but his mind was clear. His prescription of what was needed for the National Gallery was clear; he wanted a clone. This letter must have been first step in sounding out a promising young man, just as he had settled on Alex Wetmore and in January had made him third in line, behind Dr. Abbot. Incidentally, in 1933 the one-legged Dr. Holmes was still coming to work. Walcott was right, however; the old guard was almost all played out.

Walcott received a telegram that his wife had arrived safely in New Orleans, but it was small comfort. "Miss Mary[,] as we have been together almost constantly since June 30, 1914" (April 12, 1926). Walcott worked part-days at home and part-days at the office. Fortunately, Helen came in for a quick visit, and that perked him up. "Called for Dwight Morrow at the Mayflower & we look over the N[atural] H[istory] Museum with Dr. Wetmore" (April 17, 1926). Perhaps now something would happen with the endowment drive.

"Went to my office early. At home for luncheon & afternoon. Puttering with mss P.M. & writing letters in evening" (April 20, 1926). Despite a number of letters from Mary, Walcott was a lonely man. Fortunately, a distraction came after another day of puttering: Walcott was off to Philadelphia. "Attended meeting of Council of Amer. Phil. Soc. at Mr. Lippencotts 8–12 P.M." (April 22, 1926).

"Presided at meeting of Phil. Soc. 10–1 A.M. Conference on building for P.S. with Alba Johnson & Dr Dencum P.M. Reception in evening & Dr Milliken [*sic*] gave an address. One of the best I have heard him deliver[,] 'Advances in Physics in the last 15 years'" (April 23, 1926). Walcott neglected to write in his diary that it was the duty of the president to give an annual address. He had chosen to speak on the pioneering work of Langley in aviation. Published, it was only four pages (Walcott 1926) and mainly cut and paste, but it included the text of the modified label on the Langley machine. With that change, Walcott had moved his position a bit, but he was not about to give Orville Wright another inch. "Attending meetings of Phil. Soc. 9:30 A.M.–4:30 P.M. Presided P.M. when Henry F. Osborn presented portrait of Dr Scott (*Wm* B). The dinner in evening was a very pleasant affair" (April 24, 1926). Still the obsession with time and still the attention to detail; there were not so many Scott names in his circle of colleagues that Walcott would not have known that this was the vertebrate paleontologist from Princeton.

It was now NAS annual meeting time, his final attendance at that gathering, though he was to continue to be involved. Walcott carried on as a member of the building committee and as a member of the committee on forestry research. The concerns of the latter group had been publicly expressed last year (Jones 1925). Fortunately all was going well; at the autumn meeting in 1925, the committee chairman announced that the General Education Board had awarded fifty thousand dollars for a worldwide survey of research in that field. Walcott had been on the committee for the Elliott Fund since 1922 and was reappointed at this meeting.

Naturally, Walcott still carried on as chairman of the NRC division of government relations and chairman of its executive committee. "The division of Federal relations is maintained as an organization ready to function at any time in connection with scientific matters regarding which the council may be in position to aid the Government by cooperative, coordinated effort. The members of this division are designated by the President of the United States, and represent eight Government departments and about 40 Government bureaus" (Smith, 1929, 52). Just seeing that appointments were made to the committee was a major undertaking.

Walcott sandwiched in a few minutes at the si on mail but mostly attended the "large, fine meeting" of the Academy for three days. He attended the annual banquet with the Millikans, and the next night he had them and a few other close friends to dinner; at the moment, Walcott was a bit too busy to miss Mary. The Millikans left town, and Walcott began to feel "dumpy" once more. "Went to my office in morning. Left for home at noon On account of cold all over me. Developed a case of grippe & Dr John Stevens ordered me to bed. Too bad as I have [been] so well during April" (April 30, 1926).

The missing "been" in his diary entry might have been the result of fever. About all he could do the following day was jot a note to Mary, now in St. Louis. Sunday was worse and Monday almost as bad. "Mary will be home tomorrow. Am sorry to be ill as we need all possible energy to get through with the various matters at the s.i. & at home" (May 3, 1926). Duty called loud and long, but Walcott was too weak to respond.

At about the time Walcott left for the American Philosophical Society meeting, Rep. Frank Reid wrote, bringing back yet another memory of the past. "During the World War you rendered valuable and distinguished services to our country in connection with the work of the Council of National Defense. The country is just beginning to realize the importance of that work and how greatly it contributed to the success of the war. I would deem it a personal favor if you would prepare, either now or at an early date, a statement that I could release for use and publication at an appropriate time, giving your views of the importance of having prepared an adequate and comprehensive plan of national defense. Any advice or suggestions that occur to you from your war experience would be most helpful."[33] That would be a tall order for anyone, let alone a failing man who already had far too many horses to ride.

Mary arrived, which soothed his soul but did little for his body. "Neuralgia severe in pleural & body muscles. Unable to sit up with any degree of comfort" (May 7, 1926). The illness went on and on, and it was not until mid-May that Walcott was able to concentrate for a short time on his manuscript; a few more days were required for him to gain some strength. "Spent the morning at my office in the Smithsonian. Working at home in afternoon. Am glad to be able to be about & at work" (May 17, 1926). Ditto marks recorded for the rest of the week. In mid-April Robert Sterling Yard had asked Walcott to write an article. Walcott scribbled on the letter, "Tel.[ephone] him. No time at present."[34] When the National Park Association committee met in mid-May at the si, Walcott was not present.

The long illness convinced Walcott that when duty called on some matters, he should finally turn a deaf ear. He dropped a note to Robert Brookings: "I am cutting out all activities that require time, attention or thought, as I have more to attend to in connection with the Smithsonian and the completion of some research work than there are time and energy for. This will explain to you my resignation as a member of the Board of Trustees for your Graduate School of Economics and Government and Institute for Government Research."[35]

"Attending to routine & various matters connected with illustrations for my paper. At home reviewing mss P.M." (May 24, 1926). Walcott was determined that his major opus on stratigraphy of western Canada be completed. Though he took time for a meeting of the Executive Committee, to attend to a formal visit of the crown prince and princess of Sweden to the Museum, and to visit the cemetery with flowers on Decoration Day, the manuscript came first. Half of the Decoration Day holiday was spent on the illustrations.

Mary left for a quick trip to check on the progress of *North American Wild Flowers*, but otherwise Walcott's schedule was the same—that is, some time for the SI, but more, finally, for his manuscript. "Going over lists of fossil in my mss with Dr Resser A.M. Working over mss at home afternoon & evening" (June 10, 1926). Resser was helpful, but the chances are good that if Mr. Burling had been still around, the project would have gone faster. Checking identifications and localities is more than routine, and later in life Resser had a reputation for proceeding at a less than rapid pace.

Meanwhile, the Walcotts called on friends, had a couple or two in for dinner, and kept up a more private social life, as distinguished from the more formal social duties of official Washington. The Merriams were frequent visitors, but George Otis Smith, still USGS director, and John E. Lodge, still curator of the Freer, were among those who dined *en famille*. Mary left again, though by now long-distance telephone calls were so common that Walcott and his wife stayed in contact; the mention of each telephone call in his diary is an indication of the reassurance this contact brought him.

More time went into the manuscript. Not once during May or June did Walcott attend church. On a Sunday Walcott commented, "I have been working too long hours during the week & feel tired so rested read a little & slept a little" (June 20, 1926). The old machine decidedly was running down. Summer began: "Attended to correspondence & administrative matters at the S.I. in morning. Looking over items connected with illustrations for my paper at home in afternoon" (June 21, 1926). Slow or not, the Walcott machine was still going.

Walcott conferred with Resser and Charles Butts, a USGS colleague, about some of the diagrams and cross-sections in his geologic manuscript. He and Mary attended a reception for Cdr. Richard E. Byrd, who received a medal from the National Geographic Society. The endowment drive and more conferences and headaches came to the top of the heap. In the midst of this, Walcott found time for another letter to Associate Curator Bishop, still in China. It tells a little about personalities. After commenting that Mr. Lodge had taken a four-month leave of absence to return to the Boston Museum of Fine Arts and that Dr. Holmes was at work but anxious to retire, Walcott got to the heart of matters: "A suggestion was made the past winter that Mr. Lodge be appointed in charge of the National Gallery, in addition to the Freer Gallery, he employing a suitable person as an assistant. This has not been seriously considered, as it was thought that his research work and the Freer Gallery would keep him fully occupied. There is another side to it, which involved human contacts, or the meeting of the public—art amateurs, professorial artists, etc, and the presentation of the needs of the Gallery to the congressional committees; it is felt that in part at least, these duties would be more or less objectionable to him."[36]

It does not take much reading between the lines to interpret this proposed step up for Mr. Lodge as a suggestion put out by a regent or one of Freer's designated few. Walcott had no intention of following it. The word "snob" may be pejorative, but at the very minimum Lodge was far too patrician to dirty his hands with running the National Gallery of Art. Secretary Walcott had a wildly disparate team to manage.

The pace in Washington slowed for the summer. The work on illustrations for his manuscript still moved forward, mail came and went, and *North American Wild Flowers* progressed, but it was like walking with mud clinging to one's shoes—and this even though for a Washington summer the temperature so far had been cool. It was time for a little break away from the city, in a cooler climate.

The end of June, Alphonso Jones drove the Walcotts north in the Pierce Arrow. While Walcott was en route, Dorsey sent a letter, on which Walcott made notes that indicate some of his work methods. "The sheep group have been installed & make a very attractive addition to the s.i. habitat. It has occurred to me that the interest of the public would be materially increased if we could show in each side of the case some photographs of the region when these specimens were collected. The space on each side is 45 inches wide & 12 ft high. If such photos are in existence I could use 3 or 4 on each side."[37] Near the top Walcott wrote and initialed "*Desk.* Good idea. Will look it up on my return." On the margin is an initialed "Attended to" and a date stamp of July 17, 1926.

On Independence Day, Secretary Walcott reported to Chief Clerk Dorsey; Mary acted as amanuensis, so the letter is easy to read.

We had a pleasant drive to Philadelphia and passed the night at Bryn Mawr. The drive up the Hudson Boulevard & from Englewood to Alpine on the slope of the Palisades was delightful as the forest is uninjured [that is, uncut]

& the glimpses of the Hudson suggest a quiet lake. Crossing the Ferry-Alpine to Yonkers we found new concrete roads all the way to Westport except on one hill near Greenwich. We arrived at Ferry Lane 5:30 on the second day from Wash'n without hurrying or reaching speed limits.

Mail comes up from New York 4 times a day and it is only 4 minutes drive to the P.O. The Younger summer home is very comfortable & surrounded by trees & grass covered primitive lawns. Mr. Younger has been working in the garden this morning rooting out wire grass from about the sweet corn.

I have been looking over the N.Y. papers in hopes of finding a report of the conferees on the Army Aircraft bill but without success. Will you not send me a copy of the bill—also name of Asst. Sect.'y of Commerce for aeronautics.

We now plan to go from here Saturday to Bridgeport—cross by ferry to Long Island and & spend Sunday with Sidney at Quoque.

Will you not telephone to the house & ask how the work has progressed[?] If necessary you can reach me here by telegraph or telephone Westport 885.

Tomorrow we celebrate the Fourth of July at the Roger Williams place. Alphonso goes home to New Haven for the day. He has been most helpful here & we expect to catch a few bass & flounders after tomorrow. Remember us to all at the office.[38]

If comments are in order, they have to do with transportation and communication. No doubt that the roads had improved dramatically since Walcott had his first adventure with an automobile. No doubt that with four mails a day, combined with one-day service between Washington and Connecticut, information was transmitted more than half a century ago almost as fast as in the computer age. One thing that has not changed is the importance of luck when fishing: Alphonso and Walcott caught nothing. Another letter was forthcoming.

Hot here yesterday. Cool this morning. Mrs. Walcott has gone to Mt. Vernon *en re* N.A.W.F. & I am clearing up mail. We plan to go to Quoque on Long Island, New York, Saturday so send mail there care of Sidney S. Walcott up to Saturday noon. Please telephone this to Delia. We will probably start back Monday but may stop a day or two on the road.

Will you not send me here the *Press* copy of vol. 1 [of] N.A.W.F.[?] It may be in my room or up stairs in Mrs. Walcott[']s room. We visited a beautiful old garden at Saugatuck yesterday & will go to another this afternoon if Mrs. Walcott returns in time. The enclosed is interesting as it is what Wyer strenuously advocated.

The gnats are busy, so good morning.

There is a postscript. "Mrs. Walcott thinks that the book is on the bookcase in the Regents room."[39]

The faithful Harry Dorsey reported that work on the new Frigidaire refrigerator for the house was progressing, that the book had been sent, and that Delia had been notified. He also volunteered that the temperature in Washington was 107 degrees—the good old summertime. The ferry ride across Long Island Sound was uneventful, and the older folks spent Saturday night with the younger Walcotts at their summer place. Sunday, they slept late and then picnicked at Montauk Point. On Monday evening the Walcotts were in Philadelphia, and the next morning they saw the sesquicentennial exhibit, which was not like the great expositions that had been held before the war. Even with that delay, Alphonso had them home by late that afternoon.

Naturally, mail was waiting at the office, but no huge pile had accumulated. In those days every answer to a public inquiry was signed by the secretary. The number and diversity of questions asked by the public was, and remains, astounding. The public must be served, but once that was done, Walcott could get back to his own business. "Went over mss of sections with Dr. Resser 9–11:30 P.M. to correct list of fossils. Attended to mail & went home for luncheon. Occupied with mss 3–5:30 P.M." (July 15, 1926). As stated before, the identity of the fossils present in a formation gives the age of the rock. One problem was that Walcott was working in rocks younger than Cambrian, and increasingly he had to depend on the opinion of others for precise identifications and interpretation of the age.

"Called on dentist 8:30 A.M. Consultation with Dr E. O. Ulrich & C. E. Resser 9–11 en re my report on Canadian Rockies" (July 13, 1926). Dr. Ulrich was what is called a "splitter," for he could see differences among fossils that others could not; in fact, he could see differences where later work has shown that none exist. As a result he was able to make what he thought were precise correlations to a few places, whereas actually the slight differences among fossils led him to establish a more complex set of relationships among rocks than really existed. Ulrich had supreme confidence in his ability, and Walcott accepted his opinions a little too uncritically.

Perhaps it was the climate that made Walcott's head swim, and made Ulrich's pronouncements on age seem reasonable. Washington was muggy; the temperature was 102 degrees outside of Walcott's office. "The humidity is worse than the heat of Thursday. We worked as state of mind & opportunity permitted" (July 24, 1926). Sunday was too hot to sit in church; letters to Sidney and Helen were all that Walcott could manage. "At home A.M. Checking up geologic sections at Smithsonian 1:30–5 P.M. Went to Mary['s] garden on East Potomac Branch [Now Anacostia River] flats at Bennings road & spent an hour. The garden is a great source of health and good vegetables" (July 26, 1926).

"Work on mss is slow owing to difficulty of getting data for correcting fossil lists" (July 27, 1926). There will be more on this subject, and it is sufficient here to note that Walcott was compiling a short paper to summarize the deposition of the rocks in the southern Canadian Rockies. His remarks about sections and diagrams refer to that summary effort. "The warm muggy weather prevents exercising except to trim bushes etc about the yard" (July 30, 1926).

"Mr. *Wm* E. Rudge came 5 P.M. *en re* Wild Flower book. We talked it over in the evening. The Library edition is beginning to sell. We agreed to advance $10,000 to help out publication" (July 31, 1926). Mary scoured the philanthropic field hoping for a large donation so that copies could be distributed free to schools. Walcott had met John D. Rockefeller in 1900 and over the years had sent him Christmas cards, Smithsonian calendars, and an occasional letter. Mary tried her luck, and there ensued a few letters, plus discussion among Rockefeller's advisors. This was unsuccessful, and neither she nor Walcott was able to obtain financial assistance from any other source either, apart from the subscriptions to the deluxe edition, which dribbled in. Without the personal funds that the Walcotts poured into Rudge's plant, several volumes of *North American Wild Flowers* would never have come out.

How much of Walcott's own money went into the annual treks to Canada is not clear, but the SI did not cover all the expenses. The money situation was grim. From 1923 onward, Walcott had applied to the National Academy of Science for money from the Marsh Fund and the Henry Fund. Over the years, he had received grants totaling about five thousand dollars; this had been used to finance the fieldwork of Resser, visiting areas in the United States where Walcott wanted more information on stratigraphy and more detailed collections. A few dollars went into preparation of the fossils Walcott collected in Canada. If anyone knew of the need for an increase in the endowment, it was Walcott.

August began with the temperature reaching ninety-four degrees, though with Washington humidity, it is hard to tell ninety from a hundred. "At my office A.M. & home P.M. writing Cordilleran Geosyncline for Can. Rockies paper" (August 4, 1926). A thundershower eased the heat, but only for a few hours. "Weather too depressing to do effective work" (August 4, 1926). The Executive Committee consisting of Mr. Delano (a shrewd investment banker) and Representative Moore met with Walcott; he brought along Drs. Abbot and Wetmore. "This has been a tedious trying week" (August 7, 1926). Another thunderstorm developed, making Sunday a few degrees better.

"Wrote John Lodge *en re* Freer gallery & his spending the summer up in Boston. Picking up & packing up at home P.M. Geo. Otis Smith called in evening" (August 9, 1926). Here are two disparate items juxtaposed. To Walcott's way of thinking, Lodge was neglecting his duties as curator of the Freer Gallery, in that almost every year he was spending months in Boston. Whether the Freer actually suffered by his absence depends on one's viewpoint, but the slow pace first established in the setting up of public exhibits had continued.

Dr. Smith was a different matter, if only as he was the conduit whereby Walcott kept his finger on the development of natural-resources policy. As the scandals of the Harding administration began to unfold, use and misuse of federal land once more became an important issue in Congress. Whether Smith asked Walcott for advice as to what the USGS should do is not obvious, but it is hard to imagine that he did not. There were also some practical advantages for Walcott in maintaining close ties. The map in SMC volume seventy-five, number four, has four colors on a black-and-white base. No paper trail exists, but this figure is so like comparable maps printed by the USGS that it is a sure bet Smith had it printed for Walcott. Back in the days when Powell was director, the USGS had received special permission from the Government Printing Office to produce maps, and no other government agency had color presses. One certainty is that the SI did not have the money to pay for this map.

"Humidity high. Dog days" (August 10, 1926). It had been decades since Walcott had had to endure a Washington summer, and he may have forgotten that it was even hard on the poor dogs; whoever wrote "In the Good Old Summertime" never lived in Washington. Some relief was in sight, for the next day he closed up as many pending matters as possible at the Castle, and he and Mary were on the 1:05 train going north. "We are glad to get away from home as both of us are fagged" (August 11, 1926).

Before Walcott could leave Washington for a rest, the matter of Mr. Lodge had to be resolved. For six years he had spent four or more months in Boston at the Museum of Fine Arts while on salary from the Freer. Earlier that year, Walcott insisted that if this arrangement were to continue it was to be as leave without pay from the Freer. Mr. Lodge protested; he was receiving ten thousand dollars a year from the Freer and a salary from the Boston Museum at the rate of fifteen thousand dollars annually, yet he pleaded poverty; he likened his annual Boston venture to fieldwork. This approach, combined with the earlier delay in opening the Gallery and a generally elitist attitude toward the public, grated on Walcott. Nonetheless, Mr. Lodge won a round.

I submitted the question of your relations to the Freer Gallery and the Museum of Fine Arts in Boston to the Executive Committee at the meeting on August 5. The Committee considered the matter very thoroughly in its broader relations, and in view of all the circumstances, it authorized me to agree with your request for leave with pay for four months of the coming year, but in doing this, the Committee did not wish it understood that it was establishing a precedent, or that it would be followed in the future.

In arriving at this decision, the Committee had in view the question of the reorganization of the National Gallery of Art, which will probably occur the coming winter, also the relations of the Freer Gallery as a unit of the National Gallery.[40]

That Lodge won this battle did not mean that he had won the war. If the Freer became part of the National Gallery of Art, the Freer endowment would remain to support its work, but the curators would then be federal employees, to be paid at the rate of other comparable federal employees and subject to Civil Service regulations. If this arrangement were to be approved by the full Board of Regents, Lodge would earn about half his present annual salary and no longer be able to go on leave with pay for months on end and receive a second salary while he was away. It was a virtually foolproof plan for encouraging Lodge to submit a resignation. After that meeting of the Executive Committee, Walcott deserved a vacation.

Conventional wisdom was that to escape Washington heat, one did best to spend summers in Maine. John Wesley Powell had gone there, as did Richard Rathbun; Dr. Dall had a summer place; and these were just a sampling of the scientific gentlemen who extolled the state. The Walcotts took the ferry from Portland to Bar Harbor and were at Southwest Harbor by midafternoon. "Put up at Stanley House where I stopped in 1876 & 1877. The Stanley family are still running it" (August 12, 1926). Inside of two days, Mary had sketched an "Indian Pipe" and was working on a fringed orchid. "Attempted to work mss A.M. but with indifferent results. Too sleepy & languid" (August 16, 1926).

"Writing on Goodsir Trough A.M. Out on gravel beach P.M. for a sun bath & to read mss" (August 19, 1926). "At room reading A.M. *en re* geosynclines etc. After 2 P.M. Mary & I took a walk toward sea wall & back by beach. I was well tired out as result" (August 20, 1926). The weather did not agree with Walcott, as he reported to the chief clerk: "Cool these days 55°–70° in sunshine. Our room did not warm up above 65° for a week. 56° this morning so we discovered an electric reflector at Bar Harbor & all is well except that I [am] enjoying sore muscles all over. We hope that you are enjoying the cold wave. No fishing worthwhile unless one goes outside on the ocean & that will not pay for only cold & a stray haddock."[41]

Another quick note enclosed a memorandum to be typed and contained a request for the proofs of volume two of the wild flowers book. "It is 9:30 & I am sleepy. One hour past usual turning in time."[42] The area was far too chilly and damp for Walcott's aged bones. His "all is well" was bravado. "East breeze & bright sun is fine for sailing & out of door life but I haven't the strength & Mary will not go without me" (August 22, 1926). "Am not gaining strength or flesh as food & climate are against it. September may be better" (August 23, 1926). Walcott was whistling in the dark; he had seen Lura, the wife of his youth many years ago in Trenton Falls, fail, and he had seen Charlie fail, so he may well have known what was happening to him. The next day brought stomach pains; still, there was nothing to be done. It was long past time to leave Maine.

"Please hold mail on receipt of this until further instructions. We will leave here in a day or two. May go to Saugatuck Conn. for a few days but have not decided. Mr. & Mrs. Younger are away & will be at Mrs. Dimock's Bar Harbor on Sunday. Wind & fog today." Added at the end was "Friday 7 A.M. Fog, fog, fog."[43]

The Walcotts motored to Bar Harbor to see Mrs. Dimock and the Youngers. Perhaps Helen saw how bad the weather had been for her father and invited him south. On the last day in Maine, they attended the funeral of President Daniel G. Elliot of Harvard, did a little visiting, and fled. The conventional wisdom on the benefits of Maine was wrong. "We are glad to get away from S.W. Harbor as the Stanley House is most uncomfortable & weather bad" (August 27, 1926). The Walcotts settled with the Youngers at Saugatuck; "We thoroughly enjoy being where it is warm & cheerful in outlook" (August 29, 1926). Mary felt fine, and Walcott's spirits were higher, but he had picked up another cold, and it lingered on and on and on.

A few days into September, the fine weather disappeared. "Puttering about. Throat sore & muscles of back incapacitate me for any serious work. Wet outside prevents exercise in the open" (September 4, 1926). Walcott presumably felt that given an opportunity by the weather for a walk, he could still force his body to improve. On Labor Day he wrote, "Am lazy & good—for nothing" (September 6, 1926). This can be taken several ways, one of which was that his Puritan conscience was troubled because there was a manuscript to complete.

Three days later, the Walcotts had left Saugatuck and were at the Letchworth Cottage at Spring Lake Beach, New Jersey, their haunt for several past seasons. Walcott had an irritated mouth and throat to add to his stomach miseries, but that passed. The Walcotts finally had what he called a "glorious day," and thereafter, "I am gaining a little strength each day, but stomach is still weak" (September 15, 1926). The good weather continued, and Walcott scribbled a note to Washington. "Ask Arthur to take the Outlook, Science, and the magazines Atlantic Monthly, Worlds Work, Review of Reviews and Science Monthly to the Chief Clerk to be sent to us at Spring Lake Beach."[44] Walcott kept up with more than just geology.

"I am feeling much better than a week ago. Took up mss. and began to write a little. Am thoroughly tired of being in poor health" (September 20, 1926). Alphonso drove up from Washington, and his first duty was to take Mary to see Mr. Rudge. Walcott put in a few hours writing while they were away, and all ended the day with a short motor ride. The next day he was able to continue on with his writing, but the old machine was operating on limited hours, and mostly Walcott napped or rode around with Mary searching for flowers to sketch.

His muscles may have ached, but Walcott had all of his wits about him. Regent Delano wrote him suggesting that some Parke, Davis and Company stock be sold. Virtually all of the Freer endowment had been in that one stock. It made sense to diversify, but if too much stock were put on the market at one time, the price would drop. Walcott agreed to a meeting of the Permanent Committee but suggested that group obtain more information on that company's present prospects and standing in the financial community. His training in business more than half a century ago in Utica was still of use.

Near the end of the September, Walcott wrote a note to Dwight Morrow in which he was more optimistic than he had been in months. Mr. Morrow still had not agreed to head the endowment drive, though he had tried, unsuccessfully, to find a proper candidate for the position. The secretary began with a little flattery before getting to his hidden agenda.

> The Mills of the Gods grind slowly but they grind exceedingly fine, a saying that may apply to [General] Mitchell and all who made confusion most confounded in Aviation Service. Your board did a fine and thorough job and brought order out of chaos. I wish I was 40 years old and could take part in things worth doing. As it is I shall be out of most of my activities in 1927. It is a real pleasure to know that younger and better trained men have taken & will take my place. It will be a relief to be free from administrative responsibilities after 40 years of service. If you are in Washington before December I should like to have a talk with you in this connection.
>   Last spring I was more or less ill for a long time but now I am much better & feeling that life is worth living.[45]

The editing on the draft shows the care that Walcott took to make sure his letters were thought out and conveyed just the right tone. He wrote another letter to Morrow outlining his future plans:

> I wish very much to have a talk with you *en re* s.i. and my withdrawing from all executive and administrative work May *1st* 1927 when I will have completed 20 years active service as Secretary. Henry, Baird & Langley died in office but I do not think it is wise for the s.i. or for me to go on. I have writing to do that will take all my energy up to 1949. An old friend who lived over 102 wrote an essay at 76, one at 84 and another at 96. In the last he said he would not write any more but that he had sufficient energy to live and would now live to be 100 and enjoy life. *Moral*—Let us do likewise but to do it we must conserve our energies as we go along. What joy it would be to watch the evolution of democracy up to 1950. Just now I am not looking beyond 1930. I was told I might pass on at 26, again at 38 and 55 but being of an obdurate temperament I declined.[46]

The fine weather was over. "This has been a good November day. High wind, cool, raw & occasional mist" (September 27, 1926). Despite that, Walcott wrote, "Am doing a little work on mss each day" (September 30, 1926). October actually brought warmer weather, and Walcott continued his progress on the manuscript; it may have been snaillike movement, but it was progress. "This is our last day at Spring Lake. We have enjoyed our time & both feel benefitted by the sea air & good food" (October 10, 1926).

They drove south via Princeton, where Walcott "called at museum & talked with Dr Howell *en re* fossils from the 'Goodsir Trough' B.C. Canada" (October 11, 1926). Walcott had given his agnostid trilobites to Howell, and Howell had identified them. Resser and Howell had tossed back and forth with drafts of a letter Howell was to write asking Walcott for his specimens. Their worries were for nothing; as soon as Howell asked to study the specimens, Walcott had agreed.

As usual, the Walcotts stayed with the George Vauxes at Bryn Mawr. "Mary & I left 1:20. Ate our lunch by the road & at 7 P.M. drew up at our home in Washington. Found Arthur, Mollie, Annie & Delia well & ready to take care of us" (October 12, 1926). People in the Walcott household were family, not staff.

Walcott wasted no time. In the morning he met with Regent Delano to get the stock sale started. Mr. Rudge was there for lunch. Later that afternoon he met with Reverend Wood and finished up with a Board of Trustees meeting of the Church of the Covenant. It was a quick reintroduction to the Washington scene. Walcott cleared up his mail and various other matters, including items from the NACA brought to him by John Victory. With the routine caught up, he went back to the Cordillera geosyncline.

"Called at White House & told President Coolidge of my intention of resigning from N.A.C.A. & also letting up on administrative work. At Smithsonian 2–4:30 P.M. Mary & I talked over many matters in evening. We are greatly interested in Helen's prospects of a home & family" (October 16, 1926). Helen may have told them that she was in a family way. Walcott checked in with his doctor, worked on his manuscript, and presided at one more annual meeting of the Iowa Apartment House corporation. "Cleared up a number of things at office & in mss. A very good day" (October 19, 1926). The next day carried ditto marks.

Walcott submitted a formal resignation to the NACA on October 21. "Meeting of the N.A.C.A. 10:30–12:15 A.M. I was reelected chairman for a year" (October 21, 1926). Not only did duty call, but it refused to pay any attention to his wishes. "In your letter you stated that your reason for wishing to resign was that you felt a younger and more vigorous man should be Chairman. Although respectful consideration was given to your views, the members were unanimous in voting for your reelection. If I may interpret the action of the members, I would say that it was but another manifestation of unfailing confidence in your leadership and of the pride that is ours in having you at our head. In electing you for the eighth successive term we have honored ourselves and assured our organization a continuation, for another year at least, of its high and increasing prestige and usefulness."[47]

To understate a little, this is an interesting reply. Despite the argument with Orville Wright, the committee insisted that he continue. Walcott may have been hazy on technical matters, but he was a moderating force among the various air factions. The new Air Commerce Act and the decline of "Billy" Mitchell had created additional factions, and the secretary performed an invaluable function in keeping the meetings on an even keel.

Walcott was feeling fairly well, so Mary left for a quick trip to Ottawa; he worked on his manuscript and polished off the mail at the office. Mary returned safely, and all was well, except that the manuscript was not progressing because of Walcott's tiredness. "Working on mss at home in morning & administrative matters at office in afternoon. Sent letter to President Coolidge *en re* Smithsonian finances & the Budget Bureau" (October 28, 1926). Walcott was now strong enough to dine out at the home of Secretary of State Kellogg. With a little more strength came a longing for the field; he wrote a mountain climber, "I keep the copy of your work on the glistening mountains on my library table, and pick it up when I wish to get away for a brief visit to the hills."[48]

Election day came and went; since this was not a presidential year, and no one in Washington could vote anyway, the day hardly warranted a note. "Spent an hour with Dr. Resser *en re* Cambrian faunas—also Drs. Merrill & Ulrich" (November 3, 1926).

Occasionally, a flash of the old Walcott showed. Progress on his manuscript was reassuring. Fortunately, there was little at the moment in Smithsonian matters to distract him, so he could continue to spend time in research. By no means, however, did he neglect the future of the place. Strangely enough, when volume two of Mary's book was distributed to subscribers, he did not note it in his diary.

Art matters were still moving along moderately well, as Walcott wrote to Regent White: "I had a very interesting talk with Mr. Mellon yesterday afternoon. He is very much interested in the National Gallery of Art development, but whether he will take an *active* interest or not I do not know. He told me that they were paying the Director of the Art Gallery in Pittsburgh $15,000 salary, and it is very doubtful, if we wanted him, if he could be induced to leave, especially as our salary is only $5,200."[49]

Walcott complained about the lingering effects of his cold but continued "fussing with mss" for part of almost every day. "Talked with Miss Guest *en re* Mr. Lodge & Freer Gallery" (November 9, 1926); by now Walcott was determined that Mr. Lodge should go, and he was gathering his ammunition. "Attending to routine and administrative matters A.M. At home in afternoon working on mss.

A quiet evening as Miss Howard came & gave me a rub-over massage" (November 12, 1926). The massage was a new addition to Walcott's health regime, and during the last part of the year became more frequent occurrences; they seemed to help a little.

Despite the driving need to complete his research, the effort to raise funds for the SI, and the general concern to oversee the NACA, Walcott still had time for little personal kindnesses. Church attendance was by now relatively uncommon; "In afternoon went out to the Hyder farm to gather acorns for Mollie's squirrel family" (November 14, 1926). This was in keeping with his character, strange as this minor incident may seem.

"At home working on map of troughs in Cordillera Geosyncline A.M.– Attended to mail at Smithsonian P.M." (November 15, 1926). If there is a final clue needed that part 4 of SMC had changed dramatically in character from an opus to a summary, this is it. Earlier clues were Walcott's remarks about a Goodsir trough for an area west of Kicking Horse Pass, and his visit to see B. F. Howell at Princeton; Howell had become the expert on tiny pelagic trilobites that occurred in the area west of the Burgess Shale outcrop. A digression into geology is needed to explain this twenty-five-page publication and accompanying map on "Pre-Devonian Sedimentation in Southern Canadian Rocky Mountains" (Walcott 1927), but a digression will be no worse an interruption here than later, and it might be a rest from recounting administrative chores and sicknesses.

To recapitulate, sediments are deposited and hardened into rocks. A sequence may be thin, because it was deposited on a stable platform, or it may be thick because it was deposited in a subsiding area, a geosyncline. When sediments are deposited, the oldest is at the bottom of pile, and the youngest at the top—no surprises here. Formation names are given to the various rock units, and their ages are supplied by fossils they contain—no surprises here, either.

Walcott began this paper with a quick summary of the underlying Precambrian rocks, in which he still adhered to the concept of their deposition in fresh water. He then proceeded onto the main matter of deposition of younger rocks in the geosyncline. Throughout western North America, there are changes in rocks from east to west. Just beyond the foothills in the southern Canadian Rockies, the rock sequence is moderately thin and contains some gaps. The rocks thicken westward toward the Bow River Valley but are generally similar. Beyond Field, the Cambrian limestones change to shales, in which fossils are rare. Walcott did not know these rocks well and thought that in large measure they were younger, rather than lateral equivalents of the Cambrian limestones.

There are some problems with this paper, the principal ones being associated with the concept of multiple incursions of the sea from different directions.

Walcott's early work had been in Trenton Falls, New York, where thin layers can be traced along the walls of West Canada Creek. In his early work on the Colorado Plateau the same situation applied, except that layers could be recognized for hundreds of miles. In the Eureka district of Nevada and up and down the Appalachians, continuity of strata is the rule. The situation in the southern Rockies is both similar in some regards and different. To overgeneralize, in Alberta one deals with shelf deposits where the same layers can be recognized north and south. More or less at the border with British Columbia, the rocks were deposited in deeper water and are of a different lithology. In Nevada the rocks deposited in deeper water to the west are more badly faulted and displaced than in Canada; in the Appalachians rocks to the east are metamorphosed and quite difficult to interpret.

This change in facies of strata that were deposited at the same time is not always easy to comprehend and interpret. E. O. Ulrich saw different incursions of the sea, whereas later workers have considered the environment of deposition of the rocks. Walcott could understand the former concept better than the latter. As a result of Ulrich's powers of persuasion, Walcott interpreted the shallower and deeper parts of the same geosyncline as a series of distinct troughs, each with its own characteristic set of rocks and fossils. This was a direct consequence of his much less detailed understanding of the stratigraphy in the western portion of the region. This interpretation of different areas of deposition was to be unacceptable to later generations of geologists.

Another way to consider Walcott's work is in a geologic-time sense. About half the formation names he assigned are still in use. In general, these are in the Cambrian rocks. For the younger rocks, Walcott followed Ulrich in attempting to apply the time terms Ozarkian and Canadian between a shortened Cambrian and a shortened Ordovician. In discarding the Ulrichian troughs of deposition concept, the geologic profession also discarded these subdivisions of time.

Yet a different way to consider Walcott's paper is from the standpoint of the rocks. Walcott gave a minimum amount of detail as to lithology, following the practice of the time. For most uses in early-twentieth-century stratigraphy, a total thickness and an indication of whether the rocks were predominately limestone, sandstone, or shale was sufficient. During the 1920s and onward, geologists not only divided formations ever finer but paid increasing attention to the rocks and their interpreted environment of deposition. One worried whether a limestone was deposited on a reef or in a lagoon, and one differentiated dark gray from light gray units. As a generalization, Walcott's Cambrian units tended to have a similar lithology and therefore have been retained, whereas the post-Cambrian units contained a much more varied suite of rocks and have been abandoned in favor of more rigorously defined formations.

Perhaps the final way to consider this paper is as a pioneering effort to summarize the geologic history of the region in a coherent matter. The stratigraphy is more complex and the structure more complicated than Walcott thought. In the last analysis, the paper was built on too few data points and too much interpretation. On the other hand, Walcott had more stratigraphic and paleontologic information by far for the region had any other geologist of the times, and he did his best to develop an intelligible picture. It would be half a century before Canadian geologists would be able to present a more coherent picture of sedimentation in the early Paleozoic of their southern Rocky Mountains.

If Walcott had not been ill, he might have depended less on Ulrich and Resser as to the significance of some of younger faunas. If Walcott had had more uninterrupted time, he might have seen some of the fallacies in Ulrich's approach. Walcott had neither time nor stamina, and for him to have completed this paper, whether it was even partly correct or mainly right, was a triumph of determination and will. With the endowment drive and Mr. Lodge both tugging at him, it is amazing that he ever wrote a sentence.

The second half of November began with a major meeting of the Permanent Committee. Should Mr. Bishop be recalled from his work in China? Should Mr. Lodge be retained? Should the contract for the Smithsonian Scientific Series be signed? None of these matters was simple, yet in two hours, all were agreed upon.

One immediate consequence was a four-paragraph letter to C. W. Bishop, still quite active in China. There was concern about unsettled political conditions in that country, and some thought the young man should return to America in the near future. The key part of the letter was a paragraph marked in the margin as confidential.

Mr. Lodge has not yet returned from Boston, having been away since about the 15th of June. He feels that he can look after the interests of the Freer Gallery quite as well while working at the Boston Museum of Fine Arts, a view, however, that is not concurred in by the Permanent Committee of the Board of Regents. On this and other accounts it is not improbable that there will be a change in the curatorship of the Freer Gallery before the close of the present fiscal year, June 30, 1927. If this should come about, you will undoubtedly be requested to close up your work and return to Washington. This is all the more probable because the members of the Committee feel that they should have a hearing on the subject at which you would be present.[50]

Walcott now could focus again on his manuscript. "Spent two hours at Nat. Museum looking over Sawback fossils with Dr. Resser. I am slowly getting mss on Cordillera Geosynclines in order. Attended to mail & routine at s.i. Lunched at home & worked on mss P.M." (November 22, 1926). He devoted another few days in part to his research before the Vaux family came for the traditional visit. "'Thanksgiving Day.' I am thankful to be alive with a splendid wife and home. I could wish for better health but that may come in due time" (November 25, 1926).

After turkey dinner, it was back to the routine of manuscript and mail. That Sunday Mr. and Mrs. Lodge came to dinner, menu and topic of conversation not recorded. "Talked with John Lodge P.M. *en re* his relations to the Freer Gallery of Art" (November 30, 1926). The first curator of the Freer Gallery was about to leave. "Talked with John Lodge *en re* action of Regents Committee on Curatorship of Free[r] Gallery" (December 2, 1926).

Almost certainly Lodge was told of the pending decision to place the Freer under the National Gallery. One result would be that the salary of the curator of the Freer would then be lowered to that of the other curators. If this was unacceptable to Mr. Lodge, he was free to resign. Walcott was determined that conditions would change. In viewing the matter from the perspective of the Smithsonian, one has to note that at this time the institution had an annual unrestricted income of $65,000 from Smithson's original grant and $70,000 from additions funds with various restrictions. The Freer income was $190,000. Mr. Lodge had so much and the others so little that hard feelings were bound to develop. Mr. Lodge submitted his resignation.

"Our first good winter day. Cold & light snow. Called on Chief Justice Taft 10–11 A.M. *en re* meeting of Smithsonian Regents on Dec. 9th" (December 5, 1926). This may have been a Sunday, but it was better to spend the time on groundwork than in church. Walcott wanted no surprises at this meeting. The Permanent Committee met on Monday to get more affairs in order. "Meeting of Advisory Commission Nat. Gal. Art 10–12—Katherine Rhodes called *en re* resignation of John Lodge. She greatly deplores such action" (December 7, 1926). Her feeling is understandable, but in attempting to rally support, she wrote of Walcott as a weak man, an error in judgment on her part.

Walcott spent the next day getting his ducks in order. The regents' meeting went well, with prickly matters smoothed over, and there was sufficient time for the formal presentation of a bust of Alexander Graham Bell. Walcott was doing well and the next day attended the CIW board meeting, later getting to his mail.

One key letter he wrote during this period was to President Coolidge, inviting him to the great meeting planned for the coming February. There is a curious duty assigned to the president of the United States: by virtue of his office, he is head of the Smithsonian "Establishment." The Establishment includes the vice president, the chief justice, and all members of the cabinet. The Board of Regents is subservient to the Establishment, but only in the most obscure way.

The Establishment had only met twice, in the early days of the institution. Walcott proposed that it convene once more, with the regents and a few prominent individuals, to emphasize the important of the SI endowment drive. The president agreed to attend.

Visitors and papers filled his Saturday. Sunday was a raw and cold day, but that afternoon Walcott was at the Smithsonian looking over papers for a coming meeting. The Permanent Committee met Monday; "Miss Rhodes spoke to Committee *en re* Mr. Lodge & Curatorship of Freer Gallery" (December 13, 1926). Most unusually, the Permanent Committee met again the following day, but the matter before them was unusual. "The Committee accepted the resignation of Mr. Lodge as Curator of the Freer Gallery of Art. Mr. Lodge spoke on the Expedition in China" (December 14, 1926).

Whether this difficult decision with Mr. Lodge made his own health worse is uncertain, but Walcott was back at one doctor's office the next day and was called upon at home by another. "The stiffness in my neck & chest muscles continues to linger & Mary worries about me accordingly" (December 16, 1926). When it was necessary to attend dinners and other events, Mary carried on while Walcott husbanded his strength at home. "Cleaned up mail & resumed work on my mss in morning. Went to Smithsonian P.M. Handed John E. Lodge acceptance of his resignation as Curator of Freer Gallery" (December 18, 1926). That at least was a problem resolved.

Sunday was quiet except for a family dinner with Assistant Secretary and Mrs. Abbot. They may have talked over the great meeting planned for February. Ever since Walcott had slowed down, Dr. Abbot had been carrying on with the endowment drive. At a meeting that week in New York, Abbot and Morrow met with a select group to see how a slightly larger select group could be induced to come to Washington and give money.

The year was winding down, but important duties were still at hand. The week began with a hearing for the independent offices appropriation bill: "Mr. Wood. We will take up the items of the National Advisory Committee for Aeronautics. Doctor Walcott have you a general statement you wish to submit[?] Doctor Walcott. Mr. Chairman, before I go into the details of the committee work and the estimates, I should like to make a statement with relation to present conditions and developments. I am very hoarse, and if I may, I should like to ask Mr. Victory to read it for me" (Walcott 1926b, 289).

At least this was a slight improvement over the hearings in 1925, which Walcott had been too ill even to attend. A one-day break gave time to send Christmas cards before it was time for the hearings on the government bureaus under SI administration. "Mr. Wood. Doctor Walcott, do you wish to make a statement?

Doctor Walcott. Mr. Chairman, the various members who are in direct charge of these various lines of work are present, and they can explain the work that they are carrying on far better than I can" (Walcott 1926c, 334).

Thereafter Assistant Secretary Wetmore handled the affair, with help from Harry Dorsey and an assist from one or two others. Walcott had faith in his staff. Wetmore did well, beginning with a clear explanation of how underpaid were the employees of the bureaus administered by the Smithsonian relative to other government employees. He had done equally well in presentation the previous year at the hearings for the zoological park; they were under the appropriation for the District of Columbia government, and that added yet another level of problems.

The hearings were so satisfactory that for the next day it was "routine matters at the Smithsonian A.M. & at home P.M." (December 23, 1926). Walcott spent Friday morning giving out little Christmas presents at the office. "Our household, Mollie, Annie, Delia & Arthur gathered at 6 P.M. & we had our Christmas tree. All well & happy" (December 24, 1926). Christmas Day itself was fairly quiet, with a few friends in for dinner. On Sunday Walcott spoke by telephone to his children in New York and commented how pleased he was that they were established and happy.

The rest of the year continued more or less routine as in past Christmas seasons. "Cleaned up mail, dictated letters, conferred with Asst Secy. Abbot & other members of the s.i. staff in morning. At home for lunch & afternoon. A long nap & then a little study of sketches for my paper on geology of Southern Canadian Rocky Mountains. After dinner Miss Howland gave me a massage 6–9 P.M. Mary read for half an hour & then tucked me in for the night" (December 31, 1926).

Walcott's comments for the year are longer than any he recorded previously.

Mary is well but tired. Her Wild Flower book is making good headway vols. 1 & 2 being published & 3 well advanced. As a whole 1926 has been a disagreeable year for me owing to influenza attacks in Feby & April and inclement weather keeping me with colds & neuralgia most of the time. Mary has been well but worried by my condition & pressure of many duties at home & in connection with her "Book." Our children are well. Helen is in New York 136 E. *67th st.* Cole Younger is doing well at the Allied Chemical Co. Sidney & family have moved from New York to Buffalo to their former home at [blank] Auburn Ave. His N.Y. venture did not meet with success but the experience may prove advantageous to him.

The Smithsonian Institution has held its own & is a better position than a year ago. The attempt to increase the endowment has advanced but the main result is expected in 1927. I shall resign as Secretary to take effect

June 30th 1927. I am no longer able to keep up with administrative & research work & I hope to get the results of past years into shape for publication before passing out of this life. (December 31, 1926)

From the standpoint of his own publication record, only the *Annual Report* and the 1925 "Explorations" were published by the Smithsonian (Walcott 1926b); the remarks about Langley to the American Philosophical Society added a couple more pages (Walcott 1926d). On the other hand, he had been pushing along on both a summary and a large paper on stratigraphy, as time permitted. The synopsis of some of his findings over the years would be finished in less than a month (Walcott 1927).

New Year's Day was quiet. Mary made a few calls, and Walcott joined her when they visited the Tafts and the Hoovers. The radio was marvelous; they listened to the football game in Pasadena, California, and a concert in New York City. On Sunday Walcott rested, and Mary went to a Friends meeting. For several years now she had been far more active in a religious sense than Walcott, and Friends meetings in Washington were now relatively common.

Work began on the first Monday of the new year. "Studying data relative to Cordillera subsidiary troughs A.M. at home. Attending to routine at the Smithsonian P.M. The variable weather keeps my cold & neuralgia going much to my annoyance. Tooth taken out 5 P.M. Massage 8–9 P.M." (January 3, 1927). "A second tooth taken out 5 P.M. Went home & developed neuralgia & 3° of fever" (January 4, 1927). This was certainly not the best way to start the new year. Walcott signed his mail but stayed close to bed while waiting for his gums to heal. By Friday he was a bit better, but Mary ached; it is hard getting old. They both improved, and Walcott noted with satisfaction a letter from Sidney that he was getting along well in Buffalo. Life returned to normal, less a few teeth.

Walcott still had his sense of humor in writing to Regent White. "Yours of January 3 came to my office. Shortly after I had a *bad* tooth extracted. At 7 P.M. was in bed with a temperature of 102°. As the comics say 'Can you beat it?' Now, Saturday morning, I am normal, but will not go out until Monday for 'conscience's sake.'" Walcott went on to mention the importance of the regents' meeting of February 10 and concluded: "I hope that your cold has departed and that you are 'quite fit,' as our English friends say when feeling not quite up to the mark."[51]

There was another letter of January 3 wishing him the best for the new year, this one from the secretary of agriculture. "I think I speak the mind not only of the Department of Agriculture, but of all public-spirited citizens in expressing my appreciation of your interest in the forest problems that confront us in the United States. This is a matter of the greatest significance, recognized as such throughout the world, and your counsel, assistance, and cooperation are most valuable.[52] Walcott dictated a long reply, worth quoting.

> Your letter of January 3 in regard to the forest problems brings up a flood of memories that go back to the season of 1882–1883, when I spent several months in the forests of the Kaibab Plateau, north of the Grand Canyon of the Colorado. I was in a mood to appreciate and enjoy the forest, as I had been in the two previous field seasons in the mining districts of central Nevada, where the piñon pine and mountain mahogany constituted the "forest" where the trees had not been removed root, trunk, and branch to be taken to the smelters.
>
> In the course of the next few years, in connection with my geological work, I lived in the forests of the high plateaux of southern Utah, the Wasatch Mountains, and the forests of western Montana. I mention these facts because it will serve to explain to you why I took such an active interest in the forestry question, and finally succeeded in shaping matters so that a forestry law was attached as a rider to an appropriation for topographic surveying by the Geological Survey, of which I was then Director. It also led me to urge upon the administration the adoption of a forest policy, and when Secretary Wilson asked me to recommend to him a forester to take the place of Dr. Fernow, I unhesitatingly suggested to him that he send for Gifford Pinchot, who at that time was the most promising American who was at all competent to administer the Forest Service of his Department.
>
> I have been interested in keeping in touch with the development of the Forest Service and I think I can congratulate you and all members of the Service upon the wonderful record it has made and is now making. It is no longer an orphan, kicked about by disgruntled people, but is a sturdy young giant, perfectly capable of taking care of itself. I do not see that I can be of much assistance, but as far as my interest and loyal support are concerned, you may feel assured that it is with the service.[53]

"At home A.M. attending to mail & mss. Went to the office P.M. & cleaned up correspondence, etc" (January 10, 1927). The same day Walcott was reminiscing about the western forests, George and Mary Vaux came from Philadelphia for a few days. George was in town as a result of his work as a commissioner of Indian affairs; it was by no means a final, farewell visit to a sick man. "Occupied with mss & office mail at home during the day. George & Mary Vaux left for home at 3 P.M." (January 14, 1927).

"Spent the morning at the Smithsonian attending to routine & dictating letters. At home P.M. Read minutes of last Regents meeting & signed each page" (January 15, 1927). He also found time to write to Bishop, who was still in China. "Judging from the reports in the papers, the political pot and civil war are still simmering at a lively rate. I spoke to Mr. Lodge about the safety of your expedition, and was glad to learn from him that he had authorized you to close up the expedition and return at any time you thought it was advisable; also, that you had abundant funds with which to return. I presume that you have heard that Mr. Lodge resigned as Curator of the Freer Gallery, and that his resignation has been accepted to take effect June 30, 1927. This will terminate the joint curatorship of the Freer Gallery and the Oriental Department of the Boston Museum of Fine Arts."[54]

Sunday, Walcott: "Read, rested, wrote letters, fixed up mss on Cordillera secondary troughs" (January 16, 1927), and prepared to start another week at the Castle. "Talked with Ulrich & Resser 9–10:30 A.M. *en re* Cordillera Geosynclines paper" (January 17, 1927). At my office A.M. & home P.M. The cold in my neck & throat still continues as the weather is bad for me" (January 18, 1927). The clear cold weather had given way to a chilly rain a few degrees above freezing. The January thaw continued, and Mary left for an overnight visit to Philadelphia.

"A mild day. Met Mr. Mawson of Australia at the museum & showed him Cambrian & pre-Cambrian fossils. I then examined fossils from British Columbia that I collected in 1910. At home P.M. Mr. Delano called 4 P.M." (January 20, 1927). According to the late Martin Glaessner, one of the next generation who investigated Precambrian fossils, for many years Sir Douglas Mawson was to declared that he had been responsible for Walcott's death. Walcott had rushed up and down ladders dragging large specimens of the heavy algal stromatolites for Mawson to examine, as similar forms were known in Australia. It is a good story, but not quite true; the truth is that Walcott was still active after Mawson's visit.

"Talked with Ulrich & Resser about my paper on Cordillera geosyncline. Reviewing mss of Goodsir Series P.M." (January 21, 1927). Walcott also recorded receiving an injection of cold serum. He was not feeling well, but was at the office on Saturday. On Sunday, Senator Smoot and his daughter Zella were at dinner. "At home during the day. Raw & cool outside. Reread my paper on Cordillera Geosynclines" (January 24, 1927).

Walcott dictated a letter to his French colleague E. de Margerie. After thanking him for a note, Walcott wrote of his own future: "I have not published any papers for about a year, but I now have one on my table, on the Cordillera Geosynclines in the southern Canadian Rockies. This will be followed shortly by a paper on the geological formations, and later by one or more paleontological papers."[55] Walcott concluded with comments about Mary's book, its high cost, and their attempts to induce a wealthy American to buy copies so that they could be distributed to libraries. He was full of plans for the future.

A footnote in volume seventy-five, part 4, provides a little more detail. "Published posthumously. Dr. Walcott completed the manuscript only ten days before his death on February 9, 1927. The proofs have been corrected by Dr. Resser"

(Walcott 1927). Walcott was feeble but clear in mind on January 24th. If he was too ill to write in his diary after that date, it is unlikely that he added any comments of significance to the manuscript.

Two days following what would have been Walcott's seventy-seventh birthday, SMC volume seventy-five, number four, was published. In his short paper for the Geological Society of Belgium, Walcott (1925) had reported one of the basic features of the geologic history of the region, showing both the westward thickening of individual units and the more complete record of additional rock units to the west. Since that time, Walcott had had his two last field seasons. "The object of this paper is to call attention to conclusions based on further field studies and the working over since 1924 of a considerable amount of unpublished geological and paleontological data on the formation of the Cordillera Geosynclines, located in the drainage areas of the Bow, Kicking Horse, and Saskatchewan Rivers" (Walcott 1927, 148).

Another posthumous Walcott paper would appear in the fall of 1928 to complete SMC volume seventy-five, the fifth volume of his "Cambrian Geology and Paleontology." This last is a substantial publication, with nearly two hundred pages and more than sixty illustrations, many of which are fold-out photographic panoramas. The preface, dated March 19, 1928, is by C. E. Resser.

> The manuscript of this paper was left by the late Dr. Charles Doolittle Walcott in such shape that it could be satisfactorily completed. Having been associated with author in his Cambrian work for almost 13 years, and having conducted some of the investigations to obtain the necessary data used in the summary of his stratigraphic sections in the Canadian Rockies, I have undertaken the task of completing and publishing the paper.
>
> Only such alterations have been made as were contemplated by Dr. Walcott, or that have resulted from plans of procedure we had previously agreed upon.
>
> From notes and fragments, it appears that Dr. Walcott intended to add a discussion of the structure and of the paleogeography, but neither of these subjects were sufficiently developed to permit me to include the chapters. He had also planned to publish certain correlation charts that I was making, but under the circumstances it is thought best to omit them.
>
> The present report, which I feel sure will take its place among the outstanding stratigraphic papers, has had a remarkable history. It existed in partly finished form for a number of years, always about completed in Dr. Walcott's mind, but since each year's work in the field and laboratory added so much new information, and new problems arose so persistently, the date for sending it to the press was repeatedly advanced, a procedure which, considering the present status of the Cambrian studies is in no wise out of the ordinary. The remarkable thing was that Dr. Walcott, when well past the age at which many men cease to work altogether, put aside this manuscript,

took time to study the newer principles of stratigraphy, and then rewrote the entire work on the new basis; truly the mark of a great mind. (Resser *in* Walcott 1928)

This was the paper that provided the basic data on which the sedimentation summary of 1927 was based. It showed where the various stratigraphic sections were geographically, and it discussed these sections and the fossils identified. The part on Mount Robson is most complete; the other portions vary widely, many simply reproducing a section as published earlier by Walcott. It should be noted that Resser never saw the rocks in Canada with Walcott; indeed, they were never really together in the field together. Essentially what Resser could do was to cut and paste from earlier publications, admittedly not always a simple task.

Five days after Walcott's death, Resser wrote a colleague, B. F. Howell at Princeton University: "The past week has been a rather hard one for me. We had our big conference on here and it passed off well. Dr. Walcott's passing hits me hard. It had to come sometime but I was by no means ready for it now. This loads quite an extra burden on me to finish the papers in hand and to bear the entire burden of caring for inquiries concerning Cambrian matters. My plans for the immediate future are all somewhat indefinite as they will be regulated largely by Mrs. Walcott's wishes."[56] It may be a bit of an uncharitable interpretation, but these are hardly the sentiments of a younger man who has lost a much-beloved mentor and has been one of his pallbearers. Resser was to remained with the Department of Geology until his death more than a decade later. G. A. Cooper (1902–2000), who joined the staff in 1930, would commented that Dr. Resser took care of the Cambrian and Cooper took care of everything else. The sentiment in the letter does not quite match that in the preface, but an interpretation might be that one writes differently for different outlets.

New fieldwork has uncovered some errors in Walcott's work; for example, one sandstone that Walcott thought to be unfossiliferous has yielded Devonian fossils, which has modified some of his interpretations. Notwithstanding such changes, there are a few more basic points that need to be made about this publication. Walcott covered a great deal of the ground, long before the days of helicopters, and he first located many of the better sections. He found many of the fossiliferous layers in these sections that subsequently have been re-collected. Finally, Walcott's measured sections are generally accurate in thickness, as remeasuring by two generations of geologists has demonstrated.

There is one more comment to be made regarding this publication. Harry Dorsey wrote a note to Mrs. Walcott, "You asked me to give you a memorandum of the volume published last summer, PreDevonian Paleozoic Formation of the Cordillera Provinces of Canada, for part of which you spoke of reimbursing the Institution."

"The total cost was $3,579.83, which has been paid. The charge for this and some other work carried over from last year has reduced our printing fund to a point where we can no longer do much more work this year."[57] Mrs. Walcott contributed a thousand dollars to the Smithsonian.

Inasmuch as the chronological sequence has been interrupted already, it may be just as well to bring the scientific sequence to a conclusion. In 1930, Mary Vaux Walcott was in the Yoho Valley, and in writing to Secretary Abbot, she instituted Walcott's final publication:

> Yesterday I went up to the quarry & found things there in great confusion. Raymond of Harvard went there earlier in the season with permits from the Minister of the Interior granted on request of our Secretary of State. He has blasted a lot of rock, leaving everything in great confusion, so that you would hardly know the place, & took back with him five large boxes of specimens. You know in Dr. Walcott's collection there were a number of undescribed specimens, and these are what are causing me uneasiness. I think these should be described & named, as Raymond is an uncertain quantity, with Harvard swelled head, & I should very much dislike him to have any credit from our quarry which should belong to Dr. Walcott. I thought it best to write you about this but I also writing Dr. Bassler, & I think this work should be pushed [?] and a separate published at the earliest possible day. Please see what can be done about it, as soon as possible. I also hear that Raymond says he got all he wanted & will not return for further work.[58]

Mary's desire was translated into action. Five months later, Resser wrote a memorandum to the assistant secretary, through the head curator of geology. When G. P. Merrill died, Bassler was promoted to that position. "According to your request to Dr. Bassler, dated August 15, 1930, I have assembled the manuscript and illustrations dealing with the Burgess Shale which Dr. Walcott left unpublished. All that seems suitable or sufficiently complete has been included in this paper which consists of 103 typewritten pages, 11 text figures and 23 plates. Personally I doubt somewhat the propriety of printing this material, inasmuch as I fear it contains conclusions which Dr. Walcott had rejected. As you know Dr. Walcott was not a person to write a manuscript and then leave it unpublished if he was reasonably sure of the validity of his deductions."[59]

Bassler added a note to the bottom of the memorandum. "Recommended for publication. I believe Dr. Walcott delayed the publication of this manuscript because he was uncertain as to the systematic position of most of the species. In my opinion this does not lessen the value of the observations and descriptions." Assistant Secretary Wetmore forwarded the manuscript to Secretary Abbot. "It is my recommendation that if funds permit, it be published in the Smithsonian Miscellaneous Collections as promptly as possible, to be paid for from the income of the Walcott fund."[60]

Volume eighty-five, number three, of smc was issued on June 29, 1931. Resser began it with a "Preparatory Statement." "During my 13 years' association with Doctor Walcott he frequently dwelt upon the fact that he considered his papers on the Burgess shale forms rather in the form of announcements than a completed study of these wonderfully preserved fossils. He always intended to return to the study of the described species and to publish more detailed descriptions and interpretations of their form and structure. However, the stress of war times and advancing years prevented a realization of this hope. Nevertheless, from time to time, he had photographs prepared or made notes of his observations regarding structure, all of which were preserved with the collections" (Resser *in* Walcott 1931, 1). (Resser died in 1943.)

Along with describing two new genera and few species, Walcott had redescribed and reconsidered several of the Arthropoda in more detail. For the other arthropods and fossils of other groups, the work consisted mainly of reprinting original descriptions with illustrations of new specimens. In this instance, Resser probably had it right. The paper added little to Walcott's reputation, and in the long run it might have been better not to have published it. Still, the twenty- three plates provided a clue that the later collections contained some interesting specimens and that there was still more to be learned from the Burgess Shale fossils. So much for Walcott's last publication.

The first entry in Walcott's diary has been published (Yochelson 1998), so for symmetry his last entry should be mentioned. He gave the weather as cl[ou]dy 30°–39°. He then wrote "At home during the day. Raw & cool outside. Reread my paper on Cordilleran Geosyncline. 2d injection of serum at night" (January 24, 1927). The last sentence is at the bottom of the page and probably was added later.

For two more days the minimum and maximum temperatures outside are recorded. Walcott's cash outlays, mainly society dues, are listed through January 18, and there is an entry of twenty-five dollars on February 1 for the "Arch. Soc. Of Wash.," though this may have been written in earlier. Otherwise, the diary is blank. Nevertheless, Walcott was still functioning, and even functioning moderately well. The copy of one letter to Ulrich dated January 28 is annotated "The last letter signed by C.D.W."

You will have reached the allotted span of life of three score and ten on February 1, but if by reason of vitality and occupation you are to go on a decade more, I trust that it be one of the most productive periods of your long and honorable career. You are now in a position to produce far more important results than you have in the past, and I sincerely hope that health may be given you to complete the rounding out of your researches.

It is not my intention to speak disparagingly of your work in the past. On the contrary, I regard it as a monument to your ability and industry, but it is only in comparison with what I know you have in mind that the work of the future seems more important.

I congratulate you and your friends on your birthday, and join with them in wishing you good health, a clear mind, and courage to go on with your work.[61]

Earlier, Rudge had suggested producing a brochure to help sales of *North American Wild Flowers*. Walcott may not have written the original draft, but he edited it. The proof arrived just before the end of the month. Some changes in the text appear to have been made by Mary, but one change seems to be in Walcott's handwriting.

On the last day of January, Assistant Secretary Abbot wrote a short letter. "Dear Dr. Walcott: We had planned—that is all of us from the top to the bottom of the whole Smithsonian staff—to have a little meeting today to felicitate the Institution and you on the twentieth anniversary of your appointment to the Secretaryship. But little things often alter the plans of men, and as a tiny grippe germ will prevent you from being with us today, we are sending you these roses with the love and heartiest good wishes of us all."[62] Walcott did not return to the institution.

A few days later, he suffered a stroke. Near the end, Sidney and Helen came down from New York. Whether Walcott was aware that Helen was pregnant is unknown; she would have a son that summer. If Walcott had known, good family man that he was, he surely would have been happy. On Wednesday, it ended: "Doctor Walcott died twelve twenty this afternoon."[63] By coincidence, the Geological Society of Washington met that evening and became the first scientific group to be notified formally of his death.

Two days later, faithful Paul Brockett, mainstay of the NAS, elaborated on the final days to George Ellery Hale. "A week ago Friday, in the afternoon, I spent some little time with Dr. Walcott discussing matters relative to the Elliott Fund and while he seemed weak and quite different from what I had seen him, the stroke which came later on in the evening was not evident then. After the stroke it was a matter of days, and I do not think the family had any hope, owing to his weakened condition."[64] Six days later Abbot wrote: "Although he had failed for a long time, it was only within a day or two of the end that it became imminent. He suffered no pain, but sank peacefully away."[65]

On the day Walcott died in office, Acting Secretary Abbot wrote officially to President Coolidge, "It is my sad duty to inform you, Sir, the head of the Smithsonian Establishment, that Secretary Charles D. Walcott died at noon today."

"By his own previously expressed wish, and that of Mrs. Walcott, the conference proposed for Friday, February the eleventh, will be held as planned."[66] The president immediately sent his condolences to Mrs. Walcott; his letter was reprinted in most of the newspapers throughout the nation that carried Walcott's obituary. The letters and memorials received from individuals and societies that were retained in the archives form a pile an inch thick.

The Board of Regents met on the 10th, a gathering that had been planned for weeks to discuss last-minute arrangements for the February 11th conference. Little business was transacted except a resolution "that the Executive Committee be requested to arrange for a memorial meeting to be held in Washington, and for the submission at such meeting of a suitable record of the life and work of Dr. Walcott."[67]

The Smithsonian and Museum staffs held a short memorial service that day; everyone had known that Secretary Walcott was ill, but then, he had been there forever and somehow was expected to be there forever. A resolution committee headed by G. P. Merrill expressed condolences, a sense of loss, and personal comments. "He displayed to a degree that excited our greatest admiration, a capacity for the dual duties of research and administration. . . . A number of Dr. Walcott's associates present at the meeting expressed their esteem and affection for him, and their admiration for his scientific work. Among these were Dr. Keith, Mr. Newell, Dr. David White, Dr. Abbot, Dr. Wetmore, Dr. Bassler, and Mr. Victory."[68]

Walcott's funeral was on Saturday, February 12, naturally enough at the Church of the Covenant, at Connecticut and N Streets, N.W. Three clergymen conducted the services. There were a number of honorary pallbearers. "Active pallbearers, all members of the staff of the Smithsonian, will be Dr. Charles G. Abbot, acting secretary of the Institution; Dr. Alexander Wetmore, assistant secretary; Dr. William R. Mann, superintendent of the National Zoological Park; Charles E. Resser, assistant curator of paleontology; Nicholas W. Dorsey, disbursing agent, and Harry W. Dorsey, chief clerk."[69] The Dorsey brothers had served Walcott faithfully and well to the end. The interment was private, in Section L of Rock Creek Cemetery. Before the funeral, nephew by marriage George Vaux, son of George Vaux, recalled knocking back a couple of scotches with Helen.

Between the regents' meeting on February 10 and the funeral on the 12th was the gathering in the Great Hall of the Castle. The Establishment assembled for the third time in SI history. The proceedings list President Coolidge, Vice President Dawes, Chief Justice Taft, and all ten members of the cabinet. The Board of Regents was listed, with its three senators, three representatives, and six private citizens. Acting Secretary Abbot and Assistant Secretary Wetmore were there, along with forty conferees.

Acting Secretary Abbot commented on the gathering in a letter to Bishop, still in China.

Your recent letter to Dr. Walcott arrived, I am sorry to say, too late for his consideration. He gradually failed and at length passed away, on February 9, after a painless and generally conscious illness, like a candle which burns down, flickers, and goes out. The event was rendered dramatic by the circumstance that a very notable meeting of eminent men, including the President, the cabinet, the regents, various members of the Senate and House, and some of the most notable leaders in science and industrial affairs in the whole world were gathered at the Smithsonian Building on February 11 to consider the future of the Institution and the means to sustain its work. I take pleasure in sending you a copy of the proceedings of the conference, which proved to be a very inspiring occasion. The Institution had prepared excellent exhibits illustrating the types of research and publication which it was uniquely prepared to undertake with suitable means. We have great hopes that results will be highly favorable.[70]

At the conference, there was general agreement that the Smithsonian Institution did good work and could do more if it had more funding. Some sentiment was interjected to the point that in addition to seeking private funds, the Smithsonian should ask for more support from Congress. General Lord, head of the Bureau of the Budget, made the point that between 1921 and 1928 appropriations for the government bureaus under the Smithsonian had increased 55.4 percent. In a peculiar way, this too is a tribute to Walcott's ability as an administrator.

After the meeting, the Smithsonian raced to print the speeches and other proceedings; the publication was out and distributed in a month (Anonymous 1927). Unfortunately, despite the promising beginning of this conference, nothing of significance was forthcoming. In October Morrow was appointed ambassador to Mexico. The endowment drive ended before it started and was thus not a victim of the depression that began in 1929.

In death, Walcott did not forget the Smithsonian Institution. By his will Mary was given lifelong tenancy in the house on S Street, N.W., a hundred shares of apartment house stock, and his personal effects. Most of the rest of the estate went to Sidney, with one major exception. "I give and bequest to the Smithsonian Institution of Washington, District of Columbia, an establishment organized and existing under and by virtue of the laws of the United States, the sum of fifty thousand dollars ($50,000) or the equivalent in securities, at the discretion of my executors; the net income of which is to be paid to my daughter, Helen B. Walcott [Younger], during her lifetime; on her decease, this fund is to be transferred to the Charles D. and Mary Vaux Walcott Research Fund and become a part thereof, and be treated in the same manner as the original donation to that Fund."[71]

Mary and Sidney were the executors of the estate. The will posed a bit of a challenge to the Board of Regents, for in effect it made the Smithsonian a trustee for Helen. The board agreed, however, with the stipulation that the SI should not be liable for any loss. Setting up the research fund with a modest original sum in 1922, two days before he wrote his will, Walcott had effectively restricted its use with a series of provisions that now took effect. First, only the income could be spent; there would be no income while Helen lived. Second, for a hundred years after February 9, 1927, only half the income could be spent, the rest to be added to the principal. Walcott included a further hedge to allow for changing conditions, that any time after a hundred years if the principal should be reduced in value, restriction would come back into effect.

During Walcott's lifetime the fund was to be used for conducting geological and paleontological research and for publishing the results of research. Just as he had considered the future to ensure that the fund grew, he allowed for changes, provided two-thirds of the entire Board of Regents voted affirmatively. Considering the difficulties of assembling the entire Board of Regents for the annual meeting, this pretty well prevented any change in the use of the money. Even so, Walcott restricted that potentiaual future change, for if it were made it would be "with the proviso that the income of the said Fund is to be used solely for the increase and diffusion of knowledge under the director of the Smithsonian Institution."[72] Walcott the scientist was equally Walcott the shrewd businessman to the end. He intended that his money would grow to support research long after he had gone, and he planned well.

A surprise was a codicil added to the will. Should the Smithsonian ever be placed under the control of the executive branch or become a department of the federal government, Walcott's money would go to George Washington University. Whether it was the talk of a Department of Education to include the SI, or whether it was the attempt to place the NACA in the Department of Commerce, Walcott was determined that the Smithsonian would remain independent, if he could express an opinion from the grave. In his understanding, the SI was not part of the federal government; it remained a public trust, administered for the good of the people of the United States.

As befitted a distinguished scientist in a globally prominent position, informal and formal obituaries appeared in an amazing variety of journals and periodicals. A list of the more significant obituaries would fill a page. The SI held its memorial meeting January 24, 1928, with appropriate talks recounting Walcott's activities. Chancellor Taft presided. Carnegie Institution of Washington president John C. Merriam spoke first, covering Walcott's efforts with that organization; he was followed by Joseph S. Ames, chairman of the National Advisory

Committee for Aeronautics. Director George Otis Smith considered Walcott's accomplishments with the U.S. Geological Survey. In his role as NAS president, Thomas Hunt Morgan had been asked to speak but had declined, pleading a move from New York to Pasadena. Secretary Charles Greeley Abbot filled in, discussing Walcott's contributions to the Academy and the institution.

The program of Walcott's funeral service cites him as "a typical American," which he was not, but gives a fairly accurate, if slightly religiously oriented, thumbnail sketch.

> Self-educated, self-controlled, self-developed, he climbed unaided from obscurity to distinction; a clerk in a hardware store, an assistant to a geologist, an associate in the U.S. Survey, Secretary of the Smithsonian Institution, Fellow in many scientific societies in Europe and America, recipient of numberless honorary degrees from universities at home and abroad; an officer in the Church; retaining in every position his calm, quiet manner, his gentleness and geniality, his firmness and concentration, his unshaken confidence in truth and in God; thus making great contributions to the ever accumulative wealth of the world, but greatest of all in his life. (Anonymous 1927a)

Chancellor Taft summed up the man even more succinctly: "Walcott made himself. His career is a long list of arduous deeds done in helping the cause of geological science and in helping the government by a disinterested devotion to its usefulness in many scientific avenues. He was a civil servant of the highest value" (Taft 1928, 4).

Epilogues

The interest shown by scientists in the history of their science was
generated by a number of considerations. Apart from a natural curiosity,
the earth sciences are always to a certain extent historical as they search for
data to reveal variations over time as part of their elucidation of the present
and future. Similarly biologists refer to the work of their predecessors for
information on taxonomy and distribution of organisms.

—M. Deacon, 1997

AT ONE TIME, LONG AGO, it seemed that a detailed account of the various
people, and especially the organizations, with which Walcott was connected
would be an appropriate way to end his story. It did not take long to discard this
idea, and if reasons are needed, there are at least two. First, institutional history is not biography; although the line between history and current events is
unclear, when it is crossed it leads into quite a different playing field. Second,
life is finite.

Nevertheless, there is some unfinished business. Any reader who has been
dogged enough to persist to this point deserves not to be left hanging. Those
who want to know more about the history from 1904 to 1939 of the U.S. Geological Survey—which during the 1990s became officially the United States
Geological Survey—should consult the book by Rabbitt (1986). She has also
summarized the first 110 years of the bureau (Rabbitt 1989). The Bureau of
Mines was abolished by Congress in 1995; for those who want to know what it
had been doing, a study was prepared some years ago by the Congressional
Research Service, part of the Library of Congress (Agnew 1976).

The Reclamation Service was headed for some years by Newell, who generated some criticism, right or wrong. It became the Bureau of Reclamation, and
it transformed, or transmogrified, part of the West. The literature pro and con
on dams, government servants and bureaucrats, family farms, and agribusiness
is voluminous. What one reads depends on one's outlook. Nevertheless, there
is still far less in the way of newspaper stories, articles, and books on reclamation than on the trees that are under the care of the national government.

To recommend any single source for the history of the Forest Service or the Bureau of Reclamation after Walcott left the trees and waters of the United States is dangerous.

One reviewer noted the lack of psychological insight in my study of Walcott's earlier years (Yochelson 1998). Fortunately, that absence did not trouble him greatly. Still, discussing Walcott's immediate family may be a way to ease into a variety of otherwise unconnected loose ends

Family

> In short, when discussing the relations of the individual to his fellows, we are compelled to concentrate our attention upon the society in which he lives. We cannot treat the individual as an isolated unit. He must be studied in his social setting.
>
> —Franz Boas, 1928

Nothing more can be added to the relationship of Walcott to Lura Rust, his wife of long ago at Trenton Falls. Their life was a closed book except for the one brief mention when Walcott applied for a license to marry Mary Morris Vaux. Her lingering death must certainly have affected his relations with Charlie and contributed to his willingness to send him to a warmer climate in a vain attempt to cure his tuberculosis.

Helena Stevens Walcott was a fine wife. If the thirty-eight-year-old widower was nuts over her, think how she must have felt about him, to have consented to a honeymoon in Newfoundland looking at rocks. The one love letter quoted earlier is sufficient. She had four fine children, plus one stillbirth (certainly not an extreme number for the times). "Mother had studied music and painting in Dresden as a girl. She was very talented, artistic and creative, but above all, she was sweet and kindly, with a delicious sense of humor."[1] Walcott was a very busy man, but he seems to have been far more than just a provider of physical items for the family. As to when Helena was killed, those who want deep psychological insight will have to settle for three words: he was devastated.

Being a practical man, Walcott, even though devastated, the month after Helena's death took out a large insurance policy as partial protection for his family. In the Walcott files are dozens of letters from the children to one parent or the other. They alone might make an interesting study.

When one has lived in a boardinghouse for years, meets and marries the girl of one's dreams, and one's first born is a boy, one can hardly ask for anything more. Charles Doolittle Walcott, Jr., was a joy. He seems to have been serious, smart, and inclined toward the sciences; he was "Charlie" to the family, never "Junior." Walcott sent him to Utah for an extended period in the hope of improving his health. He made a fine record at Yale University.

A clinically neutral, even tepid, term for relations among siblings is "interpersonal dynamics." The way Helen wrote from overseas when Charlie died was not impersonal.

> The silence and waiting that ten days seemed so friendly and lonely and how I wanted my mother; I know how near she is, but I wanted the physical side—you know and understand?
>
> As you say my memory of Charlie is of a strong, well, *man*; he was so big and splendid—and my "big brother." I think we were all a bit in awe of him as younger than he. I can't realize not having him to "boss" me. And he used to help me so: when I did foolish things, Charlie would make me feel sorry and I'd try harder for him
>
> But he will be happier by far now and I [am] so glad he and mother are together.[2]

To be a second child is a difficult position in a family, and to be the second son is even more difficult. Sidney Stevens Walcott had a fair amount of baggage to carry. His health was more delicate than that of Charlie, and he was in Utah away from the family for a longer time than Charlie was. It must have been lonely, as can be deduced from how he saved letters from his father, and his later gathering of family photographs and memorabilia. He was diligent but never wanted to be a scientist, let alone a geologist. Although he was proud of the fossil he had found that had been named *Sidneyia*, it did not stir him toward natural history. As a lad he donated some butterflies to the National Museum, but his only other recorded donations are war uniforms.

Helen made some comments about her younger brother during her mini–grand tour of Europe: "I'm sorry that Sidney has tho't fit to go to Cornell, but he has his own life to lead and if he's going to make good he can make it just as well at Cornell as he can at Yale. Charlie is disappointed naturally[;] it shows a lot of brotherly affection that he should be. And I'm glad that Sidney is out of Washington and if he rooms with Skippy I have no comments to make. I think just being with Skippy an education in itself—if only all you boys had a little more of his ambition and strength of will power!"[3] The enigmatic Skippy cannot be traced. As to Sidney's choice of Cornell University, reasonable surmise is that the Telluride House, established by L. L. Nunn after his Olmstead, Utah, school closed, may have been a factor.

Sidney graduated and went to work for Cousin Fred in a brokerage firm. Cousin Fred wrote Walcott shortly after America entered the first World War:

It makes a fellow feel lumpy to send another man's son into training where the chances are that he will be called on to go to France and assume the risks with the rest of the defenders of civilization. . . . I had a long, very serious talk with Sidney yesterday. He is a very unusual fellow, and I am exceedingly fond of him. I feel just about as I would if he were my own. The preliminary work will of course do him a tremendous amount of good, but going to France, even as an officer, is dangerous business. I left the matter entirely to him, not urging him in any way, but I am proud that he decided as he did.[4]

Walcott responded briefly. "Yours . . . enclosing copy of your letter in relation to Sidney, at hand. I fully realize the seriousness of the situation, but believing as I do, in defending civilization and the future of the race, I cannot ask the boys to remain at home. Stuart is doing good work here in connection with the Aviation Office, but he expects to get away for training this week."[5] Sidney survived the war, but Stuart did not, giving him more emotional baggage to carry.

Notwithstanding this load, Sidney married Helen-Louise; the couple had Walcott's only grandchild during his lifetime. An early attempt to start his own business failed, but he made a career first with Dunlop Rubber in its first American plant and later in other fields. He saved a chatty four-page letter from his father written in 1922: "Love to Helen-Louise, Evelyn, and my big boy Sidney."[6] Evelyn had two daughters. Years later, Sidney and Helen-Louise retired to Florida, and as an elderly man he wrote an article about his namesake fossil.

Any parent, especially a father with a brood of more than one sex, knows that girls are different from boys. Helen Breese Walcott was not a son, or a brother. "We had a happy childhood. Father was full of stories which he told on certain stated occasions. For instance every Sunday morning we had adventures of 'Hominy Dick,' started in some vague past to make us eat our hominy, which we didn't like."[7]

She reveled in the Canadian Rockies and loved her horse, "Breese." "I would pitch my lean-to (a black rubber blanket thrown over a log) as far from the family tents as Father would allow. . . . Dad made me carry his big Colt revolver. One day he tried to tell me that I might someday meet a crazy man, who, if he tried to molest me, I was to shoot him down without hesitation. I was mildly puzzled for we rarely met anyone except an occasional hunter or trapper and they were always friendly. . . . I was never afraid or timid in the wilds, never got lost although some days I would ride strange country all day long, turning up at supper time."[8] In 1913 she climbed Mount Resplendent in the Canadian Rockies.

At Holton Arms School, after the first grading period, Helen developed a reputation for being tardy returning from recess and for doing poorly in spelling and French. Some of the comments from the principal suggest this gawky girl was on the verge of being tossed out of the school. Physically, she soon outgrew this ugly-duckling stage. Helen became tall and beautiful. She cut quite a figure during her European tour and several times drove her forty-year-old chaperon to near collapse.

On her return, she was a fine hostess for her father until Mary married her beloved Daddie. Dragged back from California just before her foolish attempt to go to New Zealand, she was exiled to the Garfield family, friends of long standing. Her Aunt Helen Sanford died, leaving her property. "Until Helen settles down, so as to know what she really wishes to do, I do not think it would be wise to tie up money in a place that she may never even visit. Helen has not found herself yet, although she is trying to do so and thinks she will work hard this winter in Cleveland."[9]

Helen did find herself, so much so that she volunteered for the hell of working in a hospital for wounded French soldiers before America was committed to the conflict. Then, just as the war was ending, even though no one knew it, she volunteered for a second stint in Europe. Several years after the war, Walcott wrote Sidney, "I was glad to have Helen home to be with us and our friends. She is gaining strength & flesh and will soon be in fine condition. Just now she has no plans altho talking about several places to go for study etc."[10] Helen went to South America with cousin Fred and his family, and she made enough paintings for a show at the Corcoran Art Gallery. She met Cole Younger, went to Paris, returned, and married him. Helen would make a nice study of how a child can worry a parent and yet develop all the promise for which one could have hoped.

Sidney should have nearly the last word on Helen. "I motored to New York with my family over Labor Day to see Walcott Younger. Both he and his mother are getting along splendidly and I think he is a fine combination of his two names. However, it is still a little early to predict positively as to his future. He seems to be starting off in great shape."[11] Walcott Younger in turn sired a daughter, for whom Helen recorded a brief history of her early life; she stopped the account after a very brief summary of her wartime service, of which she chose not to record details.

If one cannot be first in a family, sometimes being the last is a good position. Benjamin Stuart was the kid brother to the older children. Walcott was past forty-five when he was born, and Stuart was—one is tempted to use the expression—the apple of his eye. "He also assisted in British Columbia in geological work during the summer of 1907; in 1908, when twelve years old, he was placed in charge of a pack train, with a packer, operating in what is now Glacier Park in Montana and southern British Columbia. On this trip one morning I heard faint rifle shots, and upon overtaking the pack train found Stuart shooting away with a 22 gauge rifle at a grizzly bear, which was some distance down the slope below the trail. On reminding him of his danger, he said he wanted to drive the bear away to prevent a stampede of the animals" (Walcott 1918b, 91).

Helen wrote him from Rome: "Well, Tootsie, you want a line eh? Miss Horsey is in despair because I write so many letters and I write to no one but you boys. Are you still trying for Annapolis? I still hope you can get in. At any rate Tootsie—you can be doing a lot of improvement to yourself this winter if you only tried. Do some good reading. Read lives and works of great men. Tackle stuff that is hard hard—both to read and understand—but get it and you'll never regret it."[12] Helen was not as flighty as first appearances suggested.

Walcott had appealed to President Taft to issue a presidential appointment for Stuart to the Naval Academy. As a citizen of Washington, D.C., he had no senator or congressman to ask for assistance; those in Washington had taxation without representation. "I lost my right to vote in the 27th Congressional District in New York State when absent on a long exploration expedition in Utah, Nevada and Arizona in connection with the Geological Survey. . . . In view of the fact that I have engaged in the public service for the past thirty years in positions to a certain extent comparable with that of an Army or Naval Officer, I wish to ask if it would not be possible for you to waive your general rule and designate B. Stuart Walcott for examination for a cadetship at the Annapolis Naval Academy."[13] That career path did not open to him, for reasons unknown.

Stuart seems to have been a likeable young man. His grades in preparatory school were only so-so, with an average of 76, but no demerits. Grades are not everything. "As I have said before, his sterling character has been thoroughly appreciated by everybody in the school. Our only regret is that he is not been with us longer."[14] He went off to Princeton and during January 1917, his last semester, he wrote his father. In that letter, most of which was quoted earlier, he also wrote: "I have been thinking of this work in Europe for over a year now and am still very strong for it. I don't know what the effect will be on myself, but if it will be of service to others, I think that it is something I ought to do" (Walcott 1918a, 86).

After a few flying lessons, Stuart went to France and joined the French army. As we have seen, he was taught to fly by a sergeant who did not think much of Americans, after which he was stationed near, but not in, the Lafayette Escadrille. He flew for a few months before being shot down. Stuart was given a posthumous commission in the American Army Air Service.

On April 1, 1919, Walcott wrote Teddy Roosevelt's namesake son:

One of my boys who enlisted in April, 1917, is now out of the Army and living in New York. The other boy, Stuart, who was in the Western High School in Washington with your brother Quentin, is resting on a hillside in the Ardennes, having been shot down under almost identical circumstances as Quentin, in an air battle with the Huns. He and the two men he brought down are buried at the same place, and a well built cross placed over Stuart's grave bearing his name and the date. When the Huns left they burned and destroyed all the nearby peasant cottages, thus illustrating in the one case the sentimental side and in the other the brute in their nature. My daughter Helen, who is still at Toul in charge of a Red Cross Hut, visited the Ardennes and found everything as reported to me by the German Casualty Bureau at Berlin.

The number of letters of condolence concerning Stuart which are preserved in the Smithsonian Archives is incredible. Walcott donated his son's papers and medals to the Museum. Balancing the scales between pride and loss is impossible.

In 1919 the American Legion founded in Washington the Stuart Walcott Post Number 10, for the first American aviator to be killed in combat. The post's name changed twice, and then in 1997 it was merged with another and ceased independent operation.

Mary Morris Vaux Walcott

Mary attended the Friend's Select School in Philadelphia from 1869 until her graduation in 1879 with a standard Quaker education. This was a private secondary school, with tuition fees, but the enrollment included non-Quakers. Care was taken to provide proper influences for children, with a lack of exaggeration and the avoidance of trivial things in life. Although the Quakers were quite progressive about women's rights, and Mary was interested in attending Bryn Mawr College, she was bound by the social limitations of the Victorian era, and received no further education.

—C. Smith, 1989

Mary Morris Vaux had met Helena on several occasions in the western Canadian mountains. There is at least a suggestion that they had struck up the start of a friendship, for Mary's domineering father essentially cut her off from female companionship. If it was difficult for Walcott to remarry after Helena's death, it was an act of incredible courage and love for this spinster, a month short of sixty, to break away from her father and her home to marry. Helen wrote her impression of the event:

Their wedding, June 30, 1914, was a true Quaker one. . . . We sat down and nothing happened. I wanted terribly to giggle or pinch Toots (Stuart) or to whistle, *anything*. Still nothing happened. Occasionally someone coughed . . . and finally a sort of peace crept in—so that when an old lady got up and started to speak, it seemed an intrusion. She sort of prayed or talked to God—hoping Dad and Mary would find the joy and happiness they both deserved. . . . Dad, Mary and I went to New York. They put me on the train for Bar Harbor, then they took a train for the west and a summer in their beloved mountains together.[15]

Mary Vaux Walcott was a good wife, and though the word is archaic, she was a true helpmate in all his activities. These ranged from planning formal dinner parties to pounding on rocks. Helen and Mary had difficulties for several years, but thereafter they were "real family." Certainly Mary gave Walcott a clearer understanding of art and artists, along with hand coloring his lantern slides and developing his photographic negatives.

Walcott's death was not Mary's only loss in 1927; for her brother George also died. He had been one of the commissioners of Indian affairs, and Mary was appointed in his stead. She served until 1933, when the commission was abolished. She visited many reservations; Alphonso Jones later commented that he had driven her back and forth across the country nine times. That was no mean feat in the 1920s and 1930s, and it must have been especially difficult for him, quite apart from the problems connected with driving. She collected enough Navaho paintings to warrant years later a publication by a Smithsonian curator.

She flew in a plane for the first time in 1929. Mary was an early member of the Association of Women Geographers, organized in 1925, and the second president of that organization, serving from 1933 until 1939. If there was a single driving force in the building of the Friend's Meeting House a few blocks from the Walcott house, it was Mary. During her seventy-fifth year, the si published a portfolio of fifteen drawings she had made of North American pitcher plants; this portfolio and two accompanying papers on these carnivorous plants sold for twenty-five dollars. Late in life she was a prolific painter of flowers. In an interview she indicated she was still using the box of watercolors she had used when she first learned to paint. "Every sketch in that collection [*North American Wild Flowers*] and the 500 pictures I have done since, came out of my little paint-box."[16] At seventy-five, she traveled to Japan, her first trip overseas. This resulted in a display of Japanese textile prints. "She's straight and tall and graceful. She has the skin you love to touch. Her face is unlined, her eyes bright, blue and merry. Her interests are legion and varied."[17] That was how she impressed a reporter at age seventy-eight.

Mary did her best to keep Walcott's memory alive. She had a nearly complete set of his reprints bound and donated it to the library. She commissioned a biography, which lingered on for years and was never published (rumor has it that she did not like the finished product). The Depression dried up all sources of money, but Mary was good to the SI when there was a dire need, such as for $225 to procure a Chilkut basket, and $175 for a Navaho necklace. When the mountain goat group was moved to a new display, Mary paid five hundred dollars for the background painting. She contributed $350—anonymously—to buy a reprint library from the widow of a museum anthropologist who had fallen on hard times. She also donated various old Quaker costumes, along with a large number of Japanese art objects, antique furniture, and family bric-a-brac.

In partial return, the SI maintained an office for Mary, which she seldom used. The last official contact was in 1939. A show of her paintings, or portraits, of wildflowers from national parks was exhibited in the foyer of the Museum. Thereafter her pictures went to the Department of Botany and later to the National Museum of American Art.

If Mary has any monument, it is the five volumes of *North American Wild Flowers*. The first volume received rave review. "Yet now and then a book appears— whose clear distinction of quality commands immediate attention and consideration."[18] "It is a monumental work, this Audubon of the floral world."[19] To compare her effort to Audubon's *Birds of North America* is quite a compliment, but it is not overblown. Quite apart from the artistry of the flower portraits, the reproduction is remarkable. Color printing is commonplace today, but these volumes pushed the printing industry to such heights that for years the methods used were known as the Smithsonian process.

By the time volume 5 came off the press in 1929, $750,000 had been poured into the operation. Mary lent the Smithsonian money to complete the job. During the Great Depression, she was owed $53,000, plus interest. Eventually, the money was repaid and additional sales resulted in a profit of $60,000. The Board of Regents approved the suggestion of Secretary Wetmore that a Mary Vaux Walcott fund be established in the department of botany; for years it has been used to support botanical illustration, and Mary would have approved. On the fiftieth anniversary of her death, the National Museum of National History mounted a modest display of her sketches and books. This led to a large temporary exhibit in 1994 at the National Museum of American Art.

Mary did not live in the shadow of Walcott's memory. In 1936, at a meeting of Royal Society of Canada in Toronto, she spoke on wildflowers and drew an audience of two thousand. For several summers during the 1930s Mary visited friends at their summer home in St. Andrews-by-the-Sea, New Brunswick. It was there that she passed away August 22, 1940: "Mrs. Walcott's death was of course a great grief to all of us. She had a serious heart attack while visiting her friends, Dr. and Mrs. H. P. Ross at St. Andrews, New Brunswick, about ten days before the end, from which she was apparently recovering, but she passed away in her sleep on the night of the 22nd of August."[20] The faithful chauffeur Alphonso Jones accompanied the body back to Washington; she is buried in Rock Creek Cemetery next to Walcott. Alphonso returned to the Castle and eventually was put in charge of the duplicating office, in the basement.

Mary made her will in 1938. She left a great deal of money to the SI, to be added to the Walcott fund "in honor of her beloved husband." Mary did not apply the same strictures regarding the accumulation of interest that he had, but she did stipulate that her stepdaughter Helen was to receive five hundred dollars annually. When Helen died in 1965, the funds supporting this bequest reverted to the Walcott fund.

Arthur Brown

> Servant of God, well done; well hast thou fought the better fight.
>
> —John Milton, 1667

History is a field where interpretations and viewpoints abound. To some, Thomas Jefferson was among the greatest man alive; to others, he was an oversexed slave owner. If there has been one overriding problem in America during the twentieth century, it is that of race. One of the important lessons of geology is that direction is important but rate is secondary. For the last four or five decades, many Americans seem to have been heading in the proper direction, even if the rate of change is slow. The term "racist" is easy to toss around, yet even by the standards of today, let alone by the standards of the time in which he lived, Walcott was never a racist. To give some flavor of the first half of the century, consider the last paragraph of a speech Walcott gave when he visited Utica, New York, in 1912, as a local boy who had made good, very good:

> In the humanities there needs to be a fearless, thorough, scientific study of the elements entering into the great race problems of the Americas. Until the fundamental tendencies of the different races now within these areas are intelligently understood not only by the few but by the many, a practical understanding and marking out of some the most threatening social problems is impossible. The uplift of the physical, mental, and moral nature will come by the increase and diffusion of knowledge that interests and stimulates sound reasoning on existing conditions and the racial limitations of the

elements entering into the peoples of the Americas. Ethnology, anthropology, preventive medicine, education—are some of the tools that must be used in the shaping of national, community and individual life of the future. In this great work the Smithsonian Institution will take such part as opportunity and circumstances permit.[21]

Arthur Brown was classified by the u.s. census as a mulatto. Walcott's only mention of Arthur Brown's color is, as we have seen, in a letter to a new teamster who was to meet him, and it was purely for purposes of identification when Arthur arrived in a small town in Montana. Helen described what little is known of his early life:

> We went by train. Father, mother, the four children, and Arthur Brown, one of the colored messengers from the U.S. Geological Survey, who went with us as nurse, cook, general guardian and friend. We called him "Doc." Son of a slave, he had been a waiter on a dining car, had worked at the White House under Cleveland, had known Presidents and many distinguished people. His fund of stories was unlimited and his judgement of human nature exceedingly keen. Working for father he sometimes sawed fossils out of the shale that embedded them, so he was a "scientist" and in the social strata of the high yellow colored folk in Washington, that rated very high indeed. His wife Mattie was a scold. We never saw much of her unless she came to complain about Arthur. Maybe he hadn't brought home his money, maybe it was some gal, but always scolding. I guess poor Mattie had a lot on her side but we never thought much of her. Doc was devoted to father during the many, many summers he went with us—rubbing his back, when he had lumbago, nursing him when he was sick, looking after us kids. . . . He really brought us up. We could never get away anything that wasn't for quality folks, and Doc knew the real from the imitation.[22]

Although Arthur was called the cook, in the field he was the camp manager and the one who made it possible for the geologists to work. For many years he was out in western Canada early to get the gear in order and set up camp, and frequently he closed the camp and stored the equipment. Walcott trusted him implicitly; otherwise, he would not have had Arthur escort some of the younger children from the West back to Washington. During the winters, apart from his Smithsonian duties, he tended the furnace and doubled as a butler, appropriately garbed for this position.

Both George Vaux and his younger brother Henry had vivid memories of their visits to Washington. In particular, regarding Arthur Brown, he recalled, "He was the family chauffeur, complete with cap an uniform, who would meet us at Union Station, deliver us to S Street, and show up 10 minutes later in the living room completely reattired in his buttler's gear to serve the hors d'oeuvres before dinner. He would reverse the change of clothes after serving breakfast and before driving Uncle Charlie to his office in the Castle. As a child it was a constant miracle that he could change clothes so fast!"[23]

Arthur Brown eventually owned a house in Washington. It is not until 1920 that his name can be found in the scanty SI payroll records. At that time he is recorded as a messenger, at sixty dollars per month, the same $720 a year he had been paid by the USGS in 1901. At that time, he also received a six-dollar increase, presumably for cost of living, and a twenty-dollar monthly bonus, the reason unspecified. For the last eight months of his tenure he worked only part time, and one guesses he may have been ill. "In July 1928, Arthur Brown disappeared from the Smithsonian payroll. When and where he died is not known" (Yochelson 1998a).

One may compare the relationship between Walcott and Arthur Brown to that between Robert E. Peary and Matthew Henson. Henson served Peary long and faithfully; without the knowledge and trust that Henson gained from the natives, Peary would have failed as an Arctic explorer. When Henson was persuaded to put his name on a book about polar exploration written by someone else, Peary fired him and apparently never saw or communicated with him again. In marked contrast, Arthur was the loyal family retainer in the finest, old-fashioned sense of the word; Walcott was head of the household, also in the finest sense of the word.

The chauffeur who came later, Alphonso Jones, was colored; he died before the term "African American" came into vogue. This fact does not appear in Walcott's diaries or any of his letters. Considering Walcott's place in society and the racial makeup of Washington, it is a reasonable surmise that one or more of the ladies who ran the house for the Walcotts was colored, yet it must remain a surmise, as the matter is not mentioned. Race simply seems never to have been a concern to Walcott. After Mary Walcott's death, Jones returned to the SI and ended his career as head of the duplicating shop.

In some quarters today, racism and sexism are treated as equal sins; certainly, they are both sins. Walcott employed Dr. Julia Gardiner as an assistant before she joined the U.S. Geological Survey. No further discussion is needed on this point. If someone wants to make an issue of the fact that, for example, Helena Walcott never voted for president, neither did any other woman of that time in the United States.

John E. Lodge

Dr. Charles D. Walcott, who was Secretary of the Smithsonian Institution when the Freer Gallery was placed under its jurisdiction, soon began to make plans for control of the gallery and the use of its funds for his own research which was not even remotely connected with Far or Near Eastern art. He even groaned to me about the sixteen thousand dollars Mr. Platt paid for a carpet in the auditorium: "Just think of the research I could do with that money."

—A. E. Meyer, 1970

Even before Walcott died, the effort to unseat Lodge by placing the Freer under the National Gallery faltered. Regent Delano, uncle of future president Franklin Delano Roosevelt wrote the acting secretary:

I have a very high opinion of Mr. Bishop, and I have discussed with Dr. Walcott the possibility of his succeeding to the curatorship. What I feel, and what I think my colleagues on the Executive Committee feel, however, is that we are laying ourselves open to criticism if we wait until the last minute, say, May, or June, before we determine the policy we should adopt. It may be urged by those who think we should retain Mr. Lodge, that we should not let him go without knowing what we were going to do. I say this, although I feel certain that Miss Guest and the staff are entirely competent to run things for a number of months just as they did when Mr. Lodge was away last summer and fall. We have got our hands full with a good may things just at present, and I think we can let this matter ride.[24]

That was all Abbot needed to start a retreat. "As the outcome of circumstances with which I am not entirely familiar, Mr. John E. Lodge resigned from the curatorship of the Freer Gallery of Art, to take effect in June. This, with the vacancy in the secretaryship makes, as you will see, an unsettled condition of affairs."[25] The next development was obvious.

"At a meeting of the Board of Regents held March 14, it was resolved, in view of the unsettled affairs incident to the vacancy existing in the office of Secretary, due to the lamented death of Dr. Walcott on February 9, that Mr. Lodge be invited to withdraw his resignation so that the subject of his continuance in charge of the Gallery after July 1, 1928, would be subject to later consideration. After an interview with Mr. Lodge, he has acceded to the suggestion of the Board, which I communicated to him, to withdraw his resignation."[26] Following this noble gesture, Lodge continued going to the Boston Museum of Fine Arts for months at a time until 1933.

Early in January 1970, an exceptionally long article, by Agnes Meyer, concerning Freer and the Freer Gallery appeared in the *Washington Post*. Two of the four persons chosen by Freer to add to his collection without any strings attached were Mr. and Mrs. Meyer. Among other interests, Mr. Meyer owned the newspaper, and after his death his widow ran it. The article gave a different account of events.

> He [Walcott] tried to invent reasons why his rock chipping in the Western
> mountains was related to the early migrations of Eskimos and Indians from
> Asia and therefore a legitimate cause for financial support under Mr. Freer's
> Will. To all these hints Mr. Lodge was impervious and according to Mr.
> Freer's expressed wishes, rightly so. Dr. Walcott then deliberately picked a
> bitter quarrel with Mr. Lodge, of which I knew nothing, with the result that
> Mr. Lodge was obliged to resign. Dr. Walcott got the acceptance of the Board
> for this resignation without explaining to them that he, himself, had brought
> it about.[27]

It ended by presenting a somewhat different account of Lodge's reinstatement,
with the Meyers seeing Chancellor Taft, and the latter reinstating Lodge.

This piece was quite a surprise to the Castle staff and to the American art
community. Shortly thereafter, the article, essentially unmodified, was issued as
a pamphlet by the Freer Gallery (Meyer 1970). Distribution of such charges
more than four decades after the event was a matter of concern. Secretary Ripley wanted the records examined to see if the charges were correct, and the project kept the archivist busy for some time. Probably the final word on this issue
is a letter former secretary Abbot wrote in response to a query from Secretary
Ripley: "As for Mr. Lodge, I enjoyed him, as others did, for his keen wit. He frequently invited me to lunch at the Freer Gallery, and I was always glad to accept.
I thought then and do still that Secretary Walcott was one of the ablest of the
Secretaries, and who accomplished much with [the] Administration and Congress for the benefit of the Smithsonian."[28]

The National Gallery of Art

> The cultivation of art, even in directions promising practical benefits to the
> people, has never received encouragement from the national Government
> except in the privilege of copyright and patent. The erection of public build-
> ings and monuments, the decoration of interiors, the portraiture of promi-
> nent officials, and the designing of medals, coins, currency and stamps have
> furnished essentially the only opportunities for the recognition of artistic
> talent, while on the other hand, the active part taken by the Government in
> developing the material resources of the country has caused its collections
> in natural history and ethnology to grow rapidly.
>
> —R. Rathbun, 1909

There is today a National Gallery of Art, but it is a different entity from that of
the name that appeared on a 1927 SI letterhead. When Harriet Lane Johnson,
niece of President James Buchanan, died in 1903, she willed her collection of art

to the National Gallery of Art, "when one should be established." The Board of Regents then reread the 1846 act establishing the SI and decided that there was a National Gallery and that they were it. A friendly lawsuit against the temporary custodian of the Lane collection clarified the fine print, and as of 1906, when the Johnson art collection came to the Smithsonian, a National Gallery more or less existed. It was actually titled the Department of Fine Arts of the National Museum and placed under the Department of Anthropology.

After the 1865 fire in the Castle, the remaining prints and engravings had gone to the Library of Congress, and many of larger art objects had been transferred to the Corcoran Gallery. In 1896, a small part of the Castle had been reclaimed for art, and objects began to come back. A nominal exhibit of the Lane bequest existed in the U.S. National Museum, but there was no room to swing even a small cat. About all Walcott could do was appoint an advisory committee of five. Francis D. Millet, a distinguished Washington artist, destined to drown on the RMS *Titanic*, was chairman. William Henry Holmes, the secretary, was the only Museum professional to be associated with the gallery.

To backtrack a little, according to some accounts the publicity in regard to the Lane bequest was one of the points that led Freer to offer his collection to the SI in 1904. That may be so, but it may also be coincidence. It took a year for the regents to act on Freer's offer, and then only because President Roosevelt waved a big stick at them. Even a major art collection was not of much concern to them, and it is a reasonable surmise that if Walcott had not acted promptly in visiting Freer, the collection might have been lost.

As mentioned, the completion of the Museum created a great deal of space in the other facilities and much new display area. Walcott tried, and failed, to have the Castle remodeled as an art gallery. He then tried, and failed, to have Congress appropriate funds for a new arts building. As a result, the National Gallery was set up in the north hall of the Museum. On March 17, 1910, the exhibit opened to the public; it was actually the first hall of the Natural History Building that tourists were to see. For the next half-century, art occupied one-third of the first floor and spilled over into other parts, such as a large amount of statuary around the rotunda.

Freer wanted his own building, bearing his own name, and he did not want it to be subservient to any mere national gallery. It took incredible effort to keep Freer pointed in the right direction and to cajole him into starting a building before he died rather than have his estate pay for the construction. With the building actually started, Walcott kept Freer informed and urged him to visit, which he never did because of failing health. What with the various other activities that Holmes and Walcott pursued, there was not a great deal of time to collect more paintings and art objects. In 1908, Congress thrust upon them the

Horatio Greenough statue of George Washington in a toga. They virtually hid it from sight in the Castle, but today George Washington sits in the National Museum of American History, pointing upward to the higher floors of the building.

In 1920, with the Freer Gallery building nominally finished and a curator nominally interested in installing the collections, Walcott was able to have the phantom National Gallery of Art officially designated as a separate entity. That was no mean feat and one with long-range consequences, for the gallery would be a separate budget item. However minuscule this amount was, it was far better than having the money subsumed within the United States National Museum budget.

Walcott arranged for donations of art throughout his career, but late in life he corralled a series of significant donations to the National Gallery. "Also in conjunction with making the gallery an independent bureau, Secretary Walcott decided to expand the five-member Advisory Board (which had served from 1906 to 1920) to a fifteen-member Board of Commissioners";[29] this was a distinguished outside committee, for support.

In 1923 he obtained a building site from Congress, but no money. Next the regents raised money for plans. He tried several times for an appropriation for a building, failing each time but each time getting closer to the goal. It was uphill work. "There is very little hope of getting help from the Government for this building as long as the economy program is a great issue. The price of a [naval] scout cruiser would put the National Gallery of Art on its feet for centuries to come."[30] Then Walcott died.

In 1921, a few years before Walcott passed away, Andrew Mellon moved from Pittsburgh to Washington to join the cabinet as secretary of the treasury (Finley 1973). To state that he was a collector of paintings is to understate the obvious, rather dramatically. Within a few years he moved onto center stage, except that he stayed behind the curtain. Rumors and hints of an anonymous private donor who might endow a national gallery circulated in Washington. Combined with the Depression, this ended any hope of a congressional appropriation to the SI for an art building. The concept of a national gallery became clearer in Mellon's mind, and after he returned to America following his stint as Ambassador to the Court of St. James, the concept gradually moved toward fact.

"Mr. Mellon determined, therefore, to give his collection to the federal government and to offer to erect a building to house it and other works of similar quality, which might be given to the people of the United States. It was a wise decision. The building without his collection, or the collection without the building, would not have produced a National Gallery such as Mr. Mellon wished to establish" (Finley 1973, 6). By the mid-1930s, Secretary Abbot and to some extent the Board of Regents were prepared to give Mellon whatever he desired. One of the conditions of Mellon's gift of paintings and building was that the organization not bear his name but be termed the "National Gallery of Art." In a twinkling of an eye, what had been National Gallery of Art administered by the SI became the "National Collection of Fine Arts."

As a minor footnote to this story, part of the land occupied by the huge building is a plot that Walcott had arranged for Congress to donate to the George Washington Memorial Association. Mrs. Dimock assisted the effort to have the site transferred for use by the National Gallery. The trail is thus tenuous, but Walcott had a finger even in this part of the Smithsonian enterprise. The present magnificent National Gallery of Art has the SI secretary as an ex officio members of its board of trustees, but otherwise there is little connection to the Castle.

The National Collection of Fine Arts limped along through the 1930s, 1940s, and 1950s, moving to the old Patent Office Building near the end. In the 1960s, the collection disappeared and metamorphosed into the National Portrait Gallery and the National Museum of American Art.

Art and its various permutations and perturbations throughout the SI might make a fascinating study, but others are pursuing these routes; besides, a good rule to follow is "work on one book at a time."

The Smithsonian Institution

"That is my father—true father—I am illegitimate—Hugh, the duke of Northumberland. While my mother, there"—he pointed to a the portrait of a sad woman wearing many jewels—"was a Hungerford and descended from many of our kings. So what did I inherit in character from either parent[?] Well, my fortune came from my mother and, thanks to that, I could be a scientist and create this institution. All to the good, of course, but hardly an advance worthy of Darwin's attention. From my father I inherited a passion for gambling. In my time—*life*time, that is, *LIFE*—I lost a fortune at Arago. But I also had curious wins, so much that I designed the foundation of the Smithsonian to resemble a game of chance, Parcheesi. Which it is. Which life is."

—Gore Vidal, 1998

At the close of the Walcott era, eight entities were listed on the SI letterhead. Only three still exist in name, and even they are greatly transformed. The Freer and the erstwhile National Gallery of Art have been mentioned. It may be appropriate to consider briefly the fate of the other six, for the sake of the record.

In his first annual report, Walcott briefly referred to the International Catalogue of Scientific Literature, as having begun in 1901. Each country catalogued its own literature and sent the information to London, where the catalogue was published and sold. "Under the congressional allotment of $5000 for the fiscal year [1907–8], as in previous years, 28,528 references to American scientific literature were completed and forwarded to the central bureau in London for publication" (Walcott 1909c, 35). As recounted, when CIW president Woodward would not support publication during the First World War, Walcott found money elsewhere to keep this enterprise alive a while longer. Even with that help, this cooperative effort was a casualty of that cataclysm. During Walcott's tenure the letterhead continued to carry the International Catalogue as one of its components, but the project was dead.

"The Smithsonian International Exchange Service was started in 1849, and its operations have grown in scale for the few hundred packages of publications then handled annually to the 714,877 packages that passed through the service in 1939, the last year before the beginning of World War II" (Dorsey 1946, 142). Joseph Henry built a network of corespondents and exchanges, both throughout the United States and overseas. In 1867 he and A. Spofford, the Librarian of Congress, got their heads together, and the SI became the official agent for distributing government documents overseas. Addressed packages of books and papers going to a particular county were piled into a crate; when the crate was full, it was nailed shut and mailed to a group in that country that had agreed to distribute the packages. For example, each crate of packages for England might be sent to the Royal Society of London, and a crate for Scotland would be sent to the Royal Society of Edinburgh. Specimens were also occasionally exchanged through this mechanism. The system survived though two world wars and was important in rebuilding ravished libraries in Europe. During the latter part of the twentieth century, it began to falter and was finally ended in 1991. For more than a century, however, the Exchange Service did a marvelous job for "the diffusion of knowledge."

The Bureau of Ethnology was created in 1879, along with the U.S. Geological Survey. After Powell took over the USGS in 1881, he ran both and to some extent intertwined them. Following his fall from grace, "American" was added to the title. When Powell died, William Henry Holmes took over. In one of the few exceptions to Parkinson's Law, as the number of Native Americans began to dwindle, the BAE also began to dwindle. When the Natural History Building was completed, making space in the Castle, the BAE moved from the Adams Building on F Street to the west side. The last two employees transferred to the Department of Anthropology in 1961, although the bureau was apparently carried on the books until 1965. The library was merged with that of the Department of Anthropology and was designated, appropriately, the John Wesley Powell Library. The SI archives moved from the fourth floor of the Castle to the space BAE had vacated. As its final move, the archives is now in the Arts and Industries Building, the old USNM building.

The United States National Museum is gone, though the acronym USNM is still used for natural history specimens. During Walcott's day, it consisted physically of the Museum—that is, the Natural History Building, on the north side of the Mall—the Arts and Industries Building east of the Castle, and the aircraft hangar, or "tin shed," south of the Castle. As essentially his last major act, the seventh secretary, Leonard Carmichael formally opened the National Museum of History and Technology, to the west of the Museum. In 1957, these two museums were placed under the United States National Museum. In the spring of 1969, each of the growing entities of the Smithsonian complex received separate status, and the USNM vanished. A banner on that newer building now identifies it as the National Museum of American History; if anyone wants an example of the problems in metaphorically, or literally, carving something in stone, this will do.

The tin shed behind the Castle, a relic of the First World War that persisted as long as the temporary buildings on the Mall, is a prime example of a Cinderella story. It gave rise to the National Air and Space Museum, dedicated in 1976. Since the day its doors first opened, this has been the most visited museum in the world.

Of all the federal establishments run on a shoestring under the supervision of the Smithsonian, the National Zoological Park may have been in the worst shape for funds. Half the funding came from the appropriation given to the SI, and half came from the budget for the District of Columbia. Although Congress is in Washington, the city itself has not been a high-priority item. Despite yeoman efforts, the zoo deteriorated, and it was not until the 1950s, when a young child was killed by a lion, that there was a general awareness of how terrible conditions had become. Changing views on the keeping of wild animals in captivity, the spread of ideas on ecology, and concern for rare and endangered species, combined with more money, have had a salutary effect. The zoo today is quite a different place from what it was when Walcott took young Charlie to see the animals.

In 1890 the third secretary, Langley, established the Astrophysical Laboratory in a small building on the south side of the Castle. It was here that a young C. G. Abbot worked. Later, fieldwork was also undertaken in various areas, first in the United States and then elsewhere in the world, one concern being accurate measurement of the solar constant. During Abbot's tenure as secretary an important adjunct of the work was done by a Division of Radiation and Organisms, which aimed at studying the effects of sunlight on plants and animals. The division was housed in the basement of the Castle and for many years was supported by funds from the Research Corporation. As with so many aspects of American life, the laboratory was disrupted by the Second World War. The faltering laboratory was physically moved to a joint operation with Harvard University, renamed and revitalized (Jones 1965); after administrative transfers, the biological work later vanished.

One measure of change, admittedly highly artificial, is that August 9, 1946, the journal *Science* published a Smithsonian Institution Centennial Issue (Wetmore 1946). The centennial date was August 10, but that was "close enough for government work." (The specifications for museum cases and drawers began with three pages discussing the kind of wood, its thickness, number of nails, and so forth, and ended with "or close enough for government work.") The sesquicentennial was marked in part by publication of a very large book (Conaway 1995). As a comparable measure of the relative importance of natural history within the SI, a sumptuous and lavishly illustrated book, jammed with impressive color photographs, even by coffee-table standards (Kopper 1982), was followed three years later by a paperback with black-and-white illustrations (Yochelson 1985).

The eponym above is taken from a novel; accuracy is not to be expected in the midst of allegory. After all, the ghost of James Smithson can say and do whatever he wants. Still, for those interested, Arago is not a place or a game but the name of French mathematician who wrote of Smithson's gambling. The ghost may be right in that the SI is a game of chance. It has also been referred to as the "octopus on the Mall" (Hellman 1967). If one's aim is to generate heat rather than shed light, one may inquire around various parts of the SI and ask for definitions of the terms "knowledge" and "culture." Then ask if the SI has moved from concentration on one to concentration on the other. The answers obtained might be illuminating, though they would be in the sphere of current events, not history.

Secretaries Abbot and Wetmore

These are excited times. Extraordinary events occur in an area of massive popularity: Social upheavals, geopolitical disasters, scientific spectaculars, and behavioral revolutions proceed concurrently. Here, and elsewhere, the middle-aged are out of touch with the young. From the turn of the century, the United States of America had sought logically enough and by effective means, to prolong the *status quo*. The successes of conservatism have reaped unprecedented power and prosperity, but, inevitably and inexorably, the elements of dissent have propagated, until, suddenly, they threaten to upset everything. American institutions are enveloped by the problem of change. This is pronouncedly true of government; it is also true of academic institutions, and of museums.

—S. D. Ripley, 1970

Slightly less than a year after Walcott's death, Abbot moved up to Secretary. He had one immediate success, now long forgotten. "The Smithsonian Scientific Series of 12 volumes was prepared by Smithsonian curators under the editorship of the Secretary, who himself wrote two of the volumes. The series gives multitudes of scientific facts and tells in an interesting and informative way of the advance of the many branches of science cultivated by the Institution. Beautifully printed, illustrated and bound by the New York publishers, over 70,000 of these sets were sold by subscription up to 1953, yielding $518,000 in royalties to the Smithsonian. Over 3,000 sets were bought by schools for general scientific reading" (Abbot 1958, 129–30).

Walcott was a difficult act to follow, and the times were all against Abbot, with the near-total collapse of the economic system. The SI was given the crumb of a few Works Progress Administration assistants, but no public buildings were erected for the organization. Abbot did manage to have the flag tower improved to the extent that an elevator, literally the size of a phone booth, went through each floor. Each floor was then used as an office. When the elevator broke, one had to open a hatch in each floor and go down a wall ladder to leave.

There was no money for anything, which accentuated a somewhat conservative approach. Automobiles gradually became more common, and parking at the Museum became a problem. The staff offered to have the driveway between the east and west sides of the building—well below the sidewalk level and therefore moatlike—widened at their expense to allow parking. This was refused for fear it would harm the appearance of the building. Today there are two huge parking lots at this building, but there is just as much trouble finding a space. One measure of growth is that the number of SI vehicles on the Museum lot today is significantly greater than the number belonging to paid staff of the U.S. National Museum when the twentieth century began.

Secretary Abbot retired at the end of the fiscal year in 1944 and moved to an office high in the flag tower. He concentrated on the issue of a connection between sunspots and climate. Along the way he took out a patent, being at the time the oldest person to do so in the history of the Patent Office. When Abbot was in his middle nineties, the SI staff finally came up with a story about the need to repair the tower, as an excuse to move him out of it; if the elevator broke, getting him to the ground would be a major problem. A fine party was held for his hundredth birthday. In a lull between the speeches, Abbot suddenly inquired as to when "you birds" would finish the work so that he could get back to his office.

Secretary Wetmore was appointed on January 12, 1945. "During the early part of Dr. Wetmore's administration the staff of the Institution was much occupied, as it had been for a year or two previously, in matters pertaining to the wars" (Abbot 1958, 136). It was characteristic of Secretary Abbot to understate. A history needs to be assembled of the efforts of the SI staff during both world wars. The Museum was not closed in 1941, as it had been during the First World War. The staff had been to many exotic locales, and its members prepared survival manuals and ethnographic studies. One story is that the navy was concerned that the noise of snapping shrimp would complicate sonar detection. This could not be resolved, but the problem was turned around: several yeomen spent months recording shrimp, and American submarines used the noise to cover their approaches to Japanese shipping. Under certain circumstances even the most esoteric of information has value.

"Throughout the seven years of Dr. Wetmore's tenure reorganization of offices and exhibits went on. This was accompanied by needed repairs of the buildings. Paucity of funds and overcrowding of the buildings were matters of great anxiety. Some increase in appropriations was indeed granted the Institution to partially compensate for the depreciation of the dollar, but no building program went forward beyond discussion" (Abbot 1958, 136). Once more Secretary Abbot understated, for the problems faced in rebuilding after the close of the Second World War were formidable. Wetmore retired in December 1952. His successor and seventh secretary, Leonard Carmichael, was the first in that office who did not have close SI connections. If Walcott's death did not mark the end of era, Wetmore's retirement certainly did.

Alexander Wetmore moved back the Division of Birds, continuing to work and helping move the collections to the new east wing of the Museum. He did not carry on quite as long as Abbot, but in his nineties he was still in his office studying his beloved birds. "What if" is a game that never ends, but had Walcott lived six months longer, and had he designated Wetmore as his successor, perhaps the history of the institution during the late 1920s and 1930s might have been quite different.

Orville Wright

This tendency to claim for Langley what was not his was destined to show itself in a more pernicious form in the later acts of Dr. Walcott.

—F. C. Kelly, 1943

The best place to continue the action of the Wright-Walcott argument is at the point of no action. In December 1926, an airplane magazine published in Dayton, Ohio, styled the *Air City Journal*, republished Walcott's American Philosophical Society article on Langley, adding pictures of Langley's models in flight and a couple of pictures of Wright planes. The editor prefaced it with a column of his own remarks. "It came to light with the first announcements of this plan to ship the famous plane abroad that Mr. Wright had in his usual taciturn manner suffered what he felt was a keen injustice at the hands of those who have to do with the affairs of our own National Museum in Washington. . . . Public dissension influenced by Mr. Wright's statements and the willing attitude of Charles D. Walcott, present secretary of the Smithsonian Institute [*sic*] in rectifying the situation to give just consideration to both Langley and the Wrights, appears to have altered the decision of Mr. Wright to send his priceless machine to the foreign museum" ("Langley and Modern Aviation" 1926, 9). Wrong!

The day before Walcott died, Abbot wrote a regent in the House of Representatives for advice concerning a matter connected with the Freer Library and ended with different thought: "Union Calender No. 746, S. 4876, provides for a monument to be erected at Kitty Hawk, N.C. in commemoration of the 'first successful attempt in all history at power-driven airplane flight.' You are aware that the large Langley models flew approximately a mile about seven years previously, so that I should hope the inscription of the monument, if it comes to realization, would be altered to be 'the first successful human flight in all history with power-driven airplane.'"[31]

One part of the Air Commerce Act of 1926 addressed the licensing of pilots. "In an understandable gesture McCracken offered Pilot's License No. 1 to Orville Wright. Wright declined the offer. He no longer flew, he told McCracken; besides, he did not think that he needed a Federal pilot's license to show that he had been the first man to fly" (Komons 1977, 96).

On February 11, 1927, at a special NACA meeting on the occasion of Walcott's death, Joseph Ames recounted Walcott's efforts. A resolution was passed (Ames 1927), and an engrossed copy was specially prepared for the family, signed by ten of the eleven members. Orville Wright did not sign. Employees at the Langley facility contributed money for flowers at Walcott's funeral. There was an excess of funds, and a suggestion was made that with it a plaque be purchased. It was also suggested that one of the buildings be designated the Walcott Laboratory. Orville scotched that action.

Thirteen months after Walcott's death, Abbot issued a statement. He had written Wright a month before. He offered to change the label, and indeed he did. It read "Langley Aerodrome—The Original Langley Flying Machine of 1903, Restored."[32] He published an account that backpedaled to some extent on the

Langley aerodrome and included the Ames-Taylor report. When interviewed, Abbot bristled at the notion that he should admit that the si had been involved in wrongdoing.

Abbot's actions were not enough; the Wright plane went off to England. A minor point is that the Wright plane did not go to London while Walcott was alive; indeed, it was not sent immediately after Walcott died. Herewith arises a piece of wild speculation. After Charles Lindbergh flew the Atlantic, his plane, *The Spirit of St. Louis*, came to Washington, through quick action on the part of Paul Garber. Lindbergh was a national hero, and Wright was once more ignored. Just possibly, had Lindbergh not succeeded and garnered so much publicity, Wright might have softened. Whatever the reason, adverse publicity swirled around the Smithsonian for years because of the Wright plane leaving the country.

As the fortieth anniversary of the Wright flight approached, Helen wrote to her Uncle Fred, concerned that adverse remarks about her father might resume. Abbot kept trying to reconcile matters, with no result:

> At last in 1942 I wrote to Dr. Wright asking him to specify in writing what he desired. He sent me a long list of differences which he stated existed between the plane flown by Curtiss and the plane attempted to be flown for Langley in 1903. I had no means of checking these. Realizing that the fortieth anniversary of the Kitty Hawk flight by the Wrights was approaching, and also that Dr. Wright was of such an age that his death might soon irreparably prejudice the Smithsonian Institution, I prepared an article yielding to everything he asked without making any reservations toward what I thought was a fairer version. This article I sent to Dr. Wright in manuscript stating that I would publish it with such changes as he wished, but only if he would prefix to it a statement of his own that he was satisfied. This article was published in the Smithsonian Annual Report of 1942. At our next meeting of the National Advisory Committee for Aeronautics Dr. Wright pressed across the room to me as I entered, shook me warmly by the hand, said I had done all that could be asked, and that now he would be as friendly toward the Smithsonian as he had always been in Langley's administration. (Abbot 1958, 132)

Wright's three-page reply has some interesting comments. "That the last sentence [page 4] be emended to read: 'I will now, speaking for the Smithsonian Institutions, make the following statement in an attempt to correct as far as now possible acts and assertions of former Smithsonian officials that *may have been misleading* or are held to be detrimental to the Wrights."[33]

Notwithstanding Abbot's account of Wright's pleasure, the resolution was not so simple. Wright kept his own council, and no one knew his plans. It was not until after his death in 1948 that a letter was opened indicating that contrary to the stipulations in his will, the Wright plane was to be returned to the United States. When shipping conditions settled down after the disruption of the Second World War, it was returned to the United States. The Wright heirs sold it to the SI for one dollar to resolve any past or future problems of ownership, and it was hung in the Arts and Industries Building, with full ceremony and honors.

Late in life, Secretary Emeritus Wetmore recounted that on a steamship trip from Washington to Langley Field he had sat on deck with Orville Wright and persuaded him to resolve the feud. He and many others referred to the 1942 paper as "the laundry list." At this date it hardly matters who receives the credit. The original Wright plane now hangs in the National Air and Space Museum in the most prominent place; perhaps Mr. Wright would be satisfied with the accompanying label, which is simple and straightforward in crediting the Wright brothers.

The Wright controversy may have been given too much space here, but it was a defining episode for the institution. This is the only possible blot one can find on the record of Walcott's service to his country. If this was indeed a blot—an arguable point to this day—it is not a large one in the grander scheme of things.

The National Advisory Committee for Aeronautics

Langley's ghost continued to hover in the Smithsonian after his death in 1906. The new secretary of [sic] C. D. Walcott, who had guided the Geological Survey as Powell's chosen successor. By fostering the programs that became the Bureau of Reclamation and the Bureau of Mines, he made a place for himself as one of the leading architects of government science in the era of Theodore Roosevelt. The secretary and Alexander Graham Bell, a member of the board of regents, kept up the Smithsonian's interest in aeronautics largely out of respect for Langley.

—A. H. Dupree, 1957

Of the various efforts Walcott fostered, the one that seems most alien to his other activities is travel by air. The only indication of mechanical interest in his life is a patent on a railway spike and a failed local company formed to produce and market it.

There is no indication whatsoever in his daily diary of his ever having been in an airplane. As mentioned, a 1911 newspaper reported on biplane flights from the Polo grounds in Washington. "There was [sic] two pretty girls, two of the most distinguished scientists in the world, one the Secretary of the Smithsonian

Institution and the other a member of the Nobel Institute of Sweden, one man who weighed 280 pounds and several common, ordinary passengers." Under a picture is the comment, "Charles D. Walcott, Secretary of the Smithsonian, says there is nothing like it."[34] A photograph was taken of Walcott and Curtiss in the flying boat *America* when he was at Hammondsport for the tests by Curtiss of the Langley aerodrome. This may only have been taxiing around the lake; one would think that if he had been in the air over the Finger Lakes, he would have written some comment.

Walcott gave advice to the secretary of the brand-new NACA. "I have found it a very effective way to send out the minutes to the members of a committee present at any one meeting, with a request that if they have any suggestions or corrections to make, to return them promptly. In this way the reading of the minutes at the next meeting is dispensed with. A copy should then be sent to each member of the committee who was not present at the meeting, in order that they be kept posted as to what is going on."[35]

As early as 1922, Walcott was writing to the NACA Executive Board suggesting it was time for a new chairman. From the field, he sent advice to John Victory in Washington: "The thing to do with the Congressional Committee is to give them the actual facts and no expressions of opinions on what we know nothing about. Leave that to the legal minds. Constructive work is what is needed, and sacrifice of independent opinion for the general good."[36]

Ames, who succeeded Walcott as the NACA's chairman, hit exactly the right note at the memorial meeting. He called attention to Walcott's vision in setting up the NACA and the three conferences Walcott organized under its auspices before the First World War. "The conferences are mentioned particularly to show Dr. Walcott's grasp of the situation, the use he made of the National Advisory Committee for aeronautics, and his power to secure results. . . . [R]eference should be made to the fact that it was he who first clearly formulated a policy for the control and encouragement of commercial aviation. This was in 1919; and his work bore full fruit in the Air Commerce Act of 1926" (Ames 1928, 13). "I doubt if Dr. Walcott knew the meaning of such words as lift and drag, thrust and torque, pressure distribution, scale-effect, etc.[,] words occurring in the every day language of those engaged in aeronautical research. Yet Doctor Walcott organized successfully a committee whose fundamental purpose is the study of aeronautic problems . . . ; his own standards of scientific work were so high that all those working for the Committee were impressed from the beginning with the need of making their researches reach the same standards" (Ames 1928, 11).

Like other wars, the Second World War gave a great impetus to technology. Both the jet engine and the rocket motor changed concepts of space and time. "In 1915 [the NACA] had consisted of twelve committeemen and a clerk in search of a place to hold meetings. In 1957, a staff of almost eight thousand occupied three major laboratories and as many subsidiary facilities valued at $300 million" (Roland 1985, 287). The end came abruptly in 1958, when the NACA was given three months to disband. When it vanished, John Victory, employee number one, was the last person to leave. Whether he still retained the picture of Walcott, larger than that of other members of the committee unknown, but it is known that his son was named Charles Walcott Victory. The structure of the NACA was leveled, and the National Aeronautics and Space Administration grew on the foundation.

National Academy of Sciences

By this time [the 1860s], Washington had become a major scientific center. The red gothic towers of the Smithsonian Institution jutted skyward less then a mile from the White House. Henry administered the Smithsonian with the primary object of "stimulating the talent of our country to original research—in which it has been lamentably deficient—to pour material on the apex of the pyramid of science, and thus to enlarge its base." There was also the National Academy of Sciences, a private organization with a Federal charter, created in the middle of the Civil War to provide expert advice to the government.

—D. J. Kevlas, 1977

Of the various efforts Mary made to keep her husband's memory alive, the most successful involved the National Academy of Sciences. At the annual meeting in April 1928, President Albert A. Michaelson announced a gift of five thousand dollars from Mary to establish a Charles Doolittle Walcott Fund. After his work on stromatolites, Walcott had been stymied in his attempts to pursue ancient life. This fund was to "encourage and reward" achievements in knowledge of Precambrian—pardon, at the time it was pre-Cambrian—life and history.

Several interesting restrictions and provisions were attached. The award was to be worldwide in character and was limited to persons between ages twenty-one and forty-eight. It was to be made "without respect to nation, race, sex, or academic degree." The first three speak to Walcott's liberalism, and the last may reflect his lack of formal training.

The award was to be given every five years, to consist of an honorarium and a medal of "bronze or some inexpensive medal." Walcott had received gold and palladium medals, which were lovely to look at but obviously counterproductive to financing fieldwork; the money was better spent on larger honoraria to investigators. To ensure that this award was truly international, representatives of the Institut de France, the Royal Society of London, and the secretary of the

Smithsonian Institution ex officio, were to be on the committee, along with two members distinguished in Paleozoic paleontology. The two members first appointed by Michaelson were E. O. Ulrich and David White; earlier White had also been selected to write Walcott's biographical memoir for the Academy. A stroke prevented that work; many years later, thanks to Dr. Wetmore, the present author wrote the NAS languishing biographical memoir (Yochelson 1967).

There were other provisions in the deed of gift that strongly suggest Walcott's hand in crafting it; he must have prepared the details and given them to Mary. The design of the medal was to be approved by Mary, the amount of money for overhead was limited, the method of rotation of the committee was indicated, and the requirement that committee members were to serve without compensation was spelled out. As a further example of attention to detail, an escape clause was inserted allowing the council to change the provisions. The committee did indeed make changes.

"Subsequently, the terms of the Walcott bequest were modified to remove the age requirement . . . and broadened to include Cambrian paleontology" (Yochelson 1979, 287). The committee makeup and other details were also changed. Most of the earlier awards were made in the name of Cambrian studies, for little attention was being paid to the Precambrian. Allowing for that change, two decades ago a judgment was rendered: "One expects that he would have been satisfied with the selections made in his name" (Yochelson 1979, 287). Several of the more recent awards have been for investigations in the Precambrian, and it is a safe assumption that Walcott would have been pleased. The Walcott Medal exists as a premium prize in a specialized part of paleontology.

The Carnegie Institution of Washington

Walcott explained that most of the younger American scientists, thirty-five to fifty years old, were thoroughgoing collectivists, while their elders still remained loyal to the individualistic traditions of an earlier day. "In my opinion," he advised the philanthropist [Carnegie], "we might as well try to make a great research institution of the c.i. by pure individualism, as to expect success in great industrial enterprises by the individualism of 1850 to 1870." Walcott's analysis fitted nicely with Carnegie's own assessment of the social process.

—H. S. Miller, 1970

If an illustration of what this might accomplish is demanded, consider the record of the Carnegie Institution. Founded twenty years ago, it set up eight principal projects, namely: the Mount Wilson Solar Observatory; the Department of Meridian Astrometry; the Department of Terrestrial Magnetism; the Geophysical Laboratory; the Laboratory of Experimental Evolution; the Marine Biological Laboratory at Tortugas; the Desert Botanical Laboratory at Tucson; the Nutrition Laboratory at Boston. In each case the director was a man with a passionate zeal for his job, and a sound program for its accomplishment. Subordinates hardly less zealous and competent were employed. The results have been so rich that if the accomplishments and the very remembrance of the work of these eight Carnegie Institution departments were now to be blotted out, our total knowledge of astronomy would be cut in half, the magnetic charts of the sea would be unfit for navigation, the United States Army and Navy would wanted unobtainable essentials in the World War, and sociology, biology, botany, and the science of nutrition would have lacked many of their most valuable data. Besides this, there has been in these twenty years a rich flow of publications too costly for the private publisher to undertake, and many great pieces of research outside the institution have been subsidized. Such is the record of a well-endowed research institution. (Abbot 1924, 143)

In some ways this statement describes the high-water mark of the Carnegie Institution of Washington in terms of diversity of interests. The Carnegie did fairly well under John C. Merriam, who was succeeded by Vannevar Bush. During the Second World War, Bush headed the Office of Scientific Development and Research and played a major role in the setting up of the National Science Foundation. The grant system of that organization changed the face of science in America.

Activities of the CIW are now limited to a few fields. The scientists under its roof, or roofs, are among the best and show what a handful of well-supported, bright people can do. Even though much of the support still comes from Andrew Carnegie's endowment, the CIW has moved from being a grant-giving organization to a grant-seeking one. The CIW deserves to have its great successes and occasional failures documented.

The Research Corporation

Many of these fundamental inventions were not fully developed until the end of the 19th century, but then their growth was so rapid and their diffusion so intense that they have become essential parts of the 20th century environment.

—G. Sarton, 1956

The Research Corporation has had a long and complex history. It nearly foundered at the start, in part because though the concept of Cottrell was brilliant, its application to individual industrial needs was not straightforward. The hostilities in Europe increased factory production and dramatically raised the need for the electrostatic precipitator. Rather than license the technique, the RC developed its own engineers and manufactured the devices. As an aside, Cottrell temporarily headed the Bureau of Mines and then for a year was chairman of an NRC division. He settled in Washington and spent a decade in and around the Castle.

Only two RC grants are recorded as having been made during Walcott's lifetime. In 1920, five thousand went to Harvard University for cryogenics, and in 1923 the Smithsonian was given five thousand dollars, which went to Robert Goddard. Inasmuch as Goddard probably had about $200,000 total support during his lifetime, this was a significant grant.

Starting in the late 1920s, the number of grants increased. By the 1930s the RC was disbursing about fifty thousand dollars annually. This was a time when most sources of funding for science were in collapse. In 1935, the RC entered an agreement with the Massachusetts Institute of Technology to evaluate and promote patents; this same year, the patent on synthetic vitamins was donated. Others in science have followed Cottrell's lead and donated patents to the RC. Because of changes in the federal tax laws after the Second World War, the RC gave up manufacturing. As a result of the sale of these assets, RC was able to increase its fund granting to three million dollars. In 1983, the RC headquarters moved from New York to Arizona. Grant totals have increased, and, more significantly, about twenty-five investigators who were supported early in their careers by RC have gone on to be awarded Nobel Prizes.

Between 1931 and 1940, E. O. Lawrence, a physicist, at the University of California, Berkeley, received seventy-five thousand dollars in connection with development of a gadget called the cyclotron. Even those who know just a smattering of the development of atomic physics and atomic energy need no explanation. Few people would guess that an unknown great-grandfather of the nuclear-space age was interested in ancient fossils.

The Middle Cambrian Burgess Shale

To the best of my knowledge this is the fourth book to be published that considers as its main theme the Burgess Shale and its half-billion-old fauna. Is not the market place becoming a little crowded? When we consider the works already available I hope that I may persuade you. At least by the time you have finished reading this book, that not only are there new viewpoints, but by no means the last word has been written.

—S. Conway Morris, 1998

The publication of the *Guinness Book of Records* has led to many bizarre records for the world's largest, smallest, fastest, slowest, busiest, and so forth. The history of science is replete with arguments on the issue of priority, who did what first. Ancillary to this are considerations of what was most important. For example, in a television program one vertebrate paleontologist pronounced *Archaeopteryx*, the world's oldest bird to date, as the most important single fossil ever discovered. Other such provocative statements occur occasionally. "The Burgess Shale biota is the single most important fossil discovery ever made, in my judgement as a professional paleontologist and as an historian of the subject" (Yochelson 1996, 470). This may be waving a red flag at the pet areas of other paleontologists. Still, it should encourage some discussion to support or refute the statement, and that is always helpful. After all, a snail never moves forward until it sticks its neck out. To strengthen the argument as to the importance of this discovery, in 1981 the Burgess Shale quarry was designated as a UNESCO World Heritage Site. At that time this was the fifth site designated in Canada; in 1981 UNESCO had designated only eighty-five sites worldwide.

There is no need to repeat here the story of the collecting and original description of the fossils (Yochelson 1996). The many detailed scientific papers from the 1960s onward restudying this fauna are well known and easy to locate. A small handful of papers during the early 1930s touched on a few of these fossil organisms, but for nearly forty years the Burgess Shale simply sat in museum drawers. This time gap is of interest. A number of good reasons may be proposed for it: lack of funds during the Depression, the Second World War, and the growth of oil exploration, with its interest in younger rocks. An equally valid reason may be a tacit assumption by the few palaeontologists concerned with the Cambrian that Walcott had done an excellent job of description and that little more basic research was required.

What is also of interest is the discovery of the Burgess Shale in the context of Walcott's life and career. It is likely an exaggeration to suggest that collecting may have saved his sanity after the death of Helena in 1911 and the subsequent death of Charlie. It is not an exaggeration to suggest that the hard physical work and the intellectual stimulation of dramatic discovery were important in helping him put grief behind him and continue as a productive human being.

In a still larger sense, one can see in Walcott's publications a systematic program of research, even if it was not outlined in any document. He studied first, and relatively briefly, the Precambrian rocks of the southern Rocky Mountains of Canada. After his work near the turn of the century and his studies of algal masses, the Precambrian proved intractable, and there was little likelihood of much new developing from the Canadian outcrops. Then he studied the Lower

Cambrian rocks and their fossils. Next he moved the Middle Cambrian, then Upper Cambrian, the Lower Ordovician, and then he died.

Two main distractions occurred in pursuit of this program. In 1912 and 1913, he diverted his attention to the Mount Robson area. To be the first to survey the geology of the largest mountain in the Canadian Rockies is a challenge and an honor. It was reasonable to leave what he had been developing of the geologic history of the rocks to the south and plunge into rocks of the same general age, but far removed. He made some mistakes, as did Burling, who came to the area a few years later. "It is ironic that both Walcott and Burling made errors stemming from similar faults in logic when arguing their case for the position of the Lower-Middle Cambrian boundary" (Fritz and Mountjoy 1975, 120). Some of the other errors in stratigraphy were corrected by them in these later works.

The second main distraction was publication, group by group, of the Burgess Shale fossils. In the mid-1920s Walcott expressed some interest in returning to the fauna, but his fieldwork continued up the geologic column. There was not enough time to work up this new field data and to study in detail those remarkable fossils. Discovery and description of the Burgess Shale biota would be enough to make a paleontologist world famous. Walcott knew just how good the material was, but if any proof is needed that he was greatly concerned with the broader picture of biostratigraphy and regional relations, it is the work that he published after the quarried fossils had been described.

It may be repetition to indicate why the Burgess Shale is so important, but the notions are worth repeating. Nothing like it had been found before, and very few places like it have been found since. Walcott's descriptions and illustrations document several basic points, though he never dwelled on them. First, there was a great diversity of life rather far back in the paleontological record, as it was known at that time. Second, many soft-bodied organisms that had essentially no fossil record were present in the Cambrian. Third, this diverse Cambrian life was morphologically at least as complex as that in the modern seas.

There has been some mild carping that Walcott "stole" these incredible fossiles from Canada. Piffle. From 1911 on he was formally associated with the Geological Survey of Canada (Zazlow 1975) and the GSC did not have the resources, financial or otherwise, to collect, study, and publish this discovery. At the same time, Walcott would have approved of the later efforts of the GSC in reopening the quarry and the continuing efforts of Desmond Collins, Royal Ontario Museum, to increase this treasure trove of complex Cambrian life.

Wonderful Life

Positive, *adj.*, Mistaken at the top of one's voice.

—Ambrose Bierce, 1911

After being of interest to only a handful of scientists, the Burgess Shale and, to a lesser extent, Walcott were brought to general attention by a prolific, prize-winning author (Gould 1989). The prime focus of his book was to recount recent work redescribing the fossil animals. From that it derived a concept of evolution. This concept may be right, wrong, or somewhere in between, but it has been challenged (Conway Morris 1998a). In the book, Walcott was set up as a kind of straw man to be knocked down, despite early protestations of great respect for his work.

It is unlikely that comments on this book made here will have any effect. When gently taken to task by the distinguished Canadian paleontologist T. H. Clark, who had known Walcott, Gould remarked that he had enjoyed meeting the gentleman and his lecture on the Burgess Shale fossils and made a few kindly remarks overall (Gould 1990). Notwithstanding that, five years after his original remarks about Walcott's investigations, his opinion was unchanged. "The Burgess Shale fossils lay fallow in drawers in Washington, D.C., still underpinned only by Walcott's false reading of their taxonomic and anatomical variety" (Gould 1994, 4). The only reason for quixotic tilting at this particular windmill was stated by another in another context: "My case probably could have been argued more precisely and persuasively than it was, but the brunt of it was that words do have power and that we should use them with care and a sense of how others will interpret them."[37]

"All the worst of Walcott's venom poured forth, as the archives reveal, in his confidential spearheading of an extraordinary campaign against the eminent anthropologist Franz Boas in 1920. Boas, German by birth, Jewish by origin, left-leaning in politics, and pro-German in sympathy, inspired wrath from each and every one of Walcott's prejudices" (Gould 1989, 255). That is a lot of prejudices in only one sentence, and each can only have a short rejoinder.

Rudolph Ruedemann was German by birth. Charles Schuchert was born in Cincinnati, but at a time when parts of the city were more German than Germany. Presumably, Walcott was not prejudiced against all Germans. The hidden charge of anti-Semitism is a serious one but easy to refute. The messages of condolence on Walcott's death are in alphabetical order; there is a telegram at the top of the heap: "I want to express to you and all of your associates my old friends at the Institution my sympathy with them and with the Institution in the great loss it has suffered in the death of Secretary Walcott. As long as I can remember he has been a friend of the Institution even before he had official connection with it. His administration has been glorious and he deservedly rack with the great men who were his predecessors."[38] This was from Cyrus Adler, former assistant secretary and a great Jewish scholar. It is hardly what one might write at the death of an even a closet anti-Semite. Hating one individual does not make for an anti-Semite.

"Left-leaning" is harder to understand. If all Democrats are left-leaning radicals and all Republicans are right-leaning reactionaries, the Republican Walcott was prejudiced in the wrong direction. The problem with that simple analysis is that Walcott did not think much of Taft's administration and even less of that of Coolidge, yet he was a key player in the Teddy Roosevelt administration. "Pro-German in sympathy" is even harder to come to grips with, since the word "jingoistic" was also used earlier by Gould. It is unlikely that many in America on December 8, 1941, were pro-Japanese. Granted that Walcott said nasty things concerning the Germans long before America entered the war, and granted that the western allies committed their share of atrocities, it was the Germans who invaded neutral Belgium, and it was the Germans who sank passenger ships. For comparison, during the 1930s there were some jingoistic Americans who complained about atrocities committed by the Nazis.

Walcott thought Boas had impugned the presidency and America when America was at war. In his view, Boas was unpatriotic. That certainly is old-fashioned, but it is hardly a sound basis for assuming wide-ranging prejudice.

This is fairly heavy stuff, and there is no need to belabor these issues further. It may be time to lighten up. "The letters quoted above have provided some insight into his traditional social attitudes—his differential treatment of sons and daughters, his ideas on frugality and responsibility" (Gould 1989, 253–54). When viewed through the prism of a bullish stock market and a presidential impeachment trial, hallmarks of the end of the twentieth century, frugality and responsibility are beyond quaint—they are archaic.

As to differential treatment of sons and daughters, one of the points established by millennia of the study of biology is that men and women are different. Even those who are not professional biologists are aware of this discovery. Maybe Helen was deprived, but to turn the matter around, the boys were forced to study in college, while the girl was given a grand tour of Europe. Even if Helen was deprived of college, mainly by her own choice, she was not deprived each and every minute. "Mrs. Henry F. Dimock gave a coming out ball for me, the night the Yale Glee Club came to Washington. What a beautiful party it was. The big ball room lit by candles, masses of American beauty roses with stems a yard wide, and young men of the diplomatic corps in their regalia, and the Yale boys—it was a night to remember. Cole Porter launched his familiar 'Mighty like a Rose' for me that night. First he played it at intermission, then gave it to the orchestra, and it was played all though that glamorous evening."[39]

Helen's coming-out party may have nothing to do with Walcott sitting in a cold tent day after day breaking up shale. Those who actually worked on redescription of the Burgess Shale fossils were appreciative of what a marvelous scientific opportunity had been given to them on the metaphorical silver platter. Certainly they were more aware of the difficulties of interpretation and the gradual development of new ideas as they labored year after year than one who described their labor. Since Walcott's day conventions and mores in day-to-day life have changed as much as concepts of classification have changed. Based on the past record, it is likely that both will continue to change. If there is one reasonably constant feature, it is that people who come later will be positive that those who preceded them had things wrong.

Evolution

Shaped by Plato's essentialism, the Western mind has tended to think in terms of unchanging types and essences and to regard variation as fleeting and unimportant. The thinking of the dominant schools of philosophy has throughout been incompatible with an adequate consideration of the importance of variation.

To an equal extent the delay in the acceptance of Darwinism is due to the enormous complexity of the evolutionary process, which seems to defy explanation.

—E. Mayr, 1976

Gould (1989, 261–62) conveys the notion that in signing a condemnation of radicals in religious faith—that is, fundamentalists, as exemplified by William Jennings Bryan—Walcott was attempting to combine religion and evolution. The argument used is difficult to follow. What one does in one's private life and beliefs is not the same as what one writes in a scientific discourse.

Gould mentions that a statement on evolution "published in 1923, two years before the Scopes trial, bore Walcott's name as first signer." From reading this statement, which indicates that the fossil record culminates in man, "with his spiritual nature and all his God-like power," Gould derives the idea that "the creatures of the Burgess Shale must be primitive ancestors to an improved set of descendants. The Burgess Shale shoehorn was more than a buttress to a comfortable and convenient view of life; it was also a moral weapon, and virtually a decree from God" (Gould 1989, 263). Despite all the ingenious/ingenuous arguments presented by Gould, there is no scintilla of evidence whatsoever that Walcott's religious views in any way affected his study of fossils.

Interestingly, Gould quotes part of a letter that Walcott wrote to John D. Rockefeller in one context on page 254 but on page 264 quotes elsewhere from the same letter to bolster his opinion that Walcott was hidebound by religion. The letter in its entirety gives a somewhat different perspective.

It seems like going back fifty years or more to think of discussing the question of the relations of science and religion. Unfortunately, through the actions of radicals in science and in religion, men of the type of mind of William Jennings Bryan have seen a great danger coming to religion through the teaching of the facts of evolution to young men and women in high schools, colleges, etc.

A number of conservative scientific men and clergymen have been asked to sign a statement, to be given wide publicity on the relations of science and religion. The matter has been under consideration for several months. The first statements were long, more or less complicated, and with a controversial note in them. A Committee in Pasadena, California, where the science and religion controversy is very acute, has finally formulated a statement, a copy of which is enclosed. They asked me to sign this, and I see no reason why I should not do so, but I should like your opinion as a layman as to how the statement strikes you. Any opinion you might express will confidential.

I was brought up in Utica, New York, by my mother and sister who were consistent Christian women, and I have always adhered to the Presbyterian Church, as I believe in the essentials of the Christian religion and in carrying them out in cooperation with people who believe in the efficiency of the Church as an agency for the preservation and upbuilding of the human race.[40]

Whatever Walcott may or may not have been, he was emphatically not a fool. By signing a statement supporting evolution he was putting the Smithsonian Institution at risk. By obtaining the approval of an exceedingly rich, exceedingly conservative, and exceedingly religious figure, he had arranged himself an ace in the hole, should this statement bring down the wrath of Congress and hurt the government agencies under Walcott's wing.

The American scene of the 1920s was one of far less tolerance than today, not that the last part of the twentieth century showed dramatic improvement. Prohibition was the law of the land, race relations where probably worse than ever since the Civil War, and fundamentalism was a strong force. It is always difficult to reconstruct the past, be it history or paleoecology, which is one reason why interpretations vary among individuals and change through time. Accordingly, although the point may be argued, it is a reasonable presumption is that the anti-evolution crusade of the 1970s and later was far less virulent than it was half a century earlier. For Walcott to have signed any public statement supporting the concept of evolution was an act of considerable intellectual courage, not an indication that he was hidebound in his thinking. That he did it two years before the Scopes trial is something that an enthusiastic spokesman for evolution should vigorously applaud, not shrug off.

Classification

Cuvier preferred to unite the four vertebrate "classes" into one Class of the
Vertebrates and he placed at an equal level the Mollusks, the Articulata, and
the Radiata. These were the famous four *embrachemantes* which would
form the basis of all of his subsequent taxonomic work.

—W. Coleman, 1964

Classification, especially when treating of living or extinct organisms, can be a
tricky business. Classification is not engraved on stone but is subject to change
as more information becomes known and as ideas change on the relative
significance of various features. Baron Georges Cuvier's classification of invertebrates may have been an improvement over that of Linnaeus, but it was far
from what is current today. As some indication of how long it may take for higher
categories in classification to change, sixty years after Cuvier's pronouncement,
Louis Agassiz was still using Radiata.

Included within the Articulata were the organisms that today are placed in
the phylum Arthropoda. According to some authorities, arthropods are characterized by jointed appendages. It was Walcott's paper, in the centennial year
of America, that first demonstrated conclusively that an extinct group of fossils,
the trilobites, belonged to the Arthropoda. It was Walcott in 1894 who propounded the view that Crustacea and Trilobita were groups of equal standing
within the Arthropoda.

Walcott's view of 1894 was not accepted by the profession, or at least those of
its members who were biologically inclined, and in subsequent compendia the
Trilobita were considered as a subclass with the Crustacea. Like most other activities, fashion plays a part in science, especially in classification. Tinkering with
higher categories was not the fashion at the end of the nineteenth century, or
for many years thereafter. Near the midpoint of the twentieth century, George
Gaylord Simpson, a profound student of evolution, argued that there were no
extinct phyla and virtually no extinct classes.

To give a personal experience that might shed a little light on this subject, in
1977 I proposed an extinct phylum that included one genus. Granted that is an
extreme position; my proposal was received coolly, to put the best possible face
on it. As study on the Burgess Shale fossils proceeded, the notion of other high-
level groups that had gone extinct became more appealing, and suddenly extinct phyla became more fashionable. A few years later I was considered a
reactionary because I was unwilling to accept the view that a group of what
I judge to be extinct mollusks should be elevated to the status of an extinct

phylum. There is far more subjectivity in classification than most persons care to admit.

The crux of Gould's bill of particulars is that Walcott produced several diagrams in 1912 that speculated on the relationship of some of the Burgess Shale arthropods to others. Gould insists that Walcott "shoehorned" these fossils into established groups, yet Walcott consistently used the concept of new families and new orders to convey how different these fossils were. He never produced a summary paper of the Burgess Shale arthropods interpreting their interrelations. P. E. Raymond wrote such a paper, based on Walcott's work, yet he is totally ignored in the anti-Walcottian diatribe.

To summarize his accusation, Gould is upset that Walcott did not propose new classes and new phyla. The time was simply not right. This is like criticizing Shakespeare as incompetent because he spelled his name in a variety of ways. Walcott did an able job of describing remarkable new fossils. A historian is supposed to judge a person in the context of his times. Gould has judged Walcott by the context of his own notions more than half a century later.

Picturing Walcott

Scientific illustration is the production of drawings of measured accuracy and other graphic images to help the scientist-author to communicate. These illustrations should convey to the reader the same concepts that are in the mind of the author. Because they communicate subtleties and eliminate the ambiguities of language, scientific illustrations are an important, often necessary, element in precise communication.

—L. B. Isham and E. R. S. Hodges, 1989

One useful custom of the U.S. Geological Survey was to have a portrait painted of each director. It began with Clarence King, for after his death his family had financial problems, and subsidizing a painting by his half-brother was a way for the geologists to help out without being obvious. Walcott's portrait was painted, but it has been reframed in such a way that the artist's name is not to be seen; for the sake of completeness, note that the artist was Charles H. Peffer. This picture went from the Hoee Iron Building on F Street to what was then the new Interior Department building, to the John Wesley Powell Building in Reston, Virginia, where it resides in the director's conference room.

Ossip Perlma, a former Cossack cavalry officer, painted a portrait in 1917. Walcott with arms folded looks for all the world like a caricature of a capitalist; the only thing lacking is a cigar. It is not on display—perhaps "hidden away" is more appropriate—but for those who are interested, its number is 1917.6.5. This painting may have soured Walcott on foreign artists, for when Moses Dykaar, another Russian emigré, wanted to sculpt his bust, Walcott demurred. Others persuaded him, and Dykaar modeled Walcott in 1924; because it was done from life, his work is what some sculptors call a portrait. In 1928, Mrs. Walcott paid the artist a thousand dollars for the bust. For a few years before and shortly after the Second World War there was an exhibit of the secretaries was in the Castle, and it included this bust. Now the bust is somewhere safe in the old Patent Office Building, under number 1929.12.1.

The late head curator of anthropology, who had his first part-time job in the Museum in 1924, used to tell of stopping off from medical school on the afternoon of February 9, 1927, to see his mentor Dr. Hrdlička. He was summarily grabbed, given a bucket of plaster to carry, and Stewart and Hrdlička went off to the house to make a death mask of Walcott. This mask is recorded within the files of the department, but because of asbestos contamination of collections that had been stored in the attic, it was not available for examination until 1999.

Mrs. Walcott also commissioned a portrait, and William Henry Holmes commented on it:

> Yesterday I tried to advise the artist of Dr. Walcott's portrait regarding possible improvements in the likeness. It is my understanding that you were considering acceptance of the portrait for yourself personally. If, however, acceptance for the Institution is contemplated, and if the acceptance depends in any measure upon my judgement, the matter becomes in a sense official and it will be well to give my opinion in writing. It is a skillful copy in color of the photographic original and is a good likeness in the photographic sense, but can not be regarded as a satisfactory portrait judged by well established standards of portraiture. I doubt if our Gallery Commission would regard it as worthy of a place on the walls of the Gallery and it is hardly the masterpiece that the Institution should have to represent its fourth Secretary, C. D. Walcott.[41]

This is not what one would consider critical acclaim.

There was a portrait of Walcott on the second floor of the Castle with portraits of the other secretaries, showing him from the waist up (accession number s/NPG.79.66). It is credited to Elizabeth Hutton Burdette. Another 1928 portrait of Walcott, behind a desk, was done by Samantha Littlefield Hentley (s/NPG.67/136). It appears to be based on a photograph of Walcott taken approximately at the time he was president of the American Association for the Advancement of Science. Either might be the one discussed by Holmes.

In 1994, Erin Younger donated a portrait to the National Portrait Gallery which might have been more to Dr. Holmes's taste; the pose is similar to that in the photograph, but it is more lifelike. During the 1920s Walcott posed for Helen in New York, but there is no indication that a painting was completed. Cole Younger remarried after Helen died, then passed away himself; when his widow died, the house was emptied. In the attic was a boxed oil painting done by Helen with a 1928 date, her tribute to her Daddie. It is reproduced herein as the frontispiece.

Character

[George Otis] Smith's religion made him a moral man and a very high-minded one for a government bureaucrat. He did not smoke, drink, or play cards. He knew his colleagues spoke of his high ethics and called him an altruist, and he agreed with this judgement by saying that he believed in uplift and the golden rule. Of course he was hard working.

—T. G. Manning, 1978

A comment written a quarter of a century before Walcott's death tells us a little. Charles R. Van Hise, an eminent geologist on the staff of the University of Wisconsin, was being considered for the presidency of that university (which he obtained). Van Hise had worked part-time for the USGS, and Walcott had such a high opinion of him that Van Hise was his choice to follow him as USGS director; what a pity he did not accept that offer. "I should not wish to see him [Van Hise] deprived of the opportunity of carrying forward and completing the work he has on hand. From my own experience I think a man can administer a large organization and at the same time carry forward scientific work. In fact, I think it is better that he should do so."[42]

Walcott had the ability to deal with persons on all levels, from princes to plumbers. Business did not linger, as shown by a reply to a letter sent on May 19, 1919. This letter to a member of the Royal Canadian Mounted Police in Banff demonstrates his attention to the main business, his willingness to defer to the wisdom of others, his attention to detail, his chatty style, and his willingness to share items that might be of mutual interest.

Yours of May 12 is at hand. You must use your judgement in relation to bringing the horses down to Banff. Some of the men told me of their experience in crossing the Red Area high water in the spring when the ice was running in it, so I thoroughly understand why it might not be wise to attempt it until the water went down.

I am enclosing herewith the list of our horses with a description of each. I think the brand U.S. is on every one of them. Some I obtained from the U. S. Geological Survey years ago, and they possibly have U.S.G.S.

Just now matters here are rather strenuous, owing to the new Congress convening to-day which will consider making of appropriations for the several Departments under the Smithsonian and owing to the rapid development of the War Museum, which comes under its jurisdiction. I have just been discussing with the Chief Administrative Officer the question of the installation of some 16-inch guns. We will have a more or less thorough representation of all war material that can be accepted, from a Service Button to a "Tank" and big gun.

I trust that all has gone well with you and all at the Park. Please remember me to Mr. Wardell, Mr. Stuart, and friends at the Office.

P.S. Am sending you a copy of the pictures that appeared in yesterday's paper of some of the animals in our Zoological Park, and among them the group of Rocky Mountain sheep which were sent to us two years ago. You will see that they are flourishing despite the hot summers.[43]

The diesel engine from a German U-boat once was in the rotunda of the Museum, where the world's largest mounted elephant now stands. Better yet, a small plot on the east side of the Arts and Industries building where the tank once stood for a time became a playground; today it is a parking lot.

Several formal photographs of Walcott late in life show him with a flower in the lapel of his jacket. Walcott had fresh flowers on his desk each day. The story is that he had two secretaries; after flowers had been around for a day or so, they would be given to one of the secretaries. He was scrupulous in the matter of turn and turn about in presenting these bouquets. One day he is reputed to have said, "People say I am extravagant, but these are my cigarette money."

He was not swayed by honors. "I thank you for your hearty congratulations. I accept them in part for myself and largely for the American scientific men who have done such splendid work the past few years. I feel that my official connection with the [National] Academy [of Sciences] and the Smithsonian probably had considerable to do with my selection for membership in the French Academy, and rightly so, as it is a means of expressing to Americans the appreciation in which their work is held in Europe, especially France."[44]

In the fall of 1925, he received an honorary degree for the University of the State of New York (this actually exists, on paper). He wrote to Elihu Root, a regent of the university, as well as a trustee of the Carnegie Institution. Two paragraphs might be worth quoting.

While I hate to slow down in my Rocky Mountain fieldwork, there are some compensations. To me this is an attractive and wonderful world and I am thankful to have had the opportunity of passing a lifetime asking questions of Dame Nature and also taking part in a few worthwhile things.

I am looking forward to an opportunity in the future to carry on a little research work on a planet attached to a sun a million or more light years distant from our Mother Earth. What joy it will be to wander about the universe and learn something of its mysteries and discover how other humans run their worlds. I would only ask that I be guided so as not to land on the same planet with William J. Bryan and similar orators and statesmen, male or female.[45]

(For the younger generation, the last public action of Bryan was his involvement in the Scopes "monkey trial" in Dayton, Tennessee.)

Several different newspaper articles confirm Walcott's insistence that the meeting to start the SI endowment drive proceed as scheduled. It was a deathbed wish in the true sense of the phrase. Walcott was a great scientist and also a man of faith. As the editor of *Outlook* wrote, "He was a man of spiritual insight, and though he knew as a scientist how to weigh and measure he valued most highly those things that are measureless and imponderable" (Oehser 1949, 166).

Fame

Geology began when early man first picked up a stone, considered its qualities, and decided that it was better than the stone he already had.

—H. Faul and C. Faul, 1983

The first edition of *American Men of Science* carried stars on the names of the hundred most illustrious workers in each field, as determined by their peers. Three decades later, the editor revealed that these illustrious persons also had been ranked. Walcott was number three, behind G. K. Gilbert and T. C. Chamberlin; that was eminently fair.

In 1928, the Geological Survey of Canada Director expressed regret at being unable to participate in the memorial meeting. "My regret is the greater because, during his long activity, Dr. Walcott made valuable contributions to the geology and palaeontology of Canada by working in Canadian territory and by giving more than one Canadian geologist the benefit of his unexcelled knowledge of Cambrian and Precambrian palaeontology. In spirit my colleagues and I shall join you in rendering tribute to the services to science of Charles Doolittle Walcott."[46]

Those people who provide names to organisms previously unknown to the world provide a certain degree of immortality by the use of patronyms. It is impossible to determine how many species have been named in Walcott's honor. In contrast, provided one knows where to look, it is easy to find out how many genera of fossil animals have been named for him. *Walcottia* Miller and Dyer, 1878, is some sort of trail or burrow. *Walcottina* Cobbold, 1921; *Walcottaspis* Ulrich and Resser, 1930; and *Walcottella* Ulrich and Bassler, 1931, are all names for arthropods. *Walcottoceras* Ulrich and Foerste, 1935, is an early mollusk; and *Walcottodiscus* Bassler, 1935, is a strange echinoderm.

During the Depression, the Civilian Conservation Corps had two camps in the Grand Canyon, now long gone, though they were put to other uses for years after the CCC disbanded. On the south rim was Camp Powell; on the north rim was Camp Walcott. "Named in honor of Dr. Charles W. [sic] Walcott, Director of the U.S. Geological Survey and Secretary of the Smithsonian Institute [sic], who in the early '80's did the first detailed stratigraphic work in geology in the Grand Canyon, and who, as a result of his extensive studies, wrote several notable geological papers."[47] Both names were appropriate. On October 31, 1944, the Liberty ship *Charles D. Walcott* was launched. After the war the ship was scrapped.

Walcott Land is in southwest Peary Land in northern Greenland. Mount Walcott in the Theil Mountains, Antarctica, is one of a group honoring former directors of the USGS. Lake Walcott is in southern Idaho, and Walcott Creek is an obscure stream in the Precambrian outcrops of the Grand Canyon in northern Arizona. In 1996, to help celebrate the sesquicentennial of the SI, Canadian geologists arranged to have part of Mount Burgess designated as Walcott Peak. Were he to stand there today, he could see his old quarry.

In front of the SI Castle stands a statue of Joseph Henry, commissioned by Congress to commemorate the most notable American scientist of his time. Within the Natural History Building, the museum directly across the Mall, the Baird Auditorium honors the second secretary. The National Air and Space Museum contains the Langley Theater, remembering the third secretary; and the Abbot planetarium, appropriate to mark the astrophysical work of the fifth secretary. Leonard Carmichael, the seventh secretary, formally opened what is now the National Museum of American History, and it contains the Carmichael Auditorium. The Enid Haupt Garden graces the area south of the Castle where Langley's astrophysical laboratory and the tin shed stuffed with aircraft stood long ago; below this ground is the Ripley Center, commemorating the eighth secretary. The two "W" secretaries, Wetmore and Walcott, have nothing named after them among the Smithsonian complex.

Finale

Many historians of science understandably have an innate distrust of histories written by scientists who have not been trained in the methods and principals of history.

—E. Drake, 1996

The Walcott family plot is in Rock Creek Cemetery; Lura and Stuart lie elsewhere. On the large granite tombstone, Walcott's full name and dates of birth and death are incised. Added to that is one word, "Geologist." Perhaps that, in its way, says all that needs to be said on a memorial.

Historians of science occasionally mention the "Newton industry" or the "Darwin industry" to suggest the number of people who have made careers considering these personages. It is something of a shock to realize that I am the entire "Walcott industry." Let me freely concede that Walcott did not shake the world the way Newton or Darwin did, but let me also say that he deserves far better from history than he has gotten. Historians who study the administration of the federal government or the development of ideas about natural resources, to cite only two areas, would do well to dig more deeply into his career.

It is no secret to my professional colleagues that my interests as a paleontologist have been in long-dead snails. Indeed, one paleontological reviewer chided me slightly for my description of why trilobites carry the name that they do. If asked how, then, I became so enmeshed with Walcott's career, I cannot give a clear, succinct answer. Once I had learned a little about him, curiosity led me to seek more, and, being a compulsive talker, I wanted to share my interest with others. From there to writing was an short step. Once on that slippery slope, one goes all the way in order eventually to reach the end.

Emphasis herein has been on Walcott's dual, and somewhat schizophrenic, career as both a distinguished geologist/paleontologist and a dedicated leader of agencies and organizations. In my mind there is a fundamental difference between one who administers and an administrator. Walcott's concern was product, not process. More importantly, he was a good father and a good husband. Whether I have done an adequate job of conveying Walcott's life is for others to evaluate. I do know that I have done the best that I can do. In my judgment, that would have satisfied Walcott.

A reasonable way to close is with the number the old Morse telegraphers used to indicate the end of a message in the days when Walcott first began riding the rails:

$$(. . — . ———) \; 30.$$

Notes

Prologue

1. Walcott to J. W. Powell, July 28, 1881, ms 4042-c, National Anthropological Archives, National Museum of Natural History.
2. Walcott to J. B. Henderson, May 4, 1907, Smithsonian Institution Archives (hereafter SIA), Record Unit (hereafter RU) 45, box 57, folder 12.
3. Walcott to E. A. Hitchcock, Jan. 28, 1907, Walcott personnel file, United States Civil Service Commission, Records Center, St. Louis, Missouri.

1. The Kindly Years

1. Remarks by Charles D. Walcott, Secretary of the Smithsonian Institution, on the occasion of the presentation of the Hayden Memorial Geological Medal, Jan. 7, 1908, SIA, RU 45, box 60, folder 5.
2. "What Grandma did and other miscellaneous writings by Helen Walcott Younger for Catherine Ann Younger c. 1955," manuscript (hereafter "What Grandma Did"). Copy in correspondence of Ellis L. Yochelson, Walcott papers, deposited in Smithsonian Institution Archives (hereafter ELY papers).
3. Walcott to R. Rathbun, July 7, 1907, SIA, RU 45, box 60, folder 5.
4. Walcott to S. G. Dixon, Nov. 15, 1905, Academy of Natural Sciences of Philadelphia, Ewell Sale Stewart Library, archives collection number 567.
5. Remarks by Walcott, Jan. 7, 1908, SIA, RU 45, box 60, folder 5.
6. Walcott to R. Rathbun, July 26, 1908, SIA, RU 45, box 60, folder 7.
7. Walcott to C. Adler, Aug. 1, 1908, SIA, RU 45, box 60, folder 7.
8. Walcott to C. Adler, Aug. 1, 1908.
9. Walcott to Sidney Walcott, Feb. 7, 1908, ELY papers.
10. Walcott to H. Huntington, May 6, 1909, SIA, RU 7004, box 1, folder 2.
11. J. Home to C. G. Abbot, Apr. 18, 1927, SIA, RU 46, box 102, folder 7.
12. "What Grandma Did."
13. Walcott to H. Dorsey, Sept. 9, 1909, SIA, RU 45, box 60, folder 8.
14. Walcott to H. Dorsey, Sept. 14, 1909, SIA, RU 45, box 60, folder 9.
15. Walcott to R. Rathbun, Nov. 14, 1909, SIA, RU 45, box 60, folder 9.
16. J. Kruttschmidt to Walcott, Dec. 21, 1909, ELY papers.
17. *Congressional Record*, 61st Cong., 2d sess., Feb. 9, 1910, 1639.
18. O. Chanute to Walcott, Jan. 27, 1909, SIA, RU 45, box 66, folder 5.
19. Walcott to R. Bacon, Mar. 17, 1919, SIA, RU 7004, box 1, folder 2.

20. Walcott to J. Iddings, May 4, 1908, SIA, RU 7004, box 1, folder 2.

21. Helena Walcott to H. Dorsey, June 28, 1910, SIA, RU 45, box 60, folder 9.

22. Walcott to H. Dorsey, July 21, 1910, SIA, RU 45, box 60, folder 9.

23. Walcott to H. Dorsey, Aug. 5, 1910, SIA, RU 45, box 60, folder 9.

24. Walcott to H. Dorsey, Aug. 5, 1910.

25. G. Henningmoen to Ellis Yochelson, Nov. 1, 1993, ELY papers.

26. Walcott to H. Dorsey, Sept. 6, 1910, SIA, RU 45, box 60, folder 9.

27. Walcott to Sidney Walcott, "Sunday eve 1910?" [Dec. 31, 1909, or Jan. 1, 1910], ELY papers.

2. The Dreadful Years

1. Walcott to C. Schuchert, Feb. 13, 1911, Charles Schuchert Papers, Manuscripts and Archives, Yale University Library, New Haven, Conn. (hereafter Yale University).

2. Walcott to Sidney Walcott, Mar. 22, 1991, ELY papers.

3. J. C. Sproule to Ellis Yochelson, Jan. 27, 1969, ELY papers.

4. J. C. Sproule to Ellis Yochelson, Jan. 27, 1969.

5. "The Future of the National Gallery of Arts," speech by Walcott, May 16, 1911; typescript bound in *Scientific and Biographical Papers and Addresses*, National Museum of Natural History library (hereafter NMNH library).

6. R. W. Brock to Walcott, May 22, 1911, SIA, RU 7004, box 1, folder 7.

7. "What Grandma Did."

8. F. W. True to R. Rathbun, July 10, 1911, SIA, RU 45, box 60, folder 10.

9. "What Grandma Did."

10. L. Hintze to Ellis Yochelson, 20 Oct., 1998, ELY papers.

11. C. Schuchert to Walcott, Oct. 25, 1911, Yale University.

12. A. H. Clark to Walcott, 22 Nov., 1911, SIA, RU 7004, box 1, folder 1.

13. Minutes of the Board of Regents, meeting Dec. 14, 1911, SIA, RU 1.

14. Minutes of the Board of Regents, meeting Feb. 8, 1912, SIA, RU 1.

15. Walcott to C. Schuchert, Mar. 29, 1912, Yale University.

16. Walcott to C. Schuchert, May 27, 1912, Yale University.

17. H. B. Walcott to B. S. Walcott ("Tootsie"), Mar. 7, 1912, SIA, RU 7004, box 5, folder 9.

18. Walcott to A. Horsey, June 14, 1912, SIA, RU 7004, box 2, folder 1.

19. Walcott to J. Holmes, June 7, 1912, SIA, RU 7004, box 2, folder 1.

20. John Knox, untitled reminiscences, seven-page typescript. Received from Brian Norford, Geological Survey of Canada (retired); source of original unknown, copy in ELY papers.

21. Sidney Walcott, "Memories of the Canadian Rockies in 1912," manuscript, ELY papers.

22. Sidney Walcott, "Memories."

23. Walcott to H. Dorsey, Sept. 12, 1912, SIA, RU 45, box 60, folder 11.

24. C. Schuchert to Walcott, Oct. 9, 1912, Yale University.

25. "Address at dedication of the New York State Education Building," speech by Walcott, Oct. 16, 1912, NMNH library.

26. Walcott to Helen Walcott, Nov. 21, 1912, SIA, RU 7004, box 5, folder 9.

27. Walcott to Helen Walcott, Nov. 28, 1912, SIA, RU 7004, box 5, folder 9.

28. *(Brooklyn, N.Y.) Citizen*, Feb. 27, 1913.

29. O. Chanute to Walcott, Nov. 20, 1908, SIA, RU 45, box 66, folder 10.

30. Walcott to Linn Bradley, Apr. 13, 1913, SIA, RU 7004, box 1, folder 1.

31. Walcott to President [P.] Lowell, Apr. 16, 1912, SIA, RU 7004, box 5, folder 5.

3. The Healing Years

1. Clipping in pocket of 1913 Walcott diary, SIA, RU 7004, box 15, folder 5.

2. Walcott to Richard Rathbun, Aug. 31, 1913, SIA, RU 45, box 60, folder 12.

3. C. Walcott to F. Kermode, Sept. 22, 1913, SIA, RU 7004, box 60, folder 12.

4. Walcott to W. A. Parks, Mar. 30, 1915, Department of Palaeontology, Royal Ontario Museum, Toronto, Canada.

5. C. Schuchert to E. O. Ulrich, Mar. 25, 1914, National Archives and Record Service, Archives II, Record Group 57, United States Geological Survey, correspondence files.

6. Clippings in 1913 diary; sources unknown but probably from *Washington Star* and *Times-Herald* or *Post*, SIA, RU 7004, box 15, folder 5.

7. A. G. Bell to Walcott, May 2, 1910, Alexander Graham Bell papers, Manuscript Division, Library of Congress (hereafter Bell, LC).

8. G. Curtiss to A. G. Bell, Feb. 16, 1914, Bell, LC.

9. A. G. Bell and Walcott, telephone conversation, Mar. 25, 1914, phone notes, Bell, LC.

10. A. G. Bell to Walcott, Apr. 1, 1914, Bell, LC.

11. C. Schuchert to G. P. Merrill, Apr. 1, 1905, Yale University.

12. M. Collen to Walcott, Dec. 23, 1906, Department of Paleobiology, NMNH, copy in ELY papers.

13. Walcott to M. Stevenson, May 14, 1913, SIA, RU 45, box 60, folder 13.

14. Walcott to C. L. Freer, June 5, 1914, Archives of American Art, Smithsonian Institution, microfilm Freer papers, reel 4728 (hereafter Freer, AAA).

15. Clipping in Walcott diary for 1914, dated June 6, 1914, newspaper source unknown, SIA, RU 7004, box 15, folder 6.

16. Walcott to F. Strange, June 4, 1914, SIA, RU 45, box 60, folder 13.

17. Walcott to H. Dorsey, Sept. 12, 1914, SIA, RU 45, box 60, folder 13.

18. Walcott to O. C. Bradeen, Oct. 14, 1914, SIA, RU 7004, box 1, folder 1.

19. Clipping in Walcott diary for 1915, *Washington Star*, Jan. 3, 1915, SIA, RU 7004, box 19, folder 2.

20. "The Call of the Mountains," speech by Walcott, NMNH library.

21. Walcott to W. B. Parson, Mar. 9, 1915, SIA, RU 51, box 1, folder 8.

22. E. B. Wilson to Ellis Yochelson, May 23, 1961, ELY papers.

23. James Hobbins, "Walcott's Back Room," memorandum to Ellis Yochelson, Aug. 23, 1993, ELY papers.

24. E. B. Wilson to Ellis Yochelson, May 23, 1961, ELY papers.

25. Walcott to D. J. McDougall, Oct. 17, 1914, SIA, RU 7004, box 90, folder 3.

26. Walcott to D .J. McDougall, Dec. 3, 1914, SIA, RU 7004, box 90, folder 3.

27. H. Houchin to Walcott, Mar. 10, 1915, SIA, RU 7004, box 90, folder 2.

28. Walcott to W. Flaherty, May 13, 1915, SIA, RU 45, box 61, folder 1.

29. Walcott to F. K. Lane, May 13, 1915, SIA, RU 45, box 61, folder 1.

30. Walcott to R. Rathbun, July 17, 1915, SIA, RU 45. box 61, folder 2.

31. Walcott to unknown, June 21, 1915, SIA, RU 45, box 61, folder 1.

32. Walcott to H. Dorsey, Sept. 18, 1915, SIA, RU 45, box 61, folder 2.

33. H. Houchin to Walcott, July 4, 1916, SIA, RU 7004, box 90, folder 2.

34. Walcott to H. Houchin, Nov. 24, 1916, SIA, RU 7004, box 90, folder 2.

4. The Busy Years

1. "What Grandma Did."

2. "What Grandma Did."

3. "What Grandma Did."

4. Walcott to W. H. Taft, June 30, 1911, Taft papers (807), Manuscript Division, Library of Congress.

5. F. H. Seares to Ellis Yochelson, July 27, 1961, ELY papers.

6. Walcott to N. Boss, Aug. 14, 1902, Walcott member file, National Academy of Sciences (hereafter Walcott file, NAS).

7. G. E. Hale to H. Goodwin, Jan. 22, 1903, G. E. Hale file, Huntington Library (hereafter Hale, Huntington).

8. G. E. Hale to M. V. Walcott, July 14, 1929, Walcott file, NAS.

9. G. E. Hale to H. Goodwin, Apr. 29, 1913, Hale, Huntington.

10. Walcott to Woodrow Wilson, Sept. 3, 1914, Woodrow Wilson papers, microfilm roll 238, Manuscript Division, Library of Congress (hereafter Wilson, LC).

11. Walcott to W. Schmidt, May 22, 1916, SIA, RU 51, box 2, folder 1.

12. A. Minton to Walcott, Nov. 3, 1916, SIA, RU 45, box 61, folder 5.

13. R. Rathbun to C. L. Freer, Oct. 65, 1915. Charles Lang Freer Papers, Freer Gallery of Art Archives, Smithsonian Institution (hereafter Freer Archives).

14. Walcott to B. B. Lawrence, Oct. 20, 1916, SIA, RU 51, box 2, folder 1.

15. Walcott to W. Schmidt, Mar. 15, 1917, SIA, RU 51, box 2, folder 1.

16. Walcott to W. Warren, Mar. 20, 1917, SIA, RU 45, box 61, folder 6.

17. Walcott to G. Burry, June 7, 1917, SIA, RU 45, box 61, folder 7.

5. The Frantic Years

1. Walcott to H. Dorsey July 28, 1917, SIA, RU 45, box 61, folder 7.

2. Walcott to H. Dorsey, July 30, 1917, SIA, RU 45, box 61, folder 7.

3. H. Dorsey to Walcott, Aug. 11, 1917, SIA, RU 45, box 61, folder 7.

4. Walcott to H. Dorsey (received Mar. 7, 1918), SIA, RU 45, box 61, folder 8.

5. Walcott to W. F. Durand, Apr. 19, 1918, SIA, RU 45, box 19, folder 20.

6. Walcott to W. Wilson, Apr. 14, 1914, Wilson, LC.

7. Walcott to Ravenel, undated railway telegram, SIA, RU 45, box 61, folder 8.

8. Walcott to chief clerk [H. Dorsey], undated night lettergram, SIA, RU 45, box 61, folder 8.

9. Walcott to H. Dorsey, Aug. 1, 1918, SIA, RU 45, box 61, folder 8.

10. H. Dorsey to Walcott, Aug. 23, 1918, SIA, RU 45, box 61, folder 8.

11. Walcott to F. C. Campbell, Sept. 16, 1918, SIA, RU 45, box 61, folder 8.

12. Walcott to G. Smith, Jan. 13, 1919, SIA, RU 45, box 61, folder 9.

13. E. O. Ulrich to R. Ruedemann, Nov. 29, 1919, Ruedemann papers, B 0579-79, C 97/23, Manuscripts and Special Collections, New York State Library, Albany, New York (hereafter Ruedemann, NYSL).

14. *Washington Post Magazine,* Apr. 11, 1993.

15. Theodore Roosevelt to regents, prior to Jan. 24, 1906, minutes of the Board of Regents, Jan. 24, 1906, SIA, RU 1.

16. Walcott to C. L. Freer, Nov. 16, 1908, Freer, AAA.

17. Walcott to C. L. Freer Nov. 22, 1913, Freer, AAA.

18. F. H. Seares to Ellis Yochelson, July 27, 1961, ELY papers.

19. A. E. Meyer, "Charles Freer and His Gallery," *Washington Post,* Jan. 11, 1970.

20. C. L. Freer to R. Rathbun, Sept. 19, 1916, Freer Archives.

21. Walcott to C. L. Freer, Jan. 9, 1915, Freer, AAA.

22. *Evening Star,* Dec. 5, 1915.

23. *Evening Star,* June 10, 1916.

24. Walcott to C. L. Freer, Dec. 27, 1916, Freer Archives.

25. Walcott to C. L. Freer, Feb. 18, 1919, Freer Archives.

26. Walcott to C. L. Freer, Apr. 22, 1919, Freer Archives.

27. Walcott to C. L. Freer, May 1, 1919, Freer Archives.

28. Walcott to C. L. Freer, Feb. 18, 1919, Freer Archives.

29. C. L. Freer to Walcott, June 4, 1919, Freer Archives.

30. Walcott to C. L. Freer, June 6, 1919, Freer Archives.

31. Walcott to C. L. Freer, June 6, 1919.

6. The "Normalcy" Years

1. Walcott to R. Ruedemann, June 5, 1916. B 0575-79, C 97/23, Ruedemann, NYSL.

2. R. Ruedemann to Walcott, May 8, 1919, B 0575-79, C 97/23, Ruedemann, NYSL.

3. C. Schuchert to Walcott, Jan. 7, 1919, Yale University.

4. Walcott to C. Schuchert, Jan. 20, 1919, Yale University.

5. Walcott to C. Schuchert, Jan. 20, 1919.

6. C. Schuchert to Walcott, June 24, 1921, Yale University.

7. Walcott to C. L. Freer, July 13, 1919, Freer Archives.

8. Walcott to J. G. Traylor, undated but after July 22 and before Aug. 9, 1919, SIA, RU 45, box 61, folder 9.

9. Walcott to H. Dorsey, Aug. 9, 1919, SIA, RU 45, box 61, folder 9.

10. Walcott to C. G. Abbot, Sept. 5, 1919, SIA, RU 45, box 61, folder 9.

11. Walcott to W. Ravenel, Sept. 20, 1919, SIA, RU 45, box 61, folder 9.

12. H. Dorsey to Walcott, Sept. 23, 1919, SIA, RU 45, box 61, folder 9.

13. Press release, Smithsonian Institution, received from Sidney Walcott, ELY papers.

14. Walcott to A. G. Nathorst, Mar. 18, 1920, Royal Swedish Academy of Sciences, Stockholm, Center for History of Science [Now in Stockholm University Library], Inkommande brev [Incoming letters], sampling 2, Alfred Gabriel Nathorst arkiv.

15. Senate, statement of Charles D. Walcott, 66th Cong., 2d sess., volume 141 (6), 43–47.

16. "The Outlook Interview: Paul Edward Garber Talks to Deborah Churchman," *Washington Post*, Jan. 26, 1986.

17. Walcott to J. Earle, Feb. 25, 1920, SIA, RU 45, box 61, folder 10.

18. R. Ruedemann to D. White, Dec. 2, 1932, Mary Clark Thompson Medal file, National Academy of Sciences Archives (hereafter medal file, NAS).

19. J. M. Clarke to Walcott, June 2, 1919, medal file, NAS.

20. J. M. Clarke to Walcott, Nov. 4, 1920, medal file, NAS.

21. T. Spicer-Simpson to Walcott, June 18, 1922, medal file, NAS.

22. Walcott to M. C. Thompson, June 7, 1919, medal file, NAS.

23. National Academy of Sciences, minutes, Apr. 27, 1921, NAS.

7. The Fretful Years

1. Walcott to H. Bingham, May 27, 1919, SIA, RU 7004, box 1, folder 2.

2. G. E. Hale to Walcott, Jan. 3, 1920, SIA, RU 7004, box 1, folder 8.

3. C. G. Abbot to Walcott, Dec. 30, 1919, SIA, RU 7004, box 1, folder 1.

4. Walcott to S. Ahrrhenius, Dec. 31, 1919, Kungliga Svenska Vetenskapsakademien (Royal Swedish Academy of Sciences), Stockholm, Center for History of Science, Inkommande brev [Incoming letters], Svante Arrhenius arkiv.

5. *New York Times*, Feb. 27, 1919.

6. L. S. Homer to Walcott, Dec. 14, 1921, SIA, RU 7004, box 2, folder 1.

7. Comment attributed to the late Joel W. Hedgepeth.

8. *New York Times*, May 18, 1919.

9. Louis Fink manuscript on history of original National Gallery of Art and successor organizations; partial copy in ELY papers.

10. Walcott to C. Schuchert, Apr. 21, [1921], Yale University.

11. Walcott to C. Schuchert, Apr. 21, [1921].

12. Walcott to C. Schuchert, May 24, 1921, Yale University.

13. Walcott to C. Schuchert, June 3, 1921, Yale University.

14. Walcott to H. Dorsey, June 21, 1921, SIA, RU 45, box 2, folder 2.

15. Walcott to A. Brown, June 15, 1921, SIA, RU 45, box 2, folder 2.

16. C. G. Abbot to Walcott, July 7, 1921, SIA, RU 45, box 62, folder 2.

17. Walcott to C. G. Abbot, July 14, 1921, SIA, RU 45, box 62, folder 2.

18. W. Ravenel to Walcott, July 18, 1921, SIA, RU 45, box 62, folder 2.

19. Walcott to C. G. Abbot, Aug. 3, 1921, SIA, RU 45, box 62, folder 2.

20. Walcott to S. Walcott, Aug. 31, 1921, SIA, RU 45, box 62, folder 2.

21. Walcott to S. Walcott, "9 A.M. Sept. 2," SIA, RU 45, box 62, folder 2.

22. Walcott to S. Walcott, "Camp below Wilcox Pass, Alberta, Sept. 8, 1921," SIA, RU 45, box 62, folder 2.

23. Walcott to S. Walcott, "Camp Saskatchewan River, Sept. 13, 1921," SIA, RU 45, box 62, folder 2.

24. Walcott to H. Dorsey, Sept. 13, 1921, SIA, RU 45, box 62, folder 2.

25. H. Dorsey to Walcott, Sept. 20, 1921, SIA, RU 45, box 62, folder 2.

26. Walcott to C. G. Abbot, Sept. 26 [1921], SIA, RU 45, box 62, folder 1.

27. Walcott to C. Schuchert, Oct. 17, 1921, Yale University.

28. Newspaper clipping, undated, and source unknown, in Walcott diary for 1921, SIA, RU 7004, box 16, folder 6.

29. O. Wright to C. G. Abbot, June 30, 1942, SIA, RU 46, box 107.

30. *New York Herald*, Jan. 19, 1919.

31. *New York Times*, Oct. 22, 1921.

32. Board of Regents, minutes of Dec. 8, 1921, SIA, RU 1.

33. Undated clipping in Walcott diary for 1921, SIA, RU 7004, box 16, folder 6.

34. Brochure, Mar. 1, 1922, Smithsonian Institution.

35. Scrap of paper, dated Jan. 8, 1922, found in museum drawer, ELY papers.

36. W. T. Calman to Walcott, Mar. 15, 1922, Natural History Museum, London, DF/252/17.

8. The Stasis Years

1. Walcott to Sidney Walcott, Jan. 8, 1922, ELY papers.

2. Walcott to J. G. O'Brien, Feb. 1, 1922, SIA, RU 7004, box 3, folder 2.

3. Walcott to J. C. Merriam, Aug. 26, 1920, Merriam papers, Manuscript Division, Library of Congress (hereafter Merriam, LC).

4. C. G. Abbot to Walcott, Apr. 6, 1922, SIA, RU 45, box 40, folder 2.

5. Walcott to J. C. Merriam, Apr. 6, 1922 (telegram), SIA, RU 45, box 40, folder 2.

6. Walcott to C. G. Abbot, SIA undated [probably Apr. 6, 1922], RU 45, box 40, folder 2.

7. Walcott to C. G. Abbot, undated.

8. *New York Evening Post*, Apr. 24, 1922.

9. Walcott to W. Gilbert, July 8, 1922, Carnegie Institution of Washington, Trustees file.

10. S. C. Phillips, "The Phillips Family," manuscript, copy in ELY papers.

11. Walcott to E. Kirk, Jan. 21, 1921, ELY papers.

12. Walcott to J. C. Merriam, Aug. 15, 1922, Merriam, LC.

13. Walcott to G. P. Merrill, Feb. 12, 1924, SIA, RU 7004, box 1, folder 2.

14. National Academy of Sciences, minutes of Nov. 13, 1922, NAS Archives.

15. Walcott to I. Remsen, Nov. 17, 1922, SIA, RU 7004, box 3, folder 5.

16. Walcott to J. Cattell, Dec. 30, 1922, SIA, RU 7004, box 1, folder 3.

17. J. Marr to Walcott, Jan. 23, 1923, SIA, RU 7004, box 2, folder 6.

18. Walcott to J. Marr, Feb. 6, 1923, SIA, RU 7004, box 2, folder 6.

19. A. A. Michaelson to Walcott, May 1, 1923, SIA, RU 7004, box 2, folder 6.

20. Walcott to J. R. Hayford, May 6, 1923, SIA, RU 7004, box 1, folder 8.

21. Walcott to R. S. Yard, May 29, 1923, SIA, RU 45, box 40, folder 5.

22. Walcott to H. Dorsey, June 2, 1923 (from Radium Hot Springs), SIA, RU 45, box 62, folder 4.

23. *Washington Herald*, July 1, 1923.

24. Walcott to H. Dorsey, Sept. 23, 1923 (from Glacier House), SIA, RU 45, box 62, folder 4.

25. Walcott to H. Dorsey, Oct. 31, 1923, SIA, RU 45, box 62, folder 4.

26. Walcott to W. M. Davis, Feb. 7, 1920, SIA, RU 7004, box 1, folder 4.

27. *New York Times*, Dec. 27, 1923.

28. Walcott to H. Dorsey, Dec. 26, 1923, SIA, RU 45, box 62, folder 4.

🐝

9. The Up and Down Years

1. H. F. Bain to Walcott, Jan. 7, 1924, SIA, RU 7004, box 1, folder 2.
2. W. B. Greeley to Walcott, Mar. 24, 1924, SIA, RU 7004, box 1, folder 7.
3. Walcott to J. M Gibbon, June 14, 1924, SIA, RU 7004, box 1, folder 6
4. W. de C. Ravenel to Walcott, July 11, 1924, SIA, RU 46, box 62, folder 4.
5. C. Resser to Mr. Traynor, July 24, 1924, ELY files.
6. C. B. Slury [secretary to Coolidge] to Walcott, SIA, RU 7004, box 1, folder 3.
7. H. Dorsey to Walcott, Sept. 23, 1924, SIA, RU 46, box 62, folder 4.
8. *Smithsonian Local Notes* (newsletter issued every other week), Oct. 24, 1924, SIA, RU 298.
9. Marginal note by Walcott on A. Hrdlička to Walcott, Nov. 22, 1924, NAA, NMNH.
10. *Smithsonian Local Notes*, Dec. 5, 1924, SIA, RU 298.
11. Walcott to Mr. Kent, Mar. 16, 1925, SIA, RU 7004, box 2, folder 4.
12. "Statement by Secretary Walcott of the Smithsonian Institution in Relation to 'Niagara Falls: Its Power Possibilities and Preservation,'" carbon copy, no date, SIA, RU 46, box 70, folder 7.
13. Walcott to C. Barrois, Jan. 8, 1925, SIA, RU 7004, box 1, folder 2.
14. *Smithsonian Local Notes*, Jan. 30, 1925, SIA, RU 298.
15. Walcott to G. F. Kunz, Jan. 22, 1925, SIA, RU 7004, box 2, folder 4.
16. *New York Times*, Feb. 15, 1925.
17. Walcott to R. G. McConnell, Mar. 31, 1920, Government of Canada, Archives, Ottawa, Geological Survey of Canada (hereafter Canada Archives, GSC), correspondence.
18. Walcott to C. W. Bishop, Mar. 17, 1925, SIA, RU 46, box 138, folder 1.
19. Walcott to H. Williams, Mar. 10, 1925, SIA, RU 7004, box 4, folder 4.
20. Newspaper clipping, source unknown, loose in Walcott 1925 diary.
21. Walcott to F. Newell, July 10, 1902, SIA, RU 7004, box 2, folder 7.
22. F. Newell to Walcott, Mar. 29, 1925, SIA, RU 7004, box 2, folder 7.
23. Walcott to C. Camsell, Apr. 20, 1925, Canada Archives, GSC.
24. Walcott to C. Camsell, Mar. 22, 1924, Canada Archives, GSC.
25. C. Camsell to Walcott, Mar. 24, 1924, Canada Archives, GSC.
26. *New York Times*, May 1, 1925.
27. Ibid., May 2, 1925.
28. O. Chanute to Walcott, Nov. 20, 1908, SIA, RU 45, box 66, folder 10.
29. O. Chanute to Walcott, Jan. 27, 1909, SIA, RU 45, box 66, folder 5.
30. *New York Times*, May 3, 1925.
31. Ibid.
32. Ibid., May 4, 1925.
33. Walcott, scrap of paper "Aeronautics", SIA, RU 45, box 1, folder 14.
34. A. G. Bell, telephone notes, Mar. 25, 1914, Bell papers, LC.
35. A. G. Bell to Walcott, Apr. 1, 1914, Bell papers, LC.
36. *New York Times*, May 4, 1925.
37. Ibid.
38. Ibid., May 5, 1925.

39. Ibid., May 6, 1925.

40. Ibid., May 14, 1925.

41. Ibid., May 17, 1925, Sunday edition, section 9.

42. Ibid., May 30, 1925.

43. Ibid.

44. Ibid.

45. Ibid., June 2, 1925.

46. Ibid., June 4, 1925.

47. G. Abbot to O. Wright, Mar. 4, 1928, SIA, RU 46, box 1, folder 8.

48. *New York Times*, June 13, 1925.

49. Ibid.

50. Ibid.

51. SI Board of Regents, minutes of Dec. 10, 1925, SIA, RU 1.

52. Walcott to W. H. Shelley, June 13, 1925, SIA, RU 46, box 30, folder 1.

53. J. M. Clarke to Walcott, Jan. 21, 1925, SIA, RU 7004, box 1, folder 3.

10. The Last Years

1. Walcott to H. Dorsey, June 20, 1925, SIA, RU 46, box 103, folder 1.

2. Walcott to H. Dorsey, June 21, 1925, SIA, RU 46, box 103, folder 1.

3. H. Dorsey to Walcott, July 18, 1925, SIA, RU 46, box 103, folder 1.

4. Walcott to J. C. Merriam, Aug. 16, 1925, Merriam, LC, box 177.

5. H. Dorsey to Walcott, Aug. 17, 1925, SIA, RU 46, box 103, folder 1.

6. C. G. Abbot to Walcott, Aug. 28, 1925, SIA, RU 46, box 103, folder 1.

7. Walcott to H. Dorsey Sept. 4, 1925, SIA, RU 46, box 103, folder 1.

8. M. V. Walcott to E. Richards and Son, Nov. 12, 1925, SIA, RU 46, box 103, folder 1.

9. Walcott to D. S. Jordan, Oct. 3, 1925, SIA, RU 7004, box 2, folder 3.

10. Walcott to H. Dorsey, Oct. 15, 1925, SIA, RU 46, box 103, folder 8.

11. Walcott to E. M. Kindle, Oct. 31, 1925, SIA, RU 7004, box 2, folder 4.

12. J. Victory to Walcott, Sept. 9, 1925, SIA, RU 7004, box 4, folder 2.

13. Charles D. Walcott, memorandum, "Relation of the Smithsonian Institution to the National Government," four pages, SIA, RU 46, box 94, folder 9.

14. Walcott to L. B. Walton, Dec. 2, 1925, SIA, RU 7004, box 4, folder 4.

15. *Smithsonian Local Notes*, Jan. 1, 1926, SIA, RU 298.

16. Walcott to D. Morrow, Dec. 29, 1925, SIA, RU 46, box 4, folder 1.

17. Walcott to P. N. Nunn, Dec. 30, 1925, SIA, RU 7004, box 2, folder 8.

18. Walcott to H. White Jan. 5, 1926, SIA, RU 46, box 114, folder 2.

19. Walcott to H. White, Jan. 26, 1926, SIA, RU 46, box 114, folder 2.

20. *Smithsonian Local Notes*, Mar. 12, 1926, SIA, RU 298.

21. Walcott to E. Blackwelder, Feb. 25, 1926, SIA, RU 46, box 90, folder 1.

22. Walcott to G. O. Tamblyn, Feb. 23, 1926, SIA, RU 46, box 98, folder 4.

23. Walcott to H. Dorsey, Mar. 4, 1926, SIA, RU 46, box 103, folder 1.

24. Walcott to H. Dorsey, Mar. 5, 1926, SIA, RU 46, box 103, folder 1.

25. Walcott to H. Dorsey, Mar. 9, 1926, SIA, RU 46, box 103, folder 1.

26. Walcott to H. Dorsey, Mar. 19, 1926, SIA, RU 46, box 103, folder 1.

27. Walcott to H. Dorsey, Mar. 20, 1926, SIA, RU 46, box 103, folder 1.

28. Walcott to H. Dorsey, "Monday" [received Mar. 23], SIA, RU 46, box 103, folder 1.

29. Walcott to L. S. Rowe, Apr. 1, 1926, SIA, RU 7004, box 3, folder 5.

30. Walcott to F. Springer, Apr. 10, 1926, SIA, RU 7004, box 3, folder 7.

31. Walcott to D. S. Jordan, Apr. 8, 1925, SIA, RU 7004, box 2, folder 3.

32. Walcott to C. W. Bishop, Apr. 9, 1926, SIA, RU 46, box 138, folder 1.

33. F. A. Reid to Walcott, Apr. 20, 1926, SIA, RU 7004, box 3, folder 5.

34. R. S. Yard to Walcott, Apr. 16, 1926, SIA, RU 46, box 69, folder 3.

35. Walcott to R. S. Brookings, May 22, 1926, SIA, RU 46, box 114, folder 2.

36. Walcott to C. W. Bishop, June 24, 1926, SIA, RU 46, box 138, folder 1.

37. H. Dorsey to Walcott, July 1, 1926, SIA, RU 46, box 88 folder 1.

38. Walcott to H. Dorsey, July 4, 1926, SIA, RU 46, box 103, folder 3.

39. Walcott to H. Dorsey, July 8, 1926, SIA, RU 46, box 103, folder 1.

40. Walcott to J. Lodge, Aug. 9, 1926, Freer Archives.

41. Walcott to H. Dorsey, "Sunday evening" (probably Aug. 22, 1926), SIA, RU 46, box 103, folder 1.

42. Walcott to H. Dorsey, Aug. 23, 1926, SIA, RU 46, box 103, folder 1.

43. Walcott to H. Dorsey, Aug. 26, 1926, SIA, RU 46, box 103, folder 1.

44. Walcott to H. Dorsey, undated, late Sept. 1926, SIA, RU 46 box 102, folder 1.

45. Walcott to D. Morrow, draft dated Sept. 16, 1926, SIA, RU 7004, box 2, folder 6.

46. Walcott to [H.?] White, draft dated Sept. 27, 1926, SIA, RU 7004, box 4, folder 4.

47. D. W. Taylor to Walcott, Oct. 25, 1926, SIA, RU 7004, box 3, folder 8.

48. Walcott to J. M. Thorington, Oct. 30, 1926, Princeton University, Princeton, N.J., Firestone Library, Thorington Archive.

49. Walcott to H. White, Nov. 8, 1926, SIA, RU 46, box 114, folder 2.

50. Walcott to C. W. Bishop, Nov. 20, 1926, SIA, RU 46, box 138, folder 1.

51. Walcott to H. White, Jan. 8, 1927, SIA, RU 46, box 114, folder 3.

52. W. W. Jardine to Walcott, Jan. 3, 1927, SIA, RU 7004, box 2, folder 3.

53. Walcott to W. W. Jardine, Jan. 11, 1927, SIA, RU 7004, box 2, folder 3.

54. Walcott to C. W. Bishop, Jan. 15, 1927, SIA, RU 46, box 138, folder 1.

55. Walcott to E. de Margerie, Jan. 23, 1927, SIA, RU 7004, box 2, folder 6.

56. C. E. Resser to B. F. Howell, Feb. 24,1927, Princeton University, Princeton, N.J., Department of Geological Sciences.

57. Chief clerk [H. Dorsey], memorandum from Mrs. Walcott, Jan. 25, 1929, SIA, RU 46, box 103, folder 10.

58. M. V. Walcott to C. G. Abbot, Aug. 9, 1930, SIA, RU 46, box 103, folder 10.

59. C. E. Resser, memorandum to A. Wetmore through Dr. Bassler, Jan. 19, 1921, SIA, RU 46, box 103, folder 3.

60. A. Wetmore, memorandum for the secretary, Feb. 14, 1931, SIA, RU 46, box 103, folder 2.

61. Walcott to E. O. Ulrich, Jan. 28, 1927, SIA, RU 7004, box 4, folder 1.

62. C. G. Abbot to Walcott, Jan. 31, 1927, SIA, RU 46, box 103, folder 2.

63. P. Brockett to G. E. Hale, Feb. 9, 1927, Walcott file, NAS.

64. P. Brockett to G. E. Hale, Feb. 11, 1927, Walcott file, NAS.

65. C. G. Abbot to C. Manley, Feb. 17, 1927, SIA, RU 46, box 102, folder 8.

66. C. G. Abbot to C. Coolidge, Feb. 9, 1927, SIA, RU 46, box 103, folder 2.

67. C. G. Abbot to H. White, Feb. 16, 1927, SIA, RU 46, box 114, folder 3.

68. *Smithsonian Local Notes*, Feb. 25, 1927.

69. *Washington Star*, Feb. 10, 1927.

70. C. G. Abbot to C. W. Bishop, Mar. 9, 1927, SIA, RU 46, box 138, folder 1.

71. Last Will and Testament of Charles Doolittle Walcott, June 8, 1922, item 4

72. Walcott Indenture on Walcott Research Fund, June 6, 1922,

Epilogues

1. "What Grandma Did."

2. H. B. Walcott to Mrs. H. Jennings, Apr. 27, 1913, SIA, RU 7004, box 2, folder 3.

3. H. B. Walcott to B. J. Walcott, Mar. 19, 1912, SIA, RU 7004, box 5, folder 9.

4. F. C. Walcott to Walcott, Apr. 27, 1917, SIA, RU 7004, box 4, folder 4.

5. Walcott to F. C. Walcott, Apr. 30, 1917, SIA, RU 7004, box 4, folder 4.

6. Walcott to S. S. Walcott, Jan. 8, 1922, ELY papers.

7. "What Grandma Did."

8. "What Grandma Did."

9. Walcott to A. F. Stevens, Nov. 8, 1916, SIA, RU 7004, box 3, folder 4.

10. Walcott to S. S. Walcott, Jan. 8, 1921, ELY papers.

11. S. S. Walcott to H. Dorsey, Sept. 10, 1928, SIA, RU 46, box 103, folder 11.

12. H. B. Walcott to B. S. Walcott, Mar. 7, 1912, SIA, RU 7004, box 5, folder 9.

13. Walcott to W. H. Taft, Dec. 9, 1911, SIA, RU 7004, box 3, folder 8.

14. H. D. Taft to Walcott, June 19, 1913, SIA, RU 7004, box 5, folder 1.

15. "What Grandma Did."

16. *Washington Post*, Apr. 15, 1936.

17. *Washington Times*, Dec. 17, 1938.

18. *Sunday Star*, Jan. 31, 1926.

19. C. G. Abbot to H. F. Stone, Sept. 4, 1940, SIA, RU 46, box 103, folder 10.

20. *Boston Transcript*, Feb. 12, 1927.

21. Walcott, "Smithsonian Institution and the American People," speech before the Century Club, Utica, N.Y., Mar. 23, 1912, NMNH, library.

22. "What Grandma Did."

23. H. S. Vaux to Ely, June 2, 1999, ELY Papers.

24. F. A. Delano to C. G. Abbot, Feb. 4, 1927, SIA, RU 46, box 138, folder 1.

25. C. G. Abbot to C. W. Bishop, Mar. 9, 1927, SIA, RU 46, box 138, folder 1.

26. C. G. Abbott to C. W. Bishop, Mar. 31, 1927, SIA, RU 46, box 138, folder 1.

27. *Washington Post*, Jan. 11, 1970.

28. C. G. Abbot to S. D. Ripley, Dec. 9, 1971, SIA special file, "Agnes Meyer pamphlet," prepared by Charles Lytle.

29. Lois M. Fink, unpublished manuscript.

30. Walcott to Mrs. A. H. Rice, Jan. 8, 1925, SIA, RU 46, box 68, folder 5.

31. C. D. Abbot to R. W. Moore, Feb. 8, 1927, SIA, RU 46, box 114, folder 3.

32. "Offer of Secretary C. G. Abbot of Smithsonian Institution to Orville Wright," Mar. 4, 1928, SIA, RU 46, box 1, folder 8.

33. O. Wright to C. G. Abbot June 30, 1942, SIA, RU 46, box 107, folder 9.

34. *Sunday Star*, Mar. 26, 1911.

35. Walcott to H. C. Richardson, June 15, 1915, NACA files, National Archives and Record Service, Archives II, College Park, Maryland (hereafter NARS).

36. Walcott to John Victory, Aug. 24, 1924, NACA files, NARS.

37. Jonathan Yardley (column), *Washington Post*, Mar. 1, 1999.

38. C. Adler to C. G. Abbot, telegram, Feb. 10, 1927, SIA, RU 46, box 102, folder 7.

39. "What Grandma Did."

40. Walcott to J. D. Rockefeller, Jr., Apr. 5, 1923, SIA, RU 7004, box 3, folder 5.

41. W. H. Holmes to M. V. Walcott, Oct. 5, 1928, SIA, RU 7004, box 2, folder 1.

42. Walcott to B. J. Stevens, July 15, 1902, SIA, RU 7004, box 3, folder 7.

43. Walcott to H. E. Sibbald, May 19, 1919, SIA, RU 7004, box 3, folder 4.

44. Walcott to W. H. Welch, Nov. 29, 1919, SIA, RU 7004, box 4, folder 4.

45. Walcott to E. Root, Nov. 5, 1925, SIA, RU 7004, box 3, folder 5.

46. W. H. Collins to C. G. Abbot, Jan. 14, 1928, SIA, RU 46, box 103, folder 6.

47. Memorandum, Aug. 14, 1933, SIA, RU 46, box 145, folder 1.

References

Published Material by Charles Doolittle Walcott

A more complete list of Walcott's publications is given in Yochelson (1967). It lacks several papers on aviation matters that are included below; these are not in the bound set of Walcott reprints in the library of the National Museum of Natural History. Each of the separate publications in his five volumes of Smithsonian Miscellaneous Contributions *bears a general title of "Cambrian Geology and Paleontology" before its number; this is generally omitted from citations.*

1876. Preliminary notice of the discovery of the remains of the natatory and brachial appendages of trilobites. [Advanced print in Dec. 1876 of 1879]. *28th annual report of the New York State Museum of Natural History,* 89–92.

1881. The trilobite; New and old evidence relating to its organization. *Bulletin of the Museum of Comparative Zoology* 8:191–224.

1884. *Paleontology of the Eureka District.* U.S. Geological Survey, Monograph 8.

1888. Cambrian fossils from Mount Stephens [*sic*], Northwest Territory of Canada. *American Journal of Science,* 3d series, 36:161–66.

1890. The fauna of the Lower Cambrian or *Olenellus* zone. U.S. Geological Survey, *10th annual report,* 1888–89, part 1, 509–744.

1891. *Correlation Papers: Cambrian.* U.S. Geological Survey, *Bulletin* 81.

1891a. The North American continent during Cambrian time. U.S. Geological Survey, *12th annual report,* 1890–91, part 1, 532–68.

1893. Geologic time, as indicated by the sedimentary rocks of North America. *Journal of Geology* 1:639–76.

1894. Notes on some appendages of trilobites. *Biological Society of Washington, Proceedings* 9:89–97. Also published in *Geological Magazine* 1:246–51.

1898. The United States Forest Reserves. *Appleton's Popular Science Monthly* 52:1–13.

1899. Pre-Cambrian fossiliferous formations. Geological Society of America, *Bulletin* 10:199–204.

1901. Sur le formations Pré-Cambriennes fossilifères. *Congrès Géologique International, Compte rendu 8me session, Paris* 1:299–312.

1905. The Cambrian faunas of China. *Proceedings of the Washington Academy of Sciences* 7:251–56.

1907. Dr. Hamlin's relations to the temporalities of the church. *In Memoriam:* Tribute to the life and character of Rev. Tenuis S. Hamlin, D.D., pastor of the Church of the Covenant. Washington, D.C., Apr. 28, 1907.

1908.　Cambrian trilobites. *Smithsonian Miscellaneous Collections* 53 (2):13–52.

1908a.　Mount Stephen rocks and fossils. *Canadian Alpine Journal* 1:232–48.

1908b.　Statement of Mr. Charles D. Walcott, Secretary. *House of Representatives, Hap 60-K*, 105–26.

1909.　Evolution of early Paleozoic faunas in relation to their environment. *Journal of Geology* 17:193–202.

1909a.　Research and the Smithsonian Institution. *Independent*, Mar. 18, 1909, 585–86.

1909b.　Acceptance of portrait of Admiral Melville. *Transactions of the American Society of Mechanical Engineers* 31:261.

1909c.　Report of the Secretary of the Smithsonian Institution, Charles D. Walcott, for the year ending June 30, 1908. *Smithsonian Institution, annual report for 1908*, 1–86.

1910.　*Olenellus* and other genera of the Mesonascidae. *Smithsonian Miscellaneous Collections* 53 (6):232–422.

1910a.　Pre-Cambrian rocks of the Bow River Valley, Alberta, Canada. *Smithsonian Miscellaneous Collections* 53 (7):423–43.

1910b.　Abrupt appearance of the Cambrian fauna on the North American continent. *Smithsonian Miscellaneous Collections* 57 (1):1–16.

1911.　Report of the secretary of the Smithsonian Institution, Charles D. Walcott, for the year ending June 30, 1911. *Smithsonian Institution, annual report for 1910*, 5–89.

1911a.　[Discussion] Special problems and their study in economic geology. *Economic Geology* 6:71–72.

1911b.　Middle Cambrian Merostomata. *Smithsonian Miscellaneous Collections* 57 (2):17–40.

1911c.　Middle Cambrian Annelida. *Smithsonian Miscellaneous Collections* 57 (5):109–44.

1911d.　A geologist's paradise. *National Geographic Magazine* 22:509–21.

1912.　Explorations organized or participated in by the Smithsonian Institution in 1910 and 1911. *Smithsonian Miscellaneous Collections* 59 (11):1–51. ("Studies in Cambrian geology and paleontology in the Canadian Rockies" occupies pages 39–45.)

1912a.　Biographical memoir of Samuel Pierpont Langley. *National Academy of Sciences, Biographical Memoirs* 6:247–68.

1912b.　Middle Cambrian Branchiostoma, Malacostraca, Trilobita, and Merostomata. *Smithsonian Miscellaneous Collections* 57 (6):145–228.

1912c.　Cambrian of the Kicking Horse Valley, British Columbia. *Report of the Geological Survey Branch of the Department of Mines, 1911*, sessional paper No. 26, 188–91.

1912d.　Notes on fossils from Steeprock Lake, Ontario. *Geological Survey of Canada, Memoir 28*, appendix, 16–22.

1912e.　New York Potsdam-Hoyt fauna. *Smithsonian Miscellaneous Collections* 57 (9):251–304.

1912f.　*Cambrian Brachiopoda*. U.S. Geological Survey, Monograph 51. Volume 1, text; volume 2, plates.

1913. New Lower Cambrian subfauna. *Smithsonian Miscellaneous Collections* 57 (11):309–26.

1913a. The monarch of the Canadian Rockies: The Robson Peak District of British Columbia and Alberta. *National Geographic Magazine* 24:626–39.

1913b. Statement by Mr. Charles D. Walcott. *U.S. House of Representatives, House Hearings* 10 (1):372–411.

1913c. Cambrian formations of the Robson Peak District, British Columbia and Alberta. *Smithsonian Miscellaneous Collections* 57 (12):327–43.

1913d. Geological Explorations in the Canadian Rockies [in 1912]. *Smithsonian Miscellaneous Collections* 60 (30):24–31.

1913e. Statement regarding the fauna occurring in the conglomerate in the vicinity of Bic. In *Bic: Excursion Al, Excursions in Eastern Quebec and the Maritime Provinces*, by G. A. Young, 67–71.

1913f. The Cambrian faunas of China. *Carnegie Institution of Washington* 54:1–295.

1913g. An account of the exercises on the occasion of the presentation of the Langley Medal and the unveiling of the Langley Memorial Tablet, May 6, 1913, including the addresses. *Smithsonian Institution*, Special Publication 2233.

1914. *Atikokania lawsoni* Walcott. *Nature* 94:477–78.

1914a. Geologic explorations in the Canadian Rockies [in 1913]. *Smithsonian Miscellaneous Collections* 65 (8):2–14.

1914b. Dikelocephalus and other genera of the Dikelocephalinae. *Smithsonian Miscellaneous Collections* 57:345–412.

1915. The Cambrian and its problems in the Cordilleran region. In *Problems of American Geology*. New Haven, Conn.: Yale University Press, 162–232.

1915a. Report of the secretary of the Smithsonian Institution, Charles D. Walcott, for the year ending June 30, 1914. *Smithsonian Institution, annual report for 1914*, 1–34.

1915b. Geologic explorations in the Rocky Mountains [in 1914]. *Smithsonian Miscellaneous Collections* 65 (6):1–10.

1915c. A National Advisory committee for Aeronautics. Sen. doc. 797, 63d Cong., 3d sess.

1915d. Discovery of Algonkian bacteria. *National Academy of Sciences, Proceedings* 1:256–57.

1916. Cambrian trilobites. *Smithsonian Miscellaneous Collections* 64 (3):157–258.

1916a. Geological explorations in the Rocky Mountains [in 1915]. *Smithsonian Miscellaneous Collections* 66 (1):1–27.

1916b. Cambrian trilobites. *National Academy of Sciences, Proceedings* 2:101.

1916c. Evidences of primitive life. *Smithsonian Institution, annual report for 1915*, 235–55.

1916d. Relations between the Cambrian and Pre-Cambrian formations in the vicinity of Helena, Montana. *Smithsonian Miscellaneous Collections* 64 (4):259–301.

1916e. Cambrian trilobites. *Smithsonian Miscellaneous Collections* 64 (5):303–436.

1917. Report of the secretary. *Smithsonian Institution, annual report for 1916*, 1–35.

1917a. Geological explorations in the Canadian Rockies [in 1916]. *Smithsonian Miscellaneous Collections* 66: (17):1–19.

1917b. The Albertella fauna in British Columbia and Montana. *Smithsonian Miscellaneous Collections* 67 (2):9–57.

1917c. [National Academy of Sciences, Washington D.C., Apr. 16, 17, 18]. Searching for a doubtful geological zone in the Canadian Rockies. *Science* (new series) 45:355.

1917d. Statement of Dr. Charles D. Walcott, member National Advisory Committee for Aeronautics (continued). U.S. House of Representatives, Committee on Naval Affairs, NH 64-B, 527–37.

1917e. Address by Dr. Charles D. Walcott. University of State of New York, *Bulletin* 634:18–21.

1917f. National parks as a scientific asset. *Proceedings of the National Parks Conference,* 112–15.

1917g. Fauna of the Mount Whyte formation. *Smithsonian Miscellaneous Collections* 67 (3):61–114.

1917h. Story of Granny, the mountain squirrel. *Journal of Animal Behavior* 7:754–55.

1918. Geological explorations in the Canadian Rockies [in 1917]. *Smithsonian Miscellaneous Collections* 68 (12):4–20.

1918a. [Introduction to] The life story of an American airman in France. [Extracts from letters of Stuart Walcott]. *National Geographic Magazine* 33:86–106.

1918b. [Introduction to] *Above the French lines: Letters of Stuart Walcott, American aviator, July 4, 1917 to Dec. 8, 1917.* Princeton, N.J.: Princeton University Press.

1918c. Appendage of trilobites. *Smithsonian Miscellaneous Collections* 67 (4):115–216.

1919. Geological explorations in the Canadian Rockies [in 1918]. *Smithsonian Miscellaneous Collections* 70 (2):3–20.

1919a. Middle Cambrian Algae. *Smithsonian Miscellaneous Collections* 67 (5):217–60.

1920. Report of the Secretary of the Smithsonian Institution, Charles D. Walcott for the year ending June 30, 1918. *Smithsonian Institution, annual report for 1918,* 1–25.

1920a. Middle Cambrian Spongiae. *Smithsonian Miscellaneous Collections* 67 (6):261–364.

1920b. Geological explorations in the Canadian Rockies: field season of 1919. *Smithsonian Miscellaneous Collections* 72 (1):1–15.

1921. Notes on structure of *Neolenus. Smithsonian Miscellaneous Collections* 67 (7):365–456.

1921a. Geological explorations in the Canadian Rockies [in 1920]. *Smithsonian Miscellaneous Collections* 72 (6):1–10.

1921b. National Advisory Committee for Aeronautics, Statement of Dr. Charles D. Walcott. Sen. Doc. 162 (3), 58–64.

1922. Report of the secretary of the Smithsonian Institution for the year ending June 30, 1920. *Smithsonian Institution, annual report for 1920,* 1–36.

1922a. Report of the Secretary of the Smithsonian Institution for the year ending June 30, 1921. *Smithsonian Institution, annual report for 1921,* 1–24.

1922b. *Seventh annual report of the National Advisory Committee for Aeronautics.* Washington, D.C.: U.S. Government Printing Office.

1922c. Geological explorations in the Canadian Rockies [in 1921]. *Smithsonian Miscellaneous Collections* 72 (15):1–21.

1923. Geological explorations in the Canadian Rockies [for 1922]. *Smithsonian Miscellaneous Collections* 74 (5):1–24.

1924. Cambrian and Ozarkian Brachiopoda, Ozarkian Cephalopoda and Notostraca. *Smithsonian Miscellaneous Collections* 67 (9):477–554.

1924a. Ozarkian brachiopods from Novaya Zemlya: Report of the scientific results of the Norwegian expedition to Novaya Zemlya, Kristiania [Oslo] 1921. *Videnskappelskapet i Kristiania* 25:1–8.

1924b. Geological formations of the Beaverfoot-Brisco-Stanford Range, British Columbia, Canada. *Smithsonian Miscellaneous Collections* 77 (1):1–14.

1924. Walcott, C. D., and C. D. Resser. Trilobites from the Ozarkian sandstones of the island of Novaya Zemlya. Report of the scientific results of the Norwegian Expedition to Novaya Zemlya, 24:1–14.

1925. Report of the Secretary of the Smithsonian Institution, Charles D. Walcott, for the year ending June 30, 1923. *Smithsonian Institution, annual report for 1923*, 1–26.

1925a. Report of the Secretary of the Smithsonian Institution, Charles D. Walcott, for the year ending June 30, 1924. *Smithsonian Institution, annual report for 1924*, 1–26.

1925b. La discordance de stratification et la lacune stratigraphique pré-Dévoniennne dans les Provinces Cordillères d'Alberta et de Colombie Brittannique, Canada. *Livre Jubilaire, Cinquantenaire de la foundation Société Géologique de Belgique*, 119–23.

1925c. Geological explorations in the Canadian Rockies [in 1924]. *Smithsonian Miscellaneous Collections* 77 (2):1–14.

1925d. Science and Service. *Science* (new series) 61:1–5.

1925e. Cambrian and Ozarkian trilobites. *Smithsonian Miscellaneous Collections* 75 (3):61–146.

1925f. *Tenth annual report of the National Advisory Committee for Aeronautics*. Washington, D.C.: U.S. Government Printing Office.

1925g. The Langley plane. *Outlook* 140 (2):54–56.

1925h. Smithsonian: A pioneer in aeronautics. *National Aeronautic Association Review* 3 (7):99, 111.

1925i. The National Advisory Committee. *National Aeronautic Association Review* 3 (6):88–90.

1925j. John Mason Clarke. *Science* (new series) 62:558.

1925k. Joseph Henry. *Science* (new series) 62:405–8.

1926. Report of the Secretary of the Smithsonian Institution, Charles D. Walcott, for the year ending June 30, 1925. *Smithsonian Institution, annual report for 1924*, 1–27.

1926a. Geological explorations in the Canadian Rockies [in 1925]. *Smithsonian Miscellaneous Collections* 78 (1):1–8.

1926b. National Advisory Committee for Aeronautics. Statements of Dr. Charles D. Walcott. *U.S. House of Representatives, House Hearings* 450 (2):289–96.

1926c. Statement of Dr. C. D. Walcott, Secretary. *U.S. House of Representatives, House Hearings* 450 (2):334–64.

〰
🐞

1926d. Samuel Pierpont Langley and modern aviation. *Proceedings of the American Philosophical Society* 65:79–82.

1927. Pre-Devonian Paleozoic sedimentation in Southern Canadian Rockies. *Smithsonian Miscellaneous Collections* 75 (4):147–73.

1928. Pre-Devonian Paleozoic formations of the Cordilleran provinces of Canada. *Smithsonian Miscellaneous Collections* 75 (5):175–368. Published posthumously.

1931. Addenda to descriptions of Burgess Shale fossils. *Smithsonian Miscellaneous Collections* 85 (3):1–46. Published posthumously, compiled by C. E. Resser.

Other Published Sources

Abbot, C. G. 1919. *Report of the National Academy of Sciences for the year 1918.* Washington, D.C.: U.S. Government Printing Office.

———. 1922. *Report of the National Academy of Sciences for the year 1921.* Washington, D.C.: U.S. Government Printing Office.

———. 1924. Who will promote science? *Smithsonian Institution, annual report for 1922*, 137–43.

———. 1958. *Adventures in the world of science.* Washington, D.C.: Public Affairs Press.

Adler C. 1941. *I have considered the days.* Philadelphia: Jewish Publication Society of America.

Agnew, A. 1976. *The U.S. Bureau of Mines.* Senate, 94th Cong., 2d sess. Committee Print for Committee on Interior and Insular Affairs.

Albright, H. M. 1985. *Birth of the National Park Service: The founding years 1913–1933.* Salt Lake City, Utah: Howe Brothers.

Albritton, C. C., Jr. 1980. *The abyss of time: changing concepts of the earth's antiquity.* San Francisco: Freeman Cooper.

Ames, J. C. 1927. *Thirteenth annual report of the National Advisory Committee for Aeronautics.* Washington, D.C.: Government Printing Office.

———. 1928. Doctor Walcott and the National Advisory Committee for Aeronautics. *Smithsonian Miscellaneous Collections* 80 (12):11–15.

Anderson, R., and R. Richards. 1912. Proceedings of the academy and affiliated societies: Geological Society of Washington. *Washington Academy of Sciences Journal* 2:357–62.

Angell, J. R. 1920. The National Research Council. In *The new world of science: Its development during the war.* Edited by R. M. Yerkes. New York: Century, 417–38.

Anonymous. 1908. Proceedings of the Board of Regents for year ending June 30, 1907. *Smithsonian Institution annual report for 1907.*

———. 1912. American Philosophical Society. 1912. *Nature* 89:334–35.

———. 1916. Proceedings of the Board of Regents for year ending June 30, 1915. *Smithsonian Institution annual report for 1915*, 116–28.

———. 1920. Proceedings of the Board of Regents for year ending June 30, 1918. *Smithsonian Institution annual report for 1918*, 107–15.

———. 1920a. [Brief reviews]. *Nature* 106:158.

———. 1926. [Material preceeding]. Langley and Modern Aviation; Twenty-third birthday of Wright brothers' flight prompts honors to American aero pioneers. *Slipstream* 7, 12:9.

————. 1927. *Proceedings of Conference on the future of the Smithsonian Institutin. February 11, 1927.* Washington, D.C.: Smithsonian Institution. Printed by Lord Baltimore Press, Baltimore, Md.

————. 1927a. Funeral Service of Dr. Charles Doolittle Walcott. The Church of the Covenant, Washington, D.C., Feb. 12, 1927.

Arnoldi, M. J. 1997. Herbert Ward's "Ethnographic sculptures of Africans." In *Exhibiting Dilemmas: Issues of representation at the Smithsonian.* Edited by A. Henderson and A. L. Kaeppler. Washington and London: Smithsonian Institution Press, 70–91.

Baker, R. 1939. *Woodrow Wilson: Life and letters.* Vol. 7. New York: Doubleday, Dooryard.

Barrows, A. L. 1933. A history of the National Research Council 1913–1933: 1. General organization and activities. *Science* (new series) 77:353–60.

Bassler, R. S. 1921. Proceedings of the twelfth annual meeting of the Paleontological Society, held in Chicago, Illinois, Dec. 28–30, 1920. Geological Society of America, *Bulletin* 32:129–44.

Bastin, E. S. 1910. [Report on the 226th meeting of the Geological Society of Washington, Jan. 10, 1910]. The mechanical part of a paleontological monograph: Lancaster D. Burling. *Science* (new series) 31:517–18.

Bierce, A. 1911. *The devil's dictionary.* Albert and Charles Sons.

Boas, F. 1928. *Anthropology and modern life.* New York: W. W. Norton.

Briggs, D. E. G., D. H. Erwin, and F. C. Collier. 1994. *The fossils of the Burgess shale.* Washington, D.C.: Smithsonian Institution Press.

Brigham, G. R. 1919. Abstracts: Paleontology [Appendages of trilobites]. Washington Academy of Sciences, *Journal* 9:229–31.

Bargain, P. 1996. Herbert Ward 1863–1919: Explorer, writer, sculptor and collector. *The World of Tribal Arts* (Spring):48–62.

Burchfield, J. D. 1975. *Lord Kelvin and the age of the earth.* New York: Science History.

Burling, L. D. 1911. Photographing fossils by reflected light. *American Journal of Science* 31 (4):99–100.

————. 1913. Cambrian Brachiopoda. *American Journal of Science* 34 (4):194–95.

————. 1914. Early Cambrian stratigraphy in the North America cordillera, with discussion of the Albertella and related faunas. Canada Department of Mines, Geological Survey, *Museum Bulletin* 2:93–129.

————. 1916. The Albertella fauna located in the Middle Cambrian of British Columbia and Alberta. *American Journal of Science* 32 (3):469–73.

Cameron, F. 1952. *Cottrell: Samaritan of science.* Garden City, N.Y.: Doubleday.

Cavell, E. 1983. *Legacy in ice: The Vaux family and the Canadian Alps.* Banff, Alta.: Whyte Foundation.

Chen Jun-Yuan and Curt Teichert. 1983. Cambrian Cephalopoda of China. *Palaeontographica,* Abt. A, Bd. 181:1–102.

Clark, A. H. 1912. Restoration of the genus Eldonia. *Zoologischen Anzeiger* 39:723–25.

————. 1913. Cambrian holothurians. *American Naturalist* 47:488–507.

Cochrane, R. E. 1978. *The National Academy of Sciences: The first 100 years 1863–1963.* Washington, D.C.: National Academy of Sciences.

Colbert, E. 1992. *William Diller Matthew, paleontologist.* New York: Columbia University Press.

Coleman, W. 1964. *Georges Cuvier, zoologist.* Cambridge, Mass.: Harvard University Press.

Conaway, J. 1995. *The Smithsonian: 150 years of adventure, discovery, and wonder.* New York: Knopf.

Conway Morris S. 1998. *The Crucible of creation.* Oxford, U.K.: Oxford University Press.

———. 1998a. The challenge [Showdown on the Burgess shale]. *Natural History* (Dec.–Jan. 1999):48–51.

Craig, G. Y., and E. J. Jones. 1982. *A geological miscellany.* Oxford, U.K.: Orbital Press.

Crouch, T. D. 1987. The feud between the Wright brothers & the Smithsonian. *Invention & Technology* (Spring):34–46.

———. 1989. *The bishop's boys: A life of the Wright Brothers.* New York: W. W. Norton.

———. 1981. *A dream of wings: Americans and the flying machine.* New York: W. W. Norton.

Cummings, R., and S. Cummings. 1996. *British Columbia: A natural history.* Vancouver: Douglas and MacIntire.

Day, A. L. 1915. *Report of the National Academy of Sciences for 1914.* Washington, D.C.: Government Printing Office.

———. 1916. *Report of the National Academy of Sciences for the year 1915.* Washington, D.C.: Government Printing Office.

———. 1917. *Report of the National Academy of Sciences for the year 1916.* Washington, D.C.: Government Printing Office.

Deacon, M. 1997. *Scientists and the sea 1650–1900.* 2d ed. Aldershot, U.K.: Ashgate.

Dickens, C. 1859. *A tale of two cities.* London: Chapman and Hall.

Dorsey, H. W. 1946. The International Exchange Service. *Science* 104:142–43.

Drake, E. 1996. *Restless genius: Robert Hooke and his earthly thoughts.* Oxford, U.K.: Oxford University Press.

Duenwald, R. M. 1953. A note from the printer [four-page loose brochure distributed with a book]. Associated with Rickett, H. W. ed. 1953. *Wildflowers of America: 400 flowers in full color based on paintings by Mary Vaux Walcott, with additional paintings by Dorothy Falcon Platt.*

Dupree, A. H. 1957. *Science in the federal government.* Cambridge, Mass.: Harvard University Press.

Faul, H., and C. Faul. 1983. *It began with a stone: A history of geology from the Stone Age to the age of plate tectonics.* New York: John Wiley and Sons.

Fenton, C. L., and M. A. Fenton. 1931. Algae and algal beds in the Belt series of Glacier National Park. *Journal of Geology* 39:670–86.

———. 1934. Walcott's "Precambrian Algonkian algal flora" and associated animals. Geological Society of America, *Bulletin* 47:609–20.

Finley, D. E. 1973. *A standard of excellence.* Washington, D.C.: Smithsonian Institution Press.

Fletcher, T. P., and D. Collins. 1998. The Middle Cambrian Burgess shale and its relationship to the Stephen Formation in the southern Canadian Rocky Mountains. *Canadian Journal of Earth Sciences* 35:413–36.

Fritz, W. 1992. Walcott's Lower Cambrian Olenellus trilobite collection 61k, Mt. Robson area, Canadian Rocky Mountains. Geological Survey of Canada, *Bulletin* 432.

Fritz, W., and E. Mountjoy. 1975. Lower and Early Middle Cambrian formations near Mount Robson, British Columbia and Alberta. *Canadian Journal of Earth Sciences* 12:119–31.

Goodspeed, A. W. 1913. The American Philosophical Society. *Science* (new series) 39:718–30.

Gould, S. J. 1989. *Wonderful life*. New York: W. W. Norton.

———. 1990. In touch with Walcott. *Natural History* 7190:10–19.

——— 1994. Introduction: The coherence of history. In *Early life on earth*. Edited by S. Bengtson. Nobel symposium 64. New York: Columbia University Press.

Grosvenor, G. 1948. The National Geographic Society and its magazine. Foreword to *Cumulative Index to the National Geographic Magazine, 1899–1946*. Washington, D.C.: National Geographic Society.

Gulliver, F. P. 1909. The American Association for the Advancement of Science. Section E: Geology and geography. *Science* (new series) 29:747–57.

Gutstadt, A. M. 1975. Pseudo- and dubiofossils from the Newland Limestone, Belt Supergroup, Late Precambrian, Montana. *Journal of Sedimentary Petrology* 45:405–14.

Hafertepe, K. 1984. *America's castle: The evolution of the Smithsonian building and its institution, 1840–1878*. Washington, D.C.: Smithsonian Institution Press.

Hale, G. E. 1920. The possibilities of coöperation. In *The new world of science: Its development during the war*. Edited by R. M. Yerkes. New York: Century, 393–404.

Hall, N. J. 1928. Langley or Wright? *Liberty*, July 23.

Hellmann, G. T. 1967 *The Smithsonian*. Philadelphia, New York: J. P. Lippincott.

Holley, I. B., Jr. 1964. *Buying matériel for the Army Air Forces*. Washington, D.C.: Department of the Army.

Illing, V. C. 1917. Dr. Charles D. Walcott's Cambrian geology and paleontology. *Geological Magazine* 4 (6): 24–27.

Isham, L. B., and E. R. S. Hodges, 1989. Introduction. In *The guild handbook of scientific illustration*. Edited by E. Hodges. New York: Van Nostrand Reinhold.

Jones, B. Z. 1965. Lighthouse of the skies. *Smithsonian Publication 4612: The Smithsonian Astrophysical observatory: background and history 1846–1955*. Washington, D.C.: Smithsonian Institution.

Jones, L. R. 1925. Report of the Committee of the National Academy of Sciences on forestry problems. *Science* (new series) 62:5–6.

Kardiner, A., and E. Preble. 1963. *They studied man*. New York: New American Library.

Kelly, F. C. 1943. *The Wright brothers*. New York: Harcourt, Brace and Company.

Kevlas, D. J. 1977. *The Physicists*. New York: Knopf.

King, C. 1892. The education of the future. *Forum*, Mar. 13, 20–32.

Komons, N. A. 1977. *Bonfires to beacons: Federal civil aviation policy under the Air Com-

merce Act. Washington, D.C.: Department of Transportation; repr. Washington, D.C.: Smithsonian Institution Press, 1989.

Kopper, P. 1982. *The National Museum of Natural History.* New York: Harry N. Abrams.

Lawton, T., and L. Merrill. 1993. *Freer: A legacy in art.* Washington, D.C.: Smithsonian Institution Press.

Lehman, M. 1963. *This high man: The life of Robert H. Goddard.* New York: Farrar Strauss and Giraux.

Livingston, B. E. 1923. The permanent secretary's report on the Boston meeting. *Science* (new series) 57:90–128.

———. 1925. The permanent secretary's report on the fifth Washington meeting. *Science* (new series) 61:121–68.

Lodge, J. E. 1925. Appendix 3: Report on the Freer Gallery of Art. *Smithsonian Institution annual report for 1923,* 59–62.

Lord, Walter. 1955. *A night to remember.* Mettich, N.Y.: Arereon.

Lowitt, R. 1971. *George W. Norris: The persistence of a progressive 1913–1933.* Urbana: University of Illinois Press.

McCormick, A. 1928. America's banishment of the original Wright airplane. *U.S. Air Service* (Mar.):30–34.

McCurdy, J. A. D. 1913. Langley Day in Washington. *Flying* (June).

Makiewicz, C. 1992. *Obruchchevella* and other microfossils in the Burgess shale: Preservation and affinity. *Journal of Paleontology* 66:719–29.

Manning, T. G. 1979. George Otis Smith as fourth director of the U.S. Geological Survey. In *Two hundred years of geology in America.* Edited by C. J. Schneer. Hanover, N.H.: University Press of New England, 157–64.

Margerie, E. de. 1917. Rapport sur l'atribution du Prix Gaudry a M. C. D. Walcott. *Compte rendu sommarie ses séances de la Société Géologique de France* 8:100–108.

Marshall, F. F. 1926. [Editorial] Langley and modern aviation. *The Slipstream* 7:9.

Mayr, E. 1976. *Evolution and the diversity of life: Selected essays.* Cambridge, Mass.: Harvard University Press.

Mendelson, C. V., and J. W. Schopf. 1992. Proterozoic and selected Early Cambrian microfossils and microfossil-like objects. In *The Proterozoic biosphere.* Edited by J. W. Schopf and C. Klein. Cambridge, U.K.: Cambridge University Press, 867–951.

Meyer, A. E. 1970. *Charles Lang Freer and his gallery.* Washington, D.C.: Freer Gallery of Art. [Reprint of *Washington Post* article by Mrs. Meyer, Jan. 11, 1970.]

Michaelson, A. A. 1925. *Report of the National Academy of Sciences, fiscal year 1924–1925.* Washington, D.C.: Government Printing Office.

———. 1925. *Report of the National Academy of Sciences, fiscal year 1923–1924.* Washington, D.C.: Government Printing Office.

Miles, J. C. 1995. *Guardian of the parks: A history of the National Parks and Conservation Association.* Washington, D.C.: Taylor and Francis.

Miller, H. S. 1970. *Dollars for research.* Seattle: University of Washington Press.

Millikan, R. A. 1920. Contributions of physical sciences. In *The new world of science: Its development during the war.* Edited by R. M. Yerkes. New York: Century, 33–48.

Milton, J. 1667. *Paradise lost, a poem written in ten books.* London: Peter Parker, Robert Boulter, and Mathias Walker.

Morgan, K. N. 1985. *Charles A. Platt: The artist as architect.* New York: Architectural History Foundation.

Newell, F. W. 1908. The Salton Sea. *Smithsonian Institution annual report for 1907.*

Oehser, P. H. 1949. *Sons of science.: The story of the Smithsonian Institution and its leaders.* New York: Henry Schuman.

Pinsky, V. 1992. Archaeology, politics, and boundary-formation: The Boas censure (1919) and the development of American archaeology during the interwar years. In *Rediscovering our past: Essays on the history of American archaeology.* Edited by J. E. Raymen. Aldershot, U.K.: Avebury Press.

Playfair, J. 1805. Biographical account of the life of Dr. James Hutton. *Royal Society of Edinburgh, Transactions* 5, part 4:1–97.

Pyne, S. J. 1998. *How the canyon became grand.* New York: Viking Penguin.

Rabbitt. M. 1980. *Minerals, land, and geology: For the common defense and general welfare.* Vol. 2: *1879–1904.* Washington, D.C.: Government Printing Office.

———. 1986. *Minerals, land, and geology: For the common defense and general welfare.* Vol. 3: *1904–1939.* Washington, D.C.: Government Printing Office.

———. 1989. The United States Geological Survey 1879–1989. *U.S. Geological Survey, Circular* 1050.

Rathbun, R. 1909. The National Gallery of Art. United States National Museum, *Bulletin* 70. Washington, D.C.: Government Printing Office.

Ravenel, W. de. C. 1921. Appendix 1: Report on the United States National Museum. *Smithsonian Institution annual report for 1919,* 25–37.

Raymond, P. E. 1917. Beecher's classification of trilobites after 20 years. *American Journal of Science* 43 (4):196–210.

———. 1920. The appendages, anatomy, and relationships of trilobites. *Connecticut Academy of Arts and Sciences* 7.

———. 1921. Criteria for the species of trilobites. Geological Society of America, *Bulletin* 32:349–52.

Reacher, N. 1996. *Priceless knowledge?* Lanham, Md.: Rowman and Littlefield.

Resser, C. E. 1933. Preliminary generalized Cambrian time scale. Geological Society of America, *Bulletin* 33:735–56.

Rezak, R. 1957. Stromatolites of the Belt series in Glacier National Park and vicinity, Montana. U.S. Geological Survey *Professional Paper* 294-D.

Rigby, J. K. 1986. Sponges of the Burgess shale (Middle Cambrian), British Columbia. *Palaeontologica Canadiana* 2.

Ripley, S. D. 1970. Foreword to *The Smithsonian Institution,* by P. H. Oehser. New York: Praeger, v–vii.

Roland, A. 1985. *Model research: The National Advisory Committee for Aeronautics 1915–1958.* Vol. 1. NASA SP-4103. Washington, D.C.: National Aeronautics and Space Administration.

Roseberry, C. R. 1972. *Glenn Curtiss: Pioneer of flight.* New York: Doubleday.

Rothpletz, A. 1915. Über die systematische Deutung und die stratigraphische Stellung der älesten Versteinerungen Europas und Nordamerikas mit besonderer

Berücksichtigung der Cryptozoen und Oolithe: Teil I, Die Fauna der Beltformation bei Helena in Montana. *Abhandlung der Küniglichen Bayerischen Akademie der Wissenschaften Mathematische-physikalische Klasse* 28, Bd.2.

———. 1916. Über die systematische Deutung und die stratigraphische Stellung der älesten Versteinerungen Europas und Nordamerikas mit besonderer Berücksichigung der Cryptozoen und Oolithe: Teil II: Über *Cryptozoon, Eozoon* und *Atikokania*. *Abhandlung der Königlichen Bayerischen Akademie der Wissenschaften, Mathematische-physikalische Klass* 28, Bd. 2.

Sardeson, F. W. 1929. Posey in paleontology. *Pan-American Geologist* 51, 282–86.

Sarton, G. 1956. History of science. *Encyclopedia Americana*. Vol. 24, 413–17.

Schofield, C. J. 1921. The discovery of Olenellus fauna in southeastern British Columbia. *Science* (new series) 54:666–67.

Schopf, J. W. 1999. *The cradle of life: The discovery of the earth's earliest fossils*. Princeton, N.J.: Princeton University Press.

Schuchert, C. 1913. Cambrian Brachiopoda. *American Journal of Science* 35 (4):331–32.

Scott, W. B. 1939. *Some memories of a paleontologist*. Princeton, N.J.: Princeton University Press.

Seward, A. C. 1931. *Plant life through the ages*. Cambridge, U.K.: Cambridge University Press; New York: Macmillan.

Shankland, R. 1951. *Steve Mather of the national parks*. New York: Knopf.

Sheets-Pyeson, S. 1996. *John William Dawson: Faith, Hope, and Science*. Montreal and Kingston: McGill–Queen's University.

Shimer, H. 1913. Abstract of "Cambrian Brachiopoda" by C. D. Walcott. *Geologisches Zentralblat* 19:564.

Smith, C. 1989. *Off the beaten track: Women adventurers and mountaineers in western Canada*. Jasper, B.C.: Coyote Books.

Smith, G. O. 1929. Division of Government Relations. *Report of the National Academy of Sciences, fiscal year 1927–1928*. Washington, D.C.: U.S. Government Printing Office.

Spalding, P. 1915. The Botanical Society of Washington. *Science* 41:879.

Stegner, W. 1954. *Beyond the hundredth meridian*. Boston: Houghton Mifflin.

Størmer, L. 1939. Studies of trilobite morphology. Part 1: The thorassic appendages and their phylogenetic significance. *Norsk Geologisk Tidsskrift* 19:143–273.

Taft, W. H. 1928. Introductory remarks to Charles Doolittle Walcott secretary of the Smithsonian Institution 1907–1927, memorial meeting, Jan. 24, 1928. *Smithsonian Miscellaneous Collections* 80 (12):3–4.

Toulmin, S. E., and J. Goodfield, 1982. *The discovery of time*. Chicago: University of Chicago Press.

True., F. W. 1913. *A history of the first half-century of the National Academy of Sciences*. Baltimore: Lord Baltimore Press.

Tsonis, A. A. 1998 Review of *Fractal river basins*. *Science* 280:1210

Vaux, M. M. 1907. Camping in the Canadian Rockies. *Canadian Alpine Journal* 1:67–70.

Vidal, G. 1998. *The Smithsonian Institution*. New York: Random House.

Walcott, M. V. 1925–1928. *North American Wild Flowers*, 5 vols. Washington, D.C.: Smithsonian Institution.

————. 1935. *Illustrations of North American Pitcher Plants*. Descriptions and notes on distribution by E. Wherry, notes of insect associates by F. M. Jones. Washington, D.C.: Smithsonian Institution.

Walcott, S. S. 1971. How I found my own fossil. *Smithsonian* 1 (12):28–29.

Walter, M. 1992. Stratigraphic distribution of stromatolites and allied structures. In *The Proterozoic biosphere*. Edited by J. W. Schopf and C. Klein. Cambridge, U.K.: Cambridge University Press, 507–9.

Weiss, M. P., and E. L. Yochelson. 1995. Ozarkian and Canadian systems: Gone and nearly forgotten. In *Ordovician odyssey: Short papers for the Seventh International Symposium on the Ordovician System*. Edited by J. D. Cooper, M. L. Droser, and S. C. Finney. Fullerton, Calif.: Pacific Section, Society for Sedimentary Geology.

Weller, S. [signed S.W]. 1913. Cambrian Brachiopoda. *Journal of Geology* 21:568–69.

Wernert, S. J. 1989. *Our national parks: America's spectacular wilderness heritage*. Pleasantville, N.Y.: Readers Digest.

Wetmore, A. 1946. After one hundred years. *Science* 104:113–16.

Wheeler, A. O. 1911. Report of the director. *Canadian Alpine Journal* 3:179–85.

Whittington, H. B., and J. E. Almond. 1987. Appendages and habits of the Upper Ordovician trilobite *Triarthrus eatoni*. Royal Society of London, *Philosophical Transactions*, B 317:1–46.

Wilks, M. E., and E. G. Nisbet. 1985. Archaen stromatolites from the Steep Rock Group, northwestern Ontario. *Canadian Journal of Earth Sciences* 22:792–99.

Wilson, E. B. 1966. *List of the proceedings of the National Academy of Sciences of the United States of America 1914–1963*. Washington, D.C.: National Academy of Sciences.

Wright, H. 1966. *Explorer of the universe: A biography of George Ellery Hale*. New York: E. P. Dutton.

Wright, H., J. N. Warnow, and C. Weiner, eds. 1972. *The legacy of George Ellery Hale*. Cambridge, Mass.: MIT Press.

Wright, O. 1915. Stability of aeroplanes. *Smithsonian Institution annual report for 1914*, 200–216.

Wyer, S. S. 1925. Niagara Falls: Its power possibilities and preservation. [Smithsonian Institution] *Publication*, 2820.

Yard, R. S. 1919. *The new Grand Canyon National Park*. Washington, D.C.: National Parks Association.

Yochelson, E. L. 1967. Charles Doolittle Walcott 1850–1927. *National Academy of Sciences, Biographical Memoirs* 39:471–540.

————. 1979. Charles D. Walcott: America's pioneer in Precambrian paleontology and stratigraphy. In *History of concepts in Precambrian geology*, by W. O. Kupsch and W. A. S. Sarjeant. N.p.: Geological Association of Canada, 261–92.

————. 1983. Walcott's discovery of Middle Ordovician vertebrates. *Earth Sciences History* 2:66–75.

————. 1985. *The National Museum of Natural History: 75 years in the Natural History Building*. Washington, D.C.: Smithsonian Institution Press.

————. 1988. The bulletin of the Geological Society of America and Charles Doolittle Walcott. Geological Society of America, *Bulletin* 100:3–11.

————. 1989. "Geologic time" as calculated by C. D. Walcott. *Earth Sciences History* 8:150–58.

————. 1994. Andrew Carnegie and Charles Doolittle Walcott: The origin and early years of the Carnegie Institution of Washington. In *The Earth, the Heavens, and the Carnegie Institution of Washington.* Edited by G. Goode. Washington, D.C.: American Geophysical Union, History of Geophysics. Vol. 5, 2–19.

————. 1996. Washington Academy of Sciences: Background, origin and early years. *Washington Academy of Sciences, Journal* 84:184–220. [Issued in 1998.]

————. 1996a. Discovery, collection, and description of the Middle Cambrian Burgess shale biota by Charles Doolittle Walcott. American Philosophical Society, *Proceedings* 140:469–545.

————. 1997. Walcott in Scotland. *The Edinburgh Geologist* 30:7–12.

————. 1998. *Charles Doolittle Walcott, Paleontologist.* Kent, Ohio: Kent State University Press.

————. 1998a. Arthur Brown: The forgotten "assistant for all seasons." *Marrella* (7):14–18.

Yochelson, E. L., and W. E. Osborne.1999. Dr. Cooper Curtice: Unknown worker in interpreting the Cambrian of Alabama. *Southeastern Geology* 38:215–22.

Yochelson, E. L., and H. S. Yoder, Jr. 1994. Founding the Geophysical Laboratory: A scientific bonanza from perception and persistence. Geological Society of America, *Bulletin* 106:338–50.

Zahm, A. F. 1915. The first man-carrying aeroplane capable of sustained free flight: Langley's success as a pioneer in aviation. *Smithsonian Institution annual report for 1914,* 217–22.

Zaniest, A.A. 1998. Water ordering landscapes. *Science* 250:1210

Zazlow, M. 1975. *Reading the rocks: The story of the Geological Survey of Canada 1842–1972.* Ottawa: Macmillan of Canada.

Index